Disaster Management:
HAZARD AND RISK AWARENESS
- A Comprehensive Approach

Disaster Management:

HAZARD AND RISK AWARENESS

- A Comprehensive Approach

N.V.S. Raju

B.E. (Mech.), PGDIRPM, M.Tech., MBA., Ph.D.

Professor of Mechanical Engineering,
JNTUH College of Engineering, Jagitial,
Karimnagar (Dist.), Telangana State, India.

BSP BS Publications

A unit of **BSP Books Pvt., Ltd.**

4-4-309/316, Giriraj Lane, Sultan Bazar,
Hyderabad - 500 095

Disaster Management: *Hazard and Risk Awareness - A Comprehensive Approach*
by N.V.S. Raju

Published by:

BSP BS Publications
A unit of **BSP Books Pvt., Ltd.**
4-4-309/316, Giriraj Lane, Sultan Bazar,
Hyderabad - 500 095
Phone : 040 - 23445688, 23445600
e-mail : info@bspbooks.net
www.bspbooks.net

Printed at
Aditya Offset Process (I) Pvt. Ltd.
Hyderabad.

Price : Rs. 895.00

ISBN : 978-93-8830-534-1 (Paperback)

Dedicated to

The Lord Maha Siva,

The GOD -(Generator, Operator & Dissolver) of

The Disaster Management

Dr. K. Hari Kishan Raju,
M.sc., Ph.D.,
Sr. Technical Officer
CMR - Vector Control Research Centre
Indira Nagar – Puducherry – 6
Email: khkraju@gmail.com
Mobile: 9443802302

FOREWORD

Dear Professor

Congratulations on the upcoming publication of your another scholastic book. I feel it my privilege to have an opportunity to go through the very 'edutaining' book. The book is written in short an excellent and innovative way that will prize and surprise everyone.

At the outset, I can't stay without admiring the O'MY SILENT INNER VIBES- in short O'M SIV (before main text of each chapter), which hooked me from the very beginning, and the way of starting with spiritual notes and manoeuvring into nature or real world problems is amazing. The extensive explorations of the relationships between science and spirituality over the past four decades have made it evident that the sense of oneness, the key characteristic of spiritual experience, is fully confirmed by the understanding of reality in contemporary science. If mind is not scientific enough, it cannot be spiritual. If the mind does not know the world, it cannot move to something beyond the world. Knowing the world, its movements, its games, its fury, its suffering and its cunningness is very important. To understand these things deeply, your mind should be spiritually scientific or scientifically spiritual. Even, the great scientist Einstein believed that spirituality / religion without science is blind and science without spirituality / religion is lame.

The awareness of being connected with all of nature is particularly strong in ecology / environment. Connectedness, relationship, and interdependence are fundamental concepts of ecology, which are also the essence of spiritual experience. By bringing all these connections and relationships to explain the causes of disasters is excellent and very informative. Your vibes are clear and new in a way that is not only self-conscious but also universal-conscious.

Coming in to the next aspect, classification of disasters; very simple and even laymen can understand. The science behind the major disasters such as Earthquakes, Tsunamis, Volcanoes, Floods and Cyclones are covered extensively and pinpointed the significance of technocrats' roles in managing them. Inclusion of the hot and cold waves, drought, famine, pollution, wildfires, and deforestation as the disasters is appreciable and thought provoking. Keeping separate bacterial, protozoan, fungal and viral epidemics is very appropriate, even though some of these spread diseases through common transmission methods. The subtitle 'Hazard

And Risk Awareness-HARA' is an apt, with all the chapters in general, but accidents and industrial hazards and epidemics in particular.

I loved the cartoons of your book. You have a wonderful way of thinking how to balance the light, humorous, and playful with serious, raw, disaster subject. I rarely found any other author balancing the two different aspects quite so well, making me laugh in the grief while reading some of the serious matter in various chapters. I think this will help the readers grasping the subject very easily and make their heavy hearts light.

Excellently started with Kshamya Dharitri (O Mother Earth, Forgive me), covering all the disasters and concluding with Mruthyorma Amrutham Gamaya (The mitigation) is extraordinary and readers will be benefitted from your much appreciable work. Heartfelt compliments for thorough research and clear writing. I rate this book with 10 out of 10 on a 10 point scale. I look forward to reading your next informative work. Thank you.

With best wishes

Dr. K. Hari Kishan Raju

PREFACE

Saying is easier than doing. The amount of pains I felt while writing is more than the joy I experienced while teaching. The hurdles were in many forms, but finally the success of bringing out this book into the light after its beginning about five years ago, gave the immense pleasure like a mother, seeing her new born baby after having borne labor pains.

This subject 'Disaster Management' itself gives pains to teach, because one who teaches this subject needs to discuss about the number of deaths, injuries, sorrows, sad or bad moments at every line and moment of teaching, but, one thing to feel good is that it is one form of paying tributes to those misfortunate people. At the same time it gives a scope of teaching lesson of safety to alert against the human carelessness or negligence.

Another pain to the students or the teachers of this subject is that there is not even a single book available to cater the needs of UG (B.Tech.) students. There is no other option to the learners and lecturers than to take from the web resources and Wikipedia. Unfortunately, some information obtained from such sources is either incomplete or incorrect because it is not authentic. Moreover, this information of this subject so dynamically varies that today's information becomes outdated by tomorrow. So, many of my students and well-wishers forced me to write the essence of this subject. The idea of writing this book on **'Disaster Management'** was born from those suggestions.

I cannot claim it as my success, nor, I wish to take all the credit, because many hands, hearts and heads were the parts and parcels of this endeavor. Particularly, I should share the credit to all those writers and contributors to the info-banks of Wikipedia, NDMA, OSHA, CDC, Red-cross, WHO, Survey of India, and Disaster Management related websites from which I gathered information. Therefore, I cannot claim the originality of the concepts, but for the presentation. Further, I listed some names in the acknowledgements those who shared their views and suggestions, helped, assisted, guided and contributed directly or indirectly. However, the list is not exhaustive. I beg the pardon, if I miss any name inadvertently.

I believe that 'visualizing' is powerful than just 'reading' a concept or a matter. Moreover, a figure or picture or image will help memorizing the subject easily and retentive too. The efforts of my student and globally recognized cartoonist cum 3-D artist, ***Dr. Singarapu Shiva Rama Krishna (SSRK)*** along with assistance of my daughter ***Ms. Sanja Karunamayi (SK)*** and my student ***Mr. K.Raja Shekhar (KRaSh)*** through their ***cartoons*** added a new dimension, and gave life to the concepts of the subject. I am sure they will keep readers relaxed and rejuvenate the readers by relieving the stresses developed while reading. The intension of these cartoons is purely to create interest and enthuse before studying, and entertain while studying and to keeping the concepts in everlasting memory after studying. The wit and wisdom in the cartoons will be helpful to the teachers also to present these concepts during their lectures to inculcate the curiosity in students. But, definitely it is not to hurt any person or group, caste or creed or religion etc. Further, it is not intended or focused on any person(s).

Instead of giving at the end of the chapter, some questions are given under the head 'Self Assessment Interval (SAI)' at every topic or a group of relevant topics. This will help the students understand the topic better and easier. Further, it helps the students to be aware of the way how a question may be asked in an exam. However, the quiz (multiple choice questions) are not given in this book in view of cost reduction (to keep the book within the affordable price to students), but will be provided online free of cost for those who bought this book. These questions will be very useful for the students for their midterm quiz exams and for many competitive examinations for which this subject is very important such as Civil services, Forest Officers exams, Engineering Services, Groups, UPSC, TSPSC, APPSC and many more.

At the end of each chapter some ideas are given for mini-projects or major projects or as case study and to gain/ get a practical exposure.

Sufficiency is end of the growth and stops the improvement. So, any suggestions for the improvement will gratefully be acknowledged.

The most interesting feature of this book is ***'O'My Silent Inner Vibes (OM SIV)'***. The essence of the chapter is presented with a philosophical touch excerpted from various mythologies, histories and cult of Hindus, Muslims, Christians, Sikhs, Norse, Greek, and Japan including some moral stories. I heard or read from various sources that throbbed my heart and swayed through inherent feelings and also inspired me. I am sure these will give awareness as well as some motivation to the readers to come up in their lives because this subject teaches how to live i.e. what ought to do and what not to do.

The latest developments in all the fields of this subject and some noteworthy issues are given under the box item ***'Do you know?'*** These will be useful to the budding engineers to keep them advanced to speak when they are in a group and fills confidence in attending their interviews. I observed with many pupils of engineering that they treat this subject as 'read a day before the exam' and forget the very next day like 'use and throw'. Perhaps! This is because the books and teachers could not create the interest and did not insist its importance. To address this issue, every chapter is provided with ample number of some astounding facts and issues relevant to the respective chapters in the box items under the head, ***'O My God (OMG)'.*** These will create some interest and take space of the young minds on one hand and enthuse to think in new dimensions on the other hand.

This subject is systematically organized in eighteen chapters The chapters are sufficiently small and so designed (not to be long) because lengthy chapters cause boredom and readers may be scared or lose interest as they cannot make time easily to read. Further, the lecturers can plan their lecture periods with a great ease as one or two for each chapter. The first chapter deals with the anatomy and all about the planet Earth, titled as Kshamayaa Dharithri, with due apologies to the mother Earth and the second is the elements of disaster that gives an overall picture about disasters. The third chapter covers Earthquakes, while fourth chapter is about Tsunami. Volcanoes are dealt in fifth chapter where as the sixth chapter describes all about slides, i.e. Landslides, Rockslides and Mudslides etc. The seventh chapter narrates the Blizzards and Avalanches. The eighth chapter encompasses Cyclones, Hurricanes, Typhoons, Tornadoes and various types of Storms. The Floods and Soil Erosion are discussed in ninth chapter while in tenth chapter the issues of Drought and Famine are explained. The eleventh chapter covers various Industrial Hazards due to fire, chemical, explosion, nuclear and radiation. Cold waves, Heat waves and Deforestation and their effects are depicted in twelfth chapter, while thirteenth is used to discuss about Pollution and Acid Rains. The fourteenth chapter addresses all types of Accidents including, road, rail, air and marine accidents. In fifteenth chapter, the man-made disasters like Violence, Wars and Terrorism are described. The sixteenth and seventeenth chapters deal with various Bio-Hazards which include various bacterial, fungal, protozoan and viral epidemics. The final, eighteenth chapter named as Mruthyorma Amrutam Gamaya, deals with Mitigation, Rescue and Rehabilitation issues of overall disaster management. At the end of each chapter, ***review questions*** are supplemented with both ***essay type, and short answer type*** to benefit the students who prepare for the interviews and competitive exams such as Civil Services Examination such as IAS, IPS, IFS, IES in addition to those who prepare for jobs through Public Service Commission (PSC), Public Sector Units (PSU), Government Jobs including group examinations and so forth.

It will be incomplete if I do not mention the continuous help, support, encouragement and pain sharing of my wife Mrs. Prasanna, my children Ms. Srija Nataraj, Ms. Himaja Padma Priya and Ms. Sanja Karnamayi while writing this book.

Though, utmost care is taken to make this book error free, some mistakes/errors might have crept in by oversight. I request your omission and commission. Constructive criticism will be gratefully acknowledged.

Dr. N.V.S. Raju
enviousraju@gmail.com

DISCLAIMER

While writing this book, I was really moved by reading the literature of the tragedies of various disasters and calamities. So, for those who lost their lives, I thought I should pray the almighty for all those souls rest in peace. At the same time, in the process of soothing my heavy heart, I have gone through some bits and pieces of several spiritual, mythological, holy books such as Srimad Bhagavadgita, Srimad Ramayan, Maha Bharat, some bits of Hindu Purans, Holy Quran, Holy Bible and even some mythological stories of Sikh, Chinese, Japanese, Norse, and Greek. While reading those stories, inadvertently my heart started throbbing and I had a feeling of some unknown vibrations inherently. I started putting them on paper. My friends, students, well-wishers, and my critics also who read them felt interesting, and worth reading for all, particularly to the young generations. Thence, these have been named **O'My Silent Inner Vibes (OM SIV)** which have occupied the first two pages of every chapter.

These are the true excerpts from the mythological stories of various religions and beliefs (may be myths or truths) of various sections of people. With a great respect on them, I wrote these, only with the interest of teaching the morals and ethics to the young generations. Hence, it is disclaimed that they have nothing to do with the scientific and technical information of the remaining chapter that starts from the third page onward of the respective chapter. (If any person is not interested to read them, he/she may skip them and directly go to the third page of the chapter skipping the first two pages of the chapter or tear them off from your owned book).

Further, any part of this book, including the cartoons, OM SIV, OMG boxes, figures and the running text are written only to generate interest in readers and memory retention but not to hurt the feelings of any clan, creed, caste, religion, gender or a section of people. Definitely it is not intended on any particular person or a group in any form.

Further, I beg your Purdon, if any word of this book inadvertently hurts the feelings of anyone as it is not intentional.

-Author

ACKNOWLEDGEMENTS

Mathru Devobhava! Pithru Devobhava!! Acharya Devobhava!!!

At the outset I thank my parents (Late Smt. Ammayi and Sri. NVMMRaju) and all Gurus who taught me, managing myself and others, particularly in the crisis. Especially, I thank Dr. K. Narayana Rao (Retd. Prof. of OU- Former MS –AICTE), Dr. C.B. K. Murthy (Retd. Prof. of ME, JNTU), Dr. (Col. Retd.) K. P. Rao (former Principal VREC, NIET and others), Dr. A. Vinaya Babu (Retd. Prof. of CSE & former Principal, JNTUHCEH & Director, Indur Group of Institutions).

I gratefully acknowledge all my family members particularly, my wife Mrs. Prasanna Lakshmi and daughters Ms. Srija, Himaja and Sanja. Thanks for useful ideas and contributing poems from his book "TO MY FRIEND" for OMSIV by my eldest brother Dr. Nakta Venkata Raju (Neonatologist-USA). Thanks are due for the erudite suggestions given by my elder brother Mr. N.V.Srinivasa Raju (C&F, Nippon) and sisters Mrs. Hema Gangadhar Raju, Mrs. Prema Madhusudan Raju and Mrs. Suma Srihari Raju. The help and assistance of my nephews Mr. P G Prasad, Kishor, Pruthvidhar, Pradeep and Saandeep and nieces Ms Jyothi, Aruna (Dolly), Pallavi, Kavitha, Lavanya, Harika, Divya, Adithi and Sahithi are noteworthy. I wish to place on record, the encouragement given by my uncles SarvSri. C. Bhaskar Raju, K. Laxman Raju, K. Sudhakar Raju, K. Prabhakar Raju and entire Kasu and Chennamadhavuni families.

I profusely thank our Principal, Dr. N. V. Ramana (Prof of EEE), and all my fellow colleagues who have been good critiques and motivators. A few names to quote, Dr. Ch. Sridhar Reddy (Head & AsP-ME-JNTUHCEM), Dr. Suresh Arjula (AP-ME), Mr. K. Vasantha Kumar (AP-ME) and Mrs. Shailaja. M (AsP-ME) of ME Department; Dr. B. Vishnu Vardhan (P-CSE & Vice Principal, JNTUHCEM), Dr. B. Kranthi Kiran (AsP-CSE), Mr. S. Praveen Kumar (AP-ECE), Mr. B. Prabhakar (AsP-ECE), M.Uday Kumar (AsP-CSE), Dr. T. Venugopal (P-CSE), Dr. B. Sathyanarayana (AP-Chem), Dr. T. Srikanth (AP-Phy.) and many more (I beg their pardon for not listing due to space constraint).

Special thanks to **Dr. K. Hari Kishan Raju, Scientist,** Pondicherry who was source of information for the last three chapters and reviewer of the book.

I thank my former colleagues and associates (working as faculty members at various colleges/ universities) Dr. D. V. Ravi Shankar, Dr. A. Prasad Raju, Dr. K. Aparna, and my scholars Dr. P. V. Subhashini, Dr. Aleti Padma, Mr. MV Ramana Reddy, Dr. R. Vykunta Rao, Dr. K. S. Raghuram, Mr. M. Krishna (APME-MEC), Late Sri. N L Narayana and many more students who helped sculpting the book to its best.

I think, I better pray the God to shower His blessings instead of thanking my students and Ad-hoc Lecturer ME-JNTUHCEM, Mr. S. Shiva Rama Krishna, my research scholars Mr. M. Pradeep Kumar (AP-KITS Huzurabad), Dr. C.Shivraj (Ad-hoc lecturer ME-JNTUHCEJ), My daughter Ms. N. Sanja Karunamayi (SK), and Mr. K. Rajashekhar (KRASH) for cartoons and art works which have given shape and life to my ideas and the text. I also pray the almighty for the health and wealth of my daughters Ms. Srija Nataraj (M.Tech.-Structures) and Himaja Padmapriya who helped while editing and proof reading.

I also would like to acknowledge the help rendered by the Ad-hoc Lecturers of JNTUHCEJ; some names to quote, Vijay Mohan, Narsaiah, Ramkishor, Mrs. Grace Prashanthi, Vemula Swathi, M. Sravanthi, Pragnya, K. Gouthami while data compiling, scripting, editing, computerizing and data processing.

This book would not have seen any light without the encouragement of Mr. Anil Shah and Mr. Nikhil Shah. I also thank Mr. M. Vasudeva Rao, Mr. Naresh Devargave, Mrs. Sandhya, Mrs. Deepa, Mr. Hari Prasad, Mr. Santhosh, Mr. Shiva, Mr. Sham for the editing, designing, help, assistance and what not! Thanks to entire team. Finally, I thank everyone who helped me directly or indirectly and since the list is big, I printed them in my heart to remember for the life time.

Dr. N.V.S. Raju

enviousraju@yahoo.co.in

CONTENTS

CHAPTER 2

Elements of Disaster

CHAPTER 3

Earthquake

CHAPTER 4

Tsunami

CHAPTER 5

Volcano

CHAPTER 6

Landslides

CHAPTER 7

Avalanche and Blizzard

CHAPTER 8

Cyclone–Hurricane–Typhoon

CHAPTER 9

Floods and Soil Erosion

CHAPTER 10

Drought and Famine

CHAPTER 11

Industrial Hazards *(Chemical, Fire, Explosion and Radiation)*

CHAPTER 12

Heat/Cold Waves, Wildfire and Deforestation

CHAPTER 13

Pollution and Acid Rains

CHAPTER 14

Accidents in Transport *(The Manmade Disasters)*

CHAPTER 15

Violence, Terrorism and Wars *(The Manmade Disasters)*

CHAPTER 16

Bio-hazards *(Bacterial, Protozoan and Fungal Epidemics)*

CHAPTER 17

Bio-hazards: Viral Epidemics

CHAPTER 18

Mruthyormaa Amrutham Gamaya
The Response, Rescue and Mitigation

CHAPTER 1 Kshamayaa Dharithri

(Oh Tolerant Mother Earth! Forgive Me)

O'MY SILENT INNER VIBES (O'M S I V – 1)

The mother Earth has greatest tolerance that she bears all our mistakes and misdeeds. She gives us everything such as minerals, food, shelter etc. But she can smash everything if we cross our limits. So,.....

I bow to Mother Earth to save the mankind!
I pray to mankind to save the mother Earth!
Oh! Mother Earth... Forgive us and give us your blessings!

Though ploughed through your belly, you fill our stomachs fully
Though cared never gratefully, you fulfil our needs gracefully,
I stand before Thee! Maa... with folded hands
Forgive us and give us your blessings!

Even when your body is split parts and parts, you never move apart
Though made you victim of our party, But you never leave our party
I kneel down! Maa... eyes filled with tears
Forgive us and give us your blessings!

Even if your heart's 'mine' is broken, you give us gold and diamonds
Even if garbage is thrown on you! You grab in your lap and garb us
I lay down on thee! Maa... to prostrate with stretched hands
Forgive us and give us your blessings!

Despite being kicked always with our feet!
Yet, you make us walk thousands and thousands of feet!
Touching thy feet! Maa...I salute you with these words
Forgive us and give us your blessings!

Kshamayaa Dharithri! Rakshathu! Samrakshathu!! Parirakshathu!!!

Namo Prithvee Matha! – Namo Prithvee Natha!!

The God **(Prithvee Nath)** created **Prithvee Matha,** 'The Earth' as the most beautiful planet! No other planet has all the requisites for living-hood except the Earth. It has abundant water at ambient temperature; amiable atmosphere, amicable humidity and pressure conditions and what not! All 'the optimal' conditions for life are available. However, when any of these conditions go to their uncontrollable extreme level, it becomes a disaster. What a wonder! The God not only created good living conditions, but also gave right self-resisting mechanism to adjust itself to the situations.

There is a small garden which has some cats and rats. One day suddenly, one wild cat came from a nearby forest (like a disaster) and ate many rats. Then, suddenly the rat population came down drastically. The cats could not get food and even starved to death (like famine/draught to cats). Thus the cats count fell down and thence the rat hunt reduced. This favoured the raise in rat population, which in turn the cats got abundant food. Now cats started hunting more and got food. Slowly cat population went up. This is called ecological balance, which nature by itself adjusts to a natural-ecological equilibrium. So we need to maintain the status-quo and/or allow the nature to balance by itself. If we go against this principle, there is every chance that we have to pay for its fury.

Similarly, for instance, if there is a high temperature at a placė, the air at the region gets heated up and creates a depression. Then the dense air from nearby place rushes toward the depression. Thus a balance will be maintained. If this goes in a larger scale, it may become a disaster (cyclone). Thus, any disaster is for ecological balancing. If we don't let it go imbalance, or we balance it, there won't be any disaster. Thence, ...

The Ecological Balance is the Key to Disaster Prevention

1.1 THE EARTH – AN OVERVIEW

Earth, the densest planet in the solar system is the 3rd planet from the Sun. It is the only planet in the universe known to harbor life. According to radio-metric dating, the Earth is about 4.54 billion years old. But,

How safe are we on this Earth?

Are we safe on the surface of earth? What is above and below the earth?

Do we have safe environment in the air above the earth? What is inside the earth? Can we have safe environment inside the earth?

To answer the above questions, we should first know the geography and the anatomy of the earth also in addition to the ecology. Let's have a quick look on it.

Earth is revolving about its own axis and the time taken for one rotation is assumed as one day (24 hours). The Earth is oblate spheroidal and its rotation flattened along the geographic axis and bulged around the equator. Further it also rotates around the sun in an elliptical orbit due to gravitational interactions and takes 365.26 days for each rotation, called a year. The Moon is its natural satellite that rotates around the earth once in every 27.32 days (relative to the background stars) or 29.53 days (new moon to new moon), called a month approximately. Earth's axis is tilted about 23.44° from the perpendicular to the Earth–Sun plane (the ecliptic), and the Earth–Moon plane tilted up to ±5.1° against the Earth–Sun plane. Without this tilt, there would be an eclipse every 2 weeks, alternating between lunar and solar. Earth's rotation about its own axis causes day and night, Earth's rotation around Sun produces Seasonal variations and the Moon's rotation around the Earth causes ocean tides.

Chemical composition of the earth crust

Compound	Formula	Composition	
		Continental	Oceanic
Silica	SiO_2	60.2%	48.6%
Alumina	Al_2O_3	15.2%	16.5%
Lime	CaO	5.5%	12.3%
Magnesia	MgO	3.1%	6.8%
Iron(II) oxide	FeO	3.8%	6.2%
Sodium oxide	Na_2O	3.0%	2.6%
Potassium oxide	K_2O	2.8%	0.4%
Iron(III) oxide	Fe_2O_3	2.5%	2.3%
Water	H_2O	1.4%	1.1%
Carbon dioxide	CO_2	1.2%	1.4%
Titanium dioxide	TiO_2	0.7%	1.4%
Phosphorus pentoxide	P_2O_5	0.2%	0.3%
Total		**99.6%**	**99.9%**

O My God!

The diameter of the Earth at the equator is 43 km (27 mi) larger than the pole-to-pole diameter. Thus the point on the surface farthest from Earth's center of mass is the summit of the equatorial Chimborazo volcano in Ecuador. The average diameter of the reference spheroid is 12,742 km (7,918 mi). The maximum deviations of radius of sphere: 0.17% at the Mariana Trench 10,911 m (35,797 ft) below SL, while 0.14% at Mt. Everest 8,848 m (29,029 ft) above SL.

About 71% of Earth's surface is covered with water, mostly by its oceans namely, Pacific, Atlantic, Indian, Arctic and Antarctic. The remaining 29% is land consisting of seven continents, namely Asia, Europe, Africa, North America, South America, Australia, Antarctic and islands that together have many lakes, rivers and other sources of water that contribute to the hydrosphere. The Earth's poles are covered in ice (Antarctic Ice sheet and sea ice of the Arctic ice pack). Earth's interior with a solid iron inner core and a liquid outer core generates the magnetic field. Earth's lithosphere has several rigid tectonic plates that migrate across the surface driven by mantle over periods of many millions of years.

1.2 EARTH AND GEOGRAPHY

Before knowing the anatomy of earth (basic geology), what is known as 'in and out' of the earth, we now need to know a little geography to understand the earth.

For the ease of study, Earth is divided by 180º (90º on either side are poles) horizontal imaginary lines called latitudes. The middle one, called equator (0º) divides into two halves as Northern Hemisphere (NH) and Southern Hemisphere (SH). At 23° (Approx.) on either side we call Tropic of Cancer (N) and Tropic of Capricorn (S) respectively.

1.2.1 Axial Tilt: The Reason for Season

The Earth is axially tilted by 23.44° (approx.) with the axis of its orbit plane, always pointing towards the celestial poles. Due to this tilt, the amount of sunlight falling on any point on the surface changes over the year, thereby causing the seasonal change as summer in the NH when the Tropic of Cancer faces the Sun, while winter to Tropic of Capricorn in SH, and reverse in other half of the year. During the summer, the day lasts longer, and the Sun appears to move higher in the sky. In winter, the climate becomes cooler and the days are shorter. In northern temperate latitudes, the Sun rises north of true east during the summer solstice, and sets north of true west, reversing in the winter. The Sun rises south of true east in the summer for the southern temperate zone and sets south of true west.

Above the Arctic region (N. Pole), an extreme case i.e., no daylight at all for 6 months, called a polar night. In the SH, the situation is exactly reversed, with the S. Pole. Six months later, this pole will have a midnight sun, a day of 24 hours, again reversing with the S. Pole.

By astronomical convention, the 4 seasons can be determined by the solstices. In the NH, winter occurs around 21 December; summers near 21 June, spring is around 20 March and autumn is about 22 or 23 September. In the SH, the situation is reversed, with the summer and winter solstices exchanged and the spring and autumnal equinox dates swapped.

O My God!

1. Earth orbits around Sun about 150 million km (93 million mi)
2. Earth rotates in 365.2564 mean solar days, or 1 Sidereal Yr.
3. Orbital speed is about 29.78 km/s (107,200 km/h; 66,600 mph)
4. Earth's diameter is about 12,742 km (7,918 mi)
5. Solar System in Milky-way orbits about 28,000 LY from its center
6. It is about 20 LY above the Galactic plane in the Orion Arm
7. During the Devonian period (410 Mya) a year had 400 days & each day was 21.8 hrs.

1.2.2 Geographic History

It is believed that Earth's atmosphere and oceans were formed by volcanic activity and out-gassing which included water vapor. The oceans originally formed by condensation augmented by water and ice delivered by asteroids, proto-planets, and comets. By 3.5 Gya (Billion years ago), magnetic field was established that prevented the atmosphere stripping away. Continents formed by plate tectonics along with continuous loss of heat from Earth's interior. About 750 Mya (million years ago) supercontinents broke and recombined. The present pattern began about 40 Mya. High-latitude regions undergo repeated cycles of glaciations (every 40,000–100000 yrs) and the last continental glaciations occurred 10,000 years ago.

Do You Know?

The orientation (rather than the angle) of Earth's axis also changes over time, with precision in around 25,800 yr cycle due to which a sidereal year is differing from a tropical year. Both of these motions are due to variations in attraction of the Sun, Moon and Earth's equatorial bulge. The poles also migrate a few meters across Earth's surface. In addition to this motion, there is a 14-month cycle called the Chandler Wobble. Earth's rotational velocity also varies, known as length-of-day variation. Further, Earth's perihelion occurs around 3 Jan, and its aphelion around 4 July subject to the precession and other orbital factors following the cyclical patterns called Milankovitch cycle.

1.2.3 Internal Structure and Composition

The mass of Earth is approximately 5.97×10^{24} kg (5,970 Yg), mostly composed of iron (32.1%), oxygen (30.1%), silicon (15.1%), magnesium (13.9%), sulphur (2.9%), nickel (1.8%), calcium (1.5%) and aluminum (1.4%) and 1.2% trace elements. The core is composed of iron (88.8%) with small amounts of nickel (5.8%), sulfur (4.5%) and less than 1% trace elements. Mostly rock constituents are oxides of chlorine, sulfur, and fluorine along with silica, alumina, iron oxides, lime, magnesia, potash and soda.

Earth's outer layer is silicate solid crust along with tectonic plates upon a highly viscous solid mantle (called lithosphere) separated by the Moho. The thickness of the crust varies from about 6 km (under the oceans) to 30–50 km (for lands). Under this, a relatively low-viscosity layer, the asthenosphere consists of the upper and lower mantle at 410-660 km below the surface. Below this, there is an extremely low viscous liquid outer core underlain by a solid inner core. The detailed study is given in the section 1.5 of this chapter.

Earth gets external heat from sun and other celestial bodies while it gets internal heat from a combination of residual heat from planetary accretion (about 20%) and radioactive decay (80%), mainly of isotopes K-40, U-238 and Th-232. At the center, the temperature may be up to 6,000 °C (10,830 °F), and the pressure could reach 360 GPa.

1.3 ENVIRONMENT–ATMOSPHERE–WEATHER– CLIMATE

Environment of a region refers to its surroundings or conditions in which a person, animal, or plant lives or operates. It speaks about the natural world, as a whole or in a particular geographical area, especially as affected by human activity. Thus environment is a broader term that includes not only atmosphere, but also the surroundings and their states and conditions. The **natural environment** includes complete ecological functions of all living and non-living things such as all vegetation, microorganisms, soil, rocks, water, atmosphere in all forms and states occurring as natural phenomena (not artificial) and covers all the interaction of all living species, climate, weather and natural resources that affect human survival and economic activity. The term is most often applied to the Earth (or planets or celestial bodies such as stars) or some parts of Earth.

Atmosphere (in Greek, atmos means 'vapour', and sphaira, means 'sphere') is a layer of gases surrounding a planet or a material body due to gravity. Atmosphere is a subset of environment.

The atmosphere of the Earth is mostly composed of Nitrogen (about 78%), Oxygen (about 21%), Argon (about 0.9%) with carbon dioxide and other dust and gases traces. Oxygen is mainly used by most organisms for respiration, nitrogen by bacteria and to produce ammonia used in the construction of nucleotides and amino acids and carbon dioxide is used by plants, algae and cyano-bacteria for photosynthesis. The atmosphere helps protect living organisms from genetic damage by solar UV radiation, solar wind and cosmic rays.

Weather is the state of the atmosphere, to the degree of hotness or coldness, wet or dry, calm or stormy, clear or cloudy etc., and mostly occurs in the lowest level of the atmosphere i.e., the troposphere, below the stratosphere. It also refers to day-to-day temperature and precipitation, while climate is the term for the averaging of atmospheric/weather conditions over longer periods of time.

Weather is governed by differences of air pressure, temperature and moisture between places which occur due to the sun's angle, latitude and other reasons discussed in the above paragraphs of this chapter.

Climate is the statistics of weather assessed the variation patterns of temperature, humidity, pressure, wind, precipitation, atmospheric particle count and other meteorological variables in a given region over long periods. A region's climate is described by five components, viz. atmosphere, hydrosphere, cryosphere, lithosphere and biosphere. Climate differs from weather in terms of time frame i.e. weather refers to short-term conditions of these variables in a given region while climate refers long term conditions. The following table distinguishes between weather and climate clearly.

The climate of a location is affected by its latitude, terrain, altitude and water bodies and their currents. Climates are classified based on the average ranges of temperature and precipitation. The most common classification is given by Koppen-Gieger. Paleoclimatology is the study of ancient climates.

Distinction between Weather and Climate

No	Weather	Climate
1.	It is a short-term phenomenon	It is long-term phenomenon
2.	The state of the atmosphere, to the degree of hotness or coldness, wet or dry, calm or stormy, clear or cloudy etc.	The statistics of weather assessed by variation patterns in temperature, humidity, pressure, wind, precipitation, atmospheric particle count etc., in a region over long period.
3.	Described by temperature, pressure and humidity due to sun's angle, latitude and other reasons	Described by changes of temperature and pressure in 5 components, viz., Atmosphere, hydrosphere, cryosphere, lithosphere and biosphere.
4.	Study of weather is Meteorology	Study of climate is climatology
5.	It is an information of instantaneous conditions	It is an information of averaging conditions

1.3.1 Classification of Climate

Koppen-Gieger classified the climates in five broad groups as given below. However, these may be further divided into more specific subtypes based on temperature and precipitation.

(i) Humid tropics (ii) Arid

(iii) Humid middle latitudes (iv) Continental

(v) Cold polar

Since the amount of solar energy reaching Earth's surface decreases with increasing latitude, perhaps, the simplest way of classifying the climates is based on the latitudes of the region. At higher latitudes, the sunlight reaches the surface at lower angles, and it must pass through thicker columns of the atmosphere. As a result, the mean annual air temperature at Sea Level (SL) decreases by about 0.4°C (0.7°F) per degree of latitude from the equator. Earth's surface can be subdivided into specific latitudinal belts (equator to the poles) with nearly homogeneous climate as; these are

- Tropical (or equatorial) climate
- Subtropical climate
- Temperate climate
- Polar climate

1.3.2 Factors Influencing Climate (in addition to latitude factor)

Undoubtedly, climate is largely influenced by the latitude and the tilt of the earth and the climate of a region is characterized by the latitudinal aspects and features as discussed above. Though the climate can be described based on the latitudes, yet there are several anomalies, which may attributed to the local conditions and other reasons. The following are a few:

- **Nearness to oceans:** Proximity to oceans moderates the climate e.g., Scandinevian region has more moderate climate than at similar northern latitudes of N.Canada.
- **The wind direction effect:** The windward side of land gets more moderation than the leeward side. In the N. Hemisphere; the wind is west-to-east, and so western coasts would be milder than eastern. In the S. Hemisphere, wind is east-to-west, and so eastern coasts are milder.
- **The distance from the Earth to the Sun variation:** The Earth is closest to the Sun (at perihelion) in January, which is summer in the S. Hemisphere; winter for N. Hemisphere. Similarly, it is furthest away (at aphelion) in July, and so is summer in the N. Hemisphere and winter in South. Only 93.55% solar radiation of Sun falls on a given square area of land than at perihelion.
- **The heat transfer variation between land and ocean regions:** Land gets heated faster and cools faster while water gets heated slower and cools slower. This heat transfer variation makes a lot of difference in the climate. We know that there is larger land mass in the N. Hemisphere, and thence easier to heat than the seas. Consequently, summers are 2.3 °C (4 °F) warmer in the N. Hemisphere than in the Southern Hemisphere under similar conditions.
- **Altitude from Sea Level (SL):** The climate is colder at high altitudes than at sea level because of the decreased air density.
- **Tilted Earth and angle of incidence of sun rays:** Since the Earth is slightly tilted, the sun rays will not be at same angle at all places. This also, influences the climate considerably.

The highest air temperature ever measured on Earth was 56.7 °C (134.1 °F) in Furnace Creek, California in Death Valley, in 1913. The lowest air temperature measured on Earth was –89.2 °C (–128.6 °F) at Vostok Station in 1983, but satellites records read lowest at –94.7°C (–138.5 °F) at 81.8°S 59.3°E, along a ridge between Dome Argus and Dome Fuji, at 3,900 m elevation.

Above the troposphere, the atmosphere up to Karman line (supposed as boundary between atmosphere and outer space) about 100 km up is usually divided into the stratosphere, mesosphere, thermosphere exosphere and magnetosphere. These are described at length in the sections 1.4 and 1.5 of this chapter to follow.

SELF ASSESSMENT INTERMISSION (SAI – 1.1)

1. What do you understand by the terms 'Ecological System' and 'Ecological Balance'? Discuss what happens if ecological imbalance occurs?
2. Give a brief account of Geography and Ecology of Earth.
3. Do you think ecological balance is the key to disaster control? Justify.
4. Describe briefly, the formation of Earth and its geography and its environment.
5. Define and distinguish the terms environment, atmosphere, climate and weather.
6. What are the effects of axial tilt of the Earth in its rotation?
7. Give briefly, the internal structure of the Earth.
8. Distinguish between Climate and Weather.
9. What are the five components of climate? Give brief notes.
10. What are the factors influencing climate of a region? Explain briefly.
11. What is meant by atmosphere? How is it different from weather?

1.4 THE SPHERES OF EARTH

No doubt, the Earth is big sphere, but there are many big spheres on the Earth, virtually revolving around it. To get an overview of the Earth, we should understand these spheres listed below.

1. Pedosphere – concerned with the surface of Earth
2. Hydrosphere – related to the waters on Earth
3. Cryosphere – speaks about the icy regions on Earth
4. Atmosphere – connected to the weather, climate and all about air on Earth
5. Magnetosphere – means the magnetism of the Earth
6. Biosphere – The Life on the Earth

We shall now discuss about the above spheres in brief.

1.4.1 Pedosphere – The Superficial Earth

The Earth's TSA is about 510 million km^2 (197 million sq mi) of which 70.8%, i.e. 361.13 million km^2 (139.43 million sq mi), is under (sea/ocean) water containing continental shelf, mountains, volcanoes, oceanic trenches, submarine canyons, oceanic plateaus, abyssal plains, and a globe-spanning mid-ocean ridge system. The remaining 29.2% (148.94 million km^2, or 57.51 million sq mi) varies greatly from place to place and consists of mountains, deserts, plains, plateaus, and other productive and non-productive landforms. However, the tectonics, erosion, volcanic eruptions, flooding, weathering, glaciations, the growth of coral reefs, and meteorite impacts are those some of which reshape the Earth's surface over geological time.

The continental crust consists of lower density material such as the igneous rocks granite and andesitic with some basalt (a denser volcanic rock), sedimentary and metamorphic rock while the pedosphere (surface) is most abundant with soil containing silicate minerals such as quartz, feldspar, mica, etc along with carbonates like lime stone (calcite), dolomite etc.

The elevation of the land surface varies from the low point of –418 m at the Dead Sea, to a maximum altitude of 8,848 m at the top of Mount Everest while the mean height is 840 m above SL.

The total arable land is 10.9% of the land surface, with 1.3% being permanent cropland. Close to 40% of Earth's land surface is used for cropland and pasture, or an estimated 1.3×10^7 km^2 of cropland and 3.4×10^7 km^2 of pastureland.

1.4.2 Hydrosphere – The Wet Globe

The abundance of water distinguishes the Earth as "Blue Planet" from other planets of the Solar System. Earth's hydrosphere is composed of oceans (major portion-nearly 1.35×10^{18} MT i.e. 1/4400 of total Earth's mass) along with inland seas, lakes, rivers, creeks and underground waters such as wells and springs down to a depth of 2,000 m. The deepest (10,911.4 m) underwater location is Challenger Deep of the Mariana Trench in the Pacific Ocean. The oceans cover an area of 3.6×10^8 km^2 with a mean depth of 3682 m, resulting in an estimated volume of 1.332×10^9 km^3. About 97.5% of the water is saline and only 2.5% is fresh water. Most fresh water, about 68.7%, is present as ice in ice caps and glaciers. The average salinity of oceans is about 35 g/kg of sea water (3.5% salt) most of which was released from volcanic activity or cool igneous rocks. Shifts in the oceanic temperature distribution can cause significant weather shifts, such as the El-Nino (Southern shift) and La-Nino (Northern shift).

1.4.3 Cryosphere – The Cool World

The **cryosphere** (cryo refers to "cold, frost or ice" and sphere means "globe or ball") refers to those portions of Earth's surface where water is in solid form, such as sea/lake/river ice, snow cover, glaciers, ice caps/sheets, and frozen ground including permafrost. Thus, it is an integral part of the global climate system that widely overlaps with the hydrosphere. It influences surface energy and moisture fluxes, clouds, precipitation, hydrology, atmospheric and oceanic circulation. Cryology is the study of cryospheres.

1.4.4 Atmosphere – The Sphere of Air

The Earth's surface has an atmosphere averaging 101.325 KPa with a scale height of about 8.5 km. It has a composition of 78% N_2 and 21% O_2, with traces of H_2O and CO_2, and other gaseous molecules. The height of the troposphere varies with latitude, ranging between 8 km at the poles to 17 km at the equator, with some variation resulting from weather and seasonal factors. The detailed discussion is given in section 1.5 of this chapter. However, an overview is given here below.

Strictly speaking, there is no definite boundary to Earth's atmosphere as it slowly becomes thinner and fades into outer space. About ¾ of the atmosphere's mass is within the first 11 km (6.8 mi) of the surface, called the troposphere (lowest layer). Energy from the Sun heats this layer (and the surface below) causing expansion of the air. Obviously, this lower-density air rises up replaced by cooler, higher-density air, which is known as atmospheric circulation that governs the weather and climate through redistribution of thermal energy. These circulation bands are known to be trade winds in the equatorial region below 30° latitude and the westerlies in the mid-latitudes (30°–60°). In addition to this the weather and climate is characterized by Ocean currents and particularly the thermohaline circulation (distribution of thermal energy from the equatorial oceans to polar oceans).

Water vapor through surface evaporation moves up into atmosphere in circulatory patterns and as the conditions favour for an uplift of warm, humid air, this water condenses and precipitates to fall on the surface. This precipitation fall depends on atmospheric circulation, topographic features, and temperature differences of the given region. Most of the fallen water is then flows down by river systems and usually returned to the oceans or lakes. This water cycle is a vital for life on land and at the same time a chief factor of erosion.

1.4.5 Magnetosphere – The Attractive World

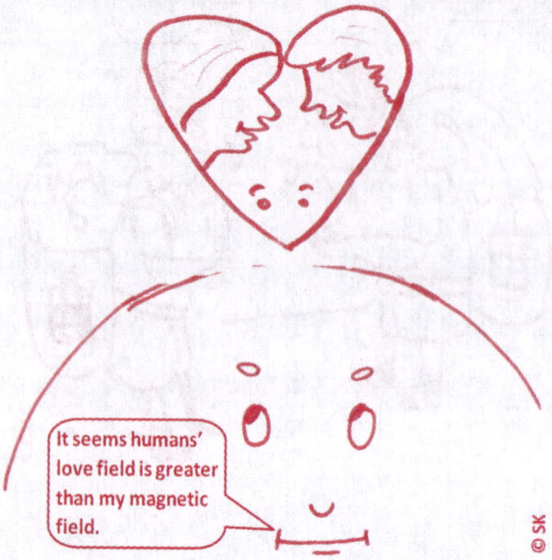

The extent to which Earth's magnetic field is felt can be termed as the magnetosphere. Since the solar rays are electromagnetic waves, the ions and electrons of the solar wind are deflected by the magnetosphere. So, the solar wind pressure compresses the dayside of the magnetosphere, while extends the night-side magnetosphere into a long tail. This considerably changes the climatic conditions in several ways.

During magnetic storms, the charged particles get deflected from the outer magnetosphere (magnetotail), directed along field lines into Earth's ionosphere, where atmospheric atoms can be excited and ionized, causing the Aurora.

Magnetic field

The Earth's magnetic field is generated in the core and extends outwards through the mantle, and up to Earth's surface, where it is, approximately, a dipole located close to Earth's geographic poles (The Earth's Geographic North is its Magnetic South and vice-versa). At the equator of the magnetic field, the magnetic-field strength at the surface is 3.05×10^{-5} T, with global magnetic dipole moment of 7.91×10^{15} T-m^3.

Gravitational field

The gravity of Earth causes the acceleration to objects due to the distribution of mass within the Earth. On the surface of Earth the acceleration due to gravity is about 9.81 m/s^2 or 32 ft/s^2 which may vary according to the height, depth, latitude, topographic and geological conditions. However, the gravitational constant described by Newton's law of universal gravitation (the force of attraction between any two bodies is directly proportional to their product of masses and is inversely proportional to the square of the distance between their centers) is given by $G = 6.674 \times 10^{-11}$ m^3 kg^{-1} s^{-2}.

1.4.6 Biosphere – The Lively World

A planet is said to be habitable if it can sustain life, even though life did not originate there. The total of the planet's life inhabit ecosystems is often called "biosphere". Earth provides liquid water environment where complex organic molecule can assemble and interact with metabolism on getting sufficient energy. Great the God's creation! The distance of Earth from the sun, its orbital eccentricity, rate of rotation, axial tilt, geological history, cycling hydrosphere,

Estimation of human land use (2000)	
Land use	**Mha**
Cropland	1,510–1,611
Pastures	2,500–3,410
Natural forests	3,143–3,871
Planted forests	126–215
Urban areas	66–351
Unused, productive land	356–445

sustaining atmosphere, and magnetic field all together contribute to the current living climatic conditions (habitable) at the surface.

The air on the earth has large influence on its biosphere while the life on Earth's has a significant impact on its atmosphere. Earth's biosphere is believed to have started about 3.5 Gya.

It is believed that the outcome of Oxygenic photosynthesis about 2.7 Gya is today's nitrogen–oxygen atmosphere, creation of aerobic organism and also the Ozone layer that permits living-hood by stopping UV radiation as well as burning up small meteors before they strike the surface, and moderating temperature. This last phenomenon is known as the Greenhouse Effect. The trace molecules such as water vapor, carbon dioxide, methane, nitrous oxide (precisely called greenhouse gases) in the atmosphere capture thermal energy emitted from the ground and thence raise the mean temperature. Without this heat-retention effect, the mean surface temperature would have been "18 °C, instead of today's +15 °C, and life on Earth probably would not exist like what is today.

The biosphere is divided into a number of biomes, inhabited by broadly similar plants and animals. On land, biomes are separated primarily by differences in latitude, height above SL, humidity and so forth. About 7½ billion humans survive on Earth and depend on its biosphere and minerals. Humans have developed diverse societies and cultures. Politically, the globe has about 200 countries.

Humans discovered the Earth's natural non-renewable resources (which can only renew over geological timescales) such as fossil fuels in the form of solids (coal), liquids (petroleum), and gases (natural gas). Also humans found mineral bodies on the earth crust for various applications. Earth's biosphere produces many useful biological products for humans, like food, fuel, wood, medicines and the recyclable organic wastes. The land-based ecosystems depend on topsoil and fresh water, while the oceanic ecosystems depend on dissolved nutrients washed down from the land.

SELF ASSESSMENT INTERMISSION (SAI – 1.2)

1. What do you understand by the terms 'Pedosphere' and 'Biosphere'? Discuss.
2. Distinguish between Hydrosphere and Cryosphere of the Earth. Describe the significance of their existence on the earth.
3. What is atmosphere? What are its components? How is useful to the livelihood?
4. What is magnetosphere? What is its significance on the earth?
5. What do you understand by the term 'Biosphere'? Explain in detail.

1.5 THE ANATOMY OF THE EARTH

The sequence of the principal layers is as shown in the following figure:

Above From Earth	Below From Earth
1. Crust	1. Crust
2. Troposphere	2. Lithosphere
3. Atmosphere	3. Aesthenosphere
4. Stratosphere	4. Upper Mantle
5. Mesosphere	5. Mantle
6. Thermosphere	6. Outer Core
7. Exosphere	7. Inner Core

A: Mohorovic discontinuity – B: Gutenberg discontinuity – C: Lehmann–Bullen discontinuity.

1.5.1 Principal Layers

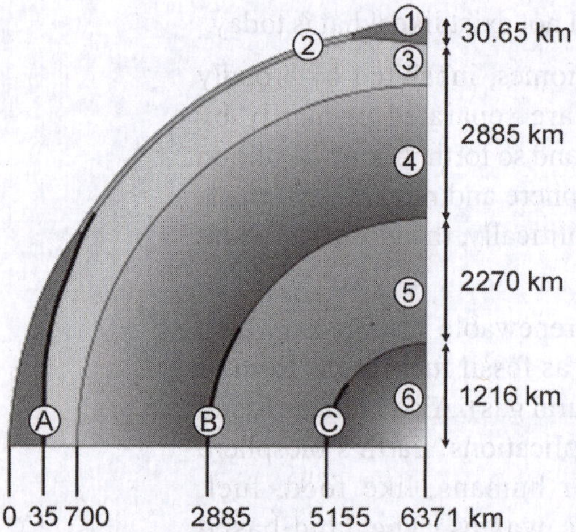

The earth is made up of several layers in spherical shells like an onion or cabbage, with distinguishable structure characterized by their physical/chemical or rheological properties. Let us understand these layers starting from the space toward the centre of the Earth.

The region above the Earth's surface, up to the space, is filled with the air having a set of spherical layers is often referred to as the atmosphere. Generally, air pressure and density decrease with altitude in this atmosphere. Of course, the temperature has a complicated profile with altitude, and may remain relatively constant or even increase with altitude in some regions. With reference to these changes, the Earth's atmosphere can be classified (called atmospheric stratification) into five main layers from highest to lowest, as given below:

1. Exosphere: 700 to 10,000 km (440 to 6,200 miles)
2. Thermosphere: 80 to 700 km (50 to 440 miles)
3. Mesosphere: 50 to 80 km (31 to 50 miles)
4. Stratosphere: 12 to 50 km (7 to 31 miles)
5. Troposphere: 0 to 12 km (0 to 7 miles)

Do You Know?

14 Lokas according to Hindu Myths

As per Hindu myths there are 14 Lokas, 7 on upper side of the Earth while 7 on downside. The seven upper lokas are Bhulok, Bhuvarlok, Suvarlok, Maharlok, Thapolok, and Sathyalok. The lower seven are Athala, Vithala, Suthala, Mahaathala, Thalaathala, Rasathala and Pathaala lokas.

Perhaps! These are the seven layers on either sides (above and below) the earth crust.

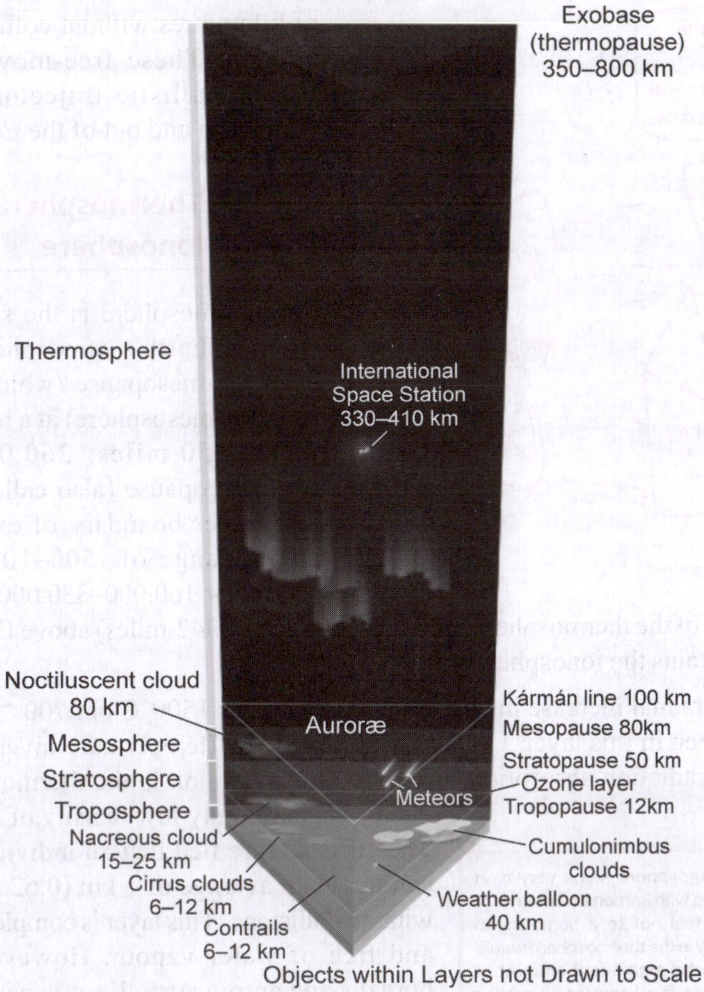

1.5.2 Exosphere

The exosphere is the outermost layer (i.e. the upper limit) extends from the exobase located at the top of the thermosphere at a height of about 700 km above SL, to about 10,000 km (6,200 miles; 33,000,000 ft). The exosphere merges with the vacuum of outer space, where there is no atmosphere.

> **Do You Know?**
>
> The exosphere is located too far above Earth for any meteorological phenomena to be possible. However, the aurora borealis and aurora australis sometimes occur in the lower part of exosphere, when they overlap into the thermosphere. The exosphere contains most of the satellites orbiting Earth.

This layer chiefly consists of very low densities of hydrogen, helium and some heavier molecules including nitrogen, oxygen and carbon dioxide closer to the exobase. Strictly speaking, the exosphere does not behave like a gas, and the particles constantly escape into space, because the atoms and molecules are so far apart that they can travel hundreds

of kilometres without colliding with one another. These free-moving particles follow ballistic trajectories and may migrate in and out of the magnetosphere.

1.5.3 Thermosphere and Ionosphere

The thermosphere is the second-highest layer of Earth's atmosphere extending from the mesopause (which separates it from the mesosphere) at a height of about 80 km (50 miles; 260,000 ft) up to the thermopause (also called exobase as it is lower boundary of exosphere) at a height range of 500–1000 km (310–620 miles; 160,000–330,000 ft). The lower part of the thermosphere, from 80-550 km (50-342 miles) above Earth's surface, contains the ionosphere.

Gradual increase in temperature (as high as 1500°C or 2700 °F) with height is seen in this layer. Unlike the stratosphere, (temperature inversion is due to the radiation absorption by ozone), the inversion in the thermosphere occurs due to the extremely low density of its molecules. The air is so rare fied that an individual molecule can travel an average of 1 km (0.62 mile; 3300 ft) without collisions. This layer is completely cloudless and free of water vapour. However the aurora borealis and aurora australis are occasionally seen in the thermosphere. The International Space Station orbits in this layer, between 320 and 380 km (200 and 240 mi).

Do You Know?

Even though the thermosphere has a very high proportion of molecules with immense amounts of energy, it would not feel hot to a human skin because the low density in the thermosphere would not be able to conduct a significant amount of energy to or from the skin. In other words, a person would not feel warm because of the thermosphere's extremely low pressure.

1.5.4 Mesosphere

The mesosphere is the third highest layer of Earth's atmosphere, occupying the region above stratosphere and below thermosphere i.e., from the stratopause at a height about 50 km (31 miles; 160,000 ft) to the mesopause at 80–85 km (50–53 miles; 260,000–280,000 ft) above sea level.

Temperatures drop with increase in height to the mesopause that marks the top of this middle layer of the atmosphere. It is the coldest place on Earth (an average temperature around “85°C; “120°F; 190 K). These are the highest clouds in the atmosphere visible to the naked eye if sunlight reflects off them about an hour or two after sunset or before sunrise (i.e. when Sun is around 4° to 16° below the horizon). This type of lightning referred to as either SPRITES or ELVES occasionally form far above tropospheric thunderclouds. The mesosphere is mainly accessed by sounding rockets. Be happy! The mesosphere is also the layer where most meteors burn up upon atmospheric entrance.

1.5.5 Stratosphere

The stratosphere is the second-lowest layer of Earth's atmosphere, above the troposphere (about 12 km; 7.5 miles; 39,000 ft above Earth's surface) separated by the tropopause to the stratopause at a height about 50 to 55 km (31 to 34 miles; 164,000 to 180,000 ft).

The pressure at the top of the stratosphere is around 1/1000 of that at sea level. It consists of the ozone layer, which is the part of Earth's atmosphere. In this layer also temperatures rise with increasing height. But, this rise is due to the absorption of ultraviolet radiation (UV) radiation from the Sun by the ozone layer, which restricts turbulence and mixing. What a wonderful Earth!

Although the temperature may be "60°C" ("76°F; 210K") at the tropopause, the top of the stratosphere is much warmer, and may be near 0 °C. The stratosphere is almost free of clouds rarely nacreous clouds are seen in the lower part where the air is coldest. Perhaps! This is the highest layer that can be accessed by an aircraft.

1.5.6 Troposphere

The troposphere is the lowest layer of Earth's atmosphere, distributed from Earth's surface to an average height of about 12 km; this height actually varies from 9 km (30,000 ft) at the poles to 17 km (56,000 ft) at the equator, with some variation due to weather. The troposphere is bounded above by the tropopause, a boundary marked in most places by a temperature inversion (i.e. a layer of relatively warm air above a colder one), and in others by a zone which is isothermal with height.

Although variations occur, the temperature usually declines with increasing altitude in the troposphere because the tropospheric heat is through energy transfer from the surface. Thus, the lowest part of the troposphere (i.e. Earth's surface) is typically the warmest section of the troposphere. This promotes vertical mixing. The troposphere contains roughly 80% of the mass of Earth's atmosphere. The layer is denser than all its atmospheric layers because a larger atmospheric weight sits on top of the troposphere and causes it to be most severely compressed. Fifty percent of the total mass of the atmosphere is located in the lower 5.6 km (18,000 ft) of the troposphere. It is primarily composed of nitrogen (78%) and oxygen (21%) with only small concentrations of other trace gases. Most of Earth's weather is due to the water vapour or moisture that comes from the surface and is basically all the weather-associated cloud genus by active wind circulation. Most conventional aviation activity takes place in the troposphere, and is the only layer accessed by propeller-driven aircraft.

Fig: Space Shuttle Endeavour orbiting in the thermosphere. Because of the angle of the photo, it appears to straddle the stratosphere and mesosphere that actually lie more than 250 km below. The orange layer is the troposphere, which gives way to the whitish stratosphere and then the blue mesosphere.

1.5.7 Other Layers

Within the five principal layers that are largely determined by temperature, several secondary layers may be distinguished by other properties:

- The ozone layer about 2 to 8 ppm, at the lower portion of the stratosphere from about 15–35 km (9.3–21.7 miles; 49,000–115,000 ft), being about 90% in the stratosphere.
- The ionosphere is ionized by solar radiation, is responsible for auroras. During daytime hours, it stretches from 50 to 1,000 km (31 to 621 miles; 160,000 to 3,280,000 ft) and includes by the mesosphere, thermosphere, and parts of the exosphere.
- The homosphere and heterosphere are defined by whether the atmospheric gases are well mixed. This relatively homogeneous layer ends at the turbopause i.e. at about 100 km (62 mi; 330,000 ft), which places it about 20 km (12 mi; 66,000 ft) above the mesopause. Above this height lies the heterosphere, which includes the exosphere and most of the thermosphere.
- The planetary boundary layer is the part of the troposphere closest to Earth's surface. The depth of this layer ranges from as little as about 100 meters on clear/calm nights to 3000 m or more during the afternoon in dry regions.

The average temperature of the atmosphere at Earth's surface is 14 °C (57 °F; 287 K) or 15 °C (59 °F; 288 K), depending on the reference.

SELF ASSESSMENT INTERMISSION (SAI – 1.3)

1. What do you understand by the terms 'Anatomy of Earth'? What are its constituents? Discuss.
2. What is "Earth's Atmosphere"? How do you classify it?
3. What is Stratification of Earth's atmosphere? Discuss briefly each layer.
4. What are mesosphere and stratosphere?
5. What are thermosphere and ionosphere? Brief out.
6. What are troposphere and exosphere? What differences do you observe between these two?
7. Distinguish between homosphere and heterosphere. Write a note on atmosphere of earth.
8. What are mesopause, tropopause, stratopause and exobase?
9. List out and briefly describe the principal layers of atmosphere above the earth.
10. Write short notes on (a) Mesosphere (b) Stratosphere (c) Thermosphere (d) Troposphere

1.6 STRUCTURE OF EARTH

Scientific understanding based on topography and bathymetry, observations of rock, volcanic material, analysis of the seismic waves, measurements of gravitational and magnetic fields and so forth, the Earth has an outer silicate solid crust, a highly viscous mantle, a liquid outer core (much less viscous than mantle), and a solid inner core.

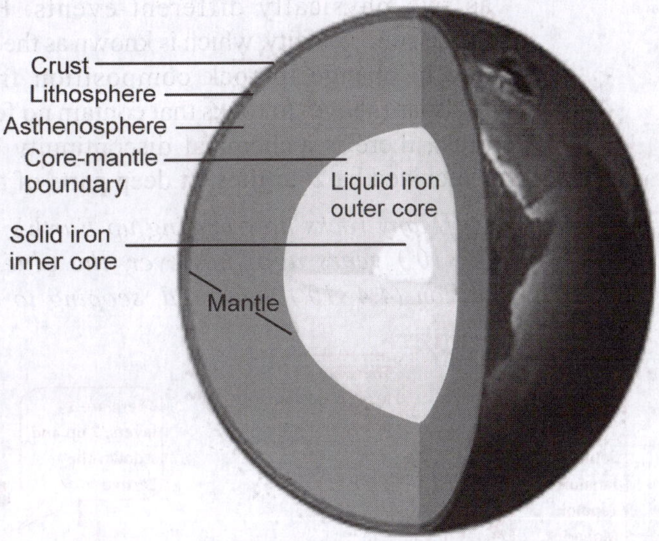

The structure of Earth can be defined in two ways: by mechanical or chemical properties. Mechanically, it can be divided into lithosphere, asthenosphere, mesospheric mantle, outer core, and the inner core. Chemically, Earth can be divided into the crust, upper mantle, lower mantle, outer core, and inner core. We shall discuss about these in detail now.

1.6.1 Crust

The crust is the outermost layer ranging from 5–70 km (3–44 miles) in depth. The oceanic crust is thin underlying the ocean basins (5–10 km) and are

Depth		Layer
Kilometers	Miles	
0–60	0–37	Lithosphere (varies between 5 and 200 km)
0–35	0–22	... Crust (varies between 5 and 70 km)
35–60	22–37	... Uppermost part of mantle
35–2,890	22–1,790	Mantle
100–200	210-270	... Upper mesosphere (upper mantle)
660–2,890	410–1,790	... Lower mesosphere (lower mantle)
2,890–5,150	1,790–3,160	Outer core
5,150–6,360	3,160–3,954	Inner core

composed of dense iron, magnesium, silicate, igneous rocks (called mafic), like basalt. The continental crust is thicker but less dense and composed of sodium, potassium, aluminium, silicate rocks (called felsic), like granite. The rocks of the crust fall into two major categories – sial (**si**licon and **al**uminium) and sima (**si**licon and **ma**gnesium) that starts about 11 km below the Conrad discontinuity (2nd order discontinuity). The uppermost mantle along with the crust constitutes the lithosphere (rocky layer). The crust-mantle boundary occurs as two physically different events. First, there is a discontinuity in the seismic velocity, which is known as the Mohorovièiæ discontinuity or Moho due to change in rock composition from rocks containing plagioclase feldspar (above) to rocks that contain no feldspars (below). Second, in oceanic crust, there is a chemical discontinuity between ultramafic cumulates and tectonized harzburgites, at deep parts of the oceanic crust.

[Many rocks now making up Earth's crust formed less than 100 million (1×10^8) years ago; however, the oldest known mineral grains are 4.4 billion (4.4×10^9) years old, scoping to estimate the age of the Earth].

1.6.2 Moho

Between the Earth's crust and the mantle is a boundary called the moho which portrays a major structural change. The **Mohorovièiæ discontinuity** (in short **moho**), discovered by Andrija Mohorovièiæ in 1909, is the boundary between the crust and the mantle of the Earth. He uncovered that there are two kinds of seismic waves produce earthquakes, the shallow slower wave arrives first, and a deep faster wave arrives second. This is due to the fact that the material of the mantle is different from that of the crust and deeper wave changed speed as it got just below the mantle. The discontinuity lies 30–40 km below the surface of continents, and less deep below the ocean floors.

1.6.3 Mantle

Earth's mantle is the thickest layer at a depth of 2,890 km. The upper mantle is divided into the lithosphere and asthenosphere. The upper and lower mantles are separated by the transition zone and the lowest part of the mantle next to the core-mantle boundary is known as the D3 layer where pressure is about 140 GPa (1.4 Matm). The mantle is composed of silicate rocks that are rich in iron and magnesium relative to the overlying crust. Though solid, due to the high temperatures within the mantle, the silicate material is sufficiently ductile to flow on very long timescales. As there is intense and increasing pressure the lower part of the mantle flows less easily than the upper mantle (chemical changes are also significant). The viscosity of the mantle ranges between 10^{21} and 10^{24} Pa·s, depending on depth.

1.6.4 Cores

The average density of surface material is about 3,000 kg/m^3 while that of the Earth is 5,515 kg/m^3. Hence, it can be concluded that denser matter exists within Earth's core. Seismic measurements show that the core is divided into two parts, a "solid" inner core with a radius of about 1,220 km and a liquid outer core up to a radius of about 3,400 km. The densities are between 9,900 and 12,200 kg/m^3 in the outer core and 12,600–13,000 kg/m^3 in the inner core.

The inner core, discovered by Inge Lehmann in 1936 is believed to be composed of iron and some nickel. According to his theory, in early stages of Earth's formation about four and a half billion (4.5×10^9) years ago, in a process called planetary differentiation, melting would have caused denser substances to sink toward the centre while less-dense materials would have migrated to the crust. The core is thus believed to largely be composed of iron (80%), along with nickel.

Thus, summarily, the Earth has an outer solid crust, a highly viscous mantle, a liquid outer core, and a solid inner core. The shape of the earth is an oblate spheroid, because it is slightly flattened at the poles and bulging at the equator. Further, the structure of the Earth has two distinct (physically and chemically different) separating layers. The boundaries between these layers were discovered by seismographs which showed the way vibrations bounced off the layers during earthquakes. The following are note worthy points.

1. The **crust** is the outermost layer of the Earth mostly made of sial (silicon = Si; aluminium = Al) or felsic.
2. The **mantle** is the layer of the Earth right below the crust made of **sima** (Si + ma for magnesium) or mafic. The mantle itself is divided into layers as listed below.
   (a) The uppermost part of the mantle is solid, and is the base of the crust generally made of the heavy rock peridotite. The continental and oceanic plates together form the lithosphere plates floating on the semi-liquid asthenosphere
   (b) Upper asthenosphere: magma
   (c) Lower asthenosphere
   (d) Lower mantle
3. The **core** is made of solid iron and nickel, and is about 5000–6000°C.
   (a) **Outer core** is a liquid layer below the mantle,
   (b) **Inner core** the very center of the Earth, is very hot but solid due to the high pressure.
   With the increasing heat and pressure makes the changes in the crystallization of minerals, such that the composition might be a kind of changing mixture of liquid and crystals.
4. The change-over, called **discontinuities** between the layers are clearly distinguishable by boundaries
   (a) Moho: A boundary that separates the earth's crust and the mantle.
   (b) Guttenberg discontinuity: This is the boundary that separates the Earth's mantle and the outer core
   (c) Lehmann discontinuity: This boundary separates the inner and outer cores of the Earth.

1.7 ARE WE SAFE ON THE EARTH?

The God has created this Earth which seems to have all good conditions and climate for living. No other planet has the habitability. But at the same time, he has created the environment around capable of mass killing, large destruction and becoming disastrous. No land on the earth is 100% safe. And the five natural forces earth, sky, water, air and fire can anytime move to extreme conditions.

1.7.1 The Present of The Earth

Large areas of Earth's surface have extreme weathers vulnerable to tropical cyclones, hurricanes/ typhoons that dominate life in those areas. (These events caused on average 11,800 human deaths per year during 1980-2000). Many places are subject to earthquakestsunamis, rockslides, mudslides, landslides, volcanic eruptions, tornados, blizzards, hot/cold waves, floods, hailstorms rainstorms, droughts, wild fires, and so on.

Many localized areas are subject to human-made air/water pollution, acid rain and toxic substances, loss of vegetation (due to overgrazing, deforestation, desertification etc.), loss of wildlife, species extinction, soil degradation, depletion, erosion and so forth. Universally agreed scientifically proven fact is global warming due to industrial (COx, SOx and NOx) emissions. Further, huge changes are predicted such as the melting of glaciersice sheets, extreme temperature ranges, significant weather fluctuation and changes in average Sea level (SL).

1.7.2 The Future of The Earth

In long-term, future of the earth, is expected to be disastrous with reference to the Sun. The following hazards are predicted (A 2008 simulation model).

- In next 1.1 Ga, solar luminosity increases by 10% and over the next 3.5 Ga by 40%.
- Surface temperature increase speeds up the inorganic CO_2 cycle,
- CO_2 concentration levels drastically go down for plants (10ppm for C4 photosynthesis) in approximately 500–900 Ma.
- Lack of vegetation leads to the loss of oxygen in the atmosphere, by which animal life becomes extinct.
- After another billion years all surface water disappear
- The mean global temperature will reach 70°C (158°F) in a billion years.
- The Earth may be habitable for another 500 Ma only.
- Nitrogen will be removed from the atmosphere in 2.3 Ga.
- Even if the Sun were eternal, 27% of the water in the oceans descends into the mantle in 1 billion years, due to reduced steam venting from mid-ocean ridges.

- The Sun becomes red giant in about 5 Ga.
- The Sun will expand to roughly 1 AU (150,000,000 km), i.e. 250 times its present radius.
- As a red giant, the Sun will lose about 30% of its mass, thence without tidal effects, Earth shifts to an orbit 1.7 AU from the Sun while the star reaches its maximum radius.
- The Sun's increased luminosity destroys life at the rate about 5,000 times of present level
- Earth's orbit will eventually decay due to tidal effects and drag, causing it to enter the Sun's atmosphere and be vaporized.

Whether the points stated in the above model are right or wrong, happen or not, it is certain that the situations predicted will very soon reach if we do not realize to save, conserve and preserve our present environment. It is high time to realize this fact and to act accordingly, otherwise our future generations will never forgive us. Of course! We cannot stop certain things which are not in our hands, but we can at least try to prevent their early arrival or postpone to the extent possible. We must set our hands together to fight against such evils and manage those aspects which are under our control.

SELF ASSESSMENT INTERMISSION (SAI – 1.4)

1. What is "the structure of the Earth"? How do you classify it?
2. What are Moho and Guttenberg and Lehmann discontinuities?
3. What are lithosphere and aesthenosphere? Briefly discuss.
4. What is mantle? What is it made up of? What differences do you observe between upper and lower mantle?
5. Distinguish between inner and outer core. Write a note on the cores of earth.
6. List out and briefly describe the principal layers below the earth's crust?
7. What are Crust, Moho, Mantles and Cores of the earth?
8. Where are Sima (or mafic), Sial (or felsic) and magma found inside the earth? What are these?
9. With reference to the earth structure write short notes on (a) Crust (b) Lithosphere (c) Discontinuities (d) Troposphere and their properties.
10. Discuss what could be the future of the Earth about a billion years later.

MINI-PROJECTS - CASE STUDIES

Search websites, books and all possible literature in print or audio/ video lectures etc., and prepare essays or presentations of the following. You discuss with your colleagues or classmates. You may conduct a competition of presentations or short-film or documentary etc.

Many natural disasters occurred in past 100 years. Search and browse them to list out the top ten. As a sample, three of the worst events of their kind are given below. Prepare a presentation for each of the following.

1. **Indian Ocean Tsunami:** The December 26, 2004 tsunami was triggered by a 9-magnitude quake under the Indian Ocean, near Sumatra. It had the energy of 20,000+ Hiroshima-type A-bombs. Across 15 countries over 230,000 were estimated to have lost their lives and 1.69 million displaced. Damages were estimated to be about $10 billion.
2. **Bhola Cyclone:** Considered to be the deadliest tropical cyclone ever, Bhola hit the then East Pakistan coast on November 12, 1970. Over 5 lakh people died. According to World Bank the estimated cost of rebuilding the ravaged areas was $188 million (1970 figure). Government mismanagement over relief operations was one of the reasons for the birth of Bangladesh.
3. **China Floods:** It was actually a series of floods that caused damage across central China during the summer months of 1931. Water levels in rivers had risen dangerously on the back of heavy rainfall. Regular cyclones worsened things. Western estimates suggest that the death toll reached 4 million.

DO YOU KNOW

The Birth of Earth...

Here is the story how mother earth was born...

Scientists believe that, we were once not alone in our orbit around the Sun – we had a "twin" planet, called Theia, (size of Mars) and was 60° away of the Big Blue Ball (Earth). About 4.533 billion years ago, Theia crashed into the Earth; most of the planet was absorbed, but a large chunk blew off and combined with materials from the planet to create the Moons. In fact, the Earth may once have had two moons. A teensy second moon, spanning ~1,200 km (750 mi) wide may have orbited Earth before it catastrophically slammed into the other one. This titanic clash can explain why the two sides of the surviving moon are so different from each other. That's the birth of the earth and now its age is above 4.5 Billion Years. **And...**

The Worth of Earth...

Here are some noteworthy points of earth.

1. For convenience of explanation, earth is assumed sphere but not exactly; it is a squashed sphere.
2. Do you have a desire of weight loss or weight gain, you don't need to do any exercise nor use any medicines, but just go to Equator to weigh less while go to Poles to weigh more.
3. Earth is 5th largest planet in terms of size and mass. Its circumference at equator is 40,075 km.
4. The diameter from the N to S pole is shorter than that across the Equator by 43 Km.
5. The point on equator moves fast, while that at N/S Pole will be perfectly still.
6. Like earthquake, there exist moonquakes also. Of course! They are less common and less intense.
7. The earth's hottest spot is in Libya at *El Azizia* that recorded 57.8 °C on Sept 13, 1922.
8. The coldest place on the earth is in Antarctica where the temperature falls to -73 °C.
9. Russia's Vostok Station as -89.2 °C on July 21, 1983 recorded the lowest temperature on earth.

10. Earth has uneven gravity. The Hudson of Canada has lower gravity than other regions.
11. The earth poles flip-flops about every 2,00,000 - 3,00,000 years.
12. Mt Everest is not the only tallest mountain. There's tie between Mt Everest and Mauna Kea.
13. Existence of water in liquid phase on earth is due to the temperature span on earth (0 – 100 ^{0}C).
14. Earth is the only planet where water can be present in all the three states or phases.
15. We are all travelling around the sun at an average velocity of 1,07,182 kmph.
16. Though earth is made up of >70% of water, it accounts for <1% of Earth's mass.
17. Earth has only one moon whereas Jupiter has highest number of (67) moons.
18. The same side of moon is always facing earth, means moon is synchronously rotating with earth.
19. Earth is the only planet not named after a Greek or Roman God.
20. Speed of rotation of earth is gradually slowing. After 140 million yrs, a day would be 25 hrs.
21. Earth is also known as Blue Planet due its bluish appearance from the outer space.
22. The extra 0.2564 day of a year (365.2564) is adjusted with an extra day in February of leap year.
23. Sea levels on Earth would rise about 60 m if all the ice in Antarctica were to melt.
24. Antarctica holds about 90% of the Earth's ice and 70% of Earth's fresh water.
25. Lake Baikal in Russia has 20% of Earth's unfrozen fresh water. It is the deepest and oldest lake.
26. The only man-made monument that is visible from the moon/space is The Great Wall of China.
27. The light that you are seeing or feeling now is approx. 8 min and 20 sec old at Sun.
28. Mawsynram, Meghalaya, India is the wettest on land of Earth with annual rainfall of 11,871 mm.
29. Dry Valleys in Antarctica is the driest on Earth, never saw rainfall from the past 2 million yrs.
30. Maldives is the flattest country.
31. Nile is the longest river (6,695 km) flowing from Burundi to Mediterranean Sea. Besides being widest, Amazon is the biggest river in terms of water flowing down. Congo River is the deepest.
32. About 1500 minerals are still undiscovered, though aware of >5000, many still unknown.
33. Some rocks on Earth move by themselves, of course minutely, but their movement is certain.
34. ***Perihelion*** ($1.471X10^{11}$m)/***Aphelion*** ($1.521X10^{11}$m) are min/max distance between Earth & Sun
35. An asteroid/comet may hit earth to devastate life, e.g. 65 million yrs ago, it wiped out dinosaurs.
36. Since recording began (1880), **2016 was the hottest year ever,** 1.69°F above mean of 20th century
37. There are 3 crater lakes – Nyos, Monoun, and Kivu, in Cameroon, on the border of Rwanda and Congo. They spit CO_2 at an enormous level and killed 100's of people in the past.
38. The peak of Ecuador's Mt Chimborazo, located just 1° S of equator and highest point on Earth.
39. **An ocean of water exists at a depth of 1,000 km under the surface of Earth.** This is important for volcanic activity, which in turn is responsible for generating soil.
40. Made of millions of tiny polyps, coral reefs are the largest living structures on Earth. But, the largest single living thing (apart from reefs) is mushroom fungus in Oregon, grew to 2,200 acres
41. The world's largest earthquake was with a magnitude of 9.5 mile in Chile on May 22, 1960. The most active eruption on Earth is Stromboli Volcano in Italy. For the past 2,000 years it has been erupting almost continuously, thence nicknamed "Lighthouse of the Mediterranean"

CHAPTER 2 Elements of Disaster

O'MY SILENT INNER VIBES (O'M S I V – 2)

"Sun rises in the east"

Is this statement correct?

Yes! You must have said the answer 'Yes'. But think once again…and then answer.

Now, you might have realized that the statement is wrong, because the sun does not rise at all and is stationary, and in fact, earth revolves around it. Then, is it wrong statement which you have been thinking true all these years? No, there is an element of truth in it, i.e. the above statement 'Sun rises in the east' is also true. It is only an ***apparent truth***, but not real. So, let us modify the statement as…***"Sun appears to be rising in the east".***

Now is it true?

Perhaps! But, why sun appears to be rising when he is not rising at all? Then, this statement again seems to have something untrue. This is because we are comparing sun with reference to earth's motion. Thus when earth is revolving around itself, we are going tangentially downward while sun appears to be moving upward. So, the statement, ***"Sun appears to be rising in the east"*** is a ***relative truth***

Once again, let us put the question, does sun rise or appear to rise in 'the east'? What is east and what is west? Are we assuming the direction of sun with reference to the east, or direction of east with reference to sun's appearance? Strictly, speaking there is no east or west. These directions are only assumptions, with reference to the sun. We call the direction where sun appears as 'East' because, the East which you see today becomes west after six months as the earth rotates to reach other side. Moreover, from India you can reach Americal from the so called east or the west. Isit not?. So, this statement is wrong as it is only an ***assumed truth***.

But, the ***actual truth*** is ***"Sun appears to be rising in a direction in the sky called east"***.

Even the above statement has a flaw. Because, if we see from the space, or say we see from an airplane, where you cannot say what is east or west or north or south, we notice that the earth is rotating around sun and sun's rays will be falling straight at some place while slant at an angle at other places of the earth and no rays at all at some other places. And this is the ***ultimate truth***.

Thus what we hear, or see may or may not be true, since it could be either apparent truth, or relative truth, or assumed truth or actual truth or an ultimate truth. [So, do not believe instantaneously, and never make hasty decisions because a lie will always spread faster than truth].

Don't believe everything you hear, see or read. There are always three sides to a story, yours, their and the truth.

"REAL EYES REALIZE REAL LIES"

(Continued)

Sometimes, we do not give an attention to certain truths. Immaterial, whether we notice or not, obey it or not, follow it or not, accept it or not, experience it or not, the truth is always truth and ultimately occurs in some form or the other.

Of course, if we notice and observe them, we can live better, longer and happier, by being prepared to face it, or avoid it or being resilient. Of my silent inner vibes, some of such truths of nature moved my heart, let me share...

Our nature is so beautiful and we are so blessed to experience and enjoy the beauty throughout the life. Great is God, gave us all, but how much life we have to enjoy this nature? How much safe is our surround?

He gave us the earth that gives food and shelter, but can crack and burst at any time to burry.

He gave us the fire that gives light and energy- but at the same time it can burn you to ash.

He gave us the water, without which you cannot live, but it can drown you to down.

He gave us the sky to shower its blessings, but it can roar and pour cats and dogs.

He gave us the air to breathe and live, which can be hot or cold or cyclone to make breathless.

Along with the wonders, he gave us thunders. Not only cakes on hearth, but also quakes in earth. Not just a small breeze and calm always, but can harm with storm sometimes.

As we all know, the above said five great forces (The Pancha-bhoothas) help us live, as long as they are in the normal range. But when even one (or more) of them shows its anger, our survival may not be in our hands and is uncontrollable. Such a situation is **DISASTER...so...**

Avani-Shanti! Anala-Shanti! Anila-Shanti! Ambu-Shanti! Ambara-Shanti! ... Shantirevashanti!

2.1 DISASTER – DEFINITION AND CONCEPT

A disaster is a consequence of a sudden event which seriously disrupts the normal function of the society or the community to the extent that it cannot subsist without outside help, such as an earthquake, flood, riots, volcanic eruptions, health epidemic or an industrial accident and so forth.

A disaster can be any tragic event stemming from events, but not just confined to earthquakes, floods, catastrophic accidents, fires, or explosions. It is a phenomenon that can cause damage to life, property and destroy the economic, social and cultural life of human beings as well as the environment.

Disaster can be defined as the event of occurrence at the expense of a group of people exposed to a hazard, leading to a serious disruption of the functioning of a society and causing human, material, economic, environmental losses that exceed the ability of the affected community or society to cope. A disaster results from a combination of hazards and vulnerability that exceeds the capacity of a society to reduce the potential negative consequences of risk.

The World Health Organization (WHO) defines disaster as "any occurrence that causes damage, ecological disruption, loss of human life, deterioration of health and health services, on a scale sufficient to warrant an extraordinary response from outside the affected community or area."

In a simple sentence, disaster is defined as untoward and worse situation causing wide spread damage which far beyond the ability to prevent or recover.

Thus, by definition, there cannot be a perfect ideal system that prevents damage, if so; it would not be a disaster. Thus a disaster, to call disaster, has to suffocate our ability to recover. Only then we call it 'disaster'.

In simplest words

'Disaster is a crisis situation that far exceeds the capabilities'-Quarentelly (1985)

2.2 NEED FOR DISASTER MANAGEMENT

Disasters are not totally discrete events. The possibility of occurrence, time, place and severity of the disaster can be reasonably and in some cases accurately predicted with the advent of technological and scientific advances. It has been established that there is a definite pattern in their occurrences and hence we can to some extent reduce the impact of damage though we cannot reduce the extent of damage itself. This demands the study of disaster management in methodical and orderly approach.

2.3 DISASTER MANAGEMENT - DEFINITION AND CONCEPT

Disaster Management can be defined as the organization and **management** of resources and responsibilities for dealing with all humanitarian aspects of emergencies, in particular preparedness, response and recovery in order to lessen the impact of **disasters.**

Disaster management is a set of programs, measures and mitigation activities carried out before, during and after a disaster so as to avoid reduce the impact or recovering from its losses.

According to Kelly (1996), Disaster management is defined as "the range of activities designed to maintain control over disaster and emergency situations and to provide a framework for helping those who are at risk to avoid or recover from the impact of the disaster".

Thence, disaster management comprises of managing resources and shouldering various responsibilities to deal with all humanitarian aspects of emergencies. This includes preparedness and avoiding before disaster, response and resisting during the disaster, and rehabilitation and recovery (i.e. rebuilding) after the disaster, all put together, helping and supporting society during emergency.

2.4 DISASTER MANAGEMENT FUNCTIONS AND OBJECTIVES

Disasters are not predictable at the same time no two disasters are alike, even though they are alike no two are identical in its volume and intensity or impact. Thence each type of disaster is unique in its characteristics. Therefore, the management functions before or during or after disaster are entirely different from those of the other types of managements. Moreover, the objective of disaster management should be directed toward service, and the functions should be humanity oriented with a great sympathy and kindness.

2.4.1 Objectives of Disaster Management

The disaster management is carried out with the following main objectives:

- Predict the occurrence of disaster (wherever possible) and caution;
- Reduce (avoid, if possible) the potential losses from hazards;
- Assure prompt and appropriate assistance to victims when necessary;
- Achieve rapid and durable recovery.

2.4.2 Functions of Disaster Management

The various functional aspects (3P/4R) of disaster management include

1. Prediction,
2. Prevention,
3. Preparedness,
4. Response,
5. Risk Reduction/Mitigation,
6. Rehabilitation, and
7. Reconstruction.

2.4.3 Desirable Characteristics of Disaster Manager

In addition to the philanthropy, kindness, and service orientation, a disaster manager is desired to possess the following characteristics.

1. **Comprehensiveness** – A disaster manager, while taking a decision, should consider all factors associated with it and has to take into account all similar hazards, all stages and phases, all those people who are connected with including the victim and all causes effects relevant to disasters.
2. **Progressiveness** – The disaster manager should have long and broad vision. He should be able to expect effect and result of a disaster and so take decisions accordingly. He should predict what could be future and take preventive measures and be prepared. The disaster-resistant and disaster-resilient communities may be formed for execution.
3. **Risk-driven** – Disaster and mitigation manager needs to take risk at times, so he should be fully aware of the risk management principles such as hazard identification, risk analysis, and impact analysis, and thence assign priorities of using resources.
4. **Integration** – Disaster management and mitigation is not a single person's job, but a collective effort. So, integrating the efforts of all levels of government and community is necessary.
5. **Collaboration** – Disaster mitigation and rehabilitation needs the support of various individuals and organizations. Collaborative working can make the disaster management effective and enables quick response. Therefore, the manager should create and establish broad and selfless relationships among individuals and organizations and build team culture, consensus, and facilitating communication.

6. **Coordination** – A good manager should synchronize the activities and unify all relevant individuals or organizations to achieving the common objective.
7. **Communicator** – Pass on the information in all required dimensions in both horizontal and vertical direction to the relevant persons.
8. **Flexibility** – The decisions taken for disaster mitigation, preparedness, prevention and control often are instantaneous or spontaneous. Hence, the disaster managers should be creative and innovative and also dynamic in solving disaster challenges. Thence, the decisions should range flexibly.
9. **Professionalism** – The disaster managers often need to face the criticism. Hence, if they use a science and knowledge-based approach, valuing education, training, coupled with experience, it can rescue the manager from such critics. Further, the manager should illustrate professionalism with the ethical practices, and use public stewardship for continuous improvement.

SELF ASSESSMENT INTERMISSION (SAI – 2.1)

1. What do you understand by the term “Disaster”? Define and explain.
2. Define the terms ‘Disaster’ and ‘Disaster Management’?
3. What are the functions of disaster management? Briefly discuss.
4. What is disaster management? What is the need for the disaster management?
5. What are the objectives of disaster management?
6. What are the desirable characteristics of disaster manager?

2.5 ELEMENTS OF DISASTER

A disaster is said to have occurred if the event/process negatively impacts human populations. On critical observation, we can understand disasters as a combination of three elements:

1. The hazard,
2. The vulnerability, and
3. The Risk.

2.5.1 Hazard

Hazard is defined as the situation having a probability of occurrence of an extreme potentially damaging natural phenomenon in a given period, in a given area by inducing fire, air, earth or water movements. However, the magnitude of the phenomenon, the probability of its occurrence and the extent of its impact can vary and, in some cases, be determined. Thus a hazard is

- an unavoidable danger or risk, even though often foreseeable.
- something that can cause unavoidable danger, peril, risk, or difficulty.
- an event that may result in adverse effect due to the absence or lack of predictability, chance or uncertainty.

Role of FEMA

The Federal Emergency Management Agency (FEMA) of US has set a basic four-stage cyclic vision of preparedness that runs through mitigation to preparedness to response, to recovery and back to mitigation in a circular planning process. Later, this overlapping, circular model has been modified by other agencies. FEMA developed courses to provide guidance for multi-hazard mitigation that focuses on creating disaster-resilient communities to reduce loss of life and property. FEMA also advises citizens to prepare their homes with some emergency essentials in the case that the food distribution lines are interrupted. For contingency, it kept ready for emergency with millions of frozen dried food packs in the form of 'meals ready to eat' (MRE's) to dispense to the communities where emergency shelter and evacuations are needed.

2.5.2 Vulnerability

Vulnerability of any physical, structural or socio-economic element to a natural hazard is the probability of getting damaged, destroyed or lost. Vulnerability is dynamic process but not because by it can be changed by integrating changes and developments of all the exposed elements. Literally, vulnerability is

- susceptible to being wounded or hurt, as by a weapon
- open to moral attack, criticism, temptation, etc.
- potential place open to assault; difficult to defend

Dimensions of vulnerability assessment

Vulnerability is assessed based on the physical socio-economic environment of the given area. Thus it can be understood, analyzed and estimated through four dimensions viz. physical, social, economic and environmental factors. A brief outline of the vulnerability assessment is given in the following paragraphs.

- ***Physical vulnerability*** – Estimation of the impacts of events on assets such as landscape, building, infrastructure, agriculture and so forth.
- ***Social vulnerability*** – Analysis of the impacts of events on highly affecting groups such as the poor/ socially backward communities, tribes, unawareness of risk.
- ***Economic vulnerability*** – Assessment of potential impacts of hazards on economic status and processes (business interruption and secondary effects).
- ***Environmental vulnerability*** – Evaluation of degraded environmental quality that limits the natural resilience to hazard effects and reduces environmental buffering of effects.

2.5.3 Risk

After the prediction of an occurrence of a disaster, the most important activity prior to the disaster mitigation is the identification of risks. Physical risk assessment implies evaluating the hazards and vulnerability.

The risk assessment is concerned with the identification of probability of occurrence of various hazards such as earthquakes, volcanic eruption, floods, riots etc. within a certain area of interest. Further, whatsoever may be the magnitude of hazard, if there is no vulnerability there will be no risk, for example an earthquake occurring in a desert where nobody resides. So, at the same time the vulnerability also significantly influences risk assessment as compared to the hazard. Thence, the risk associated at the given area depends on two major factors, the hazard (its impact) and the vulnerability. Thus the risk is the function of the two components viz. hazard component and vulnerability component.

Risk Management = f(H, V) = f (natural event) (social &regional factors) where,

H = Hazard function or hazard component i.e. the potentially damaging exogenous events whose probable characteristics and frequency of occurrence can be estimated, and

V = Vulnerability component i.e. the intrinsic characteristics of the elements at risk that determine how damaged they would be if they experienced a hazard event of some level.

Further, we know that more the exposure to the hazard, more will be the effect of hazard multiplies while the vulnerability can be minimized by improving the manageability i.e. the resistance or resilience to the hazard. Thus risk implies

- a future potential condition,
- a function of the magnitude of the natural hazard and
- a function of the vulnerability of all the exposed elements in a given moment.

And the risk is estimated by

- **R**uining probability or Ruin-ability (denoted by R or H) by occurrence of a natural event
- **I**mpact duration of hazard (denoted by I or E) that multiplies the hazard effect
- **S**usceptibility (denoted by S or V) i.e. the vulnerability to a hazard
- **K**now-how to resist (K or M) that divides the effect and so reduces the risk of hazard

R.I.S/K = (**R**uinability.**I**mpact duration) × (**S**usceptibility/**K**nowhow)

or = **(Hazard.Exposure) × (Vulnerability/Manageability) = (H.E).(V/M)**

where

Ruinability (R) or Hazard Intensity or Hazard (H)

= The probability of destruction by an event or situation

Exposure (E) or Impact duration (I) = the extent of hazard

(Effect of Hazard = Hazard intensity × Exposure time)

Susceptibility (S) or Vulnerability (V) = Possibility of damage or harm by a hazard

Knowhow (K) or Manageability (M) = Capacity to respond/resistance needed by disaster

A disaster occurs when a hazard exposes the vulnerability of individuals and communities in such a way that their lives are directly threatened or sufficient harm has been done to their community's economic and social structure to undermine their ability to survive.

SELF ASSESSMENT INTERMISSION (SAI – 2.2)

1. What are the elements of Disaster? Discuss.
2. Define the term hazard. Distinguish between hazard and a disaster.
3. What is 'vulnerability' to a hazard or disaster? How do you assess the vulnerability?
4. What is 'Risk' with respect to the disaster management? How do you evaluate the risk of a certain area?
5. Describe the terms Hazard, Vulnerability and Risk. How are they related?
6. What are Ruinability, Impact duration, Susceptibility and Knowhow of Disaster management? Establish a relation among them.

2.6 CLASSIFICATION OF DISASTERS

Perhaps! You have seen the term "Acts of God" in the 'terms and conditions' of insurance policy documents. So, in their terminology the natural disasters such as earthquake, floods etc. are the acts of god. Similarly, all other disasters which occur by the acts of man i.e. due to human ill-activities may be termed as man-made or artificial disasters. Thus intuitively disasters can be broadly classified into two categories as

O My God! - India is Disaster Prone

- About 8% of land to Cyclones
- About 12% of land to Floods
- About 55% of land to Earthquakes
- About 70% of land to Drought

1. Natural Disasters, and
2. Manmade Disasters.

We shall now discuss about these.

2.6.1 Natural Disasters

These disasters are caused by nature such as earthquakes, volcanic eruption, floods, cyclones etc. The natural disasters may occur due to some reactions inside or on the surface of the earth such as earthquakes, volcanic eruptions etc., often referred to as 'Endogenic Disasters', while the disasters that occur over and above the surface of the earth like cyclones, rainstorms, meteors etc. are called 'Exogenic Disasters'.

Depending on the root cause, these can be further classified as

(a) Meteorological,

(b) Topographical, and

(c) Environmental.

(a) Meteorological: Meteorology is the interdisciplinary scientific study of atmosphere. Meteorological phenomena are observable weather events which are explained by science. It includes extreme heat and cold winds, floods, cyclones, tsunami, eruption of volcanoes etc.

(b) Topographical: It is the study of shape and features of surface of earth and other observable objects such as planets, moons, asteroids etc. It includes avalanches, landslides, asteroids etc.

(c) Environmental: Environmental disaster is a disaster to natural environment which results in the alteration of ecosystem has led to widespread and long-lasting consequences. It affects agriculture, biodiversity, economy and human health.

2.6.2 Manmade Disasters

These are caused as a result of human related activities such as road accidents, warfare, terrorist attacks etc. The manmade disasters may be either deliberately done or inadvertently occur.

These also can be further divided into three types as follows,

(a) Technological,

(b) Industrial, and

(c) Security related.

(a) Technological disaster: These disasters occur due to malfunction of a technological structure and or some human error in controlling and handling technology. It includes oil spills, radiation leaks etc. These are often difficult to predict and may occur inadvertently also. Further, it may be the result of the people connected to the issue, as they

- Do not shoulder the responsibility
- Not willing to take the responsibility.
- Escape from the responsibility
- Ignore or do not notice the significance of certain points in the process
- Unexpected threat of technological failures

(b) Industrial disaster: These are caused in industrial companies due to accident, incompetence or by sheer negligence resulting in great damage, injury or loss of life.

(c) Security related disaster: The disasters due to lapses in security, non-compliance of safety principles, accidents, attacks by terrorists or dacoits or robbers etc. come under this category.

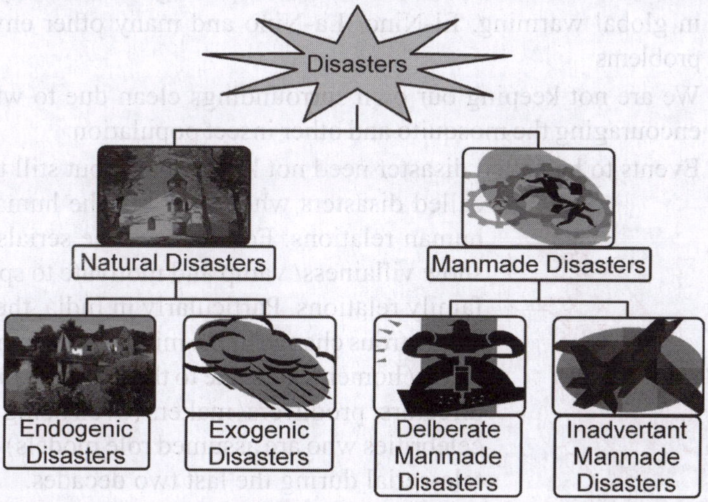

The following diagram illustrates the classification of disasters.

Natural Disasters		Manmade Disasters	
Endogenic Disasters	**Exogenic Disasters**	**Deliberate Manmade Disasters**	**Inadvertent Manmade Disasters**
Earthquake Tsunami Volcano	Cyclone/ Floods Heat/Cold wave Blizzard/Rainstorm Avalanche/ Landslide/ Rockslide/ Mudslide	Communal riots Terrorism War Bombing Dacoit	Wildfire/ Fire Hazards Chemical Hazards All Accidents Global Warming Ozone Depletion

2.6.3 Man-triggered Natural Disasters (Natural Disasters Increased by Humans)

Have you noticed that your grandmother or grandfather or great-grand parents lived happily and lived long than us? What could be the reason? Yes! They did not have much stresses. They did not have a radiation

Today, the society has become more complex, and each and every one of us is responsible for the society to get this complexity and obviously, the people are increasingly responsible, directly or indirectly, for the consequences of events previously ascribed to forces beyond their control.

For example,

- We have been using plastics and spoiling the environment. For a convenience of a little time, we are harming the environment and hence the society
- The flouro-carbons used or burnt are depleting the ozone layer resulting in global warming, El-Nino/ La-Nino and many other environmental problems
- We are not keeping our own surroundings clean due to which we are encouraging the mosquito and other insect population
- Events to be called disaster need not kill humans, but still they may be called disasters when they kill the humanity and/or human relations. For instance the serials in TV that show villainess/ vamp and motivate to spoil even the family relations. Particularly in India, there has been a disastrous change in the mind sets of females, house-wives/ homemakers due to the irresponsible sponsors/ directors/ producers/ makers (even being women and celebrities who are assumed role models) of tele-film/ tele-serial during the last two decades.

- Mobile/ cell phone or such electronic gadgets have rather become an integral part of body, without which we are unable to live. They are gaining more importance than the fundamental needs like food, water and even disastrously spoiling/ ruining the human relations besides being radiating hazard in our pockets or wallets.
- We are cutting down the trees and destroying the forests for our comforts and selfish motives, knowingly that this will adversely affect the environment and hence the society.

Perhaps! Everybody thinks that his/her contribution is only a little and negligible. But, all put together becomes considerably huge to cause a disaster. We know pretty well that all such above human acts will flair and fire up as natural disaster in long run on the society.

Are these natural hazards or man-made?

In fact, most of the disasters arising from natural hazards would not have occurred or would have had a smaller impact on communities had it not been for actions by people.

There are several evidences that the volume and effect of the natural disasters increased due to their human activities before they have occurred.

Some examples are given below

- deforestation for firewood or building materials has resulted in landslides during heavy rainfall in Central and South America
- overgrazing of cattle has allowed desertification in the Sahel
- uncontrolled housing construction close to beaches increased risks from tsunamis and storms in South-east Asian contries.
- removal of wetlands has eliminated a natural mitigating factor for the damage caused by tropical storms in Asia
- political systems have turned droughts into famine, particularly in Africa.

All these are man-triggered or man-motivated natural disasters gaining increasing importance and concern. If today's youth realizes this, the next generation can breathe well and live safe.

SELF ASSESSMENT INTERMISSION (SAI – 2.3)

1. What are the Natural Disasters? Explain causes of any two.
2. Define the term natural hazard. Distinguish between hazardous and disastrous area.
3. What is man-triggered natural disaster? Explain with examples. Suggest some counter-measures.
4. Classify the disasters. Explain each briefly.
5. Distinguish between natural and man-made disasters.
6. Distinguish between exogenous and endogenus disasters.
7. Distinguish between terrestrial and extra-terrestrial disasters.
8. With examples, discuss meteorological, topographical and environmental disasters.
9. Describe technological, industrial and security related disasters with examples.

2.7 DISASTER MANAGEMENT CYCLE

Disaster management cycle includes the following stages/ phases

1. Prediction and Prevention phase.
2. Preparedness phase.
3. Response phase.
4. Recovery/ Rehabilitation phase.
5. Risk Reduction/ Mitigation phase.

All the above phases are inter-related and even over-lapping (some authors describe the cycle in 4-phase only as mitigation, preparedness, response and recovery). Therefore, we cannot discuss each phase exclusively as a separate function. Also, it is important to note that the time period for each phase may depend on the type and severity of the disaster.

2.7.1 Prediction and Prevention Phase

Strictly speaking, prediction and prevention phase was recently added to the phases of emergency management. Most disasters are unpredictable. However, if certain precautions are taken, we can avoid or reduce the impact of the disaster. Sometimes, the disaster is predictable and the loss or damage can be minimized by taking suitable measures.

Not only prediction, but this phase, also focuses on preventing the human hazard, primarily from potential natural disasters or terrorist attacks. Preventive measures are taken on both the domestic and international levels to protect against disasters. Though every natural disaster cannot be prevented, the risk of loss of life and injury can be mitigated through strict implementation of standards of designs, environmental strategies and evacuation plans. [In Jan 2005, 168 Governments adopted a 10-yr global plan for natural disaster risk reduction called the Hyogo frame work].

2.7.2 Preparedness Phase

This phase overlaps with the prevention phase and involves in creating awareness among the population on the general aspects of disaster and on know-how to act in case of a disaster if occurs. This includes educating on warning signs of disasters, methods of safe and successful evacuation and first aid measures.

Preparedness also focuses on training/ educating people, preparing equipment and procedures for use when a disaster occurs. This equipment and these procedures can be used to reduce vulnerability to disaster, to mitigate the impacts of a disaster or to respond more efficiently in an emergency.

Planning the preparedness should be on the basis of

- the characteristics of natural disasters,
- preparedness to overcome them, and
- making preparations for evacuation and shelter.

The following steps are generally involved:

- Setting up 'Early Warning Systems' for horizontal and vertical communications.
- Providing management, and conducting rehearsals and drills for the Inter-Department Relief Team to enable it to provide assistance during natural disasters from the nearest location in the field.
- Providing training from the grassroots level organizations to the Township/ Division/State to ensure preparedness for emergency activities during natural disasters.

- Brainstorming possible solutions for different scenarios during training.
- Building safe shelters, artificial mounds and high embankments for use in times of emergency, and making evacuation plans and conducting drills.
- Stock piling food, water, clothing, supplies, construction materials, shelter and ready-made tents, tools, etc. that will be necessary during emergencies or arranging access to them and designating transportation routes.

2.7.3 Response Phase

This phase commences with search and rescue and focuses on fulfilling the fundamental humanitarian needs of the victims or affected people. This assistance may be provided by individuals or groups and organizations or national or international agencies. What is more important is the coordination, especially when several people or organizations come forward for helping.

> **O My God!**
>
> **Doctrine of Emergency Management?**
>
> Under the direction of Dr. Cortez Lawrence, (Spdt of FEMA's Emergency Mgmt Instt.), Dr. Wayne Blanchard (FEMA's Emergency Mgmt Higher Education Project) convened practitioners and academicians to frame principles of emergency management in 2007. This was the first time the principles of the discipline were codified with 8 principles used to guide the development of a doctrine of emergency management.

Generally, when the capacity of a country to respond and recover from a disaster is utilized at its full length, then upon request from the National Society, the International Federation and/or Red Cross enters and uses its regional and international resources and networks to assist.

Obviously, the first to respond and to start rescue and relief operations to a disaster are those living in the local community. So the Red Cross and Red Crescent National Societies aim at community-based disaster preparedness so as to help communities to reduce the vulnerability to disasters and boost their capabilities of countering them.

In the past, the field of emergency management and immediate response has been handled mostly by military in forefront and/or first responder background. But now, the field has been more diversified with a variety of backgrounds other than the military or first responder fields. For example, student-volunteers from educational institutions, National Cadet Corps (NCC), National Service Scheme (NSS), doctors' teams, service organizations affiliated to political parties, police, security organizations, fire department, charity organizations, employees of certain organizations, and so forth.

2.7.4 Recovery Phase

The recovery phase starts soon after the threat to human life has subsided. The prime objective of the disaster manager during this phase is to bring back the affected area to normal living conditions at the earliest possible. It is suggested to consider construction material as well as local-regional problems during the rebuilding. The most extreme events that may last up to a year or could bea war, a famine and severe epidemics, the recovery takes place inside the home. Planning for such events usually involves purchase of bulk foods and appropriate storage and preparation equipment etc.

Training is provided by local, state, federal and private organizations and ranges from public information and media relations to high-level incident command and tactical skills.

Rehabilitation

In this phase, the victims often would be in pathetic situation seeking sympathy and help. They not only need assistance for survival, but also the revival to their normal life. The Governments take necessary steps. Yet, it may not suffice to cater the needs. At this juncture, depending on the volume or effect of the disaster, the involvement of the nearby communities, local bodies, national and international societies would become a necessity. Insurance agencies have a key role to play in this phase. Sometimes, the victims may even lose their documents also along with their assets and properties. Thence insurance companies must act generously and wisely. Encouraging philanthropists and humanitarian donors is another better practice to rehabilitate the victims as well as to help the vulnerable people. In the process of rehabilitation the Governments of the states generally compel the employees of Government and public sector units and also the people above poverty line to help in monetary terms such as donating a day's salary or by charging a cess or tax etc.

In recovery phase the immediate needs of the victims is medical help and then the other equally important help could be food, water, clothing and shelter. Once these are fulfilled, they start entering the real part of this phase which is the most significant, in terms of long term outcome to get back there pre-disaster position. During this time, the victims actually realize the impact of disaster and perceive the meaning of 'the loss' they suffered.

2.7.5 Risk Reduction and Mitigating Phase

This phase is concerned with the steps taken to prevent loss of life and property during natural disasters as well as precautionary and mitigating measures. These steps vary depending on the type of disaster. For instance, the measures taken to reduce the risk of an earthquake are quite different from those for floods.

Some of the suggested measures to be taken for different disasters are given below.

1. construction of sufficient fire breaks to prevent forest fires from spreading into urban areas
2. planting trees as wind breakers and breakwaters against floods
3. planting rows of trees and groves to reduce damage from tsunami
4. using fire-proof materials in construction to reduce fire hazards
5. using earthquake resistant designs to reduce damage caused by earthquakes

Truly speaking, this phase has large overlap on the prediction & preventive phase (1st phase) since the process of risk reduction obviously focuses on preventing the occurrence. Else, this phase has to concentrate on returning the population back to pre-disaster standards of living, which is very difficult task. Also, as we know that the prevention is better than cure, putting the best efforts to prevent or avoid or warn to vacate whenever and wherever possible.

Further, certain measures needed to reduce the extent or impact of damage during the next similar disaster, have to be identified and executed. For example, after an earthquake causes damages to improperly built houses, the population usually rebuild stronger houses so as to reduce effect of earthquake if occurs thereafter. If there is a threat of tsunami, the housings is avoided near to the shore and develop a 'green belt' (a thick stretch of trees adjacent to the coast line to lessen the impact of the tsunami waves on the land). This process of lowering the impact of disaster is known as Mitigation.

Mitigation

Self help is the best help. Personal mitigation is a key to national preparedness. Individuals and families should be trained to avoid unnecessary risks. This includes an assessment of possible risks to personal/ family health and to personal property, and steps taken to minimize the effects of a disaster, or procure insurance to protect them against effects of a disaster.

The mitigation measures may be entirely different from one type to the other. Further, it may be even different from one disaster to the other within the same type also. For instance, in earthquake prone areas, mitigation measures focus on structural changes while in flood prone areas, houses may asked to construct on poles/ stilts.

The central/ state level governments have to plan, design and implement large scale mitigation measures. For example, after the monsoon floods of 2010, the Punjab government built 22 disaster-resilient villages, with 1885 single-storey homes, along with schools and health centers. Such suitable plans may be taken up all over the country.

SELF ASSESSMENT INTERMISSION (SAI – 2.4)

1. Explain various phases of disaster cycle.
2. Explain the significance of prediction and prevention phase in disaster management.
3. What is preparedness? Explain about this phase in disaster cycle.
4. Describe the role of a disaster manager during disaster phase of disaster cycle.
5. What do you understand by the terms 'Response' and 'Responsibility' with reference to the disaster management? Explain the response phase of disaster cycle.
6. Distinguish between recovery and rehabilitation with reference to disaster management. Explain the phase of disaster that deals with recovery and rehabilitation.
7. What are risk reduction and mitigation with reference to disaster management? Explain the phase of disaster that deals with these two activities.
8. Distinguish between functions before, during and after disasters. Classify the phases of disaster-cycle under these three heads (before/during/after disaster) and justify your classification with suitable examples.
9. Write a short note on disaster mitigation.

2.8 PREPAREDNESS MEASURES AT DIFFERENT LEVELS

Undoubtedly, emergency preparedness is difficult to measure. However, the following aspects can help mitigating approach to reducing the effect:

- Institutional changes.
- Enunciation of policy.
- Legal and techno-legal framework.
- Mainstreaming Mitigation into Development process.
- Funding mechanism.
- Specific schemes addressing mitigation.
- Preparedness measures.
- Community participation and capacity building.

The focus of preparedness measures ranges from an individual people/ locations/incidents to government-based state/ national/ international level planning. There are a number of stages in this planning, involving both mitigation and response.

Disasters take a variety of forms including earthquakes, tsunamis or fires. Further these may give a warning or suddenly flair up while coming. Small or big, preparedness starts with everyone's daily life and training for the same would be useful in an emergency. What is useful in an emergency is often also useful in everyday life as well. From personal preparedness, it continues on a continuum through family preparedness, community preparedness and then business, non-profit and governmental preparedness and their combinations. Whatsoever, the central idea behind preparedness is, 'to be ready' for an emergency and the basic guidance for preparedness is common irrespective of the area or a specific threat.

Many of the bigger disasters are associated with changes in climate, environment and human ecology, thereby increasing the vulnerability. They are causing greater damage, loss, and dislocation, in addition to periodic economic crises, growing inequalities, competition over scarce resources, demographic change, urbanization, migration, changing disease burdens and complex patterns of violence, thence, generating various forms of vulnerability and crisis that enhance marginalization, impoverishment and insecurity.

With the advent of technological revolution, managing human vulnerability is now better, faster, and on a bigger scale. This is possible due to the information and communication, social networking, science and technology, and the accumulation of knowledge and wealth at collective efforts. These factors, along with historic, political, economic and social shifts, have set new horizons and created new capacities for innovative problem solving. Meanwhile, people everywhere are awakening to their basic human rights and aspiring to develop and fight against vulnerabilities.

2.8.1 Role of Individuals and Local Bodies

As discussed above, mitigation is not just the responsibility of the Government, but every individual's job. Particularly, the local bodies have to shoulder more responsibility as they know the prevailing situations much better. Identifying this importance, US Environmental Protection Agency called for under the Emergency Planning to develop an emergency response plan, review the plan at least annually, and provide information about environment, climate and chemicals used in the community to local citizens. This emergency preparedness effort was successful in several aspects in preventing as well as for preparedness. Especially, it helped focusing on hazards presented by use and storage of hazardous and toxic chemicals.

The responsibilities of the local bodies should be shouldered in the following directions.

- Identifying the probable area and people who might get affected.
- Awareness on local emergency equipment and its availability/person in-charge.
- Knowledge on facilities available and requirement in respect of disasters.
- Available transportation routes in general, and of extremely hazardous substances in particular.
- Know-how of both on-site and off-site emergency response methodology and procedures.

- Schedules and training programs of emergency response and their execution.
- Preparation of emergency notification procedures.
- Thorough understanding on evacuation plans.

ROLE OF INTERNATIONAL FEDERATON OF RED-CROSS AND RED-CRESCENT (IFRC)

> FEMA (US) notes "Preparing for disaster helps everyone in the family as disasters do happen, and so identify and collect the resources needed to meet basic needs after disaster. When people feel prepared, they cope better and so do children". FEMA published a booklet called the "Threat and Hazard Identification and Risk Assessment (THIRA) Guide" in which it recommends everyone to have a 3-day survival kit that includes:
>
> - 3-day supply of non-perishable food.
> - 3-day supply of water – one gallon of water per person, per day.
> - Portable, battery-powered radio or television and extra batteries.
> - Kitchen accessories and cooking utensils, including a can opener.
> - The credit and identification cards including cash and coins.
> - Flashlight and extra batteries.
> - First aid kit and manual.
> - Extra clothing.

The Red Cross and Red-Crescent is well known for vital relief work in disasters and crises, and committed to be the world's leading humanitarian actor, and is present not just during disasters, but also much beforehand and long afterwards.

However, its presence comes out from within local communities organized through their National Societies which call upon the services of lakhs of volunteers with different skills. Nevertheless, each National Society has a unique, long-established and legally-defined auxiliary partnership with its government which enables it to decision-making and access to resources as well as to address national vulnerability. Red-Cross and Red-Crescent services are developed over a long period, and continuing to inspire setting global norms, raising standards, shaping codes of conduct, and establishing legal frameworks.

Perspective on development

National Societies, specifically National Service Scheme (NSS) in India covers small to large, short to long-range, local to national services including disease prevention and health promotion, water and sanitation, blood donations, food and nutrition, disaster preparedness, response, and recovery, social assistance, as well as protection for poor, vulnerable, and marginalized groups through promoting social inclusion, and a culture of non-violence and peace.

The developmental activities chiefly concentrate on preventing and reducing the underlying causes of vulnerability. This intent defines general objective of NSS as "to inspire, encourage, motivate, facilitate and promote at all times all forms of humanitarian activities by National Societies, with a view to preventing and alleviating human suffering, and thereby contributing to the maintenance and promotion of human dignity and peace in the world"

The IFRC's 189 member National Societies are significantly contributing to reducing the vulnerability of people living in the most hazard-prone areas of the world. In the 28th International Conference of the Red Cross and Red Crescent in Dec' 2003 at Geneva committed to a plan of action aiming at reducing vulnerability to the risk and impact of natural disasters. To reduce disaster risk, the IFRC framed three main strategies:

- to strengthen the preparedness and capacities of communities so as to better their position to respond when a disaster occurs;
- to promote activities and actions that mitigate the adverse effects of hazards; and
- to protect development projects such as health facilities from the impact of disasters.

SELF ASSESSMENT INTERMISSION (SAI – 2.5)

1. What are preparedness measures? What are the factors that influence the preparedness measures?
2. Discuss the role of individuals in preparedness and mitigation to disasters.
3. What is the role of local bodies in disaster prevention, preparedness and mitigation? Discuss under Indian environment.
4. Describe the roles of government and FEMA in disaster preparedness and mitigation.
5. Critically appreciate the role of Red-Cross in disaster management.
6. List out the items of a disaster kit as specified by FEMA.

2.9 APPROACHES TO DISASTER MANAGEMENT

There are numerous approaches available for disaster management focusing one or more of aspects such as the disaster risk reduction, vulnerability reduction, prevention, protection, quick response, best and fast recovery/rehabilitation and so forth. However, the following are the most popular.

1. Ecosystem Approach,
2. Perception Approach, and
3. Landscape Approach.

These are briefly explained below:

2.9.1 Ecosystem Approach

'Ecosystem' can be defined as "a functional interactions of a dynamic complex of plant, animal and microorganism communities and their non-living environment".

The **ecosystem approach** is a conceptual framework with the following objectives

- To resolve ecosystem issues through scientific reasoning.
- To protect and manage the environment.

- To preserve the Earth and its inhabitants from potential harm or permanent damage to the planet itself.
- To sustain and increase the capacity of environment with the preservation and management of the planet, thereby attaining the future monetary and planetary gains as by-products.

Since, the ecosystem approach incorporates the ergonomics (work science of humans), the economy (science of wealth), and ecology (science of nature) to the solution of any given problem; the above objectives can be achieved through this approach. On Dec 29, 1993, the Convention on Biological Diveristy (CBD) was signed and applied as a multilateral treaty with the purpose of achieving…

1. Biodiversity,
2. Sustainability of species diversity, and
3. Endorse genetic diversity (e.g. to maintain and endorse livestock, crops, and wildlife).

In fact, the first idea of ecosystem approach emerged in the 2nd meeting at Conference of the Parties (COP) during Nov 1995 in the Convention on Biological Diversity (CBD) where two similar terms were created namely:

- Ecosystem-based management (EBM), and
- Ecosystem management (EM).

2.9.2 Perception Approach

Humans act how they perceive. So, actions convey and/or deny the chosen information and influence ultimately to result in foreign behaviors and official actions favorable to the originator's objectives. In various ways, perception management combines truth projection, operations security, cover and deception, and psychological operations.

Climate change undoubtedly is a natural phenomenon, but it is being accelerated by human activities. To set a disaster policy based on climate change, one has to understand several factors, of which some are listed below:

- readiness to accept the climate,
- readiness to accept the change,
- readiness to accept the climate change,
- readiness to accept the reality of climate change,
- willingness to embed climate change,
- institutions' capacity,
- risk assessment, and
- management in development strategies, and so on …

All such above factors depend on the perception of the problem and associated risks. A focus on development that neglects to enhance governance and resilience as a prerequisite for managing climate change risks will, in all likelihood, do little to reduce vulnerability to those risks. Therefore, during the past few decades, 4 distinct and independent research and policy communities have been developed under this approach. These are

- disaster risk reduction,
- climate change adaptation,
- environmental management, and
- poverty reduction.

In spite of significant efforts put by actively employed the 4-communities to lower socio-economic vulnerability to natural hazards, the vulnerability is still continuing to increase considerably. More specifically, the hydro-meteorological hazards are increasingly affecting large populations with huge economic losses. Thus this approach had only limited success in lowering vulnerability. This indicates an urgent need to strengthen by collaborating, facilitating, learning and exchanging information among them. This proposes exercises that would help to structure a multi-community dialogue and learning process, which depends on perceptions.

2.9.3 Landscape Approach

Before discussing the approach let us first understand what a landscape is.

A landscape can be defined as, "a contiguous area, intermediate in size between an eco-region and a site, with a specific set of ecological, cultural and socioeconomic characteristics distinct from its neighbors".

But practically, most landscapes are social constructs and thence the understanding or interpretation of a landscape lies largely on one's own perception. Landscape as a social construct is a meeting ground between Nature and People – and these interact and create a distinct place, past and present – and how landscapes thus present a record of our natural and cultural history, tangible and intangible values providing a sense of identity.

Objectives of Landscape Approach

- Be able to explain the context, principles and relevance of landscape approaches (landscape level planning and management) for "good enough" natural resource governance,
- Be able to relate this knowledge to your professional work experiences and context,
- Assess the relevance of the landscape concept for the achievement of the most successful operation of the project.

The Landscape Approach: The key features

The landscape approach as defined by Food and Agriculture Organization (FAO) of United Nations (UN) in 2012 reads the following lines:

Landscape approach is "Dealing with large scale processes in an integrated and multi-disciplinary manner, combining natural resources management with environmental and livelihood considerations".

It is a holistic approach to conservation, a series of interdependent natural and human systems concerned with biodiversity and local economies, agriculture, eco-tourism, geo-diversity, health and social benefits of the environment. The landscape conservation has emerged in response to the challenges posed by climatic changes. This approach recommends to maintain the 'essential natural capital' by promoting the best practices in production, planning and local decision making processes to ensure the healthy provision of ecosystem services and improvement in human well-being.

This essentially focuses on

- Protection of natural capital by delineating landscape boundaries, drivers of deforestation etc.
- Sustainable production along key commodity value chains through incentivized change in production practices.
- Government and policy alignment at all levels with transparent and accountable platforms.
- Sustainable finance creating a long term funding plan for landscape, mainstream conservation incentives to government budgets, attracting private sector investments etc.
- Science based decision making by identifying essential natural capital and create capacity and incentives for protection by local community.
- Building awareness at all levels and motivating multi-stakeholder participation.
- Design, develop and implement a Landscape accounting framework so as to guide continuous measurement of key indicators and progress toward verifiable end-goal.
- Develop partnerships to drive long-term change in landscape using donor funds and services.

Ten Principles of Landscape Approach

The Convention on Bio-Diversity (CBD) in Hyderabad, India, in Nov 2012, has submitted the 10 principles of the landscape approach and have now been adopted now.

Principle 1: ***Continual learning and adaptive management***

Since, landscape processes are dynamic owing to the uncertainties in causes/ effects, the changes in landscape attributes must be intimated for decision-making to improve. Further, nonlinear relationships, external shocks, unexpected interactions and thresholds could surprise and provide an opportunity for learning, thence forming a basis for strategy revision. This learning and revision needs continual adjustment for which new knowledge is derived from multiple sources. The most practical of these sources is "adaptive collaborative management".

Principle 2: *Common concern entry point*

Problems are to be solved through shared negotiation processes with mutual trust which can be established only when objectives and values are shared. The stakeholders having different values, beliefs, and objectives can also be aligned through addressing simpler short-term objectives. Of course, every stakeholder will only join the process if judgement is favourable. So, initially consensus on objectives may be difficult, but launching the process by focusing on easy-to-reach intermediate targets may provide a basis for stakeholders to begin to work together. The work toward this first goal may create opportunities for shared learning and thence builds the confidence as well as the trust needed to address further issues.

Principle 3: *Multiple scales*

The system influences and feedbacks on multiple scales affect management outcomes, and open up under the diverse range of external influences and constraints such as synergies, flows, interactions, and time lags, as well as external drivers and demands. An understanding on these higher and lower level processes can improve local interventions, inform higher-level policy and governance, and help coordinate administrative aspects.

Principle 4: *Multi-functionality*

Landscapes and their components have several functions and applications, used in variety of ways by different stakeholders. So landscape approach takes into account of the different tradeoffs among these goods/ services.

Principle 5: *Multiple stakeholders*

Multiple stakeholders have different objectives (principle 2) and failure to cope stakeholders equitably in decision-making processes leads to sub-optimal and sometimes even unethical outcomes. Therefore, all stakeholders should be recognized, even though negotiated solutions may involve only a subset of stakeholders, which means the solutions should encompass a fair distribution of benefits and incentives. Thence, this approach needs a patient iterative process of recognizing stakeholders and their concerns and aspirations which are usually dynamic in nature. Further, there is often a need to address conflicts, and issues of trust and power.

Principle 6: ***Negotiated and transparent change logic***

As the stakeholders' trust is the scale of success of management (as discussed in principle-1), avoiding or resolving conflicts is very important. And transparency is the basis of trust (principle-2), which can be achieved through mutually accepted/ negotiated process of change backed up by good governance. This needs a broad vision on general goals, challenges, and concerns, as well as on options and opportunities. At the same time, all stakeholders need to understand and accept the general logic, legitimacy and justification for a decision, and to be aware of the risks and uncertainties. Establishing and maintaining such a consensus, becomes an important objective of a landscape approach (principle 2).

Principle 7: ***Clarification of rights and responsibilities***

Rules on resource access and land use build social and conservation outcomes and need to be clear for good management. A fair justice system allows conflict resolution and recourse. So, the rights and responsibilities of every point of action must be clear, and acceptable to all stakeholders. Clarification of conflicting claims need changes, ideally negotiated on legal grounds. A legitimate system for arbitration, natural justice and fair reconciliation should exist in case of conflict.

Principle 8: ***Participatory and user-friendly monitoring***

Information derived from multiple sources should be accessible to facilitate shared learning and integrate systems, which have to be participatory and user-friendly. If stakeholders have agreed on desirable actions and outcomes, obviously, they share an interest in assessing progress. In a landscape approach, no single stakeholder has a unique claim to relevant information, and so should be enabled to generate, gather and integrate the information to interpret activities, progress, and threats used for developing and updating the "theories of change" (principle 6).

Principle 9: ***Resilience***

Unplanned system changes are usually detrimental and undesirable. System-level resilience should be enhanced through regular monitoring. Actions have to be initiated against threats and vulnerabilities that allow recovery through improving capacity to resist and respond. Maintaining resilience can avoid deflect such threats and absorb recover from their manifestations, which is vital to sustain processes and benefits in long term. Factors contributing to system resilience reflect ecological, social and institutional attributes.

Principle 10: ***Strengthened stakeholder capacity***

The ability to participate effectively in different roles and to shoulder responsibilities can portray certain social, cultural, financial skills and abilities. The learning process of the landscape approach can improve stakeholders' capacity to judge and respond and also provides a platform to share experiences within and among sites. However, strengthening the stakeholders can largely improve the caring and sharing capabilities.

The conflicting objectives are resolved subject to changing societal desires and will vary from place to place and over time. Thus, payments for environmental services, a currently popular approach in dealing with land use conflicts, are only likely to be successful if developed with due regard to the above 10 principles. Similar issues are relevant to the implementation of the Reducing Emissions from Deforestation and Forest Degradation program, the expansion of oil palm in Southeast Asia, or the development of various mining interests in the Congo Basin. Current land use and environment conflicts often exist because of a failure to address one or more of the 10 principles.

Advantages of landscape approach

- Closer to reality than 'ecosystem approach' through identification with multi-stakeholder processes (negotiated outcomes),
- Emerging recognition of added value of the "whole" of landscape components,
- Overcome the community approach which failed to address environmental problems beyond the community sphere of interest,
- Recent surge in thinking about valuation of environmental services and linking end-user to resource manager,
- Interdisciplinary concept not claimed /dominated by one perspective.

SELF ASSESSMENT INTERMISSION (SAI – 2.6)

1. List out the approaches of disaster management. Briefly describe.
2. What are the objectives of landscape approach with reference to disaster management?
3. What are the issues on which landscape approach focuses with reference to disaster management?
4. What are the advantages of landscape approach with reference to disaster management?
5. 'Landscape approach is a holistic approach to conservation'. Critically appreciate the statement under the light of disaster management.
6. List and brief out the 10 principles under landscape approach under the backdrop of disaster management.

(continued)

7. Write a short note on history and development of landscape approach with reference to disaster management.
8. Explain ecosystem approach in light of disaster management.
9. What are the objectives and focal issues of ecosystem approach to disaster management?
10. What are the advantages of ecosystem approach to disaster management?
11. What is perception approach of disaster management? Explain.
12. List out the objectives and advantages of perception approach to disaster management.

MINI-PROJECTS

1. Identify the disasters for which your area is vulnerable and prepare the strategies to risk reduction, and preparedness. Prepare an emergency team from your NSS team and conduct drills.
2. Make a presentation on the activities of National Cadet Corps (NCC) and National Service Scheme (NSS). Establish if such organization not available with your institution.
3. Browse and write an essay on the activities of (a) Federal Emergency Management Agency (FEMA), (b) Center for Disaster Control (CDC), and (c) Red-Cross and Red-Crescent movement.

WEB – RESOURCES

- https://media.ifrc.org/innovation/about-the-red-cross-red-crescent-movement/.
- http://www.ifrc.org/en/what-we-do/disaster-management/preparing-for-disaster/risk-reduction/
- https://www.ncbi.nlm.nih.gov/pmc/articles/
- https://books.google.co.in/books
- https://en.wikipedia.org/wiki/Emergency_management

CHAPTER 3 Earthquake

O'MY SILENT INNER VIBES (O'M S I V – 3)

The myths and beliefs all over the world about how an earthquake occurs are quite funny.

Funniest of all is with an old African belief that attributes earthquakes to a wife calling the name of her mother-in-law.

An interesting story is found in Norse (Norway/ Scandinavia) mythology, as earthquakes are believed to be the violent struggling of the God. Loki, the God of mischief and strife, murdered Baldr, the God of beauty and light, and so was punished by being bound in a cave with placing a poisonous snake over his head spilling venom. Loki's wife Sigyn catches the poison with a bowl, but whenever the bowl gets filled up, she has to empty the bowl. At that time, when the poison drips on Loki's face, he jerks his head and thrash against his bonds, causing the earth to tremble.

In Greek myths, Poseidon, the God of the sea, is the cause and is so named 'the God of earthquakes'. When he is in a bad mood, he strikes the ground with a trident, causing earthquakes and other calamities. Further, it is also believed that he uses the earthquakes to punish and inflict fear upon people as revenge. Due to his unpredictable and violent behavior he is often called with the nickname "Earth-Shaker".

(Poof! Some ancient Greeks also believed that earthquakes were caused by winds rushing out from caves inside Earth).

According to Japanese myths, Namazu, a giant catfish is the cause of earthquakes, lives in the mud beneath the earth, guarded by the God Kashima who restrains the fish with a stone. When Kashima lets his guard fall, Namazu thrashes out, causing violent earthquakes.

For a long time in my childhood, I also believed a Hindu myth about the earthquake, told by my mother, which runs as below.

Earth is held by eight gigantic elephants (Ashta Dikpalakas), all balanced on the back of turtle (Koorma, the 2nd incarnation of Lord Vishnu), which itself stands on the coils of a snake (the thousand headed Aadisheshu). If any of these animals shift or move, an earthquake occurs as per Vishnu puran.

My grandmother told another story that the mother Earth (Bhudevi) is the wife of Lord Vishnu and stands on a thousand headed giant snake, 'Aadi Sheshu'. When the snake moves, the Earth shakes.

We all know pretty well that all the above stories are myths but not truths. It is unknown that when and who created these myths.

However, Thales of Miletus, 625-547 (BCE) was the only documented person who believed that earthquakes were caused by tension between the earth and water. But this is also a wrong perception.

Whatsoever, I strongly believe that the first earth quake known to us perhaps, happened during the end of Thretha Yug, (the ending period of Ramayana) when the Mother Earth

(Continued)

(Bhoomatha, the mother of Sitha) quaked (cracked) to take away her daughter Sitha. Then, King Rama tries to stop it to get back Sitha but in vain.

So, even the Lord Maha Vishnu, (incarnated as Rama, 'the complete man'), who has been being worshipped by Hindus as the God, could not stop the earthquake. After all! How can we stop! None can stop when earth is furious, it cracks and quakes. So, what we can do is only to accept what and how things occur, but for trying to minimize the losses.

No matter, whether the above one is a story or history, one 'of my silent inner vibes' is...

Pray Mother Earth – If You Have To Stay in Mirth
AUM Namo Pruthvee Matha! AUM Namo Pruthvee Natha!!
Amen

3.1 THE KING OF DISASTERS

The earthquake is the most devastating disaster of all the kinds of disasters that may ever occur on the earth. It is high time for us to know about this ***king of disasters*** to contribute to ourselves to reduce the adverse effects and/or minimize the loss or at least to be prepared if not to prevent.

Some of the most disastrous events recorded in the known history of mankind, which left no chance to minimize losses but faced the Earth's fury are …

- **Largest length, largest on Richter scale:** The 1960 Chilean Earthquake is the largest earthquake that has been measured on a seismograph, reaching 9.5 on Richter scale on 22 May 1960 with its epicenter near Cañete, Chile. Its rupture zone was over 497 miles long which caused giant ocean waves as far as 6,000 miles (10,000 km) away.
- **Highest structural collapse:** The most deadly earthquake struck Izmit, the northwest Turkey on August 17, 1999, at 3 am which consumed over 14,000 lives. The major reason is attributed to the poor constructed apartment complexes due to which each floor collapsing on the one below and sandwiched so many lives. The death toll of this single event was greater than the average annual loss of life from all earthquakes worldwide.

- **Highest and loss of humans:** One of the most deadly earthquakes recorded in history was the earthquake occurred on 23 Jan 1556 in Shaanxi province, China. More than 830,000 people died and most houses in the hillsides collapsed—and many victims were killed when the structures collapsed. Similar, the 1976 Tangshan earthquake, killed between 240,000 to 655,000 people, was the deadliest of the 20th century.
- **Longest time:** The most powerful (9.2 on Richter scale) quake occurred called the Good Friday earthquake (March 27, 1964) was centered in Prince William Sound, Alaska. It lasted four minutes and dropped streets 20 ft (6 m) below normal. It caused flooding on the coast of Hawaii, more than 3,100 miles away. Further, Alaska holds a record of experiencing quakes highest number times (top 8 of top 10 of N. America).

- **Largest under the ocean bed, largest death toll, largest area affected:** The ten largest recorded earthquakes have all been mega-thrust earthquakes; however, of these ten, occurred on the Boxing Day, the Dec 26, 2004 in Indian Ocean earthquake causing Tsunami is simultaneously one of the deadliest earthquakes in history. The earthquake even though occurred far away under the ocean, did not leave the 2.83 lack human lives on the Earth.
- **Largest number of aftershocks:** Nepal is struggling to cope with the effects of two devastating earthquakes (7.8M_w or 8.1M_s or IX on Mercalli) on the 25th April 2015, leaving over 9,000 dead, 23,000 injured and millions in need of assistance.

The above roars of the Earth on humans are only a few to quote and the list is so big which is being added by such tragedies every year, and challenging the mankind.

3.2 EARTHQUAKE – THE CONCEPT AND MEANING

Before understanding what an earthquake is, let us get clarified certain misconception and wrong perceptions about the earthquakes all over the world.

3.2.1 Wrong Perceptions on Earthquake

Some of the wrong perceptions and misconceptions are unleashed here under.

- There is a misconception that "lubricating" or filling faults with water or some other substance will reduce the quakes or the intensity. But, in fact, these injecting high pressure fluids deep into the ground trigger earthquakes to occur sooner than would have been the case without the injection. Further, this would be a dangerous act in any populated area.
- There is a common myth (particularly in New Zealand where earthquakes are common) that if several small earthquakes occur, it enhances the pressures building up to cause a big one, but this is not true. Seismologists clarify that for every magnitude 6 earthquake, there are 10 of magnitude 5, 100 of magnitude 4, 1,000 of magnitude 3, and so forth as the events get smaller and smaller. This indicates a lot of ***small earthquakes are never enough to eliminate the occasional large event***. It would take 32 magnitude 52 s, 1000 magnitude 42 s, 32,000 magnitude 32 s to equal the energy of one 6-magnitude event.
- ***March is not earthquake month***, despite what some people believe. True, on March 9, 1957, the Andreanof Islands, Alaska, felt a 9.1 temblor.

And on March 27, 1964, Prince William Sound, Alaska, — one of the biggest (9.2) ever killed 125 people and caused $311 million in property damages on Good Friday. But the next three biggest earthquakes occurred in February, November, and December. The devastating major earthquake (9.5) struck Chile on May 22 in 1960 and again on Feb. 27 in 2010. And the huge 9.3 temblor spawned the devastating Indian Ocean tsunami in 2004 occurred on December 26.

- By the way, ***there is no such thing as earthquake weather***. They seem to occur the same number of times in all different types of weather. Statistically, there is an equal distribution of earthquakes in cold weather, hot weather, rainy weather, and so on. It is impossible for the weather to affect the forces beneath the earth's surface. Moreover, the changes in barometric pressure in the atmosphere are very small compared to the forces in the crust, and the effect of the barometric pressure does not reach beneath the soil.
- There is wrong perception that soft ground shakes less than hard ground. The Greek scientist Aristotle recognized in 350 BC that **soft ground shakes more than hard rock** in an earthquake.

3.2.2 The Conceptual Framework

To understand the meaning and mechanism of earthquake, we need to understand the following statements.

- Earthquakes are the result of the vibration of Earth due to the movements on faults.
- The focus is the point on the fault surface where motion begins.
- The epicenter is the point on Earth's surface directly above the focus.

3.2.3 How does an Earthquake occur?

As we all know, an **earthquake** is the **shake** of Earth's surface.

This **shake** is because of the release of **seismic energy** in the layers/ plates of the earth.

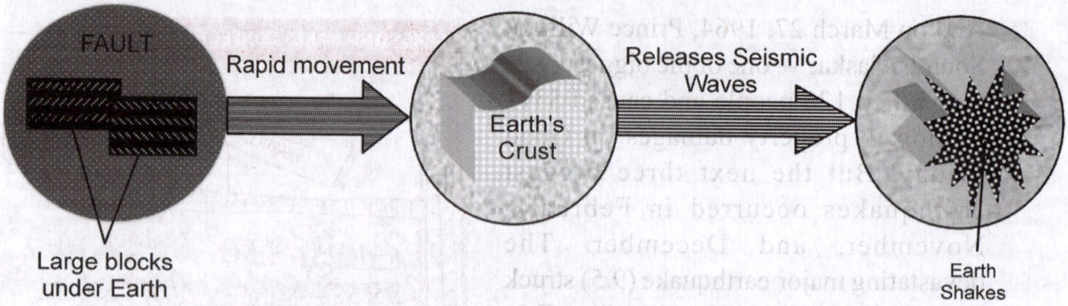

Fig. 3.1 Block diagram showing occurrence of an earthquake.

The **seismic energy** is released due to rapid movement of large blocks of the crust along a **fault**.

The **Faults** are the breaks in the crust that may be hundreds of kilometers long and extend downward 10 to 20 km (6-12 miles) into the crust.

Summarily, an earthquake occurs when Earth shakes due to the release of seismic energy by the rapid movement of large blocks of the Earth's crust along mismatches/breaks between the layers/plates of Earth, called fault. This can be better understood through a block diagram shown in figure 3.1.

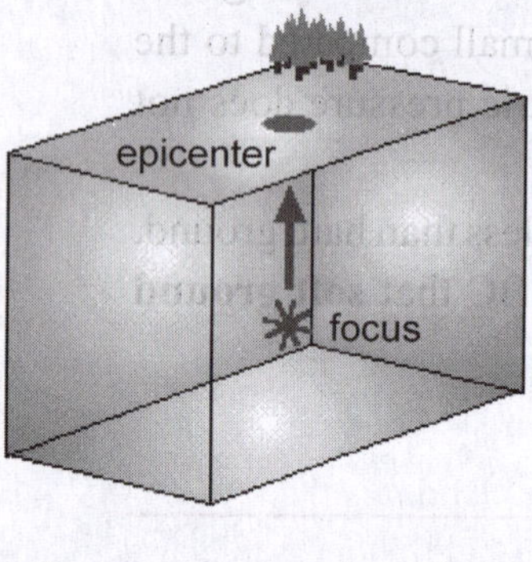

Fig. 3.2 The focus is the source of the earthquake and the epicenter is the point on the surface directly above the focus.

3.2.4 The Focus and Epicenter of Earthquake

The **point on fault surface** where movement begins, i.e. the source of earthquake, is called the **focus.** **Seismic waves** radiate outward from the **focus**. The geographic location of the point on the earth's surface directly above the focus is known as **epicenter** (Fig. 3.2). Earthquake **foci** (plural of focus) occur at a range of shallow depths ranging from the surface down to 70 km (44 miles). Less frequent intermediate (70-300 km; 44-188 miles) and deep (300-700 km; 188-438 miles) earthquakes are generally associated with subduction zones where plates descend into the mantle.

3.3 CAUSES FOR EARTHQUAKES

Although, it is known that the earthquake occurs due to the faulting movement between the tectonic plates underground, the very root causes of infuriating the movement may be attributed to the following aspects.

1. Faulting between the plates.
2. The stresses between the plates and rocks.
3. Straining (flexuring and fracturing) as described by Elastic Rebounding theory.
4. Thermal interactions by the cores.
5. Thermal stresses developed in the mantle due to minerals and chemicals seeped into the earth.
6. Sagging effect induced by dams and reservoirs.
7. Increased pore pressure in reservoirs and dams.
8. Atomic explosions and blasting activity in mining.
9. Volcanic explosions.

Whatsoever may be the cause listed above, it is the provoking feature to cause a fault. Thence, without any iota of doubt, we can say that the lion's share of the causes behind the earthquake is occupied by faulting. Hence, understanding the mechanism of earthquake needs a thorough awareness on the faults underneath.

3.4 FAULTS

A fault can be described as a fracture in the crust. Faults may exist through hundreds of kilometers in length but only the portion of longer faults shatter during the quake. The fault movement may propagate slowly or rapidly. The slow and gradual fault movement produces small earthquakes, while rapid and fast movements of faults cause catastrophes. Whatsoever, duration of ground shake in most of the quakes is for a few **seconds only** but it involves such a large region of Earth's crust that sensational amounts of energy are released. [Duration of ground shake of Izmit earthquake was 45 seconds and affected an area of approximately 100,000 sq. km].

Moreover, it is surprising to know that even the largest earthquakes are generated by a small fault offsets of less than 10 meters. The segments of faults which do not experience a quake are called **seismic gaps.** We can't be happy if the seismic gaps exist underneath the ground for not experiencing the quake, because, these seismic gaps form the potential source sites for future events.

For example, During the Izmit earthquake, the crust broke along the **North Anatolian Fault** in northern Turkey (Refer Fig. 3.3). It occurred in a 150 km

(94 mile) long gap at the western end of the Fault. But during 1939-1999, a series of large earthquakes have occurred on the fault system; each resulting from only one segment of the fault breaking at a time. Particularly, the two adjacent fault segments to the east and west broke during large earthquakes in 1963 and 1967. Believe it or not, **ELEVEN** earthquakes of magnitude **6.7 or more** occurred along the segments of this fault over the previous 60 years.

Figure 3.3 shows Earthquake sequence along the North Anatolian fault, Turkey.

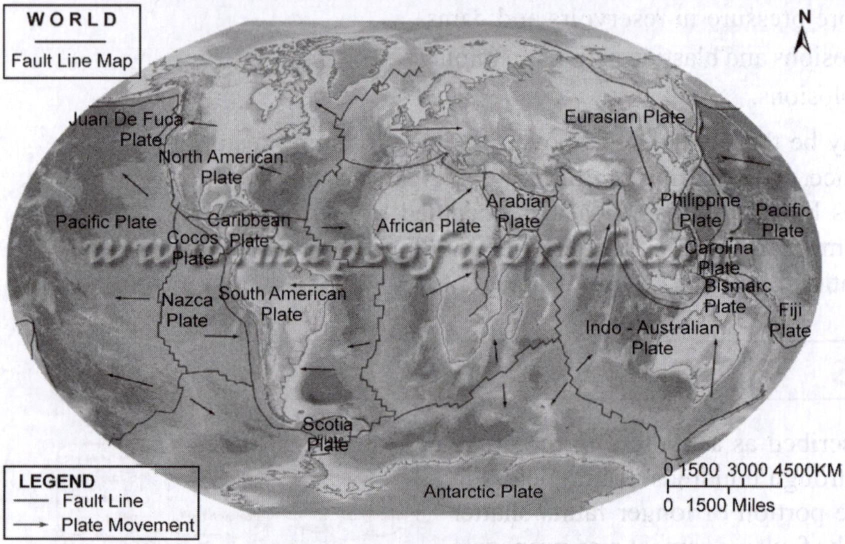

Fig. 3.3 Fault line map.

3.4.1 Fault Classification

Faults can be categorized into two types as dip-slip or strike-slip faults. The **dip-slip faults** are further classified as normal and thrust (or reverse) faults

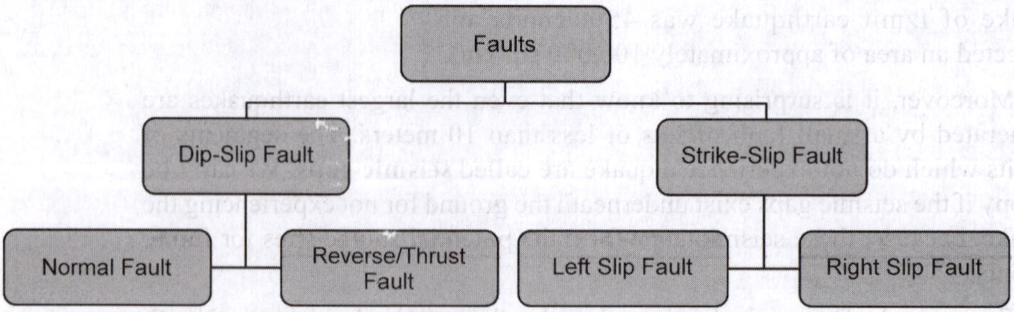

Fig. 3.4 Classification of faults.

on the basis of the relative motion of rocks across an inclined fault surface (Fig. 3.4). Similarly, strike-slip is divided into left and right slip faults. The Fig. 3.4 following shows the classfication of faults.

3.4.2 Dip-slip Fault

As described above, the break between the two blocks of rocks in layers (often called tectonic plates) is fault. This fault is said to be dip-slip fault, if it occurs along vertical plane inclined at an angle (slant) between the two blocks i.e. as if a tectonic plate slides over the other along a vertically inclined plane as shown in the figure 3.5.

The block of rocks above the fault is termed the **hanging wall (hw)** and the one lying below the fault is called **footwall (fw)**. The plane of slide is called **fault plane** and break in slope is known as a **fault scarp**. The line in horizontal plane differentiating the two walls (i.e. between the hanging wall and footwall) is known as **Fault line**. This fault can occur in two ways as normal or reverse. These are explained below. (Refer 3.5)

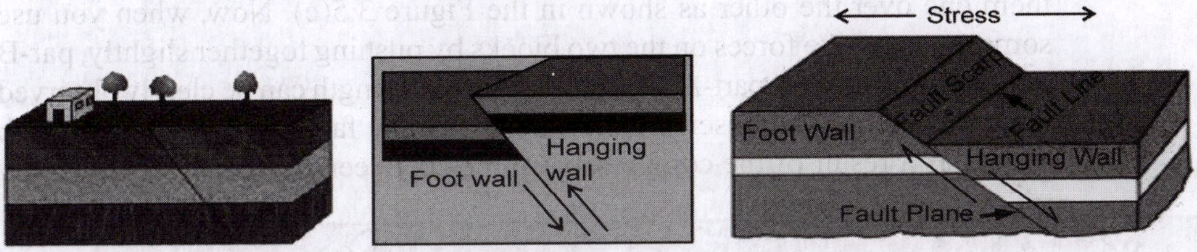

(a) (b) (c)

Fig. 3.5 Fault mechanisms.

3.4.3 Normal Fault

Inclined fault can be identified by the offset of rock layers on either side of the fault surface. If the fault is in such a way that the hanging wall moves down relative to the footwall, then it is called a **normal fault**. The normal faults are most common at ***divergent boundaries*** such as oceanic ridges, where plates break apart.

To understand this fault more clearly, do the following activity,

Take a wooden block of rectangular cross section, section it through an angle, say 60^0 along vertical plane to form two blocks, A and B. Now, keep them one over the other as shown in the figure 3.5(b). Now, when you use some longitudinal tensile forces on the two blocks to pull out slightly, and readjust by moving part B a little down, such that it seems as if part-B slides down over part-A. This represents the normal faulting *earthquake. Further, it can be clearly noticed that the length increases after sliding. Thus, the normal fault occurs as a result of the tensile forces between the tectonic plates.*

Example: North Anatolian fault

3.4.4 Reverse or Thrust Fault

In contrast to the normal fault, the hanging wall moves up relative to the footwall, then it is known as a **reverse fault or thrust fault**. This fault is the outcome of the compressive forces between the tectonic plates. In other words, the reverse faults occur most frequently at ***convergent boundaries*** where plates collide. Movement on a dip-slip fault often results in a break or Fault scarp.

Example: A scarp more than 2 meters is formed during the Hebgen Lake earthquake, Montana, 1959.

We shall understand this fault with a similar experiment as above.

Take a wooden block of rectangular cross section, section it through an angle, say 60^0 along vertical plane to form two blocks, A and B. Now, keep them one over the other as shown in the Figure 3.5(c). Now, when you use some compressive forces on the two blocks by pushing together slightly, par-B moves a little up over part-A. Further, decrease in length can be clearly observed after sliding. This represents the thrust or reverse faulting earthquake which occurs as a result of the compressive forces between the tectonic plates.

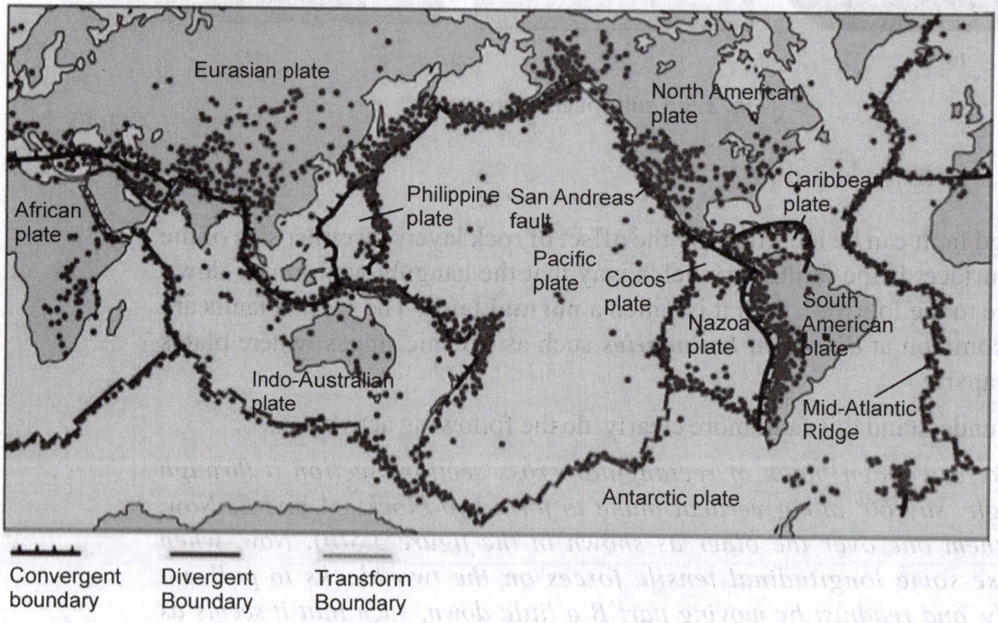

Fig. 3.6 Major earthquake belts in the world.

3.4.5 Strike Fault

This fault can be identified along vertical surface with sliding along horizontal plane between the plates. The **strike-slip faults** can be identified as left-slip and right-slip faults on the basis of the motion on vertical fault surfaces. An observer, standing on one side of the fault, sees objects on the other side of the fault move to the right for a **right-slip fault** or to the left for a **left-slip fault**. For example, a subduction zone in the eastern Mediterranean Sea marks the boundary with the African Plate to the south where two plates move in opposite directions.

These faults can also be understood by conducting a similar example given under dip-slip.

Take a wooden block of rectangular cross section, section it through an angle, say 60^0 along vertical plane to form two blocks, A and B. Now, keep them one over the other as shown in the figure 3.7. Now, when you use some shear forces on the two blocks slightly, part-A towards you while part-B away from you. Further, no change in length can be clearly observed after sliding. This represents the strike-slip faulting earthquake which occurs as a result of the shear forces between the tectonic plates.

Example: The 800 miles or 1,280 km (one of the longest) **San Andreas Fault**, California to Mexico, is a right-slip fault. In fact, the San Andreas Fault is not just one fault but it is actually made up of many faults. The San Andreas fault extends at least 20 miles vertically into the Earth. The San Andreas Fault is moving about 2 inches a year, about the same rate fingernails grow. At this rate, San Francisco and Los Angeles will be next to each other in 15 million years.

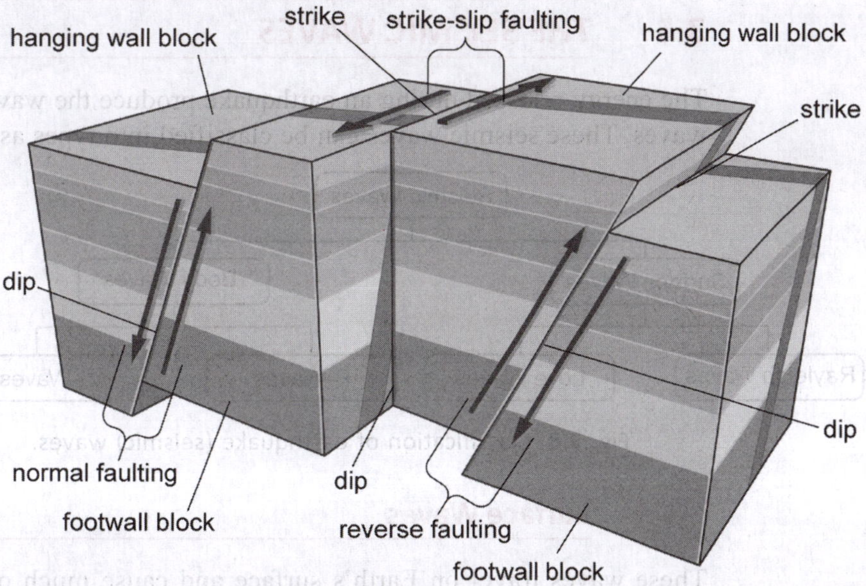

Fig. 3.7 All types of faults and their occurence .

The **North Anatolian Fault** that broke during the Izmit earthquake is also a right-slip fault and is of similar length as the San Andreas Fault. The major fault in the world are shown in Fig. 3.6 and 3.7 the above discussed faults are shown in a single figure.

SELF ASSESSMENT INTERMISSION (SAI – 3.1)

1. What is an earthquake? Explain the phenomenon of earthquake.
2. How does an earthquake occur?
3. Enumerate the causes for earthquakes.
4. What are the misconceptions about earthquakes? Discuss.
5. Classify faults and explain each briefly with neat sketches.
6. What is a fault? What is its significance with reference to earthquakes?
7. Define the following terms in the jargon of earthquakes.
   (i) Focus (ii) Epicenter (iii) Fault
8. Define the following terms in the jargon of earthquakes.
   (i) Normal fault (ii) Thrust fault (iii) Strike fault
9. Write short notes on the following earthquakes.
   (i) Chilean Earthquake (ii) Izmit Earthquake (iii) Nepal Earthquakes
10. Give a brief account on Good Friday Earthquake and Boxing-day earthquake.
11. State the causes for the occurring of earthquake.
12. What is a fault? Distinguish between normal fault and thrust fault.
13. Give the classification of faults and describe each of them in detail.
14. List out and brief out at least five the most disastrous earthquakes occurred so far.

3.5 THE SEISMIC WAVES

The energy released during an earthquake produce the waves called seismic waves. These seismic waves can be classified into types as (Refer Fig. 3.8).

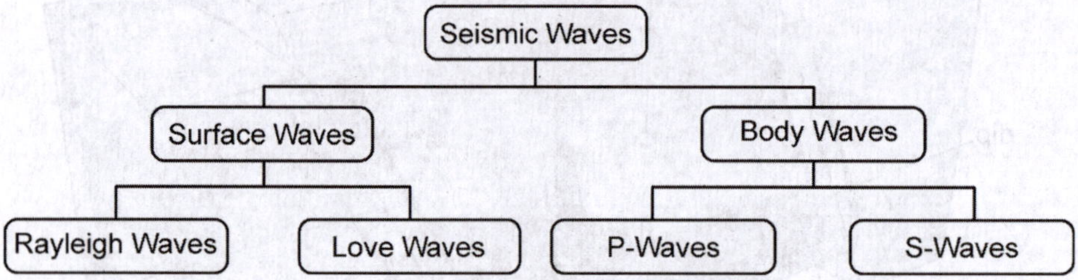

Fig. 3.8 Classification of earthquake (seismic) waves.

3.5.1 Surface Waves

These waves travel on Earth's surface and cause much of the destruction associated with earthquakes. Undulations of the land surface during an earthquake are a representation of surface waves. These waves are found in two ways as

(a) Rayleigh waves and
(b) Love waves.

(a) Rayleigh waves: Surface waves resulting in vertical motions are Rayleigh waves. These are much like waves traveling through water.

(b) Love waves: Surface waves resulting in sideways motions are **Love waves** which have no vertical component of movement.

Shock waves produced by Rayleigh waves or waves that roll through the Earth's surface—in contrast to side-to-side waves or Love waves—can travel far enough upward to cause a disturbance in the ionosphere, the layer of atmosphere about 80-480 km (50-300 miles) above Earth.

3.5.2 Body Waves

The body-waves travel through Earth's interior. These are further subdivided into **P** (primary) waves and **S** (secondary or shear) waves based upon their vibration direction and velocity. Variations in seismic wave velocity are used to infer the properties of Earth's interior. We shall not discuss about.

1. P-Waves or Primary waves
2. S-Waves or Secondary waves

1. P-waves vibrate parallel to their travel direction in the same way a vibration passes along a slinky toy (Fig. 3.9). P waves travel at speeds of 4 to 6 km per second (2.5-4 miles per second) in the uppermost part of the crust.

2. S-waves vibrate perpendicular to their travel direction, like the wave that passes along a rope when it is given a sharp jerk (Fig. 3.9). S wave velocity is 3 to 4 km per second (2-2.5 miles per second) in the shallow crust. The velocity of seismic waves is lower in loose, unconsolidated materials (sand, partially melted rock) and higher in solid materials (rock)

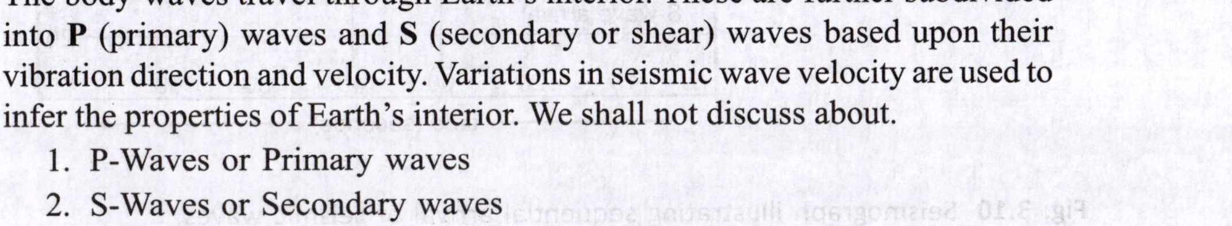

Fig. 3.9 Contrasting travel paths for surface waves and body waves following an earthquake.

the focus generates both P and S waves as a result of movement on a fault. P waves will arrive at a recording station (**seismograph station**) first because of their greater velocity, while surface waves are the last to arrive. (Fig. 3.10)

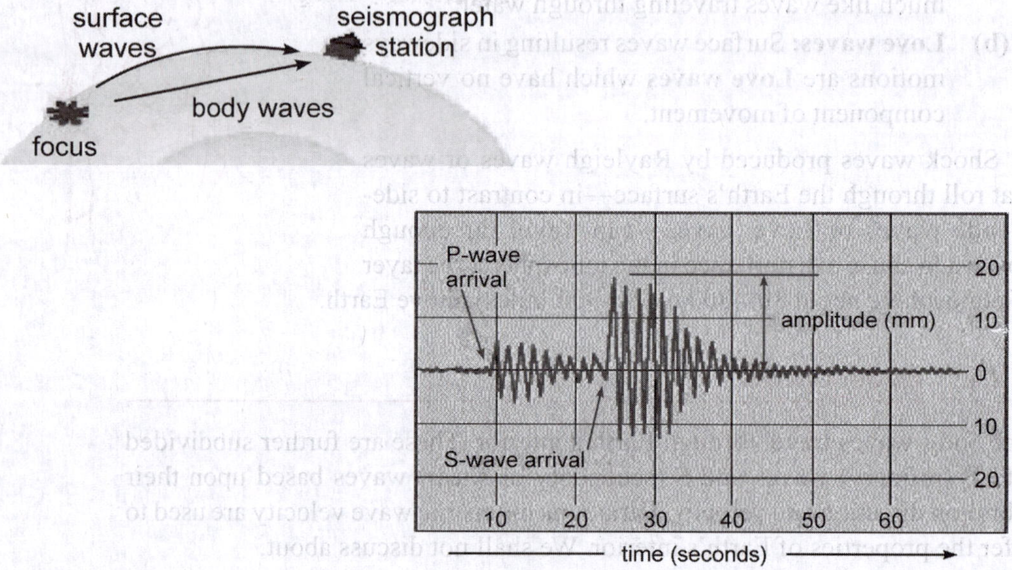

Fig. 3.10 Seismograph illustrating sequential arrival of seismic waves.

Seismic waves are recorded on a seismogram at a seismograph station. The distance of an earthquake epicenter from a seismograph station is determined by the difference in the arrival times of P and S waves at a seismograph station. Earthquake magnitude is calculated using the amplitude (height) of the S wave recorded on a seismogram. Seismic waves represent the energy released from the earthquake focus. These are summarized through the following tables.

Table 3.1 The differences between body waves and surface waves.

S.No.	Surface waves	Body waves
1.	These travel on Earth's surface	These travel through Earth's interior
2.	Undulations of land surface during an earthquake represent surface waves.	They cause tremors and vibrations in the earth
3.	Further divided into Rayleigh and Love waves	Further subdivided as P (primary) & S (secondary) waves on the basis of their vibration direction and velocity

Table 3.2 The differences between P-waves and S-waves.

S.No.	P-Waves	S-Waves
1.	These vibrate parallel to the travel direction	These vibrate perpendicular to their travel direction
2.	These are longitudinal waves	These are transverse waves
3.	P wave velocity is 4 to 6 km per second.	S wave velocity is 3 to 4 km per second.
4.	Analogous to vibration passing along a slinky toy	Analogous to the wave that passes along a rope when it is given a sharp jerk at one end

The record of an earthquake at a seismograph station is a **seismogram** (Fig. 3.10). The principal elements of a seismogram that interest seismologists (scientists who study earthquakes) are the relative size of the recorded waves and the difference in time that the first P and S waves were recorded. The amplitude of the recorded wave is proportional to the magnitude of shaking associated with the earthquake but shaking may vary with the character of the material underlying the seismograph station. On average, the kilometer distance to the earthquake is the number of seconds between the P and S wave **times 8**. Loose, unconsolidated materials (e.g., mud, sediment) may exaggerate the shaking whereas solid bedrock may result in smaller vibrations.

Figure 3.9. Analogs of P wave (upper) and S wave motion (lower). P waves are similar to the passage of a vibration through a slinky. The vibration occurs in the same direction as the wave travels. S wave motion is analogous to a vibration moving along a rope. The vibration occurs perpendicular to the direction in which the wave travels.

The difference in arrival time between P and S waves on a seismogram can be used to determine the distance of the station from the earthquake source and the amplitude (height) of the S wave recorded at the station can be used to determine earthquake magnitude (see Measurement of Earthquakes). Seismologists match the time difference with standard curves (Fig. 3.11 to determine distance from the earthquake.

In fact, it is difficult to predict epicenter of the earthquake by the data obtained at a single seismograph station because a seismogram yields only the distance from the earthquake source. The epicenter could be located anywhere along a circular arc of the calculated distance from the seismograph station. Therefore, seismologists use data from multiple stations to locating the event. The common intersection point for several circles plotted relative to different stations represents the epicenter.

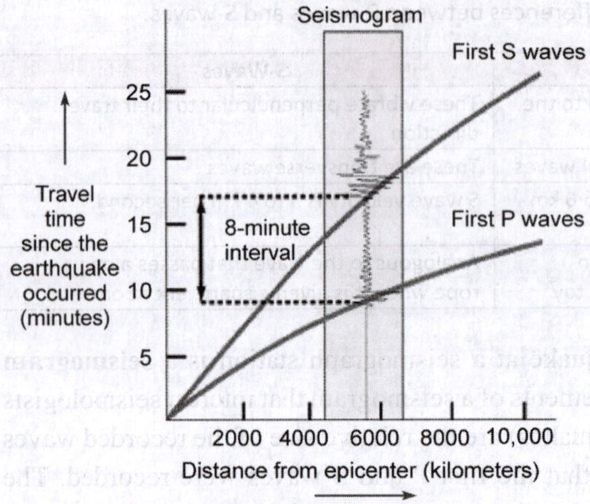

Fig. 3.11 Seismograph.

3.6 TYPES OF EARTHQUAKES

Earthquakes are classified in different ways with different bases. Most generally the bases to classify the earthquakes are the cause of origin, depth of focus and the intensity or magnitude of earthquake.

3.6.1 Based on the Cause of Origin

Based on cause of origin, the earthquakes are classified into two types. They are

1. Tectonic earthquakes, and
2. Non-tectonic earthquakes.

1. **Tectonic earthquakes:** These are the earthquakes caused by the faults that occur between the tectonic plates. The term "tectonic" is related to the "texture" and is from the Greek. The tensile or compressive or shear types of forces between the tectonic plates cause the earth to shake and thence release a seismic energy. The diagram showing the plates under the land are called tectonic maps. They indicate the earthquake prone areas and risk the involved. An example is shown in Fig. 3.12. Scientists developed the theory of plate tectonics in the mid-twentieth century. Tectonic plates move less than 3 inches (17 cm) per year. However, a tectonic plate movement of just 20 cm is enough to set off a major earthquake, such as the 6.9 Kobe-earthquake in 1995.

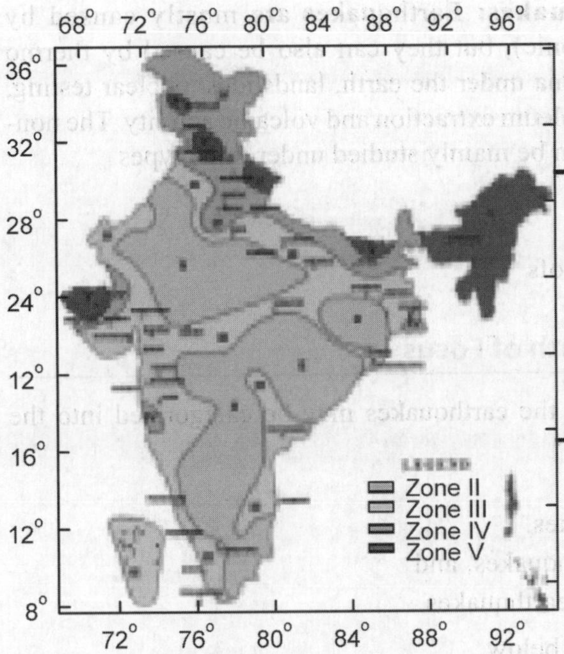

Zone	Magnitude
Zone V	Very High Risk Quakes of Magnitude 8 and greater
Zone IV	High Risk Quakes up to magnitude 7.9
Zone III	Moderate Risk Quakes upto Magnitude 6.9
Zone II	Seismic Disturbances upto Magnitude 4.9

Source: IS 1893 (Part I) : 2002 (BIS)

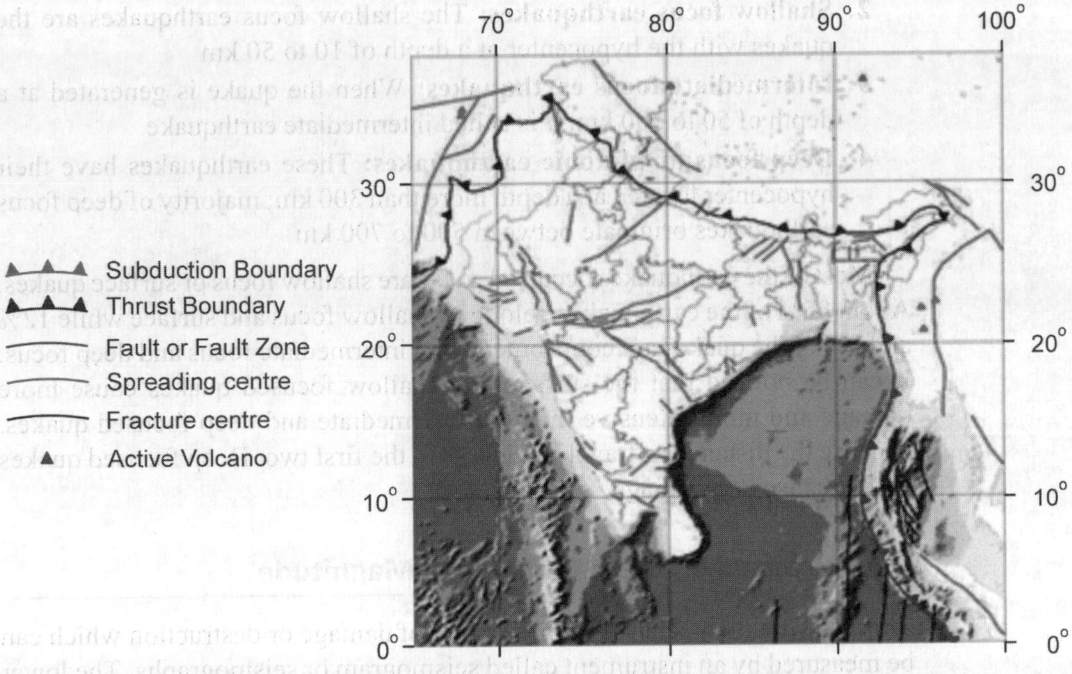

Fig. 3.12 Tectonic maps showing earthquake prone areas and risk in India.

2. **Non-tectonic earthquakes:** Earthquakes are mostly caused by geological faults (tectonic), but they can also be caused by thermo reactions/heat phenomena under the earth, landslides, nuclear testing, mine tests, mining/petroleum extraction and volcanic activity. The non-tectonic earthquakes can be mainly studied under three types
    - Surface causes
    - Volcanic reasons
    - Collapse of cavity roofs

3.6.2 Based on the Depth of Focus

Based on the depth of focus, the earthquakes may be categorized into the following four types;

1. Surface earthquakes,
2. Shallow focus earthquakes,
3. Intermediate-focus earthquakes, and
4. Deep focus or plutonic earthquakes.

These are described briefly below.

1. **Surface earthquakes:** Surface quakes occur on the surface i.e. the crust of the Earth. The depth of the focus lies below 10 kilometers.
2. **Shallow focus earthquakes:** The shallow focus earthquakes are the quakes with the hypocenter at a depth of 10 to 50 km
3. **Intermediate-focus earthquakes:** When the quake is generated at a depth of 50 to 300 km, it is called intermediate earthquake.
4. **Deep focus or plutonic earthquakes:** These earthquakes have their hypocenter located at a depth more than 300 km; majority of deep focus earthquakes originate between 500 to 700 km

Most of the earthquakes occurred so far are shallow focus or surface quakes. About 85% of the earthquakes belong to shallow focus and surface while 12% and 3% of the quakes are contributed from intermediate focus and deep focus. It can be noticed that the surface and shallow focused quakes cause more damage and more intensive than the intermediate and deep focused quakes, because the distance of travelling is less in the first two. Deep focused quakes hardly cause any damage.

3.6.3 Based on the Intensity and Magnitude

This classification is based on the degree of damage or destruction which can be measured by an instrument called seismogram or seismographs. The lower intensity values on Richter scale will not cause any damage and perhaps not even perceptible in several occasions. Furthermore, we can observe that the earthquake will not be constant and same at all the regions. The intensity gradually diminishes outwards from the origin i.e. epicenter. Thus an earthquake can show different effects at different places. It also inculcates an idea of recording by connecting the areas of same intensities as contours called isoseismic graphs. A magnitude of 3.0 or lower is nearly imperceptible. There are about 1,300,000 earthquakes per year (two per day) with magnitudes of 2.9 or lower which are going unnoticed. A quake is considered major when it registers more than 7.0 on the moment magnitude scale. Approximately one earthquake with a magnitude of 8.0 or higher occurs per year. Whatsoever the type of quake is; based on the intensity & magnitude the earth quakes are divided into following types.

1. Imperceptible,
2. Feeble,
3. Very slight,
4. Slight,
5. Weak,
6. Moderate,
7. Strong,
8. Major, and
9. Great.

The above terms are self explanatory and so not specifically explained. For details the scales of measurement may be referred.

SELF ASSESSMENT INTERMISSION (SAI – 3.2)

1. What are the seismic waves? How are they classified?
2. How are the waves produces during an earthquake?
3. Differentiate between the surface waves and body waves of earthquakes.
4. What is a seismogram? How P and S waves are used to determine earthquake epicenter?
5. Classify earthquakes and brief out each type..
6. What are the types of earthquakes based on depth of focus? Explain.
7. Explain the difference between P-waves and S-waves.
8. How are the earthquakes classified based on the cause of origin. Describe each of them.
9. "Surface & shallow focused quakes cause more damage than intermediate & deep focused quakes" Elucidate.
10. Differentiate between a Tectonic and Non-tectonic earthquakes.
11. How are the earthquakes classified based on the Intensity & Magnitude.

3.7 EARTHQUAKE MEASUREMENT

The earthquake is measured in several ways, such as the intensity (frequency of wave), effect (damage caused), the duration of quake, the number of times (frequency of occurrence), and location (epicenter) of the quake.

3.7.1 Measurement with Reference to Epicenter

The instrument used to measure the intensity of earthquake is known as seismograph or seismometer. A seismograph can capture and record the seismic waves. The relative arrival times of different seismic waves are used to ascertain the distance of the seismograph station from the origin of the earthquake. Three or more records can be used to locate the earthquake's **epicenter**. Earthquakes are often measured with reference to the epicenter location and the greatest loss is expected at this location.

Examples:

1. Nisqually earthquake (2001) occurred 53 km (33 miles) below the mouth of the Nisqually River in western Washington.
2. Loss of life in the Turkish earthquake (1999) was greatest in the city of Izmit, located close to the earthquake's epicenter.
3. Epicenter of the Nepal earthquake (2015) is located at about 80 km from Khatmandu.

3.7.2 Measurement with Reference to Damage

Over two million people were killed during the previous century by earthquakes and associated phenomena. Therefore, another method of earthquake measurement is taken by the level of destruction following an earthquake. In this method, the degree of damage is often related to more human activity than the earthquake itself. The Turkish earthquake is thus considered to be biggest quake, though not big according to the intensity on Richter scale. (Refer Fig. 3.13)

3.7.3 Measurement with Reference to Duration

The earthquake duration usually range in seconds. The large duration indicates more intensive. However, some quake, though last for more duration may not affect due to less intensity.

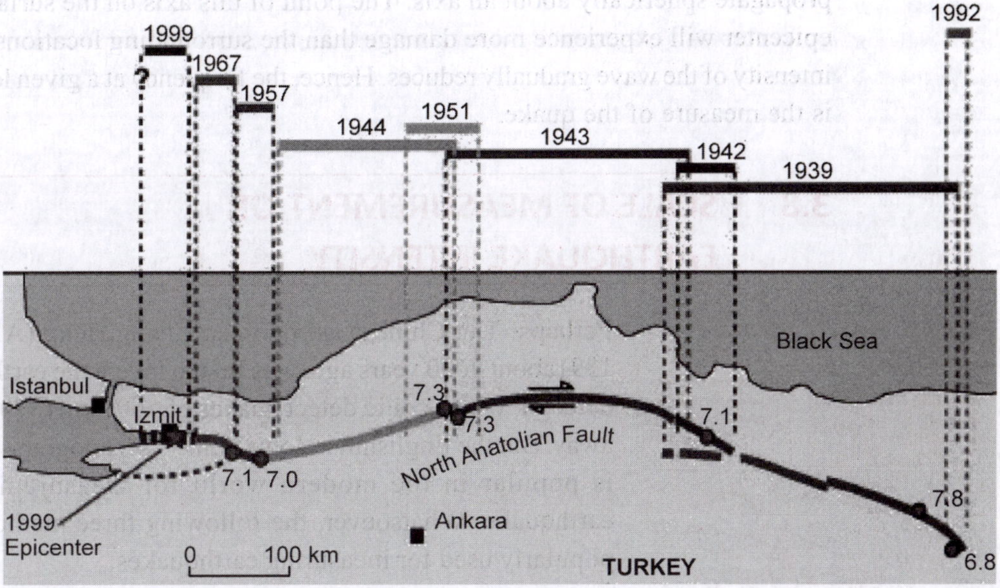

Fig. 3.13 Measurement of earthquake at Turkey/Blacksea.

3.7.4 Measurement with Reference to Frequency of Occurrence

Often, an earthquake will not stop with single wave, but a series of waves generate from the epicenter. Therefore, the earthquakes continue to come one after the other with certain gap. The duration between the two consecutive quakes may also be taken as the measure of the earthquake. This helps prediction of earthquake occurrence in a geographical region. For example, the threat of future earthquakes in heavily populated in the regions like California and Turkey. Analysis of number of past earthquakes permits finding the potential size and location of future events, but the problem is with ascertaining, when such events may occur with any degree of accuracy. The principal difficulty is that large, dangerous quakes occur at intervals measured in decades or centuries yet our record of past earthquake activity is available for only a few hundred years and is so, inadequate for exact predictions.

3.7.5 Measurement with Reference to Intensity

Earthquake distribution is far from random. Earthquakes occur on faults that are preferentially located along plate boundaries and the largest earthquakes along convergent plate boundaries. Thus the waves that travel from the focus propagate spherically about an axis. The point of this axis on the surface, i.e. epicenter will experience more damage than the surrounding locations as the intensity of the wave gradually reduces. Hence, the frequency at a given location is the measure of the quake.

3.8 SCALE OF MEASUREMENT OF EARTHQUAKE INTENSITY

Perhaps! The Chinese astronomer, Zhang Heng (A.D. 78-139) about 2000 years ago, was first to invent the earthquake detector, which could detect quakes of >600 km (370 miles) away. But the Englishman John Milne's seismograph (1880) is popular in the modern world for measurement of earthquake. Whatsoever, the following three methods are popularly used for measuring earthquakes.

1. Mercalli scale
2. The Richter scale
3. The Moment-Magnitude scale

The above three principal methods of measuring the effects of earthquakes are explained below.

3.8.1 Mercalli Scale

The Mercalli scale is not widely used but relatively easy to use and realistic since its interpretation mainly considers three reasonable factors, viz. the distance from epicenter, building materials used, and population density.

1. **Distance from the epicenter:** The intensity of earthquake decreases with increasing distance from the epicenter. Therefore, the same quake will have different effect at different places thus makes it is difficult to compare individual events. Thence, the measurement of intensity of earthquake should consider the effect due to this factor
2. **Building materials and methods:** Though quakes are of similar size, they may show different effects on two different buildings located at same place due to the strength of buildings due the material used and the building codes applied.
3. **Population density:** The effect of earthquake may prove to be more adverse if the region is thickly populated. On the other hand, the intensity of earthquake would be underestimated in sparsely populated areas. Therefore, loss to the people is yet another factor to describe the intensity of earthquake.

The Mercalli scale is more useful in ranking historical earthquakes that occurred before seismographs have become popular (after World War II). The Modified Mercalli scale also measures intensity and is often used to rank the cultural effects of historical earthquakes.

The Mercalli scale ranks intensity from I to XII (1-12) using Roman numerals. The level of destruction of the earthquake (higher values) and the effect of the event on people (lower values). The table below summarizes the characteristics of the Mercalli scale.

Table 3.3 Earthquake index on Mercalli Scale.

Index	Effects of Earthquake on People and Structures
I	Not felt by people.
II	Felt by people at rest on upper floors of buildings.
III	May be felt by people indoors. Vibrations similar to the passing of a truck.
IV	Felt indoors by many, outdoors by few. Dishes, windows, doors disturbed; walls make cracking sound. Sensation like heavy truck striking building.
V	Felt by nearly everyone; many awakened. Some dishes, windows broken. Unstable objects overturned.
VI	Felt by all; many frightened. Some heavy furniture moved; a few instances of fallen plaster. Damage slight.
VII	Slight to moderate damage in ordinary structures; considerable damage in poorly built or badly designed structures; some chimneys broken.
VIII	Slight damage in buildings designed to withstand earthquakes; heavy damage in poorly constructed structures. Chimneys, columns, walls may fall.
IX	Considerable damage in specially designed structures. Damage great in substantial buildings, partial collapse. Buildings shifted off foundations.
X	Some well-built wooden structures destroyed; most masonry and frame structures destroyed with foundations.
XI	Few, if any (masonry) structures remain standing. Bridges destroyed. Rails bent greatly.
XII	Total damage, objects thrown into air.

3.8.2 Richter Scale

It is the most popular method of measuring earthquake magnitude developed by Charles Richter in 1935 to measure shallow earthquakes in California. The early measurements simply relied on using two factors (the difference in P and S-wave arrival times and S wave amplitude i.e. the height on the seismogram).

Table 3.4 Magnitudes of ground motion and energy in Richter Scale.

Magnitude	Ground Motion	Energy Release
1	1	1
2	10	30
3	10^2	900
4	10^3	27000
5	10^4	810000
6	10^5	24300000
7	10^6	729000000
8	10^7	21870000000
9	10^8	656100000000

The Richter scale is logarithmic. Each division represents a 10-fold increase in the ground motion associated with the earthquake, and about 30-times increase in energy released. For example, a magnitude 6 earthquake has ten times as much ground motion (and releases over 30-times the energy) as a magnitude 5, 100 times as much motion (900 times the energy) as a magnitude 4; 1,000 times the motion of a magnitude 3 (27000 times the energy), and so on.

Unlike the Mercalli scale, the Richter scale is open-ended, i.e. it does not have a maximum value. However, the largest earthquakes measured with the Richter scale have magnitudes between 8 and 9. It is perhaps, due to rocks in earth crust are unable to bear the stresses required to generate earthquakes of magnitude 9 or more.

Determination of magnitude from body waves (Mb)

$$Mb = \log_{10}(a/t) + c$$

where a is the amplitude of ground motion (microns);

t is time taken for motion (seconds); and

c is a correction for distance from the epicenter and the focal depth (kilometers).

The terminology used to describe earthquakes is dependent upon their magnitude.

Comparison between Richter scale and Mercalli scale

Description	Magnitude (Richter)	Equivalent Intensity (Mercalli)	Number per Year
Moderate	5 – 5.9	VI – VII	800
Strong	6 – 6.9	VII – VIII	120
Major	7 – 7.9	IX – X	18
Great	8+	XI – XII	1

The 1906 earthquake in California was before the Richter scale, but scientists estimate it would rank as a 7.8. As much as 90% of the damage in San Francisco was from fires caused by cracked gas pipes. San Francisco burned for three days and nights. The 1906 California earthquake was one of the first major disasters to be recorded by photography.

3.8.3 Moment-Magnitude (Mw) Scale

This is a recent method that probably measures the energy release on large faults more accurately than the Richter scale. The amount of energy released depends on rock properties such as the rock rigidity, area of the fault surface and amount of movement on the fault.

Distribution of Earthquakes

> **O My God!**
>
> The 1,200 km (750 miles) long San Andreas Fault that separates the North American and Pacific Plates in California is the most active fault system in the contiguous U.S. The Izmit earthquake occurred on the North Anatolian Fault, which is of similar length and sense of movement as the San Andreas Fault.

- Earthquakes are most frequent along plate boundaries.
- The largest earthquakes are associated with convergent plate boundaries.
- Oceanic ridges are characterized by shallow earthquakes.
- Deep earthquakes (to depths of ~700 km) occur within subduction zones along convergent plate boundaries.

Formula to determine magnitude

$$M_w = 2/3 \log_{10}(M_o) - 10.7$$

Here M_o = mad,

Where 'm' is shear strength of the faulted rock,

'a' is the area of the fault, and

'd' is fault displacement.

Summarily,

- Modified Mercalli scale focuses on measuring damage and human perception of an earthquake.
- Richter scale focuses on measuring the size of the seismic waves recorded at a seismogram.
- Moment-magnitude scale focuses on measuring the amount of energy released by a quake.

SELF ASSESSMENT INTERMISSION (SAI – 3.3)

1. What are the general methods of measuring earthquake? Explain any two methods.
2. How the earthquake measurement is done with reference to epicenter?
3. Describe the measurement of earthquake with reference to Intensity and Frequency of Occurrence.
4. Differentiate between magnitude and intensity of an earthquake. How are they measured?
5. Name the scale of measurement of earthquake intensity.
6. How the Richter scale is used for measuring earthquake magnitude? Explain
7. Explain the measurement of earthquake with reference to Damage and Duration.
8. What is the instrument used to measure the intensity of earthquake.
9. Explain the Moment-Magnitude (Mw) Scale to measure the earthquake.
10. Give the comparison between Richter scale and Mercalli scale
11. List out and explain the popular methods of measuring earthquake.

3.9 EARTHQUAKE PREDICTION

O My God!

Isoseismal maps are those which show areas of equal earthquake intensity, e.g. New Madrid, Missouri (the eastern U.S.) and San Francisco, California (The western U.S.)

Often seismologists and disaster managers are concerned with the following general and fundamental questions with regard to the prediction of earthquakes.

Where do earthquakes occur?

When do they occur?

How big they would be, if they occur?

At what frequency they occur?

To obtain the answers for the above questions, the judicial and analytical thinking is required. Let us evaluate some of the points that favour the occurrence of the earthquakes:

- Earthquake magnitude is directly related to fault length. Earthquake magnitude increases with fault length i.e. to say, the longer the fault, the bigger is the earthquake.

  A good evidential support to this argument is the 1906 San Francisco earthquake (Mw 7.8, maximum Mercalli intensity of XI, the extreme) caused by rupture of 400 km (250 miles) of the San Andreas Fault and shaking lasted for 42 seconds (It struck the coast of Northern California at 5:12 a.m. on April 18, 1906 which consumed about 3,000 people and over 80% of San Francisco was destroyed and devastating fires broke out in the city that lasted for several days). In contrast the magnitude 6.7 Northridge earthquake was caused by displacement on a 14 km (9 miles) long fault segment and the duration of shaking was just 7 seconds.
- Earthquakes typically occur in areas of active faults, especially along plate boundaries.

  The active faults are shown in the tectonic diagram. There are two major faults, namely, San Andeas Fault and Anatolian Fault.
- Various instruments and satellite observations can be used to measure the buildup of strain in rocks.

  Japan's 9.0 earthquake in 2011 moved the island closer to the United States, and also shifted the planet's axis by 6.5 inches, created a massive 186-mile long and 93 mile wide rift 15 miles under the ocean. Japan's massive 2011 earthquake shifted the earth's mass toward the center, causing the planet to spin faster and shortening the day by 1.6 microseconds. The 2004 Sumatra quake shorted the day by 6.8 microseconds. Because of earthquake-prone, Japan placed high-tech sensors around the country after its 1995 quake. Japan's 2011 earthquake is the best-recorded earthquake in history. Nearly 80% of Earth's largest earthquakes occur near the "Ring of Fire," (Fig. 3.14)which is a horseshoe-shaped region in the Pacific Ocean where many tectonic plates meet. The tectonic maps obtained by satellite observations reveal the fact that the second-most earthquake-prone area is a region called the Alpide Belt, which includes countries such as Turkey, Iran, Pakistan, North India, Nepal, Tibet, and South China. The iso-seismic lines on the map can help predicting the intensity. (Refer Fig. 3.15).

An example of Alaska is given below:

Isoseismal map of 1964 Alaska earthquake showing areas with equivalent damages following the largest recorded U.S. earthquake. Locations of U.S. earthquakes causing damage 1750-1996, Mercalli intensity VI to XII. Large red squares represent locations of largest earthquakes (intensity XII). Note squares in southeast Missouri from New Madrid (1811-1812) earthquakes.

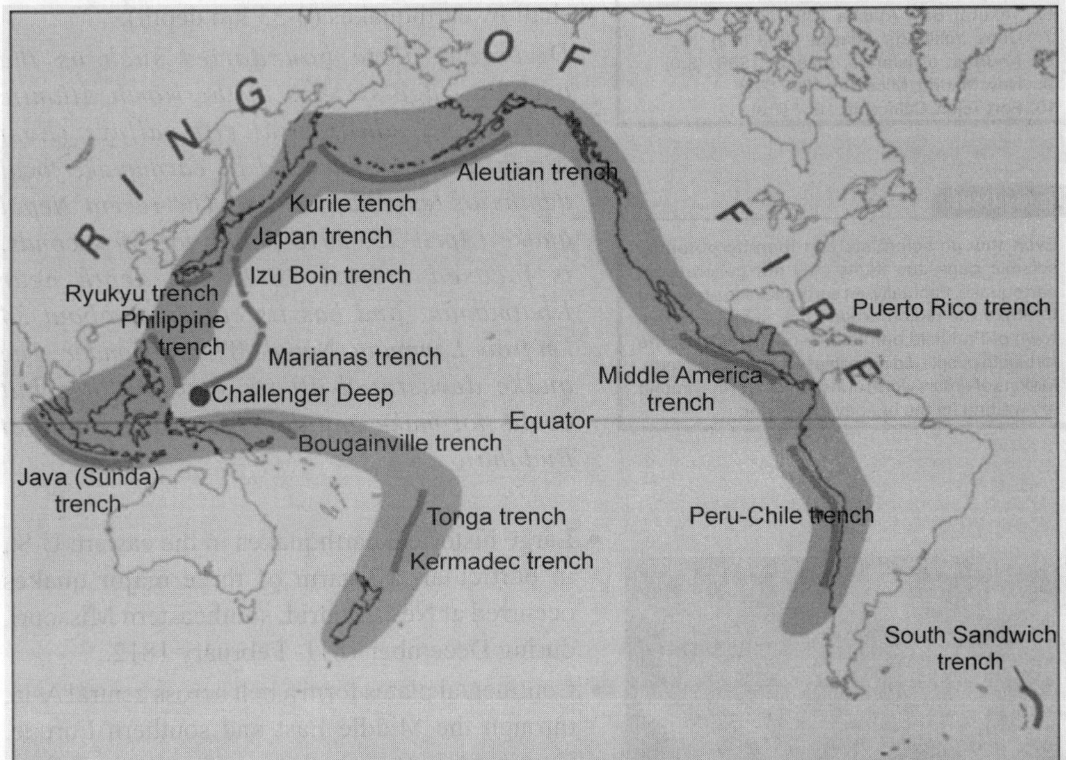

Fig. 3.14 Ring of fire (Pacific).

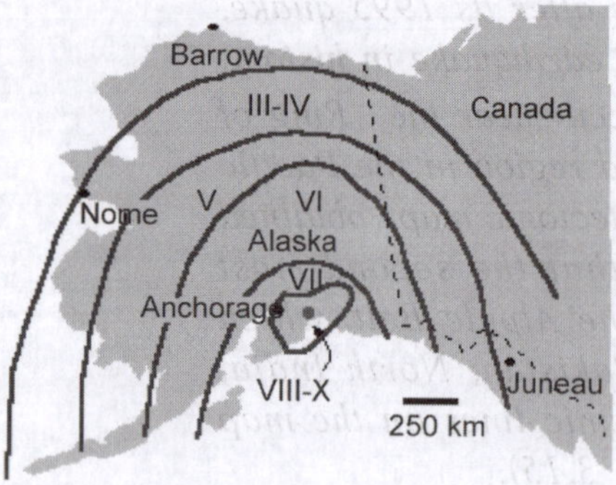

Fig. 3.15 Isoseismic lines map.

O My God!

8 of 10 largest U.S. Earthquakes in ALASKA

1. Prince William Sound, **Alaska 1964** (9.2)
2. Andrean of Islands, **Alaska 1957** (8.8)
3. Rat Islands, **Alaska 1965** (8.7)
4. Shumagin Islands, **Alaska 1938** (8.3)
5. Lituya Bay, **Alaska 1958** (8.3)
6. Yakutat Bay, **Alaska 1899** (8.2)
7. Cape Yakataga, **Alaska 1899** (8.2)
8. Andrean of Islands, **Alaska, 1986**, (8.0)
9. New Madrid, Missouri, 1812 (7.9)
10. Fort Tejon, California, 1857 (7.9)

O My God!

Even though scientists can identify potential seismic gaps, the faults may not generate an earthquake. Factually, an earthquake is predicted to strike the region around the small California town of Parkfield before the end of 1993 but the fortunate people did not witness the quake hitherto. Millions of dollars worth of instruments in the ground are waiting for the big day to register.

- Scientists predict the long-term probability of earthquakes for specific locations on the basis of information about strain accumulations and recurrence interval.

  The most earthquake-prone state is Alaska. It experienced one major quake in every 11 years (between 1899 and 1986, it experienced 8 major quakes all of which measure 8 or more on Richter scale).

- Short-term prediction, days or weeks before an earthquake, is still a long way off.

  Japan is one of the most earthquake-prone nations in the world. Thousands of earthquakes occur in Japan every year, but most of them are very weak and not predictable.

- The most devastating earthquakes are typically shallow earthquakes (0-33 km depth).

  Divergent plate boundaries such as the oceanic ridge systems in the North Atlantic Ocean and continental rift valleys (East Africa) are characterized by earthquake focal depths of less than 33 km. The recent Nepal quake (April 25, 2015 shook for 50 seconds, is focused at just 10-15 km depth near Khatmandu and has its epicenter about 34 km from Lampung, Nepal. What a wonder! The quake devastated all its surroundings but could not make any damage to the statue of Buddha).

- Large historical earthquakes in the eastern U.S., in particular, a swarm of three major quakes occurred at New Madrid, southeastern Missouri, during December 1811- February 1812.
- Continental plates form a belt across central Asia, through the Middle East and southern Europe. Continental interiors that are far removed from plate boundaries (e.g., Canada) have few earthquakes.

- A belt of shallow earthquakes are traced along the global oceanic ridge system from the center of the Atlantic Ocean, through the Indian Ocean, spread around the southern and Eastern Pacific.
- Earthquakes can occur under hot spots such as the Hawaiian Islands in the central Pacific Ocean. The largest earthquakes are associated with convergent plate boundaries.

Summarily, the tectonic diagrams can give a rough idea about the quake prone regions and the probability theory helps in prediction of the quakes by locating the seismic gaps. However, the prevention is impossible, but can minimize the loss.

- Scientists predict the average recurrence interval – i.e. the time between earthquakes of similar magnitude - for individual faults by determining the ages of offset layers of rocks and/or sediment. Analysis of time elapsed since the last earthquake and the energy released can reveal which faults gain sufficient strain for seismic activity in the near future.
- Researchers use statistical methods and probability theory to predict future damaging earthquakes on particular faults with sufficient record of seismicity. Faults with a high probability of an earthquake exhibit a lot of stored strain and a long time interval without fault movement. In 1990 a panel of experts convened by the National Earthquake Prediction Evaluation Council estimated a 67% probability for a major earthquake on one of 4 segments of the San Andreas Fault in the San Francisco Bay area between 1990 and 2020. Scientists predicted the near certainty (95% probability) of an earthquake at Parkfield, California, between 1986-1993. Parkfield, located on the San Andreas Fault, averaged a magnitude 6 earthquake every 22 years since 1857. Geophysicists distributed an array of monitoring instruments around Parkfield in the 1980s hoping to pick up a signal that would aid in predicting future earthquakes. However, the earthquake has still not occurred illustrating a potential pitfall of prediction by probability, because probability theory assumes a random occurrence of earthquakes.

3.9.1 Prequake Period – Fore-Shocks and Symptoms of Main Shock

- The history as well as the experiences, reveal that tremors of lesser magnitude occur before the main event. These are often referred to as fore-shocks. Since, these tremors are of smaller magnitude and do not damage, and even sometimes too lesser magnitude to sense the people often ignore. But, strictly

EARTHQUAKES IN INDIA (Magnitude 6+)

1950 Arunachal - China Border 8.5
1956 Anjar, Gujarat 7.0
1967 Koyna, Maharashtra 6.5
1975 Kinnaur, Himachal Pradesh 6.2
1988 Manipur - Myanmar Boarder 6.6
1988 Bihar - Nepal Border 6.4
1991 Uttarkashi – Uttar Pradesh Hills 6.0
1993 Latur - Maharashtra 6.3
1997 Jabalpur, Madhya Pradesh 6.0
1999 Chamoli, Uttar Pradesh 6.8
2001 Bhuj, Gujarat 6.9
2005 Muzaffarabad (Pakistan) & Impact in J&K 7.4

speaking, the fore-shocks are the alarms for a big one to occur. Further, it is very difficult to predict how big (magnitude), and when (the interval) that the main would occur even if the fore-shocks are noticed. Sometime they may not occur too.

However, some observations of the survivors of the earthquakes and seismologists say that-

- Animals cry or make strange sounds and move restlessly or run with fearful feelings. Particularly, the pet animals like dogs, cats etc, which can sense the seismic, ultrasonic, infrasonic, supersonic as well as the normal sound waves, can better predict these wave. They even sense the released gases from the earth before a quake. Oh God! Unfortunate that we do not understand neither their language nor they can talk in our language. But if we carefully observe their behaviour, perhaps, we may predict the occurrence of a quake.
- Birds make some characteristic sounds. They fly high. They cry with peculiar sounds.
- Before an earthquake, ponds and canals may give off a strange smell. This is caused due to the release of gases underground.
- The temperature of ground water can also become warmer, some of the seismic energy converts into thermal energy.

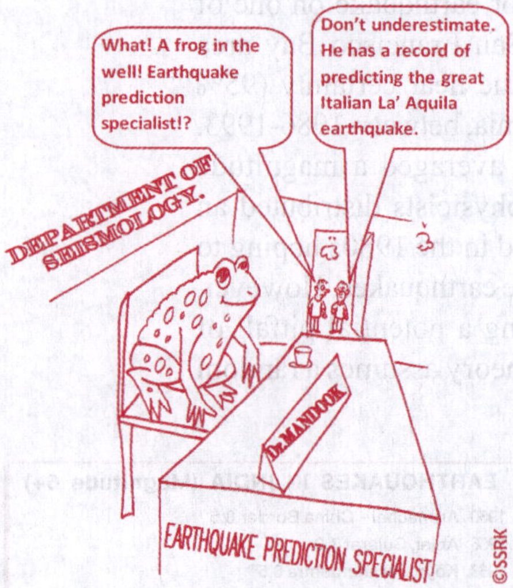

- In April 2009, British researchers when studying the common toad (frogs) at central Italy observed a mass migration of toads and just five days later, a 6.3-magnitude earthquake hit killing 308 people and causing extensive damage to the town of L'Aquila, Italy on April 6, 2009. Just after 9 days, Afghanistan experienced a quake of 5.5 which perhaps could be an aftershock. ***Think! Who is frog in the well?... The Frog? Or the Man?*** Though, thousands of fore-shocks of which more than 30 are about 3.5 had been occurring since December 2008, it was not properly forecast. Six scientists and an ex-government employee were convicted and sentenced 6-year imprisonment for the manslaughter for failing to predict and/or confusing and contradicting.
- Rachel Grant, a researcher at Open University on animal behavior surrounding earthquakes, wrote, "The toad population at the breeding site dropped to zero three days prior to the quake. A day after the earthquake, they all started coming back". He believes that toads can detect pre-seismic cues such as the release of gases and charged particles, and this can be used as a early warning system.

- In 373 B.C., historians wrote that rats, weasels and snakes made a mass exodus from the Greek city of Helice days before an earthquake destroyed the city.
- Reports include bees leaving their hive, catfish moving violently and chickens refusing to lay eggs.

Till date, seismologists can't predict when or where the next earthquake will hit, and scientists don't know what, if anything, animals sense before a quake. But what a wonder! Animals have more sensitive hearing and other senses allow them to feel vibrations that humans can't even detect or measure. But alas! They cannot help us nor to themselves.

3.9.2 During Earthquake

When the earth is quaking, depending on its intensity, the following are some events occur

- People move as if somebody is shaking or waving to and fro or left and right like a pendulum
- Cars run away uncontrolled
- Buildings shake, move to and fro, and collapse
- Objects like chairs, tables, utensils move and make sounds
- Resonating sounds are produced
- Roads and structures crack
- Bridges, dams and construction crack or break
- Fire and explosions occur and many more…

3.9.3 Post Earthquake - Aftershocks

An aftershock is an earthquake that occurs after a previous earthquake, the main shock.

- Aftershocks occur in the same region of the main shock but always smaller in magnitude.
- If an aftershock is larger than the main shock, the aftershock is re-designated as the main shock and the original main shock is re-designated as a foreshock.
- Aftershocks are formed as the crust around the displaced fault plane adjusts to the effects of the main shock.
- Most aftershocks are located over the full area of fault rupture and either occurs along the fault plane itself or along other faults within the volume affected by the strain associated with the main shock.

- Typically, aftershocks are found up to a distance equal to the rupture length away from the fault plane. The pattern of aftershocks helps confirm the size of area that slipped during the main shock.
- Aftershocks are dangerous because they are usually unpredictable, can be of a large magnitude, and can collapse buildings that are damaged from the main shock.
- Bigger earthquakes have more and larger aftershocks and the sequences can last for years or even longer especially when a large event occurs in a seismically quiet area.

Example: Nepal quakes April-May 2015: The main shock occurred on 25th April 2015 and continued aftershocks occurred throughout Nepal at the intervals of 15–20 minutes, with one shock reaching a magnitude of 6.7 on 26 April at 12:54:08 NST. It experienced over 38 aftershocks with magnitude of 4.5M_w. A major aftershock occurred on 12 May 2015 at 12:51 NST with a moment magnitude (M_w) of 7.3. The epicenter was near the China border between Kathmandu and Mt. Everest. More than 200 people were killed and more than 2,500 were injured by this aftershock. The country also had a continued risk of landslides.

3.9.4 Earthquake Swarms

Earthquake swarms are sequences of earthquakes striking in a specific area within a short period of time. They are differentiated from earthquakes succeeded by a series of aftershocks by the observation that no single earthquake in the sequence is obviously the main shock. Earthquake swarms are one of the events typically preceding eruptions of volcanoes.

Examples:

- In the U. S., the 2008 Reno earthquakes began in February and ended in November. Between February and April the swarm produced more than 1,000 quakes of small magnitude, although the largest measured 4.7
- Spanish island in the eastern Atlantic during the 2011–12 El Hierro eruption, 100s of small earthquakes were measured from July 2011 until October 2011. The accumulated energy released by the swarm increased dramatically on 28 September. The swarm was due to the movement of magma beneath the island, and on 9 October indications of a submarine volcanic eruption were detected.

- Between February 2011 and December 2011 more than 500 earthquakes were recorded during the 2011 Christchurch earthquakes, with 31 of them greater than magnitude 5.
- Near Mexicali, along the Cerro Prieto Fault, over 500 quakes and aftershocks occurred during a 2-week period in Feb 2008
- In 2013, the Santa Cruz Islands had been experiencing a large earthquake
- A Swarm with many magnitude 5 and 6 earthquakes since January and continuing into February later resulted in the 2013 Solomon Islands earthquake (8.0) on Feb 6,.

3.9.5 Earthquake Storms

An earthquake storm is a recently proposed theory about earthquakes. According to this theory, one quake triggers a series of other large quakes along the same plate boundary due to the transfer of stress along the fault system. This is somewhat similar to the idea of aftershocks, with the exception that they take place years apart. However, these series of earthquakes can ruin entire country or a geographical region. Perhaps! It might have happened during the end of the Bronze Age, and the latter part of the Roman Empire. It has been suggested that this is what may be occurring in modern day Turkey.

3.10 EFFECTS OF EARTHQUAKES

Obviously, the earthquakes from shallow depths cause greatest damage since the seismic waves travel lesser distance to reach the surface. It is quite evident from the earthquake disaster occurred at Kobe, Japan, during the 1995. Though the ground shook for only about 20 seconds, more than 5,000 people were killed, 300,000 people were left homeless, and more than 100,000 buildings were destroyed. An earthquake can release hundred times more energy than the nuclear bomb that was dropped on Hiroshima in Japan in 1945.

The **earthquake effects**, the type of damage due to earthquakes, include changes in the natural environment such as landslides, tsunami, volcano eruption but major attention is given to the impact on constructed structures.

- A major earthquake under a heavily populated area could result in thousands of deaths.
- Several effects of earthquakes could result in extensive damages.
- Ground shaking can collapse buildings.

- Uplift may raise or lower large areas of Earth's surface.
- Liquefaction in water-saturated sediment can result in the collapse and subsidence of the ground surface.
- Landslides are potential hazards on steep slopes in seismic zones.
- Tsunamis are dangers to coastal communities, particularly around the Pacific Ocean.

Sudden changes on or near the earth's surface result from earthquakes and may include:

1. **Ground Shaking:** Rapid horizontal movements associated with earthquakes may shift homes off their foundations and cause tall buildings to collapse or "pancake" as floors collapse down onto one another. Shaking is exaggerated in areas where the underlying sediment is weak or saturated with water.
2. **Fault Rupture and Uplift:** Break of the ground surface by the fault plane may form a step in the surface known as a fault scarp. Large sections of Earth's surface may change elevation as a result of uplift on an earthquake fault. Mountains east of Los Angeles were uplifted 0.3 meters (1ft) by the 1994 Northridge earthquake.
3. **Liquefaction:** Liquefaction occurs when water-saturated sediment is reorganized because of violent shaking. The sediment collapses, expelling the water, and causing the ground surface to subside.

4. **Landslides:** Earthquakes are often associated with mountains formed along convergent plate boundaries. The steep slopes present in these environments are prone to landslides when shaken.

Examples:

- Landslides became a symbol of the devastation the 2001 El Salvador earthquakes left, killing hundreds in its wake. (see adjacent figure)
- The world's worst landslide started by an earthquake occurred in 1920 in the Kansu province in China. The landslide killed about 200,000 people.
- Landslides are common following earthquakes in California.

5. **Tsunamis:** An earthquake under the ocean can cause a tsunami, which travels outward in all directions up to 600 miles (970 km) per hour, the speed of a jet. When the tsunami reaches the shoreline, it suddenly rolls up to heights of over 100 feet (30 meters) causing massive destruction.

Giant sea waves are generated by submarine earthquakes, especially noted from the Pacific Ocean. Tsunamis caused by earthquakes around the ocean's perimeter travelled thousands of miles to destroy coastal property in Hawaii.

Tsunami of 2004 Indian Ocean EQ

Examples:

- Many casualties associated with the 1964 Alaska earthquake resulted from tsunamis.
- The highest tsunami caused by an earthquake happened in Japan in 1771. A tsunami 278 feet (85 meters) high struck Ishigaki Island.
- The 9.0 earthquake that struck Japan Mar 11, 2011 was the worst earthquake in Japan's history. It generated a tsunami with 30 ft (10 m) high wave and severely damaged nuclear power plants.

The Deadliest Earthquakes in History		
Place	**Year**	**Casualties**
SW Syria	1201	1,100,000
Tangsha, China	1978	655,237
Shansi, China	1556	830,000
Ganja, Azerbaijan	1139	300,000
China	1662	300,000
Tangshan, China	1737	255,000
Aleppo, Syria	1138	230,000
Xining, China	1927	200,000
Damghan, Iran	856	200,000

6. **Avalanches:** Even avalanches are triggered by earthquake. The worst avalanche triggered by an earthquake occurred in Peru in 1070. A 250-ft (850-m) wave of ice, mud, and rock fell down the mountain in Huascaran at 250 mi (400 km) per hr. Entire villages washed away killing >18,000.
7. **Volcanoes:** Earthquakes can set off volcanoes, as were the cases in the 1980 Mount St. Helens eruption and the Mount Etna eruption in 2002.
8. **Fires:** Earthquakes can cause fires by damaging electrical power or gas lines. In the event of water mains rupturing and a loss of pressure, it may also become difficult to stop the spread of a fire once it has started. For example, more deaths in the 1906 San Francisco earthquake were caused by fire than by the earthquake itself.

Fires of 1906 San Francisco EQ

9. **Floods:** Floods may be secondary effects of earthquakes, if dams are damaged. Earthquakes may cause landslips to dam rivers, which collapse and cause floods. The terrain below the Sarez Lake in Tajikistan is in danger

> **O My God!**
>
> **Believe it or not**
> Even the largest earthquakes may be generated by relatively small fault movements due to large volumes of rock. Astounding fact is that the offsets on faults for the largest of earthquakes are **less than 5 meters.**
>
> Another amazing fact is that the accumulated movement from hundreds of thousands of earthquakes over millions of years results in the formation of mountains in association with plate boundaries.

of catastrophic flood if the landslide dam formed by the earthquake, known as the Usoi Dam, were to fail during a future earthquake. Impact projections suggest the flood could affect roughly 5 million people.

10. **Other Effects:** An earthquake may cause injury and loss of life, road and bridge damage, general property damage, and collapse or destabilization (potentially leading to future collapse) of buildings. The aftermath may bring disease, lack of basic necessities, and higher insurance premiums.

3.11 MITIGATION

Possible risk reduction measures

- **Community preparedness:** As it is not possible to prevent the occurrence of earthquake, the only method of mitigation is to be prepared. Community preparedness is vital for mitigating the impact of earthquake. The most effective way to save you even in a slightest shaking is **'DROP, COVER** and **HOLD'**. (Refer Fig. 3.16).
- **Planning:** The Bureau of Indian Standards (BIS) has published building codes and guidelines for safe construction of buildings against earthquakes. Before going for any construction, the building plans have to be thoroughly checked by the Municipality, as per code.

The 5 Strongest Earthquakes Since 1900		
Place	**Year**	**Strength (MMS)**
Valdivia, Chile	1960	9.5
Prince William Sound, Alaska	1964	9.2
Sumatra, Indonesia	2004	9.1
Sendai, Japan	2011	9.0
Kamchatka, Russia	1952	9.0

- Many existing lifeline buildings such as hospitals, schools and fire stations may not be built with earthquake safety measures. These have to be identified and their earthquake safety needs to be upgraded by retrofitting techniques.
- **Public education** on causes and characteristics of an earthquake is very important particularly in the quake prone areas. It can be created through sensitization and training programme for community, architects,

engineers, builders, masons, teachers, government functionaries teachers and students on the issues like

- o Effect of Soil type on ground shaking
- o Essential requirements in a Masonry building
- o Earthquake and preparedness measures.

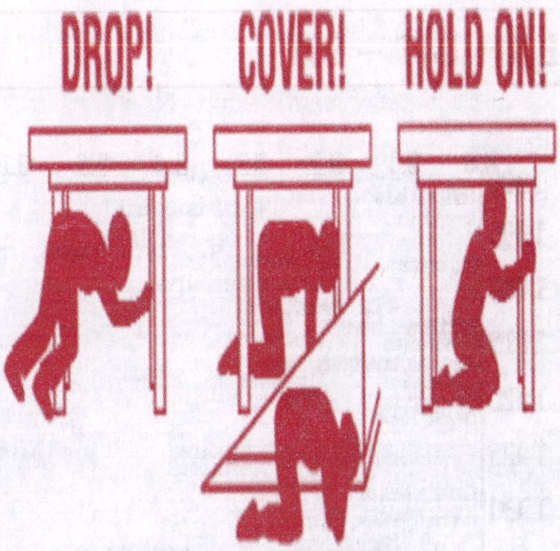

Fig. 3.16 Safety tips for (Drop-Cover-Hold).

- **Engineered structures:** Buildings need to be designed and constructed as per the building by laws to withstand ground shaking. Architectural and engineering inputs need to be put together to improve building design and construction practices. The soil type needs to be analyzed before construction. Building structures on soft soil should be avoided. Buildings on soft soil are more likely to get damaged even if the magnitude of the earthquake is not strong as shown. Similar problems persist in the buildings constructed on the river banks which have alluvial soil.

SELF ASSESSMENT INTERMISSION (SAI – 3.4)

1. What are the factors to be considered while planning the rebuilding works after a major disaster due to earthquake?
2. Describe various types of hazards and impacts associated with earthquakes?
3. Give the major earthquake prone areas (countries) in the world. Discuss why?
4. How can the earthquakes be predicted.
5. List out the areas where earthquake occurred in India.
6. What will be the effects of earthquakes?
7. What is the role of disaster manager in reducing the risk?
8. Give the three major mitigation measures to reduce earthquake risk.

MINI-PROJECTS / CASE STUDIES

1. Prepare an animation model of earthquake, and make a presentation with your voice over.
2. Browse internet and list out top ten earthquakes. Prepare an article with variety of them, such as, highest damage, highest human loss, largest time shaken, etc.
3. List out all the earthquakes occurred hither to and prepare a frequency table for each continent. Also prepare iso-seismic map of earth.

EXHIBIT – 3A

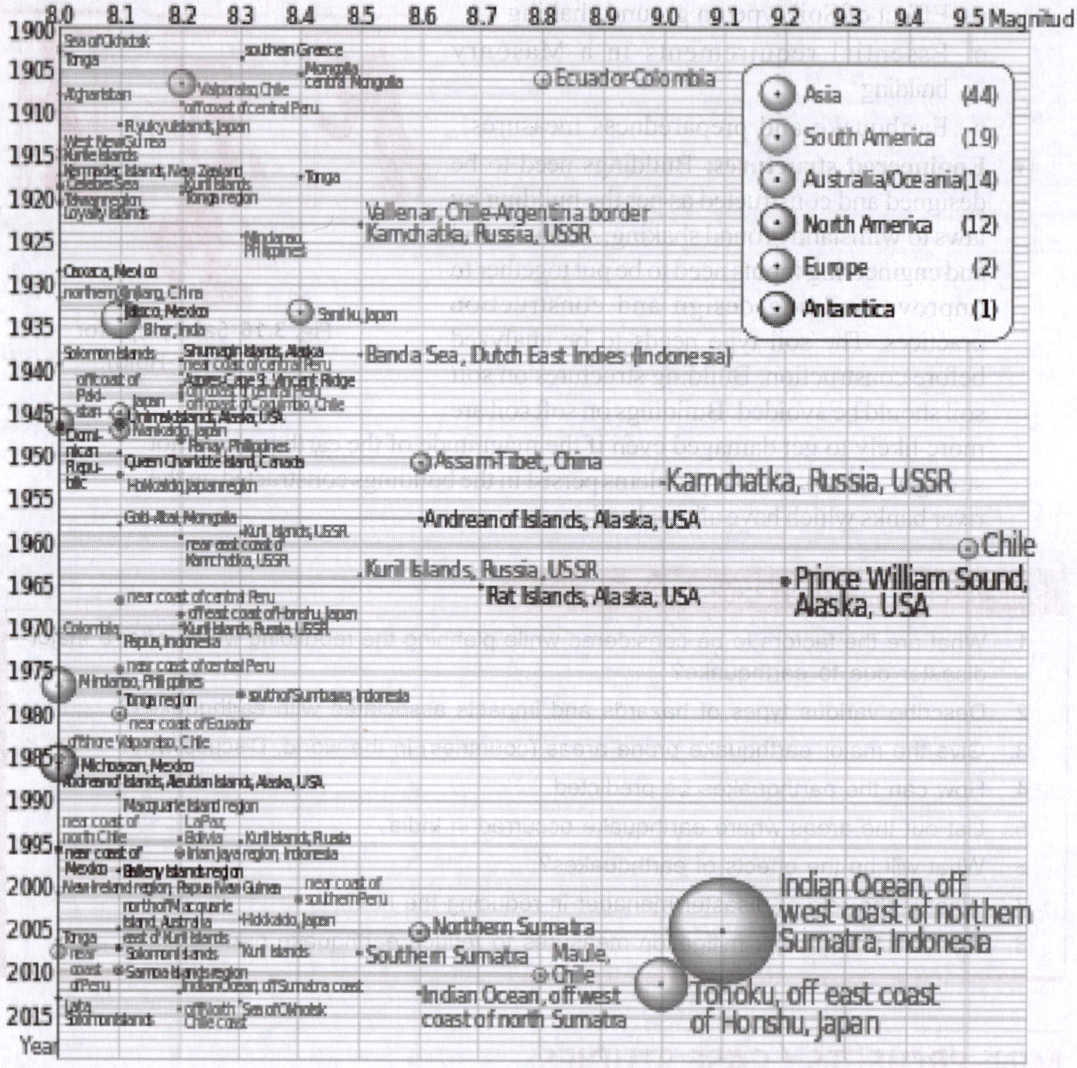

8.0 8.1 8.2 8.3 8.4 8.5 8.6 8.7 8.8 8.9 9.0 9.1 9.2 9.3 9.4 9.5 Magnitud
1900 1905 1910 1915 1920 1925 1930 1935 1940 1945 1950 1955 1960 1965 1970 1975 1980 1985 1990 1995 2000 2005 2010 2015
Year
Asia (44)
South America (19)
Australia/Oceania (14)
North America (12)
Europe (2)
Antarctica (1)
Sea of Okhotsk
Tonga
southern Greece
Mongolia
central Mongolia
Afghanistan
Valparaiso, Chile
off coast of central Peru
Ecuador-Colombia
Ryukyu Islands, Japan
West New Guinea
Kurile Islands
Kermadec Islands, New Zealand
Celebes Sea
Kuril Islands
Tonga region
Taiwan region
Loyalty Islands
Vallenar, Chile-Argentina border
Kamchatka, Russia, USSR
Mindanao, Philippines
Oaxaca, Mexico
northern Xinjiang, China
Jalisco, Mexico
Bihar, India
Sanriku, Japan
Solomon Islands
Shumagin Islands, Alaska
near coast of central Peru
Banda Sea, Dutch East Indies (Indonesia)
off coast of Pakistan
Japan
off coast of Coquimbo, Chile
Unimak Islands, Alaska, USA
Hokkaido, Japan
Dominican Republic
Panay, Philippines
Queen Charlotte Island, Canada
Assam-Tibet, China
Hokkaido, Japan region
Kamchatka, Russia, USSR
Gobi-Altai, Mongolia
Andreanof Islands, Alaska, USA
Kuril Islands, USSR
near east coast of Kamchatka, USSR
Chile
Kuril Islands, Russia, USSR
Prince William Sound, Alaska, USA
near coast of central Peru
Rat Islands, Alaska, USA
off east coast of Honshu, Japan
Kuril Islands, Russia, USSR
Colombia
Papua, Indonesia
near coast of central Peru
Mindanao, Philippines
Tonga region
south of Sumbawa, Indonesia
near coast of Ecuador
offshore Valparaiso, Chile
Michoacan, Mexico
Andreanof Islands, Aleutian Islands, Alaska, USA
Macquarie Island region
near coast of north Chile
La Paz, Bolivia
Kuril Islands, Russia
near coast of Mexico
Irian Jaya region, Indonesia
Balleny Islands region
New Ireland region, Papua New Guinea
near coast of southern Peru
north of Macquarie Island, Australia
Hokkaido, Japan
east of Kuril Islands
Northern Sumatra
Indian Ocean, off west coast of northern Sumatra, Indonesia
Tonga
near coast of Peru
Solomon Islands
Kuril Islands
Southern Sumatra
Maule, Chile
Samoa Islands region
Indian Ocean, off Sumatra coast
Indian Ocean, off west coast of north Sumatra
Tohoku, off east coast of Honshu, Japan
Solomon Islands
off North Chile coast
Sea of Okhotsk

CHAPTER 4 Tsunami

O'MY SILENT INNER VIBES (O'M S I V – 4)

That was 25th December, 2004. I was invited by my Christian friend for a beach party. We enjoyed the Christmas party till late night. We ate a lot and even buried our faces with cream over the cake. I invited all my friends to celebrate the new-year party in the next week in my city about 500 km away. I had an urgent work on the next day. So, took leave of them and left for my city, while they were planning and scheduling the events for the Boxing Day.

Oh My God! But I never thought that I would not see them again. I did not know that it was our last supper. I am not aware that it was our last meet.

Early in the morning, on the 26th December, 2004, no sooner than reaching my city, I heard the worst and shocking news of my life, that 'A gigantic giant water wall-like wave suddenly came and smashed entire coastal belt' which ate all my friends.

What a difference it made!

A day before, we ate cakes, and a day after quakes ate us

The land saw the water's anger. The Natural Disaster by water ('water' wave instigated by 'earth' quake) played 'BOXING' on land and punched on the lives of all the living-beings of the land.

For the first time, I came to know that the term TSUNAMI. I didn't hear this term thither to.

'Bloody Tsunami'! I cursed and cried.

But I wanted to know more about the TSUNAMI and in principle I understood that it has a great relation with EARTHQUAKE.

Relation between Earthquake and Tsunami

In the previous chapter, we have learnt all about earthquakes. Now if we have a quest, "does earthquake occur only on the surface of the earth? Or does it occur under the ocean?"

Since there is a surface of earth under the ocean, and there are tectonic plates and faults beneath this surface, obviously there is every chance of occurrence of an earthquake under the seabed. What if it occurs under the ocean? Yes! If the earthquake occurs on the seabed, it influences ocean water to flow onto the land. That is TSUNAMI. Thus this chapter can be treated as an extension to the previous chapter (Earthquakes).

Tsunami is generated in the earth below sea ground but effect is upon the near-shore areas on the earth due to huge and high water waves.

Another interesting point is that the word 'Su-Naami' in Sanskrit means 'Good-Named', but a big misnomer.

(Continued)

Lord Krishna's DWARAKA – The Victim of Tsunami Dwaraka, also called *Dwâravatî* (In sanskrit "many-gated"), is one of the Saptapuris (7-sacred cities) according to Hinduism, Jainism and Budhism. As per Harivamsham it is a Hindu (Sindhu) Kingdom while Mahabhaarat, Vishnupuran and Bhaagavatham, narrate as formerly called Kushasthali (place of hay and grass) of Yadavas. To secure Yadavas, on request of Lord Krishna, on proposal of Garuda, Vishwakarma built when they left the city of Mathura because of attacks of the 2 kings Kaala Yavana and Jaraasandha before the great *Mahabharat war* at Kurukshetra. When Pandavas visited Dwaraka before retiring from the world they noticed the city submerged under water after *Krishna Niryaan*. Many researches of archaeologists say 'submerge of Dwaraka' is due to a great Tsunami. Ongoing researches claim some traces and evidences found near sea shore of Sowrashtra (Gujarath).

"Lord Krishna in the Golden City" (Dwârakâ) from the Harivamsham, ca. 1600; A Gallery Art during Akbar's reign (This is believed to be drowned by a Tsunami)

4.1 TSUNAMI- CONCEPTUAL FRAMEWORK

If 'submerged Dwaraka at the end of Dwapar Yug', is not believed to be the result of a great tsunami, then the tsunami in the known history may be seen in the writings of Thucydides (426 BC).

Historians around 1600 BC thought giant waves (tsunami) caused by the eruption of Thira (also known as Santorini) destroyed Minoan civilization on Crete and related cultures in the Cyclades. However, the oldest recorded mega waves (tsunami) occurred in 479 BC that destroyed a Persian army while attacking the town of Potidaea in Greece. The Roman historian Ammianus Marcellinus described (365 AD) a sequence of gigantic waves (he didn't know the term tsunami), including an incipient earthquake devastated Alexandria.

Some deadly disasters recorded as tsunamis in the history are…

- The 1755 Lisbon earthquake and tsunami (caused by the Azores–Gibraltar Transform Fault),
- The1783 Calabrian earthquakes/ tsunamis, each causing several ten thousands of deaths
- The 1908 Messina earthquake and tsunami claimed more than 123,000 lives in Sicily and Calabria, is the biggest disaster for modern Europe.
- The 2004 Indian Ocean tsunami was among the deadliest natural disasters in human history with at least 230,000 people killed or missing in 14 countries bordering the Indian Ocean including major victims Japan, Java, Sumatra, India, Sri Lanka, Malaysia and Indonesia.
- Harappa, Mohamjudaro, Babylonian, Sumerian, and many more civilizations that have been found by the archeological departments were believed to be smashed by either tsunami or earthquake.

4.1.1 Tsunami – Meaning and Definition

When, it is not clear, but the term Tsunami, (means '*harbor waves*'), has been derived from a Japanese language, (TSU = 'harbor' and NAMI = 'waves'). Very few people know the term Tsu-nami until 2004 December 26. They thought it could be a type of storm or gigantic waves. Most people do not even know that an earthquake can occur under the sea/ ocean also.

Tsunamis are disastrous waves which often affect distant shores. The tsunami can be defined as

The Origination of	From/on	Due to
The rapid displacement of water	· ocean or · sea or · lake	· earthquake under water or · seismic activity or · faults slides or · volcanic eruptions or · under water landslides · explosions (e.g. nuclear) · large meteoroid impacts

Thus we can understand that the tsunami occurs due to seismic or volcanic or meteorological activity. Whatsoever may be the reason; the sea water swells up with a violent motion and ultimately surges over land with great destructive power. The effects of a tsunami can be unpredictable or even destructive. It can occur on seas and lakes also, but impact is not as worse as that on ocean. Ultimately it is a rapid devastating motion of water on near shores.

4.1.2 A Misconception

Tsunamis are popularly called tidal waves or sometimes ocean waves but they actually have nothing to do with the tides and ocean waves. This may because of the misconception and the confusion between various types of waves generated in seas and oceans due to atmospheric (wind), solar, lunar, gravitational activities. These waves are generated on the surface of the sea/ocean but tsunami comes from the bottom surface of the sea/ocean. More clearly, the regular waves in the sea/ocean most generally occur in two ways. These are:

1. **Ocean wave:** generated by wind
2. **Tides:** generated due to the gravitational pull of moon and sun.

But, tsunami waves have no resemblance with any of the two kinds of waves.

The geologists and scientists define tsunami waves as the third kind of waves having special characteristics and thence, they discourage to use the terms such as "mega tides, huge tides, large tides" in substitution of tsunami.

The following table clearly distinguishes the tsunami waves from the other oceanic waves.

Table 4.1 Comparison between Tsunami waves and other oceanic waves.

S.No	Aspect	Tsunami wave	Ocean wave	Tide
1.	Point of Generation	Under the sea bed (below bottom of sea/ocean)	On the surface of sea/ ocean	On the surface of sea/ ocean
2.	Cause	Seismic/ volcanic/ meteorological	Winds, (monsoon winds also)	Gravitational pull (solar/ lunar)
3.	Effect	Can cause disruption	Can cause a depression, cyclone, storm	Can cause minor problems on new moon and full moon days
4.	Strength	Huge and large	Relatively Medium to low	Relatively Medium to low
5.	Height of wave (amplitude)	Very high	High - Medium	High on selected days (once in 15 days) medium other days
6.	Frequency of occurrence	Rare occurrence	Regular	Regular
7.	Names	Tsunami waves, seismic sea wave, huge waves, mega tides, large tides	Ocean waves, Sea waves, Lahars	Tides, Waxing and Waning
8.	Structure and Movement	Vertically oriented, moves fast toward land and gets strengthened (raises high) as it reaches shore	Circular/ spiral oriented, whirl/ move straight toward land & get weakened (lows down) as reach shore	Vertically oriented, move Straight toward land and gets weakened (lows down) as it reaches shore except on selective days
9.	Speed	Very fast i.e. jet speed (about 800 kmph)	Not that fast (about 100 kmph)	Comparatively Slow
10.	Time between waves	5 to 90 minutes	In few seconds/ minutes	In few seconds /minutes

4.1.3 Tsunami – Not Just Seismic Sea Wave

The term ***seismic sea wave*** also is used to refer to the phenomenon of tsunami, particularly English speaking countries perhaps, because these waves most often are generated by seismic activity such as earthquakes. Prior to the rise of the use of the term "tsunami" in English-speaking countries, scientists generally encouraged the use of the term "seismic sea wave" rather than the inaccurate term "tidal wave".

But strictly speaking, "seismic sea wave" is also not a completely accurate term, since the term seismic refers to earthquakes only, where as a "tsunami," can occur with forces other than earthquakes also such as underwater landslides, volcanic eruptions, underwater explosions (including detonations of underwater nuclear devices), landslides, glacier calving, land or ice slumping into the ocean, meteorite impacts. Even the weather, when the atmospheric pressure changes very rapidly, can generate such waves by displacing water. Therefore, tsunami is not just seismic sea wave, but more than that. Thence the term seismic sea wave is not a substitute for the term TSUNAMI.

4.2 CHARACTERISTICS OF TSUNAMI

Ocean Waves

Tsunami Waves

Now, we understood that tsunami totally differs from ordinary ocean waves. Thence, the characteristics of tsunami waves are unique which distinguish it from other waves. These are given below (Refer Fig. 4.1 and 4.2):

1. **Produced beneath the water:** Tsunami wave are produced by underwater seismic activity or otherwise (while Ocean waves are produced by wind blowing over water).
2. **Flooding into land as huge water wall:** Tsunami normally causes flooding as a huge wall of water enters the main land (where as ordinary ocean wave hardly come on to the main land)
3. **Wave train:** Contrary to the popular belief, the tsunami is not a single giant wave but number of waves. A tsunami may consist of ten or more waves which is then called 'tsunami wave train'.
4. **Time between waves is not same:** The waves of tsunami do not occur with same duration. The time between one wave to the next vary from 5 to 90 minutes.
5. **High velocity/ Faster waves:** The tsunamis travel much faster than ordinary ocean waves. Compared to normal wave speed of 100 kmph, tsunami in the deep water of the ocean may even travel with the speed of a jet airplane - 800 kmph
6. **More strengthened as they reach land:** The shallow water waves grow tall as these approach land, they tend to rise high and get more strength (unlike ocean waves which weaken)

7. **Straight wave front (Not Whirling):** Tsunami moves like a wave front or water wall while ocean winds whirl or move spirally/circular.
8. **Rise high:** Despite of their speed, tsunami raises the water height only 30-45 cm and often passes unnoticed by ships at sea also.

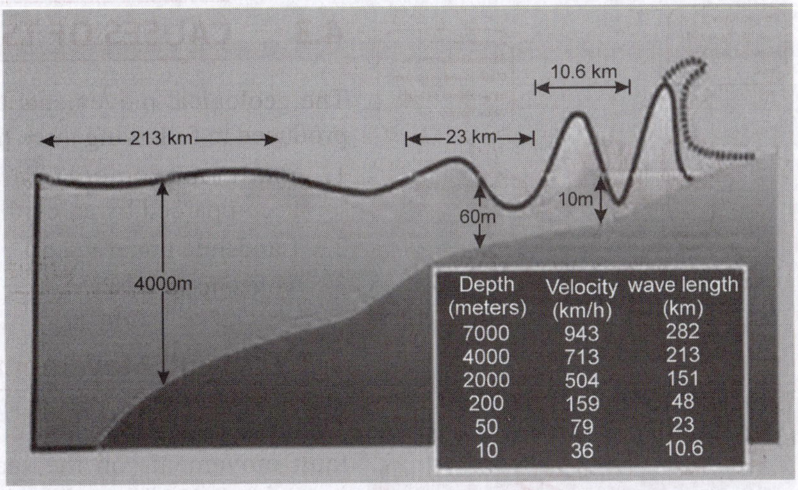

Fig. 4.1 Measurements of a typical Tsunami.

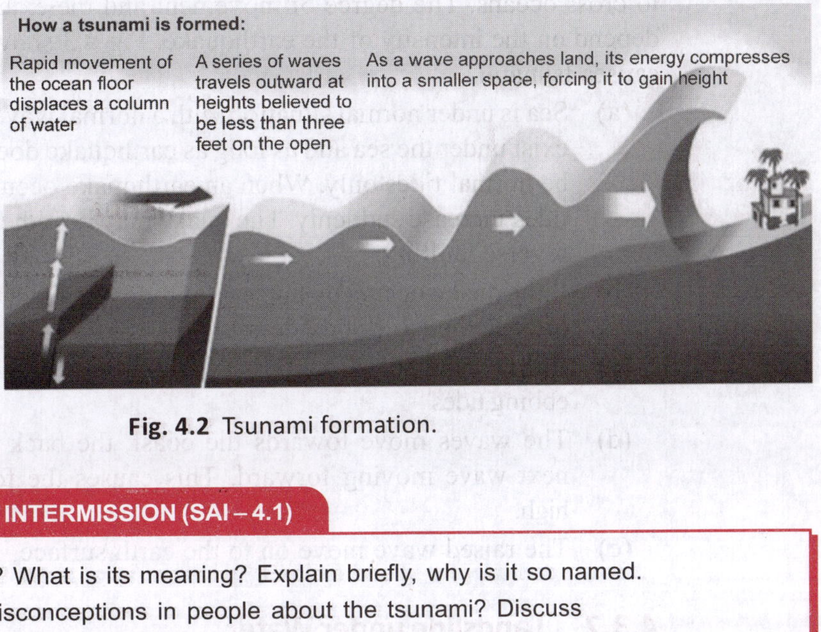

Fig. 4.2 Tsunami formation.

SELF ASSESSMENT INTERMISSION (SAI – 4.1)

1. Define Tsunami? What is its meaning? Explain briefly, why is it so named.
2. What are the misconceptions in people about the tsunami? Discuss
3. Discuss the concept of tsunami and its waves.
4. What are different types of oceanic waves? Describe briefly.
5. What are the characteristics of tsunami wave?
6. Distinguish between tsunami wave and oceanic wave?
7. 'Tsunami is a big oceanic tide'. Do you agree or disagree? Justify your answer.
8. How is tsunami different from tide?
9. What characteristics keep tsunami different from tides and oceanic waves?
10. 'Tsunami is not just seismic wave', critically appreciate the statement.

4.3 CAUSES OF TSUNAMI

The geological movements that cause tsunamis are produced in following three major ways.

1. Fault movement on sea floor (usually accompanied by an earthquake)
2. Landslide under water
3. Volcanic activity

4.3.1 Fault Movement on Sea-bed

The most common of cause for a tsunami is due to fault movements on the seabed which is usually accompanied by an earthquake. They release of large amount of energy due to a quake provides the capacity to cross oceans. The degree of movement and the extent of water displaced depend on the intensity of the earthquake. Fig 4.3 shows how an earthquake causes tsunami.

(a) Sea is under normal situation with a normal wave patterns. A fault may exist under the sea and as long as earthquake does not occur, there will be normal tides only. When an earthquake occurs at the sea floor, the tides increase suddenly. The quake may be either a Dip-slip normal or reverse faulting.

(b) If the quake occurs by normal faulting, the tides rush toward the shore, often named as flood tides only.

(c) If the quake occurs by thrust faulting, the produced waves are called ebbing tides

(d) The waves move towards the coast, the back waves overlaps with next wave moving forward. This causes the forward wave to raise high.

(e) The raised wave move on to the earth surface,

4.3.2 Landslide under Water

The second most common cause of the tsunami is a landslide either occurring under water or originating above the sea and then plunging into the water.

Examples:

- The largest tsunami ever produced by a landslide was in Lituya Bay, Alaska 1958. The massive rock slide produced a wave that reached a high water mark of 50-150 meters above the shoreline.

- The Storegga Slide in the Norwegian sea and some incidents affected the British Isles caused due to landslide or meteorological activities but are less to earthquake induced waves.

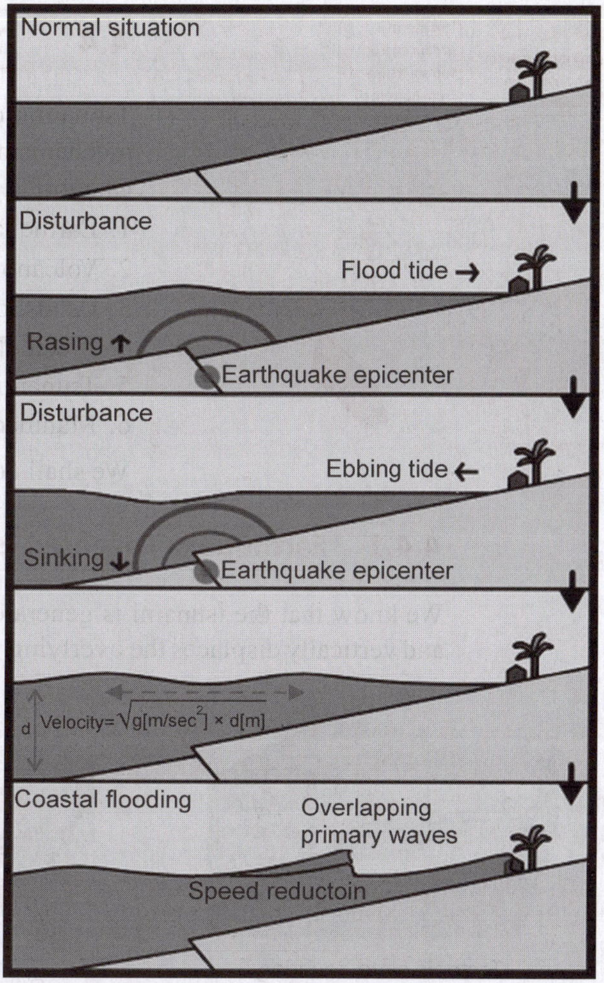

Fig. 4.3 An Earthquake causing Tsunami

4.3.3 Volcanic Activity

Volcanic activity is the third major cause of tsunami. The volcano situated near the shore or under water may be uplifted or depressed as similar as the action of a fault, or may actually explode.

For instance, the famous volcano, Krakotoa in Indonesia, exploded very violently in 1883, and produced a tsunami measuring 40 m high wave that crushed Java and Sumatra killing >36,000 people

4.3.4 Mechanism of Tsunami Generation

The general sequence of the mechanism of tsunami is as follows (Refer Fig. 4.2)

1. A considerably large disturbance (an abrupt deformation) underneath ocean due to seismic (earthquake) or volcanic or landslide or explosion (nuclear/meteorites).
2. The disturbance causes displacement of a huge amount of water or perturbation of the sea.
3. The waves formed in this way are then sustained by gravity. These waves suppress and displace the surrounding to produce a progressive wave of huge amplitude.
4. At the same time the seismic waves propagate and move these waves away from the generated point.
5. These waves move towards the shores/coastal belt and travel on to the land to cause a disaster.

Note that 'Tides' do not play any role in the generation of tsunamis.

4.4 TYPES OF TSUNAMIS

Tsunamis can be classified based the cause and mechanism of occurrence into the following four categories.

1. Earthquake Triggered Tsunami
2. Volcano Triggered Tsunami
3. Landslide Triggered Tsunami
4. Meteo-Tsunami
5. Tsunami due to Celestial Bodies
6. Manmade Tsunami

We shall now discuss these in detail.

4.4.1 Earthquake Triggered Tsunami

We know that the tsunami is generated when the sea floor abruptly deforms and vertically displaces the overlying water. And as understood in the previous

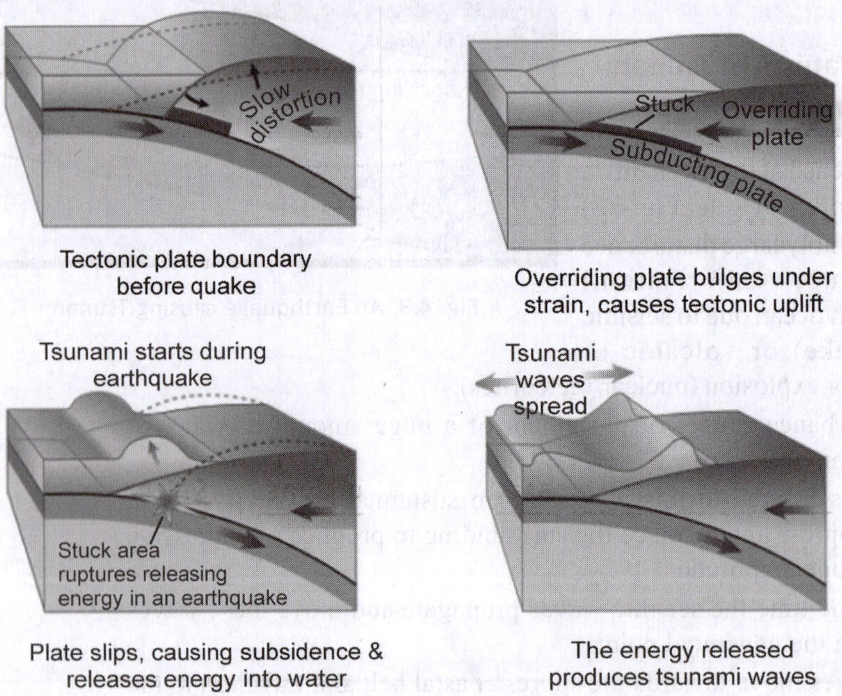

Fig. 4.4 Earthquake triggered Tsunami.

chapter – 3, the tectonic earthquakes cause the Earth's crustal deformation. Thus, if this earthquake occurs beneath the sea, the water above the deformed area would be displaced from its equilibrium position and thence generates a sequence of gigantic waves of tsunami.

Further, we know that the earthquake is dependent on the type of fault, so also, the tsunami. Some examples of earthquakes due to different types of faults/activities that caused tsunamis are given below:

- **Earthquake-Tsunami by Thrust Fault:** Since the thrust fault is associated with convergent or destructive plate boundaries, the plates move abruptly, causing water displacement due to the vertical component of movement. Some examples of this type of tsunami are given below.
    - Storegga Tsunami (about 8,000 yrs ago) originated at locations away from convergent boundaries.
    - 1929 Grand Banks, Papua New Guinea 1998 tsunamis occurred due to the earthquakes which destabilized sediments, causing them to flow into the ocean and generate a tsunami.
    - The 1960 Valdivia earthquake (M_w 9.5), the 1964 Alaska earthquake (M_w 9.2), the 2004 Indian Ocean earthquake (M_w 9.2), and the 2011 Tôhoku earthquake (M_w 9.0) are recent examples of powerful mega thrust (known as ***teletsunamis***) that crossed entire oceans.
    - Smaller (M_w 4.2) earthquakes in Japan often trigger tsunamis (called **local** and **regional tsunamis**) that can devastate nearby coasts in only a few minutes. Perhaps! The name tsunami (harbor waves) is befitting due to this.
- **Earthquake-Tsunami by Normal Fault:** Normal faults also are capable of causing displacement of the ocean-bed, but the largest of such events can only do.
- Typically related to flexure in the outer trench swell cause sufficient displacement to result in a significant tsunami,
    - The 1977 Sumba and 1933 Sanriku
    - Events occurred on April 1, 1946 Earthquake (M_w 7.8) near the Aleutian Islands, Alaska generated a tsunami inundated Hilo of Hawaii with a 14 m high (46 ft) surge by subducting (or being pushed downwards) in the Pacific Ocean floor.

4.4.2 Landslide Triggered Tsunami

A new dimension was added to the causes of tsunami in the 1950s, when it is postulated that the landslides can rapidly displace large water volumes, as energy

THE JOLT OF VAJONT

The Vajont Dam (completed in 1961) under Monte Toc, 100 km north of Venice, Italy, at 262m (860 ft), was one of the highest dams in the world. On Oct 9, an enormous landslide of about 260 million m^3 of forest, earth, and rock, fell into the reservoir at up to 110 kph (68 mph) resulting displacement of waters of 50 Mm^3 overtop the dam in a 250m (820-ft) high megatsunami wave. The floods destroyed the villages Longarone, Pirago, Rivalta, Faè and Villanova, killing 1,450 people.

transfers to the water at faster rate than the water can absorb. Thence, the giant submarine landslides could cause tsunamis. This was only theory till 1958, when a giant landslide in Lituya Bay, Alaska, produced the ever highest tsunami wave on records i.e. 524 m (over 1700 ft). Of course, the wave could not travel far, as it struck land almost immediately.

Lucky! Not more than two people fishing in the bay were killed, and astoundingly, another boat managed to ride the wave.

Another big example is with the Vajont dam, which is an eye opener to Civil Engineers of Structures and Construction while designing construction of dams. In 1963, Monte Toc witnessed a massive landslide resulting in a tsunami wave surged over 262 m (860ft) and entered the Vajont Dam in Italy. Named these waves mega-tsunami by scientists destroyed several towns and consumed about 2,000 human lives.

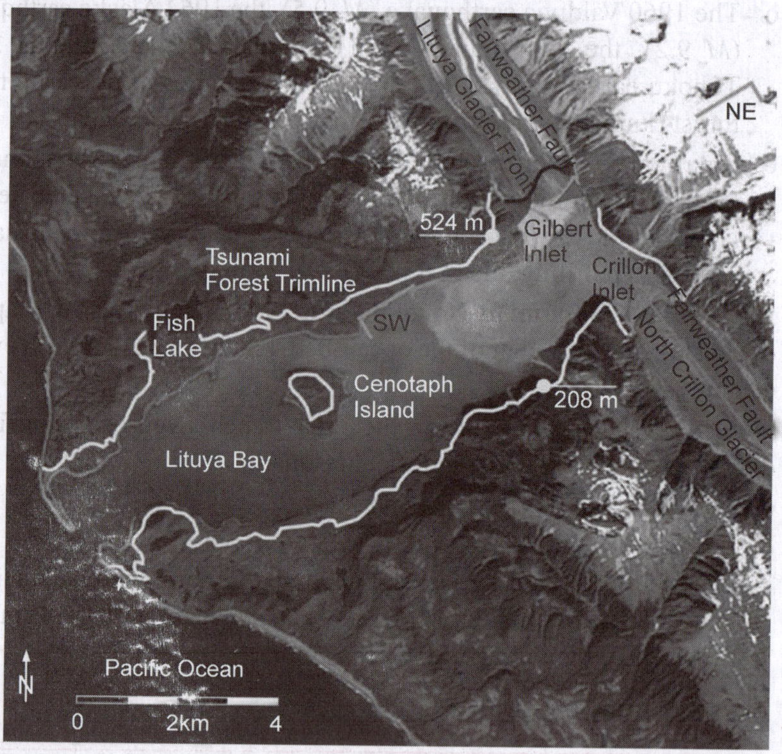

Fig. 4.5 Lituya bay and gilbert inlet-view.

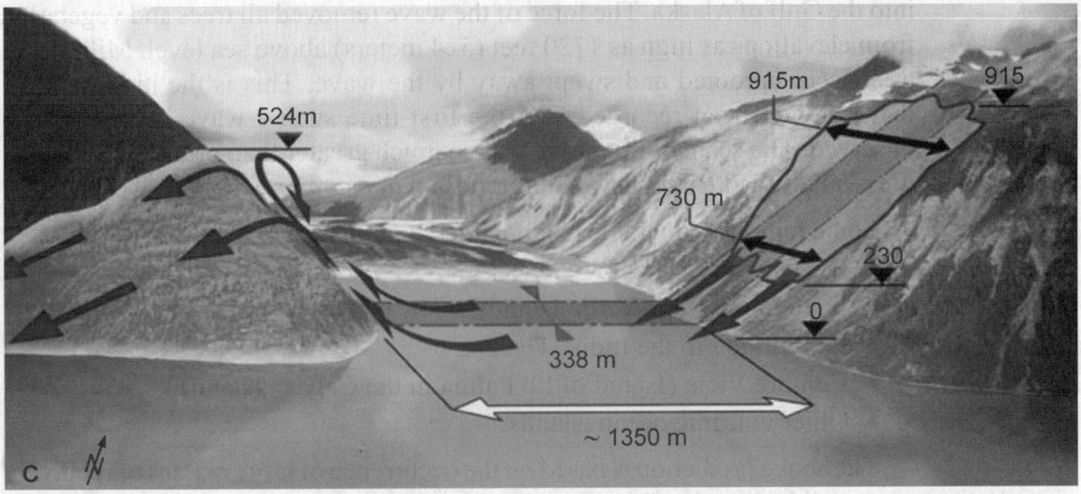

Fig. 4.6 Landslide model leading to Tsunami.

Fig. 4.7(a) Fair-weather fault-in.

Fig. 4.7(b) The land slide spot.

Lituya Bay Tsunami, The world Biggest Tsunami

On the night of July 9, 1958 an earthquake along the Fair-weather Fault-in Alaska loosened ~40 million cubic yards (30.6 Mm^3) of rock high above the NE shore of Lituya Bay. This mass of rock plunged from an altitude of approximately 3000 ft (914 m) into the waters of Gilbert Inlet. The impact generated tsunami crashed SW shoreline of Gilbert Inlet and was so powerful that it swept completely over the spur of land separating Gilbert Inlet from the main Lituya Bay. The wave continued down the length of Lituya Bay, over La Chaussee Spit and

Fig. 4.8 The Tsunami, 9th July, 1958.

into the Gulf of Alaska. The force of the wave removed all trees and vegetation from elevations as high as 1720 feet (524 meters) above sea level. Millions of trees were uprooted and swept away by the wave. This is the highest wave that has ever been recorded, and the first time such a wave had ever been observed. The scale of this wave was so much greater than ordinary tsunamis, it eventually led to the new category of *megatsunamis*.

Some regions vulnerable to landslide-tsunamis are

- Big Island of Hawaii,
- Fogo in the Cape Verde Islands,
- La Reunion in the Indian Ocean,
- Cumbre Vieja (Island of La Palma in the Canary Island)
- Other volcanic ocean islands.

The above prediction is based on the occurrence of large masses of relatively unconsolidated volcanic material on the flanks and expected development of detachment planes. However, there is growing controversy on dangerousness of these slopes are. Whatsoever, theories say that landslides can cause displacements mainly in the shallow parts of coastline and effect water enter in enclosed bays and lakes, but a landslide that can cause a transoceanic tsunami has not yet happened in the known history.

4.4.3 Volcanic Tsunami (Volcano Triggered Tsunami)

Volcanic tsunamis are caused by violent submarine explosions such as volcanic earthquakes, undersea eruptions, pyroclastic flows, caldera collapse, landslides, lahars, phreato-magmatic eruptions, lava bench collapse, and airwaves from large explosions. Waves produced by sudden displacement of water due to slope failure or phreatomagmatic explosion and collapse/ engulfment of the volcanic-magmatic chambers, can be as high as those produced by the largest earthquakes. The wave formed moves in a vertical direction and gains great speeds in deeper waters up to 650 mph. They travel over the continental shelf and crash into the land. This power doesn't decrease when they hit land though there is an extreme amount of energy when the water travels back towards its source. Nearly 5% of tsunamis are formed from volcanoes and about 16.9 % of volcanic fatalities occur from tsunamis.

On August 27, 1883, Krakatoa erupted to cause the largest and most disastrous volcanic tsunami in history with 40 m tall waves, which formed just under a minute after the explosion, and then 15 min later an air wave formed with great power. This tsunami killed over 36000 people and countless livestock. There was a 2nd explosion when the magma chamber collapsed allowing sea water to rush into, but smaller tsunami, only about 10 m in height. However, the sea levels rose and fell all over the world.

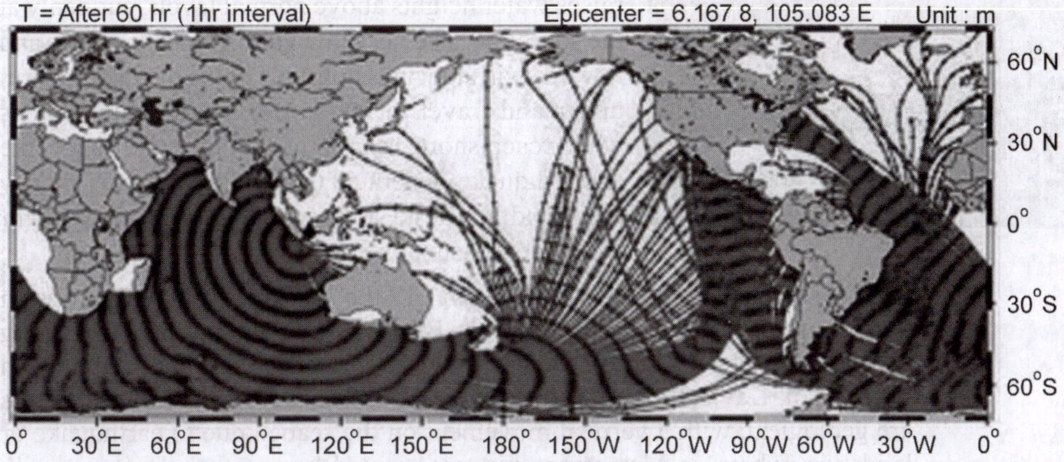

Fig. 4.9 Krakatau tsunami travel map.

La Palma (UK) volcano could erupt and spark a mega tsunami that has the potential to cause mass devastation in Britain, experts have warned.

There are also fears that Bali, (the Karangasem region of the Indonesian island) – known for its sandy beaches – could be smashed by a tsunami. As the officials declared the biggest risk from a potential volcanic eruption, locals have started packing up their possessions as they prepare to evacuate their homes nearby Mt. Agung volcano. Fears of a massive water surge were raised following an earthquake off the nearby island of Java.

4.4.4 Meteo-tsunamis (Tsunami Triggered by Meteorological Conditions)

The meteorological conditions, particularly the deep depressions like tropical cyclones, occasionally create a storm surge known as meteo-tsunami which

Table 4.1 Some Meteo-tsunami events.

Area	Country	Date	Height	Fatal
Vela Luka	Croatia	21 Jun 1978	5.9 m	0
Nagasaki Bay	Japan	31 Mar 1979	5 m	3
Pohang Harbour	Korea		0.8 m	
Kent & Sussex	UK	20 Jul 1929	3.5-6 m	2
Longkou Harbour	China	1 Sep 1980	3 m	
Ciutadella Harbour	Spain	15 Jun 2006	4 m	
Gulf of Trieste	Italy	15 Jun 2006	1.5 m	
West Sicily	Italy	15 Jun 2006	1.5 m	
Malta	Malta	15 Jun 2006	1 m	
Chicago, IL	US	26 Jun 1954	3 m	7
Daytona Beach, FL	US	3-4 Jul 1992	3.5 m	0

raises water heights above normal levels, suddenly at the shoreline. The very low atmospheric pressure and inward swirling winds uplift the dome of water to form under and travel in the storm. These water domes when reach shore, rear up in shallows and surge like an earthquake-generated tsunami that arrives shortly after landfall of the storm's eye. (Refer Table 4.1 for some meteo-tsunami events).

Meteotsunamis were also recorded in UK, the 1st officially identified was on the Cornish coastline in June 2011, when British researchers saw people walking across St. Michael's Mt. causeway suddenly found themselves standing in water. Prof. David Tappin of British Geological Survey said, "Most tsunamis are geological, with a vertical movement on the seabed due to earthquake or landslide, where as Meteotsunamis, are created by weather. Even a small, rapid change in atmospheric pressure of just a few milli-bars, can elevate the sea surface by a few centimeters. In the deep ocean it is not noticeable but when it enters shallow water whilst the weather system is moving at the same speed then the sea level increases by several meters".

Jacco Kromkamp, of the Royal Netherlands Institute for Sea Research (NIOZ), explained the mechanism of generation of meteotsunami, i.e. how the the displacement of a body of water is caused by rapid changes in atmospheric pressure.

Another best example is with the devastation of Hurricane Ike's meteotsunami storm surge over the Bolivar Peninsula in 2008.

4.4.5 Tsunami due to Celestial Bodies

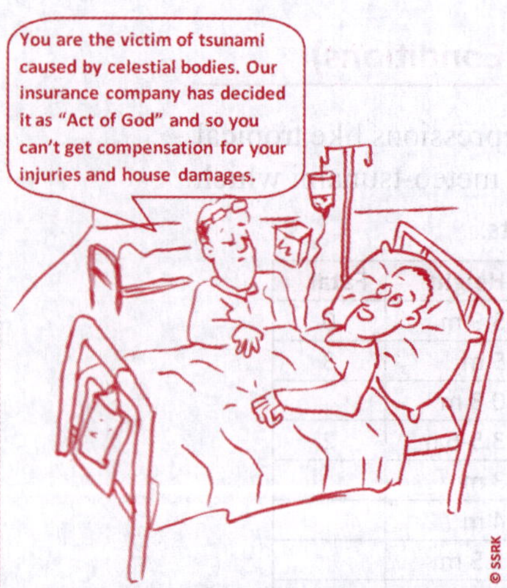

The fiction movies like 'Deep Impact' and 'Armageddon' manifested that an impact of celestial bodies on ocean can produce a devastating tsunami to affect the surrounding shorelines. Of course, Galen Gisler a scientist at LA National Laboratory in New Mexico, differed with the Hollywood portrayal of asteroid impacts in the oceans, and devastating post-impact tsunamis shown in the movies are just fictional. However, it depends on where an asteroid hits. If an asteroid hits land near a major city, we might be able to evacuate in time with the help of disaster response agencies, as it can be predicted much before with the present technology and but the damage to society, infrastructure and economy would be terrible, obviously. But if an asteroid hits oceans probably, it may not affect the lands. According to Gisler, "An asteroid impact is a point source that affects the immediate region and around only, but

to create a tsunami, it needs something that disturbs the entire water column".

An asteroid ocean impact is analogous to throwing a stone into a pond. Of course, the energy of the stone hitting the water will produce waves, but the ripples are very dispersive. In other words, they lose their energy very quickly. These dispersive waves are much localized that won't have the energy that a tsunami does. The tsunamis occur when there's large scale shift of mass in the seabed, such as while seismic or volcanic or landslide activities that cause a huge movement in a massive column of water, from the seabed to the surface and can create wavelengths of a 100 km or more, which is many times longer than the depth of the ocean (of a few km). Tsunamis aren't very dispersive and therefore don't lose energy as they travel through the ocean basin, hitting coastlines 1000's of km away, often with devastating results. They're spectacular to be sure; they would produce splashes that go up 10s of km

As per the model, water jet also protrudes from the ocean surface by a few km, producing rim waves surrounding the transient water crater reaching 400 ms in height. That's awfully high! But unless it's very close to a shore, it's not going to be very dangerous. Further, a significant fraction of the kinetic energy of the impacting asteroid will go into vaporizing huge quantities of water. Water vapour is a potent greenhouse gas goes into the stratosphere that can alter global climate for months or years.

No such incident took place in the history of tsunami hither to, so the earth has to wait till such incident occur to test the truth of the model of Gisler or the assumption of 'Deep Impact'. Till then, let us hope this type of tsunami is harmless.

4.4.6 Man-made Tsunamis

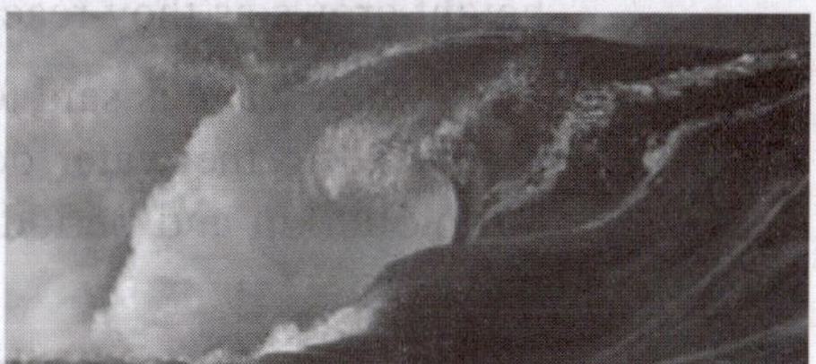

Atomic bomb Tsunami

Studies and attempts were made to generate tsunami waves as a tectonic weapon for triggering tsunami. In WW-II, New Zealand Military Forces initiated Project Seal, but the attempt failed to create small tsunamis with explosives in the area of today's Shakespear Regional Park. During WW-II use of conventional explosives, and Nuclear testing in the Pacific Proving Ground by the U.S. also gave poor results. *Operation Crossroads* fired two 20 kilotons of TNT (84 TJ) bombs, one in the air and other underwater, above and below the shallow (50 m; 160 ft) waters of the Bikini Atoll lagoon, which could produce at the most 3–4 m (9.8–13.1 ft) high waves at the shoreline when fired from nearest island about 6 km away. However, analyses of the effects of shallow and deep underwater explosions showed that the energy of the explosions doesn't easily generate the kind of deep, all-ocean waveforms as tsunamis, since most of the energy generated steam, produced vertical fountains above the water, and turned to be compression waveforms.

SELF ASSESSMENT INTERMISSION (SAI – 4.2)

1. List out the causes that trigger a Tsunami? Explain briefly.
2. Describe how seismic and volcanic activities cause a tsunami.
3. What are different types of tsunamis? Explain any two.
4. With an example discuss the mechanism involved in earthquake triggered tsunami?
5. With an example discuss the mechanism involved in volcano triggered tsunami?
6. With an example discuss the mechanism involved in landslide triggered tsunami?
7. Explain how earthquake triggered tsunami taking an example of 2004 December, 26 Indian Ocean Tsunami?
8. Can an asteroid, meteorite or comet like celestial produce a tsunami, if hits an ocean? Explain.
9. What do you understand by Meteo-tsunami? How is it caused?
10. Write a short note on man-made tsunami.
11. Explain how thrust fault and normal fault can trigger tsunami with examples.
12. Explain the cause and effects of Lituya Bay Tsunami.
13. Write a short note on the tsunami occurred in the Vajont Dam.

4.5 THE MECHANICS OF TSUNAMI

Tsunamis have a small offshore amplitude (wave height) but a very long wavelength, often hundereds of km long, while normal ocean waves have a wavelength of only 30 or 40 m, and so, may go unnoticed at sea, forming only a slight swell usually about 30 cm (12 in) above the normal sea surface. The height grows as they reach shallow water.

A water wave is said to be a shallow when its wavelength is very large as compared to the water depth. Since, the tsunamis wavelengths range from 10 to 500 km and period up to an hour, tsunamis behave as shallow-water waves.

The speed of the shallow-water waves, say *c,* depends on the water depth as: $c = \sqrt{gH}$

where *g* is the acceleration due to gravity (9.8 m/s²) and *H* is the water depth.

For example, in a deep ocean where water depth is about 4km, the waves (of tsunami) travel at a speed about 200 m/s, or more than 700 kmph.

For tsunamis generated by underwater earthquakes, the amplitude (the wave height) of the tsunami is determined by the amount by which the sea-floor is displaced.

Similarly, the wavelength and period of the tsunami can be determined by the size and shape of the underwater disturbance.

Thus, not only with high speeds, tsunamis can also travel large distances with limited energy loss.

(Further, due to variation of water depths, the crests travel at different speeds and also refract).

What happens as tsunami approaches land?

As discussed above, tsunami speed varies with the water depth and hence, the tsunami slows as the water depth decreases (The depth decreases as we move towards the coast). However, the energy flux remains nearly constant, which depends on both, wave speed and wave height. Therefore, the wave height grows which is known as shoaling. Due to this shoaling effect, a tsunami that is unnoticeable in the middle of the sea may grow high several metres near the coast.

The increase of the tsunami's wave height at shallow water is given by:

$$\frac{h_s}{h_d} = \left(\frac{H_d}{H_s}\right)^{\frac{1}{4}}$$

where h_s and h_d are wave heights and H_s and H_d are the depths in shallow and deep water respectively.

So a tsunami with a height of 1 m in the open ocean where the water depth is 4000 m would have a wave height of 4 to 5 m in water of depth 10 m. Water waves energy as they move towards onshore, so also tsunami waves of course, while the shoreward-propagating wave energy is dissipated through bottom friction and turbulence. Despite these losses, tsunamis still reach the coast with large amounts of energy.

Tsunamis may reach a maximum vertical height onshore above sea level, often called a *run-up height*, of tens of metres. Even after, the loss of the energy, tsunamis have great erosion potential, which can:

- Strip off the beaches of sand that might have taken years to accumulate
- Undermine trees and other coastal vegetation
- Inundate and/or flooding hundreds of metres inland
- Crush homes and other coastal structures.

4.6 MEASUREMENT OF TSUNAMI

In the deep ocean, a tsunami wave has small amplitude (< 1m) but very long wavelength (100s of km). So, the slope or steepness of the wave is too small to

detect by the human eye. However, the ocean observing instruments can measure this. The following are the three most popular instruments in practice to detect or/and measure tsunami.

1. Tide gauges
2. Satellite altimeters
3. DART (**D**eep-ocean **A**ssessment and **R**eporting of **T**sunamis) system
4. RADAR system

4.6.1 Tide Gauges

A '***Tide gauge***' is an instrument used to compute the height of the sea-surface by measuring the tide levels up to 1mm accuracy. It is mostly operated by the Bureau of Meteorology at the National Tidal Centres and is often named as SEAFRAME station (**SEA** level **F**ine **R**esolution **A**coustic **M**easuring **E**quipment). It consists of acoustic sensors connected to a vertical tube kept open at the lower end in water. It is analogous to the principle used by 'bat', which emits an ultrasonic sound and senses the reflection to detect an obstruction. Similarly, the acoustic sensor of the instrument emits a sound pulse from the top of the tube down on to the water surface, and reflection is sensed and drawn as a graph. Knowing the travel time of the pulse, the distance to the water level can be calculated. An example of graph sensed by acoustic sensor given in figure 4.10.

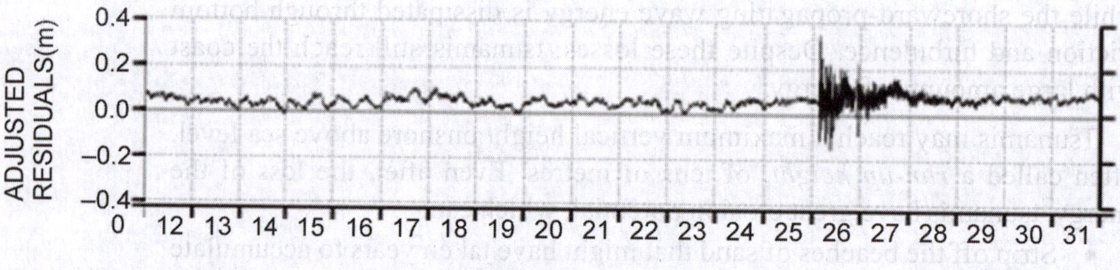

Fig. 4.10 Graph showing Tsunami sensed by accoustic sensor.

4.6.2 Satellite Altimeters

Satellite altimeters use electromagnetic pulses to measure the height of the ocean surface directly. The satellite sends the electromagnetic pulses down to the ocean surface and knowing the satellite location, the height of the ocean surface can be computed using the speed of the pulse, and the time that the pulse taken to return to the satellite.

However, the big problem with this instrument is that some satellites only move over a particular location once in a month or so. Thus, it depends on the fortune of presence of the satellite at right time and at the right place to detect tsunami. (Fortunately, during the Indian Ocean tsunami of 26th December, 2004, the Jason satellite altimeter was in the right place at the right time).

The adjacent image (figure 4.11) depicts the height of the sea surface (on either side of slant line) measured by the Jason satellite 2-hours after the initial earthquake hit the southeast of Sumatra (the epicentre) on December 26, 2004. However, the data processing took long time, and so it was less useful to warn.

4.6.3 The DART System

DART stands for **D**eep-ocean **A**ssessment and **R**eporting of **T**sunamis. This is developed by the National Oceanic & Atmospheric Administration (NOAA) in 1995.

It is not just one, but an array of stations. For example the array of stations deployed in Pacific Ocean gives detailed information about tsunamis while they are still far off shore. At each station there will be a sea-bed bottom pressure recorder, the recorder is used to detect the passage of a tsunami by recording the pressure of the water column which is related to the height of the sea-surface. This data is then transmitted through sonar to surface buoy, which would then be sent in radio wave to the Pacific Warning Centre (PTWC) via satellite.

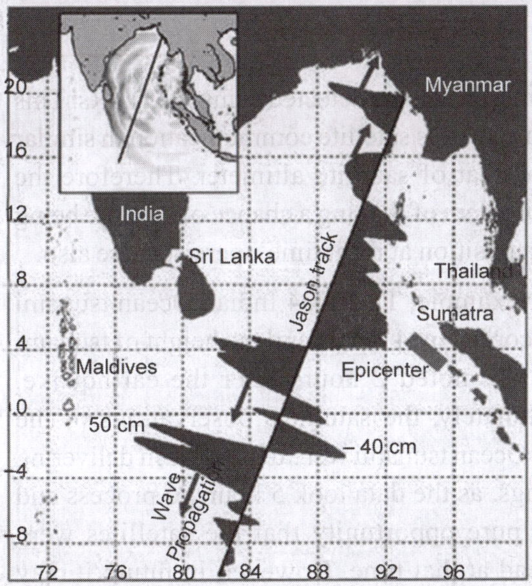

Fig. 4.11(a) Wave propagation.

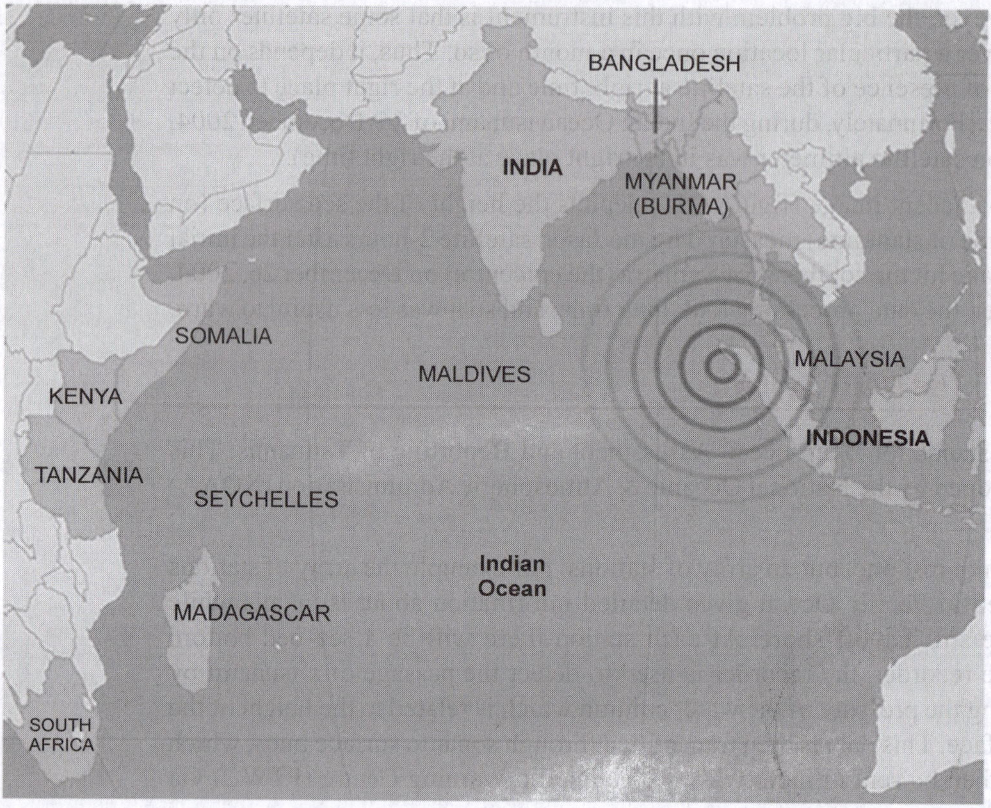

Fig. 4.11(b) 26 Dec, 2004 Tsunami sensed by Jason satellite.

> **O My God!**
>
> **O My God! – RADAR?**
>
> In 1886, German physicist Heinrich Hertz showed radio waves can be reflected from solid objects. In 1895, Alexander Popov, a physics instructor in Imperial Russian Navy School (Kronstadt), used coherer tube for detecting distant lightning strikes. He added a spark-gap transmitter and tested for communicating between 2-ships in Baltic Sea in 1897. Christian Hülsmeyer, (Germany) first used radio waves to detect "distant metallic objects" and demonstrated the feasibility of detecting a ship in dense fog in 1904. Full radar evolved as a pulsed system, in Dec 1934 by Robert M. Page, working at the Naval Research Laboratory. Though developed for navy, it is also widely used in aviation now.
>
> The word *radar* (*RADAR*) coined in 1940 by US Navy as an acronym for **RA**dio **D**etection (or **D**irection) **A**nd **R**anging occupied place in dictionaries of English and other languages as a common noun, losing all capitalization.

4.6.4 RADAR Systems

Tsunami can also be detected using RADARs. This system also uses satellite communication in similar lines as that of satellite altimeter. Therefore the same problem of 'having a chance of satellite being in right position at right time', persists here also.

For example, The 2004 Indian Ocean tsunami was recorded by 4 radars and the height of tsunami waves are noted 2 hours after the earthquake. Unfortunately, the satellites observations of the Indian Ocean tsunami were of less use in delivering warnings, as the data took 5 hours to process and it was pure opportunity that the satellites were overhead at that time. However, in future it may be possible that the space-based observation might play a direct role in tsunami warning.

One of the deep water buoys used in the DART tsunami warning system

4.6.5 Scales of Tsunami Measurement

The effect of tsunami is understood by measuring in the following two ways,

1. Tsunami Intensity Scale
2. Tsunami Magnitude Scale

1. **Tsunami Intensity Scales:** Intensity scales have been used for long time. In the early days, there were two scales in use. These are:

   (a) The *Sieberg-Ambraseys Intensity Scale (SAI Scale)*

   (b) The *Imamura-Iida Intensity Scale (III Scale)*

   The *SAI scale* was in use in the Mediterranean Sea while the III scale was used in Pacific Ocean to measure the intensity of tsunami. However, the latter scale was modified by Soloviev, who calculated the Tsunami intensity *I* as

   $I = ½ + \log_2 H_{av}$; where H_{av} is the average wave height along the nearest coast

   [This scale is termed as the *Soloviev-Imamura Tsunami Intensity Scale (SITI Scale)*, in the global tsunami catalogues compiled by the NGDC/NOAA]

   Recently, in 2013, after the close studies on tsunamis of 2004 and 2011, a new 12 point scale was proposed, the *Integrated Tsunami Intensity Scale (ITIS-2012)*, which matches closely with the modified ESI2007 and EMS.

2. **Tsunami Magnitude Scales:** Some scientists argue that the tsunami has to be measured on its magnitude rather than its intensity. Murty and Loomis proposed a scale to measure magnitude of tsunami based on the potential energy, rather than intensity at a particular location and known as the ML scale. However, owing to the difficulties involved in calculating the potential energy of the tsunami, that this scale is rarely used.

   Abe introduced the *tsunami magnitude scale*

   $$M_t = a \log h + b \log R - D;$$

   Where *h* is the maximum tsunami-wave amplitude (in m) measured by a tide gauge

   R is the distance from the epicenter, and

   a, *b* and *D* are constants used to make the M scale match as closely as possible with the moment magnitude scale.

Fig. 4.12 Tsunami warning sign.

4.7 WARNING SYSTEMS AND RISK REDUCTION MEASURES

We already understood from the previous chapter that scientists cannot exactly predict earthquakes, when and where they occur. So also, they cannot exactly predict when a tsunami will be generated. However, when the tsunami is generated in the mid-ocean, it takes time to reach the shore leaving some lead-time to warn. Though, there are tsunamis reached within minutes, but still there was a chance to predict and warn in most cases. Therefore, the tsunami warning systems (the tsunami warning sign is shown in Fig. 4.12) can help minimizing the impact of tsunami and the associated loss. There are two distinct types of tsunami warning systems. These are:

(a) International tsunami warning systems and

(b) Regional warning systems.

4.7.1 International Tsunami Warning Systems

Tsunamis have been experienced by all the oceans and in the Mediterranean Sea, but the great majority of them have occurred in the Pacific Ocean. The Pacific Tsunami Warning System (PTWS) was developed near Honolulu, Hawaii after the Hilo Tsunami, on April 1, 1946, (7.8M_w) followed by the earthquake near the Aleutian Islands, Alaska which generated 14-metre high (46 ft) surge due to Pacific ocean floor subduct (pushed downwards).

The PTWC is able to warn the countries several hours before the tsunami hits including probable arrival time and the coastal areas where the tsunami could travel in few hours.

4.7.2 Regional Warning Systems

Regional Warning Systems use seismic data of nearby earthquakes to predict the probability of a tsunami. Such systems are capable enough to provide warnings to the general public in less than 15 min. (In 1995 NOAA of US developed DART system and 6-stations were deployed by 2001 in Pacific Ocean)

Survey of India maintains a tide gauge network along the coast of India. The gauges located in major ports are shown in the figure 4.13.

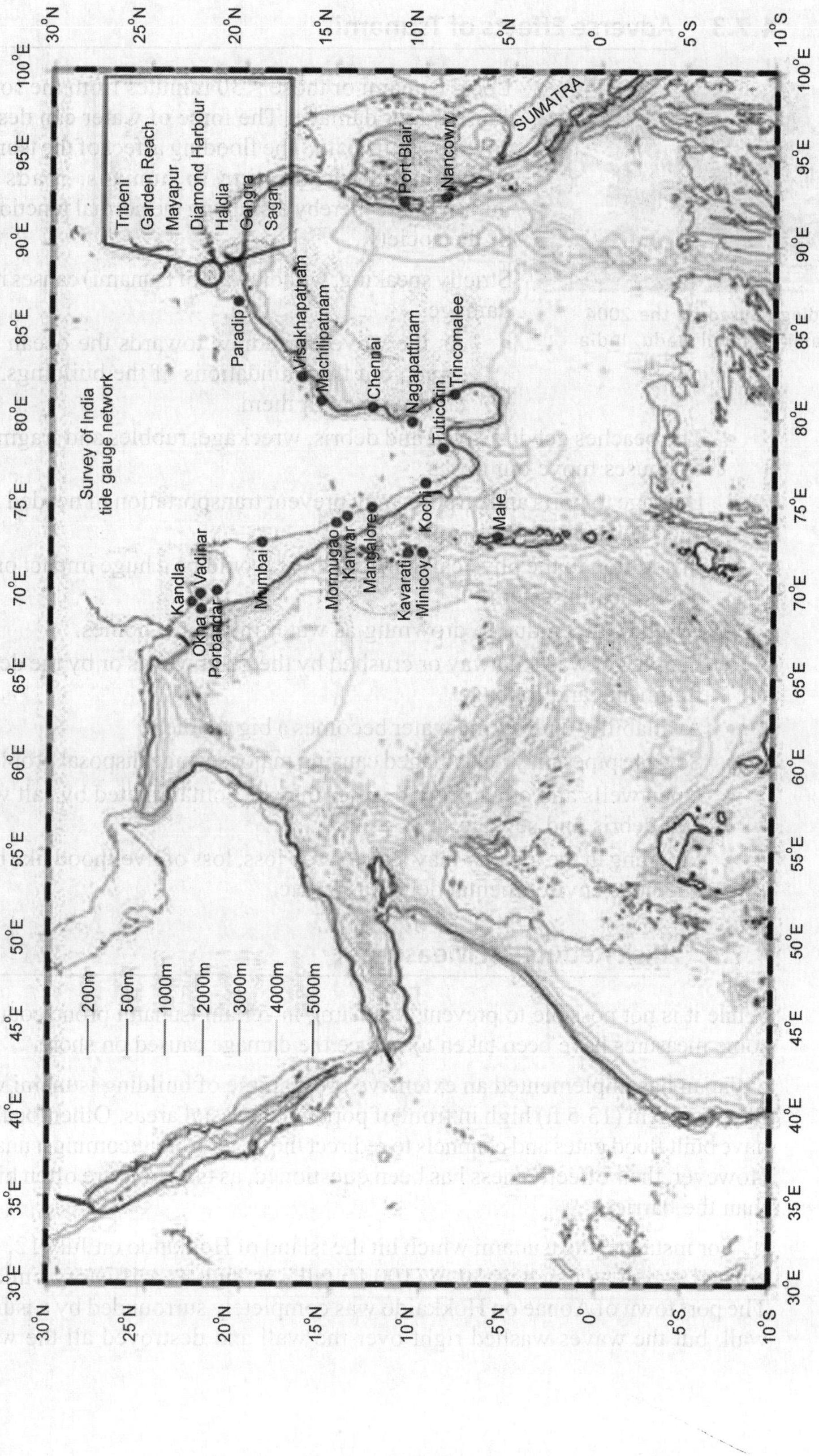

Fig. 4.13 Tide gauge network in India.

4.7.3 Adverse Effects of Tsunami

Flooding caused by the 2004 Tsunami in Tamil Nadu, India

Local tsunami or those < 30 minutes from the source cause major damage. The force of water can destroy anything in its path. The flooding affect of the tsunami causes major destruction to humans, roads and infrastructure thereby disrupting the normal functioning of the society.

Strictly speaking, withdrawal (of tsunami) causes more damage.

- As the waves withdraw towards the ocean they sweep out the foundations of the buildings, and take away with them.
- The beaches get destroyed and debris, wreckage, rubbles and fragments of houses move out to sea.
- Damage to ports and airports may prevent transportation of needed food and medical supplies.
- In addition to the physical damage, there would be a huge impact on the public health system.
- Deaths happen due to drowning as water inundates homes.
- People get washed away or crushed by the giant waves or by the debris, fragments and garbage.
- Availability of drinking water becomes a big problem.
- Sewage pipes may be damaged causing major sewage disposal problems.
- Open wells and other ground water may be contaminated by salt water and debris and sewage.
- Flooding in the locality may lead to crop loss, loss of livelihood like boats and nets, environmental degradation etc.

4.7.4 Risk Reduction Measures

While it is not possible to prevent a tsunami, in certain tsunami prone countries some measures have been taken to reduce the damage caused on shore.

Japan has implemented an extensive programme of building tsunami walls of up to 4.5 m (13.5 ft) high in front of populated coastal areas. Other localities have built flood gates and channels to redirect the water from incoming tsunamis. However, their effectiveness has been questioned, as tsunamis are often higher than the barriers.

For instance, the tsunami which hit the island of Hokkaido on July 12, 1993 created waves as much as 30 m (100 ft) tall - as high as a 10-story building. The port town of Aonae on Hokkaido was completely surrounded by a tsunami wall, but the waves washed right over the wall and destroyed all the wood-framed structures in the area. The wall may have succeeded in slowing down and moderating the height of the tsunami but it did not prevent major destruction and loss of life.

Some other systematic measures to protect coastlines against tsunamis include:

1. **Site Planning and Land Management** - Within the broader framework of a comprehensive plan, site planning determines the location, configuration, and density of development on particular sites and is, therefore, an important tool in reducing tsunami risk. The designation and zoning of tsunami hazard areas for such open-space uses as agriculture, parks and recreation, or natural hazard areas is recommended as the first land use planning strategy. This strategy is designed to keep development at a minimum in hazard areas.
   - In areas where it is not feasible to restrict land to open-space uses, other land use planning measures can be used. These include strategically controlling the type of development and uses allowed in hazard areas, and avoiding high-value and high occupancy uses to the greatest degree possible.

Tsunami walls in coastal Japan

Damaged houses constructed on the sea coast in Chennai

Tsunami in Cinema

There are several movies in English and almost all languages featured on the basis of Tsunami. There is an exclusive Hollywood movie with the title *TSUNAMI*. An Indian feature film '*Dashaavathaaram*' (2006) in which ten roles were played by Indian actor, Mr. Kamal Hasan, manifested the tsunami in the climax scene.

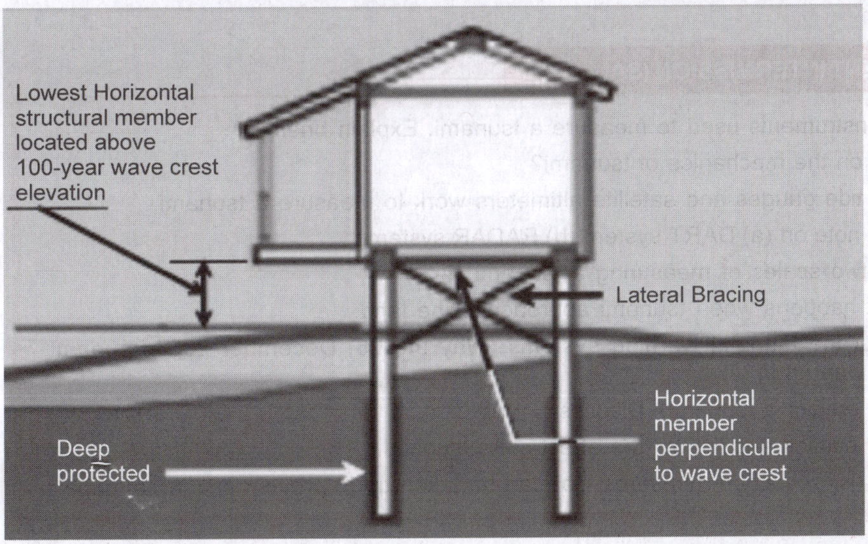

Fig. 4.14 Design solution to tsunami effect.

2. **Engineering structures** – Most of the habitation of the fishing community is seen in the coastal areas. The houses constructed by them are mainly of light weight materials without any engineering inputs (Refer Fig. 4.14). So, there is an urgent need to educate the community about the good construction practices that they should adopt such as:
   - Site selection – Avoid building or living in buildings within several hundred feet of the coastline as these areas are more likely to experience damage from tsunamis.
   - Construct the structure on a higher ground level with respect to mean sea level.
   - Elevate coastal homes: Most tsunami waves are less than 3 meters in height. Elevating house will help reduce damage to property from most tsunamis.
   - Construction of water breakers to reduce the velocity of waves.
   - Use of water and corrosion resistant materials for construction.
   - Construction of community halls at higher locations, which can act as shelters at the time of a disaster.
3. **Flood management** - Flooding will result from a tsunami. Tsunami waves will flood the coastal areas. Flood mitigation measures could be incorporated.

SELF ASSESSMENT INTERMISSION (SAI – 4.3)

1. List out the instruments used to measure a tsunami. Explain briefly.
2. Write a note on the mechanics of tsunami?
3. Explain how tide gauges and satellite altimeters work to measure a tsunami.
4. Write a short note on (a) DART system (b) RADAR system.
5. Discuss the two scales of measuring a tsunami.
6. Explain what happens when tsunami approaches the land.
7. Explain about the tsunami warning systems. Why the 26, December 2004 Tsunami could not be warned in advance.
8. How can we predict a tsunami? Discuss.
9. Identify three causes and list out the effects of a tsunami.
10. Suggest five risk reduction measures that can be taken up to prevent severe damage.

4.8 TSUNAMI IN INDIA

Because of seismic and volcanic activity associated with tectonic plate boundaries, tsunamis occur most frequently along the Pacific Ring of Fire. Though common in the Pacific Ocean, but are worldwide natural phenomena. They are possible wherever large bodies of water are found, including inland lakes, where they can be caused by landslides and glacier calving. Very small tsunamis, non-destructive and undetectable without specialized equipment, occur frequently as a result of minor earthquakes and other events.

Even though India has not faced frequent Tsunamis, still there is a need to identify the areas having the Tsunamis. The whole of the Indian coastal belt is prone to Tsunami. Table 4.2 shows incidents of tsunamis that have affected our country.

Table 4.2 History of Tsunamis in India.

Date	Location	Impact
1524	Near Dabhol, Maharashtra	Sufficient data not available
02 April 1762	Arakan Coast, Myanmar	Sufficient data not available
16 June 1819	Rann of Kachchh, Gujarat	Sufficient data not available
31 October 1847	Great Nicobar Island	Sufficient data not available
31 December 1881	An earthquake of 7.9 in the Richter scale in Car Nicobar Island	Entire east coast of India and Andaman & Nicobar Islands; 1m tsunamis were recorded at Chennai
26 August 1883	Explosion of the Krakatoa volcano in Indonesian	East coast of India was affected; 2m tsunamis were recorded at Chennai
26 June 1941	An 8.1 Richter scale earthquake in the Andaman archipelago	East coast of India was affected but no estimates of height of the tsunami is available
27 November 1945	An 8.5 Richter scale earthquake at a distance of about 100km south of Karachi	West coast of India from north to Karwar was affected; 12m tsunami was felt at Kandla
26 December 2004	Banda Aceh, Indonesia; Tamil Nadu, Kerala, Andhra Pradesh, Andaman and Nicobar Islands, India; Sri Lanka; Thailand; Malaysia; Kenya; Tanzania	The East cost of India was affected. The waves measured around 10 m high killing more than 10,000 precious lives.

4.8.1 The Indian Ocean Tsunami of 26th December 2004, (The Boxing Day Tsunami)

An earthquake of magnitude 9.0 on Richter scale occurred at the western coast of northern Sumatra in the Indian Ocean at about 1 am UTC (8 am local time) on Boxing day, the 26th December 2004 produced a tsunami, one of the biggest natural disasters in modern history which consumed over 2 lakh lives. It was the largest since the 1964 Alaska quake and 4th largest since 1900. It devastated the shores of 14 countries including Indonesia, Sri Lanka, India and Thailand with 15 m high waves, and reached even Somalia on the east coast of Africa, 4500 km west of the epicentre. The sea-level monitoring stations at Brazil and Queensland also felt the effect of the tsunami.

Tsunami memorial in Kanykumari (cape Kumarin) beach

The epicentre of the quake was located about 250 km south-southeast of the Indonesian city of Banda Aceh. It was a rare megathrust earthquake occurred on the interface of the India–Burma tectonic plates caused by the release of stresses that developed as the India plate subducted beneath the overriding Burma plate. (A megathrust earthquake is where one tectonic plate slips beneath another, causing vertical motion of the plates). The height of the tsunami varied greatly (2-3 m at the African coast at Kenya up to 10-15 m at Sumatra) depending on its distance, direction from the epicentre and other factors such as the local bathymetry.

The earthquake was also unusually large, which is about 1200 km of fault line slipped about 15 m along the subduction zone and vibrated for a period of about 10 minutes. Because the quake was in a nearly north-south orientation, the greatest strength of the waves was in an east-west direction and perhaps! Bangladesh, which lies at the northern end of the Bay of Bengal, had very few casualties despite being a populous low-lying country. It took fifteen minutes (for Indonesia & Sumatra) to seven hours (for Somalia, Kenya) to reach the various coastlines, while Sri Lanka and the east coast of India were hit roughly two hours later. Even though being closer to the epicentre, Thailand was also struck about two hours later, as the tsunami travelled more slowly in the shallow Andaman Sea off its western coast.

4.8.2 Most Vulnerable Countries to Natural Disasters

Here's a list of most vulnerable countries to all types of natural disasters, particularly to earthquakes, in the world after Japan and Alaska in the order

1. Japan
2. Alaska (USA)
3. Indonesia
4. Turkey
5. Mexico
6. El Salvador
7. Pakistan
8. Philippines
9. India
10. Nepal

The most earthquakes per unit area would probably be Tonga, Fiji, or Indonesia since they are all in extremely active seismic areas along subduction zones.

4.9 THE LAND OF RISING SUN IS THE ADDRESS FOR TSUNAMI (A CASE STUDY)

Japan, the land of rising sun, has a notorious natural disaster history, particularly with tsunami and earthquake. Believe it or not! About 1,500 earthquakes strike the island nation every year, which means about 50 in a month or 2-3 quakes everyday on average. Yes! Minor tremors occur almost on daily basis. The tremor news is as frequent as 'reading a newspaper' and as common as any 'taking tea'. Perhaps! Hardly any newspaper is found without the news of tremors on any given day. It is almost a part of their daily life. Deadly quakes are a tragic part of the nation's past. But still it is competing with the world and standing in higher positions in many aspects and fields. Thence, the following obvious question rises in our minds.

4.9.1 Why Japan has so many Earthquakes/ Tsunamis?

The reason is that this area is of high seismic and volcanic activity from New Zealand, up through Japan, across to Alaska, and down the west coasts of North and South America. If such earthquakes or volcanic eruptions occur below or close to the ocean, they may trigger high tidal waves (tsunami).

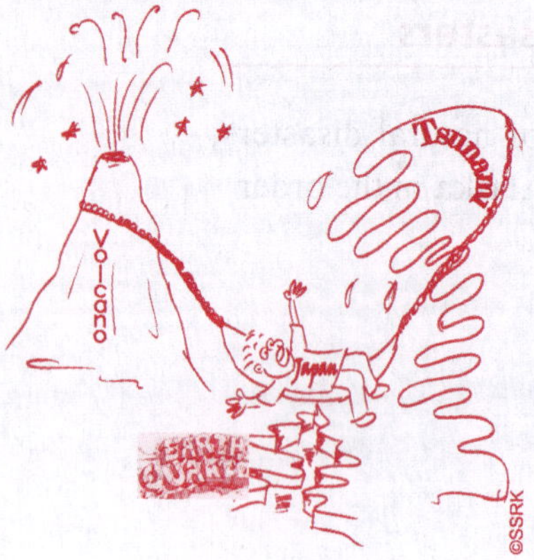

Japanese archipelago is located in an area where several continental and oceanic tectonic plates meet which known as the Pacific "ring of fire". Like adding fuel to fire, there are many volcanoes and hot springs across Japan. There are 110 active volcanoes in Japan. Of those, 47 are especially closely observed as they have erupted recently or exhibited worrying signs, such as seismic activity, ground deformation or emission of large amounts of smoke and so forth, for example, Mt. Fuji and Mt. Ontake. Further, Sakura-jima volcano, in the S-W Kyushu Island is the most active strato-volcano, which erupted recently at 2 am on May 11, 2010. Of course, it was a small scale, but the observatory recorded more than 500 eruptions in 2010.

4.9.2 Volcanic Tsunami – Mt. Unzen

Japan has many worst events due to volcanic activities in its history. Keeping the big list aside, a few notable volcanic eruptions that caused tsunami are discussed here as a sample. In 1741, W. Oshima, Japan, witnessed volcanic eruption on 29th Aug that killed 1,467 people. After 50 years of this event, Japan's worst-ever volcanic disaster occurred at Mt. Unzen, Hizen Province (Nagasaki Prefecture), Kyushu. During the end of 1791 a series of earthquakes on the W. flank of Mt. Unzen gradually moved towards Fugen-dake, which started to erupt in Feb 1792, triggering a lava flow that continued for 2 months. The earthquakes continued, shifting nearer to the city of Shimabara. Again on the night of 21 May, two large earthquakes followed by a collapse of the Eastern. flank of Mt. Unzen's Mayuyama dome, caused an avalanche that swept through Shimabara and into Ariake Bay, triggering a tsunami. It is not known whether the collapse occurred as a result of an eruption of the dome or as a result of the earthquakes. The tsunami struck Higo Province (Kumamoto Prefecture) on the other side of Ariake Bay before bouncing back. Out of an estimated 15,000 fatalities, around 5,000 are thought to have been killed by the landslide, around 5,000 by the tsunami across the bay in Higo Province, and a further 5,000 by the tsunami returning to strike Shimabara. The waves reached a height of 330 ft (100 m), making this a megatsunami. The episodes of the series of multiple disasters, (Earthquakes, Volcanic eruption, Avalanche, Landslide, Rockslide and Tsunamis) continued for more than six months like a TV serial.

4.9.3 Quake Tsunami – Nankai

Nankai, Japan, has been facing an earthquake/tsunami once in every century (100 yrs). The 1st recorded earthquake-tsunami (8.4) in Japan shore of the Kii, Shikoku and Awaji was at Nankai, on 29 Nov, 684 CE but no details of fatality available. On 26 Aug, 887 CE, in the Kyoto, a strong tsunami flooded the coast of Settsu Province (Osaka Prefecture) and Sea of Hyûga (Miyazaki Prefecture). On 3 Aug, 1361, an earthquake-tsunami (8.4 quake) washed out >1,700 houses along with 660 lives and shook many cities, islands and ports of Japan including Yuki, Awa (Minami, Tokushima). Again on 20 Sep, 1498, (the Meiô era), 7.5 eq-tsunami damaged ports in Kii Province (Wakayama Prefecture), caused 30–40 thousand deaths & smashed the building around the great Buddha of Kamakura (7 m high). On 3 Feb, 1605, in the Keichôera, a 8.1 quake and 30 m height tsunami swept much of Japan wiping >1000 houses (41%) in Hiro, Kii (Hirogawa, Wakayama), and total >5,000 drowned. On 28 Oct 1707, 8.4 eq-tsunami up to 10 m (33 ft) height at Tosa and 20 m at Tanezaki taking away total of ~30,000 lives and >29,000 houses. In 1854, The Ansei quake in S. coast of Japan (Nankai, Tôkai, and Kyushu) was actually a set of 3 earthquakes, of them 2 are of 8.4 and a 7.4 quake over of some days.

- An 8.4 earthquake on Nov 4, 1854, near Mikawa Province (Aichi Prefecture) and Tôtômi Province (Shizuoka Prefecture) produced tsunami heights of 4–6 m.
- Another 8.4 earthquake on Nov 5 hit Kii Province (Wakayama Prefecture) resulting a tsunami of 8.4 m high. It smashed 15,000 homes of which 2,598 were due to the earthquake and 1,443 people died.
- A magnitude 7.4 earthquake on Nov 7, 1854 hit Iyo Province (Ehime Prefecture) and Bungo Province (Oita Prefecture). The total result was 80,000–100,000 deaths.

The following year, the 1855 Great Ansei Edo earthquake killed nearly 10,000 people. Popular stories of the time blamed on giant catfish called *Namazu* and the Japanese era name was changed to bring good luck after 4 disastrous quakes/tsunamis in just 2 yrs.

The 1946, quake (8.4) followed by tsunami on 21 Dec, at 04:19 pm struck S.W. Japan in Nankai Trough again to claim 1400 lives. It was even observed on tide gauges in California, Hawaii, and Peru.

4.9.4 Flooding Tsunamis Struk – Sanriku

Sanriku is another most vulnerable coast in Japan. In 869 CE, a major tsunami caused flooding up to 4 km inland (from coast), destroyed the town, Tegajo, and resulted in 1,000 casualties. In 1896, on 15 Jun, 7.36 pm, a large undersea quake at Honshu (NE) triggered tsunami waves ½ hr later with a height of 100 ft (30 m) to kill 27,000 people. This repeated in 1933, on 3rd March with 8.1 earthquake + tsunami and destroyed ~5,000 homes & 3,068 lives. Iwate Prefecture lost 42% population & 98% of its buildings. The same area witnessed another hit in 2005 but no major tsunami. Tarô is now protected by tsunami wall 10 m height and over 2 km long.

4.9.5 Entire Japan – Disaster Prone

Year 1293 saw 7.1 quake with tsunami hit Kamakura, then Japan's de facto capital, killing 23,000 after resulting fires. A 7.4 quake near Yaeyama Islands in former Ryûkyû Kingdom (presently Okinawa, Japan) on 4 Apr 1771, 8 am caused no deaths, but the followed tsunami of 30-85.4 m (99-280 ft) killed >12,000 humans. Malaria & crop failures followed and took 150 yrs to get back. The years 1854 and 1855 worsened Japan with large earthquakes and tsunamis. On 1st Sept 1923, The Great Kantô eq-tsunami devastated much of Japan and surrounds within minutes with the waves of 12 m high, killed 150 people and over a lakh in fire in Atami. On 7 Dec 1944, 8.0 eq-tsunami struck Tônankai, the Pacific coast of Japan, mainly Mie, Aichi and Shizuoka Prefectures. News was unclear due to wartime (WW-II).

4.9.6 Fooling Tsunami – Aleutian Islands

In 1946, people of Aleutian Islands thought prank, but 'All Fools Day (1st Apr)-Tsunami' killed 159 in Hawaii & 5 in Alaska (lighthouse-keepers at Aleutians). It led creating the Pacific Tsunami Warning Centre (PTWC)-1949 for Oceania countries. In 1964, Niigata of Japan witnessed Eq-tsunami destroying the port & entire apartment buildings and 28 lives. On 26th May,1983, at 12 noon, 7.7 Eq-Tsunami (10m tall) in the Sea of Japan, came about 100 km into W. coast of Noshiro in Akita Prefecture, Aomori and Noto Peninsula caused 107 fatalities. The tsunami also hit Okushiri Island, more deadly 10 yrs later (12th July 1993), killed 104 people and injured 235. The tsunami (30 m high) struck within 2-5 min of the 7.8 off shore quake that ran 130 km (80 mi) and in the next hour, 13 waves arrived from multiple directions to kill ~200.

> **Web Resources** to know more
> http://ioc.unesco.org/itsu/ IOC/UNESCO International Coordination group for the Tsunami Warning System in the Pacific (ICG/ ITSU), Paris, France
> http://quake.usgs.gov/tsunami/ Tsunamis and Earthquakes, USGS, USA www.asc-india.org Amateur Seismic Centre gives details of state wise seismicity for the country and also reports on past Earthquakes/ Tsunamis.
> http://www.prh.noaa.gov/pr/itic/ International Tsunami Information Center, Honolulu, Hawaii http://www.tsunami.org/ Pacific Tsunami Museum site answers to FAQs, links, and information related to Pacific Ocean tsunamis.

4.9.7 Nuclear Tsunami – Tohoku

On 11th Mar, 2011, Pacific coast of Japan saw a 9.0-earthquake (also known as the 2011 Tôhoku earthquake) that produced a tsunami of 33 ft (10 m) high, and hugely devastated, with 18,550 killed/ missing. The highest tsunami wave recorded (at Miyako, Iwate) total height of 40.5m (133 ft). Tsunami warnings were issued to the entire Pacific Rim. In addition, the tsunami caused to precipitate multiple hydrogen explosions and nuclear meltdown (level 7 in 3 reactors) at the Fukushima-I Nuclear Power Plant (NPP) which registered 15,894 deaths, 6,152 injured and 2,562 missing across 20 prefectures, as well as 228,863 destabilized. 127,290 buildings totally collapsed, while 272,788 half collapsed and 747,989 buildings partially damaged. Damages include roads and railways and a dam collapse. About 4.4 million in NE Japan lived without electricity and 1.5 million without water. The World Bank's estimated economic cost was US$235 billion, making it the costliest natural disaster in history.

Earthquakes, Tsunamis, Volcanoes, Floods, Landslides, Rockslides, Mudslides, Avalanches, Nuclear Explosions, and what not! Japan finds a place in the history of every disaster. But…

Hats off! Still Japan finds a place in world class products and one among the top.

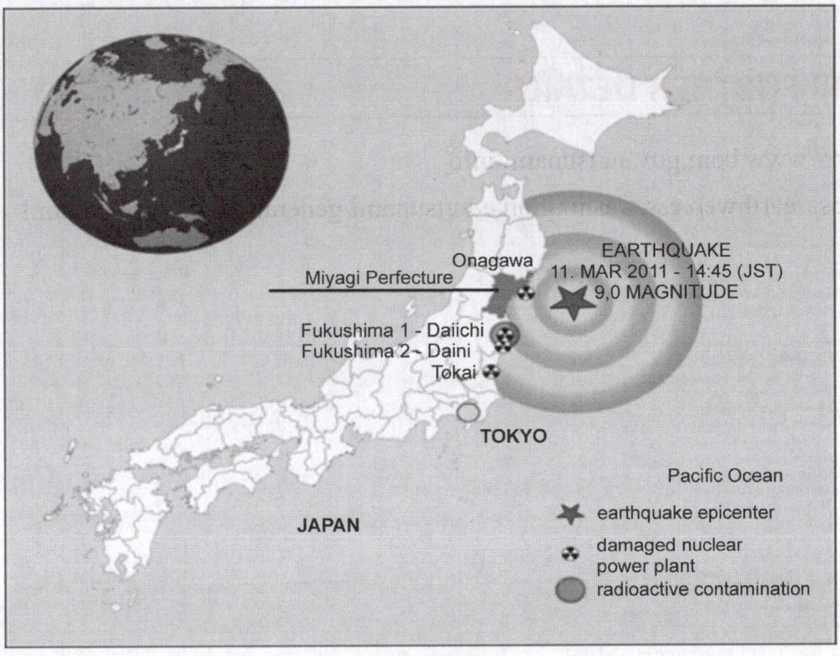

Fig. 4.16

SELF ASSESSMENT INTERMISSION (SAI – 4.4)

1. Discuss the status of occurrence of tsunami in India?
2. Write a detailed note on Boxing Day Tsunami?
3. Discuss some of the disasters, those triggered tsunamis in Japan?
4. Why is Japan highly vulnerable to natural disasters?
5. What types of disasters does Japan face mostly? Why? Explain with examples.
6. Nankai of Japan is most vulnerable to tsunami/ earthquake. Why? Explore the reasons.
7. Explain the nuclear disaster associated with the 2011 earthquake followed by tsunami at Tohoku.
8. List out at least 5 most natural disaster prone countries. Discuss why they are so.
9. Where do minor tremors occur almost on daily basis? Why?
10. 'Hardly any newspaper is found without the news of tremors on any given day. It is almost a part of their daily life'. Where does this occur? Why?
11. 'Deadly quakes are a tragic part of the nation's past'. About which nation, this statement is made? Discuss.

MINI-PROJECT/ CASE STUDIES

1. Write a report on the 2004, Dec 26 Tsunami.
2. Write a detailed note on Japan's vulnerability to all types of disasters and prepare a documentary.

FOR FURTHER DETAILS

http://www.bom.gov.au/tsunami/info/

https://earthweb.ess.washington.edu/tsunami/general/physics/runup.html

CHAPTER 5 Volcano

O'MY SILENT INNER VIBES (O'M S I V – 5)

Volcano itself is the term derived from Vulcan, the God of fire in Roman mythology. For that matter, Hindu myths also say that the volcanoes are mountains of fire (*Agni parvathas*) and the volcanic eruption is the fury of Agni, the God of fire. Almost all parts of ancient world believed that volcanic eruptions are due to supernatural causes, such as the actions of gods or demigods.

An interesting story from Hindu myths tell that at the beginning of this creation, the deities and demons, decide to churning the ocean of milk (*Ksheera Saagara Mathanam*) to get '*Amrutam*', the nectar of immortality that makes one eternal and deathless on drinking it. They used the king of serpents, '*Vasuki*' as churning rope and the mount *Mandhara* as the churning stick. While they were churning, the mountain Mandhara started sinking. Then, Lord Vishnu incarnated as the turtle (*the Kurma*, the 2nd incarnation) and rescued the operation by lifting it up.

On churning, several products, both good and bad came out. The first product came out was "Kalakuta Garalam or Halahalam", the most powerful and disastrous Poison, which can smash entire creation. Lord Shiva, for the sake of protecting the world, swallowed it and halted it at His throat, and so was named '*Garala Kantta or Sri Kantta or Neela Kantta*'. Next, Moon came out of it and is given to Lord Siva to provide cooling the heat caused due to the poison.

Then evolved, the Goddess of money and prosperity (*Lakshmi*), the precious stone (*Kousthubha*), the conch (*Panchajanya shankha*) were taken by Lord Vishnu who rescued by bearing the weight of the mountain.

Kama Dhenu, the holy cow that gives whatever (food) you want for survival was given to the seven great sages (*Sapta rishis*) for milk, curd, and ghee that is required for performing *Yagnas* for wellbeing of the world. The most beautiful never wilting flower (*Parijatham*) was taken to *Indralok*.

Later, *Airavatam*, the white elephant, which can give victory in wars and expeditions; *Kalpatharu*, the holy tree to provide shelter/ livelihood; the *Apsaras* (*Rambha, Urvasi, Menaka, Thilothama* etc.) who can provide entertainment, have come out. All these are retained by Indra, the king of deities while the 7 headed holy horse (*Uchhaishrav*) that can take you wherever you want to go (transport), was given to Bali, the leader of Demons.

Finally, on churning, *Dhanvantari* (the physician) brought the nectar of immortality (*Amrutam*).

Some bad elements also came out such as Goddess of misfortune (*Jyeshta*), the sloth (*Nidra*), the sedative drink (*Varuni*), the belligerence (*Sarang*) and so forth. People believe that the bad elements came out, are the results of ***volcanic eruptions*** of Mandhara while the poison was from the serpent's mouth.

Just a keen observation on the above story, my volcanic heart erupted and produced some vibes...

- Whether gods or demigods or humans, they churn the ocean of life to get the fundamental needs like, food of their choice (*Kamadhenu*), shelter to live (*Kalpataru*), transport to go

(Continued)

wherever they want (*Uchhaishrav*) and finally the nectar (*Amrut*) that can make them eternal (remembered forever). All are given by the almighty, and it is up to you, how you use them.

- Nothing comes easily unless you take the pains of churning. The best can come only after shedding the sweat.
- The best (*Amrut*) comes, only after the worst (*Poison*). Be ready to swallow and sustain.
- Prosperity (*Lakshmi*) and misfortune (*Jyeshta*) i.e. good & bad are together one after the other.
- *NIGHT* is always followed by a *DAY*. No lock (problem) is produced without key (solution).
- Before a victory, you may face lot of troubles, miserable failures and unbearable insults. But…
    - Troubles make you tough - welcome them, because 'when going becomes tough, tough only would be going'.
    - Failures are the steps of success and
    - Let the insults produce fire and inspire to erupting your heart at its peak.

Of course! God will rescue whenever you need. Yes! **He definitely gives what you require but not what you aspire.** So, erupt the volcanic fire to get what you aspire.

5.1 DEFINITION AND CONCEPT

In the early days, Johannes Kepler (16th-17th-century), the German astronomer assumed volcanoes as ducts for the Earth's tears. But Jesuit Athanasius Kircher (1602–1680), differed with it after witnessing eruptions of Mt. Etna, Stromboli, and the crater of Vesuvius and proposed that a central fire in the Earth caused by the burning of sulphur, bitumen and coal. Several other models were also proposed to explain volcano behavior. Until the modern theory of Earth's mantle structure (as a semisolid material) was developed, it was assumed or believed for so many years that the volcanic activity was due to chemical reactions, compression and radioactive materials and so forth.

Definition

A **volcano** is a rupture on the crust of a planetary-mass object, such as Earth, that allows hot lava, volcanic ash, and gases to escape from a magma chamber below the surface.

The study of volcanoes is called volcanology, or vulcanology.

5.2 FORMATION OF VOLCANOES – THE PLATE HYPOTHESIS

We already understood that Earth's crust is broken into 17 major rigid tectonic plates (refer chapter – 3: Earthquakes) which float on a hotter, and softer layers of its mantle. As many people think, the volcanoes are usually not created by sliding of two tectonic plates. The plate hypothesis can better describe the formation of volcanoes,

According to ***'the plate hypothesis'***, the volcanoes are formed in the three typical areas depending on where they are the plates are located with reference to the surface of the Earth. These are,

I. The volcanoes formed under ocean bed
II. The volcanoes formed under the shores/ along coasts
III. The volcanoes formed under the land

Surprisingly the above three volcanoes formations are in three distinct behaviors of the plates in the three different ways as described as the following,

Case-1: Diverging Tectonic Plates (pull apart) e.g. Mid-Atlantic Ridge

Case-2: Converging Tectonic Plates (come together) e.g. Pacific Ring of Fire

Case-3: Tension and Compression of Crust's Interior Plates, e.g., E. African Rift, Wells Gray-Clearwater volcanic field and Rio Grande Rift in N. America.

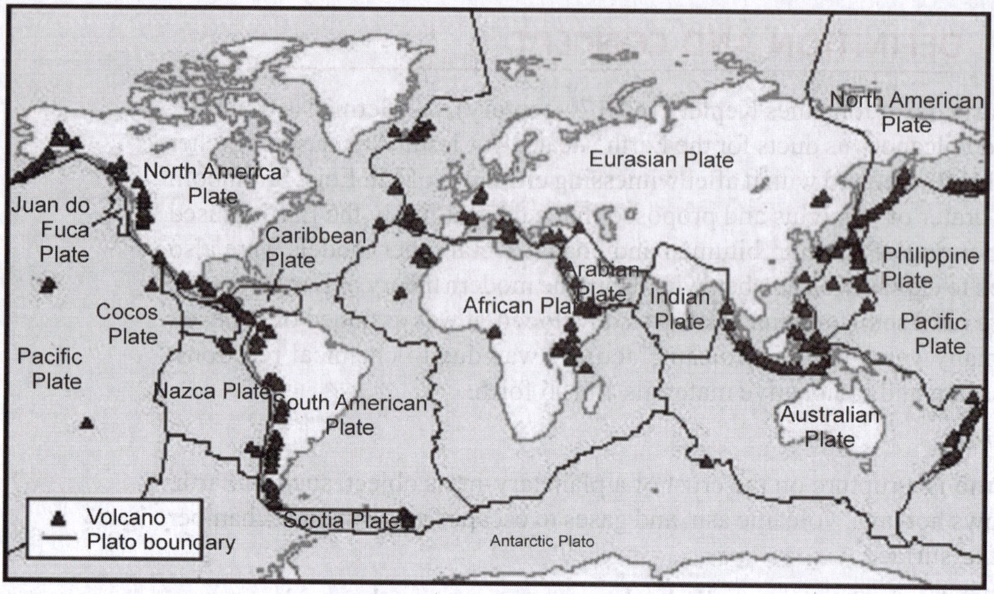

Fig. 5.1

There is yet another case as given below.

Case-4: The volcanic activities other than plate boundaries are explained as mantle plumes and are called "hotspots", (e.g. Hawaii). These are supposed to arise from upwelling diapirs with magma from the core–mantle boundary, about 3,000 km deep.

We shall now discuss about the above four cases briefly.

5.2.1 Volcanism by Divergent Plate Boundaries

These volcanoes are formed mostly at the bottom of the ocean, particularly, at divergent plate boundaries. Due to the divergence of tectonic plates in the mid-oceanic ridges, a new oceanic crust is formed by the cooling and solidifying of hot molten rock. As this crust is very thin at these ridges, the pull of the tectonic plates release pressure leading to adiabatic expansion and the partial mantle melting finally results in volcanism and creates new oceanic crust.

Since most divergent plate boundaries are at the bottom of the oceans, this type of volcanic activity is submarine, forming new seafloor. Black smokers, also called deep sea vents are of this type of volcanic activity, when the mid-oceanic ridge is above sea-level that form volcanic islands, e.g. Iceland.

5.2.2 Volcanism by Convergent Plate Boundaries

This volcanism is exhibited by the subduction zones, i.e. places of collision of two plates, usually an oceanic and a continental plate. In this case, the oceanic plate subducts or submerges under the continental plate and forms a deep ocean trench just offshore. In a process called flux melting, water released from the subducting plate lowers the melting temperature of the overlying mantle wedge, creating magma, which is very viscous due to high silica content. Thence most probably, this magma does not reach the surface and cools at depth. But when it reaches the surface, a volcano is formed. Mt. Etna in the Pacific Ring of Fire is a good example for this type of volcanism.

5.2.3 Volcanism by Tensions and Compressions of Interior Plates

These volcanoes are found on the land and formed under the crust due to tensions and compressions of plates over a period of time. The volcanic activity in the above two cases often may trigger a tsunami, whereas this normally does not. The high pressure hot liquids or gases and lava flows out when a channel is found through loose soil, digging, excavation, mining etc.

5.2.4 Hotspots

Hotspots, formed by mantle plumes are the columns of hot material rising from the core-mantle boundary in a fixed space that causes large melting. As tectonic plates move across them, each volcano becomes dormant and is eventually reformed as the plate advancing over the plume e.g. Hawaiian Islands, Snake River Plain, and Yellowstone Caldera.

SELF ASSESSMENT INTERMISSION (SAI – 5.1)

1. Define Volcano? What is its meaning? Why is it so named?
2. How do volcanoes form? Explain.
3. Explain the plate hypothesis of volcano formation.
4. What is 'Hotspot'? How is it formed?
5. Give a brief account on volcano formation below the ocean bed, below near-shore and underneath land.
6. Explain the formation of the volcanism by tectonic plate convergence and divergence. Distinguish between the two.
7. Classify the volcanoes with reference to their formation due to tectonics. Briefly describe each with an example.
8. Is there any relation between an earthquake and a volcano? Discuss.
9. Is there any relation between a tsunami and a volcano? Discuss.

5.3 CLASSIFICATION OF VALCANOES

If you ask anybody to describe a volcano…Perhaps! You would notice at least 80 to 90% would describe the volcano as a conical mountain, spewing lava and poisonous gases from a crater at its summit.

But, this is only one class among various types of volcanoes. In fact, their structure and behavior depends on a number of factors and so the volcanic features are very complicated.

They show a wide variety of external shapes and structures such as a rugged peak with 'lava dome', or as a summit crater, or with landscape features, or as a massive plateau and so forth. Surprisingly the vents that deliver volcanic material (including lava and ash) can develop anywhere on the landform. Sometimes, they may be smaller cones also like Hawaii's Kîlauea. Other interesting types are cryovolcanoes (or ice volcanoes), more so, on the moons of Jupiter, Saturn, and Neptune. Further, mud volcanoes, are often not magmatic activity.

However, for a better understanding the volcanoes can be studied by classifying them with reference to the factors by which they can be characterized such as their formation/ place of formation or the types of tectonic plates, the features and structure of the volcano, the frequency of volcanic activity, the shape/ material of lava, the type of eruption mechanism, and so forth.

Some authors classify volcanoes based on the formation and place where they form

(i) Volcanoes by Divergent Plates (or) Volcanoes under the sea bed
(ii) Volcanoes by Convergent Plates (or) Volcanoes along the sea shores
(iii) Volcanoes by Tensions/Compressions of Plates (or) Volcanoes under the land
(iv) Hotspots

These are already explained in the previous section (above 5.2) under formation of volcanoes.

We shall classify volcanoes in the other characteristics now.

5.4 CLASSIFICATION BASED ON THE FEATURES

Various types of volcanoes and their nature and features are briefly given below

1. Fissure vents
2. Shielded volcanoes

3. Lava Domes
4. Cryptodome
5. Cinder Cones
6. Stratovolcanoes
7. Supervolcanoes
8. Submarinevolcanoes
9. Sub-glacial or Mountain Tables or Tuyas
10. Mud Volcanoes or Mud domes

We shall now get awareness about the features of above types of volcanoes.

5.4.1 Fissure Vents

- The lava emerges through flat, linear fractures. Example: The fissure formed by the 1886 eruption of Mt. Tarawera.

Lakagigar fissure vent in Iceland

5.4.2 Shield Volcanoes

- These are so named because of their broad, shield-like profiles.
- They generally do not explode catastrophically.
- These are formed by the eruption of low-viscous lava
- The lava can flow for a large distance from a vent.
- These are more common in oceans than in continents, as low-viscous magma is low in silica. Example: Very common in Iceland, The Hawaiian volcanic chain is a series of shield cones.

Skjaldbreiður, a shield volcano whose name means "broad shield"

5.4.3 Lava Domes

- Lava domes are built by slow eruptions of highly viscous lava.
- Their eruption is often violent and explosive but the lava generally does not flow far from the originating vent.
- They usually form within the crater of a previous volcanic eruption. Example: Mt. St. Helens.
- They can also form independently. Example: Lassen Peak.

5.4.4 Cryptodomes

- These are formed when viscous lava forces upward to cause a bulge on the surface.

Example: In 1980 eruption of Mt. St. Helens, bulged upward due to lava, which slid-down to north side.

5.4.5 Volcanic Cones (Cinder Cones)

- Volcanic or cinder cones are formed by eruptions of mostly tiny pieces of scoria and pyroclastics and build up around the vent.
- These pieces of scoria and pyroclastics look like cinders, and so the name.
- These eruptions have relatively short-life
- Most cinder cones erupt only once.
- These are generally cone-shaped hills up to 30 to 400 m high.
- They may form as flank vents on larger volcanoes, or occur on their own.

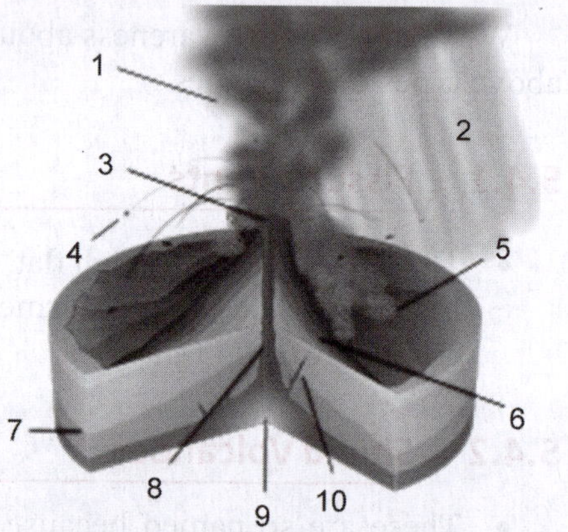

1. Ash plume 2. Volcanic ash rain 3. Lava dome 4. Volcanic bomb 5. Pyroclastic flow 6. Layers of lava & ash 7. Stratum 8. Magma conduit 9. Magma chamber 10. Dike

Examples: Parícutin (Mexico), Sunset Crater (Arizona), Caja del Rio (New Mexico) has over 60 cinder cones; Also on the surface of Mars and its Moon.

5.4.6 Stratovolcanoes (Composite Volcanoes)

- They are composed of lava and other ejections in alternate layers (called strata), so the name.
- These are tall conical mountains.
- They are also called composite volcanoes as they are created from multiple and complex structures during different kinds of eruptions.
- They are made of cinders, ash, and lava.
- Cinders and ash pile up one over the other, lava flows on top of the ash, where it cools and hardens. This process repeats.
- The ash produced by the explosive eruption pose the greatest volcanic hazard to civilizations.

- These build high pressure from the underlying lava flow (greater than shield volcanoes)
- Their fissure vents and monogenetic volcanic fields (volcanic cones) have more powerful eruptions, as they are many times under extension.
- They are steeper with slopes of 30–35° than shield volcano slopes (5–10°).
- Their loose source material (tephra) can cause dangerous lahars.
- Large pieces of tephra, called volcanic bombs even measure >4 ft (1.2m) and weigh several tons.

Examples: Mt. Fuji (Japan); Mayon Volcano (Philippines); Mt. Vesuvius and Stromboli (Italy).

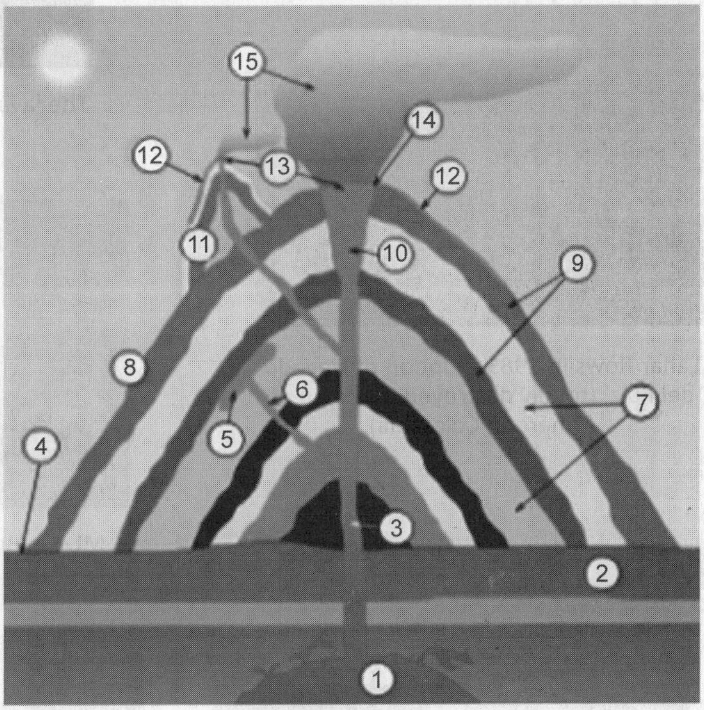

Cross-section through a stratovolcano (Not to scale)
1. Large magma chamber 2. Bedrock 3. Conduit (pipe) 4. Base 5. Sill 6. Dike 7. Layers of ash emitted 8. Flank 9. Layers of lava emitted 10. Throat 11. Parasitic cone 12. Lava flow13. Vent 14. Crater 15. Ash cloud

Izalco, at Cordillera de Apaneca volcanic range in El Salvador is the youngest and best known cone volcano erupted from its formation (1770) to 1958 almost continuously, it is nicknamed "Lighthouse of the Pacific"

Pyroclastic flows at Mayon Volcano, Philippines, 1984

The lava spine developed after the 1902 eruption of Mt. Pelée

Lahar flows in 1985 eruption of Nevado del Ruiz, (totally destroyed the town of Armero in Colombia)

Mt. Lamington following the devastating 1951 eruption

Surtsey, erupted 13 days after breaching the water. A tuff ring surrounded the vent

21 April 1990 eruption from Redoubt Volcano, Kenai Peninsula

5.4.7 Supervolcano

- It is the most dangerous type of volcano, usually has a large caldera.
- It covers enormous area, and so the name
- It is difficult to identify centuries after an eruption.
- It can severely cool global temperatures for many years after the eruption owing to the release of huge volumes of sulphur and ash into the atmosphere.

Examples: Lake Toba (Sumatra, Indonesia); Lake Taupo (New Zealand); Yellowstone Caldera in Yellowstone National Park and Valles Caldera (New Mexico); and Ngorongoro Crater (Tanzania)

5.4.8 Submarine Volcanoes

- These are common on the ocean floor and so the name.
- These erupt a thick sequences of discontinuous pillow-shaped masses formed under water, called pillow lava.
- Active volcanoes, in shallow water can exhibit their identity by blasting steam and rocky debris high above the ocean's surface.
- In the ocean's deep, the huge weight of the water above forestalls the explosive release of steam and gases. However, they can be detected by hydrophones and discoloration of water due to volcanic gases.
- Even large eruptions may not disturb the ocean surface due to the rapid cooling effect and increased buoyancy of water which often causes volcanic vents to form steep pillars on the ocean floor.
- Hydrothermal vents are common near these volcanoes, which exhibit peculiar ecosystem based on dissolved minerals.
- Over a period of time, the submarine volcanoes may create new islands or floating pumice rafts.

5.4.9 Subglacial Volcanoes or Table Mountains or Tuyas

- Subglacial volcanoes are called tuyas, named after Tuya Butte, at River Tuya and Tuya Range in N. British Columbia. (Tuya Butte was the first of this kind of eruption and so the name).

Tuya The *Tuya Mountains Provincial Park* was recently established to protect the unusual landscape lies between north of *Tuya Lake* and south of the *Jennings River* near the boundary with the Yukon Territory

- They are also called mobergs (perhaps derived from the words moving ice-bergs)
- These develop underneath icecaps.
- They are made up of flat lava which flows at the top of extensive pillow lavas and palagonite.
- When the icecap melts, the lava on top collapses, leaving a flat-topped mountain, therefore, these are also called table-mountains

Examples: Ranges in Iceland, and in British Columbia.

5.4.10 Mud Volcanoes or Mud Domes

- Mud volcanoes or mud domes are formations created by geo-excreted liquids and gases.
- The largest structures are 10 km in diameter and reach 700m high.

Pâhoehoe lava flow on Hawaii. The picture shows overflows of a main lava channel

San Miguel (volcano), El Salvador. On December 29, 2013, San Miguel volcano, also known as "Chaparrastique", erupted at 10:30 local time, spewing a large column of ash and smoke into the sky; the eruption, the first in 11 years, was seen from space and prompted the evacuation of thousands of people living in a 3 km radius around the volcano. https://kids.kiddle.co/Volcano

The Stromboli stratovolcano off the coast of Sicily has erupted continuously for thousands of years, giving rise to the term strombolian eruption

Ash plume from San Miguel (volcano) "Chaparrastique", seen from a satellite, as it heads towards the Pacific Ocean from the El Salvador Central America coast, December 29, 2013

SELF ASSESSMENT INTERMISSION (SAI – 5.2)

1. Classify Volcanoes based on their feature? Explain any four of them.
2. Describe the features of fissure vents and shield volcanoes.
3. Explain the features of lava domes and crypto domes.
4. Give a neat labeled diagram of cross-section of (a) volcanic cone (b) stratovolcano
5. Enumerate the features of stratovolcanoes. Give an example.
6. What are cinder cones? How do they form? How do they behave?
7. What do you understand by a super volcano? Discuss its features.
8. With a neat sketch explain the structure and nature of strato-volcano? Why is called composite volcano?
9. What are submarine and subglacial volcanoes? Distinguish between them. Where do they occur?
10. What are tuyas? Why are they so named?
11. Give brief note on mud-domes?
12. What do you understand by the terms table-mountains, mobergs and tuyas? Why they so named?

5.5 CLASSIFICATION BASED ON FREQUENCY OF VOLCANIC ACTIVITY

Magmatic volcanoes are popularly classified by their frequency of eruption as follows

1. Active Volcanoes – erupt regularly
2. Dormant or Inactive Volcanoes – erupt in historical times but quiet now
3. Extinct Volcanoes – not erupted in historical times

Classification of Volcanoes

The Active-Dormant-Extinct classification is practically meaningless to scientists. They use classifications which refer to a particular volcano's formative and eruptive processes and resulting shapes.

5.5.1 Active Volcanoes

Strictly speaking, there is no clear definition for "active" volcano because the lifespan of a volcano can vary from months to several million years. So, such a distinction seems to be meaningless sometimes. For instance, many volcanoes erupted number of times in the past few thousand years are not showing any signs of eruption presently. Thus, such volcanoes may be very active in their long lifespan, but by human lifespan, they are not. Further, there is no hard and fast rule or scale for measuring the frequency of eruption.

Kîlauea burns and lava entering the sea

Lava flows at Holuhraun, Iceland, September 2014

The lava arcs during Strombolian activity.

Ropey pahoehoe lava from Kilauea, Hawaii.

The following are considered Earth's most active volcanoes:	The longest currently ongoing (but not necessarily continuous) volcanic eruptive phases are:
• Kīlauea, in Hawai, has been in continuous, effusive eruption since 1983, and has the longest-observed lava lake. • Mt. Etna and nearby Stromboli, two Mediterranean volcanoes in "almost continuous eruption" since antiquity. • Mt. Yasur, in Vanuatu, has been erupting "nearly continuously" for over 800 years.	• Mt. Yasur, 111 years • Mt. Etna, 109 years • Stromboli, 108 years • Santa María, 101 years • Sangay, 94 years
Other very active volcanoes include:	
• Mt. Nyiragongo and Nyamuragira, are Africa's most active volcanoes • Nyiragongo's lava lake in Africa • Piton de la Fournaise, in Réunion, erupts frequently is a tourist attraction. • Erta Ale, in the Afar Triangle, has maintained a lava lake since at least 1906. • Mount Erebus, in Antarctica, has maintained a lava lake since at least 1972. • Whakaari / White Island, has been in continuous state of smoking since its discovery in 1769.	Some more • Mt. Merapi • Ol Doinyo Lengai • Ambrym • Arenal Volcano • Pacaya • Klyuchevskaya Sopka • Sheveluch

5.5.2 Dormant Volcanoes

It is difficult to distinguish between extinct and dormant (or inactive) volcanoes, because they may be understood as extinct when there are no written records. If so, volcanoes may remain dormant for a long period of time.

Narcondam Island, India, is classified as dormant volcano by Geological Survey of India

After being believed extinct for over 10,000 yrs Fourpeaked volcano, Alaska, Sept 2006

Right: Mount Rinjani eruption in 1994, in Lombok, Indonesia

Scientists usually consider a volcano to be erupting or likely to erupt, or showing signs of unrest such as unusual earthquake activity or significant new gas emissions. A volcano is considered to be active if it has erupted in the last 10,000 years (Holocene times). Most of active volcanoes are situated on the Pacific Ring of Fire. An estimated 500 million people live near active volcanoes.) is another timeframe for active. The Catalogue of the Active Volcanoes of the World, published by the International Association of Volcanology, uses recorded history to describe more than 500 active volcanoes.

Scientists believed that pulses of magma mixed together in the chamber before climbing upward—a process estimated to take several thousands of years. But Columbia University volcanologists found that the eruption of Costa Rica's Irazú Volcano in 1963 was likely triggered by magma that took a nonstop route from the mantle over just a few months.

Examples:

- Soufrière Hills volcano on the island of Montserrat, remained to be extinct before activity occurred in 1995
- Four-peaked Mountain in Alaska, before its eruption in Sep 2006, had long been thought to be extinct as it had not erupted since 8000 BC.
- Romans described Vesuvius as having been covered with gardens and vineyards before its eruption of AD 79, which destroyed the towns of Herculaneum and Pompeii.
- Until its catastrophic eruption in 1991, Pinatubo was unknown to people in the surrounding area.

5.5.3 Extinct Volcanoes

Extinct volcanoes are unlikely to erupt again, since the volcano no longer has a magma supply.

Examples:

- Hawaiian – Emperor seamount chain in the Pacific Ocean,
- Hohentwiel, Shiprock and the Zuidwal volcano in the Netherlands,
- Edinburgh Castle in Scotland.

Some volcanologists refer to extinct volcanoes as inactive, though the term is now more commonly used for dormant volcanoes once thought to be extinct.

5.6 TYPES OF LAVA

The eruptive product of the volcanoes is called LAVA. Volcanoes can be classified on the basis of the *composition of material erupted* (lava), as it affects the shape of the volcano. According to Cas & Wright (1987), lava can be broadly classified into 4 different compositions:

1. Felsic Lava
2. Andesitic Lava
3. Mafic Lava
4. Ultra Mafic Lava

These compositions and features of volcanoes with reference to the lava compositions are described below. (The volcanoes can also be classified into these four types based on the lava compositions).

5.6.1 Felsic Lava

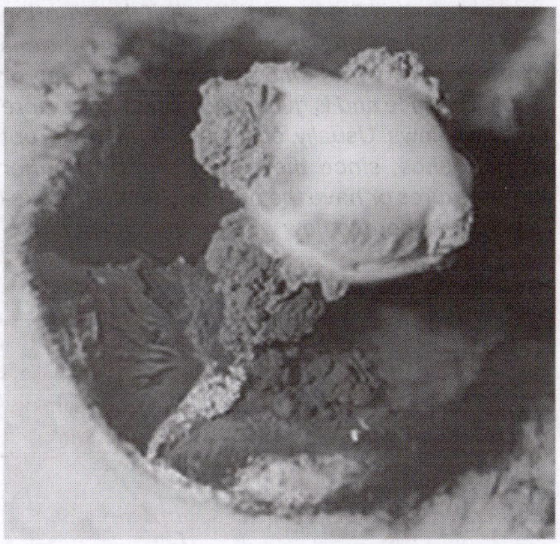

- The lava is termed 'felsic', if the erupted magma contains a high percentage (>63%) of silica.
- Felsic lava is rich in **Fe**rro materials (Fe), **Al**uminum (Al), **Si**lica (Si), **C**alcium and **C**arbon
- Felsic lavas (dacites or rhyolites) are highly viscous (but not very fluid) and are erupted as domes or short, stubby flows.
- Due to the viscousity, these siliceous magmas trap volatiles (gases) present, thence can form stratovolcanoes or lava domes to result in a catastrophe.
- Volcanic ash that is light enough to be erupted high into the Earth's atmosphere may travel many kilometers before it falls back to ground as a tuff.
- Highly hazardous Pyroclastic flows (ignimbrites) and molten volcanic ash (too heavy to go up into atmosphere) flow over the slopes and can travel far from their vents.
- Temperatures up to 1,200°C can occur in pyroclastic flows, so inflammable in their path and may deposit many meters thick layers.

Examples:

1. Lassen Peak (California) is actually a large lava dome formed from felsic lava.
2. Alaska Valley of Ten Thousand Smokes (Alaska), formed by the eruption of Novarupta near Katmai in 1912, is a thick pyroclastic flow (ignimbrite deposit).

5.6.2 Andesitic Lava

- If the erupted magma contains 52–63% silica, then the lava is of *intermediate* composition, called andesitic.
- These volcanoes only occur above subduction zones.
- Andesitic lava is typically formed at convergent boundary margins of tectonic plates, by several processes (Sea shores, island).

Example: Mt. Merapi (Indonesia)

Lava a Texture

Two types of lava are named according to the surface texture: »A»a (pronounced [È"a"a]) and pâhoehoe ([paÐÈho.eÈho.e]), both Hawaiian words. »A»a is characterized by a rough, clinkery surface with texture of viscous lava flows. However, even basaltic or mafic flows can be erupted as »a»a flows, particularly if the eruption rate is high and the slope is steep. Pâhoehoe is characterized by its smooth and often ropey or wrinkly surface and is generally formed from more fluid lava flows. Usually, only mafic flows will erupt as pâhoehoe, since they often erupt at higher temperatures or have the proper chemical make-up to allow them to flow with greater fluidity.

5.6.3 Mafic Lava

If the erupted magma contains 45–52% silica, the lava is called basaltic or mafic [rich in % of **Ma**gnesium (Mg) and iron (Fe)]. These are much less viscous and hotter than felsic lavas. Mafic lavas occur…

- when divergent plates pull apart at mid-ocean ridges, the basaltic lava erupts as pillows to fill the gap.
- Shield volcanoes (e.g. the Hawaiian Islands, including Mauna Loa and Kilauea), on both oceanic and continental crust.

5.6.4 Ultramafic Lava

The magmas containing up to 45% silica are called ultramafic lava, also known as komatiites. These are very rare; indeed, very few have been erupted at the Earth's surface, when the planet's heat flow was higher. They are the hottest lavas, and probably more fluid than common mafic lavas.

5.7 ERUPTION MECHANISMS

We have understood from the above sections that the behaviors of volcanoes vary widely. For the obvious reasons, the eruption activity also varies in a wide range between one volcano and the other. They vary in extremes, the explosive to effusive to flowing. [Ref.fig 5.2]

For example, Hawaiian eruptions exhibit by lava fountains or lava flows that are not very dangerous, whereas Plinian eruptions are large, violent, and highly dangerous and/or explosive too.

Thence, volcanoes and their eruption activities cannot be described in a single common model. Further, they show many different patterns, both effusive as well as explosive. Moreover, volcanoes neither always erupt vertically nor always from a single crater near their peak. Some are lateral and fissure eruptions. For example, Many Hawaiian eruptions start from rift zones, while some of the Surtseyan eruptions along fracture zones. However, with reference to the activity, every eruption may be characterized on a scale continuum of the two extreme eruption patterns as,

- Explosive eruption by gas-driven explosions that propels magma and tephra
- Effusive eruption by the outpouring of lava without significant explosive eruption.

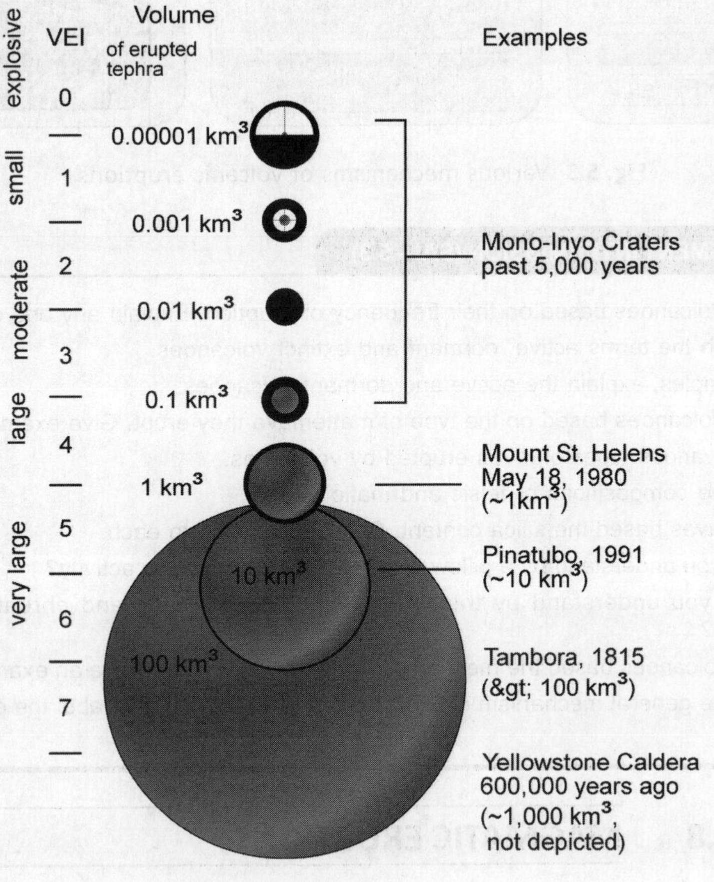

Fig. 5.2 Variation in volcanic eruption

Whatsoever, the eruption pattern is, volcanic eruptions can be explained through three main mechanisms based on some technical similarities. These are:

1. ***Magmatic eruptions*** due to gas release under decompression
2. ***Phreato-magmatic eruptions*** by chilling (i.e. thermal contraction) due to contact with water
3. ***Phreatic eruptions*** due to ejection of particles during steam eruptions

Further, each of these has some variations as shown in the following figure 5.3. Now, we shall understand these mechanisms in detail.

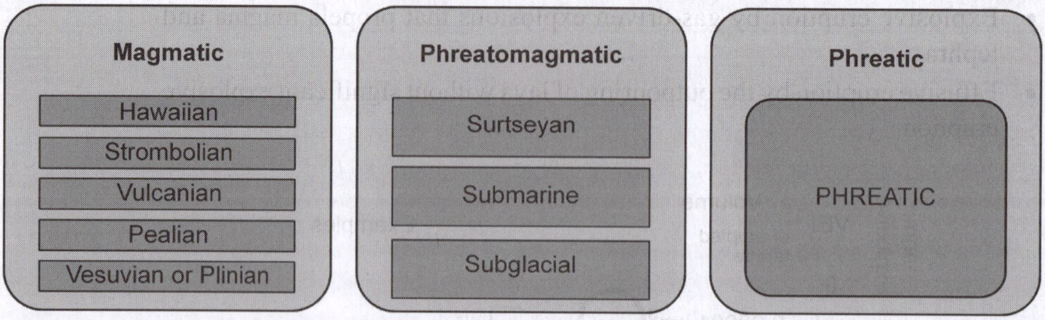

Fig. 5.3 Various mechanisms of volcanic eruptions.

SELF ASSESSMENT INTERMISSION (SAI – 5.3)

1. Classify Volcanoes based on their frequency of eruption. Explain any one of them.
2. Distinguish the terms active, dormant and extinct volcanoes.
3. With examples, explain the active and dormant volcanoes.
4. Classify Volcanoes based on the type of matter/lava they erupt. Give examples.
5. Describe various types of lavas erupted by volcanoes.
6. Explain the compositions of felsic and mafic lavas.
7. Classify lavas based the silica content. Give an example to each.
8. What do you understand by a pillow with reference to volcanic activity?
9. What do you understand by the terms magmatic, phreatic and phreato-magmatic eruptions?
10. Classify volcanoes based the mechanism (or type) of eruption. Give an example to each.
11. Explain the general mechanism of volcanic eruption. Sketch and label the cross-section diagram.

5.8 MAGMATIC ERUPTIONS

Magmatic eruptions intensity depends on the gas release under decompression and ranges from the relatively small lava fountains (Hawaiian) to catastrophic (Ultra Plinian eruption columns which is more than 30 km high, bigger than the eruption of Mt. Vesuvius in 79 that buried Pompeii).

As discussed earlier in this chapter, all magmatic eruptions are not alike. Though the magma is common, the composition is different. Obviously their erupting mechanics also differ. Some erupt with explosions while some other with effusion. Each is unique. However, using the similarities and nearness of the erupting patterns and styles, that they have shown at different locations and occasions, the magmatic eruption mechanisms can be described under the following types.

1. Hawaiian Eruption
2. Strombolian Eruption
3. Vulcanian Eruption
4. Pelean Eruption
5. Plinian or Vesuvian Eruption

All these are named after the place where they have first erupted. We shall now have a look on these mechanisms with some examples.

5.8.1 Hawaiian Eruptions

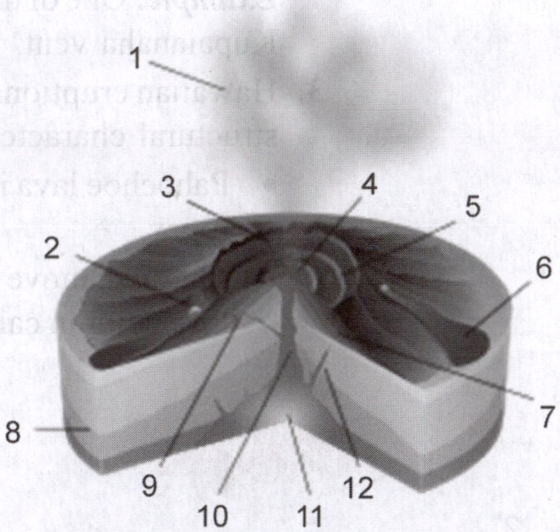

Hawaiian Eruption

1. Ash plume 2. Lava fountain 3. Crater 4. Lava lake 5. Fumaroles 6. Lava flow 7. Layers of lava and ash 8. Stratum9. Sill 10. Magma conduit 11. Magma chamber 12. Dike

Hawaiian eruptions stand as models for such type, and are often named 'Hawaiian activity'. Though, Hawaiian eruptions are so named, the eruptions in Hawaii are not necessarily restricted to this pattern.

The examples of Hawaiian eruptions include

- All the volcanoes of Hawaiian islands
- Mt. Mihara recorded the largest lava fountain ever formed on the island of Izu Oshima in 1986. The gusher (1,600 m) is more than double the height of the mountain (764 m).

These eruptions are the most silent and calm with the effusion of very fluid basalt-type lava along with low gaseous matter. The volume ejected in these eruptions is not even half of that in other kinds of eruption. The consistent small amounts of lava make large and broad as a shield volcano. Unlike many other types, these do not centralize at the main summit and often occur at vents around the summit and from fissure vents radiating out of the center.

Hawaiian activities often begin as a line of vents eruptions along a fissure, called "curtain of fire". As the lava begins to flow out from few of the vents, the activity slows down. Meanwhile the central-vent eruption often takes place as a large lava fountain either continuous or sporadic that can raise 100's of m high. Blessing in disgust is that the particles from lava fountains usually cool in the air before hitting the ground, but pile up. If the air is thick, the cooling may not be that fast, hence hit the ground still hot and accumulate in the form of spatter cones. And if rate of eruption too high, the splatter-fed lava flows.

Thus the Hawaiian eruptions can be characterized by the following features.

1. These are often extremely long lived.

   Example: Continuously since 1983, Kilauea has been erupting with rope shape (called Pahoehoe) lava. The eruptions began on 3 January with a 6 km long fissure based "curtain of fire". Later, the centralized eruptions built up on the site of Kilauea's east rift, the parasitic cone is still active.
2. Formation of active lava lakes, self-maintained pools of raw lava with a thin crust of semi-cooled rock

   Example: One of the current 5 only such lakes in the world, is at Kilauea's Kupaianaha vent.
3. Hawaiian eruptions are basaltic, and can be divided into 2 types by their structural characteristics.
   - Pahoehoe lava is a relatively smooth lava flow that can be billowy or ropey.
   - They can move as a sheet by the advancement of "toes" or as snaking lava column called A'a.

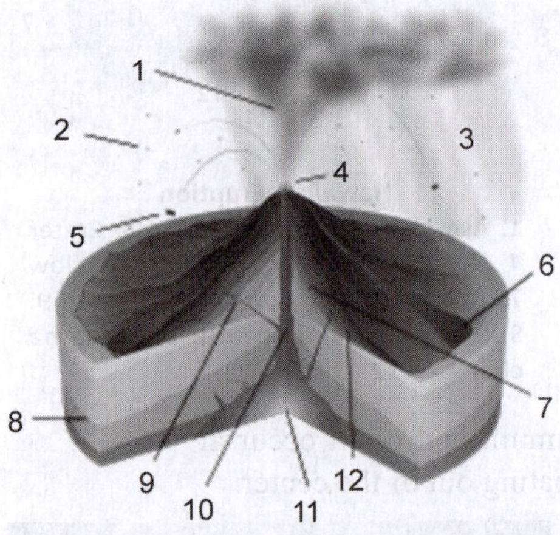

Strombolian Eruption

1. Ash plume 2. Lapilli 3. Volcanic ash rain 4. Lava fountain 5. Volcanic bomb 6. Lava flow 7. Layers of lava and ash 8. Stratum 9. Dike 10. Magma conduit 11. Magma chamber 12. Sill

5.8.2 Strombolian Eruption

Strombolian volcano has been erupting continuously for centuries and has become a model for this kind of eruption. This kind of eruptions start with small gas bubbles within the magma and as they accumulate into large bubbles, called 'gas slugs' rise through the lava column on to the surface and burst with a loud pop sound throwing magma in the air (analogous to a soap bubble). Owing to the high gas pressures in the lava, explosive eruption is continuous accompanied by the distinctive loud blasts for every few minutes.

The Strombolian eruptions are found in wide range from small blasts to large eruptive columns. Strictly speaking, 'true Strombolian' eruptions are short-lived and explode with viscous basaltic lava (mostly ends as scoria), often ejected 100's of m high into the air, but relatively passive and the non-damaging and so continue unabated for 1000's of years.

Analogous to a flower pot cracker (a type of Diwali cracker), Strombolian eruptions also eject volcanic bombs and lapilli fragments that travel in parabolic paths around the vent and accumulate to form cinder cones basaltic pyroclasts, which in turn form well-ordered rings of tephra.

The examples of volcanoes Strombolian activity include:

- Stromboli itself, is exhibiting throughout historical time continuously, and occasionally accompanied by lava flows.
- Paricutin, Mexico erupted from a fissure in a cornfield in 1943. 2 years later, pyroclastic activity started to wane and the outpouring of lava and eruptions ceased in 1952, and the final height was about 424 m. (First time, scientists could observe the complete life cycle of a volcano)
- Mt. Etna of Italy has displayed Strombolian activity in recent eruptions in 1981, 1999, 2002-03, and 2009.
- Mt Erebus (Antarctica), the southernmost active volcano in the world showing frequent Strombolian activity since 1972.

Distinction between Hawaiian and Strombolian Activities

Both being magmatic eruptions, (Strombolian and Hawaiian) the two eruptions are similar. Still there are certain features that distinguish the two as given in the Table 5.1 (adjacent).

Table 5.1 Distinction between Hawaiian and Strombolian Volcanoes.

Hawaiian	Strombolian
Silent	Noisier
Produce volcanic products such as ropy structures, snaking, Pele's tears and Pele's hair	Do not produce volcanic products
Produce large molten lava flows	Produce fewer molten lava flows
Forms a line of vents of eruption, often called 'curtain of fire'	Cracks like flower pot and form well-ordered rings of tephra.

5.8.3 Vulcanic Eruption

1888-1890 eruption of Vulcano (means volcano, named by Giuseppe Mercalli) gained the name for yet another type of eruption of highly viscous magma within the volcano that even obstructed escaping gases. Like Strombolian, the high gas pressure is built up here also, eventually pop up the cap and explode. However, unlike Strombolian, the lava particles are not projectile, due to the higher viscosity and the greater crystalline material broken off. The lava and erupted particles can rise up to 5-10 km high and the deposits are often andesitic to dacitic while other types are basaltic.

Initially Vulcanian activity is a series of short-lived explosions, lasting for a few minutes to hours and ejects are called "bread-crust bombs". However the bulk of Vulcanian deposits are fine grained ash dispersed into air.

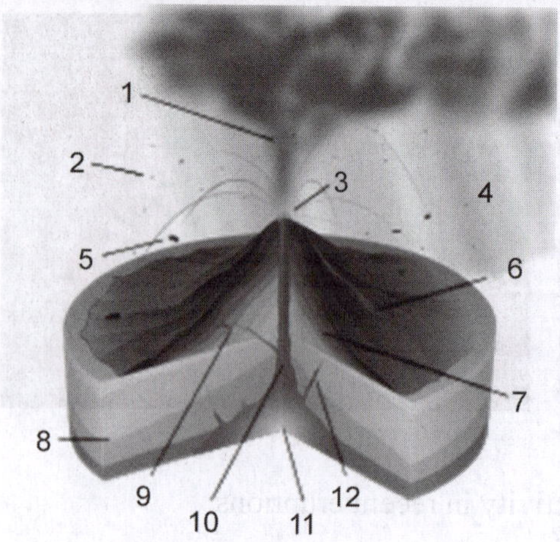

Vulcanian Eruption

1. Ash plume 2. Lapilli 3. Lava fountain 4. Volcanic ash rain 5. Volcanic bomb 6. Lava flow 7. Layers of lava & ash 8. Stratum 9. Sill 10. Magma conduit 11. Magma chamber 12. Dike

Examples of Vulcanian Eruptions:

- Sakurajima, Japan continuously since 1955
- Tavurvur, Papua New Guinea, on the Rabaul Caldera.
- Irazú Volcano in Costa Rica exhibited Vulcanian activity in its 1965 eruption.

5.8.4 Peléan Eruption

Peléan type eruptions are named after the volcano Mt. Pelé in Martinique, after occurrence of the worst natural disasters in history of eruptions in 1902, which caused a huge destruction, took away > 30,000 lives and completely destroying the town of St. Pierre. Peléan eruption is a blow out of a large amount of gas, dust, ash, and lava fragments through the volcano's central crater by the collapse of rhyolite, dacite, andesite lava dome etc. A bulge in the volcano's summit called Peléan or lava spine, appears as a warning sign on the summit and then, the material collapses forming a fast-moving pyroclastic block-and-ash flow that runs down the mountain side with very high speeds (150 kmph). Massive material slide looks like a landslide.

Tavurvur in Papua New Guinea eruption

Peléan eruptions are basically glowing pyroclastic flows, very similar to that of Vulcanian eruption, except that Peléan eruptives can bear more pressures, thence the eruption occurs as one large explosion instead of several smaller ones.

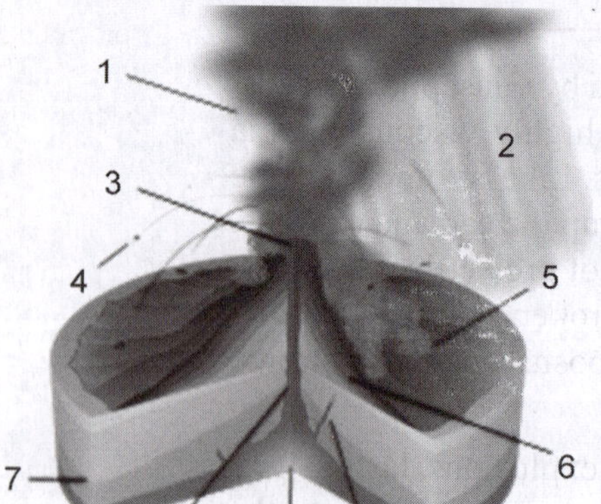

Pelean Eruption

1. Ash plume 2. Volcanic ash rain 3. Lava dome 4. Volcanic bomb 5. Pyroclastic flow 6. Layers of lava & ash 7. Stratum 8. Magma conduit 9. Magma chamber 10. Dike

Examples of Peléan activity are:

- The Mt. Pele (Martinique), proceeded by lava dome growth in 1902 erupted to devastate the island completely. It destroyed the town of St. Pierre totally except 3 survivors only.
- Mayon Volcano (Philippines) is of variety of types of eruptions of which Peléan is one. From about 40 points, it provides pathways for pyroclastic flows and mudslides recurrently to the hillside lowlands. It is the most violent disaster occurred in 1814 caused over 1200 human lives.
- Mt. Lamington experienced Peléan eruption in 1951 killing more than 3000 humans after which only it has recognized as a volcano benchmarked for large Peléan eruptions.

5.8.5 Vesuvian (or Plinian) Eruptions

Vesuvian (or Plinian) eruptions are named after Mt. Vesuvius (more specifically Pliny the Younger hence called Plinian) which erupted to bury the Roman towns, Pompeii and Herculaneum etc. The Plinian eruptions can be characterized by the following features.

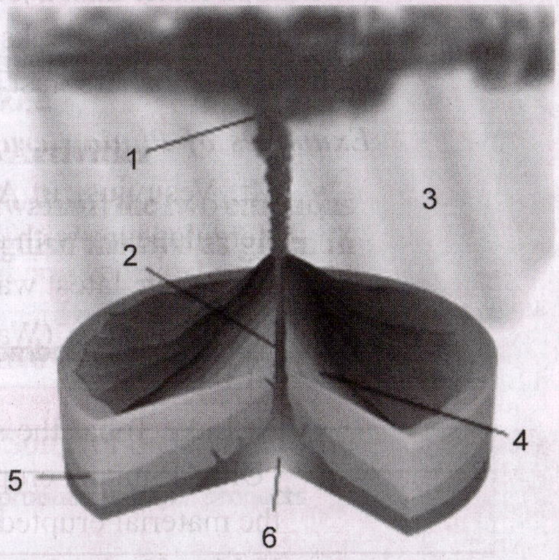

Vesuvian/ Plinian Eruption

1. Ash plume 2. Magma conduit 3. Volcanic ash rain 4. Layers of lava & ash 5. Stratum 6. Magma chamber

- It begins with the dissolved volatile gases in the magma chamber which accumulate rising through magma conduit and explode as they reach a certain size (about ¾ volume of the magma conduit).
- Eruption velocity depends on the gas contents and other local geographical factors.
- These massive eruptions reach up 2 to 45 km (1 to 28 mi) into the atmosphere.
- As it reaches higher, the plume expands and becomes less dense and moves up to the stratosphere. At the top the powerful winds move the plume away.
- These are highly explosive, highly volatile, dacitic to rhyolitic lavas and often occur with stratovolcanoes.
- These may last from hours to days.

Vesuvian eruption is similar to both Vulcanian and Strombolian eruptions, except that it has sustained eruptive column rather than creating discrete explosive events. Plinian eruptions are subjected to heavy pumice air fall which can affect an area up to 50 km^3 and the most dangerous feature is that speed

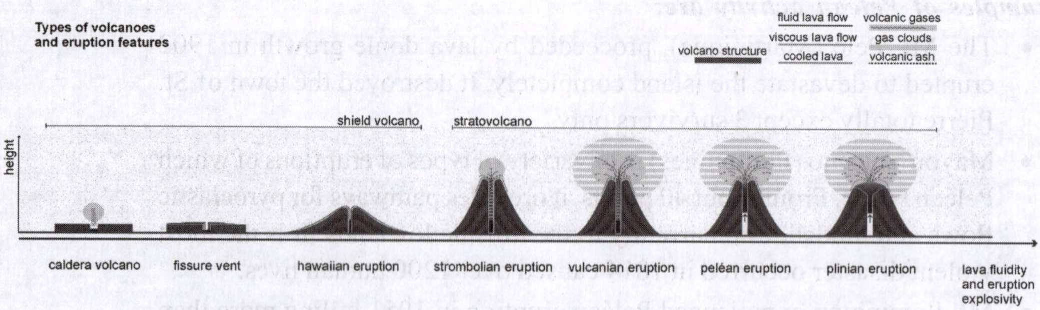

Fig. 5.4 Magnetic eruption patterns of various types of volcanoes.

(700 kmph faster than a jet) of pyroclastic flow. Further, the hot material at the summit melts snow-banks and ice deposits on the volcano, which mixes with tephra to form lahars, fast moving mudslides, landslides and avalanches.

Examples of Plinian eruptions are…

- Mt. Vesuvius, in AD 79, buried the Roman towns of Pompeii and Herculaneum with a layer of ash and tephra and erupted several times since then, latest was in 1944
- Mt. St. Helens (Washington, US) in 1980 was a Plinian eruption of VEI 5
- At Lake Toba, the strongest of this type with VEI 8 occurred (called "Ultra-Plinian" eruptions) about 74000 years ago, which is 2800 times the material erupted by Mt St. Helens in 1980
- Hekla of Iceland exemplified basaltic Plinian volcanism in 1947-48
- Pinatubo (Philippines) on 15 June 1991 produced 5 km^3 (1 cu mi) of dacitic magma, a 40 km high eruption column, and released 17 megatons of SO_2 various magnetic eruption patterns are shown in figure 5.4

5.9 PHREATOMAGMATIC ERUPTIONS

Phreatomagmatic eruptions occur by interactions between water and magma due to thermal contraction. The magmatic eruptions driven by thermal expansion is opposed by water when it comes in contact. The temperature difference between the two causes the violent water-lava interactions make up the eruption. The ejections of these eruptions are more regular in shape and fine grained due to the differences in eruptive mechanisms. Some of these eruptions are discussed in the paragraphs to follow.

5.9.1 Surtseyan Eruption

In 1963, there was an eruption of a different variety and formation of the island of Surtsey in the coastal Iceland of and so the name. A Surtseyan eruption, also called hydrovolcanic, is caused by interactions between lava and shallow-water. Because of the place of occurrence, these are the "wet" equivalent of ground-based Strombolian eruptions, but not much explosive. The water heated by lava turns to steam violently by expansion and fragments of the magma in contact into fine-grained ash. These are often found in volcanic-oceanic islands and the ejections of these eruptions are generally oxidized palagnite basalts and continuous or periodic like Strombolian eruptions.

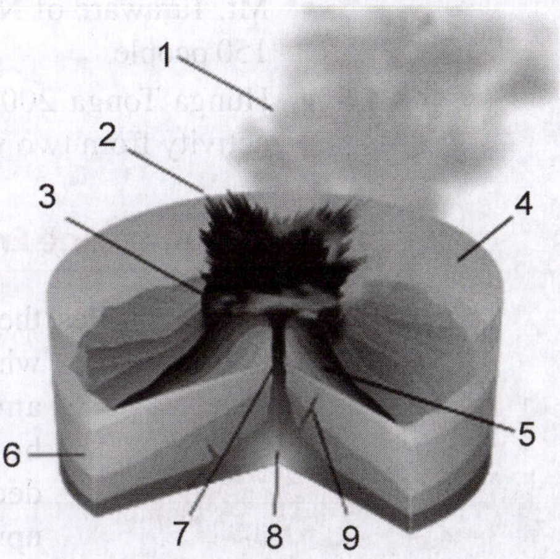

Surtseyan Eruption

1. Water vapor cloud 2. Compressed ash 3. Crater 4. Water 5. Layers of lava & ash 6. Stratum 7. Magma conduit 8. Magma chamber 9. Dike

> **A Surtseyan activity occurred in Mediterranean Sea is quite interesting. Ferdinandea, a seamount in Mediterranean Sea breached sea level in July 1831, was the source of a dispute over sovereignty between Italy, France and Great Britain. But, the volcano did not build tuff cones strongly enough to withstand erosion, and soon it disappeared below the waves after it appeared.**

The distinguishing features of this kind of eruption are

- The formation of a pyroclastic surge on the ground radially clouded
- The densest part of the cloud is nearest to the vent, forming a wedge shape
- The accumulations of wet spherical ash known as 'accretionary lapilli'
- Over a period of time Surtseyan eruptions tend to form
  - Maars i.e. broad low-relief craters dug into the ground, and
  - Tuff rings, the circular structures due to rapidly quenched lava (e.g. the 1886 eruption of Mt. Tarawere).
- Littoral cones are generated by the explosive deposition of basaltic tephra.
- They form when lava accumulates within cracks, superheats and explodes in a steam explosion, breaking the rock apart and depositing it on the volcano's flank.
- Consecutive explosions of this type eventually generate the cone.

The examples of this type of activity include:

- Surtsey volcano in Atlantic Ocean at the coast of Iceland in 1963, initially aggressive, but later, as the volcano grew out, the rising lava interacted less with the water and more with the air, until the activity waned and became more Strombolian in character.
- Ukinrek Maars, Alaska 1977, and Capelinhos of Azores 1957 are above-water Surtseyan activity.

- Mt. Taraware of New Zealand erupted along a rift zone in 1886, killed 150 people.
- Hunga Tonga 2009 (in 1988 also), showed an underwater Surtseyan activity from two vents for much of the time.

5.9.2 Submarine Eruption

As the name indicates, these eruptions occur underwater and produce seamounts which can break the surface to form volcanic islands and/or island chains. Volcanic activity near plate boundaries and mid-ocean ridges built by the decompression melting of mantle rock that rises on upwelling convection cell to the crust.

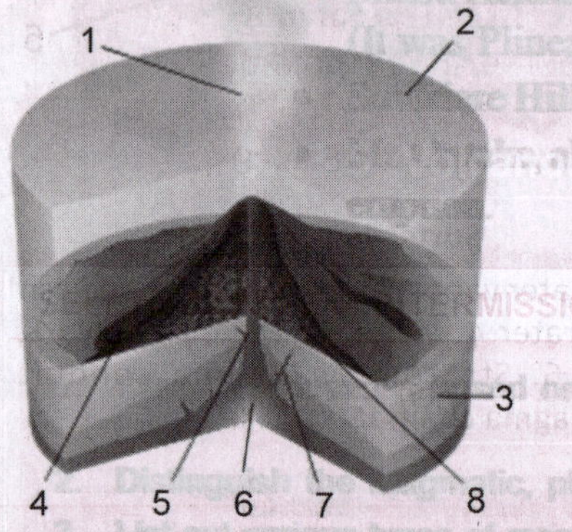

Submarine Eruption

1.Water vapor cloud 2. Water 3. Stratum 4. Lava flow 5. Magma conduit 6. Magma chamber 7. Dike 8. Pillow lava

The volcanic matter at mid-ocean ridge is basically basaltic while subduction flows are mostly calc-alkaline, which is more explosive and viscous. Pillow lava, a spiral flow is the most common underwater flow. There are about 1 lakh deepwater volcanoes, although most are beyond the active stage of their life.

Examples for submarine eruptions:

- Axial Seamount,
- Bowie Seamount,
- Davidson Seamount, and
- Loihi Seamount

5.9.3 Subglacial Eruption and Tuyas

Subglacial eruptions are due to the interactions between lava and ice, often under a glacier, at high latitude and high altitude. Not so active volcanoes often supply heat to the ice to form melt-water which can cause dangerous floods and lahars.

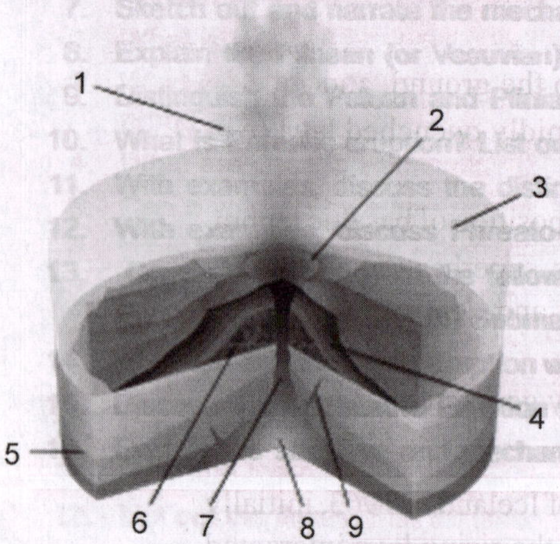

Subglacial Eruption

1. Water vapor cloud 2. Crater lake 3. Ice 4. Layers of lava & ash 5. Stratum 6. Pillow lava 7. Magma conduit 8. Magma chamber 9. Dike

The unusual flat-topped steep-sided volcanoes (called tuyas) have formed from eruptions below ice at the Tuya Butte in N.W. British Columbia, Canada. The process began with volcanic growth below the glacier and the eruptions are similar to pillow lava and when some of the lava shattered, contacted the cold ice to form a glassy hyaloclastite.

Herðubreið, a tuya in Iceland

The subglacial eruptions produce different shapes and structures based on eruptive pattern and environmental interactions. The ice distribution increases probability destabilization of other structures to cause mass landslides. The evidences can be seen in Iceland and some parts of British Columbia, Hawaii and Alaska, the Cascade Range of western N. America, S. America and even on the planet Mars. More specific examples of Subglacial Volcanoes are:

- Mouna Kea, Howaii has subglacial deposits on its summit. The eruptions might have started about 10,000 years ago, when the summit of Mauna Kea was covered in ice.
- Under the Antarctica Ice Sheet an eruption occurred about 2,200 years ago, the biggest eruption in Antarctica in the last 10,000 years. Evidences on the Mt. Hudson close to Pine Island Glacier are reported by British Antarctic Survey (2008).
- Iceland underwent an eruption under Vatnajokull ice cap in 1996, which covered 2,500 ft of ice.

5.10 PHREATIC ERUPTIONS

These are steam-blast eruptions occur when cold ground or surface water contacts with hot rock or magma and consequent superheating and explosion fractures the surrounding rock and thrusts out a mixture of steam, water, ash, volcanic bombs and blocks.

The distinguishing features of phreatic explosions are…

- They only blast out fragments of pre-existing solid rock from the volcanic conduit.
- No new magma is erupted.
- They do not always result in eruption as they are driven by cracking of rock under pressure.
- If the rock is too strong to resist the explosion, eruptions may not occur. However, cracks may be developed in the rock to become the potential for the probable future event.

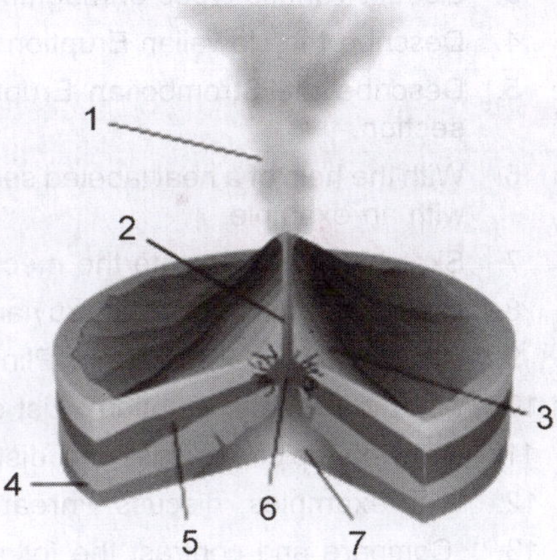

Phreatic Eruption

1. Water vapor cloud 2. Magma conduit 3. Layers of lava & ash 4. Stratum 5. Water table 6. Explosion 7. Magma chamber

- Some phreatic events may be triggered by earthquake/seismic activity.
- Phreatic eruptions form base surges, lahars, avalanches, and volcanic block flow.

- They may also release deadly toxic gas which can suffocate in a certain range.

Examples of phreatic volcanoes are…

- Mt. Bulusan, well known for its sudden phreatic eruptions.
- Poás Volcano has frequent geyser like phreatic eruptions from its crater lake.
- Taal Volcanoes, Philippines, 1965.
- La Soufrière of Guadeloupe (Lesser Antilles), 1975-76.
- Mt. St. Helens exhibited phreatic just before its catastrophic 1980 eruption. (It was Plinean ealier).
- Soufriere Hills volcano on Montserrat, West Indies, 1995–2012.
- Mt. Ontake, all historical eruptions are phreatic including the deadly 2014 eruption.

SELF ASSESSMENT INTERMISSION (SAI – 5.4)

1. Classify Volcanoes based on their mechanisms of eruption? Explain any one of each type?
2. Distinguish the magmatic, phreatic and phreatomagmatic eruptions.
3. List out various types of magmatic eruptions. Explain any two.
4. Describe the Hawaiian Eruption with the help of neat and labeled sketch.
5. Describe the Strombolian Eruption with the help of neat labeled diagram of vertical section.
6. With the help of a neat labeled sectional figure, explain the Vulcanian Eruption mechanism with an example.
7. Sketch out and narrate the mechanism of the Pelean eruption.
8. Explain the Plinean (or Vesuvian) eruptions and the mechanism.
9. Distinguish the Pelean and Plinian types eruptions.
10. What is Phreatic eruption? List out various Phreatic eruptions.
11. With examples, discuss the distinguishimg features of Phreatic eruptions.
12. With examples, discuss Phreato-magmatic eruption mechanisms.
13. Compare and contrast the following Phreatic eruptions
    (a) Surtseyan Eruption (b) Submarine Eruption (c) Subglacial Eruption
14. Describe the Surtseyan Eruption with the help of neat labeled diagram of vertical section.
15. Discuss the Submarine Eruption with labeled sketch.
16. Explain the structure and mechanism of Subglacial Eruption.

5.11 MEASUREMENT OF VOLCANIC ACTIVITY

Measurement of volcanic activity is very difficult because of its various dimensions and features. Some are frequent while others are extinct. Some are explosive while some other effusive, and so on. The volcanoes are blends of these features. Further, not all volcanoes are alike. So it is very difficult to measure strength of a volcano or compare one with the other. However, the Smithsonian Institution's Global Volcanism Program attempted to evaluate the impact of historic/ prehistoric lava flows.

5.11.1 Volcano Explosivity Index (VEI)

The Smithsonian Institution's Global Volcanism Program devised a scale to measure the volcanic activity called "***Volcano Explosivity Index (VEI)***". It is a scale graduated from 0 to 8, for measuring the strength of volcanic eruptions. This scale is similar to Richter scale for an earthquake that works on logarithmic scale where each interval represents a tenfold increase in magnitude. The vast majority of volcanic eruptions are between 0 and 2 on VEI scale.

5.11.2 Major Volcanic Eruptions (by VEI index)

VEI	Plume height	Eruptive volume*	Eruption type	Frequency#	Example
0	<100 m (330 ft)	1,000 m^3 (35,300 cu ft)	Hawaiian	Continuous	Kilauea
1	100–1000 m (300–3,300 ft)	10,000 m^3 (353,000 cu ft)	Hawaiian/Strombolian	Months	Stromboli
2	1–5 km (1–3 mi)	1,000,000 m^3 (35,300,000 cu ft) †	Strombolian/Vulcanian	Months	Galeras (1992)
3	3–15 km (2–9 mi)	10,000,000 m^3 (353,000,000 cu ft)	Vulcanian	Yearly	Nevado del Ruiz (1985)
4	10–25 km (6–16 mi)	100,000,000 m^3 (0.024 cu mi)	Vulcanian/Peléan	Few years	Eyjafjallajökull (2010)
5	>25 km (16 mi)	1 km^3 (0.24 cu mi)	Plinian	5–10 years	Mount St. Helens (1980)
6	>25 km (16 mi)	10 km^3 (2 cu mi)	Plinian/Ultra Plinian	1,000 years	Krakatoa (1883)
7	>25 km (16 mi)	100 km^3 (20 cu mi)	Ultra Plinian	10,000 years	Tambora (1815)
8	>25 km (16 mi)	1,000 km^3 (200 cu mi)	Supervolcanic	100,000 years	Lake Toba (74 ka)

* the minimum eruptive volume necessary for the eruption to be considered within the category.

\# Values are a rough estimate. Exceptions occur.

† There is a discontinuity between the 2nd and 3rd VEI level; instead of increasing by a magnitude of 10, the value increases by a magnitude of 100 (from 10,000 to 1,000,000).

5.11.3 Volcanic-Alert Level

Many people living on or near a volcano have either careless or ignorance or false beliefs that they are not at risk. To help such people and to bring awareness, the countries have adopted new alerting systems to describe the various levels and stages of volcanic activity. Some alert systems use different numbers or colors to designate the different stages. Other systems use colors and words. Some systems use a combination of both.

5.11.4 Volcano Warning Schemes

The US Geological Survey (USGS) proposed and adopted a common system nationwide for characterizing the level or seriousness and eruptive activity at volcanoes. The new volcano alert-level system classifies volcanoes now

- normal,
- advisory,
- watch or
- warning stage.

Additionally, colors are used to denote the amount of ash produced.

5.11.5 Decade Volcanoes

The International Association of Volcanology and Chemistry of the Earth's Interior (IAVCEI) has identified the 17 volcanoes under the title '*Decade Volcanoes*' across the world as the destructive eruptions and proximity to populated areas. The title '*Decade Volcanoes*' is given because the project was initiated as part of the UN-sponsored 'International Decade' for Natural Disaster Reduction. The 17 current Decade Volcanoes are given in the following table.

THE 17 - DECADE VOLCANOES

• Koryaksky volcano towering over Petropavlovsk-Kamchatsky on Kamchatka Peninsula, Far East Russia • Avachinsky-Koryaksky-Kamchatka, Russia • Nevado de Colima, Jalisco and Colima, Mexico • Mount Etna, Sicily, Italy • Galeras, Nariño, Colombia • Mauna Loa, Hawaii, USA • Mount Merapi, Central Java, Indonesia • Mount Nyiragongo, Democratic Republic of Congo	• Mount Rainier, Washington, USA • Sakurajima, Kagoshima Prefecture, Japan • Santa Maria/Santiaguito, Guatemala • Santorini, Cyclades, Greece • Taal Volcano, Luzon, Philippines • Teide, Canary Islands, Spain • Ulawun, New Britain, Papua New Guinea • Mount Unzen, Nagasaki Prefecture, Japan • Vesuvius, Naples, Italy

5.12 ADVERSE EFFECTS OF VOLCANOES

There are different kinds of eruptions explained above in this chapter. From these explanations, it is clearly understood that the effects of volcanoes mainly depend on the material of eruptions and associated characteristic features of the activity. Summing up all these, the following four volcanic activities have considerable adverse effects to the mankind and the environment.

1. Phreatic eruptions (steam-generated eruptions),
2. Explosive eruption of high-silica lava (e.g., rhyolite),
3. Effusive eruption of low-silica lava (e.g., basalt),
4. Pyroclastic flows, lahars (debris flow) and carbon dioxide emission.

All of these activities pose hazard to humans. Volcanic activity is often accompanied by earthquakes, tsunamis, landslides, hot springs, fumaroles, mud pots and geysers and so on. The following are the noteworthy adverse effects of volcanoes. (Refer Fig. 5.5)

1. Volcanic gases and Radiation
2. Famines
3. Acis Rain
4. Air Pollution and Climatic Changes
5. Other Hazards

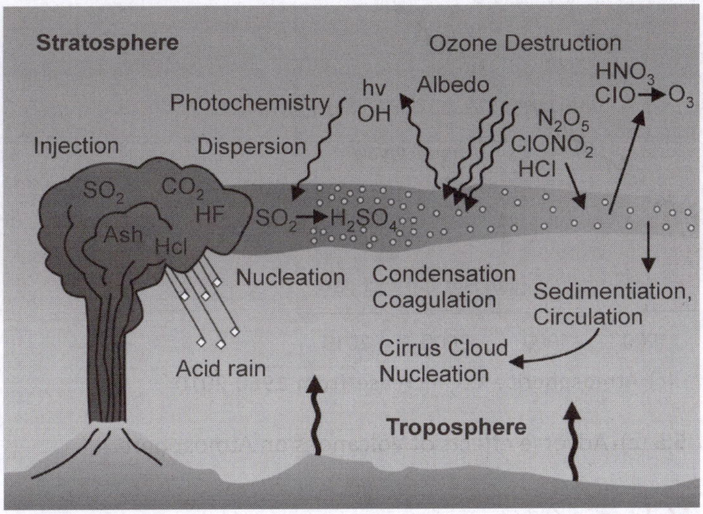

Fig. 5.5 (a) Schematic of volcano injection of aerosols and gases

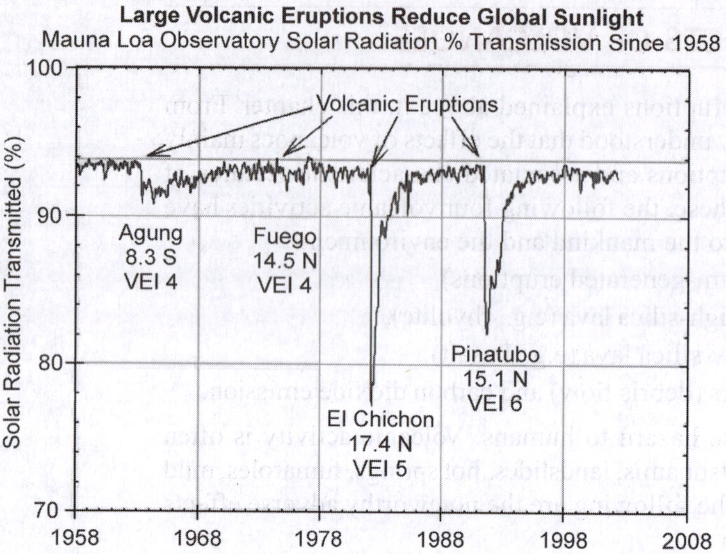

Fig. 5.5 (b) Solar radiation 1958–2008, (radiation is reduced after major volcanic eruptions)

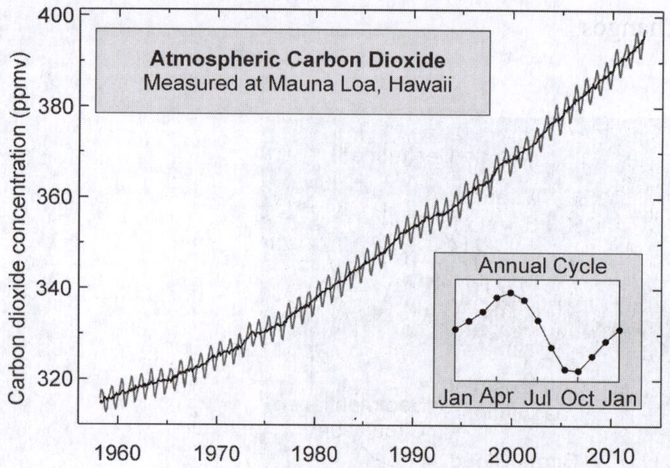

(c) Atmospherice Co_2 increase from 1960-2010

Fig. 5.5 (c) Adverse effects of Volcanoes on Atmosphere.

5.12.1 Volcanic Gases

Volcanic gases liberation varies considerably from one volcano to the other. In fact, Water vapor (H_2O) is the most abundant volcanic gas, followed by carbon dioxide (CO_2) and sulphur dioxide (SO_2), hydrogen sulphide (H_2S), hydrogen chloride (HCl), and hydrogen fluoride (HF). A large number of minor and trace gases are also found in volcanic emissions, for example hydrogen (H_2), carbon monoxide (CO), halocarbons, organic compounds, volatile metal chlorides and so forth.

Large and explosive volcanic eruptions inject the above listed gases and in addition ash (pulverized rock and pumice) into the stratosphere to heights of 16–32 km (10–20 mi) above the Earth's surface. The most significant effects of these injections arise from the conversion of sulphur dioxide to sulphurouc acid (H_2SO_3) or sulphuric acid (H_2SO_4), which may either fall as acid rains or may condense rapidly in the stratosphere to form fine sulphate aerosols that are sufficient to show impact on climate. The aerosols enhance the Earth's reflection of radiation from the Sun back into space – and thence cool the Earth's lower atmosphere (or troposphere); of course, they also absorb heat radiated up from the Earth, thereby warming the stratosphere. Several eruptions during the past century have caused a decline in the average temperature at the Earth's surface of up to ½ °F for periods of 1-3 years. The sulphur dioxide from the eruption of Huaynaputina probably caused the Russian famine of 1601–1603

5.12.2 Famines due to Volcanoes

- 70,000 years ago a super eruption created the Lake Toba on Sumatra Island in Indonesia.
- In 1815, Mt. Tambora eruption affected global climate causing the "Year Without a Summer" due to which agricultural crops and livestock are seriously destroyed in the N. Hemisphere. It is one of the worst famines of the 19th century.
- Scientists refer the volcanic eruptions for freezing winter of 1740–41 leading to the widespread famine in N. Europe.
- The biggest eruption of the Siberian Traps, is one of the largest known volcanic eruptions of the last 500 million years. It continued for a million years and is considered to be the likely cause of the "Great Dying" (estimated 90% killing of existing species).

5.12.3 Acid Rain due to Volcanoes

- Gas emission from volcanoes is the foremost natural cause to acid rain.
- Most of the hydrogen chloride (HCl) and hydrogen fluoride (HF) are dissolved in water droplets in the eruption cloud and quickly fall to the ground as acid rain.
- The injections of SO_2 during volcanic activity and conversion of sulphur dioxide to sulphurouc acid (H_2SO_3) or sulphuric acid (H_2SO_4), may result in acid rains
- Release of large amount of CO_2 can also cause an acid rain.

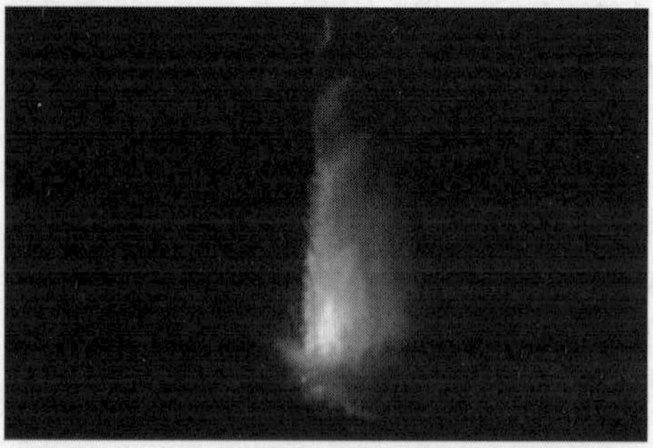

Ash plumes raised 19 km high in explosive eruption at Mt Pinatubo, Philippines in 1991.

Mount Shasta

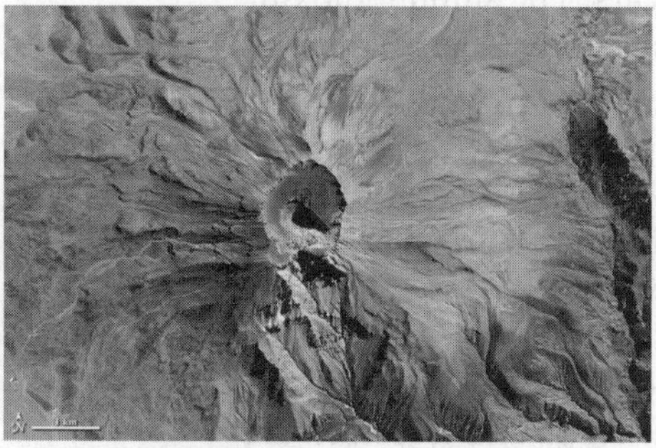

A 2007 eruptive column at Mt Etna produced volcanic ash, pumice and lava bombs

Santa Ana Volcano, El Salvador. Nested summit calderas and craters, along with the crater lake.

Ubinas Volcano of the Barren Isl, Andaman Isl, India, during an eruption in 1995. It is the only active volcano in S. Asia.

Ash plume from Eyjafjallajökull (Apr17, 2010)

5.12.4 Air Pollution and Climatic Changes due to Volcanoes

Volcanoes can be good also...

Explosive volcanic eruptions release the greenhouse gas CO_2 and thus provide a deep source of carbon for biogeochemical cycles. Volcanic eruptions also provide the benefit of adding nutrients to soil through the weathering process of volcanic rocks. These fertile soils assist the growth of plants and various crops. Volcanic eruptions can also create new islands, as the magma cools and solidifies upon contact with the water.

- Volcanic activity releases about 145 to 255 million cc of CO_2 each year.
- Volcanic eruptions may inject aerosols into the Earth's atmosphere.
- The sulphate aerosols react with chlorine and nitrogen chemical species increasing stratospheric chlorine levels, chlorofluorocarbon pollution, chlorine monoxide (ClO) generation and destruction of ozone (O_3) layer.
- The aerosols coagulate and settle in the upper troposphere to form as nuclei for cirrus clouds.
- The Earth's radiation balance is seriously affected.
- Large injections affect global climate by cooling it. (It can be identified by unusual colors during sunrises and sunsets).
- The injected ash also falls rapidly from the stratosphere which takes several days to few weeks for removal, otherwise can affect the soil properties.
- Some erupted gases are poisonous and can pollute the air and may claim lives or cause ill-health.

5.12.5 Other Hazards due to Volcanoes

A volcano is hazardous not only in the immediate vicinity of the eruption but also up in the atmosphere. The ash thrown into the air by eruptions can cause a hazard to even an aircraft, especially while a jet aircraft moves near an eruption, the particles melt due to the high operating temperature and adhere to the turbine blades resulting in their shape change, finally the operation of the turbine is disrupted.

Not kidding! History witnessed such dangerous events, of which two noteworthy events caused hazards to jet planes are:

- 1982 after the eruption of Galunggung in Indonesia, and
- 1989 after the eruption of Mt Redoubt in Alaska

Believe it or not! The 2010 eruptions of Eyjafjallajökull caused major disruptions to air travel in Europe. Nine exclusive Volcanic Ash Advisory Centers were established by the International Civil Aviation Organization to monitor such ash-clouds and advise pilots accordingly.

5.13 DISASTER PLANNING AND MITIGATION

5.13.1 Before Volcanic Eruption

At the outset, make a plan for the disaster by based on risk and danger.

- Be prepared for mudslides, flash floods, earthquakes, ash falling, acid rain and tsunamis.
- Each individual should have a disaster kit for the home and car, including
  - first aid kit
  - packaged food and water (for 3 days)
  - battery-operated radio (for news and status)
  - mobile phone (for communication)
  - flashlight
  - protective clothing
  - dust mask
  - goggles and
  - sturdy shoes
- Most important is to possess the route map of the area to know all evacuation routes.

5.13.2 During Volcanic Eruption

- Follow evacuation orders issued by authorities.
- Avoid areas downwind and river valleys downstream of the volcano.
- Close all windows and doors, put machinery inside.
- Wear a dust mask and gloves.
- Use goggles to protect your eyes.
- When ash falls, wear long-sleeved shirts and long trousers.

If you are-

- ***indoor:*** bring pet animals inside.
- ***trapped outdoors:*** seek shelter indoors.
- ***in car:*** keep car engines off.
- ***caught in falling rocks:*** roll into a ball and protect your head.
- ***caught near a stream:*** be aware of mudflows and move to higher ground.

Tavurvur in Papua New Guinea erupting

5.13.3 After Volcanic Eruption

- Cover your mouth and nose because volcanic ash can irritate your respiratory system.
- Wear goggles and protect your eyes.
- Keep your skin covered.
- Clear roofs of ash, because the ash is very heavy and can cause the building to collapse.

5.14 VOLCANOES ON OTHER PLANETARY BODIES

Not just Earth, but the other planetary bodies, such as planets, satellites etc. also are not free from volcanic activities. As there is no livelihood on these bodies the effect of the volcanoes is not a problem, even though the eruption is huge. However, the knowledge of these volcanic activities gives us an insight and a clear understanding on the mechanism and effects.

5.14.1 Volcanoes on Moon

There are no clear evidences of volcanic activity hither to on **Earth's Moon**. However, recent studies are giving scope for possession of a partially molten core and some volcanic features such as maria (the darker patches seen on the moon), rills and domes.

5.14.2 Volcanoes on Venus

Researches revealed that **Venus** has 90% basalt. The volcanism played a great role in shaping the surface of this planet. The radar sounding by the Magellan probe evidenced highest volcanic activity, Maat Mons, ash flows near the summit and on the northern flank on Venus. This planet might have undergone a major planet resurfacing event about 500 million years ago. Researchers say that the lava flows were so widespread that have not occurred on Earth also.

5.14.3 Volcanoes on Mars

Mars has many extinct volcanoes for several millions of years, 5 of which are vast shield volcanoes far bigger than any on Earth. These are named as Arsia Mons, Ascraeus Mons, Olympus Mons, Pavonis Mons and Hecates Tholus. The European *Mars Express* spacecraft said that volcanic activity might have happened recently on Mars.

5.14.4 Volcanoes on Jupiter

There is clear information about the volcanic activity on Jupiter, but the Jupiter's moon **Io** is the most volcanically active in the solar system owing to the tidal interaction with Jupiter. Io is getting resurfaced constantly by the volcanic eruptions of sulphur, sulphur dioxide and silicate rock. The lavas are the hottest known (>1,800 K or 1,500 °C) anywhere in the solar system. In Feb 2001, the largest recorded volcanic eruptions in the solar system occurred on Io. **Europa,** the smallest of **Jupiter's Galilean moons**, is yet another to have active volcanoes, but its volcanic activity is entirely in the form of water that freezes into ice on the frigid surface, known as cryovolcanism, which is most common on the moons of the outer planets of the solar system.

5.13.5 Volcanoes on Neptune

The Voyager 2 (space craft), observed cryovolcanoes (ice volcanoes) on **Triton**, a moon of **Neptune** in 1989.

5.13.6 Volcanoes on Saturn

Cassini–Huygens (space craft) found the fountains of frozen particles erupting from **Enceladus**, and **Titan**, the moons of **Saturn** in 2005. The erupted material may contain water, liquid nitrogen, dust, or methane compounds.

SELF ASSESSMENT INTERMISSION (SAI – 5.5)

1. Explain how can the strength of Volcanoes be measured?
2. What is Volcano Explosivity Index? How is devised?
3. What is Volcano-Alarm Level? Discuss about the warning schemes for alerting volcano prone areas.
4. What are decade volcanoes? Why are they so named?
5. Can a volcano be advantageous? If so, give example and describe briefly.
6. What are the adverse effects of a Volcano? Explain.
7. What are the chief contents in volcanic gases? How do they effect?
8. How is a volcano related to (a) landslide (b) tsunami (c) acid rain (d) air pollution?
9. Can a volcano be responsible for occurrence of famine and climatic change? How?
10. Can a volcano be responsible for air craft failures? If so, how?
11. Describe the procedures, DOs and DONTs in mitigation of a volcano.
12. List out the items of kit for being prepared of volcanic eruption.
13. What measures do you take before, during and after a volcanic eruption?
14. Do volcanoes exist on any other planetary bodies other than Earth? Substantiate your answer.
15. Give a brief account of volcanic activities if any on Mars, Venus and Jupiter?

CHAPTER 6 Landslides

O'MY SILENT INNER VIBES (O'M S I V – 6)

Is it a Natural Calamity?
Or a Supernatural Divinity?
We never know, my friend, we should only bow,
For, Lord is our creator, p rotector, and destroyer!

How can the auspicious be malicious? pernicious?
How can the divinity become enmity or calamity?
We never know, my friend, we should only bow,
For, Lord is our creator, p rotector, and destroyer!

Is it a massive salvation of the blessed population?
Or is it to punish the act of environment pollution?
We never know, my friend, we should only bow,
For, Lord is our creator, p rotector, and destroyer!

Is it to teach us a lesson to take every precaution?
Or warn generation to respect Nature's emotion?
We never know, my friend, we should only bow,
For, Lord is our creator, p rotector, and destroyer!
It's time to act, we must! To prevent the human error,
Let us not be "egocentric" - But be "eco-centric".
When the fence turns into an offense, where is the defense?
When the protector becomes the destroyer, who is the upholder?
When the Mountain is crestfallen, who is there to look up to?
When do the life giving rivers flood and cause bloodshed?
Where is the abode to safeguard? Who is the saviour?
We may never know, my friend, we should only bow!
For the Lord is the only answer.

GOD is our Governor! The **G**enerator, **O**perator and **D**estroyer!
We may never know, my friend, we should only bow,
For the Lord is, Omnipresent, Omnipotent, and Omniscient! Amen!
AUM Namah Shivaaya! Salutations to Lord Shiva – the auspicious!

[This is an excerpt with permission taken from the poem in the book ***"To My Friend"*** written by my brother, ***Dr. Nakta Venkata Raju, MD (USA)***, in response to the natural calamity in Himalayas (Kedarnath) Landslides and following Floods of river Ganges in June of 2013, and is dedicated to the brothers and sisters affected and afflicted by the disaster]

6.1 DEFINITION AND CONCEPT

The landslides in general, are a migration or movement of land/ earthen material from one place to the other. These happen in a wide variety of processes. Though landslide is basic phenomenon connected with mountainous regions and coastal areas, it can occur in any general low relief areas too such as

- river bluff failures,
- lateral spreading,
- cut-and-fill failures (roadway/ building excavations),
- a wide variety of slope failures associated with quarries,
- collapse of mine-waste piles (particularly coal),
- open-pit mines.

Thus, landslides may be found in offshore as well as onshore environments.

6.1.1 Definition

Landslide, (also called landslip) is a massive downward/outward ground movements like rock, silt, sand, soil, debris, artificial fill, or any combination of these.

6.1.2 The Concept

Of course, the major reason for a landslide is attributed to a slope on which the material slides down due to gravity, but there are other contributing factors to effect the landslide including affecting the original slope stability. Strictly speaking, there are several factors, such as geological, physical and human activities which are the root causes that destabilize the material and trigger to landslip before the gravity drives down the material.

6.1.3 Landslide Prediction and Hazard Analysis

An avalanche, similar in mechanism to a landslide, involves a large amount of ice, snow and rock falling quickly down the side of a mountain.

A pyroclastic flow is caused by a collapsing cloud of hot ash, gas and rocks from a volcanic explosion that moves rapidly down an erupting volcano

The purpose of studying about landslides is multi-fold.

Landslides cannot be totally stopped, but prevention or reduction of catastrophic loss is possible by landslide hazard analysis and mapping. Further, the analysis can assist development by providing the guidelines for land use planning.

6.1.4 Objectives of Landslide Hazard Analysis

The following are the objectives of landslide hazard analysis:

1. Identify the factors that trigger landslides
2. Estimate the contribution causing slope failures
3. Establish a relation between the factors and landslides
4. Predict landslide future hazard based on such relationship.

The landslide hazard analysis uses the concepts from geomorphology, geology, land use/ land cover and hydrogeology. Though several factors are considered for the mapping, GIS is the powerful, fast, effective and most apt tool as it has functions of collection, storage, manipulation, display and remote sensing. Satellite imaging can be used to characterize the landslide and plan the process of regeneration and recovery.

6.2 THE ANATOMY AND PROCESS OF LANDSLIDE

Landslides are the result by the movement of slope-forming materials. A landslide can be described through the five main parts in the order, top to bottom namely, crown, head, main body, foot, and toe. The nomenclature of landslide is shown in Fig.6.1. Around the '*crown*', the top most point of the landslide, some cracks

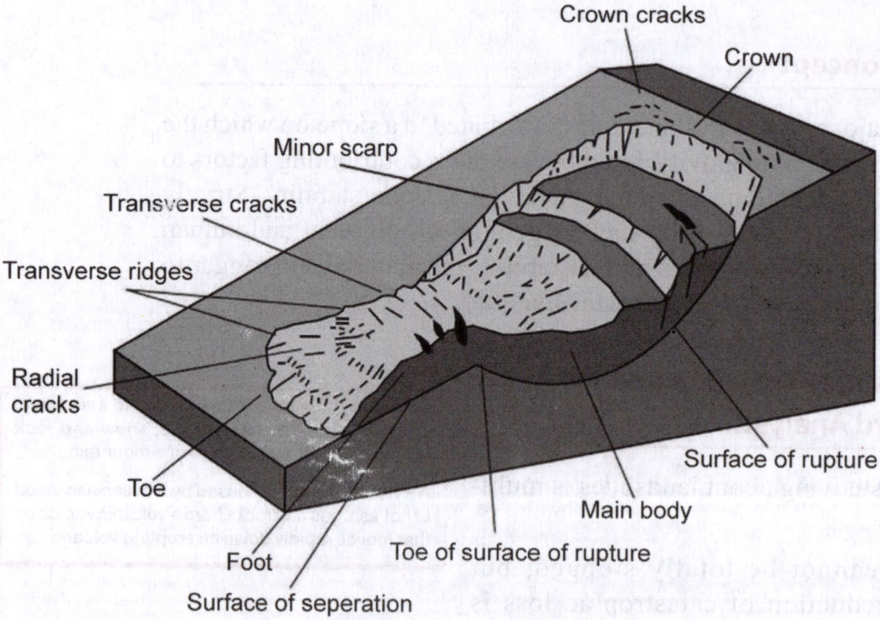

Fig. 6.1 Nomenclature of landslide.

develop before the slide occurs, which are called '*crown cracks*'. Below the crown, the sliding material known as the '*main scarp*' exerts the downward force due to weight on the part called '*head*'. Along the sideways also the sliding material exists, which aids the process. This material is called the '*minor scrap*'. Most generally the rupture occurs below the head, termed as the '*surface of rupture*' upon the main body. The lower part of this surface suffers the separation of the *'foot'* from the main body and flows toward the toe, hence known as 'surface of separation' forming and leaving the new *'toe of surface of rupture'*. During this process, the transverse cracks and transverse ridges may form along the foot and toe respectively. At the bottom upon the toe, the radial cracks also may appear. The figure associated illustrates the nomenclature of a landslide, with the generally accepted terminology describing its features.

6.3 FEATURES AND CHARACTERISTICS OF LANDSLIDES

Classifying and characterizing the landslides is very difficult due to the fact that phenomena are not perfectly repeatable. Also, they are characterized by different causes, movements and morphology, and involving genetically different material. Thus one landslide is different from the other and no two are identical. For these reasons, various differentiating factors have to be considered for landslide classification. Sometimes these factors are very subjective and may even evolve in combination with another factor also. Some of these factors are discussed in the following paragraphs.

6.3.1 Type of Movement

This is the most important aspect to characterize a landslide. Though uncertainties and confusions arise in the identification of exact type of movement, most of the movements generally observed are spoken in terms of ***slides*** or ***flows***.

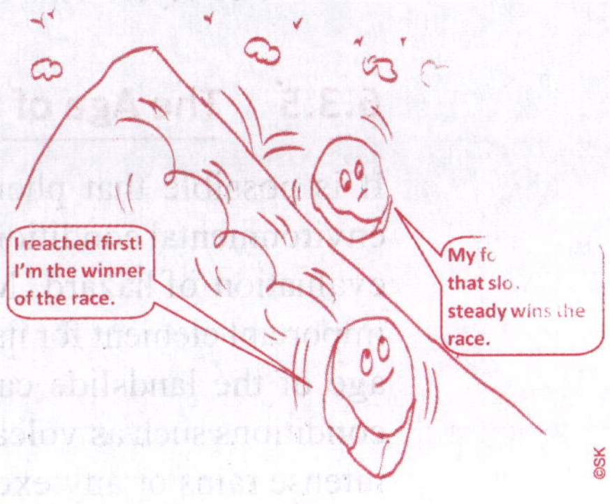

Commonly, the movement of materials would be one or more of the following types

1. Toppling
2. Falling
3. Spreading
4. Sliding
5. Flowing and
6. Creeping

6.3.2 Type of Material

The most important feature by which a landslide is distinguished is the type of material involved in the process. Rock, earth and debris are the most common terms used to distinguish the materials involved in the landslide process. However, the terms like silt, sand, broken wood and vegetation are also found while describing a landside. Some terms are interlinked and closely related, for example, if the weight of the particles with a diameter greater than 2 mm is less than 20%, the material will be defined as earth; otherwise, it is debris.

6.3.3 Speed

This feature of landslide also has a great importance in the hazard evaluation. The speed (or velocity) range of landslides varies from imperceptibly very slow to very rapid. The speed of landslide is determined on the basis of case history or site observations.

6.3.4 The Spatial and Temporal Conditions

A landslide is characterized by three main aspects as per the recommendations of the WP/WLI (1993) with reference to the spatial and temporal conditions. These are;

1. **The state:** This refers to the time in which the movement took place
2. **The distribution:** This describes, in a general way, where the landslide is moving
3. **The style:** This indicates how it is moving.

6.3.5 The Age of the Movement

It is possible that phenomena could have occurred in past under specific environmental conditions. Hence, landslide dating is an interesting topic in the evaluation of hazard. Moreover, the awareness of landslide frequency is an important element for its probabilistic evaluation, because the evaluation of the age of the landslide can help correlating the sources or triggers to specific conditions such as volcanic eruptions, occurrence of earthquakes or periods of intense rains or any excavations made near the point of occurrence.

6.3.6 Geological Conditions

This is yet another fundamental factor of the morphological evolution of a slope. Bedding attitude and the presence of discontinuities or faults etc. can give us a clear picture to estimate the slope morphogenesis.

6.3.7 Morphological Characteristics

The landslide being a movement due to changes in geological volume with a hidden side, its morphological characteristics are greatly significant in the reconstructing the technical model.

6.3.8 Geographical Location

This aspect helps locating the probable area where a landside may occur in the physiographic context. Based on this characteristic (geographical position) some authors describe landslides as "alpine landslides", "plain landslides", "hilly landslides" or "cliff landslides". Of course, it is also useful in explaining slope evolution processes.

6.3.9 Topographical Criteria

Any event is described by its address. Say, a landslide occurred at a place like Amboor in Kerala state in India. So this is referred to as Amboor, Kerala landslide. It is quite often customary to describe a landslide using the name of a site, where it happens. Thus the topographical criterion becomes very important in addressing a landslide.

6.3.10 Type of Climate

The climatic conditions have great significance in the genesis of landslide phenomena, since the rain, ice fall, moisture content in air (humidity) etc. can provoke the occurrence of landslides. As a consequence, while describing a landslide, it can be interesting to understand under what type of climatic conditions the event occurred.

6.3.11 Triggers of the Movements

In the evaluation of landslide susceptibility, the triggers of the event to happen play the major role. Both, the "internal" as well as the "external" forces are the root causes for the event occurrence.

The internal causes: Modify the material itself thereby decreasing its resistance to shear stress,

The external causes: Enhance shear stress, so that block or bodies are no longer stable.

Hence, it is important to know the triggers to make the stability to instability of a slope or surface, because these induce the movement of the mass.

SELF ASSESSMENT INTERMISSION (SAI – 6.1)

1. Define Landslide? What is its meaning? What is its significance in disaster management?
2. Discuss the process of a typical landslide with the help of labelled diagram.
3. Sketch out a general landslide and label its nomenclature.
4. What are the objectives of Landslide – Hazard Prediction & Analysis?
5. List out the features and characteristics of a Landslide.
6. How do the landslide features get influenced by the type of material and the type of movement?
7. Describe the influence of topographical and geographical factors on the features of a landslide.
8. How do morphological and geological factors characterize a landslide?
9. What is the impact of climate on landslides?
10. How do you specify a landslide? Explain.
11. Discuss the following with reference to landslides. (a) toppling (b) spreading.

6.4 FACTORS CAUSING LANDSLIDES

Undoubtedly, the main cause of landslides is related to instabilities in slopes. But, what is important is to know the reason behind causing this instability. Often, it is found one or more causes that trigger a landslide. However, one of them will be more effective depending on the situation. Various possible causes are listed in the following table (table no.6.1) under four categorical factors viz. geological, physical, morphological factors, and factors associated with human activity. A cause for a landslide may be one or a blend of two or more of the factors that may be from the same group or different also. Further, these factors are interrelated and hence one may become cause of other within the group or other group.

Causes may be considered to be generated out of the above factors to make the slope vulnerable to failure and predispose the slope to becoming unstable. Though the trigger is the single event that finally initiates the landslide, various causes inherently combine to result in a disaster. Thus landslides can have many causes but can only have one trigger, which is usually, easy to identify after the landslide has occurred.

Though rare, the trigger could not be determined even after detailed investigations in the case of Mt. Cook landslide in New Zealand 1991.

Whatsoever, an underlying cause is the nature of the material. For instance, by adding water or pressure, or shaking, the material such as mud or sand and

Table 6.1 Factors causing the instability in slope that can trigger a landslide

Geological factors	Physical factors	Morphological factors	Human activity factors
• Earthquakes create stresses that make weak slopes fail • Volcanic eruptions produce loose ash deposits, heavy rain, and debris flows • Weathered Materials e.g. heavy rainfall • Jointed or fissure materials • Sheared materials • Permeability contrasts • Adversely orientated discontinuities such as bedding, fault etc. • Material contrasts (weak/sensitive) • Groundwater pressure making the slope unstable • Erosion by rivers, glacie rs, or ocean waves makes slopes too steep • Rainfall and snow fall - rock and soil slopes are made weak through saturation by snowmelt or heavy rains • Weight from much rain or snow, stockpiling of rock or ore, from waste piles, or from buildings may stress weak slopes to failure and other structures	• Intense rainfall • Rapid snow melt • Prolonged precipitation • Rapid drawdown • Earthquake causing liquefaction • Volcanic eruption • Thawing • Freeze-thaw • Ground water changes soil pore water pressure • Surface runoff • Seismic activity • Soil erosion	• Slope angle • Tectonic uplift • Volcanic uplift • Glacial Rebound • Fluvial erosion • Wave erosion • Glacial erosion • Erosion of lateral margins • Subterranean erosion • Slope loading • Vegetation change • Erosion • Loss of vertical vegetative structure, nutrients, soil and soil structure after a wildfire • Loss of vegetation due to drought • Shrink-and-swell weathering • Deposition loading slope or crest	• Land use (constructing roads, houses etc.) • Land use pattern • Water management • Water leakage • Quarrying/Mining • Excavation • Draw-down (reservoir) • Loading • Cutting Trees • Cultivation and agricultural activities along slopes or near the slopes • Vibration due to machinery, traffic, blast s (even thunder cause failure of weak slopes) • Deforestation in shallow soils, removal of deep-rooted plants that bind the colluviums to bedrock • Pollution • Loading of slope or its crest

water changes from a gel to a sol. Thence, a material stable turns to fluid resulting in the greatest disasters, such as lahars or mudslides, happen suddenly. Further, some volcanic activity can also probe to just slide down suddenly, like in the case of Toba, Krakatoa and Mt. St. Helens.

At Surte (Sweden), 1950 quick clay slide killed one person.

6.5 THE TRIGGERS

Great majority of the landslides occurred hither to, have been initiated by one of the following triggers.

1. Snowmelt
2. Heavy or continuous rainfall
3. Rivers
4. Change in Water-level
5. Seismicity
6. Volcanic activity
7. Excavations and constructions

We shall now discuss about these.

6.5.1 Snowmelt

In cold mountain regions, snowmelt could be a landslide initiator, particularly, when there is a sudden increase in temperature due to which snow melts rapidly. This water then seeps into the ground, which may have impermeable layers below because of still-frozen soil or rock. This in turn rapidly raises the water pressure and leads to landslide activity. Further, this effect will be more serious if this warm weather is accompanied by precipitation, which accelerates the rate of defrosting.

6.5.2 Rainfall

Usually mountains and hills are associated with heavy rain fall. Which could be another trigger to initiate the occurrence of a landslide. The importance of rainfall as a trigger for landslides cannot be underestimated. Heavy or prolonged rainfall is the main trigger of landslides in majority of cases. Generally, the rainfall may be associated with a tropical cyclone or an intense thunderstorm or of a long duration rainfall with lower intensity, such as the cumulative effect of monsoon rainfall (often occurs in South Asia).

Of these, over 90% occurrences were triggered by heavy rainfall. For example, in Sri Lanka heavy rainfall in May 2003 caused hundreds of landslides, claimed 266 human lives and about 3 lakh homelessness. In the same year about two months later, the annual Asian monsoon initiated 14 fatal landslides resulting in 85 lives in Nepal.

The rainfall enhances pore water pressures within the soil on an unstable block on a slope as illustrated in figure 6.2. Motion is caused by shear stress generated by the mass of the block under gravity down the slope. Of course, the normal load offers resistance to motion, but when the slope fills with water, it develops the fluid pressure that provides the block with buoyancy, thereby reducing the resistance to the motion. (In some cases fluid pressures acts down the slope as ground water provides a hydraulic push to the landslide that further reduces the stability). Refer Fig.6.2.

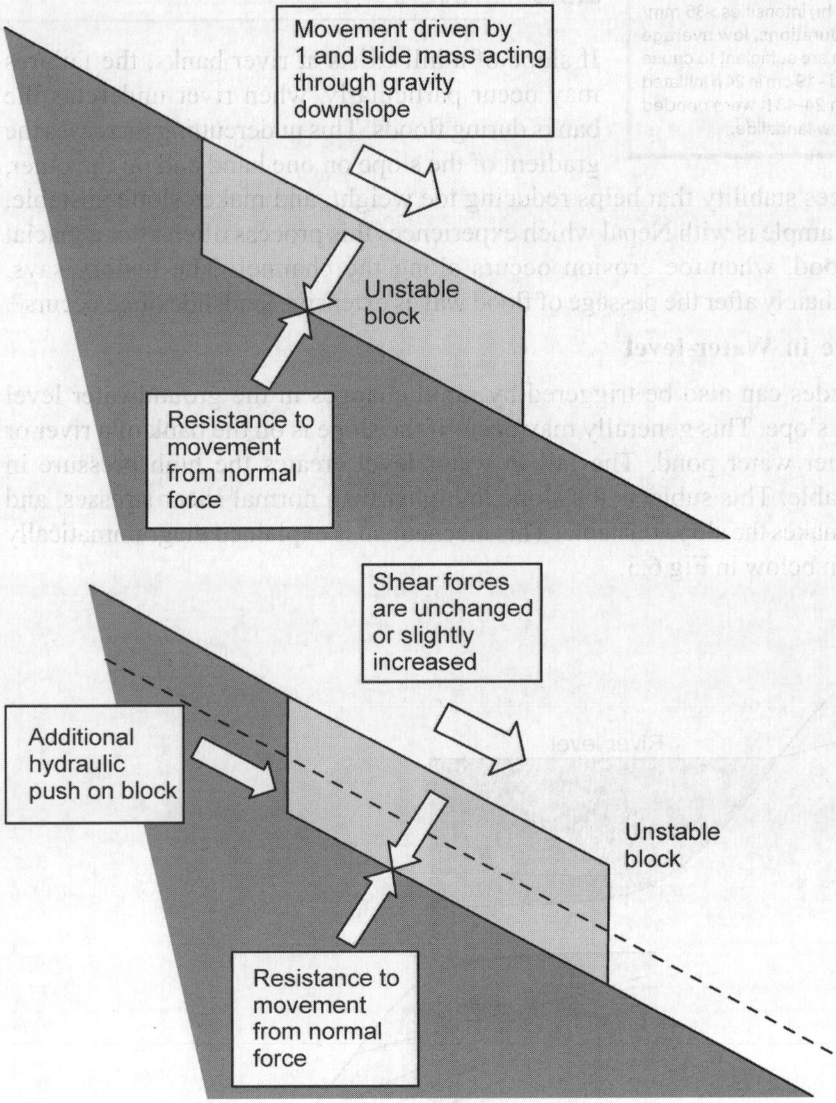

Fig. 6.2

1st figure: Illustration of the resistance in a slope system of an unstable block.

2nd figure: Illustration of the movement in a slope system of an unstable block.

> **O My God!**
>
> **Low rains longer time can also cause Landslide?**
>
> Larsen and Simon (Port Rico) found storms with a total precipitation of 10–20 cm, about 1.4 cm/h rain for many hrs, or 2–3 mm/h rain for ~100 hrs can trigger landslides. Rafi Ahmad, Jamaica, found rainfall of short duration (~1 hr) intensities >36 mm/h triggered. Long rainfall durations, low average intensities of about 3 mm/h are sufficient to cause landslide. A rainfall threshold ~19 cm in 24 h initiated failures whereas >30 cm in 24-48 h were needed to cause widespread shallow landslide.

Other reasons include the presence of high level fluids (Fluidization of debris), loss of suction in silt materials, residual soils following deforestation, undercutting toe of slope through river.

6.5.3 Rivers

If slope of a hill exists at river banks, the failures may occur particularly, when river undercuts the banks during floods. This undercutting increases the gradient of the slope on one hand and on the other, it reduces stability that helps reducing toe weight, and makes slope unstable. Best example is with Nepal which experiences this process often after a glacial lake flood, when toe erosion occurs along the channel. The history says, "immediately after the passage of flood waves extensive landslide often occurs".

Change in Water-level

Landslides can also be triggered by rapid changes in the groundwater level along a slope. This generally may occur if the slope is on the bank of a river or any other water pond. The fall in water level creates the high pressure in water table. This subjects the slope to higher than normal shear stresses, and hence makes the slope unstable. This mechanism is explained diagrammatically as given below in Fig 6.3.

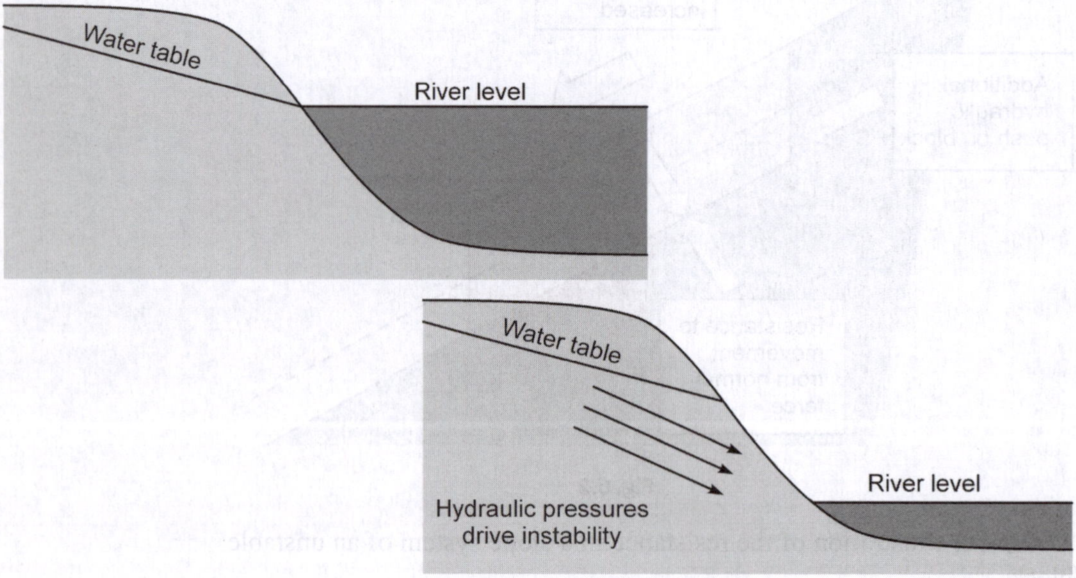

Fig. 6.3 Land slide triggered by water level changes at a river basin.

(i) Groundwater conditions when the river level is stable

(ii) When the groundwater level falls, river level falls rapidly; thence the high water level in the slope gives a hydraulic push to destabilize the slope, triggering collapse

Same is the mechanism at the sea shores also if a hill exists near shore. It is also significant in coastal regions when sea level falls after a storm tide, or when the water level of a reservoir or even a natural lake rapidly falls, e.g. Vajont failure, a rapid decline in lake level instigated a landslide that killed over 2000 people.

6.5.4 Seismicity

The seismicity is in fact, the second major factor in triggering landslides. Landslides may occur due to earthquakes as a result of the following two different but interrelated processes:

(a) Seismic shake and

(b) Liquefaction

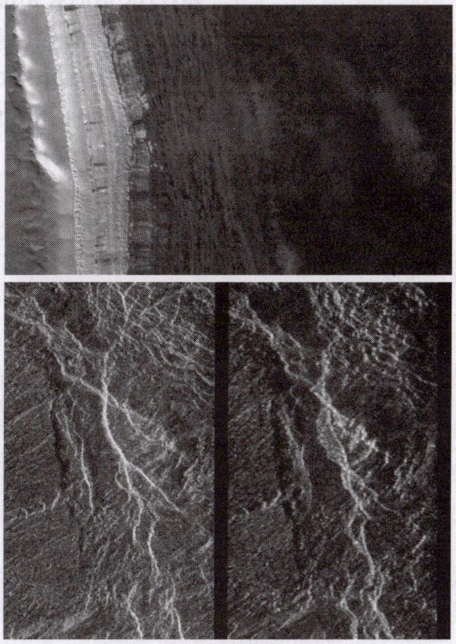

Extraterrestrial landslides

Before and after radar images of a landslide on Venus, 1990 image. Landslide in progress on Mars, 2008-02-19

Landslides have been detected on both Venus and Mars by orbiting satellites.

(a) Seismic shake: The earthquake waves pass through the rocks/hard soils whose accelerations influence the gravitational load on the slope. The vertical accelerations of seismic waves impact the normal load on the slope while the horizontal accelerations induce a shear force due to the inertia of the landslide mass, which may cause the failure of the slope. This is more disastrous at hill sides as the magnitudes of the ground accelerations would get enhanced by the so called 'topographic amplification'. Thence maximum acceleration is found at the crest of the slope or along the ridge line, i.e. to say landslide is triggered by seismic shake.

(b) Liquefaction: The earthquake waves would also through a granular material such as a soil induce a process called liquefaction, in which the shaking reduces the porosity of the material. For example, a salt bottle when you fill upto the brim, and if you shake it, you get some space due the material gets compact (porosity gets reduced) and so you can still accommodate some more salt in to it. Similarly, when the earth shakes, compacting and so reduced porosity of the granular material raises pressure in the material. In some other cases, if the granular

O My God!

During 1964 Alaska earthquake (8.6), the houses were affected by liquefaction induced lateral spread landslide in which the ground dropped on the average of 11 m and houses slid about 150-180 m

material is permeable it can change a granular material into a liquid, inducing 'flow slides' which can be rapid and damaging.

The nature of seismically-triggered landslides

The following characteristics maybe observed in the landslides triggered by seismic waves.

(i) These occur suddenly, tend to be more widespread and rapid.
(ii) Usually their morphology would not change as they occur suddenly.
(iii) Earthquake-induced landslides are often rock falls and form on steep slopes.
(iv) Rock falls, disrupted rock slides, and disrupted slides of earth and debris are the most abundant types of earthquake-induced landslides
(v) Earth flows, debris flows, and avalanches of rock, earth, or debris typically transport materials do not generally occur due to earthquake.
(vi) Landslides due to liquefaction failure uniquely limited to earthquake-induced event.

6.5.5 Volcanic Activity

It may be surprising to know that some of the largest and most devastating landslides are affiliated to volcanic activity. These happen either in association with the eruption of a volcano, or get mobilized (very weak deposits) due to volcanic activity. There are two types of volcanic landslide:

(i) Lahars (e.g. Mt. St. Helens, May 18, 1980 an earthquake of 5.1 magnitude also occurred that triggered volcano and followed by gigantic rock slide and debris avalanche).
(ii) Debris avalanches (e.g. Casita Volcano, Nicaragua, October 30, 1998).

Ferguson Slide on California State Route 140 in June '06

Trackside rock slide detector on the UPRRSierra grade near Colfax, CA

Rhine cutting through Flims-Rockslide debris, Switzerland

SELF ASSESSMENT INTERMISSION (SAI – 6.2)

1. List out the factors of causing the landslides.
2. What geological factors tend to cause landslide?
3. What human activities contribute to cause a landslide? Discuss.
4. What are the morphological factors that can cause a landslide?
5. List out the physical factors that can tend to cause a landslide.
6. List out the triggers of landslides.
7. Explain the significance of seismicity in triggering a landslide.
8. Discuss how volcanic activity is related to landslide.
9. What is the relation among the snow melt, rivers and landslides?
10. Can rivers cause landslide? Discuss.

6.6 CLASSIFICATION OF LANDSLIDES

It is very difficult to classify landslides, because the criterion chosen for categorization differs largely. Some people take the type of movement as the basis while others take the type of material that is moving down. The grade of the material, such as fine/coarse can also be chosen for classification. The translational or rotational movement can also be one of criteria in classifying the landslides. Considering all such criteria, the following table shows a summarized schematic landslide classification adopting the classification of Varnes 1978 and taking into account the modifications made by Cruden and Varnes, in 1996. Some integration has been made by using the definitions of Hutchinson (1988) and Hungr (2001).

Type of movement			Type of material		
			Bedrock	Engineering soils	
				Fine	Coarse
Topples			Rock topple	Earth topple	Debris topple
Falls			Rock fall	Earth fall	Debris fall
Lateral spreads			Rock spread	Earth spread	Debris spread
Slides	Rotational		Rock slump	Earth slump	Debris slump
	Translational	Few units	Rock block slide	Earth block slide	Debris block slide
		Many units	Rock slide	Earth slide	Debris slide
Flows			Rock flow	Earth flow	Debris flow
			Rock avalanche	-	Debris avalanche
			Deep creep	Soil creep	
Complex and compound			Combination in time and/or space of two or more principal types of movement		

Although many types of mass movements are included in the general term "landslide," the more restrictive use of the term refers only to mass movements, where there is a distinct zone of weakness that separates the slide material from more stable underlying material. The most common types of landslides based on the type movement (Refer Sec. 6.3.1)from the above table can be read as

1. Toppling
2. Falling
3. Lateral Spreading
4. Creeping
5. Flowing (Rotational/Translational)

Further, the landslide movement can be a combination of two or more of the above movement forming a complex and compound structure. These are briefly described below.

6.6.1 Toppling Landslides

"Toppling is the forward rotation out of the slope of a mass of soil or rock about a point or axis below the centre of gravity of the displaced mass. Toppling is sometimes driven by gravity exerted by material upslope of the displaced mass and sometimes by water or ice in cracks in the mass" (Varnes, 1996).

Toppling can be either due to bedrock, simply called rock-topple or some engineering materials ranging from fine earth toppling to coarse debris toppling.

Toppling failures can be differentiated by the forward rotation of a unit about some pivotal point, below the unit, under the actions of gravity and forces exerted by adjacent units or by fluids in cracks.

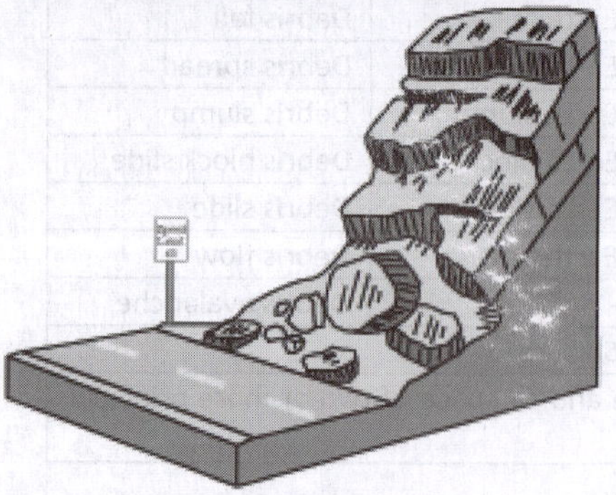

6.6.2 Falling Landslides

"A fall starts with the detachment of soil or rock from a steep slope along a surface on which little or no shear displacement takes place. The material then descends mainly through the air by falling, bouncing, or rolling" (Varnes, 1996).

"Secondary falls involves rock bodies already physically detached from cliff & merely lodged upon it"(Hutchinson, 1988)

Thus, falls are abrupt movements of masses of geologic materials, such as rocks and boulders that become detached from steep slopes or cliffs. Separation occurs along discontinuities such as fractures, joints, and bedding planes, and movement occurs by free-fall, bouncing, and rolling. Falls are strongly influenced by gravity, mechanical weathering, and the presence of interstitial water.

6.6.3 Lateral Spreading Landslides

Lateral spreads occur on very gentle slopes or flat terrain. The dominant mode of movement is lateral extension accompanied by shear or tensile fractures. The failure is caused by liquefaction,

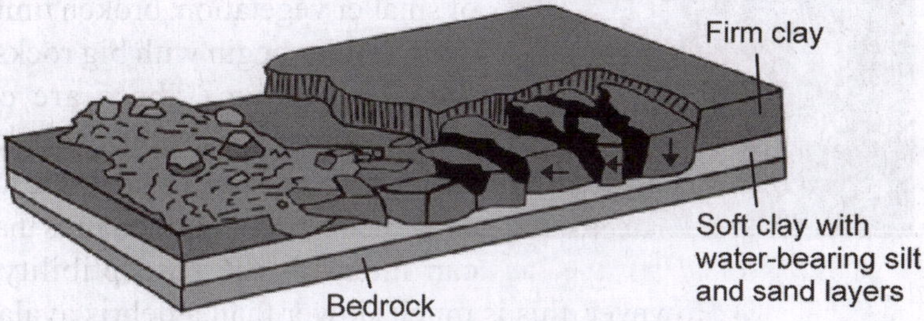

the process whereby saturated, loose, cohesionless sediments (usually sands and silts) are transformed from a solid into a liquefied state. Failure is usually triggered by rapid ground motion, like in earthquake, but can also be artificially induced. When coherent material, either bedrock or soil, rests on materials that liquefy, the upper units may undergo fracturing and extension and may then subside, translate, rotate, disintegrate, or liquefy and flow. Lateral spreading in fine-grained materials on shallow slopes is usually progressive. The failure starts suddenly in a small area and spreads rapidly. Often the initial failure is a slump, but in some materials movement occurs for no apparent reason. Combination of two or more of the above types is known as a complex landslide.

6.6.4 Flowing Landslides

The flow type landslides are majorly found in four models

(i) Debris Flow or Debris Slide
(ii) Debris Avalanche
(iii) Earth Flow
(iv) Mud Flow

We shall briefly discuss about these flow type landslides.

6.6.4.1 Debris flow (or Debris slide)

*A **flow** is continuous movement in which surfaces of shear are short-lived, closely spaced, and usually not preserved. The distribution of velocities*

in the displacing mass resembles that in a viscous liquid. The lower boundary of displaced mass may be a surface along which appreciable differential movement has taken place or a thick zone of distributed shear (Cruden & Varnes, 1996).

A combination of loose soil (50% fine), rock, and organic matter with air and water form as slurry and rapidly flow down slope. The slurry may also contain an incoherent mixture of smaller vegetation, broken timber and other debris. Usually, debris slides begin with big rocks at the top and break apart as they slide down. These are caused by the erosion and movement of loose soil or rock on steep slopes by intense surface-water flow, usually due to heavy precipitation or rapid snowmelt or rain. Further, fires that denude slopes of vegetation can intensify the susceptibility of slopes to debris flows. However, this is much slower than a debris avalanche.

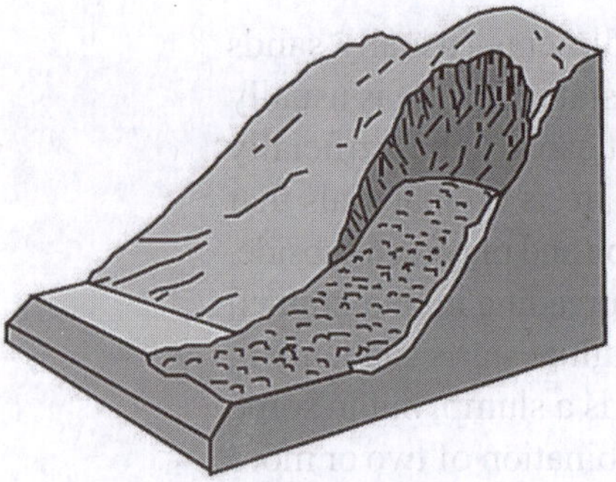

Pozzano (Castellammare di Stabia),, Quindici Sarno – Italy- Debris flow deposits & damage

6.6.4.2 Debris avalanche

This is extremely rapid debris flow and entire mass seems to liquefy as it slides down the slope. This is caused by steep slopes and saturation of material. As the debris moves down it follows a stream channel and makes a V-shape scar. Due to the high speeds they can also travel down to the foot of the slope. These are common on the submerged flanks of ocean island volcanoes such as the Hawaiian Islands and the Cape Verde Islands.

Goodell Creek Debris Avalanche, Washington Blocking Hunza river

6.6.4.3 Earth flow

Guerrero, Mexico Earth flows are down slope, fine-grained, saturated viscous materials, which move at any speed from slow to fast, ranging from 0.17 to 20 km/h (0.1 to 12.4 mph) depending on the water content. These look like mudflows, but, overall they are very slow and are covered with solid material. Moreover, they often contain clay, fine sand, silt, and fine-grained pyroclastic material.

However, they differ from fluid flows because they are more rapid. These flows are usually triggered by the pore pressures in a fine-grained mass increase. When enough is the weight of the material to support the pore water to

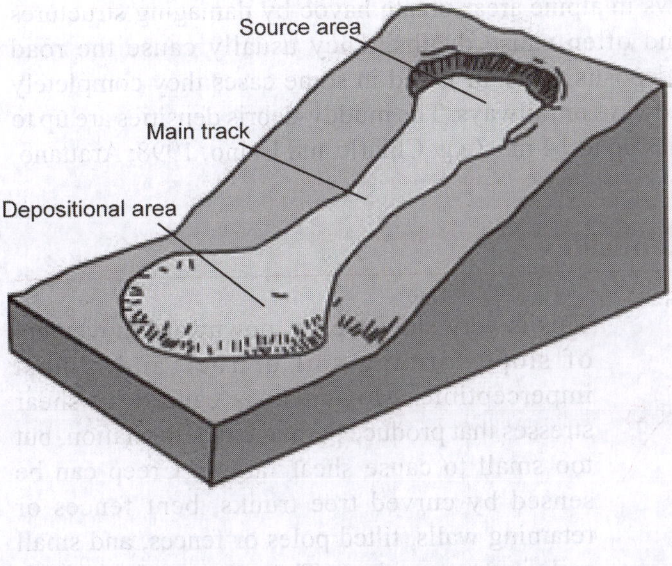

Guerrero, Mexico

significantly decrease the internal shear strength of the material. Thence, it creates a bulging lobe and advances with a slow, rolling motion. As these lobes spread out, fall of the mass increases and starts drying out, thereby lowers the overall flow velocity. The slope material liquefies and runs out, forming a bowl or depression at the head. Thus they have a characteristic "***hourglass***" shape.

6.6.4.4 Mudflow (or Mudslides)

It is slurry consisting of sand, silt, and clay, rock which is wet enough to flow rapidly. The mud-debris flows due to slope-related factors while shallow slides form stream bed like a mini-dam and results in temporary water blockage. Mud/Debris flow is often confused with flash flood, which is totally different process.

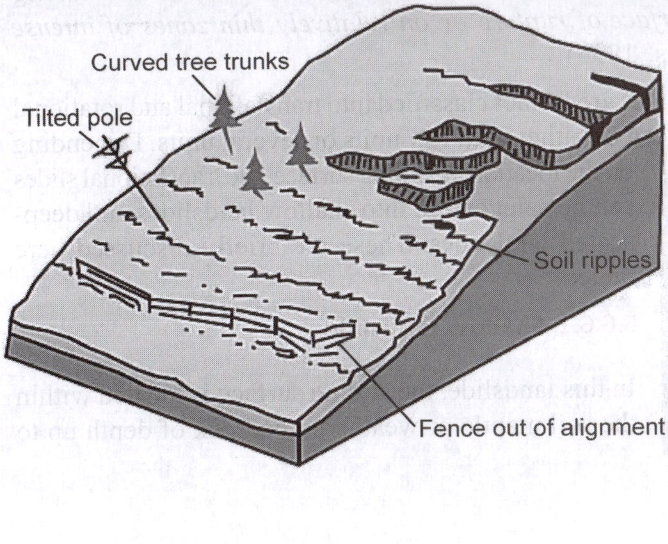

9 Nov 2001 Amboori, Kerala killed 39 people

Muddy-debris flows in alpine areas create havoc by damaging structures and infrastructure and often cause deaths. They usually cause the road interruptions, due to deposits (100s m^3), and in some cases they completely remove bridges or roadways or railways. The muddy-debris densities are up to 2 tons/m^3 and velocities up to 14 m/s (e.g. Chiarle and Luino, 1998; Arattano, 2003).

6.6.5 Creeping Landslides

This is very slow, steady, downward movement of slope-forming soil or rock and almost imperceptible. Movement is caused by shear stresses that produce permanent deformation, but too small to cause shear failure. Creep can be sensed by curved tree trunks, bent fences or retaining walls, tilted poles or fences, and small soil ripples or ridges. Three types of creep are usually found:

1. **Seasonal:** The movement is within the soil depth due to seasonal changes in moisture and temperature;
2. **Continuous:** The shear stress continuously exceeds the strength of the material; and
3. **Progressive:** The slope reaches the point of failure as other types of mass movements.

6.6.6 Sliding Landslides

"A slide is a down slope movement of soil or rock mass occurring dominantly on the surface of rupture or on relatively thin zones of intense shear strain." (Varnes, 1996)

The sliding type landslides are further classified into translational and rotational types. The translation can be either with few units or several units. Depending on the location of sliding surface, the translational slides can be categorized into shallow landslides and deep-seated landslides. These are briefly discussed here under.

6.6.6.1 Shallow landslide

In this landslide, the sliding surface is located within the soil mantle or weathered bedrock of depth up to some metres. The shallow landslides include debris slides, debris flow, and failures of road cut-slopes. However, the landslides when single large blocks of rock move slowly down slope are sometimes termed ***block glides***.

Shallow landslides usually occur at the slopes with high permeable soils on top and low permeable at bottom. The low permeable bottom soils trap the water in the high permeable soils, which create high water pressure in the top soils. Obviously, as the top soils are filled with water turn heavy making the slopes very unstable and hence slide over the low permeable bottom soils.

We can demonstrate this with the following activity.

Take a considerable amount of silt and sand and pour it on a rock-bed or cement or concrete bed. Now, if there is a heavy rain, the bedrock will trap the rain water in the topsoil i.e. silt and sand. When, the topsoil is saturated, it becomes so heavy to slide over the bedrock and that is a shallow landslide.

Example: Hotel Limone at Lake Garda. Part of hill of Devonian shale was removed to make the road, forming a dip-slope.

Talas Landslide of soil and regolith in Pakistan

Sehara, Kihô, Japan caused by torrential rain of Tropical Storm

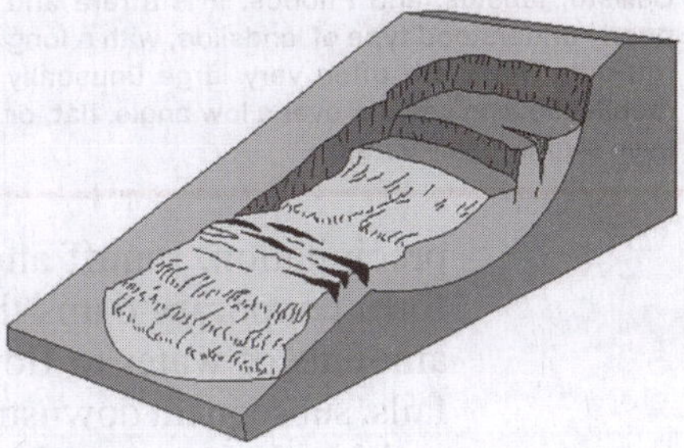

6.6.6.2 Deep-seated landslide

These have sliding surface deeply located below the maximum rooting depth of trees (Depth > 10m). They have deep regolith, weathered and/or bedrock with large slope failure and move with translation, rotation or any complex motion. They usually occur in active tectonic areas like Zagros Mountain, Iran. They usually move slowly (few meters per year). They are bigger than shallow landslides and form along a plane of weakness such as a fault (or an effect of earthquake also). They can be visually identified by concave scarps at the top and steep areas at the toe.

Before slide

6.6.6.3 Rotational & translational slides

Rotational slide is the movement of material along a surface of rupture that is curved

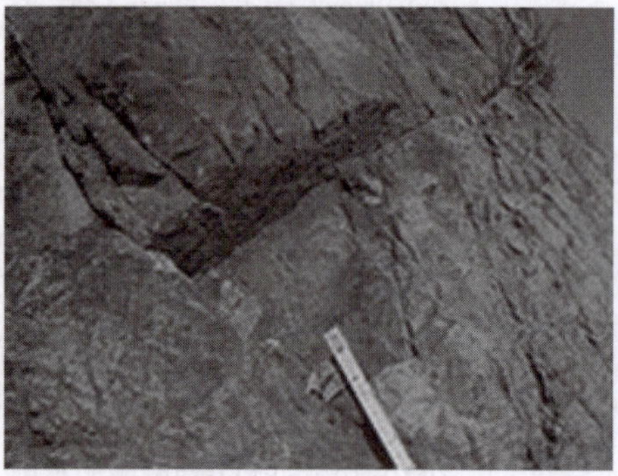

After slide

and concave while translational slide is down slope movement of soil or rock mass occurring dominantly on the surface of rupture or on relatively thin zones of intense shear strain. (Varnes, 1996)

This is a slide in which the surface of rupture is curved concavely upward and the slide movement is roughly rotational about an axis that is parallel to the ground surface and transverse across the slide.

A quick revision and comparison of various landslides is given below:

O My God!

Sturzstrom? The Mt St Helens volcanic landslide was a sturzstrom.

It (In German Sturz =fall and Strom=stream) is a unique type of landslide of soil and rock with a great horizontal movement as compared to its initial vertical drop — up to 20-30 times the vertical distance. (a normal landslide will typically travel a horizontal distance that is less than twice the distance that the material has fallen). These are similar to the flow in glaciers, mudflows, and lava flows. Sturzstroms flow across land easily, and their mobility increases when volume increases. They have been found on other bodies in the Solar System, including the Moon, Mars, Venus, Io, Callisto, Iapetus, and Phobos. It is a rare and poorly understood type of landslide, with a long run-out. These are often very large unusually mobile, flowing very far over a low angle, flat, or even slightly uphill terrain.

6.7 LANDSLIDES AND OTHER DISASTERS

Although landslides occur in multiple combinations, the following three seem to be the most common and hazardous as per the known history of the world.

6.7.1 Landslides and Floods

It is well known fact that the slope saturation by water is fundamental reason behind landslides and this can occur due to intense rainfall, snowmelt, changes in ground -, and rivers. Thus, landslides and floods are closely associated such that one may be the cause for the other, since both are related to precipitation, runoff and the saturation of ground by water. Landslides may form temporary dams that block valleys and stream channels effecting large amounts of water to flow back causing backwater flooding and, if such dam fails, subsequent downstream flooding. Further, solid landslide debris can "bulk" and block the normal stream flow creating flood environment or localized erosion. Landslide falling in a reservoir of dam reduces the capacity of reservoirs or/and causes overflows to result a flood. On the other side, a river or a stream can cut or erode soil at the banks resulting in a slope destabilization to cause a landslide.

Strange Landscape by Dallol Volcano explosion crater in Ethiopia.

6.7.2 Landslides and Earthquakes/ Tsunamis

History reveals that many mountainous areas susceptible to landslides have also experienced

Type of landslide			Speed	Slope (angle)	Control factor	Causes
FALL		Starts with the detachment of soil or rock from a steep slope along a surface with a little or no shear displacement. Material then descends through the air by falling, bouncing, or rolling (Varnes, 1996). Secondary falls involves rock bodies already physically detached from cliff & merely lodged upon it (Hutchinson, 1988)	Extremely rapid	45-90^0	Discontinuities	Vibration, undercutting, differential weathering, excavation, or stream erosion
TOPPLE		The forward rotation out of the slope of a mass of soil or rock about a point or axis below the centre of gravity of the displaced mass. It is sometimes driven by gravity exerted by material upslope of the displaced mass and sometimes by water or ice in cracks in the mass (Varnes, 1996)	Very slow to very rapid (>5m/s)	45-90^0	Discontinuities, lithostratigraphy	Vibration, undercutting, stream erosion, excavation differential weather
SLIDE	Transl-ational	Down slope movement of soil or rock mass occurring dominantly on the surface of rupture or on relatively thin zones of intense shear strain. (Varnes, 1996)	Very slow to very rapid	45-90^0	Discontinuities, geological setting	Vibration, undercutting, stream erosion, excavation differential weather
	Rotational	Move along a surface of rupture that is curved and concave (Varnes, 1996)	Very slow to very rapid	45-90^0	Morphology and lithology	Vibration, undercutting, stream erosion, excavation differential weather
SPREADS		An extension of a cohesive soil/rock mass combined with a general subsidence of the fractured mass of cohesive material into softer underlying material. The lateral extension is accommodated by shear or tensile fractures. (Varnes, 1996)	Very slow to very rapid (>5m/s)	45-90^0	Discontinuities, lithostratigraphy	Vibration, undercutting, stream erosion, excavation differential weather
FLOW	Rock- Flow	A spatially movement with short-lived, closely spaced, and usually not preserved shear surfaces. The distribution of velocities in the displacing mass resembles that in a viscous liquid. (Cruden & Varnes, 1996)	Extreme slow	45-90^0	Discontinuities, lithostratigraphy	Vibration, undercutting, stream erosion, excavation differential weather
	Rock avalanche (Sturzstrom)	Extremely fast, massive, flow-like motion of fragmented rock from a large rock slide or rock fall (Hungr, 2001)	Extreme Rapid	45-90^0	Discontinuities, lithostratigraphy	Vibration, undercutting, stream erosion, excavation differential weather
	Soil Flow	Very rapid to extremely rapid, massive, flow of saturated non-plastic debris in a steep channel (Hungr et al 2001)	Very Rapid	20-45^0	Torrent sediment, water flows	High intensity rainfall
	Debris aval anche	Very rapid to extremely rapid shallow flow of partially or fully saturated debris on a steep slope, without confinement in an established channel. (Hungr et al., 2001)	Very Rapid	20-45^0	Torrent sediment, water flows	High intensity rainfall
	Earth Flow	Rapid or slower, intermittent flow-like movement of plastic, clayey earth. (Hungr et al.,2001)	Slow to rapid (>1.8 m/h)	5-25^0	Lithology	High intensity rainfall
	Mud flow	Rapid to extremely rapid flow of saturated plastic debris in a channel, involving significantly greater water content relative to the source material (Plasticity index> 5%)." (Hungr et al.,2001)	Slow to rapid (>1.8 m/h)	20-45^0	Torrent sediments, water flows	High intensity rainfall

Pavlof Volcano in N. America is a threat to air traffic.

Yosemite Rock Fall and debris avalanche by Herb Dunn

earthquakes. Of course, the earthquakes in steep landslide-prone areas greatly enhance the probability of landslides occurrence due to ground shaking. Further, it allows rapid infiltration of water. The 1964 Great Alaska Earthquake caused a big landslide. California and Puget Sound region in Washington, USA have experienced slides, lateral spreading, and other types of ground failure as a result of earthquakes. Large rock falls also are caused by loosening of rocks as a result of ground shaking. Further, Lituya Bay of Alaska (1958) witnessed a mega tsunami also due to landslide (Ref. Chapter 4).

6.7.3 Landslides and Volcanic Eruption

Records reveal that volcanic eruption often causes the devastating landslide. Volcanic lava may melt snow at a rapid rate, causing a huge rock fall, soil, ash and water flow that accelerates rapidly on the steep slopes of volcanoes. These volcanic debris flows (also called lahars) can damage structures in surrounding areas. The 1980 eruption of Mt. St. Helens, in Washington experienced the largest and massive landslide.

SELF ASSESSMENT INTERMISSION (SAI – 6.3)

1. List out various types of landslide movements. Describe each of them briefly with the help of sketches.
2. Discuss the following with reference to landslides. (a) toppling (b) spreading
3. Distinguish between falling type and flowing types of landslides. Give examples.
4. Compare and contrast various types of landslides with reference to their movement.
5. Discuss various types of fallings in landslides. Give examples.
6. What is sturzstrom? Explain with an example.
7. Explain the terms toppling, creeping, spreading, falling and flowing with reference to landslides.
8. Discuss the relationship between a landslide and earthquake.
9. How are landslide and tsunami related? Discuss.
10. Describe the relation between a volcano and a landslide?
11. Describe the 1980 Mount Saint Helens volcanic landslide.

6.8 ADVERSE EFFECTS OF LANDSLIDES

1991 rock slide near Loggers Creek closed the Sea-to-Sky Highway for 12 days and cost $7 million for repairs.

Landslides cause property damage, injury and death and adversely affect a variety of resources such as,

- dams
- forests,
- fisheries,
- water supplies,
- drainage systems,
- sewage disposal systems,
- communication systems (cables)
- electricity distribution systems and
- transportation systems (roadways/ railways)

The landslides can cause direct cost of

- repairing structures,
- loss of valuable property,
- medical costs of injuries/ deaths,
- cost of reinstituting disrupted transportation/ communication systems,

Indirect costs such as

- lost fish,
- pollution
- lost timber,
- cattle food,
- agriculture and
- Water availability (quantity and quality)

14 major (all >20 000 m^3) debris slides occurred on Vancouver to Squamish highway since 1906. 12lives, 11bridges, and many structures damaged.

6.9 LANDSLIDE MITIGATION

Mitigation can be carried out by constructing suitable engineering structures on slopes with the objective to prevent or reduce the effect of landslides.

The landslide mitigation methods are classified by the sort of slope stabilization method used:

- Geometric methods, in which the slope of the hillside is changed
- Hydro-geological methods to lower the groundwater level or to reduce the water content of the material
- Chemical and mechanical methods to increase the shear strength of the unstable mass or to introduce active external forces (e.g. anchors, rock or ground nailing) or passive (e.g. structural wells, piles or reinforced ground) to counteract the destabilizing forces.

6.9.1 Geometry Modification

This type of measure is used if below the material to be removed, or the rock face is sound and stable. Detachment measures are carried out where there is a risk due to infrastructures or the passage of people at the foot of the hillside. The re-profiling a slope to improve stability can be obtained by

- Lowering the angle of the slope by digging out the brow of the slope, in a step-wise or
- Positioning infill at the foot of the slope by constructing gravitational structures such as gabions, or reinforced ground (i.e., concrete blocks).

6.9.2 Reinforcement Measures

A hillside can be stabilized by enhancing the mechanical strength of the unstable ground. This can be achieved in two ways:

1. The improvement of the mechanical characteristics of the ground through chemical, thermal, or mechanical treatment.
2. Insertion of reinforcement elements into the ground

6.9.3 Treatment Methods

The treatment methods are comparatively costly. The following are the generally employed treatment methods:

- Mechanical treatments to improve the mechanical characteristics of the soil volume (e.g. Jet-grouting technique).
- Thermal treatment by lighting of wood or coal fires within holes dug into the slope.
- Electro-osmotic treatment of the ground (action of a continuous electrical field).

Insertion of reinforcement elements into the ground

Types of mechanical reinforcement include:

- Anchors using geofabrics to prevent erosion
- Large diameter wells (supported by crowns of consolidated and/or reinforced earth columns)
- Integrating wells with a series of micro-drains laid out radially
- Networks of micro-piles (making up a three-dimensional grid)
- Soil nailing to stabilise natural slopes and artificial scarps (SCOUJET/SNART methods)
- Geogrids to reinforce ground
- Cellular or crib faces (supporting walls made of head grids prefabricated in reinforced concrete or wood)

6.9.4 Anchor Structure

The simplest method is to position anchors and nails in an unstable rocky hillside. This process is carried out in the following steps

- Clean out/wash the cracks
- Plaster the crack
- Predispose the injection tubes at suitable inter-axes, parallel to the crack
- Prepare the concrete mix
- Inject the mixture sequentially from bottom to top and at low pressure (1-3 atm).

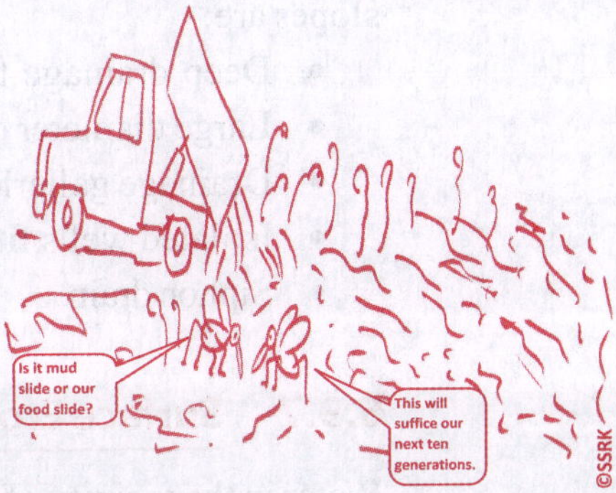

6.9.5 Shotcrete

Shotcrete (also called spray-concrete or spritzbeton) is mortar or concrete conveyed through a hose and pneumatically projected at high velocity onto a surface.

6.9.6 Drainage

Drainage systems can reduce the water level inside the hillside where there is a likelihood to become unstable, which in turn lowers pore water pressure in the ground and an enhancement in the shear strength within the slope.

Thus this system considers threefold objective:

- To prevent water entering the hillside through open or discontinuity traction cracks

- To lower the pressure near probable breakage surfaces through selective shallow drains
- To place drainage so as to reduce water pressure in the immediate vicinity of the hillside.

Various drainage techniques suitable in this context along with brief explanation are listed below to achieve the above objectives are:

Shallow drainage

Shallow drainage is facilitated through trenches cut in an unbroken length and filled with highly permeable, granular, draining material.

Deep drainage

Deep drainage is more effective but costlier than shallow drains. It modifies the filtration routes in the ground. They directly remove the water that causes instability within the hillside. Various deep drainage methods suitable to earth slopes are:

- Deep drainage trenches
- Large diameter drainage wells with sub-horizontal drains
- Drainage galleries fitted with micro-drains
- Isolated wells fitted with drainage pumps
- Siphon drain

6.9.7 Surface Erosion Control

Water in the vicinity of the hillside can erode the surface material due to runoff, which in turn weakens the slope and also triggers excess pore pressures due to the water flow. The products made of geo-synthetic materials can be used to protect and grassing of slopes subjected to surface wash. They provide two main erosion control mechanisms: reinforcement of ground surface and protection from raindrops. The following are some of these techniques used to reduce the surface erosion.

- ***Geo-mats (or anti-eroding bio-mats or bio-nets)***
- ***Geo-grids***
- ***Coir (coconut fibre) geo-textiles***.
- ***Fastening Steel wire mesh*** (for soil and rock slope stabilization).

6.9.8 Protection Measures

A boulder catching net on a trail at Multnomah Falls, Oregon, USA, erected to protect hikers from debris falling down the steep incline.

The protection of natural and quarry faces can have two different aims:

- Protecting the rock from alteration or weathering
- Protecting infrastructure and towns from rock falls.

SELF ASSESSMENT INTERMISSION (SAI – 6.4)

1. What are adverse effects of landslides?
2. Give the mitigation methods to encounter the landslides.
3. Does landslide lead to surface erosion? If so, how do you control surface erosion caused due to landslides?
4. Suggest and explain some structural modifications to mitigate from the landslides.
5. What is anchor structure? How does it help in controlling landslides?
6. Give some suggestions to modify the drainage systems to mitigating the landslides.

MINI-PROJECTS / CASE-STUDIES

1. Prepare a documentary on rockslides and landslides in Himalayas suggesting certain guidelines of mitigation and risk reduction measures for Amarnath Pilgrims.
2. Prepare demonstration set up for various types of landslides using mud/ sand/ silt etc.

DO YOU KNOW

1. Landslides also occur throughout the solar system, specifically on Mars and Venus.
2. On steep hillsides, debris flows begin as shallow landslides that liquefy and accelerate and travel at about 10 mph-35 mph. The fastest landslide ever recorded went 186 mph.
3. Volcanic eruptions can cause deadly landslides. The May 1980 eruption of Mt. St. Helens caused the largest landslide in history. A rockslide debris avalanche was as large as to fill 250 million dump trucks, travelled 14 miles, and destroyed 9 highway bridges and many things.
4. Landslides most frequent in US to kill 25-50 people every year and damage ~\$3.5 billion.
5. In Canada, a landslide moved a river bank as fast as 680m in less than half an hour.
6. The debris avalanche from the eruption formed several new lakes by damming the N.Fork Toutle River and its tributaries.
7. The consistency of debris flow ranges of watery mud to thick, rocky mud that can carry large items such as boulders, trees, and cars.

8. Areas where wildfires or human modification of the land have destroyed vegetation on slopes are particularly vulnerable to landslides during and after heavy rains.
9. Landslides vary in size, from a single boulder to thousands of tonnes of earth and debris.
10. Landslides often accompany earthquakes, floods, storm surges, hurricanes, wildfires, or volcanic activity and are often more damaging and deadly than the triggering event.
11. Mudslides usually start on steep slopes and activated by natural disasters.
12. Landslides/mudflows injure (Trauma) and/or cause tons of damage, break electrical/ water/ gas/ sewage lines that can result in injury or illness.

Top 10 Land/Rock/Mudslides based on Deaths					
No.	**Place**	**Country**	**Year**	**Deaths**	**Figure**
1.	Kansu	China	1920	Over 180,000	
2.	Khait	Tadzhikistan USSR	1949	12,000	
3.	Chiavenna Valley	Italy	1618	2,240	
4.	Rio De Janeiro	Brazil	1966, 2011	550, 600	
5.	Goldau valley	Switzerland	1806	500	
6.	Hauncavelica Province	Peru	1974	200-300	
7.	Darjeeling	India	1980	Over 250 died	
8.	Sichuan Province	China	1981	Over 240 died	
9.	Nebukawa	Japan	1923	200 died	
10.	Chungar	Peru	1971	200 died	

CHAPTER 7 Avalanche and Blizzard

O'MY SILENT INNER VIBES (O'M S I V – 7)

Just before sunrise, the clouds and sky are lighting up nicely with swathes of pink on blue.

The weather was exulting to some while upsetting some other.

February 23, 1910, Spokane Railway station...

"Your Attention Please" – Announcer said, "The Great Northern Railroad's *Spokane Express* is ready to leave for Seattle, Washington".

The train reached Wellington station, located near the base of Windy Mountain and stopped for a long time due to bad weather conditions. Soon after it started, the weather became too bad while it was just passing through the Stevens Pass, a small village in King County.

February 26, 1910, Stevens Pass...

Suddenly, a ***blizzard***... blocked the railway lines with high snow drifts in the Cascade Mountains.

Many workers attempted to clear the tracks, but the train was still stuck.

Communications were totally cut.

The area's telegraph lines had come down in the storm.

Nothing the railway personnel could do, except waiting for the storm to stop.

There was little, the passengers could do but for hoping for good morning.

February 28, 1910, Idaho (Near Steven Pass)...

Weather condition still worsened. Temperatures dropped. Thunderstorms battered the area.

Suddenly an ***avalanche***... flooded over the low-lying areas. Several miners lost lives.

At about 4:20 a.m. 50 passengers and 75 employees of Great Northern Railroad sleeping in the *Spokane Express*.

The ***avalanche*** preceded by the ***blizzard***, with shivering ***cold wave*** and severe ***snowfall*** motivated by ***rain***, followed by ***lightening*** with frightening ***thunders*** smashed down the ***Windy*** Mountain.

Alas! How terribly nature can torture humans!

Not one, but two trains are swept into a canyon by the avalanche killing 96 people.

Ill-fated! Being the remote location and the risk of further avalanches, efforts to rescue survivors and find the bodies of the dead were not completed until several days later.

The trains were buried by 40-70 ft of snow and debris. As the telegraph lines were down, the people of Wellington could not call for immediate assistance. Despite the risk of further avalanches, many people pitched in to try to dig out survivors, but in vain. Until the night of March, 2nd, no assistance from outside Wellington could reach the site. Meanwhile, 23 people had been pulled out alive, but with serious injuries.

(Continued)

Charles Andrews, a rail worker, resident of Wellington who witnessed the disaster, described the scene: "***White Death** moving down the mountainside above the trains. Relentlessly it advanced, exploding, roaring, rumbling, grinding and snapping. The Spokane Express and a mail train were both thrown from the tracks down a nearby gorge 150 ft deep. The Wellington station was wiped away*".

The incident raised several questions on how and why the blizzards and avalanches occur. One major reason was cutting down the trees on the mountainside. The nature taught a big lesson about the dangers of clear-cutting timber on mountains above towns and villages that proved to be very costly. And the title of the lesson is...

If You Deface the Nature, You Have to Face its Torture.

7.1 DEFINITION

A powder snow avalanche in the Himalayas near Mt. Everest

The toe of an avalanche in Alaska's Kenai Fjords

An avalanche is simply snow sliding down a mountainside. Other names of snow avalanche are "snowslide or snowslip". It can be compared to a landslide, or rockslide, only with the difference 'snow' instead of earth or rock. (Slides of rocks or debris, behaving in a similar way to snow, are also referred to as avalanches – see chapter- 6, Landslides).

Thus an **avalanche** (**Snowslide** or **Snowslip**) is a natural disaster defined as a rapid flow of snow down along a sloping surface.

7.2 THE CONCEPT AND CHARACTERISTICS OF AVALANCHE

What is required for an avalanche to occur is - a mass of snow and a slope for it to slide down.

Let us understand the concept of avalanche with an example.

You might have noticed the layer of snow on a car windshield after a snowfall. While the temperature remains low, the snow stuck to the surface may not slide off. But, as the temperature increases, the snow slides down the front of the windshield, often in small slabs. You may even find such an event on a cool drink bottle when you open the deep freezer door of a refrigerator and taken out. This is the concept of an avalanche on a miniature scale.

Now think big of this situation… That is avalanche!

An avalanche can be composed of many different kinds of materials along with snow depending on the region, temperature and weather. It could be loosely packed light fluffy snow, which is more dangerous than it appears or a thick "slab" tightly packed together snow. Though basically consist of flowing snow and air, the large avalanches may include ice, rocks, trees, debris and other material on the slope. Whatsoever sliding mass is, the avalanches are distinctly different from mudslides and rockslides. As an avalanche nears the bottom of the slope, it gains speed and power and hence even the smallest of snow slide can cause a major disaster.

Avalanches are most common during winter or spring but it does not mean that it will not occur in other seasons. The glacier movements causing ice and snow avalanches are the serious natural hazards in mountainous terrain throughout the year that can destruct both life as well as assets.

7.2.1 Why Do Avalanches Occur?

The snowpack on the slope cannot support itself when the weight increases sufficiently higher than bond strength. When the bond strength and the gravitational forces are equal, even a small force of any factor as described above such as a person's or animal's step or a wind or rain drops etc. can influence to loosen the snow and trigger an avalanche.

7.2.2 When/How Do Avalanches Occur?

We know that avalanche occurs hillside or mountainside as a rapid flow of snow and can occur anytime throughout the year provided the right conditions develop. However, these conditions easily and readily develop in the winter (December to April in India)

7.2.3 Where Do Avalanches Occur?

Avalanches occur on mountains with extreme snow fall or build-up. The steadily increasing winter activities along with the growth of interest in skiing result in a much greater hazard. Europe, France, Swiss mountains, Western Canada, Utah, Alaska, and Colorado are a few places among those have high probability of avalanches. All of these locations go through a freeze-melt cycle during the year at the bases of the mountains.

7.3 THE ANATOMY OF AVALANCHE

A large avalanche in N. America might release 230,000 m^3 of snow, which is the equivalent of 20 football fields filled 3m (10 ft) height with snow. Such avalanches often naturally occur when the snowpack becomes unstable and layers of snow fail. Skiers usually trigger smaller, but often it is enough to result in more dangerous snow-slide. To understand how this can happen, one should first know the anatomy of the avalanche.

An avalanche has three main parts, viz.

(a) Starting zone
(b) Avalanche track
(c) Run out zone

We now brief about these three parts of an avalanche.

7.3.1 Starting Zone

This is the most volatile region of a slope, at which unstable snow detaches (fracture) from the surrounding snow cover and starts to slide. Usually, starting zones exists at the top of slopes, but the right conditions prevail, the snow can fracture at any point on the slope.

7.3.2 Avalanche Track

It is the path or channel (called track) that an avalanche tends to move downhill. Large vertical trees or chute-like clearances can help avalanches run frequently thereby, generating their own tracks. A large pile-up of snow and debris at the bottom of the slope indicates the run of an avalanche.

7.3.3 Run-Out Zone

This is the area where the snow and debris finally come to a stall. This is the location of the deposition zone, where the snow and debris pile up the highest and can be a potential source for a snow-slide, if further slope or any favorable conditions exist.

SELF ASSESSMENT INTERMISSION (SAI – 7.1)

1. Define Avalanche? What is its meaning? What are its other names? What is its significance in disaster management?
2. Discuss the process of a typical avalanche with the help of sketch.
3. Discuss the anatomy of an avalanche? Explain about the main parts of it.
4. Explain the terms 'starting zone, track and run-out' with reference to an avalanche.
5. What are the characteristics of an avalanche?
6. Where do avalanches occur? What are the reasons for occurrence at those areas?
7. Why and when does an avalanche occur? What are the favorable conditions for occurrence?

7.4 TRIGGERS (CAUSES) OF AVALANCHES

We know that a snowpack will fail when the load (weight) exceeds the strength. Since the strength of the snowpack is extremely heterogeneous, it is very difficult to determine. It varies with properties of the snow grains, size, density, morphology, temperature, water content; and the properties of the bonds between the grains. Further, these properties may change time to time according to the local humidity, temperature, heat flux, radiation and the local wind flow. A complicating factor is the complex interaction of terrain, snowpack structure and weather as described above.

Any factor might help snow accumulation, but the snowpack fails and falls mainly due to gravity. Of course, the internal reason for failure may be increased precipitated load or weakening in the snowpack, but externally it is initiated by some triggering event. The occurrence of an avalanche may be attributed to one or more of the following most common triggers (causes).

- Most avalanches spontaneously occur during storms are triggered by *increased load* due to *snowfall.*
- The second largest reason for natural avalanches is *metamorphic changes* in the snowpack such as *melting* due to *solar radiation*
- Other natural causes include
    - *Rain*
    - *Earthquake*
    - *Rock fall* and
    - *Icefall* or *snowfall*
- Artificial triggers of avalanches include
    - *Skiers,*
    - *Snowmobilers* and
    - *Controlled explosive work*

Whatsoever the cause may be, an avalanche starts at a point with only a small amount of snow moving initially. If the snow sinters into a stiff slab overlying a weak layer, then fractures propagate very rapidly resulting in 1000's of cubic meters of snow can start moving almost simultaneously. The pattern of this snow-sliding has some variations distinctly different from one another with reference to the size, mechanism, material composition and so forth. These are discussed in the next section to follow.

7.4.1 Factors Motivating Avalanche

Several factors may encourage the likelihood of an avalanche as listed below

1. Terrain,
2. Weather
3. General snowpack conditions
4. Slope steepness
5. Slope orientation (facing north or south)
6. Temperature
7. Wind direction
8. Vegetation

The list is not exhaustive but the above are more common factors for an avalanche formation. Of course, all other factors of the above list, except the first three, can change so frequently that it may be daily or even hourly also. Further, various combinations of these factors can create low, moderate, or extreme avalanche conditions. However, terrain, snowpack, weather are considered to be the most significant factors to characterize an avalanche, and hence named as the primary elements of an avalanche by Doug Fesler and Jill Fredston who developed a conceptual model. According to them,

- *Terrain* depicts the places where avalanches occur,
- *Weather* describes the meteorological conditions that create the snowpack, and
- *Snowpack* tells the structural characteristics of snow that make avalanche formation possible.

Though the above three factors (terrain, snow pack and weather) effect avalanche mainly, the other factors such as height of the snowpack, temperature, wind speed and direction etc. also have their own significance in motivating an avalanche. However, most times these can be considered as sub-factors to the three and can be fit under one or more of these three.

Avalanches mostly occur out of cornice, the over-hanging snow above a cliff formed during snowstorms. This occurs due to strong winds, snow drifts usually in 1-2 days. The terrain factor depends on the slope angle and profile (25–45°). Further, the snow movement is determined by smoothness/ roughness of the ground and rocks under the snow. A convex slope due to more tension increases the chances of a slab avalanche. The slopes have to be avoided after storms or high wind speeds because, avalanche locations move according to wind direction.

Rapid snow build-up (> 2 cm/h) can create unstable conditions and > 30 cm build up in 24 hrs is very hazardous. Lose snow and air packets trapped under the snow enhance danger levels. Sudden temperature change, wind speed and direction also alter snow stability. Most important is human interference.

7.4.2 The Primary Elements of Avalanche

As discussed above, to describe an avalanche, we require understanding about the three primary elements:

1. Terrain
2. Weather and
3. Snowpack

Thence, we shall have a brief discussion about how these factors can portray the behavior of an avalanche through the paragraphs to follow.

7.4.3 Effect of Terrain

Effect of vegetation on avalanche

Avalanches are unlikely to occur in very thick forests, but boulders and sparsely distributed vegetation can become a weakness owing to their strong temperature gradients. Generally, avalanches follow drainages down-slope sharing drainage features. At and below *tree line*, avalanche paths through drainages are well defined by vegetation boundaries called *trim lines* that occur where avalanches have remove trees and prevent regeneration of large vegetation. Engineered drainages, like an *avalanche dam* (e.g. Mt Stephen in Kicking Horse Pass), can protect people and property by redirecting the flow of avalanches. Deep debris deposits of avalanches will collect in catchments at a run out, gullies and river beds.

The terrain is the geographical structure of the place. It gives us an idea if an avalanche can occur. For the formation of an avalanche, the terrain should have a slope shallow enough to snow accumulation but steep enough for the snow to accelerate (due to gravity after mechanical failure of the snowpack).

The snow accumulation has a relation with the angle of the slope that can grip snow against gravity, called the *angle of repose*, which depends on several of factors like dry or wet, cold or warm, crystal form, moisture content and so forth. Some forms of dry but cold snow bonds to shallower slopes, while wet and warm snow can stick to very steep surfaces also. Particularly, in coastal mountains (e.g. Cordillera del Paine region of Patagonia) deep snow packs accumulate on vertical and even overhanging rock surfaces.

The snow acceleration also can be determined by the angle of slope, which depends again on a variety of factors such as the snow's shear strength (which is itself dependent upon crystal form) and the configuration of layers and inter-layer interfaces.

As discussed above, the start zone of an avalanche must be steep enough to allow snow to accelerate. However, we can notice that the convex slopes are less stable than concave slopes, because of the tensile and compressive strengths between the snow layers. Thence the composition, shape and structure of the ground surface under the snowpack can also influence the stability of the snowpack, either being a source of strength or weakness. In addition to the above, the following points are noteworthy in the case of avalanche formation.

Slopes flatter than 25° or steeper than 60° have a lower incidence of avalanches.

- Human-triggered avalanches have the greatest incidence when the snow's *angle of repose* is 35-45°
- The critical angle, the angle at which human-triggered avalanches are most frequent, is 38°.
- When the incidence of human triggered avalanches is normalized by the rates of recreational use, however, hazard increases uniformly with slope angle, and no significant difference in hazard for a given exposure direction can be found.

Whatsoever, the rule of thumb is: *A slope that is flat enough to hold snow and steep enough to skid has the potential to generate an avalanche, regardless of the angle.*

7.4.4 Effect of Snowpack Structure and Characteristics

After ice-stuck surface is buried by snowfall, the buried ice layer can weaken upper layers to slide. The snowpack is composed of ice layers parallel to ground that agglutinate over the winter. The particles of each layer gain distinct meteorological conditions during the snow formation.

Now, if an avalanche occurs, it indicates that the snowpack has a weak unstable layer below the slab of cohesive snow. The structural factors of snowpack such as penetration resistance, grain size, grain type, temperature can be used as index to measure the established mechanical properties of the snow e.g. tensile strength, friction coefficients, shear strength, and ductile strength.

A powder snow avalanche in the Himalayas near Mt. Everest

After an avalanche, the newly fallen snow needs certain time to bond with the snow layers beneath it, particularly during very cold and dry situations. If the air temperature is sufficiently cold, the shallow snow (around rocks & plants) in the slope weakens from rapid crystal growth.

A cornice of snow about to fall. Observe the cracks in snow in area (1) and the area (3) falls, leaving area (2) as the new edge.

Avalanche path with 800 m (2,600 ft) vertical fall in the Glacier Peak Wilderness, Washington. A cornice of snow about to fall. Observe the cracks in snow in area (1) and the area (3) falls, leaving area (2) as the new edge.

The crystal structure and shape also play a significant role here. Large, angular snow crystals have lesser bonds per unit volume than small, rounded crystals that pack tightly together. Consolidation of snow is an essential condition for the occurrence of slab avalanches, but such snow is less likely to flow than loose powdery layers or wet isothermal snow.

7.4.5 Effect of Weather

Weather plays a vital role in formation of an avalanche. The following common sub-factors of weather can motivate the formation of avalanche.

Modeling of an Avalanche

Prof. Lagotala during preparation for 1924 Winter Olympics in Chamonix attempted to model. In 1955, A. Voellmy modeled On the Destructive Force of Avalanches using a simple empirical formula, treating an avalanche as a sliding block of snow moving with a drag force proportional to the square of the speed of its flow: $f = \frac{1}{2}ñõ^2$. Subsequently other factors are considered by Voellmy-Salm-Gubler and the Perla-Cheng-McClung models

Saltation Theory

In a slab avalanche, as the snow falls downhill, the slab disintegrates into increasingly smaller fragments so small that the outer layer of the avalanche, called a saltation layer, assumes fluid the characteristics. If they form too fine particles, they can become airborne and, accumulation a sufficient quantity of such airborne snow separates from the bulk to travel a greater distance as a powder snow avalanche. The studies after 1999 Galtür avalanche disaster, confirms this saltation theory.

(i) **Season and Geography:** The weather during winter seasons at high latitudes and/or high altitudes is quite motivating. It is cold enough for precipitated snow to accumulate into a seasonal snowpack and can be controlled by the critical factors such as solar heat, radiation and cooling, vertical temperature gradients in standing snow, snowfall amounts, snow types etc. Generally, mild winter weather will favor the settlement and so stabilizes the snowpack, while very cold, windy, or hot weather will weaken the snowpack.

(ii) **Freeze-Melt Cycle:** When there is a moderate solar radiation, the water and ice undergo a freeze-melt cycle, during which the snowpack strengthens in freeze-phase while weakens in melt-phase. During this process, a sudden rise of temperature may motivate an avalanche.

(iii) **Temperature Gradient:** Continuing cold temperatures can either prevent stabilization of new snow or destabilize the existing snowpack and can produce a temperature gradient in the snow with regard to the ground temperature; however, the air temperature can be much colder and when this gradient greater than 10°C variation per vertical meter of snow is persisting for more than a day, then angular crystals known as *depth hoar* or *facets* develop in the snowpack due to rapid moisture transport. The angular crystals have poor cohesiveness as well as poor adhesiveness with the surrounding snow. Thence they create the weakness in the snowpack and can cause an avalanche.

(iv) Wind Speed: Stronger winds boost up snow accumulation rate on sheltered slopes downwind. Thence, wind slab forms so quickly that weaker snow below the slab may not have time to tune to the new load. Even on a clear day also, the slope may be loaded quickly with snow due to wind blow. Here snow deposit occurs either by top-loading or cross-loading depending on wind direction (parallel or perpendicular to the plane of slope).

(v) Snowstorms: Snowstorms and rainstorms are yet other noteworthy contributors to avalanche formation. Snowstorm (Heavy snowfall) causes instability in the existing snowpack because of two reasons

(i) The additional mass adds gravitational force and

(ii) The new snow has insufficient time to bond to underlying snow layers.

(vi) Rainstorm: Rainstorm (heavy rainfall) has a similar effect. In addition to the above two reasons (adding weight and having no time for bonding), it has some more motivators like, hitting the rain drops to act as pointed impact loads; rainwater acts as a lubricant while seeping down through the snow reduces the natural friction between snow layers that holds the snowpack together. It is evident from the experiences that most avalanches occurred during or soon after a storm.

(vii) Sunlight: Sunlight during daytime can destabilize the upper layers of the snowpack rapidly thereby reduces its hardness. During clear nights, the snowpack may re-freeze. The differential radiation heat loss can motivate avalanche formation.

SELF ASSESSMENT INTERMISSION (SAI – 7.2)

1. List out the triggers of an avalanche?
2. What factors motivate an avalanche? Explain briefly.
3. Discuss the effect of terrain on motivating an avalanche?
4. How do snow pack structure and its characteristics affect the avalanche?
5. Explain the effects of weather on occurrence of an avalanche.
6. Explain the factors influencing the avalanche
7. Give short notes on the following terms with reference to an avalanche.
   (a) Freeze-Melt-Freeze Cycle (b) Temperature Gradient
8. Discuss the contribution of the following on an avalanche.
   (a) Snow and Snowstorm (b) Rain and Rainstorm
9. Discuss the contribution of the following on an avalanche.
   (a) Wind speed (b) Sunlight and radiation

7.5 TYPES OF AVALANCHES – THE CLASSIFICATION

There is no universally agreed classification of avalanches— because all avalanches are not alike. Avalanches can be classified by their size, destructive potential, initiating mechanism, composition and dynamics.

7.5.1 Classification based on Snowfall Dynamics

There are two common types of avalanches based on snowfall dynamics.

(a) Surface Avalanche and

(b) Full Depth Avalanche

(a) Surface Avalanche: When a layer of snow with different properties slides over another layer of snow, it is called surface avalanche. For example, when a layer of dry loosely packed snow slides over a dense layer of wet snow.

(b) Full-Depth Avalanche: When an entire snow cover, from the base to the surface, slides over the ground, it is known as full-depth avalanche.

7.5.2 Classification based on Type of Snow

With reference to the type of snow, the avalanches are categorized into the following types

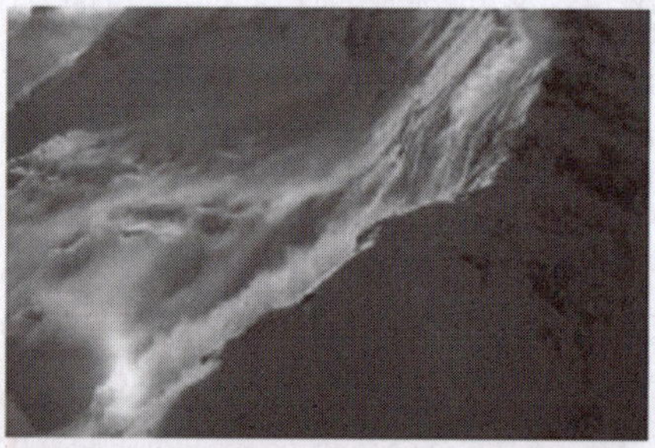

1. Slab avalanche
2. Loose snow avalanche or Powder snow avalanche
3. Wet snow avalanches

One or more also can occur simultaneously. We shall now discuss about these with a little more details.

Slab avalanches

As the name suggests, the slab avalanches have the characteristic appearance of a block (slab) of snow cut out from its surroundings by fractures. These begin as a result of instability and mechanical failure in the snowpack. They form frequently in snow that has been deposited, and re-deposited by wind. Slabs can vary in thickness from a few centimeters to three meters. Typical slab avalanche consists of the following three elements.

- A crown fracture at the top of the start zone,

- A flank fractures on the sides of the start zones, and
- A fracture at the bottom called the staunch wall.

Powder snow avalanches

The loose or powder snow avalanches or mixed avalanches are the largest avalanches that produce turbulent suspension currents composed of a powder cloud. They gradually widen as the forces on the snow exceed its strength. The snow initiation happens with fresh dry powder and once initiated, they move rapidly (>300 kmph speeds) accumulating with large mass and volume (about 10 million tons). While the avalanche moves fast enough, some of the snow mixes with the air and flows long distances along flat valley bottoms and even uphill for shorter distances.

Wet snow avalanches

In contrast to above (powder snow avalanches), these are low speed (about 10–40 kmph) suspensions of snow and water limited to the track. Perhaps! The low speed is attributed to the friction between the sliding surface of track and water saturated flow. Even though the speed of travel is low, these can generate powerful destructive forces owing to the large mass, and density. In fact, the flow can plough through soft snow and can scour boulders, earth, trees, and other vegetation. Often the scored ground in the avalanche track can be identified after the flow. They may be initiated from either loose snow or slab releases, but only occur in snow packs by water saturated and isothermally equilibrated to the melting point of water. These usually occur at the end of the winter season, that too, when there is significant daytime warming.

7.6 AVALANCHE HAZARD ANALYSIS AND RISK MEASUREMENT

The hazard level of an avalanche can be tested by the following two most popular methods

1. Rutsch Block Test (In German language, Rutsch means Slide)
2. Snow Pack Test

These are briefly described here below.

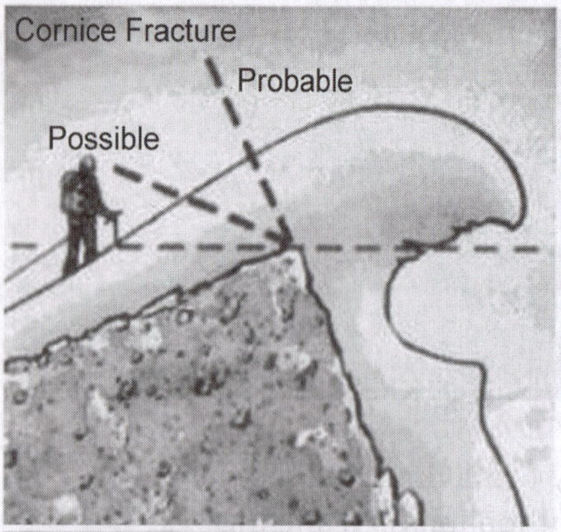

A crown fracture from a slab avalanche near the Neve Glacier in the North Cascades mountains. Extensive fracture propagation is evident

7.6.1 Rutsch-block Test

Slab avalanche hazard analysis can be done using the Rutschblock Test. A 2 m wide block of snow is isolated from the rest of the slope and progressively loaded. The result is a rating of slope stability on a seven step scale.

7.6.2 Snow Pack Test

Snow-pack test is very easy to conduct. Simply cut a square slab of snow and check the pack for layers by a shovel. If snow breaks on stepping on it, then avalanche danger is high. The snow pack test can give a fair understanding on…

- recent avalanche activity,
- fresh snow drifts and
- large snow masses and
- the accumulation pattern

The snow packing is determined by…

- depth of each footstep,
- cornice build up and
- wind patterns

7.6.3 Avalanche Risk Measurement

The avalanches are often described by the type of slope/gradient. The following names are generally used.

- *Gentle slope:* < 30°
- *Steep slope:* > 30°
- *Very steep:* > 35°
- *Extremely steep slope:* >40°

European avalanche risk table

In Europe, the avalanche risk is rated on the following scale, adopted in April 1993. Most avalanche deaths occur at risk levels 3-4 in France, while 2-3 in Switzerland.

Loose snow avalanches (far left) and slab avalanches (near center) near Mt Shuksan in North Cascades mountains. Fracture propagation is relatively limited.

15cm deep, soft slab avalanche near Heliotrope Ridge, Mt Baker in March 2010. Multiple crown fracture lines are visible in the top-middle. The foreground granular debris is due to the slab breaking up during descent.

North American Public Avalanche Danger Scale

Avalanche danger is determined by the likelihood, size and distribution of avalaches.

Danger Level		Travel Advice	Likelihood of Avalanches	Avalanches Size and Distribution
5 Extreme	4 5	Avoid all avalanche terrain.	Natural and human-triggered avalanches certain	Large to very large avalanches in many areas.
4 High	4 5	Very dangerous avalanche conditions. Travel in avalanche terrain not recommended	Natural avalanches likely; human-triggered avalanches very likely.	Large avalanches in many areas; or very large avalanches in specific areas.
3 Considerable	3	Dangerous avalanche conditions. Careful snowpack evaluation, cautious route-finding and conservative decision-making essential.	Natural avalanches possible; human-triggered avalanches likely.	Small avalanches in many areas; or large avalanches in specific areas; or very large avalanches in isolated areas.
2 Moderate	2	Heightened avalanche conditions on specific terrain features. Evaluate snow and terrain carefully; identify features of concern.	Natural avalanches possible; human-triggered avalanches possible.	Small avalanches in specific areas; or large avalanches in isolated areas.
1 Low	1	Generally safe avalanche conditions. Watch for unstable snow on isolated terrain features.	Natural and human-triggered avalanches unlikely.	Small avalanches in isolated areas or extreme terrain.

Safe backcountry travel requires training and experience. You control your own risk by choosing where, when and how you travel.

European avalanche size table

Size	Run-out	Potential Damage	Physical Size	
			Length (m)	Volume (m^3)
1 - Sluff	Small snow slide that cannot bury a person, though there is a danger of falling.	Unlikely, but possible risk of injury or death to people.	<50	<100
2 - Small	Stops within the slope.	Could bury, injure or kill a person.	<100	<1,000
3-Medium	Runs to the bottom of the slope.	Could bury/ destroy a car/ truck, small buildings or break trees.	<1,000	<10,000
4 - Large	Runs over flat areas (<30°) of at least 50 m in length, may reach the valley bottom.	Could bury/ destroy large trucks or trains, large buildings/ forested areas.	>1,000	>10,000

American and Canadian classification of Avalanche Danger Scale

In the US and Canada the following avalanche danger scale is used.

Destructive Potential		
Size	**Canadian**	**American**
1	Relatively harmless to people.	Sluff/snow slides <50m (150') of slope distance.
2	Could bury, injure or kill a person.	Small, relative to path.
3	Could bury/destroy a car, damage a truck, destroy a small building or break a few trees.	Medium, relative to path.
4	Could destroy a railway car, large truck, several buildings or a forest area up to 4 hectares.	Large, relative to path.
5	Could destroy a village or a forest of 40 hectares (Largest).	Major or maximum, relative to path.

Risk Level	Snow Stability	Flag	Avalanche Risk
1 - Low	Generally very stable.		Unlikely until heavy loads are applied on extreme steep slopes. Any spontaneous avalanches will be minor. In general, safe conditions.
2 - Limited	Only moderately stable on some steep slopes, very stable elsewhere.		May be triggered if heavy loads are applied on a few generally identified steep slopes. Large spontaneous avalanches are not expected.
3 - Medium	Only moderately or weakly stable on many steep slopes.		May be triggered on many slopes even if light loads are applied. On some slopes, medium or even large spontaneous avalanches may occur.
4 - High	Not very stable on most steep slopes.		Likely on many slopes even if light loads are applied. In some places, many medium or sometimes large spontaneous avalanches are likely.
5-Very High	Generally unstable.		Even on gentle slopes, many large spontaneous avalanches are likely to occur. https://en.wikipedia.org/wiki/Avalanche

7.7 AVALANCHE PREVENTIVE MEASURES AND MITIGATION

Preventive measures are very much necessary in areas where avalanches set a significant threat to people, such as ski resorts, mountain towns, roads, and railways. There are many ways to forestall the avalanches and reduce their effect or destruction, which can be classed into two kinds ***active*** and ***passive***.

- The active preventative measures can reduce the likelihood and size of avalanches by disrupting the structure of snowpack, while passive measures reinforce and stabilize the snowpack in situ.
- As we know, the avalanches occur in three stages as ***snow accumulation, snow failure and snow flowing***, the preventive measures also may be planned to prevent or stop these three activities.
- To prevent or reduce snow accumulation, the simplest active measure is to travel on a snowpack repeatedly as snow accumulates. This can be achieved by means of
    - boot-packing,
    - ski-cutting, or
    - machine grooming.
- Explosives extensively prevent avalanches, by triggerring smaller avalanches that break down instabilities in the snowpack and remove overburden that may produce a large avalanche.
- Explosives may be thrown manually by hand, or bombing by a helicopter, or by ballistic projectiles launched by cannons or any other suitable method.
- Passive preventive systems can be used to restrict or redirect the snow flow. For example snow fences and light walls restrict or redirect falling snow.
- If adequate density of trees is present, they can greatly weaken the avalanche. Therefore, the best mitigation plan, prevention and protection from an avalanche is growing appropriate trees in the predicted avalanche tracks,.

Danger of Avalanche = Danger of Death

After one hour, only 1/3 victims who are buried in an avalanche can be alive. The most common cause of death of these victims is asphyxiation (suffocation), wounds and hypothermia.

7.7.1 Mitigation

Precautionary measures can be taken to reduce the damage in many areas, by identifying the regular avalanche tracks and constructing artificial barriers. There are several types of most popular are given below:

- **Snow net:** It is a net strung between poles that are anchored by guy wires in addition to their foundations. These barriers are similar to those used for rockslides.
- **Snow fence:** These are rigid fence-like structures made of steel, wood or pre-stressed concrete. They usually have gaps between the beams and are built perpendicular to the slope, with reinforcing beams on the downhill side. They are costly and vulnerable to damage from falling rocks in the warmer months.
- **Avalanche dams:** These are barriers either landscaped or structures made up of concrete, rocks or earth to stop or deflect avalanches with their weight and strength. They are usually placed above a road or railway track to be protected or channelized into other barriers.
- **Earth mounds:** These are placed in the avalanche's path to slow it down.
- **Snow sheds:** Large shelters built directly in the slide path of an avalanche to protect traffic from avalanches.

O My God!

Noise Doesn't Cause Avalanche?

A very popular myth is that louder noises cause avalanches, but do not usually. The pressure of someone or something that makes the noise usually causes them but not the noise.

7.7.2 Survival, Rescue and Recovery

The simplest way to avoid getting caught in an avalanche is to recognize where it is most likely to occur. Once understood the high possibilities of an avalanche, and if its track is identified, then it is less likely to fall victim. Most avalanche tracks are obvious, appearing as an open slope, bowl or gully shape. Other common are bent or damaged trees.

Avalanche accidents can be described under 2 categories. This distinction is motivated by the observed difference in the causes of avalanche accidents in the 2 settings.

- Accidents in recreational settings, and
- Accidents in residential, industrial and transportation settings.

- In the recreational setting most accidents are caused by the people involved in the avalanche. In a 1996 study, Jamieson found that 83% of all avalanches in the recreational setting were caused by those who were involved in the accident.
- In contrast, all of the accidents in the residential, industrial, and transportation settings were due to spontaneous natural avalanches.

Disastrous avalanches occur when massive slabs of snow break loose from a mountainside and shatter like broken glass as they race downhill. These moving masses can reach speeds of 130 kmph (80mph) within 5s. Victims caught in these events seldom escape.

Avalanches are most common within 24 hrs of a storm when dumps >30 cm of fresh snow, because the quick pileup overloads the underlying snowpack, and weakens layer beneath the slab to fracture. The layers are an archive of winter weather: Big dumps, drought, rain, a hard freeze, and more snow. Thus, storminess, temperature, wind, slope steepness and orientation (the direction it faces), terrain, vegetation, and general snowpack conditions are all factors that influence whether and how a slope avalanches. The intensity of avalanche depends on the various combinations of these factors.

If caught in an avalanche, try to get off the slab. In most instances, this is not easy. Skiers and snowboarders can head straight downhill to gather speed, then try to move left or right out of the slide path. Snowmobilers can punch the throttle to power out of harm's way.

- No escape? Reach for a tree.
- No tree? Swim hard.
- The human body is 3 times denser than avalanche debris and will sink quickly.
- As the slide slows, clear air space to breathe. Then punch a hand skyward.
- Once the avalanche stops, it settles like concrete.
- Bodily movement is nearly impossible.
- Wait and hope for a rescue.
- Statistics show that
  - About 93% of avalanche victims survive if dug out within 15 min.
  - The survival rates drop fast after 15 min.
  - After 45 min, only 20-30% of victims are alive.
  - After 2hrs, very few people survive.

7.7.3 Some Facts about Avalanches

- Avalanches can reach speeds of up to 250 mph and 80 miles/hr. within about 5 seconds
- Most avalanches occur 30° - 45°, on a slope that faces the north, east and northeast directions
- Mountains, heavily forested are safer areas from avalanche occurrence.
- 89% of victims are males aged 20's and are generally skiers, snowmobilers, or climbers
- Only a few seconds after an avalanche the snow quickly turns into ice, freezing hard as cement.
- The US ranks 5th in the world for avalanche danger.
- The deadliest avalanche reported in American history was in Feb 1910, in Washington's Cascade Mountains, the avalanche swept trains away and killed 100 people.
- Loose snow avalanches account for only a small percentage of deaths and property damage. "Slab" avalanches (the most lethal) are cohesive plates of snow sliding as a unit.
- Each year avalanches kill more than 150 people worldwide.
- In 90 % avalanche accidents, the victim or someone in the victim's party causes the snow slide.
- Avalanches are caused by noise, but by the four factors: a steep slope, snow cover, a weak layer in the snow cover and a trigger.
- Avalanche risk is at its greatest 24 hrs, if followed by a snowfall of 30 cm (12 in) or more.

SELF ASSESSMENT INTERMISSION (SAI – 7.3)

1. Define an avalanche and classify according to snowfall dynamics and type of snow.
2. Describe different types of avalanches based on the type of snow
3. Explain how an avalanche can be tested?
4. What is Rustch Block test? Which feature of avalanche do you measure with this test? How?
5. What is snowpack test? What does it infer about an avalanche?
6. Write a note on Avalanche –Hazard Analysis?
7. Discuss about avalanche risk measurement. How do the US, Canada and European countries evaluate the risk of avalanches?
8. Briefly describe the various methods of avalanche mitigation?
9. Give some suggestions for survival, rescue and recovery for avalanche victims.

7.8 BLIZZARD

Some children left their homes for school happily saying Goodbye to their parents…

Some children cried that they don't want to go to school but were sent forcefully…

Some for playing with their friends… some for learning from their teachers…

The weather was pleasant….

Some went to attend the office duty, and some to the factories.

Whatsoever, public started from their homes to the town to enjoy the warmth of the day whether with working or otherwise.

But, all of a sudden, the warmer weather turned out chilled. Within a short while, strong winds started blowing. Not in night nor a dawn nor dusk, but during school hours, the cold front began to pour a powdery snow, with no time reduced the visibility, even on the open plains to zero. The storm raged… and smashed…

As a result, thousands of people—including many school children—got caught. Oh... My God! Was it a snowstorm!

No, it was blizzard! The Schoolhouse Blizzard of 1888, N American Great Plains. Jan 12–13, 1888.

O My God!

1. The first blizzard to be declared a Federal Emergency (in USA) was in 1977, affecting upstate NY and S. Ohio. The storm's accumulation was only about 12 in over 5 days, but the winds were deadly.
2. Rochester, NY is the largest city with the most snow in the US, accumulating an average of 94 in of snow every year.

Exactly after 3 months, more or less another one hit in similar lines. But it was on sailors, on Mar 11–13, 1888, one of the most severe recorded blizzards in the history of the US. On Mar 12, an unexpected northeaster buried New England and the mid-Atlantic, dropping up to 130 cm (50 in) of snow in just two days. It is named Great Blizzard of 1888, victimized thousands of people with claiming about 400 deaths, including many sailors aboard vessels by gale-force winds and turbulent seas. Believe it or not! In some parts of NY City, snowdrifts reached up to the second story of some buildings.

The history of US witnessed another fury of the nature, right on its heart, the capital city Washington D.C. and many more mega cities of US. An extremely unusual blizzard, named as Great Blizzard of 1899 attacked during 11–14, Feb on the far southern states of America including area in and around Washington, D.C., which experienced 51 hrs straight of snowfall. The port of

New Orleans was totally iced over. Nebraska reached “47 °F (“44 °C), Ohio experienced “39 °F (“39 °C), Louisiana bottomed out at “16 °F (“27 °C), and Florida dipped below 0 to “2 °F (“19 °C).

7.8.1 What is a Blizzard?

We know that what a snowstorm is. If this snow fall (snowstorm) is severe, that too, for a long period, then it is a blizzard. Thus blizzard is can be considered as a type of snowstorm. So, a ***blizzard*** is a severe snowstorm with strong sustained winds lasting for a prolonged period of time. We have another term, often get confused is ***ground blizzard.*** This is a weather condition where snow is not falling but loose snow on the ground is lifted and blown by strong winds.

Thus a blizzard is a natural disaster associated with

- strong winds and
- cold temperatures

Poor visibility due to snow blows (Characteristic of blizzard)

7.8.2 The Concept and Characteristics of Blizzard

A blizzard can be differentiated from a snowstorm with the strength of the wind, but not the amount of snow. To be a blizzard, a snowstorm must fulfill the following characteristics

- sustained winds or frequent gusts
- blowing or drifting snow
- wind speed 56 km/h (35 mph) or more
- reduced visibility to less than 400 m (0.25 mi)
- must last for a prolonged period - typically 3 or more hrs.

A severe blizzard has

- winds over 72 km/h (45 mph),
- nearly zero visibility, and
- Temperatures of -12 °C (10 °F) or lower.

Blizzards in Antarctica are associated with winds spilling over the edge of the ice plateau at an average velocity of 160 km/h (99 mph).

7.8.3 Blizzard and Ground Blizzard

Ground Blizzard is a weather condition when loose snow or ice on the ground is lifted and driven by strong winds. The primary difference between ground blizzards as opposed to a regular blizzard is that in a ground blizzard no precipitation is produced at the time, but rather all the precipitation is already present in the form of snow or ice at the surface.

7.8.4 When/How Does Blizzard occur? (Causes for Blizzard)

A blizzard is experienced in the higher latitudes where cold winds from the poles moves south and warm winds from the tropics moves north.

In order to form a blizzard, the following 3 main things must come together.

1. First, the air must be cold enough for snow to form. We also need moisture from water vapor since the cold air and water vapor create the snow.
2. Second, we need lift — warm air must rise over cold air. This occurs when the wind pulls warm air from equator towards poles, and cold air from poles towards equator.
3. The third is when warm and cold air meet, a front is formed which results in high winds and participation.

(Top) March blizzard-N' Dakota, 1966. (Middle) Blizzard whiteout-Minnesota, Mar 1, 2007 (Bottom) Drifted snow near Lancashire, UK, Jan 1963

7.8.5 Where Do Blizzards Occur?

The areas in USA and Canada are highly prone to blizzards. In the US, the places most prone are the plains states and provinces, the Great Lakes region, and the Northeastern U.S., Gulf of Mexico, Texas Panhandle and Canadian Maritimes. Blizzards over the plains often form when dry northern air collides with warm, humid southern air while the stream causes cold. In northeast, they come from hurricane force moving down from northern Atlantic Ocean and are so named Nor'easters.

7.8.6 Blizzards and Snowstorms in US

In the US, particularly, Great Plains, the Great Lakes states, and the northeastern states along the coast, blizzards often occur since the cold, dry polar air from the north to south clash with warm, humid air moving up from the south to north. These are less common in the Pacific Northwest as cold, moist air from the Pacific Ocean moves eastward to the Rocky Mountains and the Great Plains, and warmer, moist north from the Gulf of Mexico, all that is needed is a movement of cold polar air moving south to form potential blizzard conditions that may extend from the Texas Panhandle to the Great Lakes and also Hudson Bay, Southeast and New England of Canada.

Low pressure systems of the Rocky Mountains onto the Great Plains, can cause thunderstorms and rain to the south and heavy snows and strong winds to the north. These are highly vulnerable to blizzards with very low temperatures and whiteout conditions with no visible horizon. [People can become lost in their own front yards, when the door is only 3 m (10 ft) away, and they would have to feel their way back. Motorists have to stop their cars where they are, as the road is impossible to see].

7.8.7 Nor'easter – A Special Case of Blizzards

A nor'easter blizzard or simply nor'easter is a macro level storm along the East coast of US and Atlantic Canada. The name is so given by the virtue of the direction the wind coming from. The usage of the term in N America comes from the wind associated with many different types of storms some of which can form in the N Atlantic Ocean while some other form in south at the Gulf of Mexico. The term is most often used in the coastal areas of New England and Atlantic Canada.

This type of storm is similar to a hurricane in its characteristics. More specifically it depicts a low-pressure area with center of rotation at the East Coast and leading winds in the left-forward quadrant rotate onto land from the northeast. If the storm is huge, it may even sink ships at sea and cause coastal flooding or/and beach erosion.

The Great Blizzard of 1888, is the notable Nor'easter and one of the worst blizzards in US history. It drifted 1–1.3 m (40–50 in) of snow and had sustained winds over 45 mph (72 km/h) that produced snowfall more than 50ft (15 m). Rail/roads were shut down, kept people house arrested for up to a week and consumed about 400 lives, mostly in NY.

7.9 EFFECTS OF BLIZZARDS

Large amounts of snow may be drifted during sever cold. Thus wind chills occur during blizzards. The wind chill factor is the amount of cooling the human body feels due to the combination of wind and temperature. These wind chills can result in

- Hypothermia or
- Frost bite
- Breathing difficulties

The other effects include

- Extremely low temperatures have an effect on plant life too.
- Skin exposed to such severely cold condition can lose all sensitivity within minutes.
- Traffic and communication is severely disrupted.
- Power lines can collapse under the weight and power of the wind and snow.
- Food and water shortage can result if the blizzard is sustained over a long duration.
- Medical emergencies are very difficult to attend to during a blizzard.
- The visibility drops to less than 400 m during a blizzard and can lead to road accidents.
- Blizzards that last a long time can wreak havoc on life and property.
- Sometimes it may not snow during a blizzard but the snow on the ground is whipped up by sustained winds leading to poor visibility and life threatening conditions.

Blizzards can bring *whiteout* conditions for days at a time. Its effect is felt more at the places where snowfall is unusual or rare.

O My God!

Armistice Day Blizzard Was Sudden?

Took place on Armistice Day, Nov 10–12, 1940 in 1600-km-wide path (1000 mi) through the middle of US from Kansas to Michigan. The morning of the storm was warm but by midday conditions quickly changed to severe blizzard that lasted to the next day claiming 145 deaths, 1/3rd of them duck hunters who wanted to take advantage of ideal hunting conditions. Forecasters could not predict and so the hunters were not dressed ready for cold weather. When the storm started they took shelter on small islands in the Mississippi River, and the 80 km/h (50 mph) winds and 1.5-m (5 ft) waves in the single-digit temperatures moved in overnight froze them to death.

Iran Blizzard at Tochal Skiing resort, Tehran.

7.10 NOTEWORTHY BLIZZARDS

The following are some of the noteworthy blizzard events in the history.

O My God!

On Mar 29, 1881, snowdrifts in Minnesota (higher than train)

The winter of 1880–81 is the most severe winter ever known in US. Many children—and their parents—learned of "The Snow Winter" through the children's book "The Long Winter", by Laura Ingalls Wilder, in which the author tells of her family's efforts to survive. The snow arrived in Oct 1880 and blizzard after blizzard throughout the winter and into Mar 1881, causing many areas snowbound through entire winter. As was impassable Chicago and NW Railway stopped trains until the spring thaw

O My God!

November Gale, X-mas Blizzard & Super Bomb? **November Gale** (Nov 7–10), also called Great Lakes Storm of 1913, was the deadliest and most destructive ever to hit in Midwestern US and the Canadian province of Ontario, with 140km/h (90mph) wind gusts, waves 11m (35ft) high, and whiteout snow squalls, killed >250, destroyed 19 ships, and stranded 19 including *SS Edmund Fitzgerald*

N. American **Christmas day blizzard** of 1947 (Dec 25–26) was a record-breaking snowfall brought Northeast US to a standstill. No high winds, but snow fell steadily, drifts reaching 3.0 m (10 ft) killed 77.

Great Blizzard of 1978 (Jan 25–27), also called **Cleveland Super-bomb** was one of the worst snowstorms. Wind gusts approached 160 km/h (100 mph), causing snowdrifts to reach heights of 7.6 m (25 ft) in some areas, making roadways impassable.

7.10.1 1972 Iran Blizzard

The 1972 Iran Blizzard, caused > 4,000 deaths, was the deadliest blizzard in records. About 26 ft (7.9 m) of snow, completely covered 200 villages. After a snowfall lasting nearly a week, an area the size of Wisconsin was entirely buried in snow.

7.10.2 The Snow Winter of 1880–1881

The October blizzard brought snowfalls up to the 2nd floor windows of a building. No one was prepared for the deep snow so early in the season and farmers all over the region were caught before their crops had even been harvested, their grain milled, or with their fuel supplies for the winter in place. By January the train service was entirely suspended. [Railroads hired many men to digging out the tracks was a futile effort: No sooner than they had finished shoveling a stretch of line, a new storm attacked, piling up the line left their work useless].

There were no winter thaws and on Feb 2, 1881, a 2nd massive blizzard struck that lasted for 9 days. In the towns, the streets were filled with solid drifts to the tops of the buildings and necessitated tunneling for passage about town. Homes and barns were completely covered, compelled farmers to tunnel to reach for feeding their stock.

Finally, when the snow melted in late spring of 1881, the plains were flooded heavily and the massive ice jams clogged the Missouri River and compelling to break the downstream, but resulted in a ravage at downstream areas. Most of the town of Yankton, (now S. Dakota), was wiped off by the river overflow.

7.10.3 The Storm of the Century

Under the weight of snow, a tree falls next to a car in Asheville, N. Carolina

The Great Blizzard of 1993, also known as the Storm of the Century, was one of the largest cyclonic storm and unique for its intensity, massive size and wide-reaching effect. It formed over the Gulf of Mexico on Mar 12, 1993, and dissipated in the N. Atlantic Ocean on Mar 15. Moved through the Gulf of Mexico, before moving into Canada through Central America, it mainly affected the Eastern US and Cuba. Central Alabama and Georgia received 15 to 20 cm (6 to 8 in) of snow while Birmingham, Alabama, received up to 30 cm (12 in) with low pressures of 41cm (16 in). Even the Florida Panhandle reported up to 10 cm (4 in) snow, with hurricane-force wind gusts and record low barometric pressures. Between Louisiana and Cuba, hurricane-force winds produced high storm surges across northwestern Florida, which along with scattered tornadoes killed dozens of people. It caused the loss of electric power to over 10 million customers and consumed total of 310 human lives, including 10 from Cuba. Nearly 40% of the country's that time population experienced the effect directly.

7.11 MITIGATION

1. As blizzard is a severe snow storm with high winds >35 mph and visibility of <1/4 mile for >3 hrs, and can also occur after snowfall when high winds causing whiteouts (fallen snow blowing around) and snowdrifts (huge mountains of snow) and so decrease visibility, stay indoors only with doors and windows closed air-tight.
2. When a blizzard is in the forecast, you may receive a *"Winter Storm Watch,"* which means there is a possibility of a storm taking effect. You could also receive a *"Winter Storm Warning,"* which means a storm is on the way or already taking place.
3. Get prepared no sooner than you hear a storm warning. You probably lose electricity, so stock up on non-perishable foods, and keep your emergency kit ready with blankets, flashlights, extra batteries, and candles beforehand.
4. Travelling by car or on foot is highly discouraged during blizzard conditions. It increases the chance of hypothermia, accident and death.
5. If you must have to travel by car during a blizzard, then possess an emergency aid kit (water, jumper cables, road flares, tow rope, non-perishable snacks it will be very useful in case your car breaks down, you get into an accident, or become stuck in the snow.

6. To avoid hypothermia if caught outdoors during a blizzard, stay hydrated and nourished. Keep blood flowing by moving around. Also build a snow cave to block winds, which reduce your body temperature. And don't eat snow, it will make you colder!
7. While keeping yourself safe, also think about the well-being of your animals by creating an emergency plan (Save Pets).

SELF ASSESSMENT INTERMISSION (SAI – 7.4)

1. Define Blizzard? What is its meaning? Is it a type of snow storm? If not, how is it differentiated?
2. What is ground blizzard? How is different from other common blizzard?
3. Discuss the typical conditions that result in blizzard.
4. Discuss the factors favorable for a snowstorm to occur as a (a) avalanche (b) blizzard.
5. What are the characteristics of a blizzard?
6. Where do blizzards occur? What are the reasons for occurrence at those areas?
7. Why and when does a blizzard occur? What are the favorable conditions for occurrence?
8. What is a Nor'easter? Explain its meaning and concept.
9. What are the ill-effects of blizzards?
10. Describe school children blizzard-1888
11. Give some mitigation tips against blizzard.
12. Why, the Great Blizzrard-1993 is called storm of the century? Discuss.

7.12 TIMELINE OF MAJOR AVALANCHES AND BLIZZARDS

Since the list very big and hundreds of smaller avalanches and blizzards are occurring every year, it may not be advisable to list out all. However, those which made a difference to human life or environment have been given in this text.

7.12.1 Avalanches in History

- In March 1910, two avalanches occurred in the Cascade and Selkirk Mountain ranges;
  (a) Mar 1 the Wellington avalanche claimed 96 deaths in Washington State, USA.
  (b) Mar 4 the Rogers Pass avalanche killed 62 railroad workers in British Columbia, Canada.

- During WW-I (1914-18), about 80,000 soldiers died of avalanches during the mountain campaign in the Alps at the Austrian-Italian front, many of which were caused by artillery fire. And about 10,000 soldiers from both sides died in avalanches of Dec 1916 alone.
- The winter of 1950–51 was called the *Winter of Terror*, since the northern hemisphere about 650 avalanches were recorded in just 3-month period throughout the Alps in Austria, France, Switzerland, Italy and Germany causing about 265 deaths.
- In 1990 an earthquake triggered a huge avalanche that wiped out 43 in the mountain climbing camp on Lenin Peak (now in Kyrgyzstan).
- In 1993, the Bayburt, Üzengili avalanche killed 60 individuals in Turkey.
- In 1999, in Montroc, Chamonix, France, a huge avalanche slid ~300,000 m^3 snow on a 30° slope at 100 kmph (62 mph) speed to claim 12 lives in their chalets under 100,000 tons of snow, 5m (16 ft) deep. The mayor of Chamonix was convicted of second-degree murder for not evacuating the area, but received a suspended sentence.
- Till 1999, the village, Galtur in Austria was thought most safest zone, but an extraordinary avalanche disproved it by taking away 31 lives.

Blizzards in History

United States

- N. American storm complex, Late Nov 2006; Jan 2008; Oct 23–28, 2010; Dec 25–28, 2012; Oct 3–5, 2013
- N. American blizzards – Jan 27–31, 1966; Feb 14–19, 2003 (Presidents' Day Storm II); Jan 20–23, 2005; Feb 11–13, 2006; Feb 12–20, 2007; Mar 6–10, 2008; Dec 16–20, 2009; Dec 22–28, 2009 (Christmas blizzard); Feb 5–6, 2010; Feb 9–10, 2010; Feb 25–27, 2010; Dec 26–29, 2010; Jan 31-Feb 2, 2011; Dec 17–22, 2012; Jan 2015 (Feb 5–6, 2010 blizzard was a Category 3 i.e. "major" nor'easter and severe weather event).
- Nor'easter US Blizzards – Feb 8–10, 1969; Feb 6–7, 1978; Dec 10–12, 1992; Dec 6–7, 2003; Halloween Oct 28-Nov 1, 2011; Nov 7–10, 2012; Feb 7–20 & Mar 6, 2013
- Schoolhouse Blizzard, N American Great Plains, Jan 12–13, 1888 and Feb 19-Mar 6, 2013
- Great Blizzards, Mar 11–13,1888 & Feb 11–14, 1899
- Great Lake Storm, Nov 7–10, 1913
- N Dakota blizzard Mar 15–18, 1920
- Knickerbocker Storm Jan 27–28, 1922 and Dec 25–26, 1947

- Armistice Day Blizzard Nov 10–12, 1940.
- Great Appalachian Storm of Nov 24–30, 1950
- Chicago Blizzard Jan 26–27, 1967; Jan 13–14, 1979
- The Great Storm of 1975 known as the Super Bowl Blizzard or Minnesota's Storm of the Century- Jan 9–12, 1975
- Groundhog Day Gale Feb 2, 1976; and 2011
- Blizzard of January – Jan 28-Feb 1, 1977, Jan 6–10, 1996; Jan 2–4, 1999
- Great Blizzard of 1978 (also called the Cleveland Super bomb) Jan 25–27, 1978.
- 1991 Halloween blizzard Upper Mid-West US, Oct 31-Nov 3, 1991
- Storm of the Century Mar 12–15, '93 caused record impact to south & east US and Cuba.
- April Fool's Day Blizzard Mar 31-Apr 1, '97 US East Coast
- Western Plains winter storms Oct 24–26, 1997
- Colorado Holiday Blizzards (2006–07) Dec 20–29, 2006 Colorado
- Midwest Blizzard 6–8 Dec 2009 (a bomb cyclogenesis affected parts of Canada)
- Southeast US winter storm Jan 25, 2000 North Carolina and Virginia
- Hurricane Sandy Oct 29–31, 2012 caused heavy snowfall and blizzard to West Virginia, Northwest Carolina, and Southwest Pennsylvania
- New Mexico, Texas Blizzard (Goliath Storm) Dec 26–27, 2015

Canada

- Saskatchewan blizzard of 2007 – Jan 10, 2007 Canada

United Kingdom

- Winter of 1946–47 and 1962-63 in UK
- Feb 2009 Great Britain and Ireland snowfall

Other locations

- 1954 Romanian blizzard
- 1972 Iran blizzard
- Winter of 1990–1991 in Western Europe
- 2008 Chinese winter storms
- Winter storms of 2009–2010 in East Asia

MINI-PROJECT / CASE-STUDIES

1. Prepare a short-film or a documentary on avalanche with giving the precautions.
2. Prepare a short-film on blizzard, giving a message to the society.

CHAPTER 8 Cyclone–Hurricane–Typhoon

O'MY SILENT INNER VIBES (O'M S I V – 8)

During the days when the Cyclones, Hurricanes, Typhoons, Tsunamis or Floods were not yet named so, the great disaster (called Maha Pralayam) occurred which deluged the entire world by all those cyclones, rainstorms, hailstorms and floods after a 100 year famine along with drought, and heat waves, and what not (Ref: Matsya Puran).

Even the 'Book of Genesis', reads the cause of Maha Pralaya (the great deluge or disaster) to mankind's destruction as, "God saw that the wickedness of man was high on the earth, and every thought of his heart was only evil continually, which repented the Lord and grieved Him and so said, I will destroy man whom I have created from the face of the earth".

The story of Manu, reads in the similar lines with little variations in Vedas, Matsya Puran, Vishnu puran, Bhaagavatam, Aranya (11th) Parva of Maha Bharat, Agni puran and many more.

Vaivasvata Manu (Vaivasvata is the Sun God and so Manu is treated as Son of Sun) at Mt. Malaya performed tapas (austerity) for thousands of years that pleased Brahma who granted a boon. Manu, who was so concerned of mankind, asked "there will be a total destruction (Maha pralaya) after which the world will no longer exist. Please grant me the boon that I would save the world by regenerating". And Brahma readily granted. (How great humanitarian Manu is!).

At the end of Yuga (epoch) and a Kalpa (aeon equal to Brahma's day), Brahma sleeps in his night and his creation dissolves, submerging the earth and all other worlds in the cosmos in primeval ocean. A danava (demon) called Hayagriva ("horse-faced") steals the sacred Veda texts when they come out of Brahma's mouth when he yawns at the start of his night, fatigued by the creation of universe. He takes them to Pathaal, under ocean. Thence, Lord Vishnu takes the fish incarnation (Matsyavtar) to bring back the Vedas and in the process, He uses Manu to protect when he is tiny fish.

The tiny fish appears while Manu (also known as Satyavrat) was performing his ablutions in a pond. The fish appealed to Manu to protect from a bigger fish and in return promised to rescue Manu from an impending pralayam. Manu kept the fish in a pot first, but the fish grew and so a pit, and then a pond, it grew so quickly that its body occupied the entire ocean to become indestructible, in a matter of days. It was then that The Matsya (the 1st incarnation of Lord Vishnu) revealed his identity to Manu, told him about the impending destruction, and the way to save humanity. Lord Vishnu also informed Manu the time when the great deluge will occur and instructed Manu to build a ship (preparedness to the disaster-the great deluge) and fill it with animals and seeds, the two (male and female) of each kind, to repopulate the earth. (This is also seen in the flood myth from the Old Testament, God who saves Noah by instructing him to build an Ark).

On the predicted day, the devastating ***Cyclones, Rainstorms, Hailstorms and all great disasters followed by floods altogether called Maha Pralayam*** occurs and as the waters rose Manu enters the ship that he built, and also saves the 7-great sages (Saptha Rishis) along with all living species, two (male & female) of each kind. The fish then swam while Manu tied the ship to His horn with the great serpent (interpreted as Adi Sheshu at some places while Vasuki in others) as rope. The fish takes it to safe high grounds of Himalayas and instructs Manu to get off the ship and slowly descend the mountain as the water retreats. Manu does as instructed and performs Yagnya, the sacrificial fire from which he acquires a beautiful woman called Ida, to create Manavas (the generation of Manu). He also creates all beings - gods, demons and men and other movable and immovable things - by the power of his austerities, thence becomes 'the progenitor of this Earth'.

The story of a great Deluge is found in many civilizations across the globe. It is often related to the Genesis narrative of the flood and Noah's Ark. The fish motif reminds through the Biblical 'Jonah and the Whale', and similar flood myths also exist in the tales of ancient Sumer, Babylonia, Greece, the Maya of Americas and the Yoruba of Africa.

Whatsoever, the world will be regenerated after the Kalpanth i.e. after the 4th Yuganth (Kali Yug- the prevailing) as per Hindu myths. As said in Vedas or Book of Genesis, when God repents for creating this mankind due to increased sin, wickedness and the nature of harming the nature, He certainly calls for another Maha Pralayam. May it be Myth or Truth, it is cyclic. A cyclone exemplifies the fact.

SINNERS WILL NEVER BE THE WINNERS

8.1 DEFINITION AND CONCEPT

A cyclone is a rapidly rotating storm over large bodies of relatively warm water at a low-pressure center, associated with strong winds, and a spiral arrangement of thunderstorms that produce heavy rain. Based on location and strength, a tropical cyclone is named differently such as hurricane, typhoon, toophan (tufan), tropical storm (or simply storm), cyclonic storm, tropical depression, or simply cyclone.

8.1.1 Hurricane

The word *hurricane*, is often used in the North Atlantic and Northeast Pacific regions. It is derived from *huracán*, originated from Spanish storm god, Juracán. Another belief is that it derived from Mayan creator god, Huracan who is believed to have created dry land out of the turbulent waters. *Orcan* is another source word for a particularly strong European windstorm.

8.1.2 Typhoon

O My God!

On an average 86 tropical cyclones form annually worldwide, with 47 reaching hurricane/ typhoon strength, and 20 becoming intense tropical cyclones (at least Category 3 intensity on the Saffir–Simpson Hurricane Scale).

The word *typhoon*, is used in Northwest Pacific, which might have been derived from Arabic *tûfân* and also similar in Hindi/Urdu and Persian, which in turn might have been originated from Greek *Typhon*, a monster related to storm in Greek mythology. The related Portuguese word *tufão* is also derived from *Typhon*. The word is also similar to Chinese "táifçng" (fçng = wind), Japanese "taifû" and Korean "taepung".

A hurricane or typhoon is a system with sustained winds of more than 34 m/s (66 kn) or 74 mph (119 km/h). This type of cyclone generally develops a cloud-free spot with lowest atmospheric pressure at the center of circulation called eye. The eye wall size and maximum sustained wind speed for a strong tropical cyclone of hurricane or a typhoon size will measure as shown below.

Description	Metric/SI system	British system
Eye wall	16-80 km	9.9- 50 miles
Max. sustained wind speed	85 m/s (314 km/h)	185 mph (165 kn)

8.1.3 Cyclone

A **cyclone** is a closed, spiral motion of fluid rotating (cyclic) in the same direction as that of the Earth. Thus, it is characterized by inward spiraling winds, which rotate counterclockwise in the Northern Hemisphere and clockwise in the Southern Hemisphere of the Earth*.

[*Perhaps! It is because of the earth's rotation about its own axis. The air or water upon it also would tend to take the direction of whirl in the similar direction. On clear imagination we can visualize and can assign the direction as said above].

Cyclone Catarina, S Atlantic tropical cyclone Mar 26, 2004

An extratropical cyclone near Iceland on Sep 4, 2003 https://en.wikipedia.org/wiki/Cyclone

Tropical Storm 'Franklin', 2005, a strongly sheared tropical cyclone in North Atlantic basin

8.2 THE CYCLONE STRUCTURE AND TERMINOLOGY

Basically, any cyclone generates at a low-pressure area. Therefore, more or less, all the types of cyclones exhibit same structural characteristics. The structure of a cyclone can be better understood by knowing the following keywords.

1. **Cyclone:** A Cyclone is a closed, spiral motion of fluid rotating (cyclic) in the same direction as that of the Earth. It generally moves from Ocean to Earth.
2. **Cyclogenesis:** Cyclogenesis is the development of cyclonic circulation in the atmosphere (a low-pressure area).
3. **Cyclolysis or Anticyclogenesis**: It is opposite of cyclogenesis and is anticyclonic (high-pressure system).
4. **Anticyclone**: Anticyclone is the development of cyclic circulation in the atmosphere (a high-pressure area). It generally moves from Earth to Sea.

5. **Eye:** The center of cyclone generally called *eye*, is the area of lowest atmospheric pressure in the region.
6. **Pressure Gradient:** The pressure difference between the center of the cyclone (eye) and outside the cyclone is known as *pressure gradient force* or simply *pressure gradient*.
7. **Balancing Coriolis Effect by Pressure Gradient:** The pressure gradient near the eye and the force from the *Coriolis Effect* must be approximately balanced; otherwise the cyclone collapses by itself due to the difference in pressure.
8. **Contra Solem (Direction of winds):** Because of the Coriolis Effect, the cfd wind whirl around the cyclone is counterclockwise in the Northern Hemisphere and while it is clockwise in the Southern Hemisphere. Often this cyclonic circulation is referred to as *contra solem*.
9. **Landfall:** *Landfall* is said to have occurred when storm's center has crossed the coastline.

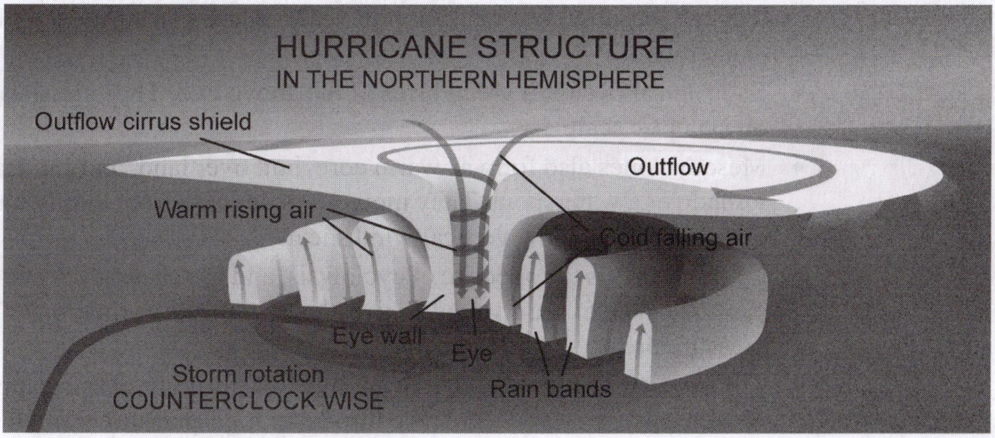

8.3 CYCLOGENESIS – THE FORMATION OF CYCLONE

Cyclogenesis is the development of cyclonic circulation in the atmosphere (a low-pressure area). It can occur at various scales, from the microscale to the synoptic scale. The mechanisms of tropical cyclogeneses are distinctly different from those of mid-latitude cyclogeneses. Tropical cyclogenesis develops through a warm-core cyclone, because of convection in a favorable atmospheric environment.

8.3.1 Requirements for a Tropical Cyclogenesis

Water temperatures of at least 26.5°C (79.7°F) are necessary down to a depth of at least 50 m (160 ft) to destabilize the overlying atmosphere so as to sustain convection and thunder-storms. Tropical cyclones generally form at more than 555 km (345 mi) or 5° of latitude away from the equator, to allow the Coriolis Effect to deflect winds in order to blow toward the low pressure center and create a circulation. The majority of cyclogenesis occurs between 10-30° latitude away of the equator, and 87% forms no farther away than 20° north or south.

Thus there are 6 main requirements for tropical cyclogenesis:

1. Significant warmth in sea surface temperatures,
2. Atmospheric instability,
3. High humidity in the lower to middle levels of the troposphere,
4. Sufficient Coriolis force to generate a low-pressure center,
5. Preexisting low-level focus or disturbance, and
6. Low vertical wind shear.

Summarily, the formations of different kinds of cyclones are as follows.

- Extratropical cyclones take shape as waves along weather fronts. Later they shape up as cold core cyclones. They are found on synoptic scale.
- Tropical cyclone is a latent heat driven, warm core, thunderstorm activity that can be observed on synoptic scale. They can turn up as highly dangerous.
- Subtropical cyclones are hybrids of the above two. They are also found on synoptic scale.
- Mesocyclones also form as warm core, but, over land, and can lead to a tornado or a waterspout. They more often develop from highly unstable environment and low vertical wind shear.
- Cyclogenesis is the opposite of cyclolysis, and has an anticyclonic (high-pressure system) equivalent which deals with the formation of high-pressure areas—Anticyclogenesis.
- The surface low has a variety of ways of forming. Topography can force a surface low when dense low-level high-pressure system ridges in east of a north-south mountain barrier.

Further, cyclones transform from one form to the other among extratropical, subtropical, and tropical phases if right conditions prevail.

8.3.2 Formation

Cyclones form anywhere, but usually between 30 and 60° latitude from the equator, either through cyclogenesis or extra tropical transition.

Extra tropical cyclones occur along linear bands of temperature (or dew point) gradient with significant vertical wind shear, and so described as baroclinic cyclones.

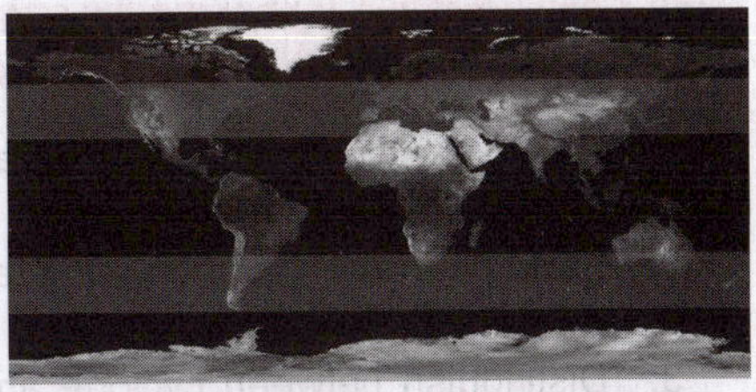

Probable regions of extratropical cyclone formation across world

Initially, cyclogenesis, or low pressure formation, occurs along front zones near a favorable quadrant of a maximum in the upper level jet stream known as a jet streak. The favorable quadrants are usually at the right rear and left front quadrants, where divergence continues.

Due to divergence, air rushes out from the top of the air column and forces convergence in the low-level wind field, thence increases upward motion within the column. This motion causes atmospheric pressure at ground level to lower as the upward air motion counteracts gravity, reducing the weight of the atmosphere at that location. Thus the lowered pressure strengthens the cyclone (a low pressure system).

When the cyclone strengthens, the cold front sweeps towards the equator and moves around the back of the cyclone. Meanwhile, it's associated warm front forwards slowly as the cooler air ahead of the system being denser. Consequently, the cyclone occludes, since the pole-ward portion of the cold front overtakes a section of the warm front, forcing a tongue, or trowel of warm air up. Finally, the cyclone becomes baro-tropically cold and weakens.

3-tropical cyclones of 2006 Pacific typhoon season appeared at different stages of development. The weakest (left) is only in the most basic circular shape. A stronger storm (top right) showed spiral banding and increased centralization, while the strongest (lower right) has developed an eye.

8.3.3 Multiple Storm Interaction - Fujiwhara Effect

Though rare, a 3rd component of motion occurs and involves the interaction of multiple tropical cyclones. When 2 cyclones approach each other, their centers will begin orbiting cyclonically about a point between the 2 systems. Depending on their separation distance and strength, the 2 vortices may orbit around one another or spiral into the center point to merge. When the vortices are of unequal size, the larger vortex will dominate while smaller orbits around it. This phenomenon is Fujiwhara effect, named after Sakuhei Fujiwhara.

SELF ASSESSMENT INTERMISSION (SAI – 8.1)

1. Define Cyclone? What is its meaning? What are its other names? What is its significance in disaster management?
2. Is Hurricane or Typhoon same as Cyclone? If same, why are they named differently? If different, how do they differ?
3. Distinguish between cyclone and anti-cyclone.
4. What is cyclo - genesis? What are the requirements for a tropical cyclo - genesis?
5. Distinguish between cyclogenesis and cyclolysis.
6. Write notes on the following terms under the back drop of cyclones. (a) Coriolis Effect (b) Pressure Gradient (c) Contra Solem (d) Landfall (e) Fujiwhara effect
7. Explain how does a cyclone generate?
8. How do tropical, subtropical and extra-tropical cyclones generate?
9. List out various parts/ components of a cyclone. Discuss briefly.
10. Sketch a structure of hurricane/ cyclone and label it.
11. What is Fujiwhara effect? Explain.

8.4 CHARACTERIZATION OF A CYCLONE

A cyclone can be characterized by the following aspects

1. Cyclonic Wind directions and cyclonic movement
2. Wind Field and Wind circulations
3. Eye and Eye wall
4. Intensity - Wind speeds and radius

We shall now discuss about these aspects.

8.4.1 Cyclonic Wind Direction and Movement

Now, we can characterize a cyclone by two directions of motions viz. the direction of whirlwinds of cyclone and the direction of the cyclone itself. These two motions feature oppositely in the two hemispheres of the Earth.

Let's see how they feature...

In the Northern Hemisphere, the cyclonic motion may be either northward or westward.

Suppose, the cyclone is moving towards north, then the fastest winds of the cyclone relative to the surface of the Earth move towards east side.

If the cyclone is directed towards west, then the winds move towards north. This is opposite in the Southern Hemisphere.

If you can imagine just opposite to the above, they may be called *anticyclones*.

Remember, anticyclone generates at a high pressure area and the wind flow around an *anticyclone* is opposite to that of a cyclone i.e. clockwise in the northern hemisphere, and counterclockwise in the southern hemisphere.

We often get confused between cyclone/anticyclone directions, winds directions, Northern/ Southern hemispheres. These directions and motions are summarized and tabulated here below (Table 8.1) for a better clarity.

Table 8.1 Directions of Cyclone/Anticyclone and Winds in both hemispheres.

Hemisphere	Northern Hemisphere		Southern Hemisphere	
Type/Movement	Cyclonic movement	Winds movement	Cyclonic movement	Winds movement
Cyclone	Northward ↑	Eastward→	Southward↓	Westward←
	Westward←	Northward↑	Eastward→	Southward↓
Anti-cyclone	Southward↓	Westward←	Northward ↑	Eastward→
	Eastward→	Southward↓	Westward←	Northward↑

8.4.1.1 Cyclonic Movement

The movement of a tropical cyclone (i.e. its "track") is typically approximated as the sum of two terms: "steering" by the background environmental wind and "beta drift".

8.4.1.2 Environmental Steering

It is the movement of the storm with the background environment, similar to "leaves carried along by a stream". The tropical cyclone motion is first-order simply as the advection of the storm by the local environmental flow often known as the "steering flow".

8.4.1.3 Beta Drift

In addition to environmental steering, a tropical cyclone will tend to drift slowly poleward and westward, a motion known as "beta drift". This motion is due to the superposition of a vortex, such as a tropical cyclone, onto an environment in which the Coriolis force varies with latitude, such as on a sphere or beta plane. It is induced indirectly by the storm itself, the result of a feedback between the cyclonic flow of the storm and its environment. This effect occurs even if there is zero environmental flow.

8.4.2 Wind Field

The 3-dimensional wind field in a tropical cyclone can be understood by two types of 'circulations' named as "primary" and "secondary". The primary circulation is the rotational part of the flow; it is purely circular. The secondary circulation is the overturning (in-up-out-down) part of the flow; it is in the radial and vertical directions. The primary circulation has the strongest winds and is responsible for the majority of the damage a storm causes, while the secondary circulation is slower but governs the energetics of the storm.

In a tropical cyclone, the near-surface wind field rapidly rotates radially inwards about its central axis. At its outer edge, the air could be almost calm; but will have a non-zero absolute angular momentum because of Earth's rotation. Since the air flows radially inward, by the principle of law of conservation of angular momentum, it rotates cyclonically (counter-clockwise in N. Hemisphere, and clockwise in S. Hemisphere). At the inner radius, air starts moving upward to the top of the troposphere, and interestingly, this radius is coincident with the inner radius of the eyewall. These winds are the strongest near-surface winds, and hence termed as the *radius of maximum winds*. As they move up from the storm's center, they form an axisymmetric shield of cirrus clouds.

Thus the low wind speeds at centre, rapidly increase moving outwards up to the so called 'radius of maximum winds', and then radially decrease more gradually as they move to further larger radii. Further, vertically also, winds are strongest near the surface and decay with height within the troposphere. [In addition, the wind field shows spatial and temporal variability as result of the effects of localized processes, like thunderstorm activity and horizontal flow instability].

8.4.2.1 Primary Circulation: Rotating Winds

In a tropical cyclone, the primary rotating flow is caused due to the conservation of angular momentum by the secondary circulation. Absolute angular momentum on a rotating planet M is given by $M = \frac{1}{2} fr^2 + vr$ where f is the Coriolis parameter, v is the Azimuthal (i.e. rotating) wind speed, and r is the radius about the axis of rotation. The first term $\frac{1}{2} fr^2$ is planetary angular momentum onto the local vertical i.e. the axis of rotation. The second term vr is the relative angular momentum of the circulation itself with respect to the axis of rotation. Since the planetary angular momentum vanishes at the equator (where $f = 0$), tropical cyclones hardly occur within 5° of the equator.

At low levels, air flows radially inward cyclonically so as to conserve the angular momentum. At the same time, near tropopause, the rapidly rotating air flows radially outward. This cyclonic rotation reduces and finally changes sign at large radius, and results in an anti-cyclone at upper-level. Thus, this vertical structure can be characterized as a strong cyclone at low levels while as a strong anti-cyclone near the tropopause. Further, according to principles of hydrostatic and thermal wind balance, this system is warmer at its center than in the surrounding environment at all altitudes (i.e. "warm-core") with the maximum pressure drop at the surface.

8.4.2.2 Secondary Circulation: A Carnot Heat Engine

The energy for a tropical cyclone comes from the evaporation (i.e. latent heat) of water from the ocean surface, which recondenses into clouds and rains when the warm moist air rises and cools to saturation. This energetic system can be considered as a natural and atmospheric Carnot heat engine. This can be described as the four stages here below:

O My God!

A tropical cyclone releases heat energy at the rate of 50 to 200 exajoules (10^{18}J) per day, equivalent to about 10^{15} watt or 70 times the world energy consumption of humans and 200 times the worldwide electrical generating capacity, or to exploding a 10-megaton nuclear bomb every 20 minutes.

1. Inflowing air near the surface acquires (latent) heat via evaporation of water at the temperature of the warm ocean surface (during evaporation, the ocean cools and the air warms).
2. The warmed air rises and cools within the eyewall while conserving total heat content (latent heat is simply converted to sensible heat during condensation).
3. Air outflows and loses heat via infrared radiation to space at the temperature of the cold tropopause.
4. Air subsides and warms at the outer edge of the storm while conserving total heat content. The first and third legs are nearly isothermal, while the second and fourth legs are nearly isentropic.

This 'in-up-out-down' overturning flow, is known as the secondary circulation.

8.4.3 Eye and Eye-wall

The two main parts of the cyclone are eye and eye-wall. Hurricane Isabel (2003) during Expedition 7 of the International Space Station saw the eye, eye-wall surrounded by rainbands as characteristics of tropical cyclones and hence the name.

1. The *eye* is
   (i) produced by suppression of cloud formation due to an air sink in a mature tropical cyclone
   (ii) calm and free of clouds, even though the sea is extremely violent

(iii) normally circular in shape
(iv) about 30–65 km (19–40 mi) in diameter

2. Smallest eye observed is 3 km (1.9 mi) and largest is 370 km (230 mi)
3. The cloudy outer edge of the eye is called the "eyewall"
4. The eyewall expands outwards with height, looks like an arena football stadium, hence often referred to as *stadium effect*
5. At the ***eyewall***
   (i) the greatest wind speeds occur,
   (ii) air rises most rapidly,
   (iii) clouds reach to their highest altitude, and
   (iv) precipitation is the heaviest
6. The heaviest wind damage happens when a tropical cyclone's eyewall passes over land.
7. The eyewall may vary over time in the form of eyewall replacement cycles, particularly in intense tropical cyclones
8. Outer rainbands form an outer ring of thunderstorms that slowly moves inward
9. When the primary eyewall weakens, the tropical cyclone weakens temporarily
10. Eventually at the end of the cycle, the outer eyewall replaces the primary one at which the storm may return to its original intensity.

8.4.4 Intensity

O My God!

Weather Bomb?

During cyclonic conditions, the atmospheric pressure drops quickly if there are strong upper level forces. If these pressures drop >1 millibar/h, the process is called explosive cyclogenesis, and the cyclone is called a weather bomb. The rapid pressure drop in these bombs may go up to 980 millibar under favorable conditions. The stronger the upper level divergence over the cyclone, the deeper will be the cyclone.

Storm "intensity" is defined as the maximum wind speed in the storm, generally taken as 1 or 10-minute average at the standard reference height of 10 meters. Storm size plays an important role in estimating the damage caused by a storm. Storm size is measured in variety of ways in terms of radius such as

- the radius of maximum wind,
- the radius of 34-knot wind (i.e. gale force),
- the radius of outermost closed isobar (ROCI), and
- the radius of vanishing wind

The tropical cyclones occur in a large range of sizes, from 100–2000 km as measured by the radius of vanishing wind. They are largest on average in the northwest while smallest in the northeast of the Pacific Ocean basin. Based on the radius of outermost closed isobar, the cyclones are often named as follows.

Name of Cyclone	Radius of Outermost Closed Isobar	With Reference to Latitude
Very Small or Midget	Less than 222 km (138 mi)	Less than 2°
Average Size	333- 570 km (207-416 mi)	3-6°
Very Large	Greater than 888 km (552 mi)	Greater than 8°

8.5 THE LIFE CYCLE

A cyclone's life cycle is generally 2 to 6 days. The life cycle of a cyclone consists of four stages as follows:

1. Initial stage,
2. Incipient stage,
3. Maturity stage, and
4. Occlusion stage.

8.5.1 The Initial Stage

At this stage, the polar and the tropical air flow on the opposite sides of the polar front blow parallel to the isobars and the front. Here, we find two air masses on the polar front, viz. cold air mass to the north and warm air mass to the south.

The flow of air is from east to west in the cold air mass to the north of the polar front while it is opposite (i.e. from west to east) in the warm air mass to the south of the front, thereby producing the wave disturbance. We can observe a perfect equilibrium that keeps the front quasi-stationary. Here, the wedge of cold air mass lies under the warm air and there is no wind shift. However, along the slant surface of discontinuity (where the opposing air currents meet), there will be a sudden change in the direction of wind, often called *wind-shear*.

8.5.2 The Incipient Stage

In the second stage, a wave forms on the front. Cold air turns to south and warm air to north. The encroachment of each air mass into the domain of the other, influence the pressures to readjust making the isobars almost circular in shape.

A cyclonic circulation begins around a low centre at the apex of the wave. The whole cyclonic vortex moves along with the winds in the warm-air region nearly with the speed of the geostrophic component of the wind. The new depression developing at the crest of the wave is called the *nascent cyclone* and this process of the birth of a new cyclone is often called cyclo - genesis.

8.5.3 The Maturity Stage

At this stage, the intensity of cyclone increases and also the curvature and amplitude of the wave increase. The air in the warm sector begins flowing from the southwest towards the colder air flowing from the southeast. Thus, the cyclone is fully developed.

There are well marked warm and cold sectors. Obviously, the warm air moves faster than the cold air which is in perpendicular direction to the warm front. Strictly speaking, the warm air is moving into a region previously occupied by the cold air. At the rear side of the cyclone, cold polar air under- runs the air of the warm sector, thus generating a cold front. These fronts are convex in the direction of its movement.

There is an ascending air along the entire surface of discontinuity and if the rising air mass is moist, it will be cloudy and precipitates along the warm as well as cold fronts. The precipitation released at the warm front is more widespread and steady, while it is confined to a narrow zone at the cold front. Since the position of the cold front advances faster, the warm sector becomes gradually narrower attaining maximum intensity, which is referred to as the maturity of the cyclone and then the occlusion begins.

8.5.4 The Occlusion Stage

This is the final stage, at which the cold front advances and overtakes the warm front resulting in the formation of an occluded front near the apex of the wave where both warm and cold fronts are closest. Gradually this occlusion comes down to the open part of the two fronts. Thus, the warm portion slowly gets off and finally the two cold air masses mix across the front by which the occluded front gets eliminated leading to diffusion of the cyclone. Generally, the life span of a single frontal cyclone is about 5-7 days.

SELF ASSESSMENT INTERMISSION (SAI – 8.2)

1. Describe the features/aspects that can characterize a Cyclone.
2. Explain the effect of cyclonic wind direction and cyclonic movement on the nature of the cyclone.
3. Distinguish between a cyclone and anti-cyclone with reference to wind directions.
4. What is the significance wind field and wind circulation on characterizing a cyclone?
5. Discuss the terms steering flow and beta drift with reference to cyclones.
6. Explain the effect of rotary winds in characterizing a cyclone.
7. The secondary wind circulation in a cyclone is the great natural Carnot Engine. Explain.
8. What are Eye and Eye-Wall of a cyclone? Explain.

(continued)

9. What is intensity? How does it signify and dignify a cyclone?
10. What is a Weather Bomb? When does it form?
11. Distinguish clearly between the wind movement and cyclone movement.
12. Give the various stages of a Life Cycle of a Cyclone. Explain.
13. Define the terms wind shear and nascent cyclone.
14. List the stages of life-cycle of a cyclone. Explain the maturity stage of a cyclone.

8.6 CLASSIFICATION OF CYCLONES

The cyclones can be studied under two categories as

(i) Cyclones identifiable on synoptic scale – Surface-based Cyclones

(ii) Cyclones not identifiable on synoptic scale – Meso-scale Cyclones

The cyclones that can be identified on synoptic scale are further classified as surface based cyclones, Polar cyclones and TUTT cell. The cyclones which are not identifiable on synoptic scale are called Meso-scale cyclones. The classification of cyclones is diagrammatically shown below:

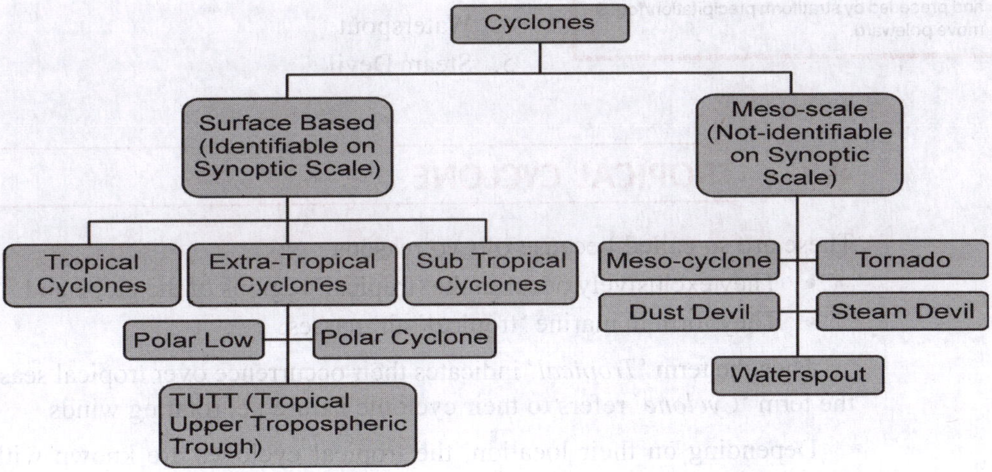

Classification of Cyclones

We shall now discuss these types of cyclones briefly

8.6.1 Surface-Based Types- Identifiable on Synoptic Chart

These cyclones are identifiable in synoptic charts. There are three main kinds of surface-based cyclones:

1. Tropical cyclones
2. Subtropical cyclones
3. Extratropical cyclones
   (a) Polar Low
   (b) Polar Cyclone
   (c) TUTT

> Some interesting/important/noteworthy points about cyclones -
> - Large-scale cyclones are centered on low atm. pressure areas.
> - The largest low-pressure systems are cold-core, called extratropical cyclones which lie on the synoptic scale.
> - Warm-core cyclones like tropical and subtropical cyclones also lie within the synoptic scale.
> - Mesocyclone, tornado & dust devil lie within smaller mesoscale.
> - Upper level cyclones exist without the surface low and form from base of TUTT during summer in N Hemisphere.
> - Extratropical cyclones form as waves in large regions of enhanced mid-latitude temperature contrasts (baroclinic zones).
> - Baroclinic zones contract to form weather fronts when the cyclonic circulation closes and intensifies.
> - Weather fronts separate two air-masses of different densities.
> - Air masses separated by front may differ in temp. or humidity.
> - Strong cold fronts feature narrow bands of thunderstorms and severe weather. They move from west to east.
> - Warm fronts form east of the cyclone center and preceded by stratiform precipitation/fog, & move poleward.

8.6.2 Meso-scale Cyclones- Not-Identifiable on Synoptic Chart

The following are not identifiable on synoptic charts and are hence categorized under meso-scale cyclones.

1. Mesocyclone
2. Tornado
3. Dust Devil
4. Waterspout
5. Steam Devil

8.7 TROPICAL CYCLONE

These are so called because of two reasons

- They exclusively occur in the 'tropical' regions of the globe and
- They form in marine 'tropical' air masses.

Thus the term '*Tropical*' indicates their occurrence over tropical seas, and the term '*Cyclone*' refers to their cyclonic nature i.e. rotating winds

Depending on their location, the tropical cyclones are known with the following names

- Cyclone – South Pacific and Indian Ocean
- Hurricane – Atlantic Ocean
- Typhoon – Pacific Ocean

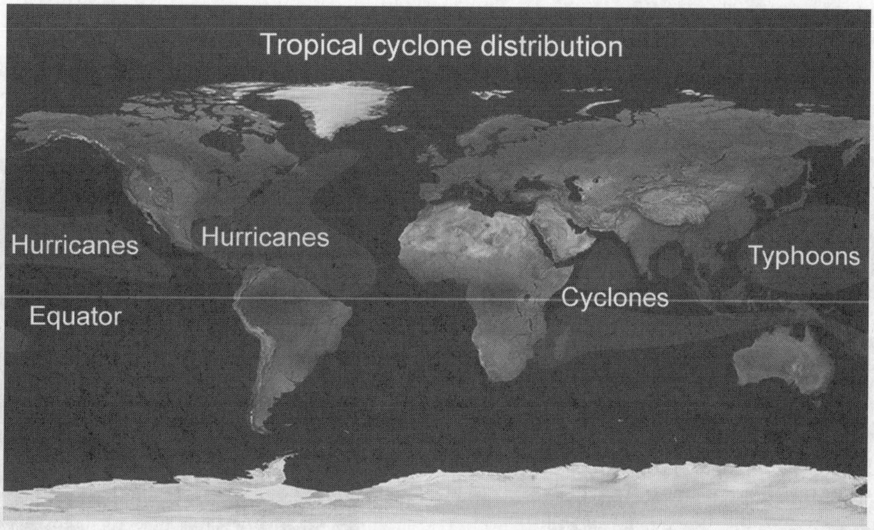

Depending on their strength, these tropical cyclones are known with the following names

- Tropical storm
- Cyclonic storm
- Tropical depression

North Indian Ocean cyclone

South Pacific cyclone

Pacific Typhoon

Atlantic Hurricane

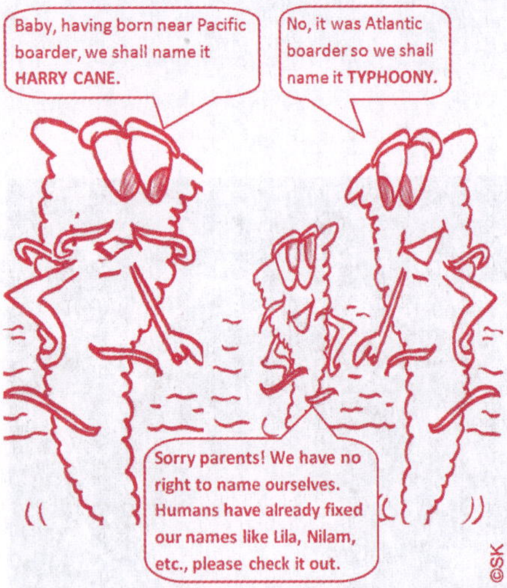

8.7.1 Features/Characteristics of a Tropical Cyclone

- A tropical cyclone generates on large water bodies or oceans of tropical regions only.
- It takes birth at a low-pressure center in heavy water bodies such as oceans.
- It is generally associated with numerous thunderstorms, strong winds and flooding rain.
- The environment at the center of this cyclone is warmer than the surroundings at all altitudes, thence they are called "warm core" systems.
- It occurs when moist air rises, and thence condenses into water vapor due to heat release.
- They form a spiral winds that rotate in counterclockwise direction in the N Hemisphere while clockwise rotation in the S Hemisphere of the globe. (Strictly speaking both are in the same direction as that of the Earth's rotation).
- The opposite direction of circulation is due to the Coriolis Effect.
- The strong rotating winds are due to the conservation of angular momentum imparted by the Earth's rotation as air flows inwards toward the axis of rotation. So, they rarely form within 5° of equator.

- Tropical cyclones have diameter between 100 and 4,000 km (62 and 2,485 mi).
- This energy source varies with regions due to horizontal temperature contrasts.
- In addition to strong winds and rain, tropical cyclones are capable of generating high waves, damaging storm surge, and tornadoes.
- It weakens rapidly over land where they are cut off from their primary energy source.
- Coastal regions are particularly vulnerable to damage from a tropical cyclone as compared to inland regions.
- Heavy rains associated with these cyclones can cause significant flooding inland.
- They can cause storm surges and extensive coastal flooding up to 40 km (25 mi) from the coastline.
- Though their effects on human populations are often devastating, tropical cyclones can relieve drought conditions.
- Heat away from the tropics transport toward temperate latitudes, which can modulate regional and global climate.

8.7.2 Effects of Tropical Cyclones

As discussed above, these cyclones are characterized by extremely powerful winds and hence the following effects may be found.

- They can cause heavy rain fall.
- Heavy rains associated with this kind of cyclones can produce significant flooding inland.
- They are also capable of generating high waves and even damaging storm surge. These storm surges can produce extensive coastal flooding up to 40 km (25 mi) from the coast.
- As they develop over large bodies of warm water, they lose their strength as they move over land.
- The strong winds associated with a tropical cyclone can damage the coastal belt significantly while inland regions are relatively safe since it goes on weakening.
- They can ruin lands, agriculture and even human/animal lives near the coastal areas, the tropical cyclones, bless in disguise, can relieve drought situations inland.

Important to note is that the heat and energy are carried away from the tropics and transported toward temperate latitudes to keep a balance of the global atmospheric circulation mechanism. Thence, tropical cyclones help maintaining equilibrium in the Earth's troposphere.

Many tropical cyclones develop when the atmospheric conditions around a weak disturbance in the atmosphere are favorable. Others form when other types of cyclones acquire tropical characteristics. Tropical systems then move winds in the troposphere and if the conditions favor, the tropical disturbance intensifies to develop an eye. Otherwise, if the conditions deteriorate or the tropical cyclone makes landfall, the system weakens and dissipates.

A tropical cyclone can turn out to be extra-tropical as it proceeds toward higher latitudes when its energy source changes from heat released by condensation to differences in temperature between air masses.

A tropical cyclone is usually does not become subtropical during its extra tropical transition.

Subtropical storm Gustav 2002

Subtropical Storm Andrea in 2007

8.8 SUBTROPICAL CYCLONES

A **subtropical cyclone** has blend of characteristics of tropical and extratropical cyclones. It is a weather system that has some characteristics of a tropical cyclone and some characteristics of an extra-tropical cyclone.

Before 1950s, meteorologists were not clear if the subtropical cyclones are tropical or extratropical cyclones, and used terms such as quasi-tropical and semi-tropical to describe these cyclone hybrids. By 1972, the US National Hurricane Center officially recognized this as a separate cyclone category. Gustav, Sep 9, 2002 Subtropical cyclone in Atlantic Basin is the 1st the official subtropical cyclone of the list.

8.8.1 Features/Characteristics

- They often occur between the equator and the 50th latitude.
- They have broad wind patterns with maximum sustained winds located farther from the center than tropical cyclones.
- They exist in areas of weak to moderate temperature gradient.

- They form initially as extratropical which have colder temperatures higher than normally found in the tropics.
- The sea surface temperatures needed for their formation are lower than the tropical cyclone threshold by 3°C (or 5°F) i.e. lying around 23°C.
- These cyclones are more likely to form outside the traditional bounds of the hurricane season.
- Although subtropical storms rarely have hurricane-force winds, they may become tropical in nature as they are basically warm-core.
- From an operational point of view, a tropical cyclone is usually not considered to become subtropical during its extra-tropical transition.

8.9 EXTRATROPICAL CYCLONE

An **extra-tropical cyclone** is a synoptic scale low-pressure weather system that does not have tropical characteristics. Forecasters and common people describe them as "depressions" or "lows". From space, extra-tropical storms have a characteristic "comma-shaped" or 'English alphabet – e-shaped" cloud pattern.

synoptic chart of an extratropical cyclone at UK and Ireland. The blue arrows between isobars indicate the direction of the wind, http://frbrstore.com/prevailing-westerlies/a-fictitious-synoptic-chart-of-an-extratropical-cyclone-affecting-the-uk-and-ireland-the-blue-arrows-between-isobars-indicate-direction-wind while the "L" symbol denotes the centre of the "low". Note the occluded, cold and warm frontal boundaries.

8.9.1 Features/Characteristics

- This type of cyclone generally occurs outside of the tropics, in the middle latitudes of the planet.
- It is a storm that derives energy from horizontal temperature differences, which are typical in higher latitudes.
- They are also called "mid-latitude cyclones" in view of their area of formation, or "post-tropical cyclones" where extratropical transition has occurred.
- These are almost daily occurring phenomena which along with anti-cyclones, drive the weather over much of the Earth.
- These are associated with fronts and horizontal gradients in temperature and dew point known as "baroclinic zones".

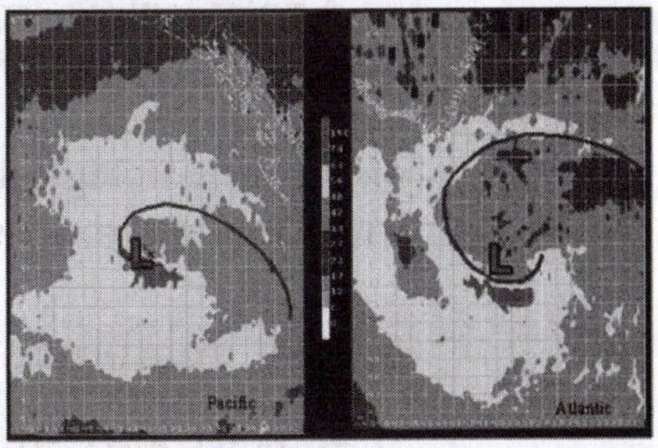

Extra-tropical cyclones over the ocean

Cyclone Catarina (not Katrina) is the 1st recorded South Atlantic cyclone on Mar26, 2004, struck South Brazil with winds of Category 2 on Saffir-Simpson Hurricane Scale. In fact, it was initially felt as extratropical, but later classified as tropical.

- Although these are always classified as baroclinic since they form along zones of temperature and dew point gradient within the westerlies, they can sometimes become barotropic late in their life cycle when the temperature distribution around the cyclone becomes fairly uniform with radius.
- A tropical cyclone can transform into extratropical as it moves toward higher latitudes, if its energy source changes from heat released by condensation to differences in temperature between air masses
- Though not frequently, an extratropical cyclone can transform into a subtropical storm, and from there into a tropical cyclone, if it dwells over warm waters and develops central convection, which warms its core.
- Extratropical cyclones can also be dangerous if their low-pressure centers cause powerful winds over high seas.
- *Nor'easter* is a typical extratropical cyclone occurs during wintertime.

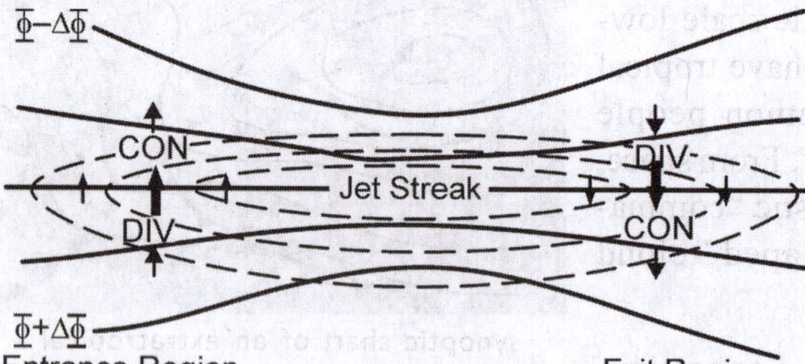

Line diagram showing formation of an extra tropical cyclone.

8.10 POLAR LOW

Polar lows are also known with names Polar Mesoscale Vortex, Arctic Hurricane, Arctic Low and Cold Air Depression. (Now-a-days the term 'polar low' is used for the more vigorous systems with near-surface winds of at least 17 m/s).

A polar low is a small-scale, short-lived atmospheric low-pressure system (depression) found over the ocean areas pole-ward of the main polar front in both the Northern and Southern Hemispheres. Polar lows were first identified on the meteorological satellite imagery that became available in the 1960s, which revealed many small-scale cloud vortices at high latitudes.

8.10.1 Features and Characteristics

- Polar lows are cold-core and hence may be treated as a subset of extratropical cyclones.

- Also, they are part of the larger class of mesoscale weather systems.
- During winter, if cold-core lows in the mid-levels of the troposphere reach "45°C ("49°F) they move over open waters leading to a polar low due to deep convection.
- During the winter, the most active polar lows can be seen over certain ice-free sea areas near the Arctic (e.g. Norwegian Sea, Labrador Sea and Gulf of Alaska).
- Polar lows while they make landfall dissipate rapidly.
- Southern (Antarctic) systems are relatively weaker than their northern counterparts because of the smaller variations of air-sea temperature around the continent.
- Though weak, vigorous polar lows are seen over the Southern Ocean.
- They can move horizontally for more than 1,000 km (620 mi).
- They persist for not more than two days.
- It is difficult to detect them using conventional weather reports and so hazardous to high-latitude operations, such as shipping and gas and oil platforms.

Polar low over the Barents Sea on Feb 27, 1987

Subtropical Storm Andrea in 2007

8.11 UPPER LEVEL TYPE

Under upper level type, we come across to kinds of cyclone viz - Polar cycloner and TUTT. We shall now discuses about these.

8.11.1 Polar Cyclone

Polar Cyclone is also known as **Sub-polar**, or **Arctic Cyclone** or **Polar Vortex.** Following are the characteristic features of Polar cyclone

Features/Characteristics

- Polar cyclone is a vast area of low pressure that strengthens in winter and weakens in summer.
- It is a low-pressure weather system, usually ranges to move 1,000–2,000 km (620 – 1,200 mi).

- The air circulates counterclockwise in N hemisphere and clockwise in S hemisphere
- In N Hemisphere, the polar cyclone has two centers on average, one is near Baffin Island and the other over northeast Siberia.
- In S hemisphere, it is located near the edge of Ross ice shelf near 160 west longitude.
- If polar vortex is strong, westerly flow descends to the Earth's surface.
- If polar cyclone is weak, significant cold outbreaks occur.

8.11.2 Tropical Upper Tropospheric Trough (TUTT) Low

These are upper tropospheric cyclonic vortices, which generate when upper cold lows break off from the base of the Tropical Upper Tropospheric Trough (TUTT) under specific conditions, therefore named as TUTT lows or TUTT cells.

Features/Characteristics

- They often generate in the mid-ocean of the Northern Hemisphere during the summer.
- They move slowly from east-northeast to west-southwest
- A weak inverted surface trough within the trade wind is generally found below them.
- They usually extend up to 20,000 feet in altitude.
- They may also be associated with broad areas of high-level clouds.
- Downward development results in an increase of cumulus clouds and the appearance of a surface vortex.
- Rarely they become warm-core, resulting in the vortex turning into a tropical cyclone.
- Upper cyclones/troughs that trail tropical cyclones can cause additional outflow channels and intensify them.
- Due to the outflow jet, tropical disturbances can generate or deepen upper troughs/ lows.

8.12 MESOSCALE CYCLONES

Mesoscale convective systems starts at surface lows initially as warm core and grows like a wave along the front while the low positioned at the crest. Around the low, cyclonic flow forms to push polar air equator-ward west via its trailing cold front, while warmer air pushes poleward low via the warm front. Obviously, the cold front moves quicker than the warm front and so, "catch up" with lower air-mass at ahead of the cyclone while the higher density air-mass sweeping in behind the cyclone. An occluded front forms at this point and pushes the warm air mass upwards into a trough of warm air aloft, which is also known as a trowal.

Mesoscale cyclones are not identifiable on synoptic chart. The following are various types of mesoscale cyclones that are not identifiable in synoptic charts.

8.12.1 Mesocyclone

A **mesocyclone** is a vortex of air, 2 to 10 km (1.2 to 6.2 mi) in diameter within a convective storm. Air rises and revolves around a vertical axis, usually in the same direction as low-pressure systems in both northern as well as southern hemispheres. They are most often cyclonic, i.e. form at a localized low-pressure region within a supercell. Such storms can feature strong surface winds and severe hail. Mesocyclones often occur together with updrafts in supercells, where tornadoes may form. About 1700 mesocyclones form annually across the US, but only half produce tornadoes.

8.12.2 Tornado

A **tornado** is a rapidly rotating air column, which is in contact with both the surface of the Earth and a cumulonimbus (rarely base of cumulus) cloud.

The wind speeds of most tornadoes are below 180 kmph (110 mph), and are about 80 m (250 ft) diameter, but can travel a several kilometers before dissipation. In extreme cases, the wind may get the speeds be up to 480 kmph (300 mph), with 3 km (2 mi) in diameter, and travel >100 km.

Tornadoes have been found on every continent except Antarctica. How ever, the vast majority occur in USA, more specifically Tornado Alley region. Tornadoes can be predicted and detected well before by Storm Spotters or Pulse-Doppler radar by identifying patterns in velocity and reflectivity, hook-echoes or debris balls. Several scales are devised for rating the strength of tornadoes such as Fujita scale (rates damage caused F0-F5), Enhanced Fujita Scale (EF0 - EF5), TORRO scale ranges (weak T0 to most powerful T11). Doppler radar data, photogrammetry, and ground swirl patterns (cycloidal marks) can also be used to determine intensity and assign a rating.)

A wedge tornado, a mile wide, at Binger, Oklahoma in 1981 (Source: Wikipedia)

Tornado at dissipating stage at Okhlahama; (Source: Wikipedia)

Multiple vortex tornado)

Gustnado

Tornadoes are also called with some general names such as **twisters**, **vayupralayam, whirlwinds, or** simply **cyclones** (but strictly speaking, **cyclone** is a low-pressure area in the center around which winds blow counterclockwise in North and clockwise in South).

Tornadoes occurs in many shapes and sizes, and are most generally seen in the form of a condensation funnel generated from base of a cumulonimbus cloud, with a cloud of rotating debris and dust under it. Based on these shapes and underlying features, tornadoes are named in variety of ways such as ***multiple vortex tornado***, ***landspout*** and ***waterspout***. Other meso-cyclones which exhibit tornado-like phenomena are gustnado, dust devil, fire whirls, and steam devil.

8.12.3 Gustnado

A *gustnado*, or *gust front tornado*, appears like 'rolling cloud', is formed if fast moving cold, dry outflow air is blown from a thunderstorm through stationary, warm, moist air near the outflow boundary. If low level wind shear is sufficiently strong, the vertical or diagonal rotation contacts with the ground what is known as a gustnado. It is a small vertical swirl associated with a gust front or downburst but not connected with cloud base. This is why; there is a debate, if gustnadoes are considered as tornadoes. They feature in small areas with heavier rotational wind. (Gustnado)

8.12.4 Waterspout

Water Spout

Waterspouts are characterized by a spiraling funnel-shaped wind current, connecting to a large cumulus or cumulonimbus cloud. Though categorized under tornadoes (non-super cellular), which develop over bodies of water, there is disagreement if they are true tornadoes. The reason is that unlike tornadoes, these spiral columns of air commonly spawn in tropical areas near to the equator, but rare at high latitudes. Further, these are weaker than most of their land counterparts, while stronger versions generated by mesocyclones.

8.12.5 Land Spout

A *landspout*, also called *dust-tube tornado*, in fact, is not associated with a mesocyclone. Perhaps! It is so named as it is characterized as a "fair weather waterspout on land". Waterspouts and landspouts are similar in characteristics, with reference to relative weakness, short lifespan, and a small, smooth condensation funnel that generally do not reach the surface. Land spouts also create a distinctively laminar cloud of dust as they touch the ground, owing to their different mechanics from true mesocyclone tornadoes. Of course, they are generally weaker than classic tornadoes, but can produce so strong winds that cause serious damage.

Water spout at Florida Keys 1969; (Source: wikipedia)

8.12.6 Dust Devil

A *dust devil*, also known as a *whirlwind* is relatively long-lived, strong and well-formed that forms on a hot day when a strong convective updraft is formed near the ground. A dust devil ranges from small (half a metre wide and a few metres tall) to large (>10 m wide and >1000 m tall). It resembles a tornado in vertical swirling column of air, but, forms under clear skies and is not stronger than even the weakest tornadoes. If there is enough low level wind shear, the column of hot, rising air develops a small cyclonic motion seen upon the ground. The primary motion is vertically upward. They are not considered tornadoes as they occur during fair or hot weather and have no relevance with any clouds. Dust devils are generally harmless and seldom result in major damage, but rarely may grow large enough to be threat to both people and property.

A Land Spout

Dust Devil

8.12.7 Steam Devil / Smoke Devil

Formation of *steam devil*, also called *smoke devil* involves steam or smoke but not high wind speeds. It is a gentle vortex over calm water or wet land seen as rising whirl of water vapour. Steam devils only make a few rotations per minute having a rotating updraft between 50–200 m wide. Steam

Smoke/steam devil at Mongolian coalmine

devils or smoke devils are very rare at other areas but most often possible to occur at hot springs, deserts and smokestacks of a power plant. This can occur over water, when cold air passes over relatively warm water. These are not dangerous to cause any damage.

8.12.8 Fire Whirl

Fire Whirl(s) is a small-scale, tornado-like circulation that occurs near any intense surface heat source such as wildfires or a hot wave. These are also not considered tornadoes, but for one exception, that can occur very rarely when it connects to a pyro-cumulus or other cumuliform cloud above. Fire whirls usually are not strong as compared to tornadoes associated with thunderstorms, but can cause significant damage.

SELF ASSESSMENT INTERMISSION (SAI – 8.3)

1. Define Cyclone? Classify cyclones based on synoptic scaling.
2. Describe the features and characteristics of tropical cyclones?
3. What are the effects of tropical cyclones?
4. Explain the features and characteristics of sub-tropical cyclones?
5. Narrate the features and characteristics of Extra-tropical cyclones?
6. What is a polar low? What are its features and characteristics?
7. What is a polar cyclone? What are its features and characteristics?
8. Distinguish between polar low and polar cyclone.
9. What are meso-scale cyclones? Brief out various meso-scale cyclones?
10. What is a tornado? Where and how does it occur?
11. What are waterspout, dust devil and steam devil?
12. What is TUTT? Explain its features and characteristics?

8.13 EFFECTS OF CYCLONE

Unlike the effects of other disaster which are found after occurrence, the effects of cyclones appear well before its occurrence. We often see rains, even far away from shores as an effect of a forthcoming cyclone. Thus the effects of cyclones are listed under two sub-heads as follows.

8.13.1 Before Landfall

Tropical cyclones at sea (before landfall) can cause

- large waves,
- heavy rain,
- flood and
- high winds,
- disrupt international shipping and,
- shipwrecks.

Tropical cyclones stir up water, leaving a cool wake behind them, which causes the region to be less favorable for subsequent tropical cyclones.

O My God!

Cyclones on other planets

Cyclone on Mars, imaged by Hubble Space Telescope

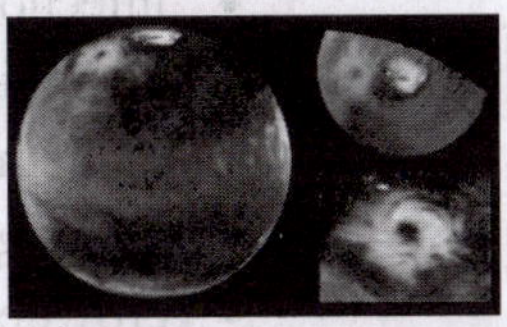

Cyclones can occur on other planets also, such as the Small Dark Spot on Neptune. It is about 1/3 the diameters of the Great Dark Spot and received the nickname "Wizard's Eye" as it looks like an eye with a white cloud in the middle. Mars has also exhibited cyclonic storms. Further, the Great Red Spot is described as the inverse phenomenon, an anticyclone.

8.13.2 After Landfall

On land (after landfall), strong winds can

- cause tropical cyclone deaths
- interrupt infrastructure, leading to
    - power outages,
    - destruction of communication systems
    - bridge destruction,
    - obstructions and damage to transport systems (roadways) and
    - hampering of reconstruction efforts.
- damage or destroy vehicles, buildings, bridges, and other outside objects,
- damage to agriculture
- severe shortage of food and water for humans and cattle
- turns loose debris into deadly flying projectiles
- the storm surge, or
- the increase in sea level due to the cyclone, is typically the worst effect from landfall of tropical cyclones,

- vertical wind shear at its periphery, spawns tornadoes. (Tornadoes can also be spawned as a result of eyewall mesovortices, which persist until landfall)
- over the past two centuries, tropical cyclones have been responsible for the deaths of about 1.9 million people worldwide.
- some species of plants and vegetation die due to the excess salt.
- carry toxins and acids harmful to the humans, animals and the environment
- the flooding water can also spark many dangerous oil spills.
- large areas of standing water caused by flooding lead to
  - infection,
  - mosquito-borne illnesses
  - epidemic diseases
  - drainage blocks
  - crowded evacuees in shelters increase the risk of disease propagation

8.13.3 Merits

Tropical cyclones also help

- Wetting the land far away from the coast
- Provide good rains for agriculture and
- Prevent drought/famine
- Maintain the global heat balance by moving warm, moist tropical air to the middle latitudes and polar regions, and
- By regulating the thermohaline circulation through upwelling
- The storm surge and winds of hurricanes stir up the waters of coastal estuaries,
- Favour fish breeding locales
- Spurs redevelopment, greatly increasing local property values
- Salt is introduced to many freshwater areas and raises the salinity levels too high for some habitats to withstand
- Some are able to cope with the salt and recycle it
- Some species of plants such as coconut and other vegetation grow well due to the salt.

8.14 FORECASTING, PREPAREDNESS AND MITIGATION

Certain things will not be under our control. Cyclone is also one of such uncontrollable disaster. We cannot stop nor prevent nor postpone the occurrence

Tropical cyclone basins and official warning centre		
Basin	**Warning Center**	**Area of Responsibility**
	Northern Hemisphere	
N. Atlantic E. Pacific	US National Hurricane Center US Central Pacific Hurricane Center	Equator northward, African Coast – 140°W Equator northward, 140°W-180
W. Pacific	Japan Meteorological Agency	Equator-60°N, 180-100°E
N. Indian Ocean	India Meteorological Department	Equator northward, 100°E-45°E
	Southern Hemisphere	
SW Indian Ocean	Meteo France Reunion	Equator-40°S, African Coast-90°E
Australian region	Badan Meteorologi, Klimatologi, dan Geofisika Papua New Guinea National Weather Service Australian Bureau of Meteorology	Equator-10°S, 90°E-141°E Equator-10°S, 141°E-160°E 10°S-36°S, 90°E-160°E
S. Pacific	Fiji Meteorological Service Meteorological Service of NZ	Equator-25°S, 160°E-120°W 25°S-40°S, 160°E-120°W

of a cyclone. What we can do is only to predict, forecast and get prepared for minimizing the loss or damage. Today, with the advancement of the technology, the forecasting the occurrence of a cyclone has become somewhat simple. Some of the methods of predicting the cyclonic activities are listed below.

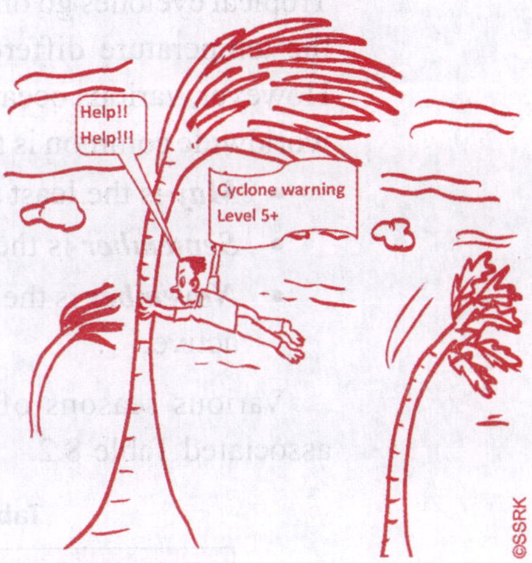

- Tropical cyclones far from land can be traced and tracked at every 15 to 30 minutes before intervals by weather satellites that capture visible/infrared images from space
- As a storm approaches land, land-based Doppler Weather Radar can be employed, particularly, during landfall, it can show storm's location and intensity every minute
- In real-time, storm intensity can be measured by sending specially equipped reconnaissance flights into the cyclone. In the Atlantic basin, such flights (4-engine turboprop cargo aircrafts such as WC-130 Hercules and WP-3D Orions) are regularly flown by US government. These fly directly into the cyclone and take direct and remote-sensed measurements of pressure, temperature, humidity and wind speeds etc.
- A new history is created in 2005 hurricane season with Remotely Piloted Aerosonde (a small drone aircraft), which has flown over Tropical Storm Ophelia that passed through Virginia.

- A similar mission was also successfully conducted in the western Pacific Ocean.
- High-speed computers and sophisticated simulation software permit forecasters to produce computer models that predict tropical cyclone tracks based on the future position and strength of high- and low-pressure systems.

8.14.1 Cyclone Information and Warning Mechanism

There are 6-Regional Specialized Meteorological Centers (RSMCs) worldwide, designated by World Meteorological Organization (WMO) and are responsible to track and issue bulletins, warnings, and advisories about tropical cyclones in their assigned areas of responsibility. In addition, there are 6- Tropical Cyclone Warning Centers (TCWCs) that provide information to smaller regions.

8.14.2 Cyclone Season (Period)

Tropical cyclones go on to peak stage in late summer all over the world because the temperature differences between land and sea surface are the highest. However, various ocean basins have their own specific seasonal patterns. But worldwide common is that,

- ***May*** is the least active month,
- ***September*** is the most active month.
- ***November*** is the only month in which all the tropical cyclone basins are active.

Various seasons of tropical cyclones worldwide are given here in the associated Table 8.2.

Table 8.2 Season lengths and averages.

Season lengths and averages				
Basin	**Season start**	**Season end**	**Tropical Storms**	**Hurricane**
N-Atlantic	Jun1	Nov30	12.1	6.4
E-Pacific	May15	Nov30	16.6	8.9
W-Pacific	Jan1	Dec31	27.0	17.0
N-Indian	Jan1	Dec31	4.8	1.5
SW-Indian	Jul1	Jan30	9.3	5.0
Australian region	Nov1	Apr30	11.0	
S-Pacific	Nov	Apr30	7.4	4
Global	Jan1	Dec31	86.0	46.9

8.14.3 Landfall

Landfall is said to have occurred when storm's center has crossed the coastline. However, the conditions of storm may be experienced on the coast and inland much before landfall, if so, it is said to be a *direct hit* on coastline. Thence, emergency planning and preparedness, actions should be initiated and scheduled from the moment certain wind speed or intensity of rainfall reaches land, but not to wait till landfall occurs.

8.14.4 Dissipation-Factors

Tropical Storm 'Franklin', 2005, a strongly sheared tropical cyclone in North Atlantic basin

A tropical cyclone can cease to possess tropical nature in several ways.

- On moving over land, it gets deprived of the warm water that is needed to power itself, and so rapidly losing strength. This is the reason for most strong storms also lose their strength very quickly after landfall.
    - It mostly becomes disorganized within a day or two, or
    - It may sometimes turn up into extra-tropical cyclones.
    - There is a chance to regenerate, if it manages to get back over open warm water, e.g. Hurricane Ivan.
- Even for a short time also, if it remains over mountains/hills, the weakening accelerates. The Western Ghats and Eastern Ghats in South Indian coastal line in India are good examples to demonstrate this.
- However, it is unfortunate that though cyclonic activity is dissipated, many storm fatalities occur in mountainous terrain, because the diminishing cyclones let loose their moisture resulting in heavy downpour/rainfall. This may lead to deadly floods and mudslides (e.g. Hurricane Mitch, 1998)
- A tropical cyclone can dissipate because, when it moves over waters below 26.5°C (79.7°F), it will lose its tropical characteristics (warm core with thunderstorms near the center). Of course, it is a good sign but we cannot be very happy, because the traces of low-pressure areas still remain. This may persist for several days before totally losing their identity. This activity is quite common in the Eastern N-Pacific.
- Weakening of the storm can occur if it experiences vertical wind shear, which can move away the convection and heat engine from the center.

- However, its interactions and merging with a nearby frontal zone, can convert tropical cyclones to extratropical cyclones within 1–3 days.
- Even after a tropical cyclone turns out as extra-tropical or dissipates, it can still have tropical storm force (rarely hurricane/typhoon force) winds and drop several inches of rainfall.
- This activity is sometimes found in the Pacific and Atlantic Oceans when they reach the west coast of N. America and Europe (they are known as *European windstorms*) e.g. Hurricane Iris,1995.

- A cyclone may also merge with another area of low pressure, evolving into a larger area of low pressure. This may strengthen the resultant system, even though it may no longer be a tropical cyclone.
- Remember: Without warm surface water, the storm cannot survive.

8.14.5 Artificial Dissipation

A futile effort was made in 1947 on a hurricane of east of Jacksonville, Florida, but it change the route to smash into Savannah, Georgia. This effort taught a lesson that seeding operation is not a good idea unless the storm had a less than 10% chance of making landfall within 48 hours, because there is so much uncertainty about the behavior of the storms.

During 1960s and 70s, the US government tried to dissipate hurricanes artificially through 'Project Stormfury' by seeding with silver iodide (AgI). It was assumed that this seeding can supercool water in the outer rain-bands to freeze, and thence collapse the inner eye-wall, ultimately to reducing the winds. One such experiment was done on the winds of Hurricane 'Debbie', which dropped up to 31%, but Debbie regained its strength after each of the two rounds of seeding. It was discovered that this is due to 'eyewall replacement cycles' automatically happen in strong storms. This discovery led the project to be dropped raising doubts on the result of the earlier attempts. (Finally, it is inferred that silver iodide seeding cannot effect sufficient amount of super cooled water in the rain bands of a tropical cyclone).

A study during the 2000s hypothesized that large amounts of dust can reduce the strength of tropical cyclones.

Research is going on with various other approaches such as

- towing icebergs into the tropical oceans,
- covering the ocean in a substance that inhibits evaporation,
- dropping large quantities of ice into the eye at very early stages of development (so that the latent heat is absorbed by the ice, instead of being converted to kinetic energy that would feed the positive feedback loop), or

- Blasting the cyclone with nuclear weapons.
- Project Cirrus even involved throwing dry ice on a cyclone.

But, all these approaches missed a simple logic: tropical cyclones are simply too large and short-lived with unpredictable behavior for any of the weakening techniques to be practical.

Tropical Storms in Popular Culture and Media

Tropical cyclones appeared in many different types of media, including films, books, television, music, and electronic games. May they be fictional or real or simulated, the following are a few among the most popular.

- George Rippey Stewart's *Storm*, a best-seller published in 1941, is thought to have influenced meteorologists on their decision to assign female names to Pacific tropical cyclones.
- The film, *The Perfect Storm*, described the sinking of the *Andrea Gail* by the 1991 Perfect Storm.
- Hurricanes are featured in serials such as *The Simpsons*, *Invasion*, *Family Guy*, *Seinfeld*, *Dawson's Creek*, *Burn Notice* and *CSI: Miami*.
- The film *The Day After Tomorrow (2004)* demonstrated actual tropical cyclones and features "hurricane-like", albeit non-tropical, Arctic storms.
- Movie, *Pie* also demonstrated the tropical storm.

And many more.....

8.14.6 Safety Precautions and Mitigation

Since, the effects of cyclones are felt in two phases i.e. before landfall and after landfall (refer previous section 8.13, of this chapter), the safety precautions, preparedness and mitigation should be designed under three heads viz. before, during and after cyclone. These are described in the paragraphs to follow.

Before Cyclone

- Rehabilitation centers should be prepared in advance
- proper warning system must be employed to make people alert.
- Try to know the nearest cyclone shelter/ safe houses and safest route to reach these shelters.
- Do not get panic by listening to rumors.
- Medical kit should be kept in reach for first aid.
- Food stocks should be maintained for sufficient number of days.
- Check the walls, pillars, doors and windows to see if they are secure. If not, repair those at the earliest. In case of tin roofs, check the condition of the tin and repair the loose points. Cover the mud walls with polythene or coconut leaves mats or straw mats on a bamboo frame. Bind each corner of the roof with a plastic rope in case of thatched roof.
- Trim dry tree branches, cut off the dead trees and clear the place/ courtyard of all debris, including coconuts and tree branches.
- People in area prone to storm surge should be located safe high ground or shelter.
- Identify the spot where you can dig holes to store food grains, seeds, etc. in polythene bags.

During cyclone

- Clear your property of loose materials that could blow about and cause injury or damage during extreme winds.
- If your area is prone to storm surge, locate safe high ground or shelter.

- Keep important documents, passbook, etc. in a tight plastic bag and take it along with your emergency kits if you are evacuating.
- Keep a list of emergency addresses and phone numbers on display. Know the contact telephone number of the government offices /agencies, which are responsible for search, rescue and relief operations in your area.
- Disconnect all electrical appliances and turn off gas.
- If the building starts crumbling, protect yourself with mattresses, rugs or blankets under a strong table or bench or hold on to a solid fixture (e.g. a water pipe)
- Listen to your transistor radio for updates and advice.
- Beware of the calm 'eye'. If the wind suddenly drops, don't assume the cyclone is over; violent winds will soon resume from the opposite direction. Wait for the official "all clear".
- If driving, stop – but well away from the sea and clear of trees, power lines and watercourses. Stay in the vehicle.

If evacuation is in progress:

Based on predicted wind speeds and storm surge heights, evacuation may be necessary. Official advice may be given on local radio / TV or other means of communication regarding safe routes and when to move.

- Wear strong shoes or chappal and clothing for protection.
- Lock your home, switch off power, gas, water, and take your emergency kit.
- If evacuating to a distant place take valuable belonging, domestic animals, and leave early to avoid heavy traffic, flooding and wind hazards.
- If evacuating to a local shelter or higher grounds carry the emergency kit and minimum essential materials.

After the cyclone:

- Do not go outside until officially advised it is safe.
- Check for gas leaks. Do not use electric appliances, if wet.
- If you have to evacuate, or did so earlier, do not return until advised. Use a recommended route for returning and do not rush.
- Beware of fallen power lines, damaged bridges, buildings and trees, and do not enter the flood waters.
- O bey all warnings and do not go sightseeing.

Role of government:

- There is a need to improve the forecasting of storm impacts over both the short term like numerical weather prediction and longer term (climate projections) timescales.

- Storm impacts like the consequences of heavy or persistent rainfall or high wind, such as groundwater, pluvial and coastal flooding; ground stability, including landslides; and coastal erosion demand the impact models and storm predictions are better linked in order to better inform policy and enable preventative measures to mitigate risks associated with such storms.
  - Predictive capability with respect to extreme wind and precipitation.
  - Knowledge about the change in the frequency and intensity of storms under global warming conditions and
  - Improve knowledge of the coastal sea surface response to extreme storm conditions so that proper precautions are taken in advance.

8.15 NAMING OF TROPICAL CYCLONES

If you want to speak about a particular cyclone, how do you describe it?

When you want to compare two cyclones you witnessed, how do you call them?

Perhaps! You refer them as 'the earlier one and the present one' or 'the old and new' or with the dates and/or place that they have hit.

Suppose, two cyclones hit more or less at the same place and during same period, then how do you make a mention of these? Further, how do you describe your forecast or warning?

These questions raise the need for concept of naming cyclones that occur time to time.

This need was first identified by Clement Wragge, the Meteorologist of Queensland Government, who used personal names for weather systems from 1887 till his retirement in 1907. However, the system of naming the tropical and subtropical cyclones by the places or things they hit to identify them, has been discarded after the retirement of Wragge, until it was revived during latter part of WW–II.

From then onward, the naming of the weather systems has been kept in practice by various warning centers mainly, to provide the ease of communication between forecasters and to remove confusions in officials as well as the general public about forecasts, watches and warnings on tropical and subtropical cyclones. Moreover, the systems can last a week or longer and more than one can occur simultaneously or sequentially at the same time or/and same place. Thence, these names can give more clarity about which storm is being talked about.

Formal naming schemes and naming lists have been introduced and developed for the Indian Ocean, N Atlantic, Eastern, Western, Central and South Pacific basins and Australian region. Names are given in sequence as per the predetermined lists with one (1), three (3), or ten (10)-minute sustained wind speeds of more than 65 km/h (40 mph) depending on which basin it originates. The naming institutions in various basins and their area of responsibility are shown in the following table.

Retiring or withdrawing or a change of a name of a tropical cyclone from the various tropical cyclone naming lists is permitted on request of a committee member of the World Meteorological Organization request, when a consensus or majority of members agree that the tropical cyclone has attained a special notoriety, such as causing a large amount of deaths, damages, impacts or for other special reasons. However, any tropical cyclone names assigned by the Papua New Guinea National Weather Service are automatically retired regardless of any damage caused. The replaced name is then put forth the committee for voting, however, these names may be accepted or rejected and replaced with another name for various reasons. Often, these reasons could be the spelling and pronunciation of the name or the similarity to the recent name or on another list of names and the length of the name for modern communication channels like social media.

Table 8.3 Tropical cyclone naming institutions

Basin	Naming institution	Area of responsibility
	Northern Hemisphere	
N Atlantic	US National Hurricane Center,	Equator northward, African Coast-140°W
E Pacific	US Central Pacific Hurricane Center	Equator northward, 140°W-180
W Pacific	Japan Meteorological Agency PAGASA (Unofficial)	Equator-60°N, 180-100°E 5°N-20°N, 115°E-135°E
N Indian	India Meteorological Department	Equator northward, 100°E-45°E
	Southern Hemisphere	
S-W Indian	Mauritius Meteorological Services Météo Madagascar	Equator-40°S, 55°E-90°E Equator-40°S, African Coast-55°E
Australian region	Indonesian Agency for Meteorology, Climatology and Geophysics Papua New Guinea National Weather Service Australian Bureau of Meteorology	Equator-10°S, 90°E-141°E Equator-10°S, 141°E-160°E 10°S-36°S, 90°E-160°E
S Pacific	Fiji Meteorological Service Meteorological Service of New Zealand	Equator-25°S, 160°E-120°W 25°S-40°S, 160°E-120°W
S Atlantic	Brazilian Navy Hydrographic Center (Unofficial)	Equator-35°S, Brazilian Coast-20°W

Some interesting points about naming of cyclones are given below

- There are no retired names within the South-West Indian Ocean, as they are not used more than once and fresh naming lists are developed every year.
- There are no naming lists for the Mediterranean and to the east of 120W of the Southern Pacific areas since Tropical cyclone is rare to form.
- Within the North Atlantic Ocean, tropical or subtropical cyclones are named by the National Hurricane Center (NHC/RSMC Miami), when they have intensified into tropical storms with winds of at least 34 knots (39 mph; 63 km/h).
- There are six lists of names with NHC which rotate every six years and begin with the first letters A toW used, skipping Q and U, and alternating between male and female names.
- The names of significant tropical cyclones are retired from the lists, with a replacement selected at the next meeting of WMO's Hurricane Committee.
- If all of the names on a list are used, storms are named after the letters of the Greek alphabet.
- When a tropical depression becomes intensive storm toward the north of the Equator between 140°W and 180° it is named by the Central Pacific Hurricane Center (CPHC) from the Hawaiian four lists maintained by WMO's hurricane committee, rotating in a sequence regardless of year without repetition.
- Tropical cyclones with 10-min sustained winds of at least 34 kn (39 mph; 63 km/h) within the Western Pacific are given international names sequentially irrespective of year from the 5-lists prepared by the ESCAP/WMO Typhoon Committee.
- If a moderate tropical storm occurs between Africa and 55°E then Météo Madagascar will name it, while if it is between 55°E and 90°E then the Mauritius Meteorological Service names it.
- Since 1963, Philippines' PAGASA has been independently operating its own naming scheme for tropical cyclones that occur within its own self-defined 'Philippine area of responsibility' from its four different lists of 25 names rotated every 4-years with retiring (> 1 billion loss or/and >300 deaths) significant tropical cyclones within the Philippines. If main list is exhausted, auxiliary list is considered.
- Within the North Indian Ocean between 45°E –100°E, tropical cyclones are named by the India Meteorological Department (IMD/ RSMC New Delhi), if they have 3-min sustained wind speeds of at

least 34 knots (39 mph; 63 km/h). There are 8-lists used in sequence, not rotated, but the significant are retired.

- When a tropical cyclone develops below 10°S between 90°E and 160°E, then Australian Bureau of Meteorology (BoM) which operates from 3 centres (Perth, Darwin and Brisbane) assigns in alphabetical order of its list in rotating order irrespective of year.
- For the cyclones developed between the Equator-10°S and 90°E-141°E, Indonesia names them in sequence from list A, while list B provides names for those which are removed or retired from list A.
- Papua New Guinea National Weather Service (NWS, TCWC Port Moresby) assigns the names for a tropical cyclone occurring between the Equator – 10°S and 141°E – 160°E, from list A in sequence which are automatically retired after being used irrespective of any damage caused and List B contains names to replace.

The names proposed are annexed for reference.

8.15.1 Notable Tropical Cyclones

Tropical cyclones that cause extreme destruction are rare, although when they occur, they can cause great amounts of damage or thousands of fatalities. However, the N Indian cyclone basin has historically been the deadliest basin.

Here, are the worst and deadliest tropical cyclones/hurricanes/typhoons on record.

- The 1970 Bhola is the deadliest tropical cyclone killed > 3 lakh lives on Nov 13 with its powerful storm surge striking the densely populated Ganges Delta of Bangladesh.
- Typhoon Nina killed nearly 1lakh in China in 1975 and resulted in a 100-year flood that caused 62 dams including the Banqiao Dam to fail.
- The Great Hurricane of 1780 is deadliest in N Atlantic, claimed ~22,000 lives in Lesser Antilles
- Hurricane Katrina, Aug 2005, is the costliest worldwide, damages exceeding $100 billion and killed about 1,836 people on striking Louisiana and Mississippi.
- Hurricane Sandy is the 2nd most destructive tropical cyclone in US history, with damages of $68 billion and with repair costs of $37.5 billion
- Hurricane Ike is the 3rd most destructive tropical cyclone in U.S history.
- The Galveston Hurricane of 1900 is the deadliest in US, killed ~12000 lives in Galveston, TX.
- Hurricane Mitch killed >10,000 lives in Central America, is the 2nd deadliest Atlantic hurricane.
- Hurricane Iniki in 1992 recorded as a Category 4 hurricane, was the most powerful storm hitting Kauai, Hawaii killed 6 people, and damaged US $3 billion. Kauai was also struck by Hurricanes Dot (1959) and Iwa (1982).

- Pauline & Kenna are the most destructive Eastern Pacific hurricanes severely damaged Mexico
- In Mar 2004, Cyclone Gafilo struck northeastern Madagascar as a powerful cyclone, killed 74, affected >2 Lakh, and was the worst cyclone to affect the nation for more than 20 yrs.
- Typhoon Nancy in 1961, recorded wind speeds of 185 knots (95 m/s) or 215 mph (346 km/h)
- Typhoon Paka on Guam was recorded at 205 knots (105 m/s) or 235 miles per hour (378 km/h). Had it been confirmed, it would be the strongest non-tornadic wind ever recorded on the Earth's surface, but the reading had to be discarded since the anemometer was damaged by the storm.
- Typhoon Tip in the northwestern Pacific Ocean in 1979, reached a minimum pressure of 870 hectopascals (26 in Hg) and maximum sustained wind speeds of 165 knots (85 m/s) or 190 mph (310 km/h).
- Tip, however, does not solely hold the record for fastest sustained winds in a cyclone. Typhoon Keith in the Pacific and Hurricane Allen in the N Atlantic currently share this record with Tip
- Tip was also the largest cyclone on record, with tropical storm-force winds 2,170 km (1,350 mi) in diameter.
- The smallest on record, having a landfall is Tropical Storm Marco, in October 2008, hitting Veracruz with storm-force winds only 37 km (23 mi) in diameter.
- Hurricane John hold the record for the longest-lasting (31 days) in 1994 and also for the longest-tracked tropical cyclone in N Hemisphere, which had a path of 13,280 km (8,250 mi).
- Cyclone Rewa of the Dec 1993 and Jan 1994, S Pacific and Australian region had one of the longest tracks in the S Hemisphere, travelling a distance of over 8,920 km (5,545 mi)
- Tropical Storm Thelma in Nov 1991 killed thousands in the Philippines,
- Hurricane Paul in 1982, killed around 1,000 people in Central America.

SELF ASSESSMENT INTERMISSION (SAI – 8.4)

1. What are the effects of cyclone during and after occurrence?
2. Can Cyclone be advantageous? If so, how?
3. What are adverse effects of a cyclone? How do you counter them?
4. Describe the process of the preparedness and precautionary measures for a cyclone?
5. Give an action plan for mitigation before, during, and after a cyclone.
6. Explain the factors which can dissipate a cyclone.
7. Explain the importance of cyclone information system in forecasting and warning.
8. Which period is called the cyclone season? Why?
9. Discuss the role of Government in mitigation of a cyclone.
10. What is a landfall with reference to the cyclone? Explain.
11. Who gives the names to cyclones? How are the cyclones named?
12. Give a detailed note on the last three cyclones attacked India.

MINI-PROJECTS / CASE STUDIES

Case-1

(Primary information given below is an excerpt from Deccan Chronicle, Dec12, 2016 and other web news sources)

- **Laila-2010:** In **2010**, after a gap of two decades the south-eastern part of India was hit by two 'severe' cyclones within a gap a few months; The first being Cyclone Laila entered along the coast of the Bay of Bengal. Total deaths in Sri Lanka, Andhra Pradesh and Tamil Nadu mounted to 65 and cost of damage reached a total of USD 117.49 million. Fishermen, who set out in about a 100 boats, were lost at sea, according to fisheries department sources.
- **Jal-2010:** Following Cyclone Laila, Cyclone Jal formed in the Pacific Ocean on **3rd Oct 2010**. Torrential rains poured in Thailand causing extensive flooding which led to the demise of 59 people and similarly claimed four more lives in Malaysia. Subsequently, Jal proceeded towards Andhra Pradesh where, through timely warnings 70,000 people were evacuated from villages where damage was expected to be the highest. On 9th Nov, the 54 people dead due to the storm. The Centre then promised 20 kg of rice and 5 L kerosene to each family in flood-affected areas with Rs. 2 lakhs also to be given as compensation to the families of the victims. The total damage estimated by the Indian government was USD 53.55 million with Visakhapatnam district suffering a damage of USD 18.53 million, Nellore district suffering a damage of USD 22.59 million and Prakasam district suffering a damage of USD 12.43 million.

QUESTIONS

1. Write a report exploring the reasons for the second major disaster of the year – 2010?
2. Laila and Jal are not just national (India) disasters, but are international issues affecting the countries like Sri Lanka, Malaysia and Thailand. So, viewing the cyclones as an international issue, write a technical paper or a management article suggesting improvements and modifications in internal and international disaster prevention and response policies.

Case - 2

- **Phailin-2013:** Originating and named in Vietnam, Cyclone Phailin hit the peninsula in **Oct 2013**. The cyclone hit Andhra Pradesh and resulted in the evacuation of 64,000 people from low-lying areas. A total of 134,426 people were eventually evacuated. Power and communication lines went down across the district. With one casualty, the damage amounted to USD 8.1 million in Andhra Pradesh alone. Other affected states like Odisha, Jharkhand and neighbouring states recorded losses up to USD 688 million. Odisha recorded as 44 people dying due to storm related accidents. [http://www.freepressjournal.in/india/list-of-cyclones-that-have-hit-india-in-recent-times/986291]
- **Hudhud-2014:** The last time a cyclone of Vardah's scale breached from the Bay of Bengal was in **Oct 2014** when Cyclone Hudhud originated from the Andaman Islands and snowballed IV cyclone, being dubbed as 'Extremely Severe.' It proceeded to hit the Indian states of

Andhra Pradesh, Chattisgarh, Madhya Pradesh, Odisha. The estimated damages were approximated to a total of USD 3.4 billion and death toll 124. Unlike most Bay of Bengal storms that dissipate quickly over land, Hudhud has been the only tropical cyclone whose remnant ever reached as far north as the Himalayas. The cyclone further proceeded up north to trigger ***an avalanche*** in Nepal. On October 15th, the Prime Minister of India, Mr. Narendra Modi announced USD 136 million awarded as aid for affected areas in Andhra Pradesh. [http://www.deccanchronicle.com/nation/current-affairs/121216/list-of-major-cyclones-that-have-hit-india-over-the-last-few-years.html?fromNewsdog=1]

QUESTIONS

1. Do you think the mitigation and response actions adequate? If not, what are your suggestions?
2. Collect the information about the effects before and after the cyclone in surrounding states of Andhra Pradesh and Odisha. Write a report on mitigation, response and rehabilitation actions state and central governments for the indirectly affected people.
3. Bring out the connections and relations among one another of cyclones, floods, avalanches, blizzards, cold waves, rainstorms, earthquakes and tsunamis. Write a technical paper or managerial article as one trigger of the other.

Case - 3

- **Nada-2016:** More recently, Cyclone Nada threatened the peninsula (India) in late **Nov 2016**. As the states geared up, the cyclone fizzled out with its landfall in Tamil Nadu. But, heavy winds were encountered. Schools were shut for 2 days to acts as storm shelters for the citizens. Unfortunately, 12 deaths were still blamed on the storm.
- **Vardah-2016:** Made a landfall in Tamil Nadu and Andhra Pradesh turning from 'very severe' to 'severe', at category-1 strength and weakened with sustained winds of 80-90 kmph. Schools have been closed and India's labour department has issued an advice, requesting companies to allow employees to work from their homes. Fishermen too, have been advised to stay away from waters. In addition, the agricultural sector has been hit severely with widespread destruction of banana plantations, papaya groves and rice paddies.

QUESTIONS

1. If you were a disaster manager or collector of district affected, what actions do you take? Prepare an action plan.
2. Collect the information about the effects before and after the cyclone to estimate the loss and damage. Critically analyze how they affect the economy of the country/state and living cost of people in and around the state.

Case - 4

Collect Images of all types of cyclones (extra tropical/tropical, subtropical, mesoscale etc…including all types of tornadoes, gustnado, water/land spout, dust/steam devils) and prepare a gallery to exhibit in a college day celebrations) [If possible include images of other disasters also..]

List of Atlantic tropical cyclone names

Year											
2016	Alex	Bonnie	Colin	Danielle	Earl	Fiona	Gaston	Hermine	Ian	Julia	Karl
	Lisa	Matthew	Nicole	Otto	Paula	Richard	Shary	Tobias	Virginie	Walter	
2017	Arlene	Bret	Cindy	Don	Emily	Franklin	Gert	Harvey	Irma	Jose	Katia
	Lee	Maria	Nate	Ophelia	Philippe	Rina	Sean	Tammy	Vince	Whitney	
2018	Alberto	Beryl	Chris	Debby	Ernesto	Florence	Gordon	Helene	Isaac	Joyce	Kirk
	Leslie	Michael	Nadine	Oscar	Patty	Rafael	Sara	Tony	Valerie	William	
2019	Andrea	Barry	Chantal	Dorian	Erin	Fernand	Gabrielle	Humberto	Imelda	Jerry	Karen
	Lorenzo	Melissa	Nestor	Olga	Pablo	Rebekah	Sebastien	Tanya	Van	Wendy	
2020	Arthur	Bertha	Cristobal	Dolly	Edouard	Fay	Gonzalo	Hanna	Isaias	Josephine	Kyle
	Laura	Marco	Nana	Omar	Paulette	Rene	Sally	Teddy	Vicky	Wilfred	
2021	Ana	Bill	Claudette	Danny	Erika	Fred	Grace	Henri	Ida	Joaquin	Kate
	Larry	Mindy	Nicholas	Odette	Peter	Rose	Sam	Teresa	Victor	Wanda	
Sources for tropical cyclone names.											

EASTERN PACIFIC OCEAN

List of Eastern Pacific tropical cyclone names

Year												
2016	Agatha	Blas	Celia	Darby	Estelle	Frank	Georgette	Howard	Ivette	Javier	Kay	Lester
	Madeline	Newton	Orlene	Paine	Roslyn	Seymour	Tina	Virgil	Winifred	Xavier	Yolanda	Zeke
2017	Adrian	Beatriz	Calvin	Dora	Eugene	Fernanda	Greg	Hilary	Irwin	Jova	Kenneth	Lidia
	Max	Norma	Otis	Pilar	Ramon	Selma	Todd	Veronica	Wiley	Xina	York	Zelda
2018	Aletta	Bud	Carlotta	Daniel	Emilia	Fabio	Gilma	Hector	Ileana	John	Kristy	Lane
	Miriam	Norman	Olivia	Paul	Rosa	Sergio	Tara	Vicente	Willa	Xavier	Yolanda	Zeke
2019	Alvin	Barbara	Cosme	Dalila	Erick	Flossie	Gil	Henriette	Ivo	Juliette	Kiko	Lorena
	Mario	Narda	Octave	Priscilla	Raymond	Sonia	Tico	Velma	Wallis	Xina	York	Zelda
2020	Amanda	Boris	Cristina	Douglas	Elida	Fausto	Genevieve	Hernan	Iselle	Julio	Karina	Lowell
	Marie	Norbert	Odalys	Polo	Rachel	Simon	Trudy	Vance	Winnie	Xavier	Yolanda	Zeke
2021	Andres	Blanca	Carlos	Dolores	Enrique	Felicia	Guillermo	Hilda	Ignacio	Jimena	Kevin	Linda
	Marty	Nora	Olaf	Patricia	Rick	Sandra	Terry	Vivian	Waldo	Xina	York	Zelda
Sources for tropical cyclone names.												

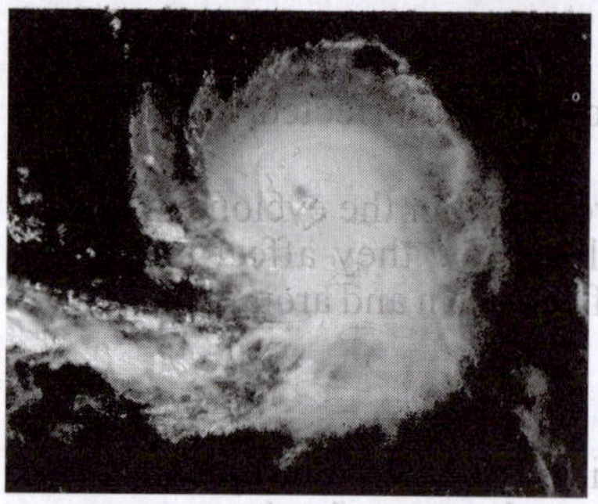

Image of Hurricane Joaquin nearing peak strength in early Oct'15

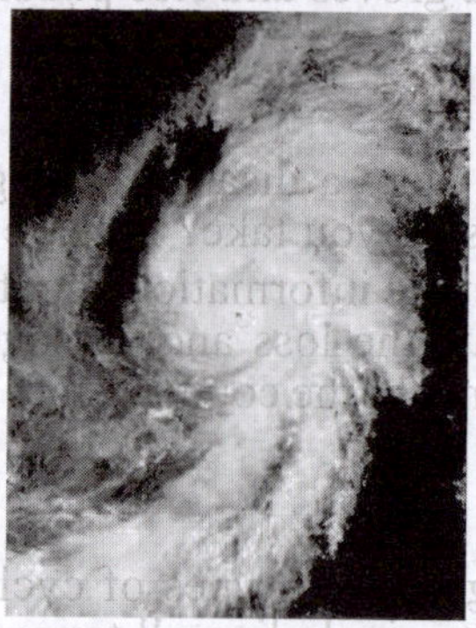

Hurricane Patricia in 2015, the most intense system in the East Pacific Basin

Pewa and Unala near the International Dateline in Aug'13

Typhoon Damrey in 2000, the first name assigned by the JMA

Typhoon Hanna (Soudelor) approached Taiwan in 2015

Cyclone Chapala over in the Arabian Sea at peak strength during late-Oct'15

Bruce was the 1st tropical cyclone to retain its name when moving into S-W Indian Ocean basin

Cyclone Palm in Mar'15, the strongest tropical cyclone in the South Pacific according to wind speeds

List of Central Pacific tropical cyclone names (140°W to 180°)

List	Names										
1	Akoni	Ema	Hone	Iona	Keli	Lala	Moke	Nolo	Olana	Pena	Ulana	Wale
2	Aka	Ekeka	Hene	Iolana	Keoni	Lino	Mele	Nona	Oliwa	Pama	Upana	Wene
3	Alika	Ele	Huko	Iopa	Kika	Lana	Maka	Neki	Omeka	Pewa	Unala	Wali
4	Ana	Ela	Halola	Iune	Kilo	Loke	Malia	Niala	Oho	Pali	Ulika	Walaka

List of Philippine region tropical cyclone names

2016 Main	Ambo	Butchoy	Carina	Dindo	Enteng	Ferdie	Gener	Helen	Igme	Julian	Karen	Lawin	Marce
	Nina	Ofel	Pepito	Quinta	Rolly	Siony	Tonyo	Ulysses	Vicky	Warren	Yoyong	Zosimo	
2016-Auxiliary	Alakdan	Baldo	Clara	Dencio	Estong	Felipe	Gomer	Heling	Ismael	Julio			
2017 Main	Auring	Bising	Crising	Dante	Emong	Fabian	Gorio	Huaning	Isang	Jolina	Kiko	Lannie	Maring
	Nando	Odette	Paolo	Quedan	Ramil	Salome	Tino	Urduja	Vinta	Wilma	Yasmin	Zoraida	
2017 Auxiliary	Alamid	Bruno	Conching	Dolor	Ernie	Florante	Gerardo	Hernan	Isko	Jerome			
2018 Main	Agaton	Basyang	Caloy	Domeng	Ester	Florita	Gardo	Henry	Inday	Josie	Karding	Luis	Maymay
	Neneng	Ompong	Paeng	Queenie	Rosita	Samuel	Tomas	Usman	Venus	Waldo	Yayang	Zeny	
2018 Auxiliary	Agila	Bagwis	Chito	Diego	Elena	Felino	Gunding	Harriet	Indang	Jessa			
2019 Main	Amang	Betty	Chedeng	Dodong	Egay	Falcon	Goring	Hanna	Ineng	Jenny	Kabayan	Liwayway	Marilyn
	Nimfa	Onyok	Perla	Quiel	Ramon	Sarah	Tisoy	Ursula	Viring	Weng	Yoyoy	Zigzag	
2019 Auxiliary	Abe	Berto	Charo	Dado	Estoy	Felion	Gening	Herman	Irma	Jaime			

INTERNATIONAL NAMES

List of Western Pacific tropical cyclone names

List	Contributing Nation													
	Cambodia	**China**	**North Korea (DPRK)**	**Hong Kong**	**Japan**	**Laos**	**Macau**	**Malaysia**	**Micronesia**	**Philippines**	**South Korea (ROK)**	**Thailand**	**United States**	**Vietnam**
1	Damrey	Haikui	Kirogi	Kai-tak	Tembin	Bolaven	Sanba	Jelawat	Ewiniar	Maliksi	Gaemi	Prapiroon	Maria	Son-Tinh
	Ampil	Wukong	Jongdari	Shanshan	Yagi	Leepi	Bebinca	Rumbia	Soulik	Cimaron	Jebi	Mangkhut	Barijat	Trami
2	Kong-rey	Yutu	Toraji	Man-yi	Usagi	Pabuk	Wutip	Sepat	Mun	Danas	Nari	Wipha	Francisco	Lekima
	Krosa	Bailu	Podul	Lingling	Kajiki	Faxai	Peipah	Tapah	Mitag	Hagibis	Neoguri	Rammasun	Matmo	Halong
3	Nakri	Fengshen	Kalmaegi	Fung-Wong	Kammuri	Phanfone	Vongfong	Nuri	Sinlaku	Hagupit	Jangmi	Mekkhala	Higos	Bavi
	Maysak	Haishen	Noul	Dolphin	Kujira	Chan-hom	Linfa	Nangka	Soudelor	Molave	Goni	Atsani	Etau	Vamco
4	Krovanh	Dujuan	Mujigae	Choi-wan	Koppu	Champi	In-fa	Melor	Nepartak	Lupit	Mirinae	Nida	Omais	Conson
	Chanthu	Dianmu	Mindulle	Lionrock	Kompasu	Namtheun	Malou	Meranti	Rai	Malakas	Megi	Chaba	Aere	Songda
5	Sarika	Haima	Meari	Ma-on	Tokage	Nock-ten	Muifa	Merbok	Nanmadol	Talas	Noru	Kulap	Roke	Sonca
	Nesat	Haitang	Nalgae	Banyan	Hato	Pakhar	Sanvu	Mawar	Guchol	Talim	Doksuri	Khanun	Lan	Saola

NORTH INDIAN OCEAN (45°E – 100°E)

List of Northern Indian Ocean tropical cyclone names

List	Contributing Nation							
	Bangladesh	**India**	**Maldives**	**Myanmar**	**Oman**	**Pakistan**	**Sri Lanka**	**Thailand**
1	Onil	Agni	Hibaru	Pyarr	Baaz	Fanoos	Mala	Mukda
2	Ogni	Akash	Gonu	Yemyin	Sidr	Nargis	Rashmi	Khai Muk
3	Nisha	Bijli	Aila	Phyan	Ward	Laila	Bandu	Phet
4	Giri	Jal	Keila	Thane	Murjan	Nilam	Viyaru	Phailin
5	Helen	Lehar	Madi	Nanauk	Hudhud	Nilofar	Ashobaa	Komen
6	Chapala	Megh	Roanu	Kyant	Nada	Vardah	Maarutha	Mora
7	Ockhi	Sagar	Mekunu	Daye	Luban	Titli	Gaja	Phethai
8	Fani	Vayu	Hikaa	Kyarr	Maha	Bulbul	Pawan	Amphan

SOUTH-WEST INDIAN OCEAN (AFRICA – 90°E)

List of South-West Indian Ocean tropical cyclone names

Season	Names												
2015–16	Annabelle	Bohale	Corentin	Daya	Emeraude	Fantala	Gao	Hassina	Inacio	Juma	Ketiwe	Lalelani	Moabi
	Naima	Octave	Piera	Quizito	Richard	Sofia	Tatiana	Umboni	Vela	Wayne	Xaba	Yazid	Zenani

List of Indonesian tropical cyclone names

List A	Anggrek	Bakung	Cempaka	Dahlia	Flamboyan	Kenanga	Lili	Mangga	Seroja	Teratai
List B	Anggur	Belimbing	Duku	Jambu	Lengkeng	Melati	Nangka	Pisang	Rambutan	Sawo
	Sources for tropical cyclone names.									

List of Papua New Guinea tropical cyclone names

List A	Alu	Buri	Dodo	Emau	Fere	Hibu	Ila	Kama	Lobu	Maila
List B	Nou	Obaha	Paia	Ranu	Sabi	Tau	Ume	Vali	Wau	Auram

List of Australian tropical cyclone names

List A	Anika	Billy	Charlotte	Dominic	Ellie	Freddy	Gabrielle	Herman	Ilsa	Jasper	Kirrily
	Lincoln	Megan	Neville	Olga	Paul	Robyn	Sean	Tasha	Vince	Zelia	------
List B	Anthony	Bianca	Courtney	Dianne	Errol	Fina	Grant	Hayley	Iggy	Jenna	Koji
	Luana	Mitchell	Narelle		Peta	Rubina	Sandra	Tim	Victoria	Zane	------
List C	Alessia	Bruce	Catherine	Dylan	Edna	Fletcher	Gillian	Hadi	Ivana	Jack	Kate
	Lam	Marcia	Nathan	Olwyn	Quang	Raquel	Stan	Tatiana	Uriah	Yvette	------
List D	Alfred	Blanche	Caleb	Debbie	Ernie	Frances	Greg	Hilda	Isobel	Joyce	Kelvin
	Linda	Marcus	Nora	Owen	Penny	Riley	Savannah	Trevor	Veronica	Wallace	------
List E	Ann	Blake	Claudia	Damien	Esther	Ferdinand	Gretel	Harold	Imogen	Joshua	Kimi
	Lucas	Marian	Noah	Odette	Paddy	Ruby	Seth	Tiffany	Vernon	------	-----

List of South Pacific tropical cyclone names

List A	Ana	Bina	Cody	Dovi	Eva	Fili	Gina	Hagar	Irene	Judy	Kerry	Lola	Mal
	Nat	Olo	Pita	Rae	Sheila	Tam	Urmil	Vaianu	Wati	Xavier	Yani	Zita	
List B	Arthur	Becky	Chip	Denia	Elisa	Fotu	Glen	Hettie	Innis	Joni	Ken	Lin	Moses
	Nisha	Opeti	Pearl	Rene	Sarah	Troy	------	Vanessa	Wano	------	Yvonne	Zaka	
List C	Alvin	Bune	Cyril	Daphne	Eden	Florin	Garry	Haley	Isa	June	Kofi	Louise	Mike
	Niko	Ola	Pam	Reuben	Solo	Tuni	Ula	Victor	Winston	------	Yalo	Zena	
List D	Amos	Bart	Colin	Donna	Ella	Frank	Gita	Hali	Iris	Jo	Kala	Leo	Mona
	Neil	Oma	Pami	Rita	Sarai	Tino	------	Vicky	Wiki	------	Yolande	Zazu	
List E	Aru	Bela	Cook	Dean	------	------	Garth	Hart	------	Julie	Kevin	------	------
	------	------	Pearl	Rex	Suki	Troy	------	Velma	Wanita	------	Yates	Zidane	
	Source for tropical cyclone names												

Tropical cyclone classifications							
The Beaufort scale	1-minute sustained winds	10-minute sustained winds	NE Pacific & N Atlantic NHC/CPHC	NW Pacific JTWC	NW Pacific JMA	N Indian Ocean IMD	SW Indian Ocean MF
0–7	<32 knots (37 mph; 59 km/h)	<28 knots (32 mph; 52 km/h)	Tropical Depression	Tropical Depression	Tropical Depression	Depression	Zone of Disturbed Weather
7	33 knots (38 mph; 61 km/h)	28–29 knots (32–33 mph; 52–54 km/h)				Deep Depression	Tropical Disturbance
8	34–37 knots (39–43 mph; 63–69 km/h)	30–33 knots (35–38 mph; 56–61 km/h)	Tropical Storm	Tropical Storm			Tropical Depression
9–10	38–54 knots (44–62 mph; 70–100 km/h)	34–47 knots (39–54 mph; 63–87 km/h)			Tropical Storm	Cyclonic Storm	Moderate Tropical Storm
11	55–63 knots (63–72 mph; 102–117 km/h)	48–55 knots (55–63 mph; 89–102 km/h)			Severe Tropical Storm	Severe Cyclonic Storm	Severe Tropical Storm
12+	64–71 knots (74–82 mph; 119–131 km/h)	56–63 knots (64–72 mph; 104–117 km/h)	Category 1 hurricane	Typhoon			
	72–82 knots (83–94 mph; 133–152 km/h)	64–72 knots (74–83 mph; 119–133 km/h)			Typhoon	Very Severe Cyclonic Storm	Tropical Cyclone
	83–95 knots (96–109 mph; 154–176 km/h)	73–83 knots (84–96 mph; 135–154 km/h)	Category 2 hurricane				
	96–97 knots (110–112 mph; 178–180 km/h)	84–85 knots (97–98 mph; 156–157 km/h)	Category 3 major hurricane				
	98–112 knots (113–129 mph; 181–207 km/h)	86–98 knots (99–113 mph; 159–181 km/h)				Extremely Severe Cyclonic Storm	Intense Tropical Cyclone
	113–122 knots (130–140 mph; 209–226 km/h)	99–107 knots (114–123 mph; 183–198 km/h)	Category 4 major hurricane				
	123–129 knots (142–148 mph; 228–239 km/h)	108–113 knots (124–130 mph; 200–209 km/h)					
	130–136 knots (150–157 mph; 241–252 km/h)	114–119 knots (131–137 mph; 211–220 km/h)		Super Typhoon		Super Cyclonic Storm	Very Intense Tropical Cyclone
	>137 knots (158 mph; 254 km/h)	>120 knots (140 mph; 220 km/h)	Category 5 major hurricane				

CHAPTER 9

Floods and Soil Erosion

O'MY SILENT INNER VIBES (O'M S I V – 9)

"The students of a college (where I worked earlier) went on an industrial tour, were enjoying the water on a Sunday afternoon at downside of a popular dam in a narrow canyon. Without any observed rainfall, suddenly a flash flood came and the flow rate increased from about 50-1500 ft^3/s (1.4-42 m^3/s) in just one minute and took away eight (8) of them. Two larger floods occurred earlier at the same site within a week, but no one was at the waterfall on those days."

I was so disturbed on hearing this news. A little later, when I put on my Television (TV), a tale from Bhagavatham was featuring on the screen and while I was watching, my heart produced some vibes silently inside to the answer the quest. The story was going on as follows.

The villagers were making huge preparations as usually for the annual offering to Indra. Krishna saw this and questioned his father Nanda about it. He debated with the villagers about what their right job (Karma) and righteousness (Dharma) truly were. He argued that the farmers, as a part of their duty, should concentrate on farming and protection of their cattle. He continued to say that all human beings should merely do their 'Karma' and follow 'Dharma', to the best of their ability and not to pray or conduct sacrifices for natural phenomenon, nor against nature. The villagers were convinced by Krishna's words, and took him into confidence and did not proceed with the special puja (prayer).

Indra was furious to this act and invoked the clouds in the sky to pour 'cats and dogs' and schemed to flood the region with a rainstorm lasting for 7 days and 7 nights. While huge waters drown flooded to the village, all the villagers were feared and came to Krishna.

In reply, Krishna lifted Mountain Govardhan, under which all the animals and people took shelter, saved from the rains of Indra's fury. Indra finally accepted defeat and recognized Krishna as supreme. Krishna asked villagers to perform Puja (prayer) to Mt. Govardhan) instead of to Indra, the natural god that had been giving food, firewood, medicines and all those required for their lives and even sheltered during the rainstorm. Then onward, with Govardhan Giri Puja, (Dhantheras) the day after Diwali, has been celebrated as a memory of Krishna defeated Indra, the deity of thunder and rain. This aspect of Krishna's life is mostly glossed over - but it actually represents many truths of life. Here are those of my S-I-Vs...

1. It represents the victory over the 'ego'. It tells not to perform '*sacrificial*' worship to please Indra (the ego), but to perform what you have to. Thus, it sets up the basis of 'Karma' philosophy (detailed in Bhagavad Gita), i.e. do your duty correctly, honestly, particularly with nature.
2. It preaches the Dharma... '*Dharmo Rakshati.. Rakshitah*', which means 'If you protect dharma, it protects you'. Obviously, if you do not follow the dharma (a righteous system), it naturally revolts. So protect the dharma of nature, environment and its features, else you will see its anger.
3. May it be rainstorm or floods or any disaster, it is the result of our failure to either safeguard the nature's dharma or not performing the right karma (i.e. doing against what you ought to do).

(Continued)

4. So, behave like right human to protect the 'Dharma' (the feature of nature) by doing right 'Karma' (the right job) so that the Dharma will protect you like Krishna lifting Mt. Govardhana.
5. Some irresponsible persons of the situation did not do the karma correctly.

   Do not curse! Take the nature as it comes! Do not show your anger to destroy the nature! Because… It is much more superior and much senior (ancient) to you.

   The only option left with us is to **Respect the 'Dharma' and Respond as per 'Karma'**!

9.1 DEFINITION AND CONCEPT

The word "flood" might have come from the old English *flod*, but its roots with nearest meaning are seen in several languages such as *Flut* (German), *vloed* (Dutch), *fluctus*, *flumen* (Latin) and so on. The English words like *flow* and *float* also seem to be closely comparable with flood.

9.1.1 Definitions

Floods occur when water covers dry land usually caused due to prolonged or very heavy rainfall, severe storms or tropical cyclones, or the excessive monsoonal (wet season) rains in the tropics or snow-melt or dam failure.

According to the European Union (EU) Floods Directive…

A flood is said to have occurred when water covers a land which is not normally covered by water.

Simply, a flood is an overflow of water that submerges land which is usually dry.

9.1.2 How do Floods Occur?

Flood may occur as an overflow of water from water bodies, such as a river or lake or tides in which the water tops over or breaks levees. It is the result of water escaping its usual boundaries. It may occur due to an accumulation of rainwater on saturated ground in an aerial flood. The following are the most common possibilities of flooding.

1. Floods occur in rivers when the water flow rate exceeds the channel capacity of the river, more specifically at bends or meanders in the waterway.
2. When the size of a lake or a water body significantly varies with seasonal changes in precipitation and snow melt, they flood out to damage property or consume the lives of humans or domestic animals.
3. In the event of tsunamis or water surge, the ocean water may flood out on the land through huge tides

Often the land on the riverside or lake side is usually flat and fertile. Also rivers provide easy travel and access to commerce and industry. So humans tend to live there. In the event of floods, they often cause damage to homes, agriculture and businesses if they are in the natural flood plains of rivers. However, river-flood damage can be minimized by moving away from rivers and other water bodies. Some floods develop slowly, while others suddenly such as flash floods which develop in just a few minutes even without visible signs of rain. Further, floods can be local, impacting a neighborhood or community, or very large, affecting entire river basins.

Contemporary picture of the flood that struck the North Sea coast of Germany and Denmark in October 1634.

People seeking refuge from flood in Java. ca. 1865–1876.

Flooding of a creek due to heavy monsoonal rain and high tide in Darwin, N Territory, Australia.

Jeddah Flood, covering King Abdullah Street in *Saudi Arabia*.

Flooding near Key West, Florida, US from Hurricane Wilma's storm surge in October 2005.

Flooding in a street of Natal, Rio Grande do Norte, Brazil in April 2013.

Flash flooding caused by heavy rain falling in a short amount of time.

Floods in Hyderabad for even a small rain (NDTV, 27 Sep-2016)

Therefore, peopie who live in low-lying areas, or close to rivers, creeks or major storm-water drains are usually at risk from flooding. Heavy rains and storms in one area can cause flooding in another. When the water level of local rivers and streams rises it can cause them to overflow, sometimes spilling out over thousands of kilometers.

9.2 ORIGIN OF CAUSING FLOODS

Flooding can be caused by a range of situations. However, if their origin can be treated as the cause for flooding, then these can be categorized under the following five heads.

1. Seawater flood
2. Tidal flood
3. Run-off from rivers
4. Failures or overflowing of dams/ reservoirs
5. Urban drainage

We shall discuss about these now.

9.2.1 Seawater Floods

Coastal areas usually experience the floods when a cyclone or severe storm hits and causes a surge of sea water. Though rare, tsunami is also worth to mention under this head that causes huge flow of water into the coastal areas.

9.2.2 Tidal Floods

These floods occur due to high tides that coincide with higher than normal river levels. The high tides higher than normal river levels cause these floods.

9.2.3 Run-Off from Rivers

This is the most common reason for flooding which occurs when river carries more water than its capacity. This may be due to a huge snow-melt or heavy or continuous rainfall (river run-off may also occur by a dam failure or sudden release, but this is taken as a separate head here).

9.2.4 Failures or Overflowing of Dams/ Reservoirs

These floods occur when dams fail or start to overflow. Strictly speaking, these floods are the consequences of the run-off, excess flow of water than the river capacity. Therefore, these can be categorized under run-off floods, however, due to magnitude of the disaster, severity of damage and frequency of occurrence, they are studied under a separate head.

9.2.5 Urban Drainage

Failures in drainage systems may cause floods often referred to as flash floods. If the drainage system is not planned and designed properly, the flash flooding becomes a serious problem. It can make the people caught in storm-water drains, trapped in their cars or even swept off the roads by water.

9.3 TYPES OF FLOODS

The types of floods can be understood under the following five heads.

1. Areal floods
2. Reverine or channel floods
3. Estuarine floods
4. Urban floods
5. Catastrophic floods

Now we shall discuss about these briefly.

9.3.1 Areal Floods

Floods can occur on flat or low-lying areas when water is abounded by rainfall or snowmelt more rapidly than it can either infiltrate or run off. The water abundance may also be due to intense rain from one or a series of storms. The excess water accumulates in place, sometimes to hazardous depths. Soil of surface becomes saturated, and thence stops infiltration. The water table is usually shallow and floodplain. The slow or very less infiltration may also be due to frozen ground, rock, concrete, paving, or roofs. As the overland flow depends on the surface slope, the areal flood starts in flat or no-slope areas like floodplains, particularly in local depressions which are not connected to a stream channel.

9.3.2 Riverine (Channel) Floods

The riverine floods are the floods caused by rivers or channels. There is no river on this earth, which has never flooded. Floods occur in all types of rivers and stream channels; no matter it is the smallest or largest, narrowest or widest or deepest, short-lived or long-lived. When overland flow occurs on tilled fields, it usually results in a muddy flood and the sediments are picked up by runoff which can be carried as suspended matter or bed load. Localized flooding may be caused or aggravated by drainage obstructions also. Landslides, ice, debris and beaver dam may also provoke flooding activity.

The riverine floods can occur in three types based on the lead time, these are:

(a) Slow-rising or Slow-onset
(b) Rapid-rising or Rapid-onset and
(c) Flash floods

(a) Slow rising / Slow-onset floods: These floods may take days to build-up, but can last for weeks or even months. They usually occur due to increased tides or overflows of rivers or dams. Slow-rising floods most commonly occur in large rivers with large catchments. The reasons for the increase in flow may be attributed to sustained rainfall, rapid snow melt, monsoons or tropical cyclones.

The damage caused by slow-onset floods includes:

- major loss of livestock
- rural towns being cut-off and isolated
- crop damage
- damage to roads and railways.

Example: Inland rivers in the vast, flat areas of Western Australia, central/western New South Wales and Queensland often flood.

(b) Rapid rising or Rapid-onset floods: Rapid-onset flooding occurs more quickly than slow-onset. These floods are usually more devastating and pose a greater risk to loss of life and assets, as there is generally less lead time to take preventive action from a faster, turbulent and more dangerous flow of water. Often, this type of flooding can affect most of major towns and cities.

Rapid flooding often occurs on

- Smaller rivers,
- Rivers with steep valleys,
- Rivers that flow over impermeable terrain or normally-dry channels.

The causes may be attributed to localized convective precipitation (severe thunderstorm) and/or sudden release of water from an upstream impoundment created behind a dam, landslide, ice-melt, avalanche or glacier.

(c) Flash floods: Flash flooding results from relatively short, intense bursts of rainfall, often during thunderstorms. Flash floods may also occur due to failures of drainage systems or failures of dams or tsunamis. After entering floodwaters, the people are often evacuated away on foot or by vehicles. These floods can cause significant damage of property and major social disruption. They are a serious problem, particularly, in urban areas where drainage systems are often unable to cope with large amounts of water in a short time.

Flash floods are the most common flood type in normally-dry channels in arid zones, (known as *arroyos* in the southwest U.S). Usually, the flood water that first arrives is depleted as it wets the sandy stream bed. Thus the leading edge of the flood moves more slowly than later and higher flows. Thence, the rising limb of the hydrograph becomes quicker as the flood moves downstream.

9.3.3 Estuarine and Coastal Floods

Flooding in estuaries is usually caused by a combination of wind driven sea tidal surges and low atmospheric pressure, and they may be even worsened by high upstream river flow.

Coastal areas may be flooded by storm events at sea, resulting in waves over-topping defenses or in severe cases by tsunami or tropical cyclones. A storm surge, from either a tropical or extra-tropical cyclones falls in this category. As these are already discussed in the previous chapters, it is curtailed here. Chapters of Earthquake, Tsunami and Cyclone may be referred for examples and other details.

9.3.4 Urban Flooding

This is relatively recently identified disaster despite events have been occurring through centuries of flood history. Urban flooding is the overflow on land and/or property in a built environment, particularly in densely populated areas, often triggered by huge rainfall and incapability of drainage systems. Although sometimes urban flooding is triggered by events such as flash flooding or snowmelt, it is characterized by its repetitive and systemic impacts on communities owing to some manmade faults done knowingly unknowingly. In addition to the potential overflow of rivers and lakes, snowmelt, stormwater; the water released from damaged water mains may mount up on property and in public rights-of-way, seep through building walls and floors, or backup into buildings through sewer pipes, toilets and sinks.

The urban flood flow is hazardous to both the people and infrastructure. The recent research has considered the criteria for safe evacuation of individuals in flooded areas. Some recent examples are

- Vaison-la-Romaine (France) in 1992,
- Nimes (France) in 1998
- New Orleans (USA) in 2005,
- Rockampton, Bundaberg, Brisbane in Queensland (Australia) during the 2010–2011 summer
- Hyderabad, Telangana, India -2016

9.3.5 Catastrophic Floods

Catastrophic flooding is usually associated with major infrastructure failures such as the collapse of a dam, but they may also be caused by drainage channel modification from a landslide, earthquake or volcanic eruption (such as Vajont dam failure, Himalayan landslides followed by floods etc.). Examples include outburst floods and lahars. As these are already dealt in previous chapters, they are not discussed here again.

SELF ASSESSMENT INTERMISSION (SAI – 9.1)

1. Define Flood? What is its meaning? What is its significance in disaster management?
2. How do floods occur? Discuss.
3. Based on the origin of causing floods, briefly describe different floods. Explain any two in detail.
4. Where do floods generate? Explain about sea water flooding?
5. Describe flooding due to failure of dams/ reservoirs with examples.
6. Classify floods and explain about riverine floods in detail.
7. Explain about urban floods? Discuss its causes and effects.
8. What are slow, rapid and flash floods? Discuss.
9. How do you classify the floods based on the lead time they provide before reaching peak level?
10. What are estuarine floods? Where and how do they occur?

9.4 FACTORS AFFECTING THE FLOODING

The floods are mainly caused and due to stop and/or coincidental factors. We shall discuss these now.

9.4.1 Up-slope Factors

The floods depend mainly on three factors of water reaching drainage channel from natural precipitation and controlled/uncontrolled reservoir release,

1. amount of water
2. location of water, and
3. timing of water that the flow at downstream locations.

The above three aspects again depend on

- evaporation,
- percolation through soil,
- temporary sequestering as snow or ice, and
- rapid runoff from surfaces such as rock, pavement, roofs, and saturated or frozen ground.

Time of Concentration indicates the critical duration of peak rainfall and is defined as the time needed for runoff from the distant point of the upstream drain area to approach the point of the drainage channel that controls flooding of the area of interest. For a drainage structure of roof or a parking lot, the critical duration of intense rainfall may be only a few minutes, but for river basin it is a cumulative rainfall and if occurs for several days, it could be too critical.

9.4.2 Down Slope Factors

Down flowing water obviously experiences the effects of downstream conditions whose final destination is often the ocean or a lake. However, the significant tidal fluctuations in coastal and estuarine flooding may cause variation in water elevation (Less foreseeable events such as tsunamis and storm surges may also influence, but only in large bodies of water).

We know that the geometry of the flow channel can control the elevation of flowing water. The effectiveness of flood channel geometry may be changed by the following common methods:

- growth of vegetation,
- accumulation of ice or debris, or
- construction of bridges, buildings, or levees within the flood channel.

9.4.3 Coincidences

Extreme flood events often result from coincidence such as

- unusually intense, warm rainfall,

- by melting heavy snow pack,
- producing channel obstructions from floating ice, and
- releasing small impoundments (at dams)

Coincidentally extensive flooding may be caused more frequently than anticipated by considering only precipitation runoff flow within unobstructed drainage channels. The heavy flows move uprooted woody vegetation and flood-damaged structures and vehicles (like boats and railway equipment etc.) due to which debris modification of channel geometry is common. Some of the causes include-

- The storage effect in urban areas with transportation corridors created by cut and fill.
- If the culverts are blocked by debris, they convert into impoundments and flow may be diverted along streets.
- Redistribution in streets during storm events and the implication on flood modeling.

Examples:

1. Many villages were seriously affected when rain pushed the rivers of northwestern Bangladesh over their banks in early Oct 2005
2. Queensland floods 2010-11 in Australia
3. The streets of Hyderabad of India get inundated for small rain also
4. Ghaghat and Atrai Rivers on Oct 12, 2005 spread across the countryside in USA

9.5 EFFECTS OF FLOODS

The various primary and secondary effects of floods are listed below.

9.5.1 Primary or Immediate Effects

The following are the immediate (often called primary) effects of flooding

1. Loss of life of humans and pet animals (Refer Table 9.1).
2. Damage or failures or cracks to
   - buildings and other structures,
   - bridges,
   - sewerage systems,
   - roadways,
   - creeks and canals.
3. Damage or interruption to
   - power transmission and
   - sometimes power generation,

Table 9.1 The deadliest floods worldwide with death tolls > 1 Lakh.

Deaths (Lakh)	Event	Location	Year
2.5–3.7	1931 China floods	China	1931
9–20	1887 Yellow River (Huang He) flood	China	1887
5–7	1938 Yellow River (Huang He) flood	China	1938
2.31	Banqiao Dam failure, result of Typhoon Nina, ~86,000 died from floods & ~1.45 Lakh died during subsequent disease.	China	1975
2.3	Indian Ocean tsunami	Indonesia	2004
1.45	1935 Yangtze river flood	China	1935
1.0+	St. Felix's Flood, storm surge	Holland	1530
1.0	Hanoi and Red River Delta flood	N Vietnam	1971
1.0	1911 Yangtze river flood	China	1911

- knock-on effects due to the loss of power

4. Loss or inconvenience in
   - drinking water treatment and
   - water supply,
   - severe water contamination
5. Damages to sewage disposal facilities and lack of clean water as it combined with human sewage
6. The flood waters raises the risk of waterborne diseases, such as
   - typhoid,
   - giardia,
   - cryptosporidium,
   - cholera and
   - many other diseases depending upon the location of the flood
7. Increases difficulty to operate help-lines (due to damage to transmission lines, power and telecommunications etc.)
8. Enhances difficulty to provide emergency health treatment (due to damage/blockage of roadways).
9. Flood waters inundate agricultural, farm land due to which
   - The lands become non-cultivatable and
   - Loss of crops from being planted or harvested,
   - Entire harvests for a state can be lost
   - Shortages of food is caused for both humans and farm animals
   - Some trees fall down on roads
   - Some species may not survive (by prolonged flooding)
   - Some big trees also are affected by their rotten or damaged root systems

9.5.2 Secondary and Long-term Effects

1. A common after-effect of severe flooding is price hike due to food shortage (e.g. during 1980 & 2013, floods in Andhra Pradesh, India caused a price hike of rice four fold in the following year)
2. Economic hardship due to rebuilding costs (e.g. floods in Chennai, India in Nov 2015)
3. A temporary decline in tourism (e.g. flooding on river Ganges and Yamuna blocked Amarnath pilgrims several times)
4. The psychological imbalances and adverse effects, particularly when deaths, serious injuries and loss of property occur. (e.g. flood victims of Bangladesh, India in the year 2006)
5. Urban flooding often causes chronic wetting of houses, which leads to an increase in respiratory problems and other related illnesses.
6. Urban flooding also has significant economic implications for affected neighborhoods.

[According to Federal Emergency Management Agency (FEMA) of the US, about 40% of small businesses never reopen their doors following a flood. It is estimated that wet basements lower property values by 10-25% and are cited among the top reasons for not purchasing a home. Insurance is available against flood damage to both homes and businesses in the US].

Is it always bad news?

Floods can have both positive and negative impacts. Sometimes floods can bring welcome relief for people, livestock and areas experiencing drought conditions. Flooding can also be a natural way for wetland areas, swamps and native waterways to survive. Underground aquifers and soils with high salt levels also benefit from floods.

Those who have coins they enjoy rain or flood.
Those who have notes need umbrella or shed.

©SK

9.5.3 Benefits

Though floods cause many adverse effects, sometimes more frequent but smaller flooding can also bring many benefits, such as

- recharges ground water,
- makes soil more fertile and
- enhances nutrients in some soils.
- raises water resources particularly in arid/semiarid regions (where precipitation can be very unevenly distributed throughout the year)

- kills pests in the farming land
- brings freshwater into wells, lakes, reservoirs and stored water resources
- play a great role in maintaining ecosystems in river corridors
- plays a key role in maintaining flood plain biodiversity
- spreads nutrients to lakes and rivers, which can lead to increased biomass
- improves fisheries for a few years
- higher viability of hydro-power and a renewable source of energy

The periodic small flooding has been the main reason for maintaining the well-being of humans. They are called boons of the respective country. Here are some examples -

The Tigris Euphrates River	– Western Asia (Syria, Iraq, and Persian Gulf
The river Nile	– Egypt
The river Indus	– Pakistan
The river Ganges	– India
The Yellow River	China

9.6 FLOOD SAFETY PLANNING AND MITIGATION

While planning for flood safety, the designers and town planners should bear the following points in mind.

1. At the outset, as we know water flows down, the best defense to floods is to choose higher ground.
2. The place chosen for living-hood should have critical community-safety facilities, such as hospitals, emergency-operations centers, and police, fire, and rescue services, built in within the reachable vicinity to have least at risk of flooding.
3. If it is inevitable to construct the structures, such as bridges, towers, flyovers and community buildings etc. in flood hazard prone areas, they should be designed to withstand flooding.
4. Areas having risk for flooding could be put to valuable uses that may be abandoned temporarily as people retreat to safer areas in the event occurrence of a flood.

Flood safety planning involves many aspects of analysis and engineering, some of which are given below:

- map the inundated areas
- observe of past and present flood heights and inundated areas,
- flood heights for future flood scenarios, (forecasting)
- statistical analyses
- insight into hydrology and hydraulics
- long-term land use plan and regulation
- engineering design and construction of structures to control or withstand flooding
- intermediate-term monitoring, forecasting, and emergency-response planning, and
- monitoring, warning system and response operations mechanisms
- promote education, policies, and activities to control
- mitigate current and future losses, costs, and human suffering caused by flooding
- protect the natural and beneficial functions of floodplains - all without causing adverse impacts

9.6.1 Control

1. Floods can be controlled by careful management through appropriately halting or holding or storing the water to prevent waterways from overflowing their banks. Often the following methods are employed as defense for flood control.
   - detention basins,
   - lakes (natural/artificial)
   - check dams
   - levees,
   - bunds,
   - reservoirs, and
   - weirs
2. When the above defenses fail, emergency measures may be used to try to stem floods such as
   - sandbags or
   - portable inflatable tubes

3. Coastal floods may be controlled (like in USA, Europe, Japan) by
    - sea walls,
    - beach nourishment,
    - barrier islands and
    - other coastal defenses
4. In the riparian zone near rivers and streams,
    - erosion control measures have to be taken by slow down the flow
    - reversing of the natural forces that cause many waterways to meander over long periods
5. Flood controls like dams can be constructed and maintained to reduce the occurrence and severity of floods and its after-effects.
6. In areas prone to urban flooding,
    - build up and maintain green-infrastructure or sustainable urban drainage systems (SUDS) (i.e. reducing impervious surfaces in streets, parking lots and buildings through natural drainage channels, porous paving, and wetlands etc.)
    - the drainage lines and creeks should be inspected on regular intervals and repair works should be undertaken immediately
    - expansion of man-made sewer systems should be planned and executed and
    - storm-water infrastructure has to be built.
7. Areas identified as flood-prone can be converted into parks and playgrounds that can tolerate occasional flooding.
8. Efforts are to be made to retain storm-water on site
9. Base height of buildings/constructions should to be elevated
10. Floods can stopped or diverted or reduced and hence protected by flood-walls and levees, or be other designs to withstand temporary inundation. (flood-wall image)
11. Property owners can also invest in solutions themselves, such as re-landscaping their property to take the flow of water away from their building and installing
    - rain barrels,
    - sump pumps, and
    - check valves

9.6.2 Source of Flood Information and Flood-Forecasting

The flood-forecasting is made based on the most commonly used information listed below:

- Historical (past) records

- Geological and geographical information
- Hydrology and soil characteristics of the area
- Drainage system
- Real-time knowledge and experience
- Radar Information
- Weather forecasting information

9.6.3 The Analysis of Flood-information

Collection of flood data is very important, particularly in the areas identified as flood-prone, such as river banks, coastal belts and low-lying areas. The information of series of annual maximum flow rates is to be collected and analyzed statistically to estimate the recurrence interval. The estimates from many sites in similar hydrologic regions can also be related to measurable characteristics of each drainage basin. (This forms an indirect estimation of flood recurrence intervals for stream reaches without sufficient data for direct analysis).

It is always a better idea to maintain a long time-series of historical data (even 100 years or more) that relates stream flows to past rainfall events in order to make the most accurate flood forecasts for waterways. This historical data coupled with real-time knowledge about volumetric capacity in catchment areas, such as spare capacity in reservoirs, ground-water levels, sewage and the degree of saturation of area aquifers can help assessing to result in the most accurate flood forecasts.

Radars also can estimate the rainfall, particularly in the coastal areas. Even the general weather forecasting techniques can also give fairly good forecasting about floods. In areas where good quality data is available, even the likely time of occurrence (arrival), duration, intensity and height of a flood can also be prognosticated with reasonably good accuracy with a good amount of lead time. Now-a-days with the advent of computerization, the instrumentation is available to predict the key locations under risk along the waterway, the time of arrival and return period and other characteristics. Many developed countries developed the mechanism and systems to protect the urban areas at risk of flooding against a 100-year flood.

9.6.4 Benefits of Analysis of Flood-information and Forecasting

Anticipating floods well in advance can allow taking precautions and alarming people so that they can be prepared for flooding conditions. Some of such precautions (benefits) are listed below.

- Farmers & peasants can move animals from low-lying areas and
- Utility services can be put in place
- Emergency provisions may be re-routed or reorganized
- Transport and other essential services may be diverted through alternate routes or alternate modes/methods if needed
- Provision is made to have enough resources available ahead of time to respond to emergencies when they occur
- People can evacuate areas to be flooded.

9.6.5 Global Flood Monitoring System (GFMS)

A computer tool, Global Flood Monitoring System (GFMS), is available online that can map flood conditions worldwide. It is accessible from anywhere in the world to determine when floods may occur in their area. GFMS uses precipitation data from NASA's Earth observing satellites and the Global Precipitation Measurement (GPM) satellite. However, the rainfall data from GPM is combined with a land surface model that includes vegetation cover, soil type, and terrain to determine how much water is seeping (into the ground), and how much water is flowing. The statistics for rainfall, stream-flow, water depth, and flooding can be viewed every 3 hours, at each 12 km grid point on a global map. Usually, the forecasts for these parameters is mapped for 5 days into the future. Users can zoom in to see inundation maps (areas estimated to be covered with water) in 1 km resolution.

At extremely high flows, or vortices are formed by large volumes of rapidly rushing water, which cause extreme local erosion, plucking bedrock and creating pothole-type geographical features called Rock-cut basins. (Example: Flooding of glacial Lake Missoula, created the channeled scablands in the Columbia Basin of E Washington).

SELF ASSESSMENT INTERMISSION (SAI – 9.2)

1. Define Flood? What are the factors motivate the floods?
2. What are up-slope factors to cause floods? Discuss.
3. What are down-slope factors to cause floods? Discuss.
4. What do you understand by coincidences to be the factor for causing floods? Explain what coincidences cause flooding?
5. Describe causes for flooding with examples.

(continued)

6. What are effects of flooding?
7. List out the short-term effects and long-term effects of floods.
8. Can floods be beneficiary? If so, what are its benefits?
9. Give a detailed flood safety plan and mitigation methods to protect, to be prepared, to control and to rehabilitate.
10. What is flood forecasting and flood information? Where do you get this?
11. What is flood information analysis? What are its benefits?
12. What is Global Flood Monitoring System (GFMS)? Where do you get it? How is it useful?
13. Discuss the effect of floods on land degradation and soil erosion.
14. Discuss the relationship between the following pairs
    (a) Cyclones and Floods (b) Tsunami and Floods
    (c) Floods and Landslides (d) Floods and Soil Erosion

9.7 SOIL EROSION

Soil erosion is a naturally occurring phenomenon of soil degradation on any type of land. Soil erosion occurs due to currents of water and wind, and is a slow process that continues unnoticed, or it may occur at an alarming rate causing serious loss of top soil. The loss of soil from fields may lead to reduce the crop production capacity and affect the surface water quality and damaged drainage network.

Definition

Soil erosion is the displacement of upper layer of soil, and is one form of soil degradation.

9.8 FACTORS INFLUENCING SOIL EROSION

There are many factors which influence the process of soil erosion, some go noticed while some unnoticed; these are discussed below:

9.8.1 Climate

The climatic factors such as amount and intensity of precipitation, rainfall, wind speed etc. form key in governing soil erosion by water. Moreover, the relationship is stronger if heavy rainfall occurs particularly, when the soil's surface is not well protected by vegetation. Other climatic factors such as average temperature and temperature range may also affect erosion, via their effects on vegetation and soil properties. In general, given similar vegetation and ecosystems, areas with more precipitation (especially high-intensity rainfall), more wind, or more storms are expected to have more erosion. Owing to their higher importance in soil erosion, we shall briefly discuss about these two factors (rainfall and wind speed).

(a) Rainfall: Precipitation is the most important factor causing erosion. Erosion depends on the amount, duration, intensity and frequency of rainfall. The dashing rain drops on soil, loosen the soil granules, detach and separate into fine particles, thereby, increase the flow ability. In some regions (e.g. the mid-west USA), rainfall is the primary determinant of erosion, with higher intensity rainfall generally resulting in greater soil erosion by water. Even, the size or velocity of rain drops is also an important factor since, the larger and higher-velocity rain drops have greater kinetic energy, and thus their impact will displace soil particles by larger distances than smaller, slower-moving rain drops. In other areas (e.g. W Europe), runoff and erosion result from relatively low intensities of stratiform rainfall onto previously saturated soil. In such circumstances, rainfall amount rather than intensity is the main factor determining the severity of soil erosion by water.

(b) Wind Velocity: Obviously, the stronger the winds, greater will be erosive potential, thence wind velocity is directly proportional to intensity of erosion. Wind erosion requires strong winds, particularly during times of drought when vegetation is sparse and soil is dry and so is more erodible. [The detailed discussion on soil erosion by wind is made in the next section 9.9.2].

9.8.2 Slope and Topography

As a known fact, the water flows down due to the flow ability supported by gravitational force. The slope accelerates erosion as it increases the velocity of the flowing water. This increases the erosion of soil at upper levels

The topography of the land determines the velocity at which surface runoff will flow, which in turn determines the erosion by the runoff. During heavy rains, the longer, steeper slopes (particularly, in case of inadequate vegetative cover) are more susceptible to very high rates of erosion besides becoming vulnerable to mudslides, landslides, rockslides and so forth.

9.8.3 Vegetation

Vegetation acts as an interface between the atmosphere and the soil. It covers up the soil and forms a protective canopy that safeguards from the beating and dispersing action of the raindrops. Further, it also acts as a mechanical obstruction to flowing water, thence reduces erosion. It also enhances the permeability of the soil to rainwater, thus decreasing runoff. The roots of plants reinforce by interweaving naturally with other roots that bind the soil together to provide high strength reducing the vulnerability to the erosion. Further, they protect the soil from winds, thence the lowered wind erosion. So, obviously, the removal of vegetation encourages the rate of surface erosion.

9.8.4 Tillage

Proper tillage enhances the infiltration and permeability of the soil, thereby reduces the erosion. However, excess tilling can expose the soil to erosion, particularly by wind.

9.8.5 Nature of the Soil

The nature of the soil plays a great role in determining the erosion of rainfall, particularly with reference to its texture, structure, organic matter, composition, moisture, and compaction of soil, amounts and kinds of salts present, presence of hard pan or rock in the soil and presence of high water table.

- Sediments with clay would be more resistant to erosion than those with sand or silt, as the clay acts as binder.
- Soil with organic matter is also more resistant to erosion, since they coagulate soil colloids and create a stronger, more stable soil structure.
- The water present in the soil before the precipitation sets limits on the amount of water that can be absorbed by the soil.
- Wet, saturated soils will not absorb much rain water, leading to higher levels of surface runoff and thence higher erosion for a given volume of rainfall.
- Compact soil is less permeable to water, and thence the amount of water that flows away as runoff. More the compacted soils, larger amount will be surface runoff.

9.8.6 Moisture in Soil and Seepage

The high water table under the soil restricts the infiltration and permeability, which in turn permits more flow of water on the surface, thence enhances erosion. Otherwise also, long continuous rainless periods loosen the soil and thus the soil gets exposed to erode by wind.

9.9 CAUSES OF SOIL EROSION

Soil erosion is the creeping death and in large majority of the cases, the causes of soil erosion are directly related to improper land use and hence can be claimed as entirely man-made.

The following are main causes for soil erosion:

9.9.1 Deforestation

Deforestation is the foremost motivator for soil erosion. For example, the removal of vegetation cover has caused large erosion in Western Ghats, Uttar Pradesh and in Himachal Pradesh.

In fact, in an undisturbed forest, the mineral soil is protected by the layers called *leaf litter* and *humus*. They absorb the impact of rain drops as they are porous and permit the rainwater to percolate into the soil beneath, instead of runoff. The roots of the trees and plants reinforce and bind soil particles, preventing from erosion. Further, the vegetative cover retards of the raindrops before falling on ground and as well restricts the flow. Thus, deforestation enhances the erosion rates by removing the humus and litter layers from the soil surface, and also the vegetative cover that binds soil together.

Globally, one of the largest contributors to erosive soil loss in the year 2006 is the slash and burn treatment of tropical forests. For example, Madagascar high central plateau, comprising about 10% of that country's land area was degraded soil to become less and less fertile.

9.9.2 Inappropriate Cultivation Methods

Agro-engineering studies have shown that inappropriate cultivation can also cause the soil erosion. For instance, in the recent past, in Nilgiris (India), tuber crops (potatoes and ginger) have been cultivated where neither the slopes were terraced and nor used any other anti-erosive measures. Moreover, the forests on slopes were removed to facilitate the plantation crops. These faulty methods of cultivation caused soil erosion and landslides also.

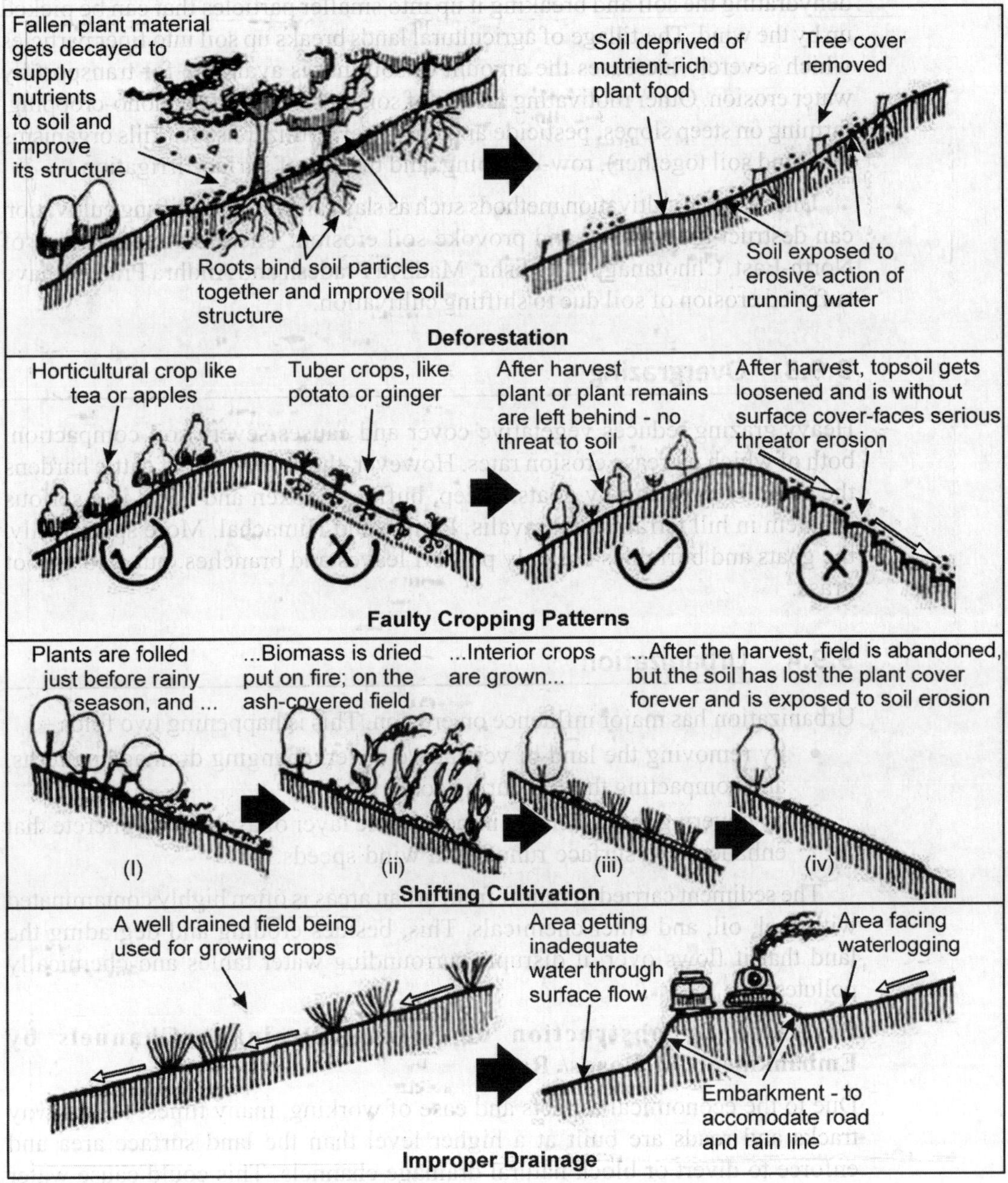

Fig. 9.1 Various causes of soil erosion.

Unsustainable cultivation practices are the single greatest contributor to the global increase in erosion rates. Tillage increases wind erosion rates, by dehydrating the soil and breaking it up into smaller particles that can be picked up by the wind. The tillage of agricultural lands breaks up soil into finer particles which severely increases the amount of soil that is available for transport by water erosion. Other motivating factors of soil erosion could be mono-cropping, farming on steep slopes, pesticide and chemical fertilizer usage (kills organisms that bind soil together), row-cropping, and the use of surface irrigation.

Uneconomic cultivation methods such as slash and burn or shifting cultivation can destruct the ecology and provoke soil erosion. The mountain terrains of North-East, Chhotanagpur, Odisha, Madhya Pradesh and Andhra Pradesh have suffered erosion of soil due to shifting cultivation.

9.9.3 Overgrazing

Heavy grazing reduces vegetative cover and causes severe soil compaction, both of which increase erosion rates. However, the movement of cattle hardens the soil. Overgrazing by goats, sheep, buffaloes, oxen and cows is a serious problem in hill terrains of Aravalis, Punjab and Himachal. More specifically, the goats and buffaloes not only pull off leaves and branches, but also uproot grass.

9.9.4 Urbanization

Urbanization has major influence on erosion. This is happening two fold:

- by removing the land of vegetative cover, changing drainage patterns, and compacting the soil during construction;
- by covering the land in an impermeable layer of asphalt or concrete that enhances the surface runoff and wind speeds.

The sediment carried in runoff from urban areas is often highly contaminated with fuel, oil, and other chemicals. This, besides eroding and degrading the land that it flows over, it disrupts surrounding water tables and chemically pollutes.

Diversion or obstruction of Natural Drainage Channels by Embankments of Roads/ Rails

Due to the economical aspects and ease of working, many times, the railway tracks and roads are built at a higher level than the land surface area and enforce to divert or block natural drainage channels. This could cause water log on one side while water loss on the other and ultimately contributes to erosion.

9.9.5 Improper Surface Drainage

The improper surface drainage causes water log occurs in low lying areas which in turn loosens the top-soil and thence makes it prone to erosion.

9.9.6 Wildfires

Though sometimes natural but often man-made, wildfire destructs the forests, thereby the protective canopy due to plants and vegetation on land surface is cleared, resulting exposure of soil to erosion.

9.9.7 Climate Change

The warmer atmospheric temperatures are observed over the past decades leading to a more vigorous hydrological cycle, and more extreme rainfall events. Climatic change is resulting in the rise in sea levels thereby increasing coastal erosion rates.

SELF ASSESSMENT INTERMISSION (SAI – 9.3)

1. Define Soil Erosion? What is its relationship with floods?
2. What factors to can influence or motivate soil erosion? Discuss.
3. What are climatic factors to influence soil erosion? Discuss.
4. How do rains and winds affect soil to erode? Explain.
5. Explain the role of vegetation in soil erosion process
6. Explain how soil erosion depends on the nature of soil.
7. Discuss the effect of the following on the soil erosion
   (a) Tillage (b) Topography
8. Describe causes for soil erosion with examples.
9. How is deforestation responsible for soil erosion?
10. How does urbanization cause soil erosion? Explain with examples.
11. How do cultivation methods responsible for soil erosion?
12. Discuss the effect of the following on the soil erosion
    (a) Over grazing (b) Global Climatic Changes (c) Wildfires (d) Drainage system

9.10 TYPES OF EROSION

Various types of soil erosions are discussed below.

9.10.1 Erosion by Water

Rainfall, and thence the surface runoff produces soil erosion by water, which may appear in several ways as described below:

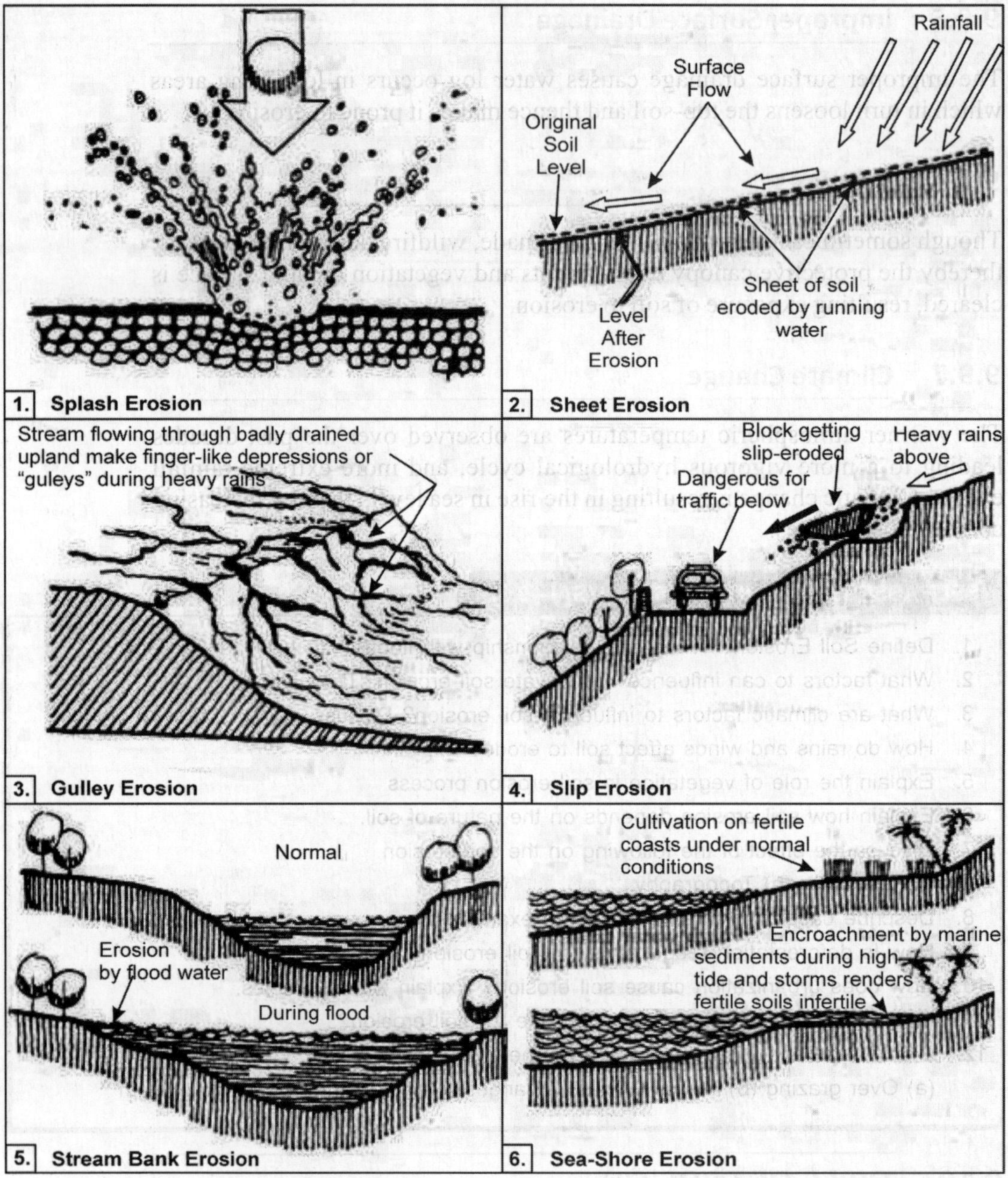

Fig. 9.2

1. **Splash Erosion:** This kind of erosion happens if the falling raindrops splash on the soil, and hammer the surrounding soil into flowing mud. The impact of a falling raindrop creates a small crater in the soil, ejecting

soil particles. The distance these soil particles travel can be as much as 0.6 m (2 ft) vertically and 1.5 m (5 ft) horizontally on level ground. Surface runoff occurs if the soil is saturated, or when the rainfall rate is sufficiently greater than the rate of infiltration of water into the soil. Further, when the runoff acquires adequate energy, it transports loosened soil and sediment down the slope.

2. **Sheet Erosion:** This type of erosion is said to be occurred when soil is a thin layer is removed uniformly from the entire surface area. However, the movement of soil by splash erosion is the basic reason behind the sheet erosion. Simply, it is the transport of loosened soil particles by overland flow.
3. **Rill Erosion:** Rill erosion is an intermediate stage between sheet or gully erosion. It occurs if the run-off water, laden with soil flowing along the slopes, forming fingerlike channels and refers to the development of small, fleeted, grooved flow paths which function as both sediment source and sediment delivery systems for erosion on hill-slopes. Generally, where water erosion rates on disturbed upland areas are greatest, rills are active.
4. **Gully Erosion:** This kind of erosion occurs when runoff water accumulates and rapidly flows in narrow channels during or immediately after heavy rains or melting snow, removing soil to a considerable depth. In other words, when the volume of concentrated run-off increases and acquires more velocity on slopes, the rills enlarges into gullies. On furtherance of this, gullies convert into ravines, which are sometimes 50 – 100 ft deep. In India ravines cover about 10 million hectares.

Eroded gully in Dead Sea (Israel), excavated by floods from the Judean Mountains within a year.

The above four types of water erosions are mainly due to rain, Of these, splash erosion is generally seen as the first and least severe stage in the soil erosion process, which is followed by sheet erosion, then rill erosion and finally gully erosion (the most severe of the four).

5. **Slip Erosion:** Slip erosion is caused by landslides i.e. big masses of soil and rock slip down, and damage the fields in the foothills and/or cause obstructions in transportation and communication. The effect of slip erosion is often localized.

6. **Valley or Stream Erosion:** This occurs due to continued water flow along a linear feature such as streams and rivers shift or alter their courses by cutting one bank and depositing the silt loads on the others. Further, the flash floods can accelerate the damage. For example, the river Kosi in Bihar has changed its course westwards by 100 km within the last 100 years.

   In the early stage, this erosive activity is predominantly vertical, the valleys have a typical **V** cross-section and the stream gradient is relatively steep. When some base level is obtained, the erosion switches to lateral, which widens the valley floor and creates a narrow floodplain. The stream gradient becomes nearly flat, and lateral deposition of sediments make the stream rush across the valley floor. In all stages of stream erosion, the most erosion occurs during floods owing to the more and faster-moving water carry a larger sediment load. Moreover, during such processes, it is not only the water that erodes, but also the suspended abrasive particles, pebbles and boulders can erode a surface, which is known as *traction*.
7. **Bank Erosion:** This is the wearing away of the banks of a stream or river. This is distinguished from changes on the bed of the watercourse, which is referred to as *scour*. Erosion can measured by inserting metal rods into the bank and marking the position of bank surface on the rods at regular intervals.
8. **Thermal erosion:** This is the result of melting and weakening permafrost due to moving water. It can occur both along rivers and at the coast. For example, the Lena River of Siberia is suffered thermal erosion, as the portions of the banks are composed of permafrost-cemented non-cohesive materials. This erosion occurs when the weakened banks fail in large slumps. The arctic coasts are susceptible to thermal erosion (guess why?).
9. **Sea Shore Erosion:** This occurs by the striking action of strong waves. This kind of erosion is found along beaches, sea shores due to the oceanic waves.

9.10.2 Erosion by Wind

Wind erosion is major geo-morphological force, particularly in arid and semi-arid regions and is also chief contributor for

- land degradation,
- evaporation,

- desertification,
- harmful airborne dust, and
- crop damage

Wind Erosion

Árbol de Piedra, a rock in the Altiplano, Bolivia sculpted by wind erosion

Wind erosion is of two primary varieties: 1.Deflation and 2. Abrasion

1. **Deflation:** The deflation is said to be done when wind picks up and carries away loose particles. This is further divided into three categories:

   (a) Surface creep: *Surface creep* refers to larger, heavier particles sliding or rolling along the ground. This is the slow movement of soil and rock debris by gravity which is usually not perceptible. More specifically, in surface creep, the dislodged soil particles, usually of the order of 0.5-1.0 mm (0.02-0.04 in) in diameter roll or slide by wind along the soil surface.

   (b) Saltation: Particles are lifted a short height into the air, and bounce and saltate across the surface of the soil

   (c) Suspension: Very small and light particles are lifted into the air by the wind, and are often carried for long distances.

   Saltation is responsible for the large majority (50–70%) of wind erosion, followed by suspension (30–40%), and then surface creep (5–25%). Silty soils tend to be the most affected by wind erosion; silt particles are relatively easily detached and carried away. Wind erosion is much more severe in arid areas and during times of drought. (Example: Soil loss due to wind erosion is 6100 times greater in drought years than in wet years in Great Plains).

2. **Abrasion:** Surfaces are worn down as they are struck by airborne particles carried by wind. The abrasion on one hand causes the soil erosion, while it raises air pollution on the other. Further, it alters the air density motivating the pressure changes to cause depressions, tornado or dust devils etc.

9.10.3 Erosion by Human Activity

While erosion is a natural process, human activities have increased by 10–40 times the rate at which erosion is occurring globally. As discussed above (in section 9.10) intensive agriculture, deforestation, roads and buildings, anthropogenic climate change and urban sprawl are amongst the most significant human activities to stimulate erosion.

Excessive (or accelerated) erosion causes both "on-site" and "off-site" problems.

On-site impacts include the loss of the nutrient-rich upper soil layers, and finally desertification. This is exhibited in two major ways as

- decrease in agricultural productivity and
- ecological collapse on natural landscapes,

Off-site effects include

- sedimentation of waterways and
- eutrophication of water bodies,
- sediment-related damage to roads and houses.

However, there are many prevention and remediation practices that can curtail or limit erosion of vulnerable soils.

9.10.4 Erosion by Mass Movement and Slumping

Mass movement refers to the landslides, rockslides and mudslides which is the downward and outward movement of rock and sediments on a sloped surface, mainly due to the force of gravity [Any perceptible down-slope movement of rock or sediment is often referred to in general terms as a landslide, or rockslide as discussed in chapter-6 of this book]. Mass movement is an important part of the erosion process, and is often the first stage in the transport of weathered materials in hilly terrain. It moves material from higher elevations to lower elevations where other eroding agents such as streams and glaciers can then pick up the material and drive it to further lower elevations.

Slumping is yet another soil eroding activity that occurs on steep hillsides along distinct fracture zones, often within materials like clay. Once released, it runs quite rapidly downhill. These will often appear as a spoon-shaped isostatic depression, in which the material has begun to slide downhill. In some cases, the slump is caused by water under the slope weakening it. In most cases it is due to poor engineering along highways where it is a regular occurrence.

9.11 EFFECTS OF SOIL EROSION

The major effects of soil erosion are listed below

9.11.1 Land Degradation

About 85% of land degraded acreage is blamed on water and wind erosion. Each year, about 75 billion tons of soil is eroded from the land—i.e. about 13–

40 times faster than the natural rate of erosion and nearly 40% of the world's agricultural land is seriously degraded. For example, as per the UN, the fertile soil of Ukraine is lost every year because of drought, deforestation and climate change. In Africa, if this continues, the continent might be able to feed just 25% of its population only by 2025, as per Ghana-based Institute for Natural Resources in Africa. The loss of soil fertility is yet another problem decide over usage of chemical fertilizers, which may lead to further water and soil pollution, rather than to allow the land to regenerate.

9.11.2 Reducing Organic Matter and Soil Structure

The upper layer of soil contains the organic matter and as other nutrients. When this is subjected to erosion, it decreases the content of this fertility, making the soil structure impoverished.

9.11.3 Loss of Soil

When the top-soil, the most fertile section, is lost by erosion due to formation of gullies and ravines, valuable agricultural lands are lost.

9.11.4 Decline in Soil Capacity

As the soil is removed from field, the available plant food along with mineral material is carried away and the ability of the land to supply moisture for plant growth is reduced. Thence, the soil capacity or yield is lowered.

9.11.5 Deposition of Sand and Gravel on Agricultural Lands

The wind-borne sand covers upon the arable lands and makes them unfertile. Crops get affected seriously due to soil erosion by sand storms.

9.11.6 Sedimentation of Aquatic Ecosystems

Soil erosion is the leading global cause of water pollution, due to the excess sediments flowing into the world's waterways. The sediments themselves act as pollutants, as well as being carriers for other pollutants, such as attached pesticide molecules or heavy metals.

The effects of increased sediments adversely affect aquatic ecosystems. Silt suffocates the fish, also reduces their food supply, and causes major respiratory issues for them as sediment enters their gills. The biodiversity of aquatic plant and algal life is reduced, and invertebrates are also unable to survive and reproduce. Though the sedimentation event itself might be relatively short-lived, the ecological disruption caused by it often persists long into the future.

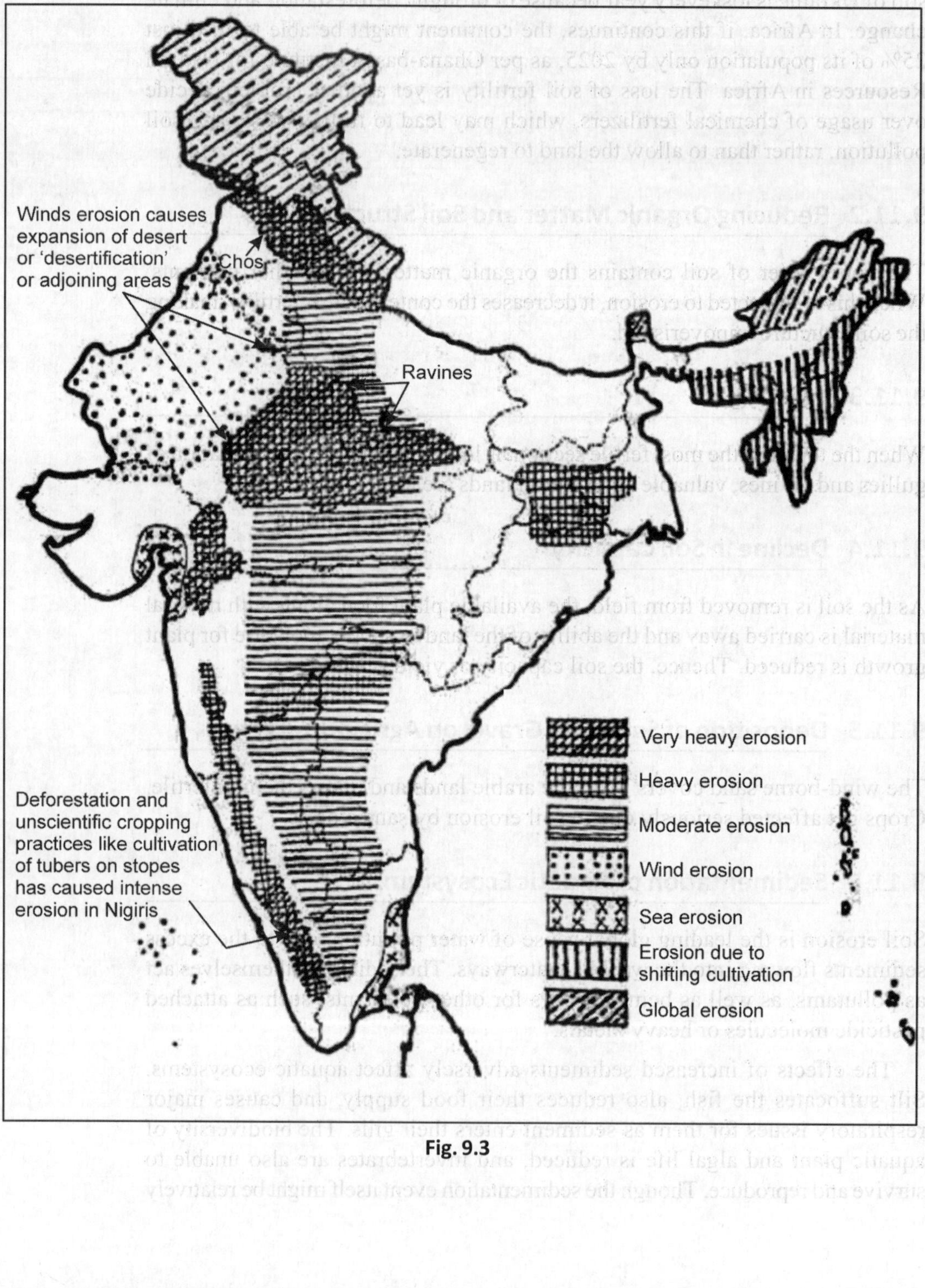

Fig. 9.3

9.11.7 Airborne Dust Pollution

Soil particles in the form of "dust" lifted up during wind erosion of soil are main source of air pollution. These airborne soil particles are often contaminated with toxic chemicals such as pesticides or petroleum fuels, posing ecological and public health hazards as they later land, or are inhaled/ingested. Further, dust from erosion can suppress rainfall and change the sky color from blue to white, leading to an increase in red sunsets. Believe it or not! Dust events are found to decline the health across the Caribbean and Florida, since the 1970s.

9.11.8 Flooding of Streams

In catchment areas of streams soil erosion takes place due to deforestation resulting in silting of streams and reservoirs. This reduces the capacity of the water bodies to carry large volumes of water, as they happen during the rainy season making the streams more prone to flooding. For example, River Brahmaputra has been exposed to siltation due to deforestation in the hills, and so, in Brahmaputra valley, the flooding became a common annual event.

9.12 MAJOR SOIL EROSION CHALLENGES IN INDIA

In India, about 80 million hectares (MHa) of land area is under the threat of soil erosion, out of which 43 MHa area is actually affected. In Madhya Pradesh, Rajasthan, Maharashtra and Punjab, about 15% of the total land is suffering from soil erosion. Believe it or not! The annual loss of fertility by erosion is 20 times faster than what is lost by growing crops. Each year, 10,000 hectares is getting eroded. Approximately 145 million hectares area in India is in need of conservation measures. Following are some noteworthy places most subjected to soil erosion.

- ***Nilgiris*** suffered widespread erosion by potato cultivation on steep slopes without proper terracing.
- ***Gujarat, Maharashtra, Karnataka, Madhya Pradesh, Uttar Pradesh and Rajasthan*** *and also along* ***Yamuna and Chambal*** have Gullies or Ravines eroded nearly 10 MHa area.
- ***Hoshiarpur in the Mt. Shivaliks*** in north India is experiencing soil erosion vis-à-vis landslides.
- ***Some parts of Punjab, Madhya Pradesh, Maharashtra, Andhra Pradesh, Telangana and Karnataka*** have low/uncertain rainfall that are scanty, ill-distributed and highly erosive with undulating topography, high wind velocity and shallow. Soil erosion is heavy in these areas usually due to heavy downpours or wind from August to October.

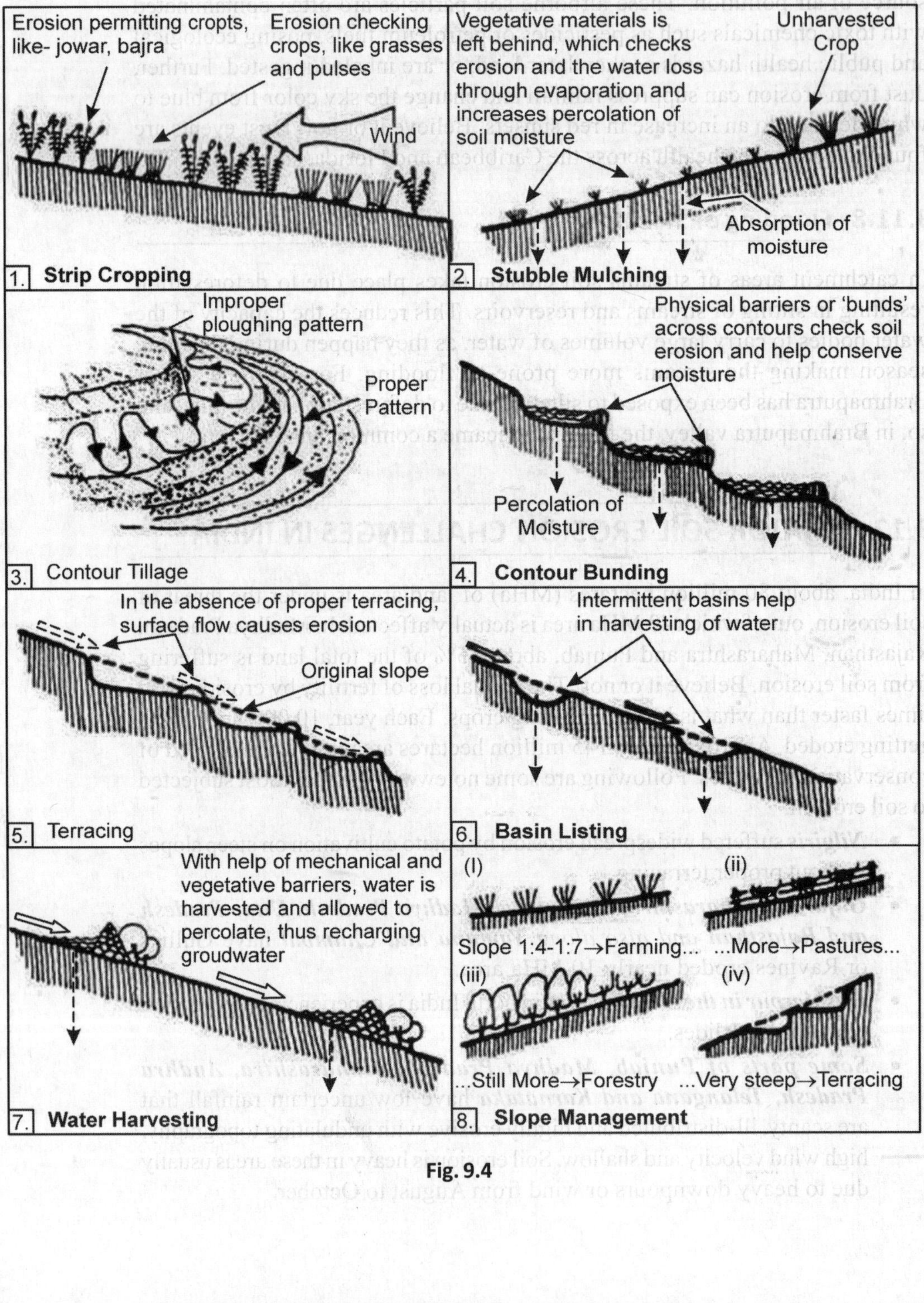
Erosion permitting cropts, like- jowar, bajra
Erosion checking crops, like grasses and pulses
Wind
1. Strip Cropping
Vegetative materials is left behind, which checks erosion and the water loss through evaporation and increases percolation of soil moisture
Unharvested Crop
Absorption of moisture
2. Stubble Mulching
Improper ploughing pattern
Proper Pattern
3. Contour Tillage
Physical barriers or 'bunds' across contours check soil erosion and help conserve moisture
Percolation of Moisture
4. Contour Bunding
In the absence of proper terracing, surface flow causes erosion
Original slope
5. Terracing
Intermittent basins help in harvesting of water
6. Basin Listing
With help of mechanical and vegetative barriers, water is harvested and allowed to percolate, thus recharging groudwater
7. Water Harvesting
(I)
(ii)
Slope 1:4-1:7→Farming...
...More→Pastures...
(iii)
(iv)
...Still More→Forestry
...Very steep→Terracing
8. Slope Management

Fig. 9.4

- ***Rajasthan*** is subjected to desertification by wind erosion, coupled with loss of surface cover in the Aravalis, posing a challenge ecological balance to the country today.
- ***Saurashtra region of Gujarat*** is facing coastal erosion by sand movement from the coast due to which the ports, once flourished are now covered with advancing sand-dunes.

9.13 METHODS TO PREVENT SOIL EROSION

The conservation of soil and water and controlling the soil erosion can be either biological or mechanical or managerial or combinations of these. These are briefed out below.

9.13.1 Biological Measures

The following are biological methods to control soil erosion

1. **Improve the Existing Surface Cover:** Cover cropping through groundnut or a fodder crop or grasses like dub, kudzu, pans can restrict the erosion.
2. **Strip Cropping:** Under this method the erosion-permitting crops (jowar, maize) and erosion checking crops (grasses, pulses) are grown in alternate strips so that the erosion checking strips hold the flowing water/soil.
3. **Crop Rotation:** This is the most common method followed by the peasants, in which two or more different crops are harvested in sequence in a field for maintaining the soil fertility. However, continuous growing of clean-cultivated crops (e.g., tobacco) causes more erosion; therefore, an appropriate rotation should be maintained with densely planted small grains, spreading legume which can control the soil erosion.
4. **Stubble Mulching:** This method advises to leave crop residue or vegetative litter on the land. This not only protects surface against erosion but also conserves moisture, favours infiltration and thus reduces evaporation.
5. **Use of Organic Manures:** Soil structure can be improved by organic manures such as cow dung, green manure, farmyard manure etc. Granular and crumby structures enhance infiltration and permeability in the soil and conserve soil moisture.
6. **Preventive Measures**: Prevention is better than cure. Therefore reducing or forestalling

Terracing at OOTY, India best way to prevent soil erosion

the soil eroding factors can help. The following are a few preventive measures.

(a) Check overgrazing,

(b) Reduce surplus cattle,

(c) Stop shifting-cultivation

(d) Prevent forest fires.

9.13.2 Mechanical Measures

The following mechanical measures can be applied to control erosion.

1. **Contour Tillage:** All tillage operations have to be made at right angles to the slope of the land so that each channel intercepts the flowing water and permits to soak into the soil.
2. **Contour Bund:** The slope of the land can be broken into smaller, more level compartments by constructing suitable mechanical structures along contours so that each bund holds the rainwater within each compartment.
3. **Terracing:** If the slope is steeper, flat platforms or terraces have to be built in steps in a series along the slope so that the water can be retained on each terrace and utilized for the crops.
4. **Proper Drainage Channels and Plugging the Gullies**

A windbreak

(The row of trees) planted next to an agricultural field, acting as a shield against strong winds. This reduces the effects of wind erosion, and provides many other benefits.

(a) **Basin Listing:** Small basins have to be scooped out at regular intervals on slopes so that the run-off can be checked and water can be conserved.

(b) **Water Harvesting:** The water is trapped or channeled into low-lying areas so as to check the run-off. This can also acts as a flood control measure.

(c) **Scientific Slope Management:** Proper farming can be carried out, if the slope is in between 1:4 and 1:7; if the slope is more, pastures have to be developed; if it furthermore, forestry operations may be considered; if it is still more, then terracing may be needed before cropping. Whatsoever, the cropping is to be taken up as per the nature of slope.

9.13.3 Managerial Methods

1. **Keep soil covered yearlong:** Bare soil is more vulnerable to erosion than soil with ground cover. It is better if at least 30% of grazing land

has ground cover. After harvesting a crop, better leave the residue as mulch, if go not, go with hardy winter crops.

2. **Plant trees to prevent landslides and soil erosion:** Tree roots are the best tools to reduce soil loss, particularly when soil is too susceptible for erosion or steeper slope. However, mulch or grass yield best results in case of bare ground.
3. **Reduce tillage:** Deep and frequent tillage may generate a layer of compact soil vulnerable to erosion by water, and topped by loose soil can be eroded by wind easily. So, better a zero-tillage approach by deep planting device or if not feasible, a ridge-till or mulch-till system can work the lower soil levels untouched. Further, it curtails the erosion due to vehicle traffic too.
4. **Protect weak crops with strip cropping:** Crops with weak roots or sparsely planted are more vulnerable to erosion. Strip plantation i.e. alternating with strips of an erosion-resistant crop such as dense grass or legumes can protect better. Plant the crops along a contour in the slope. As far as possible, plant the crops perpendicular to the prevailing wind.
5. **Practice wet season spelling:** Grazing land is not erosion-resistant if cattle are permitted to graze throughout the year. So, it is always a better idea to close off the entire wet season so that grasses rejuvenate themselves.
6. **Control downhill runoff with flumes:** The points where the concentrated runoff approaches a slope are more vulnerable to erosion. So, a paved flume, or lined channel may be built to guide the water to a safe drainage system. It is better to build these at gully heads. However, building flumes on slopes steeper than 1.5:1 (3:2) is not suggestible.
7. **Avoid soil compaction:** Soil is compressed by foot and vehicle traffic, reducing its porosity and makes vulnerable to water runoff. The following are few suggestions for minimizing this effect:
   - Demarcate permanent pavements/gangways/walkways with paving stones, stepping stones, or cleared paths. Observe and monitor people to be on the walkways only.
   - Do not permit to walk over wet soil, because it compacts more easily.
   - Create concrete drive way instead of driving over bare ground.
   - Add compost, rotted manure or other organic matter to motivate earthworms to aerate soil.

SELF ASSESSMENT INTERMISSION (SAI – 9.4)

1. What are various types of water-driven Soil Erosions? Explain with neat sketches.
2. What are splash and sheet erosions? Discuss.
3. What are Rill and Gully erosion? How do they occur? Give examples.
4. Discuss different types of soil erosion that may occur during flooding or flowing water.
5. Give a brief notes on the following soil erosion
   (a) Slip erosion (b) Valley erosion (c) Thermal Erosion (d) Sea-Shore erosion
6. How do winds erode soil? Explain the terms deflation, surface creep, saltation, suspension and abrasion.
7. Explain the effect of various human activities causing soil erosion process.
8. Explain the effects of soil erosion.
9. How is soil erosion related to land degradation? Explain some controlling measures.
10. Give various biological measures to control soil erosion.
11. Explain the mechanical and managerial methods to control soil erosion.
12. Discuss the relationship of the following with soil erosion
    (a) Flooding (b) Pollution (water/air) (c) Climatic Changes
13. How can soil erosion be responsible to water and air pollution.
14. Write short notes on the following with reference to soil erosion
    (a) Contour Till and Contour Bund (b) Wind Breaks (c) Terracing (d) Stubble Mulching
    (e) Crop Rotation
15. Write a note on major areas in India

MINI-PROJECTS / CASE STUDIES

1. The urban areas and cities in India are facing severe urban floods problem during rainy seasons (for example: Hyderabad, Mumbai). Identify the low lying areas in city of your interest and explore the reasons and remedies to overcome this problem. Choose a small location and implement your idea.
2. Choose a hillside or river bank and place (or any vulnerable place of your choice) the metallic rods at the probable soil erosion places on the riverside. Mark the level of soil in regular intervals and estimate the rate of soil erosion. Prepare a report with proposals to prevent the erosion. Also enumerate the causes and effects through Ishikawa diagram.

CHAPTER 10

Drought and Famine

O'MY SILENT INNER VIBES (O'M S I V – 10)

Hiderigami, the *God of drought*, a mythical species of *Yôkai* (Ghost) in Japanese folklore, is is 60-90 cm long, with eyes on top of head and moves as fast as wind, whose acts range diversely from malicious to mischievous, or occasionally give fortunes to those who encounter. In more or less similar lines, Hindu myths refer '*Jyeshta devi*' as the goddess of drought/ famine and misfortunes.

A similar species is found in Chinese myths ***Han-Ba*** or ***Nü-Ba***, or simply ***Ba*** ("Ba" is actual name, while the *nü* refers to feminine and ***han*** means "drought"), whose story is interesting.

After a long preparation, Chiyou made many weapons, and gathered many monsters, and attacked Huang Di, the Yellow King. Huang Di sent Yinglong, a flying dragon who caused great floods to trap Chiyou. Chiyou fielded Feng Bo (the wind god) and Yu Shi (the rain god) and countered by weather wizards, and Yinglong's army lost in dizzying storm. Then, Huang Di, sent his daughter, the Goddess ***Ba*** to battle. In black clothes, bald, and radiating great light and heat, she came and used her power, to dissipate the storm. Thus Huang Di won and killed Chiyou.

Though Hanba and Yinglong had great achievements, they could not return to the heavens, as they lost their godly power. So Yinglong stayed in the south of China, where there will be water and rain, while Ba remained in North. The 3ft height drought deity, Ba after the event, walked naked and wandered as fast as the wind in the northern parts of the earth and cursed to cause a drought. For that matter, wherever she appeared there would be a drought, so Nüba is also called drought demon. Thence, rain ceremonies were/are held in many regions of China to drive Ba out of the region with a belief that rain would then be sure to commence as soon as she goes away.

During the time of **Emperor Zhenzong,** it was rumoured that the Hanba struck and took all the water of Yanchi. The Emperor then sought help of Celestial Master Zhang, who sent Guan Yu. Yu fought for 7 days to defeat the monster and was titled "Yi yong wu an wang" (Righteous Brave Military Peace Kin). The 13th of 5th month in Chinese calendar, henceforth Chinese celebrated Guan Yu's day praying for the banishment of demons, plagues, and for rain, and thought that on that day it must rain, and if it does not, prayers would certainly be answered.

In Hindu myths also, ***Indra***, the king of Swargalok (Heaven) and the Devas (deities) is the god of lightning, thunder, storms, rains and rivers as is the most referred deity in *Rigveda*. He kills the great symbolic evil, ***Vritrasura*** *(means Enveloper, as he enveloped the waters of universe in his stomach causing drought)*, the large serpent shaped demon of drought who obstructs human prosperity and happiness. Indra, riding on White Elephant (Airavath) destroys Vritra and his "deceiving forces", with his thunderbolt (the weapon, Vajrayudham made up of backbone of Dadhichi, the great sage) and thereby brings rains and the sunshine to humankind. [The battle was an inspiration to many Hollywood movies including Matrix-3, Anacondas, Jaws and many more]

In Hindu epics, there are several references of performing *Yagnyas* (sacred fire with enchanting the *Mantras*) for the sake of rains. We often hear the word '*Swaha* (wife of *Agni*)' while pouring the ghee into the holy fire of *Yagnya*. The term '*Indrashchme*' while pouring water

(Continued)

or milk (*Abhishekam*) on the *Siva Lingam* (or holy idols) signifies the God of Gods, Indra accompanied to invoke other Gods. The Hindu traditions believe that '*Agni*' sends our offerings to the God through *Swaha*, while the God gives us coming in the form of '*Indra*'.

Even the recent researches also reveal the rains can be got by some artificial methods like cloud seeding (*Megha Madhanam*) which is analogous to that of a *Yagnya*.

Either Ba of Chinese or Indra of Hindus in several mythological stories is referred to as an interrupter of tapas, or egotists, or/and some negative shaded roles. But, in fact, (s)he is the representation of the powers produced by the senses (the Indriyas), the stories preach us to control the senses. Thus, worshipping Ba/ Indra does mean controlling our own Indriyas. Unfortunately, the most people do not realize this inherent meaning of such stories. [In fact, Indra, the God of lightening, thunders and rain, means, he is the Controller or King of emotions produced due to the clouds (the doubts and illusions) produced in external and internal senses]

So, Invite Indra's Control – Drive out Han-Ba's Patrol.

But, of course, Indra is not worshipped, due to his Sins. When Indra killed Brahman Rakshas, after a great tapas, seeks advice of Lord Vishnu, As it is an irreversible sin, he is advised to reduce the impact by distributing it to Vedic God's pious creations, the Jananies (Birth givers) namely, The Earth, Ocean, Trees and Women (and so are God's equivalents to worship). This (sharing of sin) resulted in Earth to crack, Ocean to wave, Trees to ooze milk, and Women to menstruate.

Women are pious creations of God, and are pure except for the curse of Indra, which made them impure and forbidden to visiting temples and holy pilgrimages only during the menstrual cycle. Another great thing about women is that, there is a tradition to bow down with upper torso to touch the ground (prostrate) in front of God, but women are not allowed to do so. The reason is to offer dignity and respect to women, and not to insult the Womb (treated as very sacred) of women. More than that, as God cannot stay everywhere, so, He created mother. The, often-quoted (Manusmriti-3.56) saying,

"Yatra naryastu pujyante ramante tatra Devata, Yatraitaastu na pujyante sarvaastatra falaah kriyaah" - **means, 'wherever women are respected, the deities reside there and where they are not respected, all actions remain unfruitful'.so...**

"Respect to Women" drives out droughts and invites deities.

Rare is the Famine by revering the Feminine.

10.1 THE CONCEPT AND CHARACTERISTICS

A **drought** is said to be prevailing in a given region if it experiences a period of below-average precipitation causing prolonged shortages of its water supply, whether atmospheric, surface or ground water that considerably influences the ecosystem and agriculture of the affected region.

10.1.1 Features and Characteristics

- A drought can occur for any period, short or long ranging from few weeks to months or even years.
- Short or long, the intense drought can cause substantial damage and harm to the local economy.
- The water resources such as watering holes, wells, lakes, rivers dry out completely.
- Weather will be hot with no or low humidity.
- Birds, snakes, wild life and other creatures migrate.
- Ruining of agricultural crops is clear indication of the drought.
- Severe scarcity of food and water are the basic characteristic symptoms of drought.
- The people and living-stock starve.
- Droughts are often associated with hot and dry weathers.
- The cattle deaths due to starvation and dehydration are common occurrences.
- In the tropical regions, the dry seasons motivate the probability of developing a drought, consequently bush fires and may lead to wildfires also. Thus dry seasons and wildfires are the indicators for drought conditions.
- The heat during this period speeds up evaporation of water and so can significantly

Contraction/Desiccation cracks in dry earth.

O My God!

The most prolonged (longest) drought ever in the world occurred in the Atacama Desert in Chile (400 Years).

worsen drought conditions. Thus, abnormally high rate of evaporation for a long period is an indicator of drought.

- This heat can cause the health problems to the humans, particularly to the old age, children, and diseased or physically weak. Thus increased number of registrations of hyperthermia, heat strokes etc. in the hospitals and health centres can hint forthcoming drought.
- Many plant species, such as the family Cactaceae (cacti or cactus), adapt like reduced leaf area and waxy cuticles to withstand drought conditions. Some others survive dry periods as buried seeds.
- Semi-permanent drought produces arid biomes like deserts and grasslands or with alien trees.

Prolonged droughts have caused mass-migrations and humanitarian crises. Most arid ecosystems have inherently low productivity.

10.2 CAUSES FOR DROUGHT

Drought is basically caused due to prolonged hot weathers and low precipitation. Various causes triggering the drought are listed below:

1. Dry Seasons
2. Precipitation Deficiency
3. Climate Change
4. Erosion
5. El Niño
6. Human activities (against nature)

10.2.1 Dry Seasons

The tropical regions have distinct wet and dry seasons due to the movement of the inter-tropical convergence zone or monsoon trough. Sometimes the dry season abnormally prolongs, which is manifested by its low humidity, with wells, lakes, watering holes and rivers drying up. Thence, many grazing animals like deer, zebras, elephants and wildebeest are obviously forced to migrate due to the lack of water and feed to more fertile places. Even the reptiles, monkeys and other living stock leave in gangs for more convenient areas. Lack of water in the plants causes bushfires and lead to wildfires too.

Another noteworthy issue is that water vapour gains more energy with increasing temperature. So, more water vapour is needed to increase relative humidity to 100% at higher temperatures or temperature falling to the dew point. Hot periods increase evaporation and evapo-transpiration from plants (alien), and worsen drought conditions.

10.2.2 Precipitation Deficiency

Before understanding this cause, one should first know what precipitation is and how it occurs.

Precipitation means the water seepage into the ground which may be found in the following ways

- falling as liquid water,
- liquid water that freezes on contact with the surface, or
- water in the form of ice

The process of precipitation occurs in the following three models:

(i) ***Convective process*** by huge vertical motions that can cause the overturn of the atmosphere in that location within an hour and cause heavy precipitation

(ii) ***Stratiform process*** involves weaker upward motions and less intense precipitation over a longer duration and

(iii) ***Orthographic rainfall.***

If these factors are not in favour of sufficient volumes to reach the surface for enough time, it may result in a drought. In addition the drought conditions may be motivated by

- a high level of reflected sunlight
- above average to high pressure systems, winds carrying continental rather than oceanic air masses
- ridges of high pressure areas can prevent or restrict the thunderstorm activity or rainfall over a certain region
- when a region is in drought, feedback mechanisms such as local arid air, hot conditions that promotes warm core ridging, and minimal evapo-transpiration can worsen drought conditions.

O My God!

LOESS?

Loess means a homogeneous, non-stratified, calcareous, fine-grained, silt, porous, friable, slightly coherent, pale yellow/buff, Aeolian (windblown) sediment, often stands in either steep or vertical faces and develops into highly rich soils. Widespread, tens of meters thick blanket deposits generally occur over areas of 100's of sq. kms. If climate favours, these are agriculturally most productive but geologically unstable due to erosion. So, windbreaks (like big trees and bushes) are often planted to control the erosion. Moreover, the erosion is severe in arid areas particularly, during drought period. The Great Plains of US estimates the soil loss by wind erosion is 6100 times greater during drought than in wet seasons.

10.2.3 Climate Change

Changes in global climate can also trigger a drought. The global warming leads to increased rainfall (*AthiVrushti*) and consequently floods in some areas while no rain fall (*AnaaVrushti*) leading to drought in some areas. Small or large, every individual who was born on this world is responsible in this aspect. Everybody should feel minimum responsibility to better the world.

10.2.4 Erosion

In arid climates, the main source of erosion is wind. Erosion (refer previous chapter for more details) can be the result of material movement by the wind. The wind can lift small particles and move to another region (deflation). Suspended particles within the wind may impact on solid objects causing erosion by abrasion (ecological succession). Wind erosion generally occurs in areas with little or no vegetation, often in areas where there is insufficient rainfall to support vegetation.

10.2.5 El Niño

Effects of El Niño and Motivation to Drought Conditions

> **O My God!**
>
> Due to the El Niño, Singapore underwent the driest Feb 2014 (since records began in 1869), with only 6.3 mm of rain fall in the month and temperature reached month's highest ever (35°C) on 26 Feb.

1. Some regions experience hotter and drier weather during El Niño

   Examples: Amazon River Basin, Colombia, Central America, south-central Africa, mainly in Zambia, Zimbabwe, Mozambique, and Botswana experience dry hot weather
2. Winters are warmer and drier than average conditions

   Examples: Northwest and Mideast and Midwest of northern US experienced reduced snowfalls during winter (Dec-Feb).
3. El Niño results in decreasing air quality dramatically and encourages bush fires.

   Examples: Increased bush fires, worsened haze in Southeast Asia and Northern Australia.
4. Drier-than-normal conditions in all seasons during the El Niño

   Examples: Queensland, Victoria, New South Wales, and eastern Tasmania (particularly, from Jun to Aug)
5. Extended summer seasons that triggers drought conditions.

   Examples: As warm water spreads from the Indian Ocean and the W Pacific to the E Pacific, it causes extensive drought in the W Pacific area.

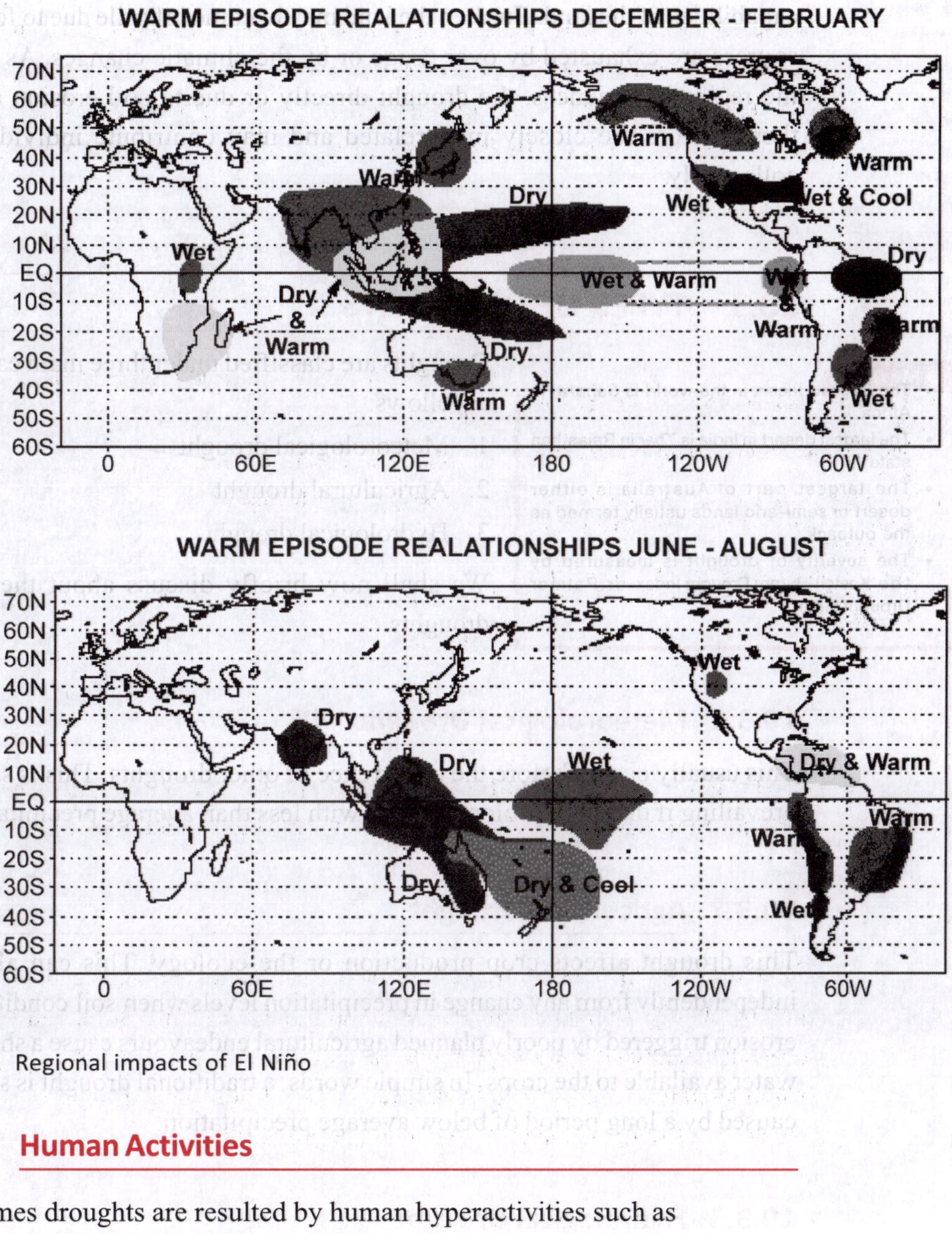

Fig. 10.1 Regional impacts of El Niño

10.2.6 Human Activities

Sometimes droughts are resulted by human hyperactivities such as

- Over farming/Excessive irrigation
- Deforestation/Desertification
- Pollution due to bad practices of disposals of chemicals/wastes
- Acid rains, explosions and nuclear testing etc.

The above activities drastically lower the water capturing and water storing capabilities of the land. Further, the land may become infertile due to fertilizing sources are exhausted by over usage or by the climatic changes. As a result, the region experiences, the drought directly or due to soil erosion also. All these factors are closely inter-related and may contribute individually or collectively.

10.3 TYPES OF DROUGHTS

O My God!

- The largest desert in the world is *Sahara*, in Africa
- The largest desert in India is *Thar* in Rajasthan state
- The largest part of Australia is either desert or semi-arid lands usually termed as the outback
- The severity of drought is measured by the Keetch-Byram Drought Index or Palmer Drought Index.

Droughts are classified under three main categories as follows:

1. Meteorological drought
2. Agricultural drought
3. Hydrological drought

We shall now briefly discuss about these three droughts.

10.3.1 Meteorological Drought

This usually occurs before the occurrence of other droughts. This is said to be prevailing if there is a prolonged time with less than average precipitation.

10.3.2 Agricultural Drought

This drought affects crop production or the ecology. This can also arise independently from any change in precipitation levels when soil conditions and erosion triggered by poorly planned agricultural endeavours cause a shortfall in water available to the crops. In simple words, a traditional drought is said to be caused by a long period of below average precipitation.

10.3.3 Hydrological Drought

This occurs when the water reserves/sources (like aquifers, lakes and reservoirs) fall below the average. These show up more slowly owing to the reason that stored water is used but not replenished. Like an agricultural drought, this is also triggered by loss of rainfall.

SELF ASSESSMENT INTERMISSION (SAI – 10.1)

1. Define Drought. What is its meaning? Do you consider it as a disaster? What is its significance in disaster management?
2. What are the types of droughts? Enumerate the causes.
3. Distinguish between meteorological, hydrological and agricultural droughts.
4. What are the causes which lead to cause a drought?
5. Explain how the changes in climatic conditions can cause a drought.
6. List out the features and characteristics of a drought.
7. What is an El Nino? How is it responsible to cause a drought?
8. Can drought occur by human activities? Enumerate such activities, if so.
9. What are dry season and precipitation deficiency? Explain their effects.
10. What is relation between soil erosion and drought? Discuss.

10.4 FAMINE

A **famine** is a state of severe and deep scarcity of food. This phenomenon is usually associated or followed by regional malnutrition, starvation, epidemic, and increased mortality.

Famine Defined

Famines are defined on the basis of three different categories

- food supply-based,
- food consumption-based and
- mortality-based.

Some definitions of famines are:

- ***Blix*** – Widespread food shortage leading to significant rise in regional death rates.
- ***Brown and Eckholm*** – Sudden, sharp reduction in food supply resulting in widespread hunger.
- ***Cuny*** – (named after Fred Cuny, US Disaster Relief Specialist) A set of conditions that occurs when large numbers of people in a region cannot obtain sufficient food, resulting in widespread, acute malnutrition.
- ***Ravallion*** – Unusually high mortality with unusually severe threat to food intake of some segments of a population.
- ***Scrimshaw*** – Sudden collapse in level of food consumption of large numbers of people.

10.4.1 The Concept

Famine means a severe food crisis. People die for food or kill for food. The hunger can make the people criminals. Further, a famine can be so devastating that it can even destabilize the economy of the country. The starvation of people makes them desperate to an extent of sacrificing long-term prosperity for the short-term survival by killing their pet animals, leading to lowered production in subsequent years. They even eat their seed, sacrificing next year's crop. Once those means had been exhausted, they would take to the road in search of food. Or it would frustrate them to commit suicide.

Otherwise, they would be compelled to migrate to the cities/town where they would become the victims of cashing the situation. With the confusion and desperation of the migrants, crime would often follow them. Some people resort to banditry in order to acquire enough to eat.

One famine would often lead to difficulties in the following years and lowered production and causes food insecurity because of lack of seed stock or disruption of routine, or perhaps because of less-available labour.

10.4.2 Distinction between Drought and Famine

We often get confused between the terms 'famine' and 'drought' most of us consider as one and the same. Perhaps! This is because, these two generally come together. Yes! Where there is drought, there is certainly famine or that where there is famine, there must be drought.

But, an element of truth is that there is a large difference between a famine and a drought. In fact, famines and droughts are caused by various conditions and factors that sometimes have nothing to do one with the other.

Drought is mainly caused by weather conditions and its consequent effects and may be defined in three ways (Refer section 10.3 of this chapter).

Meteorological drought is a reduction in rainfall below a scientifically specified level that may occur in a season, month, or even day.

Hydrological drought may be caused by meteorological drought or otherwise, when a body of water, such as a stream or lake, falls below a certain amount and occurs as a dry year.

Agricultural drought occurs when there is a significant reduction in crop yield, such that it may fall to a certain level considered to be a drought and may occur due to meteorological and/or hydrological drought, or even from other reasons such as insufficient access to fertilizer or some other necessary ingredient to produce yield.

Thus, drought can be understood as a situation of low production or a period of dry season caused mainly due to weather conditions (usually hot/dry).

Now, let us understand what famine is.

Famine is a decline in availability of and/or access to food. Of course, mostly this is caused by one of the three kinds of drought. Obviously, if there is insufficient water or fertilizer to produce a staple crop, the resulting drought may thence lead to famine. Yet, it is not necessarily the drought that causes such a famine.

Thus, for a famine to occur, irrespective of weather conditions, there must be insufficient availability of or access to food. Even though there is a drought in one year, if adequate food is made available famine can be prevented. Further, though there is no drought and food is not available to a section of people of a certain area/region due to some other reasons, still it is a famine. This point highlights the importance of access to food. Therefore, it is to be noted that inadequate management of a drought may lead to famine since drought affected people have less purchasing power, and thence, unable to gain access to the available foodstuffs.

Famine often follows drought, but it need not necessarily be a cause and effect relationship. So, the difference (between famine and drought) lies in the complexity of this relationship which in turn depends on

- The conditions and factors that surround local circumstances,
- Government responses to drought.,
- On causes of the drought and
- How communities handle their alternate food supplies.

Difference between Drought and Draught

We often get confused between these two words. The **'gh'** in drought is silent and rhymes with shout and out while the **'gh'** in draught is pronounced like **'f'** in flower and fool. So, draught is pronounced like the word draft. In American English, draught is even spelt draft.

Drought means a period of continuous dry weather, and thence there will not be enough water to meet the needs of drinking and agriculture.

Draught has several meanings (i) a rough script before finalizing a document (ii) a breeze or light wing (iii) an unwanted current of air that comes into a place like, during winter nights, cold air manages to get into the house even when we have all the doors and windows closed (iv) a dose or mouthful drink.

Usage: Droughts are very common in some parts of Africa.

I could feel the cold draught coming through the windows.

The executive committee is preparing the draught of resolutions to be passed in the general body meeting.

10.4.3 Famine Code – Famine Level Indicator by Food Insecurity

The experiences of famine relief organizations throughout the world over the 1980s and 1990s resulted in the two major developments to determine the severity of a crisis:

- the "livelihoods approach" and
- the increased use of nutrition, particularly of children, as a quantitative measure of the severity

Perhaps! The first attempt to scientifically predict and assess a famine was developed by the British in the 1880s on the basis of food security in the process of mitigate its effects. The Famine Commission issued a series of government guidelines and regulations on how to respond to famines and food shortages called the ***'Famine Code'*** which finally passed into law in 1883 under Lord Ripon, which has become a code for ***"Indian Famine Code"*** (India was under the British rule).

The Famine Commission used 'Food Insecurity' as the basis and issued the code in terms of scarcity. The code defined "Scarcity" as

- three consecutive years of crop failure,
- crop yields of one-third or one-half of normal,
- large populations in distress,
- a rise in food prices above 140% of "normal",
- the movement of people in search of food,
- widespread mortality,
- the loss of wages from lack of employment of agricultural labourers and artisans.

Based on the above symptoms, the codes listed in three stages of food insecurity:

- near-scarcity,
- scarcity and
- famine,

The early warning system developed by the Turkana people in northern Kenya also has three levels, but links each stage to monitor the region to a pre-planned response to mitigate the crisis and prevent its deterioration

Since 2003, many organizations in famine relief, including the World Food Programme and the US Agency for International Development, have adopted a five-level scale measuring intensity and magnitude. The intensity scale uses both livelihoods' measures and measurements of mortality and child malnutrition to categorize a situation as

- food insecure

- food crisis
- famine
- severe famine and
- extreme famine

The number of deaths determines the magnitude designation, with under 1000 fatalities defining a "minor famine" and a "catastrophic famine" resulting in over 1,000,000 deaths.

10.5 THEORIES AND CAUSES/REASONS FOR FAMINE

Most commonly, famine and food shortages occur due to

- lack of food production/availability
- difficulties in food distribution
- increased population
- natural climate fluctuations and
- extreme political conditions related to oppressive government
- riots, unrest and/or warfare.

Considering the above causes, there are some theories propounded to explain the causal mechanism of famines. The following theories are more popular and noteworthy.

10.5.1 Food Availability Decline (FAD) Hypothesis

The basic assumption in this hypothesis is that the central cause of all famines is due to decline in food availability. Until 1981, Food Availability Decline (FAD) hypothesis was the conventional explanation for the cause of famines. But, the studies of recent famines have raised quite interesting questions on the decisive role of FAD. The main question is why only a certain section of the population such as the peasants and the agricultural labourer were the victims of famines while others were insulated from famines in the same region. The FAD could not explain this quest.

This necessitated exploring the causal mechanisms with wider outlook.

10.5.2 Theory of Failure of Exchange Entitlements (FEE)

Since, the Food Availability Decline (FAD) hypothesis failed to explain why agri-labour only affected while others are unaffected by famines, this theory is proposed to suggest the causal mechanism for starvation. This theory includes many variables other than just decline of food availability.

The fundamental proposition of this theory is that 'the famines are results of entitlements', thence named as the "Failure of Exchange Entitlements (FEE)".

As per this theory, a person may own various commodities that can be exchanged in a market for the other commodities needed, which would happen via trading or production or a combination of the two. Thence, based on the dominating characteristics of the two in the exchange, all the exchanges can be described under one of the two titles named as 'trade-based or production-based entitlements'. Under this backdrop, this theory (FEE) views famines as a breakdown in the ability of the person to exchange the entitlements.

This means, a famine is the inability of an agricultural labourer to exchange his primary entitlement, i.e., labour for food. Therefore, the failure of FAD theory can be explained by this theory successfully as "those who are to exchange the entitlements are not affected while those who are unable to exchange are affected".

The concept also suggests considering the risk factors, such as global climate change, drought, El Nino, low or no rainfall/ precipitation, etc. as additional challenges of the land's ability to produce food, potentially leading to famine. As some elements make a particular region more vulnerable to famine, the FEE theory also includes the vulnerability factors too as the causes for FEE that finally results in a famine. The vulnerability factors include poverty, education levels (illiteracy), population growth, social commitments, cultural barricades, an inappropriate social infrastructure, a suppressive political regime, and a weak or under-prepared government and so forth.

10.5.3 Climate and Population Pressure

This theory speaks through two facets, first being the external pressure i.e. climatic changes while the second is internal pressure i.e. population. We can notice here that the climatic changes are uncontrollable as they are by and large natural occurrences, but the population is controllable, if the government takes a suitable policy.

All are not Sundays and all days are not good. All days are not alike; some may be shiny while some may be rainy. So, you have to plan for a rainy day. Thence, changing weather patterns have to be closely monitored by the country's governments and forecast so as to plan for crisis in advance. The inefficiency to predict, the inability to act according to situation and the ineffectiveness of governments in dealing with crises, would reflect as droughts and famines. This is one side of the famine face.

Looking at the other facet of famine, we can notice that many famines are caused due to imbalance between the production of food and the population (the consumers of food). More specifically, this happens when population exceeds the country's carrying capacity. History witnessed several famines due to agricultural problems such as drought, crop failure, or pestilence while population growth was not controlled.

There is an interesting link between these two famine causing factors (climate and population). Even though there is a failure of a harvest due to change in climatic conditions, such as drought, large numbers of people continue to live in the same place and do not evacuate unlike in case of other disasters such as floods, cyclone, tsunami etc. Even if they evacuate, it may occur to some extent, that too, very slowly. Since the production of reduced, but the population is not proportionally reduced, the carrying capacity of the land has temporarily dropped radically. This can trigger a famine. Famine is often associated with subsistence agriculture. Surprisingly, the total absence of agriculture in an economically strong area does not cause famine. For example, Arizona, US (even countryside also) import the vast majority of their food, since it produces sufficient economic goods for trade. For that matter all urban areas come under this category.

In addition to above, famines have also been caused by volcanism. For example, the 1815 eruption of the Mt Tambora volcano in Indonesia caused crop failures and famines.

10.5.4 State-Sponsored Famines

No surprise! There are many cases in the history witnessed famines because of government policy. Examples include, Ukraine famine in 1932, the Great Leap Forward in China in 1958, N Korea in the mid-1990s, Zimbabwe in the early-2000s.

In 1932, under the USSR, Ukraine experienced one of the largest famines, which consumed 3-7 million lives for state sponsored famine. It was named Holodomor, saying that it was a deliberate repression to eliminate protesters of collectivization. Grain quotas were imposed forcefully on the rural peasants. The Soviet government did not provide any food for victims nor accept foreign aid, and the brutal terror contributed to the widespread famine.

In 1958 in China, Mao Zedong's Communist Government initiated the Great Leap Forward campaign, aiming at rapid industrialization. The government forcibly took control of agriculture and just enough grain was left for the peasants that led to starvation in many rural areas while export of grain continued. The government refused to acknowledge the problem and the resulted famine is attributed to unintended consequences, thereby further contributed to more deaths. It is one of the most deadly famines hither to, which ate about 20-45 million human lives.

10.5.5 Other Reasons

Strictly speaking, the famines will be associated with more than one cause, in any proportions and are inter-related as well. In the recent past (during the first decade of 21st century) Somalia, famine occurred because of a failed state. It is attributed to several causes including

- Crop failure,
- Population growth,
- Increased food demand,
- Imbalance in supply and demand,
- Change in climatic conditions and
- Government policies.

In addition, the wars and epidemic diseases such as the Black Death helped to cause hundreds of famines in Europe during the Middle Ages, including 95 in Britain and 75 in France. In France, the 100 Years' War, crop failures and epidemics reduced the population by two-thirds.

The current consensus of the scientific community is that the aerosols and dust released into the upper atmosphere causes cooler temperatures by preventing the sun's energy from reaching the ground. The same mechanism is theorized to be caused by very large meteorite impacts to the extent of causing mass extinctions.

SELF ASSESSMENT INTERMISSION (SAI – 10.2)

1. Define Famine. What is its meaning? Do you consider it as a disaster? What is its significance in disaster management?
2. What is a famine? What are its other names? What are their meanings?
3. Enumerate the causes for the occurrence of a famine.
4. Distinguish between drought and a famine.
5. What is the difference between drought and draught?
6. List out the features and characteristics of a famine.
7. What is a famine code? Explain.
8. Explain The Food Availability Decline (FAD) Theory of famine. What are its drawbacks?
9. Explain The Food Exchange Entitlement (FEE) Theory of famine. What are its drawbacks?
10. Can famine occur by human activities? Enumerate such activities, if so.
11. What is relation between drought and famine? Discuss.

10.6 FAMINE FUTURE AND FUTURE FAMINE

Droughts and famines have significant impact on environment, agriculture, health, economy and social aspects of the region, where it occur. However, the effect varies according to vulnerability.

10.6.1 Effects (Consequences) of Drought/ Famine

Droughts may lessen the quality of water due to scarcity and/or increased contamination of remaining water sources. This may lead to cause a famine.

Common consequences of drought include:

- Reduced crop growth or production yield
- Lowered carrying capacity for livestock
- Famine due to lack of water for irrigation
- Deaths due to hunger and thirst (too little water to support food crops and drinking water)
- Malnutrition, dehydration and related diseases
- Social unrest and civil wars
- Wars, conflicts, scuffling, and fighting for natural resources, particularly for water and food
- Rising crime rate by frustrated people
- Dust bowls (a sign of erosion), further erode the landscape
- Dust storms hit the area and cause to suffer from desertification and erosion
- Habitat damage, affecting both aquatic and wildlife
- Mass migration, resulting in internal displacement and international refugees
- Reduced electricity production due to reduced water flow through hydroelectric dams
- Shortages of water for industrial applications
- Snake or prisonous species migration which may result in snakebites
- Wildfires, bushfires which may cause injuries of even death of humans and wildlife.
- Exposure and oxidation of acid sulphate soils due to fall of surface/ groundwater levels.

10.6.2 Threat of Drought

According to a UN climate report, the Himalayan glaciers that are the principal dry-season water sources of Asia's biggest rivers - Ganges, Indus,

Brahmaputra, Yangtze, Mekong, Salween and Yellow - could disappear by 2350 as temperatures rise and human demand rises. About 2.4 billion people live in the basins of the Himalayan Rivers flowing across India, China, Pakistan, Bangladesh, Nepal and Myanmar. These nations should be very precautious as the coming decades may more likely see floods followed by droughts. Particularly, India could experience the drought by the Ganges, which is the biggest source of water for drinking and agricultural irrigation for more than 500 million people. Beware! Whenever there is any shortage (or even due to pollution) in the flow of water, the drought may flair up.

Similarly, the west coast of N America, getting much of its water from glaciers in mountain ranges of the Rocky Mountains and Sierra Nevada, also could be affected.

10.6.3 Risk of Famines

- Nearly 40% of the world's agricultural land is seriously degraded.
- A report (2007) in the newspaper, *The Guardian*,
- If current trends of soil degradation continue in Africa, the continent might be able to feed just 25% of its population by 2025.

  - UNU's Ghana-based Instt. for Natural Resources.
- The next generations would see rising food prices without relief and massive starvation on a global level.

  – Dale Allen Pfeiffer (Geologist)

The above statements clearly indicate the alarming status of water resources and the threat of famines in the near future. Water scarcity is prevailing in numerous smaller countries, and may soon do the same in larger countries, such as China or India. US, Canada and Mexico are also not exceptions in this regard. The water tables are falling in almost all countries due to overconsumption. Obviously, it leads to water scarcity and curtail in grain harvest.

After China and India, there is a 2nd tier of smaller countries with large water deficits —Algeria, Egypt, Iran, Mexico, and Pakistan. The first four of these already import a major share of their grain. Only Pakistan seems to be marginally self-sufficient. But with a population growth by 4 million per year, it will also soon turn to the world market for grain.

10.7 PREVENTION, MITIGATION AND RELIEF

Drought and Famine are global problems with which hundreds of millions of people are suffering. Unlike other disasters, this disaster is slow and comes undercover. Though it is predictable, often it goes either unnoticed or given least importance till it flairs up to severe level. Perhaps! This may be attributed to the inhumane of certain rich sector of people who do not give attention to forward planning for the poor farmers and labourers who are often the victims of the famines and droughts.

It is most unfortunate and pathetic, if people die out of starvation and non-availability of food or water. The history filed several pages of such situations for Ethiopia; one such is with the famines of 1980s that had a big death toll. Also Asian famines of the 20th century have produced huge death tolls. African famines are characterized by widespread destitution and malnutrition, with heightened mortality confined to young children. The most widespread is found in Sub-Saharan Africa, with exhaustion of food resources, over-drafting of groundwater, wars, internal struggles, and economic failure. These famines cause widespread malnutrition and impoverishment. All these episodes teach us lessons.

Famine is a serious threat of Africa and Asia. In July 2005, Famine Early Warning Systems Network categorized Niger, Chad, Ethiopia, S Sudan, Somalia and Zimbabwe under emergency status. In Jan 2006, the UN Food and Agriculture Organization warned Somalia, Kenya, Djibouti and Ethiopia for danger of starvation of severe drought and military conflicts.

(In 2006, Sudan's Darfur issue was the most serious humanitarian crisis in Africa).

As discussed above, the famines are sometimes triggered by misguided economic policies, political design to impoverish or marginalize certain sectors of people, or of warfare activities. According to the economist Amartya Sen the liberal institutions that exist in India, including competitive elections and a free press and media, have been doing a great job to preventing famine in the country since independence. Still, the threat of drought and famine are persisting owing to environmental economics.

Looking at the demographic aspects, mortality due to famines and droughts seems to be concentrated over children and the elderly. Records reveal that male mortality is more than female, even in India and Pakistan where there is a male longevity advantage at normal times.

10.7.1 Methods of Prevention and Protection from Drought

The prevention and protection from the drought is much of the responsibility of the people than the government. People can effectively mitigate much of the impact of drought through appropriate irrigation methods and crop rotation. However, the government should bring awareness in its citizens. Further governments should shoulder the responsibility of relief activities and rehabilitation, strategies for drought protection, mitigation or relief include:

- ***Rainwater harvesting*** - Collection and storage of rainwater from roofs or other suitable catchments.
- ***Transvasement*** - Building canals or redirecting rivers for irrigation in drought-prone areas.
- ***Water recycling***- Wastewater (sewage) treatment and purification for reuse.
- ***Outdoor water-use restriction*** - Regulating the usage of sprinklers, hoses or buckets on outdoor plants, filling pools, and other water-intensive home maintenance activities.
- ***Drought monitoring*** - Continuously checking rainfall levels and regulating current usage levels.
- ***Land use*** - Planned crop rotation to minimize erosion and guiding farmers to plant less water-dependent crops in drier periods.
- ***Desalination*** - Sea water treatment and conversion to be used for irrigation or consumption.
- ***Constructing Dams*** - Dams and reservoirs can supply required water during period of drought.
- ***Cloud seeding*** - An intentional weather modification for inducing rainfall.

10.7.2 Norman Borlaug's Green Revolution – A Famine Preventive Solution

Norman Borlaug, father of the Green Revolution, saved >billion worldwide from starvation.

The Green Revolution was widely viewed solution to drought and famine in the 1970s and 1980s. Between 1950 and 1984, the concept of hybrid high-yielding crops transformed agriculture around the globe and grain production increased by 250%. Of course, there is a criticism on the concept that it requires more chemical fertilizers and pesticides that can harm the environment. Keeping away, the matter of the truth in harming the environment, it could feed more people and save from famine deaths of starvation. However, problems associated with intensive agriculture such as groundwater over-drafting and overuse of pesticides and other agro-chemicals can trigger a drought.

10.7.3 Food Security - Famine Preparedness Solution

Long term solution to famines is to improve food security. This is achieved through investment in not only on employing the modern techniques and methods in agriculture, fertilizers and irrigation procedures, but can also include strategic national food storage and use of alternate foods. The entire human population could be fed with alternate foods even in the event of global catastrophe. Moreover, the World Bank is also restricting government subsidies for farmers, and increasing use of fertilizers as opposed by some environmental groups because of its unintended consequences particularly concerned on its adverse effects on water supplies and habitat. However, supporting farmers in areas of food insecurity, through supplying free or subsidized seeds, and fertilizers that scientifically recommended can increase food harvest and reduces food prices. Thus food security and thence the preparedness to the famines can be sought by

- Applying modern techniques in agriculture
- Identifying and using alternate foods
- Using the scientifically recommended fertilizers
- Governments motivating the farmers by subsidizing or free seeds and fertilizers
- Paying the farmers the reasonable price for the grains produced without exploitation
- Food stocking and storing at national level

10.7.4 Evan Fraser's Lines of Defense – A Mitigation and Relief Solution

Evan Fraser, a geographer at University of Guelph in Ontario, Canada, explored the patterns of climatic changes, which may cause future famines. Based on past records, he drew the following three "lines of defense" to protect a community's food security from environmental change.

1. Diverse ecosystems with well managed soils high in organic matter tend to be more resilient.
2. Wealth and skills of individual households: (If households have savings or skills they can do all right despite affected by bad weather/ drought).
3. Governments or NGOs or Charities must be willing and able to put efforts for effective relief.

O My God!

Frederick C Cuny?

Cuny, born on 14, Nov 1944 is an American Disaster Relief Specialist and a great humanitarian is a Civil Engineer from A&M University, Texas. His dream was (fighter pilot) not fulfilled as he couldn't pass language requirement to get into Officer's Candidate School. He was involved in many humanitarian projects. It's a mystery that he disappeared (1995) in Chechnya while negotiating ceasefire. He wrote a great book on famine.

He stated that the chances of saving lives under relief operation greatly reduce when food is imported because by the time it arrives many people will have died. US Law needs buying food at home rather than where the hungry live, is inefficient because nearly half of what is spent goes for transport. Fred Cuny further pointed out "studies of every recent famine have shown that food was available in-country — though not always in the immediate food deficit area" and "even though by local standards the prices are too high for the poor to purchase it, it would usually be cheaper for a donor to buy the hoarded food at the inflated price than to import it from abroad."

On close observation of the above lines of defense, the first line speaks for prevention, second one speaks about preparedness while the third on relief and recovery (mitigation). Fraser argues that if an ecosystem is resilient enough, it can resist weather-related shocks. But if these shocks beyond the limit of the ecosystem's line of defense, then the household needs to employ the skills and savings. If a problem is too big even for the household, then the government or charities or certain institutions/ organizations may intervene to put their best efforts for the relief and help effectively as third line of defense. Evan Fraser attributes any situation of failure of encountering a famine as a failure of one or more of above three lines of defense. Hence, understanding climatic changes can ease the assessment of local socio-economic and environmental factors for predicting a famine and/or drought in the future

10.7.5 Relief Technologies

Providing relief to the famine affected people is fundamental duty of the Government and is minimum responsibility of every human being on humanitarian grounds. The relief technologies include

- immunization,
- improved public health infrastructure,
- general food rations
- supplementary feeding for vulnerable children

For people in a drought living a long way from to markets, delivering food may be the most appropriate way to help. Deficient micronutrients can be provided through fortified foods such as peanut butter sachets or locally significant non-perishable food packs as feed in humanitarian emergencies as they can be eaten directly from the packet, do not require refrigeration or mixing with scarce clean water, can be stored for years vitally, and can be absorbed by ill children also.

In most cases, the famine is associated with malnutrition, and some diseases such as diarrhoea, malaria etc. World Health Organization (WHO) recommends malnourished children and adults who also have diarrhoea have to drink rehydration solution, and continue to eat, in addition to antibiotics, and zinc supplements. There is a special oral **Re**hydration **So**lution for **Mal**nourished called 'ReSoMal' which has less sodium and more potassium than standard solution. Zinc supplements often can help reduce the duration and severity of diarrhoea, and Vitamin A can also be helpful. The WHO stresses on the importance of 'continuing to eat and drink', in its 2005 publication stating: "Food should *never* be withheld and the child's usual foods should *not* be diluted. Breastfeeding should *always* be continued".

10.8 UNFORGETTABLE DROUGHTS AND FAMINES – SOME CASE STUDIES

Famines did not exempt any continent. Any famine has miserable stories behind it. Every famine annoyed total mankind whether affected directly or indirectly. For that matter, it definitely annoys even unaffected as it touches the element of humanity. Therefore, a famine cannot be categorized as significant or insignificant. However, a few of the famines considered as the most worst in the known history are discussed here below.

1. The Great Irish Famine 1845-49: The first and worst famine in the recorded history in 19th century (Europe)
2. The Great Leap Forward -1958-61: The worst of 20th century (Asian)
3. The African Famines (Ethiopian Famine – 1980-82): The latest worst famine (Africa)
4. Great Bengal Famines (1770 & again in 1943): the worst famines in the history of India

10.8.1 Great Irish Potato Famine 1845–49

It was the worst famine of 19th century in Europe occurred during 1845-49 when the potato crop failed in successive years due to late blight (a disease that destroys both the leaves and the edible roots, or tubers of the potato plant) caused by the water mold *Phytophthora infestans*.

The potato had become a staple crop in Ireland by the 18th century, as it was a hardy, nutritious, and calorie-dense crop and also relatively easy to grow in the Irish soil. By the early 1840s almost half the Irish population—particularly the rural poor were dependent almost totally on the potato for their diet. Even the rest of the population also used to consume potato in large quantities. This heavy reliance on potato made the Irish vulnerable to famine.

The Irish tenant farmers struggled both to provide for themselves and to supply the British market with cereal crops during early 19th century. Many farmers long existed at just the survival level, given the small size of their allotments and the various hardships including the land resisted for farming in some regions.

A stain of *Phytophthora* arrived accidentally from N. America in 1845, and unfortunately, in same year Ireland had unusually cool moist weather, which favoured the blight and hence resulted as much of that year's potato crop rotted in the fields. The partial crop failure multiplied in the subsequent years and became devastating in 1846–49. Alas! Every year, the potato crop was almost completely ruined by the blight.

The British government's response and the efforts of relief did not suffice. The PM Sir Robert Peel (Conservative) permitted the export of grain from Ireland to Great Britain, and did what he could to provide relief in 1845 and early 1846. He authorized the import of corn (maize) from the US that helped avert some starvation.

Then, Lord John Russell (Liberal), assumed power in June 1846, and continued Peel's policy of grain exports from Ireland but took a laissez-faire approach by which the financial burden of providing for the starving farmers was thrown upon the Irish landowners themselves through local poor relief and British (absentee) landowners. Perhaps! This produced a dilemma and taken the problem in new direction and further worsened.

It is a known fact that the tenant farmers are not able to pay rents. But the landlords usually provide from the rents received, soon ran out of funds to support them. The result was obvious that millions of Irish tenant farmers and labourers were forced to leave or thrown out during the years of the crisis. The 1834 British Poor Law (enacted in 1838 in Ireland), supported the workhouses rather than relieving the famine. British assistance was limited to loans, to fund soup kitchens, employment on road building and other such public works. Further, the Irish disliked the US imported cornmeal, and reliance on it resulted in nutritional deficiencies.

Further, due to weather conditions, the first shipment did not arrive in Ireland until the beginning of Feb 1846. The maize corn was then re-sold for a penny a pound.

The impoverished Irish peasantry, lost the purchase power and could not use foods of their farms, since they had to continue (throughout the famine) to export grain, meat, and other high-quality foods to Britain. The government's grudging and ineffective measures to relieve the famine's distress intensified the resentment of British rule among the Irish.

The famine proved to be a watershed in the Ireland and as a consequence of the famine, Ireland's population of 8.4 million in 1844 fell to 6.6 million by 1851. About a million people starved to death or suffered from typhus and other famine-related diseases. About 2 million emigrated and went on decline in the following decades owing to the overseas emigration and lower birth rates. By the time Ireland's independence in 1921, its population was barely ½ of what it had in the early 1840s.

10.8.2 Great Leap Forward – The Largest Famine

Yet another manmade famine is the largest famine of the 20th century, and almost certainly of all time, the 1958–61 Great Leap Forward famine in China. The immediate causes of this famine lay in Mao Zedong's ill-fated attempt to transform China from an agricultural nation to an industrial power in one huge leap. Communist Party cadres across China insisted that peasants abandon their farms for collective farms, and begin to produce steel in small foundries, often melting down their farm instruments in the process. Collectivisation undermined incentives for the investment of labor and resources in agriculture; unrealistic plans for decentralized metal production sapped needed labor; unfavorable weather conditions; and communal dining halls encouraged overconsumption of available food. Such was the centralized control of information and the intense pressure on party cadres to report only good news—such as production quotas met or exceeded—that information about the escalating disaster was effectively suppressed. When the leadership did become aware of the scale of the famine, it did little to respond, and continued to ban any discussion of the cataclysm. This blanket suppression of news was so effective that very few Chinese citizens were aware of the scale of the famine, and the greatest peacetime demographic disaster of the 20th century only became widely known twenty years later, when the veil of censorship began to lift.

The exact number of famine deaths during 1958–61 is difficult to determine, and estimates range from 18 to at least 42 million people, with a further 30 million cancelled or delayed births. It was only when the famine had wrought its worst that Mao was forced to reverse agricultural collectivisation policies, which were effectively dismantled in 1978. China has not experienced a famine of the proportions of the Great Leap Forward since 1961.

10.8.3 Africa, The Address for Droughts and Famines

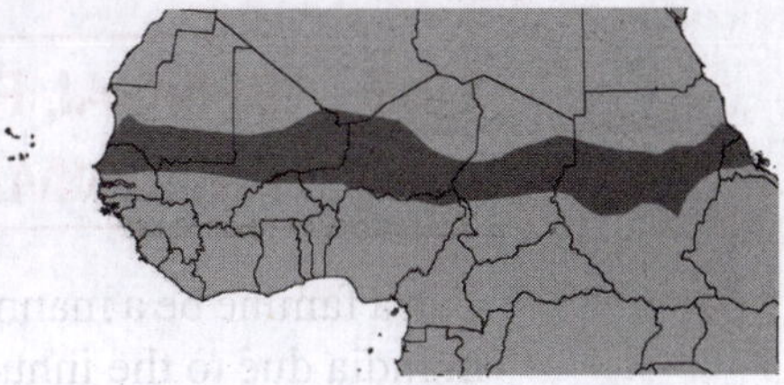

Famine-affected in the western Sahel belt during the 2012 drought.

Africa is highly susceptible to climatic fluctuations, and suffers lowered food production by droughts. Other agricultural problems include soil infertility, land degradation and erosion, swarms of desert locusts that destroy whole crops, and livestock diseases. Desertification is increasingly problematic: the Sahara reportedly spreads up to 48 km (30 mi) per year.

The most of the famines were caused by a combination of drought, misled economic policies, and conflicts. For instance, the 1983–85 famine of Ethiopia and Sudan was the result of all these three. In Sudan also, drought and economic crisis clubbed with denials of food shortage by the then-government of President Gaafar Nimeiry, took out 2.5 Lakh lives.

1998 Sudan famine experienced human rights abuses. AIDS is yet another factor that showed long-term economic effects on agriculture by lowered workforce. At the same time, it overburdened the poor public, and created new vulnerabilities to famine.

In Africa, if current trends of population growth and soil degradation continue, the continent might be able to feed just 25% of its population by 2025, according to United Nations University (UNU)'s Ghana-based Institute for Natural Resources in Africa.

SELF ASSESSMENT INTERMISSION (SAI – 10.3)

1. Define Famine. What do you understand by the captions- 'famine future – future famine'? Discuss.
2. Discuss the effects of a famine.
3. Discuss the threat of drought and risks of famine in the context of India.
4. Describe the methods and measures of mitigation of drought/ famine.
5. Explain the methods to prevent and protect from a drought/ famine.
6. Explain how food security can become a solution to prevent drought/ famine.
7. Explain the principles of Evan Frazer's lines of defense of famine.
8. What is Green Revolution? What are its objectives? How does it help preventing the famine?
9. Write a short note on relief technologies of famine.
10. Explain the causes and effects of Great Irish Potato Famine.
11. What do you understand about the famine caused by 'Great Leap Forward'? Discuss.
12. 'Some parts of Africa are considered as the addresses for droughts and famines'. Critically Comment on the statement.

10.9 BENGAL FAMINE OF 1943 – A MANMADE HOLOCAUST: A CASE STUDY

Can a famine be a manmade disaster? Yes! Here is one of such famine occurred in India due to the inhumane considered as partially manmade.

The **Bengal famine of 1943** was a major famine in the Bengal province in British India during WW-II. About 2.1 million people died first from starvation and then from diseases. Millions were impoverished by the crisis of social fabric and moved toward economic inequality.

The reasons for the famine are attributed to

- inefficient agricultural practices,
- increased population and
- population displacement, de-peasantisation through land grabbing
- natural disasters (cyclone, storm surges and flooding, and rice crop disease)

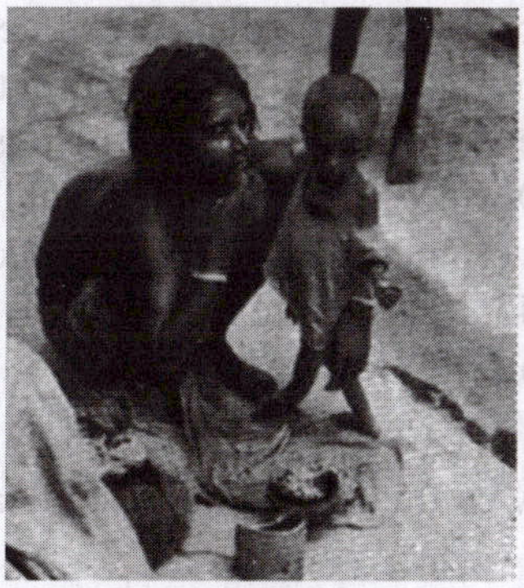

Images: *The Statesman* on 22 Aug, 1943 showed famine conditions in Calcutta which changed world opinion on colonialism.

- malnutrition and lack of health care
- unsanitary conditions and diseases such as cholera, malaria, smallpox, and dysentery
- consequences of war:
  - initial warfare activities,
  - general war-time inflation of both demand-pull and monetary origin,
  - loss of rice imports due to Japanese occupation of Burma (Now Myanmar),
  - near-total disruption of Bengal's market supplies and
  - transport systems by pre-emptive, defensive scorched earth tactics of the Raj
  - the "denial policies" for rice and boats

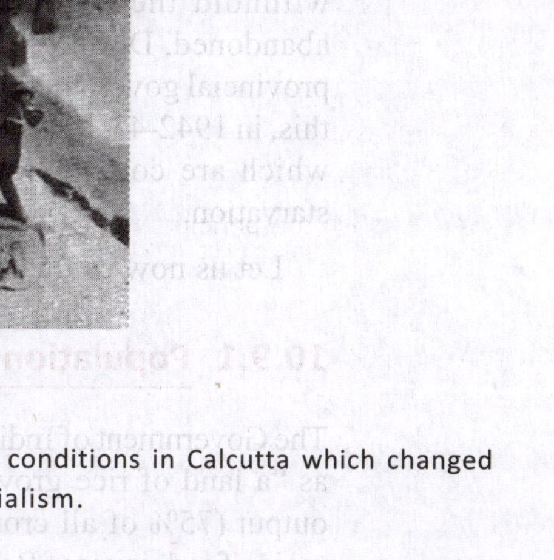

- massive inflation brought on by repeated policy failures,
- war profiteering,
- Speculation and hoarding,
- the government prioritised military and defense needs over those of the rural poor,
- allocating medical care and food immensely in the favour of the military, labourers in military industries, and civil servants only.

All of the above factors were compounded by restricted access to grain, inter-provincial trade barriers, and denying to international sources by the War Cabinet of Great Britain. The government was slow to supply humanitarian aid. Price controls created black market and encouraged cautious sellers to withhold their stocks, and the prices soared when the controls were abandoned. Despite having a long-established, detailed Famine Code, the provincial government never formally declared a state of famine. In addition to this, in 1942-43, in the context of WW-II, the Bengalis faced numerous shocks, which are complex and sometimes sudden. Millions were vulnerable to starvation.

Let us now evaluate the above said causes how they led to famine.

10.9.1 Population Growth Vs Land Shortage/ Agro-productivity

The Government of India's Famine Commission Report (1945) described Bengal as "a land of rice growers and rice eaters". Rice dominated the agricultural output (75% of all crops) and produced 1/3rd of India's rice. Fish was the 2nd major food source. Bengal was very densely populated rose by 43% (from 42.1 million to 60.3 million) between 1901 and 1941 (Population growth rate increased by 2.8% from 1911-21; by 7.3% from 1921-31, and 20.3% from 1931-41). The reason for the high excess mortality of 1943–45 was a soaring population levels, a shortage of land in Bengal, and stagnant (or lowered) agricultural productivity in India.

Prior to 1920, the food demands could be met Bengal's growing population by bringing undeveloped lands under the plough. Probably around 1930s, Bengal experienced an acute shortage of land and a chronic shortage of rice which necessitated import of food grains and a decrease in average consumption levels (In 1930 Bengali diet was the least nutritious in the world). Taken together, the rising population and falling productivity created a long-term decline in food availability - reported by the Famine Inquiry Commission of 1945.

10.9.2 Rural Credit and Land-grabbing

The system of land tenureship in India (particularly Bengal) was very complex, and the land rights and the resulting power were very unequally among three diverse economic and social groups; large landowners or *zamindars*, the upper-tier "wealthy peasant" *jotedars*; and the lower socio-economic levels, the *ryot* (peasant) smallholders and dwarf-holders, *bargadars* (sharecroppers) and agricultural labourers. *Zamindars* and *jotedars* were protected by legal and customary status and rights, while the bottom were actually cultivating the soil, with small or no landholdings and also had no rights due to no written records. They laboured under power and suffered persistent and increasing losses even after worked over-time.

During the early decades of 20th century, the power and influence of *zamindars* fell while *jotedars* rose by a rent crisis. *Jotedars* made profits and empowered in the villages by making debt bondage through their two dictating roles: grain/jute trading, and money lending to the sharecroppers/ agri-labour and ryots (small-farmers).

A large economic and social blow occurred due to their land-grabbing and occupancy rights of the ryot through both legal and coercive means and even political means (e.g. Midnapore and 24 Parganas). Further, land-grabbing was through the manipulation of the informal credit market and exploitation of their weakness of resorting to informal local lenders for the life-needs such as weddings, religious ceremonies, births, or deaths, particularly, expenses during lean months between harvests, and so were "compelled to sell their lands (along with the means of production such as seed or cattle for ploughing) at deflated prices during post-harvest glut, in order to pay loans taken during the pre-harvest 'starvation' season". Even the small landholders and sharecroppers were kept under litigations or defeated to forfeit in auctions at a low price. (Recall: The Nuxalite movement started at Nuxalbury of Bengal, why?)

Two contemporary reports, the Report of the Land Revenue Commission of Bengal (1940) and the field survey published in Mahalanobis, Mukherjea & Ghosh (1946) agreed the above facts.

> **O My God!**
>
> **Eastern Sunday Raid?**
>
> Named Easter Sunday Raid, in Apr 1942, Japan attacked Colombo and Trincomali in Ceylon (now Sri Lanka) and destroyed even Vizag. The fall of Rangoon cut off the routine import of rice to India and Ceylon. India's supply deficit in rice totalled 1.75 M tons. Famine Commission reported the most affected as Bombay, Madras, Cochin and Travancore. The price of rice in Sep 1941 was already 69% higher than in Aug 1939. The fall of Burma increased demand of rice. ***Under pressure from the*** UK, ***Bengal continued to export rice to Ceylon for months afterward***. Further, during 1942–45, there was large increase in Military build-up, inflation, and displacement.

> **Soil and Water Supply during 1943-44**
>
> The soil of E. Bengal (occupied by Japan), abundant for irrigation from monsoon rains, was unique for growing large amounts of high quality jute, while lesser quality was grown in smaller quantities in W. Bengal. During the famine, jute-producing districts suffered higher mortality rates. Furthermore, the W. Bengal suffered water supply also (Guess-Why?).

10.9.3 Japanese Invasion of Burma – Refugees to India (Feb–Apr 1942)

When Japan conquered Burma in Dec 1941, it set off >½ million Indians living in Burma. After the bombing of Rangoon many Indians left by sea for ports in

Bengal. In Jan 1942, before the Fall of Rangoon, another 70,000 Indians left by sea for Madras and Calcutta. However, most Indians, 4.5-5 lakhs trekked overland to India. Of these, about 1-2 lakhs through the Arakan hills in W. Burma, and up along coastal waters, to Chittagong in E. Bengal. Of the remaining Indians, 2.2 lakh trekked up the lower Chindwin river valley to reach Manipur, and 3rd group through the upper Iravathi river valley, arrived Assam.

Unfortunately, priorities changed, when the military became the focus. Author Hugh Tinker wrote, "The troops arrived: pushing the refugees aside, laying hands on all supplies, and utilizing all available military transport."

During journeys, some Indians were subjected to extortion, robbery, and violence. About ½ lakh Indians refugees died. In Bengal, a witness before Famine Commission, recalled in 1945, the "hair-raising stories of atrocities and sufferings". This motivated participation in the Quit India movement of Aug 1942.

10.9.4 Denial Policies (Mar 1942)

Feared of Japanese attacking through the eastern border of Bengal, British India as a pre-emptive measure, launched two "denial policies" to prevent or impede the expected invasion by denying access to food supplies or transport (+other resources) from eastern India. But, it impacted to develop a famine or/and compounded the crisis.

Denial of Rice: This was carried out in 3 southern districts along the coast of the Bay of Bengal that were expected to have surpluses of rice – Bakarganj (or Barisal), Midnapore and Khulna. In March 1942, Governor Herbert, by orders of UK, ordered that surplus stock of paddy (rough, unhusked rice) and other food items to be removed or destroyed in 3 districts immediately and urgently. Some rice was destroyed, but some paddy was purchased by government agents and stored in various locations. Of course, no need to mention, how huge fraud, corruption and coercive practices went on.

Denial of boats: On demand of the military to deny Bengali vehicles to any invading Japanese army, it was implemented in the districts readily accessible via the Bay of Bengal and the larger rivers, and the main ports of Chittagong and Calcutta. The 3 rice-denial districts were affected, as were 9 others: Hooghly, Howrah, 24 Parganas, Jessore, Faridpur, Tippera, Dacca, Noakhali, and Chittagong. It authorised the Army to confiscate, relocate or destroy any boats large enough to carry more than ten persons; Tools and instruments were also seized. The confiscation of ~46,000 rural boats severely disrupted river-borne labour, supplies and food, and livelihoods of boatmen and fishermen. Transport costs hiked, local industries collapsed. The Army took no steps to distribute food rations. Moreover, artisans and other groups were kicked out. Adding fuel to fire, the white ants ate the currency notes.

A Blow on blow! In Jan 1942, Punjab banned exports of wheat, which increased the perception of food insecurity and led Calcutta to raise the demand for rice. Further, the prioritised distribution of food/ medicine etc., [80% for priority (military) and 20% for non-priority (civil)] in Aug 1942 aggravated and led to **Civil unrest and Quit India Movement.** (The Tamluk unrest lasted for a month from 8 sep 1942 for 18000 boat destruction)

Refusal of Imports - 1942–44: From late 1942 through at least early 1944, several high-ranking government officials and military officers made repeated requests for food to be imported from outside India, but the War Cabinet persistently either rejected the requests outright or bargained them down to a fraction of the original amount.

10.9.5 Natural Disasters in Oct 1942

Later in the same year, Bengal has seen hell on the earth when five natural disasters struck: first, the winter rice crop was afflicted by a lengthy and virulent outbreak of fungal brown spot disease (caused by the fungus *Cochliobolus miyabeanus*). During this outbreak, a cyclone and 3-storm surges in October ravaged croplands, destroyed houses, and killed 1000s. The cyclone also dispersed high levels of fungal spores widely across the region, increasing the spread of the crop disease.

The winter crop of 1942 was ravaged, as unusually warm, cloudy, and humid climatic conditions and above-average rainfall lasted 2 months later than average. During critical stages of the rice crop's maturation, a massive disease spores occurred and the fungus reduced the yield even more than the cyclone.

> **O My God!**
>
> **Bengal Famine In Art & Movies?**
>
> The famine has been a theme in novels, films and art. The novel *Ashani Sanket* by Bibhutibhushan Bandyopadhyay is a story of a young doctor and his wife in rural Bengal during the famine. Filmed with the same name (English title: *Distant Thunder*) by Satyajit Ray (1973) is listed in *The New York Times Guide to the Best 1,000 Movies Ever Made*. Other well-known are the novel *So Many Hungers!* (1947) by Bhabani Bhattacharya and 1980 film *Akaler Shandhaney* by Mrinal Sen. A Bengali play about the famine, *Nabanna*, was written by Bijon Bhattacharya and staged by the Indian People's Theatre Association (IPTA), directed by Sombhu Mitra (1944) and later by Bohurupee under the direction of Kumar Roy (1948). IPTA also staged the play in several parts of the country to collect funds for famine relief. A contemporary sketch book of iconic scenes of famine victims, *Hungry Bengal: a tour through Midnapur District in November, 1943* by Chittaprosad, was immediately banned by the British and 5000 copies were seized and destroyed. One copy was hidden by Chittaprosad's family and is now in the possession of the Delhi Art Gallery. Another artist famed for his sketches of the famine was Zainul Abedin.

The Bengal cyclone (16 Oct 1942) in Bay of Bengal, landed on Contai, Midnapore and 24 Parganas, reportedly caused extensive damage and ~40,000 fatalities. Then on Oct 16–17, three storm surges destroyed the seawalls of Midnapore and flooded large areas of Contai and Tamluk. Waves swept an area of 450 mi^2 (1,200 km^2), floods affected 400 mi^2 (1,000 km^2), and wind and torrential rain damaged 3,200 mi^2 (8,300 km^2) kept 2.5 million in a hell on the earth. 7,400 villages were partly or wholly damaged by the storm, and standing flood waters remained for weeks in at least 1,600 villages. Cholera, dysentery and other water-borne diseases flourished. 527,000 houses and 1,900 schools were lost. Over 1000 mi^2 of the most fertile paddy land was totally smashed.

Cyclones, floods, plant disease and warm, humid weather, war, political policies combined with famine had a substantial impact on Bengalis to remember 1942-43 most deadly years. Further, Dec 1942 saw Air raids Japan on Calcutta created havoc. 1942–43 witnessed speculative buying, exploitation, price shocks and policy failures such as rice and boat denial, ban on exports etc.

Finally, despite having a long-established and detailed Famine Code available to plan for aid, the provincial government never formally declared a state of famine. The official explanation was wartime political goals, inter-provincial trade barriers and provision of other types of relief efforts.

10.9.6 Famine and Diseases

The sandy soil of E. Bengal and the lighter sedimentary soil of the Sunderbans (where Ganges enters Bay of Bengal) drained more rapidly after the monsoon than the heavy clay regions of W. Bengal. This obviously, raised malaria (the biggest killed during the famine) and other epidemics lasted for a month long in the areas with slower drainage. (Do you remember?- Ronald Ross conducted research here and found the medicine for malaria)

The depleted refugees fell victim to disease, initially to dysentery, smallpox and malaria, and later to cholera (during evacuation, 70–80% were ill, and 30% gravely). From Apr 1942, with refugees from Burma entering India in large numbers, the medical establishment was insufficient in E. India to monitoring serious contagious diseases. Rural areas lacked access to safe water supplies scoped for epidemic of waterborne diseases, cholera compounded by un-sanitized areas.

The famine saw two waves of excess mortality. In the first when victims of starvation overfilled the emergency hospitals in Calcutta in Nov 1943. The second was with diseases during December. The two waves also interacted and amplified each other, increasing the excess mortality. Malaria was the biggest killer (Jul 1943 to Jun 1944), the monthly deaths of malaria was of

125% over the previous 5 yrs; in Dec 1943 alone it was 203%. Dysentery and diarrhoea were directly from famine, through consumption of poor-quality food or deterioration of the digestive system due to malnutrition. Cholera is a waterborne disease due to poor sanitation and contaminated water or food; and brought on more by social disruption than malnutrition (carried by escapees from Burma and erupted during October cyclone and floods). Smallpox was an airborne disease due to crowded living.

10.9.7 Social Disruption

Deep and widespread social disruption disintegrated families with abandoning wives and children, child-selling, infanticide, and both voluntary and forced prostitution. Lines of small children begging stretched for miles outside of cities; at night, children could be heard "crying bitterly and coughing terribly... in the pouring monsoon rain ... stark naked, homeless, motherless, fatherless and friendless. Their sole possession was an empty tin. A schoolteacher in Mahisadal witnessed "*children picking and eating undigested grains out of a beggar's diarrheal discharge*".

The disposal of dead bodies was a chronic problem for the government and the public. People tied a rope around the necks and dragged them over to a ditch. Many died by the roadside –The skulls and bones were everywhere in the months following the famine. Certainly, not exaggeration! Jackals and vultures scavenged on indisposed human remains. Sometimes this happened even before the victims had fully expired. Corpses were stacked along the streets of Calcutta; millions were thrown into sources of drinking water such as rivers and canals.

10.9.7.1 Exploitation of Women and Children

Indian refugees from Rangoon to Mandalay on to India, Jan 1942

Some orphans who survived the Bengal famine of 1943

Mother with child on Calcutta street

Vultures and Jackals at human remains

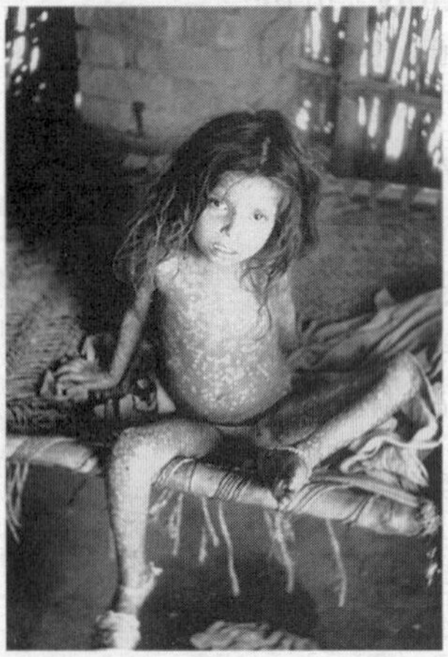

Malaria, cholera, virulence, smallpox swept the hunger-stricken

A mother and child

The exploitation of women, sales of women and girls peaked. Even before the famine, sexual exploitation of poor, rural, lower-caste and tribal women by the *jotedars* had at times been socially sanctioned, and during the crisis, women turned to prostitution in great numbers. A section of contractors made a profession of selling girls to military. There were places in Chittagong, Comilla and Noakhali where women sold themselves literally in hordes, and young boys as pimps for military.

Believe it or not! In late 1943, entire boatloads of girls were for sale in ports of E Bengal. Young girls were sent to wealthy landowners overnight in exchange for a little money or rice or sold them outright into prostitution; girls were sometimes tempted with sweet treats and kidnapped by pimps. Very often, the girls lived in constant fear of injury or death, but the brothels were their sole means of survival. Woman who had chosen or been forced to become a prostitute could not expect any social acceptance or a return to her home or family and thence became permanent outcastes in a society. In addition to lakhs of children orphaned, many were victimised by their own mothers and fathers. Sometimes they were sold as household servants, and grew up as domestic slaves. They were also purchased by sexual predators. Children were abandoned by the roadsides or at orphanages, dropped down wells, thrown into rivers, or buried alive. How pity it is!

> **O My God!**
>
> **Role of Newspapers**
>
> Calcutta's leading English newspapers were *The Statesman* (British-owned) and *Amrita Bazar Patrika*. In the early months, the government applied pressure on newspapers to "calm public fears about the food supply" and that there was no rice shortage. *The Statesman*, initially published editorials attributing the famine solely to speculation and hoarding. News of the famine was also subject to strict war-time censorship – even use of the word "famine" was prohibited. *The Statesman* later remarked that the UK government "seems virtually to have withheld from the British public knowledge that there was famine in Bengal at all".
>
> In Jul-Aug 1943, these two newspapers published detailed and increasingly critical accounts of the depth, its impact on society, and the nature of British, Hindu, and Muslim political responses. For example, a headline in *Amrita Bazar Patrika* that month warned "The Famine conditions of 1770 are already upon us", alluding to an earlier Bengal famine that caused the deaths of 1/3rd of Bengal's population. It also published an editorial cartoon showing starving peasants gazing at distant international food aid ships with the caption "A Mirage! A Mirage!" *The Statesman*'s reportage pointed as the famine was "man-made".
>
> A turning point in news coverage regarding the famine came on 22 Aug 1943, when *The Statesman* published a series of graphic photographs of the starvation and suffering. These changed the international perceptions and sparked international media. The photos of human suffering under British rule marked the end of colonial rule. The decision by editor Ian Stephens to publish the photographs was described as "a singular act of journalistic courage and conscientiousness, without which many more lives would have surely been lost".

10.9.7.2 Cloth Famine

Furthermore, it raised a curtain for new kind of famine - **Cloth Famine -** left nearly the entire population of the poor Bengali naked or clothed in scraps through the winter.

The British military consumed nearly all the textiles produced in India by purchasing Indian-made boots, parachutes, uniforms, blankets, and other goods at steep discount rates. Therefore, robbing of graveyards for clothes, disrobing of men and women in out of way places for clothes and minor riots here and there were common scenes. Some women committed suicide for want of cloth. Thousands of men and women couldn't go out for usual work for want of a piece of cloth to wrap round their loins. Many women "took to staying inside a room all day long, emerging only when it was their turn to wear the single fragment of cloth shared with female relatives".

10.9.7.3 Poor Sanitation

The famine leading to widespread unsanitary conditions, catastrophic hygiene standards spread diseases. The "cloth famine" saw a scarcity of clean clothing. Conditions in hospitals were indescribably bad with horrible state of the wards and patients, the ubiquitous filth, and the lack of adequate care and treatment, suffering from acute emaciation, with 'famine diarrhoea' and so forth. No dictionary can supply sufficient terms to describe the worst sanitary conditions.

O My God!

Winston Churchill Said Indians 2nd Worst?

By early 1942, US president Franklin Roosevelt and Chinese leader Chiang Kai-shek expressed support for the nationalist cause in India. In Britain itself, the Labour Party had been committed to a peaceful transfer of political power in India to an elected Indian body. British PM Winston Churchill responded to with autonomous political status for India like the then Canada and Australia. But Gandhi's stance was that the British should leave India immediately. On 8 Aug 1942, the INC, at Bombay, called 'Quit India movement'. However, the British authorities, overnight, imprisoned the entire senior leadership of Congress, for nearly 2 yrs. Without its leadership, it moved into a grassroots to sabotage factories, bridges, telegraph and railway lines, government property, post-offices and police stations, and threatened the British control over India. In response, 52 army battalions of British nationals/Gurkhas forcefully and rapidly suppressed the movement, arresting millions of Indians, killing 2,500, publicly flogging many, torturing entire villages and patrolling with air force bombers. For a short time, disruption of communications isolated Assam and Bengal from the rest of India. According to historians Bayly and Harper, Winston Churchill himself had a visceral hostility toward India; "The prime minister believed that Indians were the next worst people in the world after the Germans. Their treachery had been plain in the QIM. The Indians he would starve to death as a result of their own folly and viciousness."

Winston Churchill

10.9.8 Relief Efforts

Government aid was rare to rural poor; directed most of its cash and grain to the relatively wealthy landowners and urban *bhadraloks*. The response was meagre, and relief efforts were very limited until April 1943. There was rampant corruption and nepotism in the distribution of aid; often half of the goods supplied disappear into the black market or the hands of friends or relatives.

A Man-Made Holocaust

While famines were not uncommon in India throughout history, largely because of periodic droughts or monsoons, except the tragedy of Bengal famine.

British PM David Cameron expressed regret for the Jallianwala Bagh massacre of 1919 in Amritsar (British soldiers mercilessly killed ~400 unarmed Indian men, women and children), but the PM omitted to refer Britain's role in Bengal famine of 1943, which consumed 3 million deaths of starvation and malnutrition in the Indian province of Bengal which is a far greater massacre than Jallianwala Bagh incident. It is man-made disaster that has been largely forgotten by the world.

Indian MP and an agricultural scientist M. S. Swaminathan blamed the then UK government to the plight of starving people of undivided Bengal.

In the prior year, 1942, when Japan seized Burma, an important rice exporter, the British bought up massive amounts of rice but hoarded it. The famine only ended because Bengal thankfully delivered a strong rice harvest by 1944.

Dr. Gideon Polya, an Australian biochemist, called the Bengal famine '***a man-made holocaust***'. "The British brought an unsympathetic and ruthless economic agenda to India," he wrote. He further noted that the "loss of rice from Burma and ineffective government controls on hoarding and profiteering led inevitably to enormous price rises, in Dacca (E. Bengal) increase is 4-fold during Mar-

Oct 1943. Bengalis to purchase food suffered immensely and about 30% of labour died in the famine."

Image of Midnapore famine victim from Chittaprosad's *Hungry Bengal*; 5000 copies were burnt by Indian police. The caption read "His name was Kshetramohan Naik."

Many scholars of both India and Great Britain blame Winston Churchill, the Britain's inspiring wartime leader for the devastation by the famine. In 2010, Bengali author Madhusree Mukherjee in her book, "Churchill's Secret War", explicitly blamed Churchill for worsening the starvation in Bengal by diverting food away from Indians and toward British troops around the world. She described how wheat from Australia (which could have been delivered to starving Indians) was instead transported to British troops in the Mediterranean and the Balkans. Even worse, British colonial authorities (under Churchill's leadership) actually turned down offers of food from Canada and US. "If it was other than Churchill, relief would have been sent, and the famine wouldn't have occurred at all", she added, "Churchill's attitude toward India was quite extreme, and he hated Indians".

Churchill when first received a telegram from the British colonial authorities in New Delhi about the rising toll of famine deaths in Bengal, simply he regretted that nationalist leader Mahatma Gandhi was not one of the victims. Later at a War Cabinet meeting, Churchill blamed the Indians themselves for the famine, saying that they "breed like rabbits". His attitude toward Indians was crystal clear when he told Secretary of State for India Leopold Amery: "I hate Indians. They are a beastly people with a beastly religion."

10.9.9 Amartya Sen, The Witness of Bengal Famine 1943

Amartya Kumar Sen, (born 3.11.33) is an Indian economist and philosopher, conferred with Adam Smith prize (1954), prestigious Nobel Prize (1998) for Welfare Economics and the highest Indian honour, Bharat Ratna (1999), working since 1972 in UK and US (presently in Harvard University) has contributed to welfare economics, social choice theory, economic and social justice, economic theories of famines, and indexes of the measure of well-being of citizens of developing countries. Sen is a Bengali Baidya in Santiniketan in W Bengal, India, on the campus on Rabindranath Tagore's Viswa-Bharati University, to Ashutosh Sen and Amita Sen. The name, Amartya Sen (= immortal leader) was given by Tagore. While at Presidency, Sen was diagnosed with oral cancer, and given a 15% chance of living 5 years but, survived with radiation treatment. In 1953 he moved to Trinity College, Cambridge, where he earned a 2nd B.A. in Pure Economics in 1955 with 1st Class topping the list.

O My God!

Concept of "capability"?

Sen's development economics and social indicators is the concept of "capability" in his article "Equality of What". He argues that governments should be measured against the concrete capabilities of their citizens. He says, top-down development always trumps human rights as long as the definition of terms remains in doubt (Is a "right" something that must be provided or that simply cannot be taken away?).

Sen in his book, *Poverty and Famines,* in *An Essay on Entitlement and Deprivation*, (1981), says famine is not just because of lack of food, but also due to inequalities built into mechanisms for distributing food. Sen contends the Bengal famine was due to an urban economic boom that hiked food prices and millions of rural workers starved to death as their wages did not keep up.

Mostly during famine, food supplies are not significantly reduced. In Bengal, food production in the previous year was higher than in previous non-famine years. Thence, he raises several social and economic factors, like declining wages, unemployment, rising food prices, and poor food–distribution, which led to starvation. His capabilities approach focuses on positive freedom, a person's actual ability to be or do something, rather than on negative freedom approaches, which are common in economics and simply focuses on non-interference. In the Bengal famine, rural labourers' negative freedom to buy food was not affected. However, they still starved because they were not positively free to do anything, they did not have the functioning of nourishment, nor the capability to escape morbidity.

As a 9 yr-old boy, he witnessed the Bengal famine of 1943, which killed 3 million Indians. This staggering loss of life was unnecessary, Sen later concluded. He argues that there was sufficient food available in Bengal, but the prices of food rapidly rose too high to rural landless labourers including service providers to buy food. Other factors include British military acquisition, panic buying, hoarding, and price gouging, all connected to the war in the region.

He wrote a controversial article in *The New York Review of Books* entitled "More Than 100 Million Women Are Missing", analyzing the mortality impact of unequal rights between the genders in the developing world, particularly Asia. In 1998, Sen redefined the capability approach in his book *Development as Freedom*. Sen argues that development should be viewed as an effort to advance the real freedoms that individuals enjoy, rather than simply focusing on metrics such as GDP or income-per-capita. Sen was inspired by violent acts he had witnessed as a child leading up to the Partition of India in 1947. On one morning, a Muslim labourer named Kader Mia stumbled through the rear gate of Sen's family home, bleeding from a knife wound in his back. Because of his extreme poverty, he had come to Sen's primarily Hindu neighbourhood searching for work; his choices were the starvation of his family or the risk of death in coming to the neighbourhood. The price of Kader Mia's economic unfreedom was his death. This experience led Sen to begin thinking about economic unfreedom from a young age.

In *Development as Freedom*, Sen outlines five specific types of freedoms:

1. ***Political freedoms:*** the ability of people to have a voice in government and to be able to scrutinize the authorities
2. ***Economic facilities:*** both the resources within the market and the market mechanism itself. Any focus on income and wealth in the country would serve to increase the economic facilities for the people.
3. ***Social opportunities:*** the establishments that provide benefits like healthcare or education for the populace, allowing individuals to live better lives.
4. ***Transparency guarantees:*** allow individuals to interact with some degree of trust and knowledge of the interaction.
5. ***Protective security:*** the system of social safety nets that prevent a group affected by poverty being subjected to terrible misery.

Before Sen's work, these had been viewed as only the ends of development; luxuries afforded to countries that focus on increasing income. However, Sen argues that the increase in real freedoms should be both the ends and the means of development.

Welfare economics seeks to evaluate economic policies in terms of their effects on the well-being of the community. Sen, who devoted his career to such issues, was called the "conscience of his profession". His influential monograph *Collective Choice and Social Welfare* (1970), addressed problems related to individual rights (including formulation of the liberal paradox), justice and equity, majority rule, and the availability of information about individual conditions, inspired researchers to turn their attention to issues of basic welfare. Sen devised methods of measuring poverty that yielded useful information for improving economic conditions for the poor. For instance, his theoretical work on inequality provided an explanation for why there are fewer women than men in India and China despite the fact that in the West and in poor but medically unbiased countries, women have lower mortality rates at all ages, live longer, and make a slight majority of the population. Sen claimed that this skewed ratio results from the better health treatment and childhood opportunities afforded boys in those countries, as well as sex-selective abortions.

Governments and international organizations handling food crises were influenced by Sen's work. His views encouraged policy makers to pay attention not only to alleviating immediate suffering but also to finding ways to replace the lost income of the poor—for example through public works—and to maintain stable prices for food. A vigorous defender of political freedom, Sen believed that famines do not occur in functioning democracies because their leaders must be more responsive to the demands of the citizens. In order for economic growth to be achieved, he argued, social reforms—such as improvements in education and public health—must precede economic reform.

In 2009, Sen published a book *The Idea of Justice* based on his welfare economics and social choice theory, and also his philosophical thoughts.

On 19 July 2012, Sen was 1st chancellor of Nalanda University (NU). Sen received over 90 honorary degrees from universities around the world.

Sen has been called "the Conscience of the profession" and "the Mother Teresa of Economics" for his work on famine, human development theory, welfare economics, the underlying mechanisms of poverty, gender inequality, and political liberalism. However, he denies the comparison to Mother Teresa, saying that he has never tried to follow a lifestyle of dedicated self-sacrifice. Amartya Sen also added his voice to the campaign against the anti-gay Section 377 of the Indian Penal Code. A 57-minute documentary named *Amartya Sen: A Life Re-examined* directed by Suman Ghosh details his life and work.

SELF ASSESSMENT INTERMISSION (SAI – 10.4)

1. Describe the factors that led to cause the Great Bengal Famine - 1943.
2. Explain the effect of WW-II on the Bengal Famine-1943.
3. How does Japan's invasion of Burma (now Myanmar) affect Bengal Famine–1943? Discuss.
4. How was the land-use system during British India colonial Bengal Province? How did it lead to cause a famine?
5. Write a detailed note on Bengal-Famine-1943.
6. What is cloth famine? Describe in the backdrop of Bengal Famine-1943.
7. Discuss how Bengal Famine helped enhancing participation in Quit-India Movement – 1942.
8. Explain the role of News papers during the Bengal Famine-1943.
9. Write a note on the effect diseases and sanitation during famine taking an example of Bengal Famine – 1943.
10. Discuss the effect of natural disasters on Bengal Famine during British India.
11. Discuss the attitude of Winston Churchill, the British PM during British Indian colonial rule toward the famine occurred during 1943.
12. Describe the exploitation that prevails during famines, particularly with women and children and poor peasants/tenant farmers taking an example of Bengal Famine-1943
13. Some people told 'Bengal Famine-1943 is a manmade Holocaust'. Do you agree or disagree? Substantiate with some points to support your argument.
14. Explain the views of Amarthya Sen on famine (particularly, Bengal Famine-1943). Do you agree with his views? Discuss.
15. Discuss the effects of Bengal Famine-1943.

Droughts and Famines in History

Some of the well-known droughts in the history are given below:

- 12-yr severe drought smashed Australia, Victoria & Tasmania (no historical precedent available)
- 1900 India drought: estimated deaths 2.5 - 3.25 million.
- 1921–22 Soviet Union (SU) drought: >5 million suffered from starvation
- 1928–30 Northwest China: > 3 million deaths by famine.
- 1936 and 1941 Sichuan Province China: 5 and 2.5 million deaths respectively.
- 2006, Sichuan Province China: about 8 million humans & 7 million cattle faced water shortage.
- 1997–2009 Millennium Drought-Australia: severe water crisis (plants desalinated for the 1st time).
- Drought affected some areas of Karnataka, India in 2012.
- 2005 drought in Amazon basin was the worst drought in 100 years.
- 1984-85, 2006, 2011 Recurring droughts in E Africa led to desertification and created grave ecological catastrophes, food shortages and famine.

Almost every continent in the world has experienced a period of famine in the history. Some countries, particularly in sub-Sahara Africa, continue to have extreme cases of famine.

Perhaps! Famine was first eliminated in Holland and England during the 17th century, by the commercialization of agriculture and implementation of improved techniques to increase crop yields.

- By the 1590s, Holland grew as one of the most commercialized agricultural systems in Europe, through rapid urbanization in late 16th - early 17th centuries to maintain a steady food supply
- By 1650, English agriculture also was commercialized. The last famine in England was in 1623
- In East Europe, famines occurred during late the 20th century.
- The Great Famine in Ireland, 1846–51, due to the failure of potato crop over a few years, resulted in 10 lakh deaths and another 20 lakh refugees fleeing to Britain, Australia and US. It was one of the 1st to feature intervention of government response.

O My God!

The Darfur conflict in Sudan and Chad had decades of combination of drought, desertification and overpopulation. The nomadic Arabs (Baggara) searching for water took their livestock to the land occupied by non-Arab farmers

- During the 20th century, ~70 million people died from famines across the world, of which ~30 million died of 1958–61 in China
- The most notable famines of the century is the 1942–1945 disaster in Bengal, famines in China in 1928 and 1942, and a sequence of famines in the SU, including the Soviet famine of 1932-1933, caused by the policies of Stalin.
- A few of the great famines of the late 20th century were: the Biafran famine in the 1960s, the Khmer Rouge- famine in Cambodia in the 1970s, the N Korean famine of the 1990s and the Ethiopian famine of 1984–85.
- In 1680s, famine extended across the entire Sahel,
- In 1738 half the population of Timbuktu died of famine.
- In Egypt, 1687-1731, 6 famines of which the one in 1784 cost it ~1/6th of its population.
- The Maghreb experienced famine and plague in the late 18th and early 19th century.
- There was famine in Tripoli in 1784 and in Tunis in 1785.
- Angola from 16th century had great famines on average every 70 years; followed by epidemic disease, killing 1/3 or ½ of the population, and destroying the demography.
- In 20th century Congo recorded deaths up to 10 million from brutality, disease and famine.
- Nigeria has greater vulnerability to famine and severe drought struck in 1913.
- The Ethiopian Great famine afflicted (1888-1892) roughly 1/3rd of its population.
- In Sudan the year 1888 is remembered as the worst famine in history.
- Himba; 1910-1911, the "drought of the omutati seed" or *omangowi*, means the people ate fruit of a vine; 1914-1916 droughts are *katur'ombanda* or *kari'ombanda* means "the time of eating clothing"
- In the 20th century: The famine in Rwanda during WW-II and the Malawi famine of 1949
- From 1967-1969 large scale famine occurred in Biafra and Nigeria due to a government blockade of the Breakaway territory. About 1.5 million people died of starvation.
- Famine recurred in early 1970s; Ethiopia and W. African Sahel suffered drought and famine.
- Famines in Sudan in late-1970s, 1990 and 1998 depopulated 21%, including 60% of them infants.

- In the 1980s, large scale multilayer drought occurred in Sudan and Sahelian regions of Africa.
- In 1992 Somalia war zone with no effective government, police, or basic services after the collapse of Siad Barre's dictatorship, coincidentally a massive drought caused >3 lakh deaths
- Recent famines in Africa include the 2005–06 Niger food crisis, the 2010 Sahel famine and the 2011 E Africa drought in which 0.5-1.5 lakh people died.
- In 2012, the Sahel drought put >10 million people deaths due to a month-long heat wave.
- The Great Leap Forward famine-1958–61 in China was the largest of the 20th century
- From 1333-1337 a terrible famine killed 6 million Chinese. The 4 famines of 1810, 1811, 1846, and 1849 killed >45 million people.
- Japan experienced >130 famines during 1603-1868.
- The Taiping Rebellion-1850-1873 caused drought & famine to depopulate China by >30 million
- The Great North China Famine 1877–78, Catastrophe depopulated 9.5-13 million in province of Shanxi as grains ran out; desperate starving people stripped forests, fields & their houses for food.
- In 1975, Pol Pot of Khmer Rouge took over Cambodia and applied communism; drove all urban people to the countryside to work on communal farm; about 1-3 of total 8 million people died of malnourishment and exhaustion of the famine by negligent government.
- Famine of N Korea in the mid-1990s, had unprecedented floods. The industrial state depended on massive inputs from the SU and China. When the Soviet collapsed and China switched trade to a hard currency, N-Korea's economy collapsed and agricultural

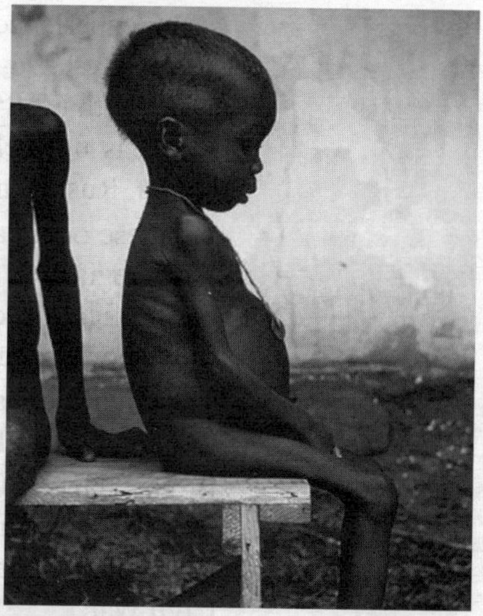

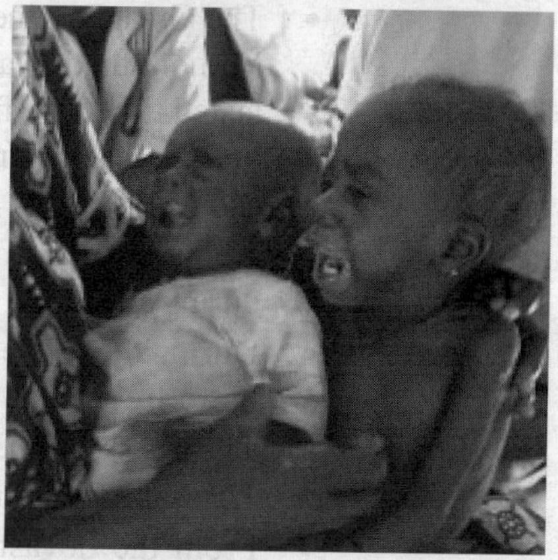

The Nigerian infants during the 2005 famine, Maradi Niger

Skulls of victims of famine in Cambodia, caused by the Khmer Rouge.

sector experienced a massive failure in 1995–96, expanding to full-fledged famine by 1996–99 causing 24-42 million deaths directly by the famine along with 60-85 million unnatural deaths between 1993-2008. Still N-Korea is not self-sufficient of food and depends on China, Japan, S-Korea, Russia and the US.

- Japanese occupation during WW-II caused the Vietnamese Famine of 1945, registered 2 million deaths, (10% of the then population). Following the unification of the country after the Vietnam War, it experienced a food shortage in the 1980s.
- The Great Persian Famine of 1870–71 killed 1½ million (¼th population) in Persia (now Iran).
- In the early 20th century an Ottoman blockade of food exported to Lebanon caused a famine which killed up to 4.5 lakh Lebanese Maronite Christians (~1/3 population), more people than the Lebanese Civil War.
- The Great Famine of 1315–1322 was the first major food crisis in Europe. Millions died. Starting with bad weather in 1315, widespread crop failures lasted till 1317, from which Europe did not recover until 1322. It was a period of extreme crimes, disease and mass death, infanticide, and cannibalism.
- About 100 famines in Britain (and France also) killed > 5 lakh people during 1315–131.
- During the Little Ice Age i.e.15th-18th century, famines in Europe became more frequent.
- The worst famine since 1600, the great famine in Finland in 1696, killed 1/3 of its population
- From the devastating harvest failures during 1618-21, Italy couldn't recover for centuries.
- Serious famines in the late-1640s and less severe in the 1670s occurred in Italy.
- In France, 2 famines made worse by ongoing wars (1693-1710) that killed >2 million people.
- In 1690s, Scotland experienced famine which reduced the population of Scotland by >15%.
- The Great Famine of 1695–97 killed 1/3 of Finnish and ~10% of Norway's population.
- The Finnish famine of 1866–1868 killed 15% of the population.
- 1740–43 saw frigid winters and summer droughts, led to famine across Europe. The winter 1740-41 was unusually cold, probably due to volcanic activity.

- The Great Famine, in 1770-71, killed about 10% Czechs and 2.5 Lakh inhabitants.
- There were only 16 good harvests and 111 famine years in northern Italy from 1451 to 1767.
- During the terrible famine of 1680, ~80,000 of total population of 2.5 lakh died in N. Italy.
- According to Bryson (1974), there were 37 famine years in Iceland between 1500 and 1804.
- In 1783, the lava of volcano Laki in Iceland caused little direct damage, but ash and SO_2 wiped of ¾th livestock. The following famine killed ~10,000 people i.e. 1/5th of population.
- Russia had droughts/ famines in every 10-13 years. It had 11major famines between 1845 and 1922, the worst being the famine of 1891–92.
- Famines (*Holodomor)* in Volga, and Ukrainian and N Kazakh USSR's during the winter of 1932–1933 consumed ~6million lives.
- The last major famine in USSR was in 1947 due to the severe drought and mismanagement of grain reserves by the Soviet government.
- The 872 days of the Siege of Leningrad (1941–1944) had famine resulting one million deaths.
- W Europe during WW-II in Netherlands, the *Honger-winter* of 1944 killed ~30,000 people.
- The 1877–78 *Grande Seca* (Great Drought), the Brazil's worst event, caused ½ million deaths.

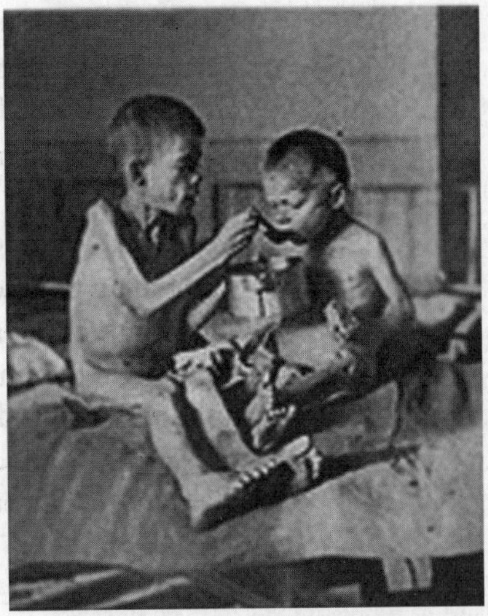

Starving Russian children during the famine of 1921–22, which killed ~5 million

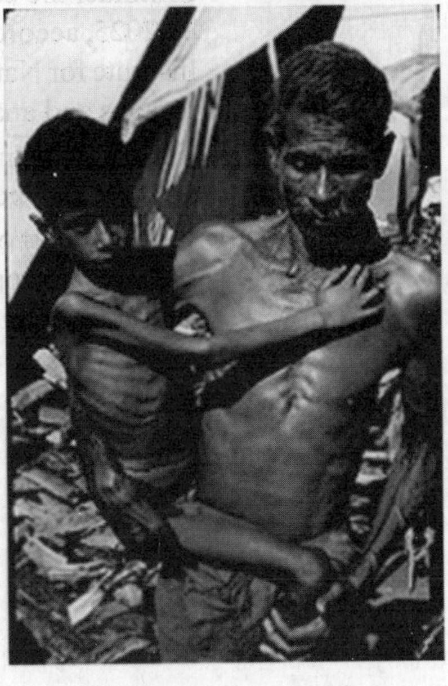

A child suffering extreme starvation in India, 1972

Notable Droughts and Famines in India

Owing to dependence entirely upon the monsoon rains, India is vulnerable to crop failures, which upon occasion deepen into famine.

- 14 famines occurred in India between the 11th and 17th centuries (Bhatia, 1985).
- During 1022–1033 Great famines in India entire states were depopulated.

- Famine in Deccan killed at least 2 million people in 1702-1704.
- As per B.M. Bhatia ~25 major famines spread through Tamil Nadu, and Bihar and Bengal during the latter half of the 19th century.
- The first, the Bengal famine of 1770, took ~10 million, 1/3 of Bengal's then population.
- The Great Famine of 1876–78, recorded 6.1 to 10.3 million deaths
- The Indian famine of 1899–1900, killed millions of people.
- The famines were ended by the 20th century with the exception of the Bengal Famine of 1943–44 even without crop failures —killed 1½-3 million Bengalis during WW-II.
- In 1966, US allocated 9 lakh ton grains to fight the famine in Bihar. Starvation & disease of 3yr drought consumed 1½ million lives

MINI PROJECTS / CASE-STUDIES

1. "In Africa, if current trends of population growth and soil degradation continue, the continent might be able to feed just 25% of its population by 2025, according to United Nations University (UNU)'s Ghana-based Institute for Natural Resources in Africa". Elaborate by exploring various reasons and analyzing them.
2. Go through Amarthya Sen's concept of 'Welfare Economics'. Discuss on his views how welfare economics is related to famine.
3. Write a report on Bengal Famine – 1943 with causes and effects. Prepare a power point presentation and discuss among your colleagues/ classmates on efforts to mitigation.

CHAPTER 11

Industrial Hazards

(Chemical, Fire, Explosion and Radiation)

O'MY SILENT INNER VIBES (O'M S I V – 11)

The ever biggest intentionally and deliberately caused fire accident (wildfire) could be the one set by Krishna-Arjuna on Khandava forest in Dwapar Yug (the period of Mahabharat), while another biggest unintentional psycho-social fire accident set by Lord Hanuman who set entire Lanka on fire in Threta Yug, (the period of Ramayan).

Khandava Vanam (Khandavaprastham) was an ancient forest in the west of Yamuna River, (today's Delhi territory). Pandavas cleared this forest to construct their capital city called Indraprastha. This forest was earlier inhabited by Naga tribes led by a king named Takshaka. Arjuna and Krishna cleared the forest by setting up a huge wildfire displacing the inhabitant of the forest, particularly the snakes (Nagas), which was the root cause of the enmity of the Naga Takshak towards the Kuru kings who ruled from Indraprastha and Hastinapura. The Mahabharata states that Indra was the deity protecting Khandava forest, and so named Indraprastha. When the forest was being burnt, Indra attacked Arjuna with his thunder bolt (*Vajrayudham*), injuring him. But, for the destruction of environment and damage to bio-diversity, the wildfire did establish a kingdom. Of course, the generations of Pandavas had paid for this act (Thashak took revenge on Parikshit). So, your today's act may affect generations.

In the other story of Ramayan, Rama, the prince of Ayodhya, is exiled to the forests for 14 years, accompanied by his wife Sita and brother Laxman. Ravana, the demon king of Lanka, who also wanted to wed Sita, and also raged by seeing Shurpanakha's ears and nose cut decides to take revenge and so kidnaps Sita. While on search of Sita, Rama meets Hanuman.

Hanuman, a great devotee of Rama undertakes the mission of finding Sita. He flies over the Indian Ocean to land on Lanka, where he finds Sita. He proves his identity, by giving her Rama's ring and asks to come with him but Sita refuses and tells him to inform Rama to come soon to take her back.

(Continued)

On his return journey he is arrested and produced in the court of Ravana. As tail is his main strength, Ravana orders Hanuman's tail to be set on fire. Hanuman then breaks his bondage and flies away. ***But, with his tail on fire he sets the whole city of Lanka ablaze.*** After setting fire to the whole town, Hanuman leaps away from the island and extinguishes the fire of his tail in the Indian Ocean.

Hanuman is considered as the most wise and intellectual, but could not stop his emotions, and set a **psychosocial fire hazard/ accident** that left the entire innocent citizens of Lanka to become victims of fire including Sita.

- Also at the same time, it is the result of the decision taken by the so called most intellectual Ravan Brahma who could not control his anger against the ambassador, Hanuman.
- Real fire-fighting is to control one's own anger.
- It tells us the moral not to take hasty decisions under emotions.
- Think a while, when you are operating with fire or any hazardous materials, if it causes any inconvenience to surround, the mankind and the environment.
- Your anger is your real enemy which can cause you ill healthy to become hyper tensed (High BP)
- '**ANGER**' is the greatest '**FIRE**' and is the real trigger for a 'HAZARD' or a 'DISASTER'.

FIRE IS A VERY GOOD SERVANT, BUT A VERY BAD MASTER.

11.1 THE CONCEPT AND MEANING OF HAZARD

The term 'Hazard' might have been derived from the French word 'hasard' or the Arabic word 'az-zahr', which means chance or luck. A hazard in literature means a state or event or an object of the potential to threaten the surroundings and environment and/or can affect people's health adversely. Environmental hazards range from man-made riots and pollution to naturally occurring storms, volcanic eruptions and earth quakes.

Definition

"A dangerous condition or event that can threaten or have the potential to cause injuries, or consume life or damage property or the environment" is called a hazard.

It will be convenient to understand more about the hazards by classifying them.

11.1.1 Classification of Hazards

Hazards are broadly classified into two categories in two ways

The first way is

1. Natural Hazards and
2. Man-made hazards

The second way of classification is

1. Social Hazard and
2. Industrial Hazards

This chapter focuses on the industrial hazards, particularly with regard to chemical, fire, explosions and radiations, however, the other are briefed for a ready reference and awareness.

Natural Hazards

These hazards are due to the natural phenomena such as meteorological, geological or even biological origin. Cyclones, tsunamis, earthquakes and volcanic eruption etc. come under this category. Hazards caused by both natural and man-made phenomenon like landslides, floods, drought, and fires also are categorized in this class.

Manmade Hazards

The hazards caused due to human negligence are called the man-made hazards. These are associated with industries or energy generation facilities and also include explosions, leakage of toxic wastes, pollution, structural failure, wars and accidents. Man-made hazards can be categorised into mainly four types. They are:

- Chemical hazards (leakages, pollution, contamination etc.)
- Physical hazards (road/water/air accidents, environmental changes etc.)
- Biological hazards (bio-mass waste, medical waste, agricultural disposals, epidemics, bio-weapons, diseases etc.)
- Psychosocial hazards (communal riots, wars, faction etc.)

11.2 INDUSTRIAL HAZARDS

Industrial hazards are mainly man-made. One of the most concerning environmental issues is that the industries release huge amounts of toxic gases such are carbon mono oxide (CO), sulphur dioxide (SO_2) and many other chemicals into the atmosphere. When the levels of these chemicals increase it results in the destruction of the mankind in terms of social, economic, and cultural aspects.

Another related issue is the usage and handling of the toxic substances. If any fire catches, the industry, and the nearby villages are seriously affected. Also due to the increased number of the industries the pollutants in the air are also increasing enormously resulting in converting a normal environment to a hazardous. Serious disasters since last 2 decades, due to the so called 'GLOBAL WARMING, are signalling the gravity of the problem and posing a global challenge. There is a dire necessity to take care of the industrial hazards though it may not appear to be urgent need because they do not show their impact immediately. But the result can be seen by the future generation who may not lead a peaceful life. "Save the environment and save the earth."

11.2.1 Most Concerned Issues and Challenges

In addition to the industrial accidents and the hazardous operations by their very nature, the usage and handling toxic and corrosive chemicals, fires, explosives and inflammable/ radiating materials are the major health and safety hazards encountered in the operations of chemical and particularly pharmaceutical, plastic, fertilizer and chemical related industries. The most worrying issues with such industries having a hazardous environment, is that they may cause disasters either immediately or in future. The following are some of such most concerning issues.

- Release of chemicals into the atmosphere
- Release of chemicals into the water
- Explosions
- Fire spreading
- Sometimes the extinction of many species
- Causing noise pollution
- Deforestation
- Disturbance to the ecosystem
- Plastics usage and disposal

11.2.2 Classification of Industrial Hazards

Whether natural or manmade, if the above listed activities occur in the premises of an industry, they are often claimed as industrial hazards.

Whatsoever, the industrial hazards may be categorized in the following way.

- Chemical and Gas Hazards
- Fire Hazards
- Explosion Hazards
- Radiation Hazards
- Biological Hazards
- Water and other Hazards

We shall now discuss the above in detail in the paragraphs to follow.

SELF ASSESSMENT INTERMISSION (SAI – 11.1)

1. Define 'Hazard'? What is its meaning? Explain with an example.
2. How do you classify hazards? Explain each of the types of hazards briefly.
3. Distinguish between natural and manmade hazards. Explain briefly with example to each
4. Distinguish between social and industrial hazards. Explain briefly with example to each
5. What do you understand by the term 'Industrial Hazard'? Classify industrial hazards.
6. What are the most concerned and challenging issues with reference to hazards and disasters in industrial environment? Discuss.

11.3 CHEMICAL HAZARDS

O My God!

- The Indian Chemical Industry contributes to 6.7% of the GDP.
- Indian Fertilizer Industry is the 4th largest in the world.
- India is 2nd largest (1st is Japan) Pesticide manufacturer of Asia.
- Indian Pharma industry is the largest in developing world

Chemicals may exist in any form such as solid, jelly (semisolid), liquid, vapour and gas. A chemical substance is a material with a definite chemical composition. Handling of large quantities of hazardous chemicals in installations, isolated storages and during transportation, poses grave risk of sudden release of copious quantities of toxicants. This may adversely affect the communities in and around the area as well as the environment. There are about 30 million chemical compounds and new chemicals are being discovered and added to the list daily. These aspects have been increasingly posing high risk to the mankind while challenging the governments and scientists.

An estimated 7 lakh existing chemical products, and hundreds of new ones being introduced annually and about 32 million workers are exposed to one or more chemical hazards posing a serious problem for exposed workers and their employers.

11.3.1 Hazard Communication Standard

Chemical exposure can result in several health problems such as heart diseases, damage to central nervous system, kidney and lungs, sterility, cancer, burns, rashes and so forth. Some chemicals even cause fires and explosions and/or major/ catastrophic accidents. And most disgusting thing is that most of the employees and even employers know little or nothing about them. Owing to these aspects of health problems and adverse effects, the Occupational Safety and Health Administration (OSHA) issued the Hazard Communication Standard that the employer must give the employees full awareness about the hazards and of the workplace chemicals to which they would be exposed and the care that they must take. The basic objective of the standard is

- to ensure employers and employees aware of work hazards and
- how to protect themselves so as to help reducing the incidence of illness and injuries.

11.3.2 Responsibilities of Managements of Chemical Industries

The chemical hazards are often posed by

- toxic germicides (e.g. formaldehyde and glutaraldehyde) and
- sterilising chemicals (e.g. ethylene oxide) or
- reacting gases (e.g. carbon monoxide and sulphur dioxide etc.)

Having understood, the type of chemicals and the type of the hazards they pose, the managements of the industries should monitor and control for preventing their consequential acts in the form of accidents and disasters. Therefore, the management of the industries have to establish a special team for the chemical hazard area monitoring and control with the following primary responsibilities:

- to define and demarcate the hazardous area
- to clearly communicate the causes and effects of the hazard
- to identify which materials pose the hazards and create awareness on them
- to monitor the occupational hygiene
- to monitor and control by the path of entering the human body
- to identify the factors that make the area/ humans vulnerable to hazard
- to apply the counter measures to prevent or control the probable hazard

11.3.3 Chemical Hazard Area Monitoring and Control

In order to discharge the above responsibilities, the management needs to study the nature and the process of the hazard converting into disaster. This involves the following three important points.

- The sending (or hazard generating) point i.e. the hygiene of the work area and associated risk,
- The entering point or the path through which the hazardous chemicals enter human body and
- The receiving point i.e. the vulnerability/susceptibility of humans working in hazardous area.

Occupational hygiene monitoring

In order to assess the adequacy of control measures, one has to first measure how much a worker is exposed to chemical germicides, sterilising gases and toxic materials. Generally, in the large scale industries (especially chemical), hazard areas involve high pressure steam and hot water, moving parts in washing, filling, capping, and packaging equipment, and also high noise levels with repetitive manual tasks. At these points, a close monitoring and control mechanisms have to be established through regulating the associated hazardous mechanical, electrical, pneumatic or thermal energy. It is important to strictly disallow any personnel without adequate training on safety precautions. Usually, some contract workers may perform special operations of production or engineering tasks, particularly in pharmaceutical plants without proper training. This may lead to an accident because chemicals have no mercy. So, contract workers should be carefully supervised (even after training also), so that, in any case they do not violate safety rules during their work with the hazardous chemicals such as toxic, reactive, flammable or explosive materials and also while processing the exothermic and high pressure substances which may lead to the loss of life.

Some chemicals have the potential to cause explosion and fire and lead to serious accidents. Some chemicals may not explode, but can cause health problems in a long run by continuous exposure or overexposure and some other may act indirectly. Therefore, it is very essential to maintain high hygiene surrounds and the occupational area at below harming level.

Monitoring by path of entering human body

Although high hygiene is maintained, and utmost care is taken, the people may get exposed to chemicals. The exposure to severe chemicals may lead to many health effects such as heart diseases, central nervous system damage, kidney and lung damage, sterility, cancer, burns, rashes and so forth. The people exposed to the chemicals must have awareness on how these diseases are caused and from where these diseases enter their bodies. This would help reducing the risk and use the countermeasures to prevent and protect them. Self help is the best help.

There are three main ways by means of which hazardous chemical enter the body. They are

- **Respiratory tract:** Absorption of chemicals through the respiratory tract through inhalation.
- **Eyes and skin:** Absorption or the injection of the chemicals through eyes and skin.
- **Digestive tract:** Absorption of chemicals through digestive tract.

One has to first know the chemical with which he/she is working can enter the body and thus design suitable safety equipment, such as cap or helmet for head, goggles for eyes, mask for nose and apron for skin etc.

Monitoring the people through total health check-up with reference to the above three paths in frequent intervals can give better insight into the intensity of the problem and enables acting at right time. Of course! The degree of danger varies from chemical to chemical and according to the form of the chemical and factors such as the following

- Toxicity of the chemical
- Physical properties such as acidic nature and flammability
- The environment in which it is encountered.
- The way it is used.

Vulnerability to Toxic Chemicals

Even though the work environment is hygienically maintained and all safety precautions are taken to prevent the entry of chemicals into human body, yet, the ailment can be caught by the person working in the area if he/she is too susceptible to such chemicals. This is because of the variation in the resistivity of individuals. Those who have less resistance may catch up the health problems fast and easily. The following are the most common factors that can make susceptible to toxic chemicals

- Genetic factors
- Age (old age or too young)
- State of Health
- Hypersensitivity or Allergy
- Personal Hygiene
- Personal habits such as smoking.
- Pregnancy & lactation.

11.3.4 Common Hazardous Chemicals and their Effects

All forms of a chemical are not harmful. For example in case of lead, water flowing in the lead pipe is not harmful. When the pipe breaks and when lead gets mixed in the flowing water and if this water is consumed it results in severe health problems.

A chemical may be hazardous even in its solid state. For example individuals who are sensitized to nickel may develop dermatics from skin contact with the metal. While some of the chemicals are not hazardous alone but are hazardous when they come in contact with the other substances or the chemicals.

The chemical agents, which are supposed as hazardous, can be classified into three categories as organic, inorganic and gases. The most common hazardous chemicals and their effects are listed below. However, the list is not exhaustive.

Organic Hazardous Chemicals

The following are most common organic hazardous materials

- Aliphatic Hydrocarbons such as Cyclohexane, n-Hexane, Methyl pentane
- Aromatic Hydrocarbons such as Benzene, Styrene, Toluene & Xylene.
- Halogenated Hydrocarbons – Halothanes, Vinyl Chloride. Tetrachlorethane, Carbon tetrachloride, Trichlorethylene (TCL)
- Amides, Phenols, Amino & Nitro derivatives - Aniline, Nitroglycerine, Trinitrotoluene (TNT)
- Alcohols, Glycols & derivatives- Ehtylene glycol, Methanol
- Ketones (Acetone) and Aldehydes (Formaldehyde)
- Asphyxiants such as Acrylonitrile, Carbon Monoxide, Cyanide & Aliphatic Nitriles.

General Areas of Exposure of Organic Compounds

Degreasing, metal machining, painting, welding, wood working & printing.

Health Effects of Organic Compounds

- Occupational Dermatitis
- CNS depressants
- CVS disturbances (especially CS_2)
- Nephro toxic
- Bone Marrow Depression & Leukaemia
- Carcinogenesis
- Chromosomal aberrations
- Skin Irritation
- Eye Irritation
- Inhalation Effects
- Ingestion Effects
- Carcinogenicity
- Mutagenecity

Inorganic Hazardous Chemicals

The inorganic hazardous chemicals are categorized under three groups as given below:

- Metals e.g. lead, mercury and their compounds
- Non-metals e.g. suphur, phosperous
- Metalloids e.g. arsenic, antimony

The common inorganic chemicals considered to be hazardous are: Lead, Mercury, Antimony, Arsenic, Barium, Beryllium, Cadmium & Chromium compounds, Fluoride, Manganese, Nickel etc.

Areas of Exposure and Effects of common hazardous Inorganic Materials

Material	Probable Area of Exposure	Probable Effects (health problems)
Lead	Lead Storage Batteries, Pottery enameling & glazing, Polyvinyl Plastics, Inorganic Lead, Mining & Smelting, Lead Paints, Lead stabilizers, Glass manufacture, Fire arms	Peripheral Neuropathy, Anaemia, Nephrotoxicity, GI Spasm, Treated with Chelating agents such as BAL, EDTA & Penicillamine
Mercury	Scientific Measuring Instruments (Thermometers/ barometers/ Transformers/ Rectifiers); Mercury Vapour Lamps & Storage batteries; Amalgams for Dental use & Jewellery; Seed Dressings & as Pesticides	Stomatitis, Gingivitis, CNS Dysfunction, Erethism, Tremors, Chronic Nephritis
Phosphorus	Phossy Jaw, matches, pesticides, fertilizers, crackers	Irritant, Peripheral Neuropathy Haemolytic
Arsenic	Smelting, Pesticides, Weed Killer, Metal smelting, refining, in manufacturing of chemicals & electronic equipment	Irritant, Peripheral Neuropathy Haemolytic
Manganese	Dry Electric batteries, steel industry	Parkinson's Syndrome, Psychosis, Pneumonitis
Cadmium	alloy in Welding, batteries, Dentistry, pigments, paints, pesticides	Nephrotoxic, Emphysema
Nickel	Steel industry	Dermatitis
Chromium	Steel industry	Chrome Ulcers, Necrosis of Nasal Septum

Organo-Inorganic Hazardous Chemicals

These are poisonous and may enter through skin absorption & GI tract. These can be classified as follows:

- Pesticides such as Baygon, Carbaryl, Chlorphenoxyacetic acid derivatives, Endrin, Hexachlorbenzene, and others such as Carbon Disulfide, Diethylstilboesterol & Ethylene Oxide
- Insecticides & Fungicides – Pyrethrum & Pyrethrins (Mosquito Coils), Organochlorine Compounds such as DDT, Lindane, Dieldrin & Aldrin, Organophosphate compounds such as Parathion, Dichlovos, Carbamates & Organic Mercurials.
- Herbicides - Arsenicals, Dinitrophenol, Dinitro Orthocresol, Phenol herbicides, Paraquat, Diquat, Phenoxy herbicides.

- Rodenticides & Fumigants -Calcium Cyanide, Methyl bromide, Phosphine, Anticoagulants.

Gaseous Hazardous Chemicals

Gases are generally categorized in three classes as follows.

- Inert gases - Act by displacing O_2 -Anoxic Anoxia, e.g. Methane
- Irritant gases - Flourine & its compounds, Ammonia, Sulphur Dioxide, Ozone, Phosgene.
- Gases with systemic poison effects- Carbon Monoxide (Toxic Anoxia), Carbon Disulfide (Chemical Anoxia), Acetylene, Hydrogen Cyanide & Cyanide Salts, Cyanide (Bitter almonds smell), Benzaldehyde (sweet almonds smell)

More specific health effects caused by various gases are listed below.

- Halogen Gases - Irritant effect on Upper Respiratory Tract.
- Flourine could cause Flourosis, Fits & Coma.
- Ammonia - Irritant, Bronchospasm, Pulmonary Oedema & Respiratory Arrest
- Sulphur Dioxide SO_2 - Lassitude, Chronic Bronchitis, Loss of Smell.
- Ozone - Irritant, emphysema, Pulmonary Fibrosis.
- Phosgene - Pulmonary Oedema, Fibrosis & Emphysema
- Carbon Monoxide - Anoxia, Headache, Cough, Paralysis, Sensory Loss, Parkinsonism, Death.
- Hydrogen Sulphide - Irritant, Loss of Smell, Giddiness, Unconsciousness, Death.
- Hydrogen Cyanide - Extremely Poisonous, Bitter Almond Smell, Dermatitis, Headache & Weakness at low conc. Breathlessness & Coma.
- Acetylene - Fume Fever

General Precautionary Measures to Prevent/Control of Exposure at Worksite

- Substitution (material)
- Segregation (material)
- Enclosure (protective)
- Ventilation
- Wet Methods
- Personal Protective Devices
- Monitor Work Environment
- Monitor Exposed Workers
- Education

- Supervision
- Enforcement of rules
- Emergency Measures

11.3.5 Prevention, Protection, Mitigation and Management of Chemical Hazards

The following methods may be adapted for prevention, protection and mitigation of chemical hazards.

- Removal from further Exposure / Evacuation
- Detoxification e.g. Chelating agents
- Supportive Therapy - Oxygen & I.V. Fluids.
- Increase Awareness about
  - the Industries in the area
  - the nature of chemicals being used, stored and transported
  - the hazards and treatment procedures in the event of exposure.

Management to Overcome Exposure to Chemicals

- **Resuscitation:** Restoration of life of one who is apparently dead collapsed or shocked refers to resuscitation. Along with many medical emergencies supportive care must be provided.
- **Symptomatic treatment:** Acute over exposure may result in a variety of signs and symptoms that require general supportive medical management regardless of the specific agent.
- **Removal from exposure:** The first and the foremost important step is to remove the person from the exposure. Lifelines and air respirators are first aid.
- **Decontamination:** A person or the victim whose skin or clothing has been contaminated requires immediate removal of garments and shoes. Then showering with soap and water, including attention to the fingernails and scalp i.e., head is advised.

SELF ASSESSMENT INTERMISSION (SAI – 11.2)

1. What is a chemical? What is a hazard? What is chemical hazard? What is its significance in disaster management?
2. What is a 'Hazard Communication standard'? Explain its objective.
3. What is Occupational Safety and Health Administration (OSHA)? What is its role with regard to the chemical hazards?
4. What types of chemicals exist in a large scale industry? Discuss briefly.

5. Explain the role of management of a chemical industry with regard to reduce chemical hazards.
6. Discuss the method of hazard area monitoring and control with regard to chemical industries.
7. What do you understand by 'hygiene monitoring' and 'vulnerability to toxic chemicals'?
8. Describe the paths through which the chemicals enter the human body.
9. Enumerate the hazardous organic chemicals. Explain their effects on human health?
10. Enumerate the hazardous organo-inorganic chemicals. Explain their effects on human health?
11. List out the hazardous gaseous chemicals. Explain their effects on human health?
12. List out the general precautionary measures to avoid or reduce the chemical exposure?
13. Enumerate the methods of protection, prevention and mitigation of chemical hazards.
14. What are the factors that influence the susceptibility/vulnerability of humans to chemical hazards?

11.4 GAS HAZARDS

Usually, in the chemical industries severe volatile and flammable liquids are employed. These liquids get vaporised at room temperature and may catch fire to result in a fire accidents causing loss of life and property. Thence, the storage and the handling of these gases need a special attention. In order to secure and safeguard from the gases or volatile liquids, we must first understand the nature and properties of such materials and also how they affect.

The gases used in industries are often classified under four generalized categories

1. Combustible/ Explosive gases
2. Toxic gases
3. Suffocating gases and
4. Dust (This is a special case of gas hazards)

We shall now look at the natures of these general types of gases and their influence used in industries:

1. **Combustible/ Explosive gases:** These gases catch fire. Some are too volatile with very low fire point (the temperature at which catch fire) and catch fire even with a small flash, like switching on a tube light in the room (e.g. Liquefied Petroleum Gas – LPG), while some other require

an ignition (e.g. methane). These form an explosion hazard, hence should be maintained below the lower explosive limit.

2. **Toxic gases:** These gases may or may not burn, but inhaling causes suffocation or ill-health or even death. For example the carbon mono oxide (CO), when inhaled reacts with iron (Fe) in haemoglobin of blood and arrests the blood flow, thus leads to death. The gases like carbon dioxide (CO_2) or sulphur dioxide (SO_2) may not kill but cause suffocation and burning sensation in the lungs due to their acidic nature. Overall, they are hazardous to human health and so proper arrangement must be made so that the exposure of the worker should be avoided or limited to below harming level.
3. **Suffocating gases:** These gases may not affect directly but, are treated as a source of indirect health hazard. These gases may be neutral like argon (Ar) or passive such as nitrogen (N_2) or Nitrogen oxides (NO_x), but cause suffocation or breathlessness. They displace oxygen (O_2) and thus cause deficiency of breathing oxygen.
4. **Dust:** Dust is composition of finest solid particles mixed in the air. When the maximum size of the particle is not more than 500 mm, it is called dust. Though rare, dust can also cause hazards, often categorized as a special case of gas hazards. Sometimes the dust may even explode, referred to as dust bomb or dust explosion.

11.4.1 Dust Explosion

The dust particles accumulate to form a '**dust cloud**' if the combustible material such as carbon, sulphur, phosphorous etc. are present in the dust, then it acts as a '**dust bomb**'. When sufficient oxygen for the combustion is supplied by the air, and also the heat supplied by the sun light or any spark occur, the dust cloud burns rapidly. This rapid combustion of the dust cloud is called '**dust explosion**'. Dust of starch and dextrin besides organic substances in the pharmaceutical industry, dust of coal mines are extremely hazardous.

Factors impacting a dust explosion: The following factors influence the dust explosion

(a) Particle size.

(b) Chemical properties of a dust.

O My God!

Innocents Die for Ignorance of Intellectual Industrialists?

here have been many more incidents of a relatively minor nature. One such was a Petroleum tanker accident on the highway near Mumbai. Spillage of the chemical on to the road came to the attention of the local impoverished tribal population, who started collecting the liquid, presuming it to be cooking fuel. A spark led to a conflagration consuming the lives of innocents. Such incidents focus the vulnerability and the need for Risk assessment of transportation of Hazardous chemicals. Other frequent accidents occur when workers descend into empty confined spaces such as disused Wells, Food silos, Sewage channels etc, due to presence of noxious gases like H_2S & CO. Many a lives have been lost and even those who tried to save the victims, due to lack of knowledge, have fallen prey to the same gas exposure.

(c) Moisture content.

(d) Cloud dispersion.

11.4.2 Prevention and Mitigation

Gas hazards can be largely prevented by careful handling and alerting through proper communication such as sign boards in vulnerable places. Recent developments in electronics and remote sensing are providing a reasonably good solution to the gas leakage, gas explosion problems through the gas sensors.

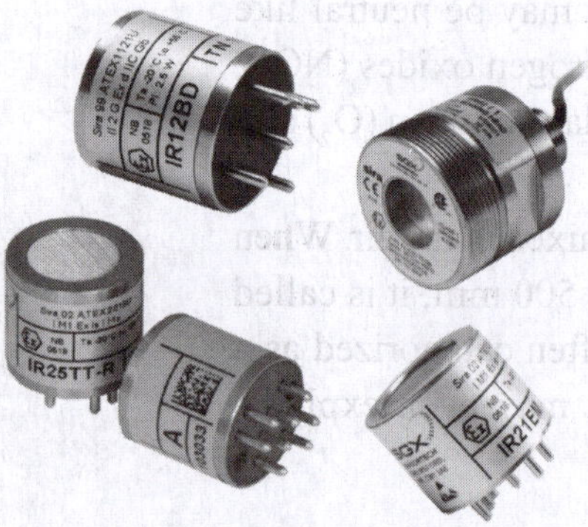

Gas Sensor Placement

This is another best way of avoiding gas hazards and dust explosion. Gas sensors should be placed in the places where the gas/dust accumulation is maximum. They should be close to possible gas source. Accessibility and maintenance issues should be considered.

Dust Management

Dust explosion can be prevented in the following three methods using the concept fire triad (source, combustible material and supporter of combustion).

1. Avoid the development of explosive mixtures.
2. Replace the atmospheric oxygen by inert gas or using inert dust.
3. Prevent the occurrence of effective ignition source.

Red Page in the Annals of Occupational Health - BHOPAL GAS TRAGEDY, INDIA-1984

The worst ever industrial tragedy known was due to gross negligence of a pesticide manufacturing company and incompetence of the government authorities. Over 5 lakh people were exposed to the deadly methyl iso-cyanate (MIC) and other chemicals leaking from the plant of Union Carbide Co. (UCC) India Ltd at Bhopal, India on the night of Dec 2-3, 1984. The leaked gas spread over the town through air and water killed 8000 people within 2-weeks and injured 5.5 lakh of which about 4000 were permanently disabled (blind). Though UCC had been warned before of potential leakages, no real efforts were made to improve the situation.

The gas (being heavier than air) started entering into the homes of the unwary population. Many panicked and ran out of houses also got crushed in stampedes. Around 5 lakh were estimated to be exposed to the gas & around 20,000 have died as a result. Over 1.2 lakh continue to suffer from the effects of the disaster. Doctors and Hospitals were unaware of the nature of the Gas, nor were they informed of the proper treatment of the inhalation of MIC gas, being merely asked to give cough medicine & eye drops. Had they been informed about the same, proper treatment could have been instituted & a lot of lives could have been saved.

Post Bhopal Gas Disaster

The Bhopal disaster taught a lesson and sharpened the focus on the unprecedented potential of hazardous chemical release in terms of loss of life, health, injury and evacuation. It created a compelling evidence to approach disaster management and chemical safety. The disaster awakened to call an era of restructuring and inducting new hazardous chemical control systems and procedures all over the globe.

The following are the after-effects of the disaster.

- Factories Act, 1948 was amended to assign responsibility for workplace safety to the occupier.
- Environment Protection Act was introduced in 1986.
- The Manufacture, Storage & Import of Hazardous Chemicals Rules, 1989 have been framed.
- The Chemical Accidents, Emergency Planning, Preparedness and Response, 1996 was introduced.
- The growth of the chemical sector has led to increase in the manufacture, storage and use of Hazardous chemicals (Hazchem) resulting in enhanced threats of accidents.
- There are around 1790 Major Accident Hazard units in the country, handling large number of chemicals as raw materials, in processes, products and wastes with flammable, explosive, corrosive, toxic and noxious properties. All these are instructed to follow the codes of safety.

O My God!

Toxicology?

Toxicology is concerned with poisons and their effect the body. The toxicity of a substance is determined by chemical composition, concentration, particle size (inhaled), physical state, routes of absorption (Inhaled, skin contact or ingestion), presence of other poisons (Additive effects) and duration of exposure

Measurement of Toxic Substances

- **Threshold Limit value (TLV):** Time weighted (average) concentration of an airborne substance to which workers could be safely exposed over an 8-hr working day throughout the life time.
- **Maximum Allowable Concentration (MAC)** Peak or Max. conc. of an airborne substance to which workers could be safely exposed.
- **Body Limit values (BLV):** Conc. of the substance in body fluids such as blood & urine below which no toxic effects should occur.

SELF ASSESSMENT INTERMISSION (SAI – 11.3)

1. What are different types of gases which pose the hazards in industry? Discuss briefly.
2. Explain how the combustible/ explosive gases can create chemical hazards.
3. What are toxic gases and suffocating gases? Discuss how they can make an environment hazardous.
4. What is 'Dust'? Discuss how dust can make an environment hazardous.
5. What is dust explosion? How does it occur? List out the factors favouring dust explosion.
6. Describe how gas hazards can be prevented/ mitigated.
7. Write a detailed note on Bhopal Gas Tragedy – 1984.
8. Enumerate the after effects of Bhopal Gas Tragedy – 1984.
9. Do you think the cause is shear negligence of management of UCC for Bhopal Gas Tragedy – 1984? Justify your answer.

11.5 FIRE AND EXPLOSION HAZARDS

Fire is a very good servant, but a very bad master. As long as it is under control, it serves a lot of useful purposes, but, once it goes out of control, it can be disastrous.

Threats to fire safety are referred to as fire hazards. A fire hazard may include a situation that increases the likelihood of a fire or may obstruct escape in the event a fire occurs.

Fire/explosion hazards most probably occur due to the potential ignition source created through

- Spontaneous combustion and
- Electrical equipment without explosion-proof.

Of course! The severity of the burning depends on the intensity of fire during the explosion time.

Definition

Fire accident can be described as the one which arises in consequence of an act of some human agency unintentionally, or which happens by some natural cause, without human agency.

11.5.1 Causes of Fire and Fire-prone Areas

The most common sources of fire hazards or fire accidents are:

(i) ***Electrical systems***

- Overload
- Heat produced in wiring/ connections

- Failed components
- Short circuits

(ii) ***Cooking/Pantry Area***

- Cooking gas/oil leakage followed by spark
- Cooking appliances – electric stoves, kerosene stoves, ovens
- Improper use/ maintenance of gas stoves
- Exterior cooking equipment like Grill Fire
- Heating appliances - wood burning stoves, fireplace, furnaces, boilers, portable heaters
- Kitchen fires due to unattended cooking, frying, boiling, simmering etc.

(iii) Other Areas in House

- Combustible storage areas with insufficient protection
- Combustibles near equipment that generates heat, flame or sparks
- Household appliances - clothes dryers, curling irons, hair dryers, refrigerators, freezers, Leaking Batteries, cell phones
- Electronic and electrical equipment

(iv) ***Smoking***

- Smoking (Cigarettes, cigars, pipes, lighters, beedi, etc.) in/ around inflammables
- Hot ashes falling on combustible materials
- Personal ignition sources - matches, lighters

(v) Lamps, Crackers and Fireworks

- Erratic operation of crackers,
- Unsafe practices, environment while using fireworks in festive seasons
- Candles and other open flames
- Lamps and lighting used in Festivals (like Deewali/ Ramzan/ Christmas) and celebrations (e.g. Marriages/ birthdays/ election winning/ national holidays etc.)

(vi) Industrial Hazardous Area

- Welding zone
- Fire produced due to friction between moving parts
- Fuel storage area
- Chimneys that concentrate creosote
- Combustible storage areas with insufficient protection
- Combustibles near equipment that generates heat, flame or sparks
- Electrical wiring in poor condition
- Improper operations and maintenance of ovens, furnaces and hearths

- Equipment that generates heat and utilizes combustible materials
- Flammable liquids and aerosols
- Flammable solvents and rags soaked with solvent placed in enclosed trash cans
- Fireplace chimneys not properly or regularly cleaned

(vii) Environmental Effects

- Hot summer environment
- Heat radiations
- Heat waves
- Lightening
- Meteors, asteroids etc

11.5.2 Fire Triangle

The three essential elements for fire namely, combustible material, supporter of combustion and the ignition source, are often called *Fire Triangle* or *fire triad*. Thus the fire triangle specifies the necessary conditions for occurring a fire hazard or accident.

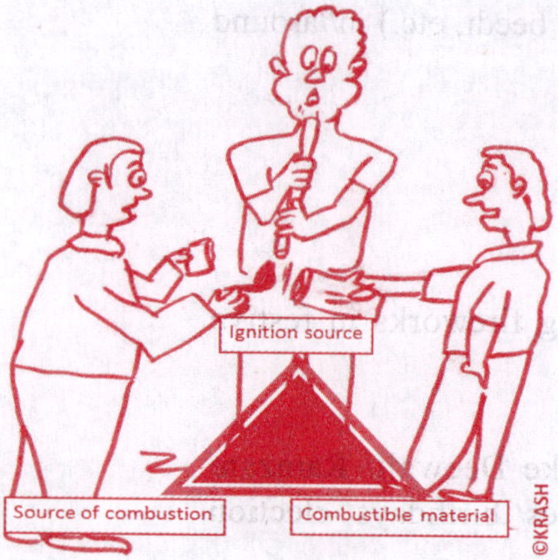

Conditions Needed For Fire

For a fire to take place, the following three conditions must exist:

1. A combustible material (Fuel)
2. A specific temperature (ignition source)
3. An aid of burning (supporter of combustion, mostly oxygen)

Example: Coal is the combustible material, burns when the sufficient temperature (fire pint) is given and the atmosphere provides the oxygen.

Fire can occur if and only if all the three elements of the fire triangle are present. However, sometimes one element can aid or provoke the other also.

Fire-fighting

We know that each of the three elements (fire triangle) have to be present to start a fire, and also for the fire to continue. This forms the fundamental principle behind all fire-fighting techniques.

To control a fire, the only way to extinguish it is to remove at least one element of the fire triangle. Sometimes, we may have to simultaneously attack two elements also because sometimes one arm could aid the other arm. Moreover, by trying simultaneously fight two arms, we can achieve the results faster and more efficiently. Of course, it is a matter of experience and the situation that determines which element(s) to be attacked. Usually, fire-fighters try to remove that element which is the easiest to remove.

11.5.3 Control of Fire and Explosion

The following points should be considered with a view to reduce the fire and explosion hazards

- Careful plant layout demarcating the explosion-prone areas and necessary plan to overcome.
- Specific choice of constructional material that can reduce fire and explosion hazards.
- Fire resistant brick walls to limit the effect of explosion.
- The roof design to lift easily under an explosive force.
- Sufficient fire alarms, temperature alarms, fire fighting equipment and sprinkler system.
- Avoiding possible sources of fire due to unnecessary ignition sources such as welding, spark, and smoking.
- Design, curing methods, curing time etc. during building construction.
- Exit points in the building.
- Safety and fire protection organization, Fire alarms, Sprinkler system, Fire extinguishers equipment and their positioning.

Fire Safety Measures

Prevention is better than cure. So, it is always a good idea to prevent the occurrence of fire accident. Thus, fire safety measures are intended to prevent ignition of an uncontrolled fire (before occurrence), and to limit the development and effects of a fire after it starts.

Fire Safety in Constructions

Fire safety is often a component of building safety. Fire safety measures in constructions include those which are

- Planned during the construction of a building
- Implemented in structures that are already standing
- Taught to occupants of the building

11.5.4 The Role of Fire Department

The fire safety officers of fire department have the following major roles to play

1. **Creating awareness in people and/or training them:** The fire safety officers often use students of schools/colleges to educate on Fire Safety

topics. The Chief Fire Prevention Officer would normally train newcomers to the Fire Prevention Division and conducts the drills or presentations.

2. **Fire prevention:** Fire prevention is an important function of fire department. Its primary objective is to educate the public about precautions to prevent potentially harmful fires, and about escaping, surviving and fire-fighting. It is a proactive method of reducing emergencies and the damage caused by them. Students are often the primary resource for fire prevention. Fire-fighters will generally visit schools/ colleges and teach/ train students about the basics of fire prevention. Seniors would have pre-planned escape routes and access to emergency exits. Juniors are trained by mock-drills. Workshops are conducted in schools for educating on the causes and effects of fires and how to deal with them. Fire prevention education can be in the form of videos, pamphlets, banners, booklets, placards, flags and so forth. Generally, the messages and lessons are in the form of ***DOs and DON'Ts*** or ***simple tips***.
3. **Inspecting buildings and observing the fire code:** They inspect buildings for violations of the Fire Code. Conducting oneself with the provisions of the fire code is depends on the occupants and operators of the building provided they are aware of the applicable regulations. The Fire safety officers have to
   - Conduct fire drills at regular intervals throughout the year
   - Periodically inspect buildings for violations of fire code
   - issue orders to comply
   - prosecute/ close the buildings that do not comply, until the deficiencies are corrected
   - condemn it in extreme cases
   - Maintain a high level of training and awareness of occupants and users of the building to avoid obvious mistakes, such as the propping open of fire doors.

Some of the ***Fire Code for Buildings***

- Do not exceed the maximum occupancy in any part of the construction.
- Maintain fire exits and signage at appropriate positions (exit signs pointing to them that function in a power failure)
- Comply with electrical codes to prevent overheating and ignition from electrical faults or problems such as poor wire insulation or overloading in wiring, conductors or other fixtures with more electric current than they are rated for.
- Place/install and maintain right type of fire extinguishers in easily accessible places.

- Do not store flammable materials in certain areas of the facility. If you have to store take all precautions as per norms.
- Store and/ or use hazardous materials in secured places (e.g. solvents in spray booths).
- Ensure that spray fireproofing remains undamaged.
- Obtain and maintain a complete inventory of fire stops.
- Maintain fire alarm systems for detection and warning of fire.

Some tips for fire prevention

Risk

Elder people and children are considered as "risk" group, especially in hazardous situations.

Stop, Drop and Roll

If one's clothing catches on fire, the most effective method of extinguishing the fire is to stop, drop to the ground, and roll back and forth to smother the flame. Never run, because running around will simply fan the flames.

Let Smoke Detectors Work

Smoke detectors reduce the chances of death in a fire by half.

Most deaths due to fire occur at night when people are sleeping. Even just one smoke detector can reduce the chances of death by almost 50%. Nearly half of all fire survivors remember hearing their smoke alarm. History says that fire deaths decreased by half since the invention of the smoke detector.

The most common cause of smoke detector failure is missing or disconnected batteries. Nuisance alarms are the most common reason for deliberately disconnecting batteries. Missing, disconnected, or dead batteries account for 73% of smoke detector failures. There are more homes with no working smoke detectors than the homes without any smoke detectors at all. It is advised that

- Smoke detectors should be installed on every level of a home.
- Change your batteries twice a year.
- Clean your detectors also.
- Replace the entire unit every ten years.
- Disconnecting your batteries, for any reason, is dangerous and illegal.
- Don't just leave to do something else

No Negligence with fire related equipment

One of the most common reasons for fires is how people often leave stoves, ovens, toasters, clothing irons, barbecues, mosquito coils, lamps, and candles unattended.

Fire-fighters are your friends

The two most critical jobs of a fire-fighter are to search and rescue. For young children often scared at seeing fire-fighter in bunker gear breathing with an air tank. So, the parents should remove the fear in their children and see that the child can get used to or trust a fire-fighter. The parents should take their children to fire station, police station etc., at least once in a year and explain their duties and responsibilities. Furthermore, being able to walk up and touch the fire-fighter can reassure the child that he or she is a real person. They must tell, 'fire-fighters are your friends'.

Don't play with fire

Playing with fire causes many unnecessary emergencies. It hurts and kills many people. Moreover, it invites false alarms, besides wasting the valuable manpower and other resources, which otherwise could be a desperate need of a real emergency. Even sometimes it may cost the lives of fire-fighters because the history reveals that most of the fire-fighter deaths occurred while responding to the calls. False alarms, waste valuable manpower and resources, which may be needed desperately at a real emergency. Also, any time fire-fighters ride trucks, they are at risk. 18% of fire-fighter deaths occur while responding to calls.

11.5.5 Top Fire/Chemical Accidents in the World

> O My God!
>
> **Fire-Fighting?**
>
> Fire departments any nation primarily promotes and educates by working with all levels of the government, services and other fire prevention and safety organizations to promote fire prevention activities and also by partnering with the Government. These are downloadable and printable. All of the information is free of cost. A few of the available guidelines with fire fighting division are: Cooking Precautions, Escape Plan, using Fire Extinguishers, Smoke Alarm etc. they are available in Official Website of Govt. of India (nidm.gov.in)

The nature has been testing our skill and will of survival with many natural calamities devastating thousands of lives and property. There have been several instances of human actions being a reason of many calamitous accidents either. Since the industrial revolution in the 18th century, almost every part of the world faced such incidents due to the negligence or technical default or accidents claiming millions of lives till date. The world's worst industrial disasters related to fire during the last century are given below:

1. **Courrièrs Mine Disaster, France-1906:** Couriers mine disaster is the worst mining accident in Europe claiming lives of 1099 miners and many children on Mar 10, 1906 in N. France. The two hypothesized causes for the event are:

   (i) an accident during handling of mining explosives and

   (ii) ignition of methane by naked flame of a minor's lamp.

   Both have evidence favouring them.

2. **The Halifax Explosion, Canada-1917:** The largest man-made explosion before the development of nuclear weapons occurred in the Richmond district of Halifax, Canada when a cargo ship fully loaded with wartime weapons collided with a Norwegian ship Nov 6, 1917. Soon after the collision, a fire was produced and ignited the explosives on the cargo resulting in a huge explosion killing about 2000 people and injuring 9000 by fires, and collapsed several buildings. The explosion also resulted in a Tsunami which resulted in further causalities including 5 children and wiped out an entire community.
3. **Opal Explosion, Germany-1921:** Opal Explosion, Germany is the one of the biggest chemical disasters happened in the Opal, Germany plant of BASF, the world's largest chemical company, on Sep 21, 1921 when a tower silo storing 4500 tons of a mixture of ammonium sulphate [$(NH_4)_2SO_4$] and ammonium nitrate (NH_4NO_3) fertilizer exploded. It killed about 600 people and injured >2000, >80% of all buildings in Opal were destroyed that made >6500 people homeless. The exact cause of the accident is still unknown as all died in the explosion. However, investigations say that an inaccurate estimation of sulphate-nitrate could be a reason. A few months before the incident the manufacturing process had been changed that lowered the humidity level which could be another reason for the explosion.
4. **Benxi Hu Colliery Explosion, China-1942:** The gas and coal-dust explosion in the jointly controlled Japanese and Chinese Benxi-Hu Colliery is world's worst coal mine disaster ever, consuming 1549 people (>1/3rd of miners) on Apr 26, 1942. The explosion flames raged out of the mine shaft entrance. The Japanese workers of the mines are blamed of raising the death toll as they tried to lessen the fire underground by shutting off ventilation and sealing pit without fully evacuating it thence trapping many Chinese workers underground to suffocate. An investigation later by the Soviet Union revealed that only some people died from the explosion while most died due to the closing of ventilation after the initial explosion.
5. **Exxon Valdez Oil Spill, Alaska-1989:** Exxon Valdez Oil Spill, Alaska is the most devastating human-caused environmental disaster claiming a huge aquatic life when on Mar 24, 1989, Exxon Valdez, an oil tanker targeted to Long Beach, California, hit the Bligh Island Reef, Prince William Sound, Alaska, spilling 2.6 – 7.5 lakh barrels of crude over the next few days. Immediate effect of the spill was the deaths of about 2.5 lakh seabirds, at least 2800 sea otters and 100's of other sea creatures. By 2010 there was still an estimated 23000 gallons of Valdez crude oil in Alaska's soil, breaking down at less than 4% per year. The spill continued to affect the sea animals in Alaska till date as a higher death rate and reduction in reproduction of many species have been noted since then.

6. **Enschede Fireworks Disaster, Netherlands-2000:** Enscheda Fireworks Disaster was a calamitous, killing 23 people, injuring 940 and destroying over 1500 buildings as the fireworks exploded at the SE Fireworks depot on May 13, 2000 in Enscheda, Netherlands. Fire began in the work area of the central building at the depot where around 900kg of fireworks were stored. The fire then spread to two full containers stored illegally outside the building. The ignition exploded 177 tons of fireworks. Surprise is that SE had been audited and was reported that it met all safety regulations and inspected as safe by the Dutch authorities only a week prior to the explosion. Is it not the sheer negligence of Dutch authorities?

SELF ASSESSMENT INTERMISSION (SAI – 11.4)

1. "Fire is a very good servant, but a very bad master", critically appreciate the statement in the backdrop of fire hazards.
2. Define fire hazard and explosion? List out various possible causes and fire prone area in an Industry.
3. What is meant by 'fire triangle'? Explain.
4. What is 'fire triangle'? How is it useful for fire fighting?
5. List out the control measures for fire and explosion.
6. Describe the role of Fire-Department in preventing, protecting and controlling fire hazards/ accidents.
7. List out the provisions for fire prevention and control under building code in constructions.
8. Suggest the fire protection and prevention measures for (a) household fire accidents (b) industrial fire accidents.
9. Describe any three of the world top fire accidents.
10. Recall a fire accident you witnessed or heard, after describing the situation; discuss the causes and effects of it?
11. Identify the fire prone areas at entire campus where you are working / studying and place some placards or posters written with precautionary measures.
12. Meet the officials of fire department in your vicinity and conduct an interview of their experiences, functions and procedures.

11.6 ATOMIC EXPLOSION

"Explosion" is a violent release of energy (generally mechanical, nuclear or chemical) bursting out due to pressure. There are several kinds of explosions that cause much damage to the health, life and assets. The following are the most notable types of explosions

1. Bomb explosion and terrorism
2. Atomic/Nuclear explosion
3. Chemical explosion
4. Coal/Petro explosions

Of all the above, nuclear/atomic explosion is highly disastrous as many people were killed and injured seriously.

Definition of Atomic Explosion

Atomic explosion occurs when the energy releases suddenly/rapidly from a high speed Nuclear Reaction due to nuclear fission or fusion or a multistage cascading combination of the two. The following is the distribution of the total energy during atomic explosions.

- 40-50% to the blasting
- 30-50% to thermal radiation
- 5% to ionizing radiation
- 5-10% to the mass of explosion

11.6.1 Causes of Atomic Explosion

As the explosion occurs due to the sudden release of energy from massive elements of fissionable material or radiation or radioactive material into the environment, it can greatly damage the whole environment over a wide geographic area leading to great destruction of human civilization. This type of explosion usually occurs in the nuclear reactors whose purpose is to generate electricity.

The following are the major causes of atomic explosion

- Sudden release of fissionable or radioactive materials or radiation into the environment.
- Poor safety measures
- Improper transporting of nuclear waste that poses risk of pollution and environment contamination
- Improper storage of radioactive elements in nuclear power plants causing radiation
- Non standard operations and also mismanagement of nuclear reactor
- Poor instrumentation
- Lack of well trained staff

- Unreliable instruments
- Errors in procedures of operation

11.6.2 Effects of Atomic Explosion

- Many people severely suffer from the radiation. The atomic explosion if occurs can effect on human life as per the following 3 stages.
  - In the 1st stage (1st-9th week), among the affected, 90% get direct deaths due to thermal injuries and about 10% due to the super lethal radiation exposure and some blast effects
  - At 2nd stage (10th-12th week), death period are from ionizing in median lethal rap LD50
  - In the last stage (13th-20th week), there may be a hope in the people for surviving
- In addition to atomic radiation, thermal radiation also greatly affects due to enormous release of energy in the form heat.
- Fallow had a great effect on the atomic explosion. Fallow means a mushroom cloud created in human body by a nuclear explosion
- There would also be long term effects so adversely on atmosphere and climate by the explosion that humans cannot survive
- The soil will be completely damaged. It will not be useful for the cropping for 100 years.

Earth had a great damage by the explosions. Save the Earth for your future generations.

11.6.3 Prevention Methods for Atomic Explosion

The following are the precautions taken for the prevention of atomic explosion

- Nuclear safety is very essential in these days of atomic culture. "PREVENTION IS BETTER THAN CURE".
- The unauthorized access to the activities involving nuclear/atomic substances must be strictly prohibited by the governments of the nations and have to adhere to the international code.
- Government must take effective measures through the security forces and monitor keenly, so that the disasters won't happen.
- Governments should enforce insurance schemes and make it mandatory. A separate monetary fund is to be created for helping in the event of any accident.
- Extraction process and also storage strategy are to be followed with the utmost concentration.

- As storage source also can also be used as a weapon, the army should be enough to protect the storage substances.
- Major source of atomic explosion is nuclear power generation, with good engineering skills. Power generation should be done efficiently and prevent explosion
- Countries should understand and the need to evolve peace, and also safety and secure nuclear technology. The nuclear energy should be properly be used for human development but not to kill the innocents.

11.6.4 Previous Calamities of Atomic Explosion

The major atomic explosions occurred in different places of the globe include, Tokaimura, Fukushima, Hiroshima and Nagasaki of Japan, St. Laurence (France), SL-1 experimental power station (USA), Goinana accident (Brazil), Three mile accident, Wind scale fire (UK), Kystym and Chernobyl (Ukrain, Russia). Brief notes of these are given below.

1. **Tokaimura Atomic Explosion-1999:** This is one of the most dangerous atomic explosions occurred in Japan in 1999. The disaster struck when some people working in the plant decided to place a high quality Uranium in precipitation tank. It consumed 56 workers life and the most painful thing is that 21 civilians were also exposed to high doses of radiations.
2. **Goiana Accident, Brazil-1987:** This is also one of the major atomic explosions occurred in Brazil in 1987. This accident in the state of Brazilian, Egoais occurred because of the radioactive contamination. An old radio therapy had been stolen from the abandoned hospital site in the hospital. 4 people were killed. Among 112,000 people examined, 249 had significant levels of radioactive material in or on their body.
3. **Chernobyl Disaster, Ukraine-1986:** The disaster occurred at Chernobyl Nuclear Plant, Ukraine is considered to be the worst nuclear power plant disaster ever (named as level 5 by the International Nuclear Event Scale, INES) when the explosion and fire released huge quantities of radioactive particles into the atmosphere that spread over the western USSR and Europe. On Apr 26, 1986, a fire started at the reactor-IV of the plant as a result of a series of stem explosions occurred during an emergency shutdown due to an unexpected power surge during a test. The disaster claimed 54 workers instantly and over the years about 4000 died of diseases of radiations and affected 18 billion people of Russia.
4. **Buenos Era Explosion, Argentina-1984:** This is also one of the dangerous atomic explosions occurred in Argentina in 1984. A worker had some errors in his operations during fuel plate recognition led him die two days later. They had planned some excursion with 3*10 fissions at the RA-2 facility with operator. It was absorbed by 2000 rad of gamma

and 1700 rad of neutron radiation. About 17 people outside of the reactor room received high doses of radiation.

5. **Saint-Laurent Disaster, France-1969:** The most dangerous civil nuclear disaster in the French history occurred in 1969. Uranium of 50 kg placed in the gas cooled reactors started melting that led to an explosion.
6. **SL-1 Experimental Power Station, USA-1961:** This explosion occurred in Idaho, USA in 1961. An experimental nuclear reactor had explosion and killed 3 operators. It occurred due to improper removal of the control rod and also responsible for absorbing neutrons in the reactor core. It was named most fatal event in the USA that released 80 curies of iodine-131.
7. **Wind Scale Fire, UK-1957:** This is also one of the major atomic explosions occurred in UK on 10th Oct 1957. It was named as the worst disaster in the Britain history. This was ranked level 5 in the International Nuclear Event Scale (INES). They had prepared 2 piles in the British atomic bomb project. On October 1950, the first pile had been active, on June 1951 the second pile was active. This explosion took place when the reactor of unit-1 caught Fire. Cancer cases of 240 had been linked to the fire.
8. **Kyshtym Disaster, Russia-1957:** This was the disaster occurred in Russia in 1957 at Mayak. It was a radiation contamination Accident, reprocessing plant in the Soviet Union. It was named at level 5 by the INES and was identified as the 3rd most dangerous disaster ever recorded in Russia. This explosion happened in the town of Ozyorsk which was a closed city that was built around the Mayak plant. Mayak orozyorsk had not marked on the maps and so the disaster had named kyshtym.
9. **Hiroshima And Nagasaki Atomic Bomb Blasts-1945:** It was the most dangerous and the worst disaster due to atomic explosion happened in the WW-II. Lakhs of people died due to this manmade (deliberate) disastrous explosion. During the final stage, US, with the consent of UK put forth Quebec Agreement, and dropped nuclear weapons on the Japanese cities of Hiroshima and Nagasaki in Aug 1945. The 2-bombs killed about 1.3 lakh people.

The bombings role in the Japan surrender and their ethical justification still beat – The World War-II

The Europe had concluded war when Nazi Germany signed its instrument of surrender on May 8, 1945. The Japanese refused to accept demands of the allies for unconditional surrender and so the pacific war continued. Together with in the UK and China, the US called for unconditional surrender of the Japanese armed forces in the Potsdam declaration on July 26, 1945-the alternate being prompt and the destruction. In July 1945, the allied Manhattan project successfully detonated on atomic bomb in New Mexico desert and by August, 2-alternate designs were made with the specialized silver plate varnish of the Boeing B-29 super fortress that could deliver them for Tinian in the Mariana Islands.

On 6th Aug, the U.S dropped a Uranium gun type atomic bomb (A LITTLE BOY) on Hiroshima. American president Harry S. Truman called for Japans surrender 16 hrs later, warning them to "***expect a rain of ruin from the air, the like of which has never been seen on this earth***". 3 days later, on Aug 9, the US dropped Plutonium impulsion type bomb (FAT MAN) on the city of Nagasaki. Within the first 2-4 months, the bombings killed 1-1.5 lakh people in Hiroshima and 39,000-80,000 in Nagasaki, roughly half of the deaths in each city occurred on the 1st day. The radiation effects, and other injuries, compounded by mental shocks, sickness and malnutrition affected severely in both cities, while the most of the dead were innocent civilians. 6 days later (on Aug 15) after the SU's declaration of war, Japan announced its surrender to the allies. On Sep 2, it signed the instrument of surrender, effectively ending WW-II.

SELF ASSESSMENT INTERMISSION (SAI – 11.5)

1. "Prevention is better than cure", critically appreciate the statement in the backdrop of nuclear explosions.
2. Define explosion. What are different types of explosions? Briefly describe.
3. Define atomic explosion. List out various causes for atomic explosion
4. Describe the causes and effects of atomic explosions.
5. What are the consequences of an atomic/nuclear explosion?
6. List out the preventive measures for atomic explosion.
7. Describe any three of the world top calamities of atomic/nuclear explosions.
8. Recall nuclear accident occurred recently in Japan. Collect the information of the accident and prepare a report.
9. Recall the situation of atom bomb attack on Hiroshima and Nagasaki of Japan. Collect the information of the accident and prepare a report or write a one act play.
10. Describe the Chernobyl incident and discuss its causes and effects.

11.7 RADIATION (RADIOACTIVITY) HAZARDS

Radioactivity can be of either natural or artificial, originates from the transformation of the structure of matter that emits ionising rays (alpha, beta, and gamma). They pose a major danger to humans and the environment. Depending on the strength of the radiation received, the effect may range from serious biological damage to provoking apparent lesions (burns, organic lesions) to delayed biological damage, which show effect after several years in the form of cancer or hereditary genetic malformations. This means, if a person is exposed to radioactive radiation, he or his son/ daughter or even grandson/ granddaughter may also be affected.

It is therefore important not to expose human beings and the environment to ionising rays by putting all unnecessary efforts for preventing or limiting the radiation level to the minimum.

11.7.1 Causes and Origins/ Sources of Radioactivity Hazard

There are most diversified origins for producing radioactivity. The following are most common causes for a radioactive rays spreading and contaminating the air are

- During the production of radioactive substances,
- During transportation of radioactive substances
- Storage of radioactive substances
- From a nuclear accident
- By terrorist acts,

O My God!

The most disastrous Weapons?

The use of nuclear weapons can result in the ultimate disaster and is the biggest threat to mankind. The primary and secondary radioactivity provoked by such weapons can devastate by their destructive effects of electromagnetic radiations, luminous and thermal, and mechanical effects of the pressure, which are proportionate to the power of the weapon and the altitude at which it explodes.

- From the fall of a satellite
- Due to a fault in a nuclear power station,
- The use of nuclear weapons
- Due to irresponsible storage or disposal of nuclear waste and weapons

The characteristics of the radioactive radiation are strange and their contamination of the air are quite unpredictable to determine how much area (localised or affecting vast regions) and how long (temporary or long lasting). Further, it depends on

- the intensity of radiation (depends on the type of radioactive substance)
- the quantity of release
- the half-life of radioactive substance
- the duration of release
- the spread of particles by the wind
- the prevailing meteorological conditions

11.7.2 Preventive and Protective Measures

The radioactivity disaster, if at all occurs; can be surely attributed to manmade disasters, whether it is accidental or deliberate. In the present scenario of scientific and technological advancements, it is certainly possible to prevent as well as protect from the harmful consequences of radioactivity.

Further, the international law is specifying the measures to be respected for protecting humans and the environment from ionising radiations from the various known sources, may it be intentional (criminal) or unintentional. This necessitates legislating with regard to the protection against radiation (radioprotection). If need be, it must be the peaceful use of nuclear energy and the protection of the population in case atomic weapons are used on the national territory or abroad in situations of armed conflict.

Since the radioactivity has some advantageous uses and its application is gaining importance in certain areas such as medical field in curing cancer-like diseases, nuclear power plants for producing nuclear energy and so forth, some organizations are permitted to use these materials under the licence. However, they are obligated through the radioprotection. In other words, all users or owners of radioactive substances of any sort, or those responsible for installations and instruments emitting ionising radiations, to take all measures that are required to protect the life and physical integrity of persons exposed to radiation.

11.7.3 Protective Measures and Obligations

The licence may be granted to use radioactive material under the following main obligations and conditions with regard to the protective measures:

- Determining and observing exact dosage limits of exposure to radiation.
- Imposing medical measures for persons exposed to radiation because of their profession.
- Medical applications of radiation.
- Responsibility of enterprises, particularly with reference to research, purely in the technical uses of radioactivity and proper disposal of radioactive waste.
- Observation of the environment and protection of the population against radioactivity.
- Checking the radioactivity of food products.

11.7.4 Protective Measures at Nuclear Power Plants

In the case of nuclear power plant, the protection of the population, the environment and the areas surrounding is the prime responsibility of the industry as well as the government. When radioactivity reaches a dangerous level, the strict implementation of permanent and complementary protective measures is only the option.

The security of nuclear plants is ensured mainly by a series of precautions, such as

- the enclosure of combustible elements,
- the covering of reactor's pressure tank,
- the steel security casing and
- the concrete security fence round the plant.

When a serious accident occurs, such as the emission of rare gases and particles, a distinctive alarm system can be triggered within an area of a 5 to 20 kms radius, either simultaneously over the whole area or by individual sectors.

11.7.5 Intervening and Alarming Organizations

The governments usually establish some bodies called 'intervention and alarm organisations or departments' for the purpose of alerting when the radioactivity increases to a critical level and also intervening as and when required. It also enables the population to be protected during non-conventional wars if atomic or chemical weapons are used. The intervening organization continuously monitors and keeps on surveillance to asses of the surrounding radioactivity in collaboration with the regional authorities and security services. In case of increased radioactivity, the intervening organisation directly subordinates to the government (Ministry of Defense or Internal affairs or Home) to observe the overall preventive and protective measures. Thus, as a part of its job, it uses a countrywide network of radiation detection equipment such as network of sirens, to measure and warn about radioactivity and toxic chemical substances as well as guiding general public by the national radio or TV channel on 'how to react and behave to the situation'.

11.7.6 Intervention and Rescue Measures

No sooner than an accident by ionising rays occur that can harm the humans and the environment, the operator and the responsible authorities should immediately start implementing the planned intervention/ rescue measures such as:

- Dealing as quickly as possible with the causes of the accident and triggering the security measures capable of reducing the damaging effects.
- Informing the government officials concerned.
- Informing the regional and local authorities immediately.
- Alerting the security services and instructing them to guide the needy.
- The radioactivity monitoring organization, the national alarm centre will be alerted
    - to proceed to assess the radiological situation by means of the various services and devices in existence, and
    - to propose which protection measures to implement.
- Immediately warning the population of any great increase in radioactivity and
- Publicising the official rules of behaviour which it is expected to follow.
- Taking refuge in the civil protection shelters or basements and in respecting the principles of individual and common protection.

If a nuclear disaster occurs such as the explosion of a nuclear weapon, the political authorities and their management organs should shoulder the responsibility of the management of protection, search, rescue and assistance (supplies, medical assistance, evacuation) operations at the local or regional level in coordination with the available civil and military means along with intervention required (equipment, material etc.). Further, the technical coordination will be ensured by specialists in nuclear protection. International cooperation may be sought through the International Atomic Energy Agency (IAEA) based in Vienna (Austria).

11.7.7 Instructions to People

The following are the general precautions and safety measures to be observed by every individual.

When there is a potential danger

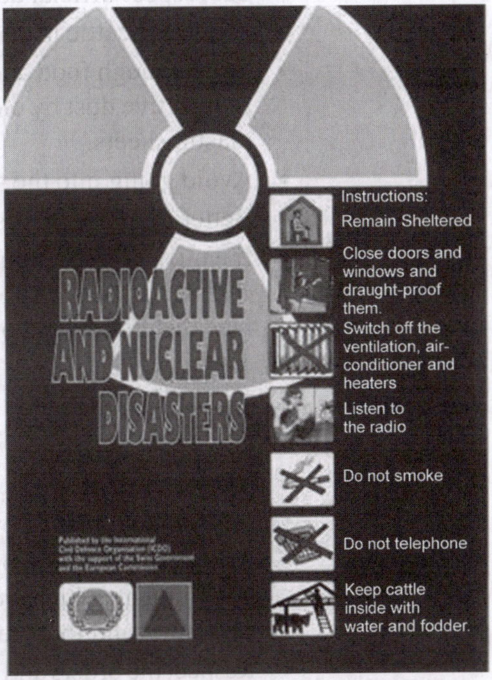

- Know and respect the regulations regarding the production, transport, handling and storage of radioactive substances
- Observe if there is the symbol of "danger or/and radioactive" shown on containers if so, make a note of it and follow appropriate instruction given therewith.
- Know the acoustic radioactivity alarm signals and the way to react.
- Always keep a family emergency kit ready. The kit should include identity cards, personal documents and personal medicines. Also food stock to suffice few days, in case you are instructed to stay indoors.
- Plan and organise your safe stay in a civil protected shelter or a basement, more important if you are residing in the neighbourhood of a nuclear power plant.
- Farmers and livestock owners should study the special recommendations on how to react and behave in case of a dangerous increase in radioactivity.

When the level of radioactivity increases

- Keep calm, do not panic. Remember! Tensions or stresses or shocks cannot save you.
- Listen to the radio and respect the suggested rules of behaviour.
- Stay in your house, in the civil protected shelter or the basement if possible.
- Close the air vents. Otherwise, stay inside, close all doors and windows, seal off all exterior openings and turn off the ventilators, air conditioners and room heaters, which run on the principle of free convection.
- If outside, protect your mouth and nose with a wet cloth and seek refuge in the nearest shelter or building.
- Do not telephone as this overloads the system.

- Follow the orders of the civil protection, fire service, police, or other intervening services.
- Eat only food stored inside a building, such as tinned food or preserves and bottled water and drinks. In principle tap water remains drinkable, but respect official advice.
- Assemble cattle in a barn or stable and shut all openings leading outside.
- Store enough food and water to last several days, and protect them from radioactive dust by closing all air vents and cover these with blankets or plastic sheets.
- Avoid going into the stricken area
- Better do not use cars so as not to slow down emergency vehicles.
- If a nuclear explosion occurs, shelter behind a very solid wall if you are outside. If this is not possible, lie down in a ditch or behind an embankment, face the ground and protect your face with your arms. Do not remain in a vehicle.

After the Accident

- Obey the instructions of the authorities and the intervening organs (civil protection).
- It is unlikely that an evacuation of the population will be necessary.
- Evacuation would be decided at the highest political level of the government, which would then organise it and involve civil and military personnel and their resources.
- Respect the orders and implementation modalities given by the authorities.
- Taking all necessary precautions, help neighbours and persons in difficulty such as the injured, children and the aged.
- Collaborate if need be with the intervening services.

11.8 BIOLOGICAL HAZARDS

This includes medical waste or samples of a microorganism virus or toxin that can impact human health. It can also include substances harmful to animals. Biological hazards cause a lot number of diseases like,

Brucellosis: It is generally seen in the dairy farm workers. Symptoms of this disease are fever, arthritis, and enlarged spleen etc.

Byssinosis: It is generally seen in workers working in the textile industries. It is caused due to the inhalation of the cotton fibre, dust over a long period of time. Symptoms of this disease are cough, breathlessness, slight fever and bronchitis.

Other such diseases are baggosis and loco motor disorder.

In addition, the epidemics and bio-weapons can be included in this category of hazards. A detailed study of these hazards is coved in separate chapters 16 and 17 of this book.

11.9 PREVENTIVE MEASURES TO REDUCE THE INDUSTRIAL HAZARDS

Both industry and Government have equal responsibility in preventing and reducing the industrial hazards. Of course! Each individual also has equal responsibility to protect and help preventing the disasters.

11.9.1 Role of Industries

The following are some of the preventive measures which an industry should take to prevent industrial hazards.

- Managements should clearly demarcate safe and unsafe zones, smoke zone etc. with clearly visible sign boards. Workers should be given adequate training of safety measures before entering the work site.
- Fire extinguishers and fire exits should be provided.
- Materials which pollute the environment should not be used.
- Waste products from the industries should not be released into sea or the nearby water bodies.
- Harmful chemicals should not be released into the air.
- Industries should be built in the places where there are no houses.
- Industries should be built according to the norms which are laid by the government.

11.9.2 Role of Government

- Frequent check on the level of pollutants being emitted from the industries/ vehicles.
- Observe rules that the industries should not work for more than the prescribed working hours.
- Licensing only to those industries whose infrastructure provides all the preventive measures including the fire exits, and extinguishers.

- Take certain measures to decrease pollution.
- Implement plans to plant trees in the most polluted area.
- Allow only limited number of industries in the manufacturing.
- Safety should also be provided by the industry management to its workers
- Ensure whether the safety rules are being adhered to.

SELF ASSESSMENT INTERMISSION (SAI – 11.6)

1. "A stitch in time saves nine", critically appreciate with reference to radiation hazards.
2. Define radioactivity. Briefly explain about radiation hazards.
3. Explore and explain various origins causing radioactivity radiation.
4. Describe the causes and effects of radiation hazards.
5. What are the consequences of exposure to radioactivity?
6. List out the preventive and protective measures for radioactivity.
7. On what factors the radiation (radioactivity) depends? Discuss.
8. List the protective measures and obligations on the licensed users of radioactivity.
9. What is an intervening and alarming organization? What are its objectives and functions?
10. What are the instruction to be given to (or to be followed by) people when

    (a) when there is a potential for radioactive radiation (b) when radioactive radiation is increasing (c) after a nuclear accident occurred and spread radioactive radiation
11. What are bio-hazards? Brief out.
12. Describe the Chernobyl incident and discuss its causes and effects.
13. Describe the preventive, protective and controlling mechanisms to reducing accidents in an industry? What is the role of the management of industries in this regard?
14. Describe the controlling mechanisms to reducing accidents to be observed in an industry? What is the role of the management of industries in this regard?

MINI-PROJECTS/ CASE STUDIES

1. Visit nearest industry or the one with which you are more familiar, and identify the hazardous areas. Prepare a report with suggesting some more safety measures. Use the following steps.
    (a) Identify the Industries (chemicals/explosives) in your area
    (b) Study the nature of chemicals being used, stored and transported.
    (c) Understand the hazards and treatment procedures for exposure.
2. Collect the norms from https://www.osha.gov/Publications/ regarding industrial hazards and safety measures and prepare a presentation.
3. Prepare a video presentation with clipping or photos Bhopal gas tragedy and present it before your colleagues/ classmates.
4. Collect various nuclear/ industrial/ chemical accidents (at least top 10) and prepare a gallery to exhibit on a selected day.

CHAPTER 12

Heat/Cold Waves, Wildfire and Deforestation

O'MY SILENT INNER VIBES (O'M S I V – 12)

Salutations to Sun God!

Salutations to Thee, O Sun God,
The Lord of light and shade.
Thou are the cause of "cause and effect"
With zodiac sign, "lion" – Thou are effulgent.

Worshipped by many saints and sages,
Thou bless us with health and wealth at all stages.
O Sun! 'Friend' of all and a 'friend' of lotus flower',
Thine son - Karna, is a hero with valor and great donor.

Destroyer of sins, devourer of all errors and mistakes,
Dispeller of darkness and ignorance, unaffected by eclipse.
Crest jewel of all stars and planets like Earth and Moon.
Gem of the Day! Thou are praised by all enlightened men.

Riding a chariot with seven days as horses,
Thou witness all our thoughts and actions!
We praise Thee in "Saurashtra" tune!
With a beautiful golden hue, Thou shine!

Thou are the abode of truth and infinity,
Thou guide us to the path of eternity,
The divinity encompassing the "Trinity",
Almighty embracing all gods in entirety.

O Sun! Thou can devastate,
The entire universe with scorching heat,
O Sun! Thou can demolish,
The whole world if we are selfish.

[Excerpted from 'To My Friend' by Dr. Nakta Venkata Raju's, Free Translation of Dikshitar kriti in Sanskrit- sUryaMurtE NamostutE – Raaga – Saurashtra]

We can't imagine the Earth and the life on it without Sun. Thence Sun is the visible God, as He gives us light, heat, health, and what not! Photosynthesis is an essential feature of any crop. Solar energy forms important component in daily utility. For that matter, Sun is the source of

(Continued)

energy required for the life of any species. As long as the Sun gives the heat and light within the tolerant range i.e. neither a bit more (heat wave) nor a bit less (cold wave), we live on this world, if not we leave this world. This chapter deals with the situations, what if the Sun (heat) outrages or out of ranges.

SUN IS POWER OF NATURE - SUN IS DRIVER OF FUTURE
Aum – Surya Narayanaya Namah!

12.1 HEAT WAVE

Heat wave is defined as an excessive hot weather condition, which may be accompanied by high humidity, specifically in oceanic climate countries.

A heat wave is often measured with reference to the usual weather in the specified area. Thus a weather condition may not be considered as hot at a normally hot area while the same may be treated as hot at a normally cold area. The hot-climate-people feel a temperature cold, which cold-climate-people say hot.

So, which is cold? Which is hot?

12.1.1 The Concept and Definition

Let us conduct a small experiment to understand the concept.

Take three bowls, Say A, B and C. Fill the Bowl A with ice cold water, Bowl B with normal water (at room temperature) and Bowl C with hot water. Now, put your left pointing finger in Bowl-A while the right pointing finger in Bowl-C. Keep for a minute or two. Now take out both and keep both in Bowl-B. How do you feel?

Yes! You would feel the normal water hot with your left finger while the same normal water seems to be cold on your right finger. So do you say the normal water, hot or cold?

So, also it is very difficult to say about a weather condition as hot or cold. Now imagine the 'water in Bowl' is weather and the 'finger' is you, you can understand the concept of a hot wave or cold wave. If your routine weather is cold like in Bowl-A, the variation such as in Bowl-B can act as heat wave, while the same variation for Bow-C can act as a cold wave.

Heat wave around the Globe

In Netherlands, Belgium and Luxembourg a heat wave is defined as a period of at least 5 consecutive days in which the maximum temperature in De Bilt exceeds 25°C (77°F), provided that on at least 3 days in this period the maximum temperature in De Bilt exceeds 30°C (86°F). In Denmark, a national heat wave (*hedebølge*) is defined as a period of at least 3 consecutive days of which period the average maximum temperature across more than 50% of the country exceeds 28°C (82.4°F) – the Danish Meteorological Institute further defines a "warmth wave" (*varmebølge*) when the same criteria are met for 25°C (77°F) temperature, while in Sweden, a heat wave is defined as at least 5 days in a row with a daily high exceeding 25°C (77°F).

In US it is usually defined as a period of at least 2 or more days of excessively hot weather, while in Northeast, it is 3 consecutive days where the temperature exceeds 90 °F (32.2°C), but not always as this ties in with humidity levels to determine a heat index threshold. The same does not apply to drier climates. A heat storm is a Californian term for an extended heat wave. Heat storms occur when the temperature reaches 100°F (37.8°C) for 3 or more consecutive days over a wide area (millions of sq. miles).

In Adelaide, Australia, a heat wave is defined as 5 consecutive days at or above 35°C (95°F), or 3 consecutive days at or over 40°C (104°F).

Thence, the hot/heat wave or cold wave is defined not only by the temperature, but, it is also described by considering variations 'routine weather' to 'extremes of a season'. And hence, an equivalent heat wave of a certain area may be completely ignored and may be treated as a routine weather in another area. However, the extraordinary spells of heat too may occur once a century, which you cannot rule out and cannot take it easy.

Further, the high heat on one day cannot be assumed a heat wave and if extends for a prolonged period it leads to a drought.

Moreover, the humidity is another factor to claim a period as heat wave period.

Definition

A peer-reviewed definition from the *Glossary of Meteorology* refers heat wave as 'a period of abnormally and uncomfortably hot and usually humid weather'.

According to Frich Heat Wave Duration Index, heat wave is said to be occurring if the daily maximum temperature of 5 or more consecutive days exceeds the average maximum temperature by at least 5°C (9°F), as compared to the normal period referred to climate of 1961–1990.

In 1900, A. T. Burrows rigidly defined a "hot wave" as a spell of three or more days on each of which the maximum shade temperature reaches or exceeds 90°F (32.2 °C). (Realistically speaking, the comfort criteria for any region depend on the normal conditions of the region).

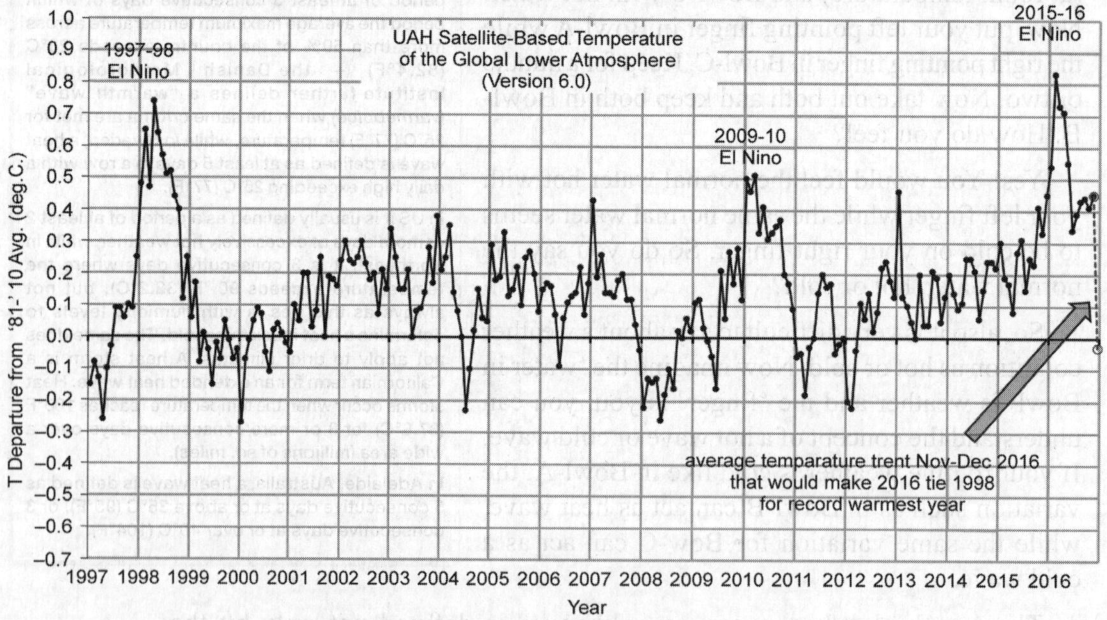

Fig. 12.1(a) Temperature anomaly for last two decades.

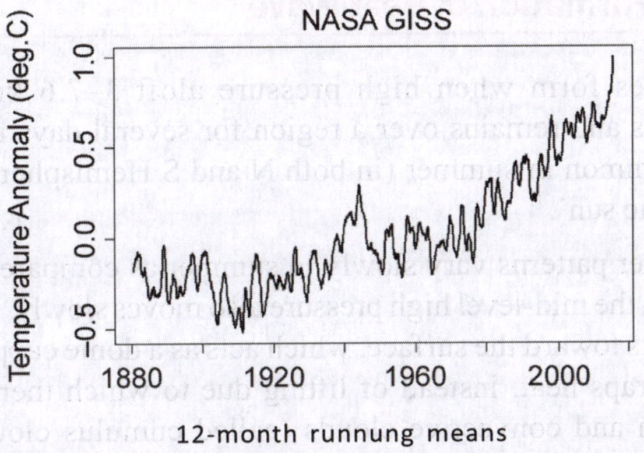

Fig. 12.1(b) Variation of average global temperature from 1880-2000.

12.1.2 Severity and Measurement

Heat wave conditions are described by the maximum daytime temperature and minimum night time temperature rising above the threshold for a particular region. Thus the length of time above that threshold defines the particular level.

Heat Levels

The MET Office in England and Wales operates a Heat Health Watch system by placing each Local Authority region into 1 of 4 levels as follows:

Level-1: Normal summer conditions.

Level-2: 60% or higher risk that the temperature will be above the threshold levels for 2 days and the intervening night.

Level-3: The temperature has been above the threshold for the preceding day and night, and there is a 90% or higher chance that it will stay above the threshold in the following day.

Level-4: If conditions are more severe than those of the preceding 3 levels.

The response and service is associated with the level of the severity.

The heat index table prepared by NOAA National Weather Service can be quite useful in measuring and determining the severity of Heat Wave.

12.1.3 Formation of Heat Wave

Heat waves form when high pressure aloft 3–7.6 km (10000-25000ft) strengthens and remains over a region for several days up to several weeks. This is common in summer (in both N and S Hemispheres) as the jet stream 'follows the sun'.

The weather patterns vary slowly in summer as compared to those in winter. Obviously, the mid-level high pressure also moves slowly. Under high pressure, the air sinks toward the surface, which acts as a dome capping the atmosphere. This cap traps heat, instead of lifting due to which there will be almost no convection and convective clouds (called cumulus clouds) with minimum probability of rain. If this continues, the heat at the surface builds up that is experienced as heat wave by humans.

12.1.4 Adverse Effects of Heat Waves

Heat wave is considered extreme weather and is dangerous since the heat and sunlight may overheat the human body. It can affect in several ways, but the major hazards are:

- Severe heat waves cause catastrophic crop failures,
- Loss of life of pet animals
- Deaths due to heat stroke (hyperthermia)
- Burns and Rashes to human body
- A Dehydration, dizziness and giddiness
- Weight loss
- Diarrhoea, vomiting, headache
- Large power outages due to increased use of air conditioning or low hydro-electric power generation.

O My God!

- The highest official temperature (51.5 °C) was recorded in South Africa in a summer during a Bergwind occurred along the Eastern Cape coastline.
- In the Eastern US a heat wave occurs when a high pressure system generates in the Gulf of Mexico.
- Global Warming enhances the probability of occurrence of heat waves.

12.1.5 Health Effects

Hyperthermia, also called heat stroke, is common during the heat wave period with the sustained high temperature and humidity. Usually sweating becomes absent in 80–100% of those affected. Most commonly the older adults, very young children, and those who are sick or overweight are highly susceptible for heat-related illness. The chronically ill and old are often found requiring medications for the diseases that interrupt the heat dissipation of the human body such as diuretics, antipsychotics, anti-hypertensive and anti-cholinergics etc.

Various probable ailments that occur during the heat wave are tabulated here below:

No	Effect of Heat Wave	Characteristics/Symptoms	Treatment/Prevention
1.	Heat Edima	- Transient swelling of the hands, feet, and ankles - Often secondary to increased aldosterone secretion that enhances water retention.	- No specific treatment is required - Resolves as patient gets acclimated to the warmer environment after some days.
2.	Heat Edima with peripheral vasodilation and venous stasis	The excess fluid accumulates at dependent areas of extremities	- Wearing support stocking and elevating the affected legs.
3.	Heat Rash or Prickly Heat (leading to dermatitis)	- Maculopapular rash with acute inflammation and blocked sweat ducts. - Sweat ducts become dilated and rupture, & small pruritic vesicles - Affects areas of the body covered by tight clothing. - Leads to chronic dermatitis or bacterial infection, if it persists	- Prevention is the best therapy - Wear loose-fitting clothes Initial treatment is to use chlorohexidine lotion to remove desquamated skin - Itching is treated with systemic antihistamines. - Antibiotics are used if infection occurs.
4.	Heat Cramps (may lead to hypo-natremia that induces cramps in stressed muscles)	- Severe pains, involuntary spasms of large muscle groups due to strenuous exercise. - Occur after intense exertion. - Often occurs to those who exercise heavily while sweating and replenishing fluid loss with non-electrolyte water.	Rehydration with salted fluids for rapid relief. - Mild cramps are treated with oral 2% salt solutions, while severe cramps need I.V. isotonic fluids. - Sport drinks are a good source of electrolytes.
6.	Heat Syncope	- Orthostatic hypotension that can precipitate near-syncopal episode due to intense sweating - Leads to dehydration followed by peripheral vasodilation and reduced venous blood return in the face of decreased vasomotor control.	- Cooling and oral rehydration therapy or isotonic I.V. fluids. Avoid long exposition to heat - Move to a cold place - Lie down if found symptoms - Wear support stockings and engage in deep knee-bending - Moving helps venous blood return
7.	Heat Stroke or Hyperthermia Heat Exhaustion (leading to Heat Stroke or Hyperthermia) Diarrhoea, headache, nausea, vomiting, dizziness, tachycardia, malaise and myalgia	- Often forerunner of heat stroke - Exhaustion resembles heat stroke, except that the neurologic function remains intact. - Excessive dehydration and electrolyte depletion - Loose motions, nausea, vomiting etc.	- Cooling and replenish with fluids. - Needs oral and IV isotonic fluids - Needs to take rest, - Drink plenty of fluids for 2–3 hours - Avoid the heat for several days. - If this advice is not followed it may lead to heat stroke

One public health measure for heat waves is to set-up air-conditioned public cooling centers.

12.1.6 Physiological, Psychological, Sociological and Environmental Effects

Ergonomic studies reveal that excessive hot environment causes the humans to strain faster. This stress can cause reduced performance of their work at the same time it causes loss of appetite and weakens the body. It obviously affects the workmanship.

Not only physical stress, but also, the excessive heat causes psychological stress, to a degree which affects performance by spoiling working moods and developing irritation or restlessness. It causes the physical as well as mental fatigue. Reports say that it is also associated with a raise in violent crime. High temperatures can promote conflicts both at the interpersonal level and at the societal level. In almost all societies, it is reported that the crime rates are going up when temperatures shoot up, particularly violent crimes such as assault, murder, and rape. Furthermore, in politically unstable countries, high temperature is one of the aggravating factors that led to civil wars.

Believe it or not! The high temperatures significantly affect income also. A study (in US) confirmed that economic productivity of individual days declined by about 1.7% for each raise of Celsius degree above 15°C (59°F).

Wildfires due to Heat Waves: A threat to Environment

Heat waves are often associated with drought, in which case, the vegetation dries out and leads to bushfires and wildfires. In tropical countries, such as India and gulf countries this is very common. The deadly 2003-European heat waves raged through Portugal, destroying over 3,010 sq. km (1,160 sq mi) or 301,000 hectares (740,000 acres) of forest and 440 sq. km (170 sq mi) or 44,000 hectares (110,000 acres) of agricultural land and the loss was estimated at € 1 billion.

A surprising paradigm is that wildfire can become a cause to form a heat wave (how?).

12.1.7 Physical Assets Damage and Power Outage

Heat waves can also damage the physical assets including power outage due to burning of power grids and transformers.

Physical Assets Damage

Various possible damages may be noticed in the following ways and list is not exhaustive.

- The huts and constructions by materials of low melting point or combustible materials, burn or catch fire

- The roads and highways buckle and melt.
- The water lines to burst due to thermal expansion.
- The power transformers to detonate, causing fires.
- The fish plates expand and rail tracks buckle and kink leading to slowing down traffic. This leads to delays and even cancellations of service. (Sun kink is a serious problem in Southern US, Canada, Middle East, etc.)

Power Outages

Hot temperatures enhance the electricity demand. Fans, air coolers and air conditioners get strained and overheated. Also they cause overload on transformers leading to burning. If a hot spell extends to 3 or more days, and if the night temperatures do not cool down, the thermal mass in houses and buildings retain the heat from previous days. The heat so built-up adds an extra load on air conditioners/ coolers resulting in higher consumption of electricity, thence raise the demand.

On the other hand, the water sources dry out and the generation of hydro-electricity comes down. Thus the reduced power production and increased demand do not match resulting in power outages. The power cuts may disturb the public life in several ways as discussed above.

> **O My God!**
>
> **America is Hot?**
>
> - The highest deaths (2190) in US during the decade of 1990s is due to heat waves (while 880 due to floods and 150 due to hurricanes).
> - The number of deaths due to heat waves alone is greater than total fatalities caused due to all other disasters in USA (according Eric Klinenberg)
> - 1995 Chicago heat wave is the worst, which lasted for 5 days and killed 600 people.
> - Average fatalities per year due to only heat waves in US are 400.
> - The most worst so far, the 2003 European Heat Wave killed > 70000

- In several states of India, the power cuts in summer are very common ranging from 4-8 hrs a day.
- During the 2006 North American heat waves, the homes and businesses underwent powerless for about 5 days in California, Los Angeles and other nearby areas due to failure of electrical transformers.
- The 2009 South Eastern Australian Heat Wave severely disrupted public life in Melbourne as it blew transformers and overloaded a power grid.

12.1.8 Underreporting and "Harvesting" Effect

It is most likely highly underreported fatalities often due to non-availability of reports or misreporting. A *short-term forward mortality displacement*, often known as 'Harvesting Effect' is observed during a heat wave. It has been observed that for some heat waves, there is a compensatory decrease in overall mortality during the subsequent weeks after a heat wave. The compensatory

decrease in mortality indicates those who would have died in the short term anyway by illness due to heat wave.

12.1.9 Preventive Measures

Concern is now focusing on predicting the future likelihood of heat waves and their severity. In addition, since in most of the world, the large majority of those suffering the impacts of a heat wave will be inside a building, and this will modify the temperatures they are exposed to, there is the need to link climate models to building models. The time series technique, forecasting techniques in the literature of statistics may be employed in addition to simulation models to predict the future weather. The future mortality due to heat waves could be reduced or prevented by two dimensions

1. buildings have to be better designed to modify the internal climate, and
2. the occupants are better educated about the issues, so that they can take timely action.

Further, the Government has to inform the weather status through all channels of TV and Radio under four levels such as Caution, Extreme Caution, Danger and Extreme Danger (similar to that of alerting in the case of cyclones, tsunami or floods etc.)

SELF ASSESSMENT INTERMISSION (SAI – 12.1)

1. Define heat wave. How does heat wave form?
2. Can heat wave be called disaster? Can a heat wave at one region be a normal temperature at other? Justify your answer.
3. What is meant by 'Heat Wave'? When do you call a climatic condition as heat wave?
4. What are the levels of Heat wave?
5. List out the adverse effects of Heat Wave.
6. List out various health effects of Heat Wave and describe their symptoms and treatments.
7. List out the provisions for heat wave prevention, protection and control under building code in constructions.
8. Discuss the physiological, psychological and sociological effects of heat wave.
9. Explain the following aspects under effects of heat wave on human beings.
   (a) Physiological (b) Physical (c) Psychological (d) Socialogical
10. How does the heat wave affect the nature and environment? Discuss its relation with wildfire and drought?
11. Does heat wave cause a wildfire or wildfire cause heat wave? Discuss.
12. Give some examples to describe how heat wave can damage the physical assets? How can it affect the public utilities?
13. What is 'Harvesting Effect' with reference to 'Heat Wave'? Explain.
14. Suggest some preventive/ protective measures to overcome heat wave.

12.2 COLD WAVE

A **cold wave,** also known as a *cold snap* is a weather phenomenon that is exhibited by a sudden cooling of the air. In Hindi (India), it is called with the names, *Sheethal Hawa, Sheeth Leher, Thandi Hawa, Aakasmik Thand.*

Definition

As per the US National Weather Service, a cold wave is defined as a rapid drop in temperature within a 24-hour period requiring enhanced protection to agriculture, industry, commerce, and social activities.

12.2.1 Cold Wave Occurrence

The occurrence and the severity of the cold wave depends on two factors

- the geographical region and
- period of year

For example: The cold wave can occur in the winter season in US and the national average temperature dropping is below 18°F (-8°C).

12.2.2 Cold Wave Severity

The severity of a cold wave is determined by

- the rate at which the temperature falls, and
- the minimum to which it falls.

12.2.3 Cold Wave Vs Heat Wave

Which wave can cause more fatalities, 'Heat Wave' or 'Cold Wave'?

Which wave is more dangerous 'Heat Wave' or 'Cold Wave'?

Which is more harmful to humans – 'Hyperthermia' or 'Hypothermia'?

Yes! It may be surprising to know. It is true that cold weather can cause more deaths than that of hot weather due to the contributing factors of hypothermia i.e. the after effects of low temperatures such as cold, flu, pneumonia etc. However statistics show that in developed countries, more deaths occur during a heat wave than in a cold snap while these numbers are significantly higher in undeveloped regions.

12.2.4 Effects of Cold Wave

The following effects may be found with the cold waves:

I. Direct effects

- Deaths and injuries to livestock and wildlife since the exposure to cold requires more caloric intake for all humans as well as animals
- If a cold wave is accompanied by heavy and persistent snow, grazing animals may be unable to reach needed food and die of hypothermia or starvation.

O My God!

The two extremes of Hot and Cold simultaneously occurred in US

Feb 2015 N. American cold wave – The Siberian Express (not the Polar Vortex) broke the outstanding temperature records in both sides. Extreme hot records were broken in the western half of the US while extreme cold records were broken in the eastern half. In addition, excessive snowfall at Tupelo, Mississippi, Huntsville, Alabama, Shreveport, Louisiana, Flagstaff, Arizona and Freezing temperatures at Miami, Florida. The extended cold wave covered every US state except Florida with snow by Mar 1, 2015, and all water bodies east of Rocky Mountains were totally frozen. The Winter Storm, Thor hit entire nation with Kentucky the hardest (as massive snow buried Kentucky, its Governor Steve Beshear declared Emergencies twice). Shortly after Thor, hard-hit cities Owensboro, Kentucky, Nashville, Tennessee recorded snowfall and subzero on the night of 5-6, March, 2015.

II. Indirect effects

- Increased demand and thence the cost of foodstuffs to feed livestock
- Due to anomalous expansion of water (4°C to 0°C), even some poorlyprotected indoor plumb lines may rupture causing serious damage to property.
- Freezing of poorly insulated water pipelines indoor and outdoor
- Water mains may break and water supplies may become unreliable
- Increased demand for electrical power
- Abnormal hike of fuel cost
- Failure of the generation of hydro-electrical power due to the freezing of water
- Some metals become brittle at low temperatures, thence the automobiles may fail when antifreeze fails or motor oil gels affecting the transportation system (more likely to occur in some places of Siberia and Canada).
- Fires become even more hazardous during extreme cold since, the air during a cold wave is denser and thus contains more oxygen, so causes a more intense fire
- Fire fighting becomes more difficult due to frozen water.
- Unexpected freezes and frosts (particularly in mid-latitude zones) kill plants during the early or most vulnerable stages of growth results in crop failure causing a famine.
- It is deadly to plants, and thence can cause drought due to dead biomass.

The history witnessed the Year without summer in 1816 in USA. Several years during the 1810s recorded numerous crop failures.

12.2.5 Countermeasures

- Internal plumbing can be wrapped, and persons should often run water continuously through pipes.
- Energy conservation is a must during cold wave, as people (especially the poor and elderly) may require such measures collecting in communal shelters.
- The homeless may be arrested and taken to shelters, only to be released after hazard abates.
- Hospitals should be alerted and prepared for admitting victims of frostbite and hypothermia;
- Schools and other public buildings can be converted into shelters.
- With the help of forecast, people may be alerted to stock up on food, water, and other necessities before a cold wave.
- Some may migrate to places of milder/ better climates, at least during the winter, which is to be encouraged.
- Suitable stocks of forage can be stored for livestock before cold waves.
- Livestock in vulnerable areas may be shifted or slaughtered.
- Water may be sprayed on vulnerable crops/ plants, which will paradoxically protect the plants by freezing by absorbing the cold from surrounding air.
- Clothing should be appropriate with sufficient number of layers if it is needed to go outside.
- Stock candles, matches, flashlights, and portable fuel for cooking and firewood as necessary.
- People should be cautious to use charcoal fires for cooking/ heating within an enclosed dwelling, since it is extremely dangerous and poisoning by semi-burnt fuel (produces CO).
- Extreme cold requires that fuel-powered machinery to be run continuously (example: In some places of Siberia)
- Children and the elderly adults must remain aware of the effects of exposure to cold.

12.2.6 Notable Cold Waves in the History

Contemporary cold waves (since 2001)

- Feb 2015 and Nov 2014 N. American cold wave – the three named winter storms (Astro, Bozeman, and Cato) were the hardest hit that did not allow Buffalo and NY to celebrate Thanksgiving.

- Early 2014 N. American cold wave – during Jan 2–11, the central and eastern US and Canada witnessed -37°F or-88°C, i.e. colder than at the Poles, which continued till early April.
- Dec 2013 N. American cold wave – During Dec-1-10, the polar vortex weakened and the jet stream shifted southward causing abnormally cold temperatures in central US. A snowfall of 0.1in (2 mm) on Dec 6th in the Dallas–Fort Worth metroplex broke the 1950 record.
- Spring 2013 N. America and Canada witnessed sudden cold wave and extended up to April, with four named winter storms (Walda, Xerxes, Yogi, and Zeus) at Minnesota and the Dakotas. Minnesota's winter even prolonged up to May with one more winter storm (Achilles).
- Early 2012 European cold wave – consumed at least 590 human lives blew -35°C (-31°F). Ukraine is the worst hit, with over 100 deaths.
- Winter of 2010–2011 in UK and Ireland, known as 'The Big Freeze', was the coldest December (winter) for 31 years with an average temperature of 1.51°C (34.72°F) and the coldest of the season "1°C (30.2°F), broke the previous record of 0.1 °C (32.18 °F), in Dec 1981.
- 2009-2010 European Cold Wave – heavy snowfall across Europe caused travel disruptions to British Isles, France, Germany, Austria, Italy, Poland, the Baltic States, Ukraine and Russia and consumed at least 90 lives. It was the coldest and longest spell for 30 years in the UK, whilst the Italian Alpine peaks reached –47°C (–52.6°F).
- Jan 2009 European Cold Wave, recorded below 0°C (32°F) was the deadliest to Germany, France, Italy, Romania and Spain. The snow and ice caused closure of schools, delays in airports and frozen everything that made life stand-still. In early February another cold front brought heaviest snowfall to Europe including the UK, France and Italy.
- Feb 2008 Alaska Cold Wave was the coldest of 8 years, with Fairbanks -45.6°C (–50°F) and Chicken, Alaska at –57.8°C(–72°F) was just 4.4°C(8°F) below the record of lowest.
- 2007 Argentine cold wave along with low pressure systems during 6–9 July, and the entry of a massive polar cold snap below –32 °C (–26 °F) resulted in at least 23 deaths with severe snowfalls and blizzards.
- 2005-2006 European cold wave shivered Europe and Russia with the coldest record since the 1970s. Snow fell heavily in unusual places also, such as in Southern Spain and Northern Africa.
- 2004-2005 Southern Europe cold waves have shown a very rare ice storm (0.001 probability occurrence). Spain, North Portugal and Morocco also recorded freezing temperatures.

- 2004 Jan cold outbreak, Northeast US – Boston, New England had the coldest January -6.8°C (19.7°F) since 1893. The mean -6.3°C (20.7°F) has broken the earlier record -2.7°C (27.2°F). Virginia Beach had an unusually long, below freezing weather. Some areas of North-NY saw 150 inches (3.81 m) of snow in a month.

20th Century Cold Waves

- 1997 Northern Plains Cold Air Outbreak–Jan-97 was one of windiest across the Northern US with wind chills touching -62.2°C (-80°F). North Dakota witnessed 90 inches (2.29 m) snow.
- 1996 Great Midwest Cold Outbreak–showed -51.1°C (-60°F) the coldest Jan-Feb to Minnesota.
- 1995 White Earthquake in southern Chile –Two consecutive cold fronts in August buried many cows and sheep in snow and some livestock starved due to fodder scarcity.
- 1989 recorded coldest December in central and eastern US that caused a 'White Christmas'.
- 1985 Great West cold Air Outbreak – entire February month saw the contiguous US' 2nd-coldest temperature of -56.1°C (-69°F) in Peter Sinks, Utah.
- Dec-1983 Great Plains Cold Wave – is the coldest ever Christmas. Minneapolis recorded an average temperature for the month of 3.7 °F (-15.7 °C), the coldest on record.
- 1982 cold Air Outbreak – The AFC Championship Game, held in Cincinnati was nicknamed as 'Freezer Bowl' due to -59°F (-50.6°C) wind chill. The week's event was called Cold Sunday.
- Winter of 1968–69 in Central Asia – Central Asia and Western Siberia recorded the coldest winter, and severe blizzards and avalanches, numerous plant deaths and record spring flooding.
- 1966 Western Canadian Cold Wave – Jan'66 was the coldest (in Yukon) which continued till March, and Winnipeg saw most severe winter snowstorm on record.
- 1962–63Winter of UK – It was the coldest for 223 years in England, which was accompanied by strong easterly winds and the freezing of rivers and streams.
- 1956 European Cold Wave – Feb'56 was the coldest month of 20th century with average of 0°C (32°F) in Western Europe.

SELF ASSESSMENT INTERMISSION (SAI – 12.2)

1. Define cold wave. How does it form?
2. Can cold wave be called disaster? Can a cold wave at one region be a normal temperature at other? Justify your answer.
3. What is meant by 'Cold Wave'? When do you call a climatic condition as cold wave?
4. List out the adverse effects of Cold Wave.
5. List out various health effects of Cold Wave and describe their symptoms and treatments.
6. Enumerate the effects and counter measures of cold wave.
7. Which is more disastrous- a heat wave or a cold wave? Discuss.
8. Does heat wave cause a wildfire or wildfire cause heat wave? Discuss.
9. Give some examples of cold waves occurred globally.
10. 'Two extremes of hot and cold occurred'. Where and when? Discuss
11. Distinguish between heat wave and cold wave, with reference to their causes and effects.
12. Are heat and cold waves natural or manmade? Discuss.

12.3 DEFORESTATION

Deforestation is "the process in which forests are used extensively for the man kind resulting in wide in forest ecology of environment". Deforestation (also called desertification) is one of the major problems the world is facing in this present era.

Notable Examples of Deforestation

The most victims of deforestation are the tropical countries including Indonesia, Bangladesh, Sri Lanka, India, Pakistan, China, Libya, Malaysia, Laos and Ghana where deforestation occurring highly. A few places undergone deforestation are exemplified here below.

1. Philippines: 90% of the country's forest has been lost.
2. Central America: Only 40% of the original forest remains.
3. Nigeria: During 1990 to 2005, 70% of forests are no more.
4. Ethiopia: In past 50 years, 98% of the forests of country vanished.
5. Brazil: In 2008, Brazilian govt. reported a record rate of deforestation in Amazon.

12.3.1 Causes of Deforestation

The major reasons of deforestation are:

- Due to wildfires (Discussed elaborately in the next section of this chapter)
- To live luxurious life. Rich people buy the luxurious household furniture such as cots, chairs, tables, sofa, antiques etc. They may even hunt forest animals for acquiring horns (deer), nails and skin (tiger), ivory (elephants) etc. and feel them as a mark of prestige.
- To fulfil the needs and desires such as making articles, household articles, people cut down the forests. This may not be a mistake, but going to any extent for this is affecting the environment.
- Population growth demanding more land and housing-needs occupy the forest land and convert it as residential land.
- Smugglers are cutting the trees recklessly. This is the biggest concern particularly with the costly wood such as Sandalwood, Teak and Rosewood and in Asian countries.
- Governments are also removing the forests to implement their new constructions, roads, industries etc. and urbanization.
- Rural people use trees for their daily needs such as firewood, campfires etc. and even some dhabhas (roadside restaurants in the outskirts of a city) are using as fire wood.
- Certain medicines, rubber, paper production and for some constructional purposes, forest is the main source for the industrialists and contractors.
- Countries to show them as developed, are trying to build very large constructions like airports, stations and industries etc. for which they are eradicating the forests without having the concern toward the upcoming dangerous situations.

In these present days people are becoming so selfish that they don't think and care for future generations. Due to this irritating, immoral and inhuman (because it is at the cost of harming to future generation) actions, a movement called "CHIPKO" was raised.

12.3.2 Ecology is Permanent Economy - CHIPKO Movement

This was the movement started in Northern Himalayan segment of Uttara khand in April 1973. The base of this movement is that the contractors when

came to that village and started cutting the forest, the women of the village came and hugged the trees. They put their bodies in between the tree and the contractor's axe and obstructed them to cut. This tells "how much they know the importance of trees and how they loved the trees".

The above incident inspired the whole country, mainly **Sunder Lal Bahuguna** who started the movement CHIPKO. The word Chipko means "stick" or "to hug". In the presence of Bahuguna people foot-marched 5000 km during 1981-1983. And the main slogans were "Ecology is Permanent Economy" and "what do the forests bear - soil, water and pure air". This movement is the first step against the deforestation in India and made S L Bahuguna a famous leader.

Adverse Effects of Deforestation

Deforestation is a small thing to our eyes until we get the effect of that one. This deforestation can affect whole life also but slowly. The main effects are

- ***Effect on life-gas***: The trees play a great role in the air–life cycle by absorbing Carbon dioxide (CO_2) and releasing Oxygen (O_2) which is essential for human life (breathing air) without which we can't live. Deforestation makes affects this cycle and makes human life miserable.
- ***Effect on Shelter and Living hood***: Some people (particularly tribal people) make use of forests for their shelter, and also as the source to food by hunting or fruits etc. by deforestation, they lose their source of living hood.
- ***Effect on Water-cycle***: Trees play key role in getting rainfall. Without trees there is an impact on water cycle (rain fall), and one can't imagine life without water.
- ***Effect on Nature and Health***: Good nature and greenery gives good health. Perhaps! The ancient emperor Ashoka, who appears in Indian history, realized and materialized this fact. He is named for plantation of trees in the lines of Indian history.
- ***Effect on Global Warming***: Trees obstruct the sun rays when they fall on earth. By this earth doesn't heat higher due to which Global Warming doesn't happen.
- ***Effect on Greenhouse Gases***: Releasing of Greenhouse gases can be controlled by the trees and forests.
- ***Deforestation Leads to Drought***: Deforestation is the main cause for drought. This is the fact proven several times in history.

- ***Effect on Ecosystem***: Trees and forests are has its own impact on Ecosystem.
- ***Effect on Soil Erosion***: Forests can reduce the adverse effects of the floods and thence the flowing of soil that leads to 'Soil Erosion'.
- ***Effect on Economy of the Nation***: Government can make profit by selling the trees and by make them as tourist places. The national economy is seriously affected by the deforestation.
- ***Effect on Wood and Food***: Forests provide two major products viz. Wood and Food. Decline in the wood for every constructional purposes wood is compulsory. Deforestation causes the declining of wood.
- ***Effect on Forest Productivity***: Not only wood and food, but also several products come out of forests. In some places persons make the extraordinary idols and toys with wood which portray the creativity and culture of that place. (Examples: Nirmal toys in Telangana state and Kondapalli toys in Andhra Pradesh of India). Further, there are many products produced from forest such as medicines, clothing, furniture, fuels, paper, rubbers, adhesives and so forth. The deforestation can affect all these productions.
- ***Irreversible Environmental Changes***: Due to deforestation environmental conditions will change undesirably. This highly affects the human lives. And we can't control those environmental conditions easily.
- ***Increased Pollution***: The air pollution can be reduced by the trees as they can attract the dust and dirt and the particulate matter can settle and on the leaves of trees. Pollution increases by lacking of trees and forests.

12.3.3 Preventive Measures

Preventive measures are very important to know, as they help to prevent and face an undesirable situations caused. So, let us explore some important points to prevent the deforestation.

By Government

- Bring the awareness in the people, mainly who live near the forest and rural areas.
- Conduct the awareness programmes by the specialised persons.
- Provide security and vigilance on the places where deforestation is highly occurring.
- The stringent and serious laws have to be framed on the name of deforestation and implemented strictly.

- If at all a single tree is to be cut for any need then proper permission is to be taken by the person justifying the action and/or paying penalty and see that it is compensated by planting two trees. This is known as the Reforestation. Reforestation is in our hands. US and many European countries have been implementing this strictly.
- Take serious actions on smugglers.
- Encourage tree lovers with suitable awards.

By Individuals

- Recycled items may be used as far as possible to prevent deforestation up to some extent.
- Every person has to take part in plantation programmes in their village.
- Using of coal or other than fire wood for cooking is helpful to prevent the deforestation.
- Everyone should support and co-operate the tree conservation organisations.
- If at all we have to cut a single tree for our needs then we should plant the two trees. This known as the Reforestation. This is in our hands. US and many European countries have been implementing this strictly.

SELF ASSESSMENT INTERMISSION (SAI – 12.3)

1. What is meant by 'deforestation'? Explain.
2. Define 'deforestation'. List out various possible causes for deforestation.
3. What are the causes and effects of deforestation? Prepare a causes and effect diagram.
4. What is 'desertification'? What are its adverse effects?
5. 'Ecology is permanent Economy' - Critically appreciate the statement in the light of CHIPKO movement.
6. 'What do forests bear – Soil, Water and Pure Air', What do you understand by this slogan? Discuss.
7. What is CHIPKO movement? Explain its background and objectives.
8. What is the role of Government in preventing deforestation?
9. What are the uses of forests?
10. Describe the role of individuals in preventing, protecting and controlling deforestation.
11. List out some notable cases of deforestation and their effects.
12. Suggest the uses of forests for (a) household (b) industrial purposes.
13. Conduct a competition for writing slogans on deforestation. Identify the areas in the entire campus where you are working / studying and place some placards or posters written with slogans to save forests.
14. Visit the officials of forest department in your vicinity and conduct an interview of their experiences, functions and procedures.

12.4 WILDFIRE

Bushfires are a common in generally hot and dry climate and pose a great risk to life and infrastructure throughout the year, though mostly during hotter months of summer and spring. As per fossil records and human history, the wildfires can occur in periodic intervals. Though, wildfires can cause extensive damage, both to property and human life, they also have various beneficial effects on wilderness areas.

12.4.1 Features and Characteristics

A **wildfire** is an uncontrolled fire of combustible vegetation that usually occurs in the countryside area. Depending on the region, type and size of vegetation being burnt, and the regional language being used, there are several names to describe this phenomenon, such as **wild-land-fire, brush fire**, **bush fire**, **forest fire**, **desert fire**, **grass fire**, **hill fire**, **peat fire**, **vegetation fire**, and **veldfire.** Wildfires range from wild to mild. The wild may be as large as, an uncontrolled disaster that burns through 100 to 100,000 acres or more, while mild may be as small as ¼ acres or less.

Wildfires feature distinguishingly different from other fires as they occur specific outdoors in large areas such as grassland, woodlands, bush land, scrubland, peat land, and other wooded areas, which otherwise would have been a source of fuel, or combustible material or cattle food. Unlike other fires, buildings and manmade structures are usually not involved except when a wildfire spreads near to communities. The causes of wildfires vary and the outcomes are always unique. Wildfire behaviour and severity result from the combination of factors such as available fuels, physical setting, and weather. Thus, all wildfires can be characterized in terms of their physical properties, the fuel type, and the effect to that weather.

Summarily, a wildfire differs from other fires by the following features/ characteristics

1. The large size,
2. The speed at which it can spread out from its original source,
3. It can change direction unexpectedly, and
4. Its ability to jump gaps such as roads, rivers and fire breaks.

A wildfire in California on Sep 5, 2008

Wildfires are characterized in terms of

1. Cause of ignition,
2. Physical properties (such as speed of propagation),

3. Combustible material present, and
4. Effect of weather on the fire

12.4.2 Causes for Wildfire

Lightning-sparked wildfires during summer in Nevada

Wildfires are 'quasi-natural' hazards, since they are not entirely natural (like volcanoes, earthquakes and tropical storms) and not always by human activity alone. The 5-major natural causes of wildfire ignitions are

1. Lightning,
2. Volcanic eruption,
3. Heat wave
4. Sparks from rock falls, and
5. Spontaneous combustion.

The 5- most common human sources of wildfires are

1. Carrying inflammables,
2. Discarded cigarettes,
3. Camp fires
4. Sparks from equipment, and
5. Power line arcs (like short circuit)

In shifting cultivation, the land is cleared quickly and farmed until the soil loses fertility, for which slash and burn clearing is least expensive way. Forested areas cleared by logging encourage the dominance of flammable grasses, and abandoned logging roads overgrown by vegetation may act as fire corridors.

The most common cause of wildfires varies throughout the world.

- In Canada and northwest China, lightning is the major source of ignition.
- In the US and Australia, the source of wildfires can be both lightning strikes and human activities such as machinery sparks, controlled agricultural burning, camp fires and cast-away cigarette butts.
- In Mexico, America, Africa, Southeast Asia, Fiji, and New Zealand, wildfires occur due to human activities such as agriculture and land-conversion burning.
- Human carelessness is a major cause of wildfires in China and in the Merranean Basin.
- Annual grassland fires in S. Vietnam is due to US military burning operations using herbicides, explosives, and mechanical land clearing during the Vietnam War.
- Human involvement is a major contributor in other parts of the world.

(a) (b) (c)

(a) A surface fire in the western desert of Utah, US; (b) Charred landscape after math of a crown fire in the North Cascades, U.S.; (c) Experimental fire in Canada

12.4.3 Types of Wildfires (With Reference to Type of Fuel and Fire Movement)

Overall, 4-types can be generally characterized by their fuels and the fire movement as follows:

1. Ground Fires
2. Crawling or Surface Fires
3. Ladder Fires
4. Canopy or Crown or Aerial Fires

These are briefly described below

1. **Ground Fires :** These fires occur on roots, duff and buried organic matter, susceptible to ignition due to spotting. They burn by smouldering, and can burn slowly for days to months.

   Example: Peat fires in Eastern Sumatra and Indonesia, which resulted from a rice-land creation project that unintentionally drained and dried the peat.

2. **Crawling or Surface Fires:** Crawling fires are so named because the fire moves as if a reptile is crawling on the surface. These are fuelled by low-lying vegetation such as leaf and timber litter, debris, grass, and low-lying shrubbery.

   Example: After a land is cultivated, before next crop, the residue is burnt. This burning is often a crawling. Also the wildfires in forests following a heat wave crawl.

3. **Ladder Fires :** These fires look as if the fire is climbing or coming down. They consume material between low-level vegetation and tree canopies, such as small trees, downed logs, and vines. Kudzu, Old World climbing fern, and other invasive plants that scale trees may also motivate ladder fires. The wildfires spread varies depending on the flammability of material present and its vertical arrangement. Topography, land shape, sunlight and water may also be the factors.

Example: Fuels uphill from a fire rapidly dry out by the fire than those downhill, and thence burning logs may roll downhill thereby igniting the other fuels.

4. **Crown or Canopy or Aerial Fires:** These fires burn (with the support of air) suspended material at the canopy level, like tall trees, vines and mosses, generally called *crown fire* or *crowning*. This depends on density of suspended material, canopy height/continuity and sufficient surface to reach tree crowns. Even before the flames of a wildfire arrive at a given region, heat transfer from the wildfire front warms the air to 800°C (1,470°F), which pre-heats and dries flammable materials, cause materials to ignite faster and allows the fire spread faster.

   Example: High-temperature and long-period surface wildfires may encourage *flashover* or *torching* the drying of tree canopies and subsequent ignition from below.

12.4.4 Fire Triangle of Wildfire

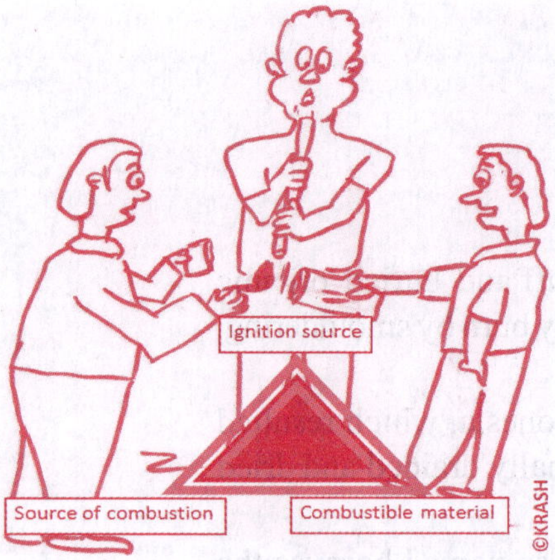

As discussed in the previous chapter (Refer Chapter-11, Industrial Hazards Section 11.5.2 Fire Triangle), without any exception, wildfires also occur when all of the necessary elements of a *fire triangle* come together in a susceptible area i.e. when a sufficient heat (ignition source) is brought in contact with vegetation (combustible material) and has an adequate supply of oxygen from the ambient air (supporter of combustion). Moisture content prevents ignition or reduces the spread, since high temperatures are needed to evaporate any water within the material. Therefore, dense forests are less susceptible to wildfires as they usually provide more shade, resulting in lower ambient temperatures and greater humidity. Whilst, less dense forests such as grasses and leaves are easier to ignite as they contain less water than denser material such as branches and trunks. Though plants continuously lose water by evapo-transpiration, it is usually balanced by absorption from soil, humidity or rain. If this balance is not maintained, plants dry out and hence become inflammable, usually a consequence of drought.

12.4.5 Wildfire Front

A wildfire *front* is the portion sustaining continuous flaming combustion, where unburned material meets active flames, or the smouldering transition between unburned and burned material. The front, as it approaches, heats both the surrounding air as well as the woody material through convection and thermal radiation in the following sequence.

1. Wood is dried as water is vaporized at a temperature of 100°C (212°F).
2. The pyrolysis of wood at 230°C (450°F) releases flammable gases.
3. Wood can smoulder at 380-590°C (720-1,000°F) depending on the grade.

Wildfire front in Nevada

Wildfires have a rapid *forward rate of spread* (FROS) in dense, uninterrupted fuels with a speed up to 22 kmph (14 mph) in grasslands and 10.8 kmph (6.7 mph) in forests. Wildfires can move tangential to the main front to form a *flanking* front, or burn in opposite to the main front by *backing*. Further, they may also spread by *jumping* or *spotting* as winds and vertical convection columns carry *firebrands* (hot wood embers) and other burning materials through the air over roads, rivers, and other barriers (called *firebreaks*). Torching and fires in tree canopies motivate spotting, and dry ground fuels that surround a wildfire are especially vulnerable to ignition from firebrands. Spotting generates *spot fires* as hot embers and the firebrands ignite fuels downwind. No surprise if spot fires occur even 20 km (12 mi) from the fire front.

Large wildfires affect air currents in their vicinities due to *stack effect*, i.e. large wildfires create powerful *updrafts* and the air rises (as it is heated) and this pulls new, cooler air from surrounding areas in *thermal columns*. The vertical differences in temperature and humidity favour the formation of *pyro-cumulus clouds*, strong winds, and *fire whirls* with the force of tornadoes at high speeds (>80 kmph or 50 mph).

12.4.6 Wildfire Vs Environment

The environment and wildfire are greatly related because, they influence each other.

A bird eats ants when it is alive while the ants eat the same bird when it is dead.

Soap is required to wash oiled hands while oil is needed for manufacturing the soap.

A similar paradigm prevails in between the wild fire and environment.

The impact of climatic changes such as El Nino, heat waves etc can aggravate the wildfires while the wildfire can change the climate. It is interesting to know the relations among these issues. We shall now discuss about these briefly.

A wildfire in Venezuela during a drought

1. **Effect of Heat Waves, Drought and Climate Changes on Wildfire:** The risk of wildfires increases by heat waves, droughts, cyclical climate changes (El Niño, La Niño) and regional weather patterns such as high-pressure ridges. Further, the aged precipitation followed by hot periods can create longer fire sessions too. However, one element does not always cause wildfire. For instance, wildfires will not occur even during a drought unless associated by other factors, such as lightning (ignition source) and strong winds (mechanism for rapid spread).
2. **Effect of 'Day' and 'Night' on Wildfire :** Of course! It is a fact that intensity increases during daytime which can raise rate of burning of smouldering logs five-fold on normal day. Further, Lower humidity, increased temperatures, and increased wind speeds can favour the situation. Sunlight heats the ground during the day and moves air-currents uphill. Again at night as the land cools, the air currents travel downhill. A beautiful fanning occurs on wildfires by these winds and often the fire follows the air currents over hills and through valleys. Perhaps! This is why fires in Europe occur frequently during 12–2 p.m.
3. **Effect of Wildfire on Climate :** Wildfires can also have considerable effect on climate change. The amount of carbon released into the atmosphere increases and vegetation growth supports it, by which overall carbon uptake by plants is enhanced. As a result, such fires in the rainforest, along with drought and human involvement, could cause destruction on huge scale. The ash hence produced can destroy available organic nutrients, causing an increase in water runoff, erosion of other nutrients, thence generating flash flood conditions.

   Example: A 2003 wildfire in the N. Yorkshire Moors destroyed 2.5 km^2 (600 acres) of heather and the underlying peat layers. Afterwards, wind erosion stripped the ash and the exposed soil, revealing archaeological remains dating back to 10000 BC.

A Pyrocumulus cloud produced by a wildfire in Yellowstone National Park

4. **Effect of Wildfire on Weathering (of Rocks):** The thermal heat from wildfire cause significant *weathering* of rocks and boulders, heat can rapidly expand a boulder and cause *thermal shock* resulting in failure of an object's structure.
5. **Effect of Wildfire on Atmosphere and Pollution:** The Earth's weather and air pollution reside mostly in troposphere, (up to a height of about 10 km or 6 mi). The vertical lift of a

thunderstorm or pyro-cumulo-nimbus can be raised in large wildfire area that can propel smoke, soot, and other particulate matter to lower stratosphere. The previous, notion and belief that particles in stratosphere came from volcanoes, is proven wrong when smoke and other wildfire emissions are found in them. Since, pyro-cumulus clouds can reach 6,100 m (20,000 ft) over wildfires. Satellites traced smoke plumes for height >1,600 km (1,000 mi).

Wildfires cause major impacts on atmospheric pollution too. Wildfire emissions contain fine particulate matter that can cause cardiovascular and respiratory problems. Increased fire by products in the troposphere can increase ozone concentration beyond safe levels.

Example: The forest fires in Indonesia in 1997 have released 0.81-2.57 giga tonnes of CO_2 into the atmosphere, which is 13%–40% of the annual global CO_2 emissions from burning fossil fuels. The sooty clouds increased absorption of solar radiation during winter by 15%.

> **O My God!**
>
> **Wildfire in World History**
>
> Minor allusions to wildfires find place in the Bible. The ancient Hebrew, Greek, and Roman writers know such fires, but not so keen in the uncultivated lands where wildfires occurred. Wildfires were used in battles as early thermal weapons. It was documented by Germany in 1290 in Odenwald and in 1344 in Black Forest. In Spain during the 1550s, sheep husbandry was discouraged in certain provinces by Philip II due to harmful effects of fires. In 17th century, Americans used fire for cultivation, signalling and warfare. Scottish botanist David Douglas used fire for tobacco cultivation; to hunt deer and rabbits; and to improve foraging for honey. Charcoal found in sedimentary deposits of the Pacific coast of America, suggests that more burning occurred in the 50 yrs before the Spanish colonization of Americas. In post-WW-II Baltic region, socio-economic changes led more stringent air quality standards and bans on fires that eliminated traditional burning practices.

Smoke trail from a fire seen from Swifts Creek, Victoria, Australia, 11 Jan 2007

12.4.7 Plant Adaptation

In wildfire-prone ecosystems, plants adapt to the local fire regime, such as physical protection against heat, increased growth after a fire event, and flammable materials that encourage fire.

Examples:

1. Grasslands in Western Sabah, Malaysian pine forests, and Indonesian *Casuarina* forests are resulted from previous periods of fire.
2. Sequoia release seeds from their cones, and clear the soil and canopy for new growth.
3. Frequent fires favour herbaceous plants while infrequent fires favour species of Bahamian dry forests

12.4.8 Human Involvement

Deliberate wildfires on Khun Tan Range, Thailand, lit by local farmers every year to promote the growth of mushroom

The human involvement with fire on wildlife and forests dates back from ages. The use of fire for agricultural and hunting purposes during Paleolithic/ Mesolithic ages changed the original landscapes. Woods were gradually replaced by smaller vegetation that helped travel, hunting, seed-gathering and planting. At the same time it is enhancing the risk also.

In the mid-19th century, Australians widely used fire for ground clearing, hunting, and to regenerate plant food in a method named fire-stick farming.

In US, in 2010, ~1.4 million acres were burnt by human-caused wildfires, and ~2 million acres by natural, while in 2011, ~5.4 million acres by human-caused and only ~3.4 million acres by natural. A 2015 study reveals that the fire risk in California is due to human-induced climate change.

SELF ASSESSMENT INTERMISSION (SAI – 12.4)

1. What is meant by 'wildfire'? Explain.
2. Define 'wildfire'. List out various possible causes for wild fires.
3. Is 'Wildfire' a natural or manmade hazard? Substantiate your answer.
4. Distinguish between a fire accident and a 'wildfire'? What are the characteristics of wildfires?
5. Draw a cause and effect diagram for wildfire.
6. What are different types of wildfires, with reference to the fuel and the fire movement? Briefly describe.
7. Describe the effect of wildfire on environment and effect of environment on wildfire.
8. Establish the relationships among the wildfires, deforestation, heat waves and drought.
9. What is 'fire triangle'? How is it applicable to wildfire?
10. What is wildfire Front? Explain.
11. Explain the human involvement in wildfire and their effects.
12. Meet the officials of Gas supply station in your vicinity and conduct an interview of their experiences, functions and procedures regarding Safety and Security.

12.5 WILDFIRE RISK

Wildfire risks are the chances of start in or reach of a wildfire to a particular area and the potential loss of humans and assets. Risk depends on various factors such as human activities, weather patterns, content of wildfire fuels, availability of resources to suppress a fire and so forth. The main wild fire risks are briefed out in the paragraphs to follow.

12.5.1 Human Induced Risk

> **O My God!**
>
> **A new twist in wildfire health risks?**
>
> Former uranium mining sites burnt over in the summer of 2012 near N. Fork, Idaho, raised problem from the residents and officials of Idaho State Dept of Environmental Quality on the potential spread of radiation in the smoke, since those sites had never been completely cleaned up from radioactive remains.

Though wildfires are considered to be mostly naturally occurring events that aid in promoting forest health as well, yet, the human induced changes in geography and climate are enhancing the risk. Further, the consequence of suppressing wildfires result in an overgrowth in forest vegetation, thence provide excess fuel that increases the severity, range, and duration of a wildfire. Global warming and climate changes increase temperatures and hence, more chances of droughts and also contributes to an increase in wildfire risk.

12.5.2 Risk to Residential Surroundings

Though residential areas surrounding wildfires are exposed to lower concentrations of chemicals, still they are at a greater risk for indirect exposure through water or soil contamination. Exposure to residents is greatly dependent on individual susceptibility. Particularly, due to already compromised body systems, children (>5 yrs), the elders (>60 yrs), smokers and pregnant women are at greatest risk even at low chemical concentrations and even for relatively short exposure periods.

The Air Quality Index (AQI), a public resource, developed by US Environmental Protection Agency (EPA) provides national air quality standard concentrations for common air pollutants. This index can be used as a tool to check their exposure to hazardous air pollutants in visibility range.

12.5.3 Risk due to Destruction

The most adverse effect occurs due to destruction of property and biomass. In addition, the hazardous chemicals released while burning of wild-land fuels can significantly impact human health. The exposed smoke directly goes through respiratory tract by inhalation of air pollutants, while wildfire debris may act indirectly by contaminating soil and water.

The smoke consists of chiefly, carbon dioxide and water vapour and other components such as carbon monoxide, sulphur dioxide, formaldehyde, acrolein, poly-aromatic hydrocarbons, benzene and some small (<ϕ2.5μm) suspended solid particulates and liquid droplets. Of these, carbon monoxide (CO) and fine particulate matter are the major health threats. Other chemicals are also hazardous but found in too low concentrations to cause detectable health effects. Of course, carbon dioxide is high in concentration, but has low toxicity. Whatsoever, risk due to destruction depends on the degree of exposure of wildfire smoke to an individual, which in turn depends on the severity, duration, intensity of exposure of smoke and proximity of the fire.

12.5.4 Risk due to Particulate Matter

Particulate matter (PM) is composed of particles of dust and liquid droplets causing air pollution. There are in 2 categories of PM based on the diameter of the particles, viz. Coarse (2.5-10 μm ϕ) and fine particles (< 2.5μm ϕ), both can be inhaled. Coarse particles are filtered by the upper airways and can cause eye/ sinus irritation, sore throat and coughing while the fine particles are more dangerous as they are deposited deep into the lungs and are absorbed into the bloodstream. This is more hazardous to children, old and those who have asthma, chronic obstructive lung disease (COLD), chronic obstructive pulmonary disease (COPD), cystic fibrosis and cardiovascular conditions. The fine particle in wildfire smoke can cause bronchitis, exacerbation of asthma or COPD, and pneumonia. (Symptoms: breathlessness and wheezing, chest pain, rapid heart rate and fatigue).

12.5.5 Risk due to Carbon Monoxide (CO)

Risk due to carbon monoxide (CO) needs a special mention here, since it is a colourless, odourless gas found in the highest concentration at close proximity to a smouldering fire and is a serious threat to human health, particularly, to fire-fighters. CO in smoke inhaled, goes into the lungs where it is absorbed into the bloodstream (forms as phosgene) and reduces oxygen supply to the body's vital organs. It can combine with iron in the blood to form complex compound and becomes reason to obstruction of blood flow. It causes headache, weakness, dizziness, chest pain, cardiac arrhythmia, confusion, nausea, disorientation, visual impairment, coma and even death. Believe it or not! About 1/5th of deaths of heart attacks occurred to wildfire fire-fighter deaths in the last two decades are attributed to this cause.

Though uncommon, psychiatric diseases, mental shocks, post-traumatic stress disorder (PTSD), depression, anxiety, phobias and disorders in both adults and children can also happen.

12.6 WILDFIRE MANAGEMENT

The management and mitigation of wildfire involves the following stages

1. Prevention
2. Detection
3. Suppression
4. Monitoring and Controlling

5. Fire-fighting
6. Cost-Benefit Analysis

These are explained in detail through the following paragraphs.

12.6.1 Prevention

Prevention is always better than cure. So, it is better to use the pre-emptive methods of reducing the risk of fires and its severity and spread. These include,

- establishing supervising agencies to manage air quality,
- maintain ecological balances,
- protect resources and
- limit the effects of future uncontrolled fires.

The prevention of wildfire requires considering both the causing factors by nature as well as human involvement and hence needs to be alert every minute.

Since, most (90-95%) of forest fires are related to human involvement, the policies can be framed to control and monitor the sources of human-caused arson, accidental ignition, or the uncontrolled use of fire in land-clearing and agriculture such as the slash-and-burn farming.

Next to human involvement, only fuels have great impact on fire risk and behaviour. So, the control over fuels make preventive job easy.

Wildfires usually happen under the combined effect of two or more the natural factors such as topography, fuels, temperature, pressure, humidity, wind velocity, heat waves, weather changes and so forth. Therefore, preventive measures are to be designed and monitored dynamically according to the varying combinations of the natural factors.

12.6.2 Detection

Fast detection is essentially important for wildfire fighting. Early the detection, early will be the response, and the ability to prioritize fire danger. In the earlier days, Fire lookout towers were used and fires were communicated though telephones, news messengers, carrier pigeons, and heliographs. 1950s witnessed Aerial/ land photography through instant cameras and in 1960s, infrared scanning was developed for fire detection. However, information analysis was often delayed due to inadequate communication technology. The satellite based fire information has started from the Yellowstone fires of 1988.

Presently, hotlines, fire lookout towers, ground/aerial patrols, and mobile communication are used for early detection of forest fires. But still, accurate human observation and timely action is questionable owing to operator fatigue, time of day/night, season of year, geographic location, reach-ability, transportation facility and so forth. Electronic and computer systems have gained popularity during recent part as a remedy to human operational errors.

A surprise is that a recent trial of 3 automated camera fire detection systems in Australia concluded "...detection by the camera systems was slower and less reliable than by a trained human observer".

Of course, Global Positioning System (GPS) in association with aerial monitoring through planes, helicopters, unmanned automatic vehicles (UAV) and satellite communication systems may be effective alternative solutions for detection, prevention and protection.

12.6.3 Suppression

Extinguishing operation against wildfire

Wildfire suppression depends on the technologies available in the vicinity of the wildfire. In the areas where high technologies are not available, the techniques used can be as simple as throwing sand/ water or beating the fire with sticks. In developed nations, the fire suppression methods use advanced technological knowledge and capacity depending on intensity of the fire and the need. These techniques include silver iodide (AgI) to encourage snow fall, fire retardants and water dropped onto fires by unmanned aerial vehicles, planes, and helicopters and so forth.

Though fire suppression cannot completely extinguish, the great majority of the wildfire is controlled. Fighting wildfires can become deadly, when it changes direction unexpectedly and jump across fire breaks. Intense heat and smoke can lead to disorientation and loss of appreciation of the direction of the fire, which can make fires particularly dangerous.

Example:

1. The 1949 Mann Gulch fire in Montana, USA, 13 smokejumpers died when they lost their communication links, became disoriented and fire overtook them.

2. The Australian Feb 2009 Victorian bushfires lost at least 173 people, over 2,029 homes and 3,500 structures as they became engulfed by wildfire.

12.6.4 Monitoring and Controlling

Wildfire though has adverse effects, still it is useful to mankind in certain aspects provided, it should be under control.

Merits of Wildfires

The frequent and periodic burning of vegetation has the following merits

- Maintains high species diversity
- Limits the surface fuel accumulation, and thence prevents major events
- Reduces the risk of crown fires.
- Increases the safety and security to the mankind particularly from snakes, poisonous species
- Using strategic cuts of trees, fuels may also be removed by hand-crews to
    - clean and clear the forest,
    - prevent fuel build-up, and
    - create access into forested areas.

The above merits indicate that the wildfire under control is permissible. Jan Van Wagtendonk, a biologist writes, "the most effective treatment for reducing a fire's rate of spread, fire-line intensity, flame length, and heat per unit of area". The following are the two strategies employed under wildfire monitoring and controlling programs around the globe

A prescribed burn in a *Pinus nigra* stand in Portugal

- *Wild-land fire use*: Under this strategy, any fire of natural causes is allowed to burn but monitored.
- *Prescribed or Controlled burns*: Under this strategy, the fire is ignited by government agencies under prescribed less dangerous weather and controlled.

12.6.5 Fire-Fighting and Safety

Fire fighters face several life-threatening hazards including heat stress, fatigue, smoke and dust, along with the risk of injuries such as burns, cuts and scrapes, animal bites etc.

Hot weathers pose the risk of heat stress in the form of feeling heat, fatigue, weakness, vertigo, headache or nausea, which can grow as heat strain, increased

> **O My God!**
>
> A case study on the exposure of wildfire smoke among wildfire-fighters reveals significant levels of CO and respiratory irritants above OSHA permissible exposure limits (PEL) and ACGIH threshold limit values (TLV) and 5-10% are overexposed. The study obtained exposure concentrations for a fire-fighter over a 10-hour shift spent holding down a fire-line. He was exposed to a wide range of CO and respiratory irritant (combination of particulate matter 3.5 μm and smaller, acrolein, and HCHO) levels. CO levels reached up to 160 ppm (OSHA PEL is 30 ppm) and the TLV irritant index value reached 10 (limit value is 1).

heart rate and/or body temperature and thence heat-related illnesses, such as dehydration. Rest, cool water, and occasional breaks are crucial to mitigating the effects of heat stress.

Fire-fighters are at the highest risk for acute and chronic health effects from wildfire smoke exposure. As a part of occupation, they are usually exposed to hazardous chemicals at a close proximity for longer periods. Smoke, ash, and debris also cause serious respiratory hazards. The smoke and dust of wildfires may contain gases such as carbon monoxide, sulphur dioxide and formaldehyde, and particulates such as ash and silica. To reduce smoke exposure, wildfire fighters should rotate as whenever possible, and avoid downwind fire-fighting, use equipment, and minimize mop-up. Camps and command posts should also be located upwind of wildfires. Protective clothing and equipment is a must. Fitness programs, medical screening programs can reduce the risks.

Other hazards include slips, trips and falls, burns, scrapes and cuts from tools and equipment, being struck by trees, vehicles, or other objects, plant hazards such as thorns, poison ivy, snake and animal bites, vehicle crashes, electrocution from power lines or lightning storms, and unstable building structures.

12.6.6 Fire Retardants

Fire retardants help slowdown wildfires, coat fuels, and reduce oxygen availability as desired by the fire-fighting situations. Usually, they contain ammonia, nitrates, phosphates and sulphates, and other chemicals. They (specifically nitrogen and phosphorus compounds) have a fertilizing effect on nutrient-deprived soils and thus create a temporary increase in vegetation. The choice of application of retardant depends on the magnitude, geographical location and intensity of the wildfire. Retardants are often applied when

- It is occurring at inaccessible geographical regions
- When land fire-fighters could not approach a wildfire or
- Human safety and structures are endangered
- It needs protection of structures and vegetation (usually applied ahead of wildfires) as a precautionary fire defense measure.

Though fire retardants are greatly useful in fire fighting, they have adverse effects too. Some of the adverse effects of retardants are listed below:

1. The aerial fire retardants can change soil chemistry.
2. They reduce nutrients in the soil by increasing the acidity of soil, and water quality through leaching, eutrophication, or misapplication.
3. Dilution factors, including water body size, rainfall, and water flow rates lessen the concentration and potency of fire retardant.
4. Wildfire debris like ash and sediment clog the rivers and reservoirs increasing the risk for floods and erosion that ultimately leads to slow and/or damage water treatment systems.
5. They affect on land, water, wildlife habitats, and watershed quality.

12.6.7 Cost-Benefit Analysis of Wildfire Management Strategies

Finally, it may confuse us whether wildfire is advantageous or disadvantageous. Whether a particular wildfire at a specified area has to be allowed or not? If wildfire has occurred, did it cost or benefit? These questions are always under debate unless a cost-benefit analysis is conducted. The following table can provide various aspects that cost or benefit and can be used as guidelines for conducting a cost benefit analysis.

Strategy	Costs	Benefits
Suppression	• Labour-intensive • Needs high level planning and very expensive • Some methods are inefficient (e.g. aeria retardant drops) • Increases intensity and likelihood of future wildfires. • Inhibits natural ecological processes in many cases	• Reduces human health impacts • Protects forest and agricultural resources • Saves private dwellings and commercial buildings
Prescribed fire	• Expensive to implement • Needs skilled workforce to implement • Needs high level of planning • Affects human health (e.g. smoke causes asthma/allergy) • May go out of control and burns large areas	• Provides habitat for wildlife • Improves forest • Enhances agricultural resources • Reduces hazardous fuel loading • Mimics natural process but needs more control
Mechanical Fuels Reduction	• Needs heavy machinery (so more fossil fuel consumption, compaction etc.) • Expensive to implement • Cannot mimic natural processes	• Can provide habitat for wildlife • Improves forest and agricultural resources • Reduces hazardous fuel loading • Doesn't produce heavy smokes

O My God!

In 1937, the US President Franklin D. Roosevelt initiated a nationwide fire prevention campaign, focusing the role of human carelessness in forest fires. Later posters of the program featured Uncle Sam, characters from the Disney movie *Bambi*, and the official mascot of US Forest Service, Smokey bear (based on the "Uncle Sam/ Lord Kitchener" poster by artist Albert Staehle in collaboration with writer and art critic Harold Rosenberg).

12.6.8 Notable Wildfires

- Peshtigo Fire 1871 most loss of life in a US wildfire.
- Great Fire of 1910 in the USA shaped 20th century wildfire policy
- Landes Forest 1949 wildfire in South West France; 50,000 hectares (500 km^2; 190 sq mi) of forest land were burnt - and 82 people killed.

Some other wild fires include, 2003 Portuguese wildfires, 2009 SE Australia bushfires, 2010 Bolivian forest fires, 2010 Russian wildfires, 2011 Texas wildfires, 2013 Beaver Creek Fire.

SELF ASSESSMENT INTERMISSION (SAI – 12.5)

1. "Fire is a very good servant, but a very bad master", critically appreciate the statement in the backdrop of wildfires.
2. Enumerate various risks involved with wildfires. Suggest some remedies to reduce the risk.
3. What is meant by 'risk'? Explain about the human induced risk to wildfires.
4. Describe the risk involved with wildfire to the surrounding living areas.
5. Do you think wildfire is advantageous or disadvantageous? Discuss with supporting examples.
6. What is wildfire management? What are its phases? Explain each phase briefly.
7. Explain the ways and means to prevent wildfire.
8. Suggest the wildfire protection and prevention measures.
9. Describe some notable wildfires and their effects.
10. What are the merits of wildfires?
11. Write short notes on
    (a) Wildfire detection (b) Wildfire suppression (c) Wildfire monitoring and controlling.
12. Describe the health effects and safety measures to be taken on fire-fighters against wildfires.
13. What are fire retardants? What are its merits and demerits.
14. Explain the aspects of cost-benefits analysis of various wildfire management strategies.
15. Meet the officials of fire department in your vicinity and conduct an interview of the safety and experiences of fire fighters against the wildfires.
16. Recall a wildfire you witnessed or heard, after describing the situation; discuss the causes and effects of it?

MINI-PROJECTS/ CASE STUDIES

1. Divide into some teams with your classmates/ colleagues and visit the nearest villages to give awareness about the natural disasters (such as heat/ cold waves or any other to which the area is vulnerable) and the precautions that they have to take in such situations. Prepare a report of the facilities/ mitigation plans and send them to the district collector or the relevant authority.
2. Visit the nearest villages and explain them the effects of the deforestation and wildfires. Write an article or make documentary on deforestation, taking reference of CHIPKO movement.
3. Visit a fire station and interview the fire station officer. Conduct their drill at your premises and ask them to give awareness to your colleagues/ classmates.

DO YOU KNOW

Cold wave

1. As per Guinness Records, the largest snowflake was 15'wide, 8'thick in Fort Keogh, Montana on Jan 28, 1887.
2. Fear of snow is called Chionophobia.
3. Snowflakes are actually translucent, not white. Snow appears white because it is a bunch of individual ice crystals arranged together. Light when falls on snow, bounces all around the ice crystals and the "colour" of all the frequencies in the visible spectrum combined in equal measure is white.
4. Every winter, at least a septillion (=1 followed by 24 zeros) snow crystals fall from sky.
5. The menopause is significantly higher in winter than in spring or autumn.
6. Average snowflake fall is at ~3mph. 10inches of snow will melt down to only 1inch of water.
7. The most snow ever recorded in 24 hr in the US was at Silver Lake, Colorado, in 1921 at 76 inches. 2nd is Georgetown, Colorado, in Dec 4, 1913, at 63 inches.
8. Mt. Baker ski area in Washington holds the world record for largest snowfall at 1,140 inches of snow during the 1998–99 winter. A single snowstorm can drop 39 million tons of snow.
9. Since the first Winter Olympics, Chamonix, France, 1924, no country in S. Hemisphere hosted, or even been an applicant to host the Winter Olympics hither to.
10. The coldest temperature ever recorded was -123° C at Vostok Station in Antarctica in 1983.
11. Thanks to hydrogen bonding, all snowflakes have six sides
12. The coldest winter on earth occurs at the Polar Plateau in Antarctica with mean temp -72.9°F.
13. In 1974, Russia recorded -96°F in Siberia. Russia being the coldest, Canada, Mongolia, Finland, and Iceland are in the top 5 in the world.
14. Winter is a major character in several movies, including *The Thing* (1982, 2011), *Whiteout* (2009), *The Day after Tomorrow*(2004), *The Colony* (2013), *Alive* (1993), *Wind Chill* (2007), *Frozen* (2010, 2013), and *The Grey* (2011). The Disney movie *Frozen* (2013) is the highest-grossing animated musical film of all time and 9th highest-gross film with a worldwide box office gross of $1.097 billion.

Heat waves

1. If a pet stays outdoors during extreme heat, it means they have cold water and an area out of the sun where they can cool off. For pets, spending time in a hot car can be super dangerous. Hang signs to remind pet owners not to leave their furry friends in hot cars.
2. Heat waves kill more Americans than any other natural disasters. In July 1995, Chicago, Illinois experienced a heat wave that caused over 700 deaths. Midwest could endure similar heat waves up to 3 times a year by 2100 if greenhouse gas emissions continue.
3. Urban areas often experience higher temperatures during the summer, referred to as "Urban Heat Island". This is due to buildings, roads, and other infrastructures absorbing solar energy, resulting in higher temperatures. Heat waves can cause blackouts and power outages, especially in areas that experience the urban heat island effect.

Wildfires

1. A peat fire is an uncontrolled fire. Wildfires often occur in unpopulated areas.
2. Fire-fighters also refer to these disasters as surface fires, dependent crown fires, spot fires, and ground fires.
3. "Crown fires" are spread by wind moving quickly across the tops of trees. "Running crown fires" are even more dangerous because they burn extremely hot, travel rapidly, and can change direction quickly.
4. Lightning strikes the earth million times a day. 10-20% of these can cause fire.
5. 90% of all wildfires are started by humans.

Deforestation

1. Forests cover 30% of the earth's land.
2. 1.5 acres of forest is cut down every second. The total world forest loss till date is 7.3 million hectares/year. Estimated that within 100 years there will be no rainforests. 4500 acres are cleared every hour by forest fires, bull dozers etc. The rate of deforestation equals to loss of 20 football fields every minute. 50% world's tropical forests have already been cleared.
3. There are more than 121 natural remedies in the rain forest which can be used as medicines.
4. The over exploitation of forests is making it extremely difficult to replant a new ecology.
5. 25% cancers fighting organisms and 20% world's oxygen are produced in Amazon forest.
6. 1.6 billion of the globe depend on forest products for livelihood and adding to deforestation
7. The world's forests store 283 billion tons of carbon present in the biomass.

O My God!

Paper industry is 4th largest in producing greenhouse gas, major contributor to deforestation. Half of world's timber and up to 70% of paper is consumed by Europe, US and Japan alone. On an average, a person in the US uses more than 700 lb of paper every year. A lot of paper and cardboard is used unnecessarily for packing. This means more tree felling. US, Japan and Europe realized this fact and footing their steps toward paperless transactions. Deforestation has considerably stopped in places like Europe, Pacific, N America and some parts of Asia due to lack of agricultural land. So, let us take an oath to reuse paper and plastic bags to discourage deforestation. Use canvas or paper bags as another alternative. Pick products which require less packaging. Support eco-friendly companies buying their products that promise more durability in an inexpensive way. Be active and plant trees- May it be at your homes, backyards or join any organization keen on stopping deforestation. Boycott companies who do not care for environment and support organizations that care about the environment at the cost of fighting back for the evergreen trees.

CHAPTER 13 Pollution and Acid Rains

O'MY SILENT INNER VIBES (O'M S I V – 13)

Let us recall a story from the moral stories of Akbar-Birbal.

One day King Akbar said, "Birbal! My people are very obedient and loyal to me. They love me very much that they blindly honour my words and follow my orders"

Birbal smiled and replied, "Jahanpanah! This is true to some extent only. But there is a fear of you, and no one is that loyal, if the fear is absent"

Akbar could not agree on this, and wanted to test Birbal's statement. So, he ordered Birbal to prove it.

Next day, Birbal announced that King would be going for hunting, and people should pour a pot of milk in a tub kept in the courtyard. When Akbar returned, he found no milk in the tub, instead there was only water. Disappointed Akbar couldn't do anything, but to accept Birbal. But still he had a doubt, if people have fear of him.

Then Birbal said, "Jahanpanah! This time you announce that you will come back and suddenly inspect the tub yourself and if anybody is found not pouring milk, he would be punished to death". The King did as Birbal said. Once again the tub was kept in the courtyard. This time when King returned from the hunting, he found the tub overflowing with milk.

Birbal said, "Jahanpanah! I told you, it is the fear which made people to obey you. The first time the order was given by me on your behalf, and they did not have any fear. Also, everybody thought that, 'all will pour milk and it would not make any difference, if he/she poured the water in the tub full of milk'. Further, there was nobody to check it. But the second time, they knew that you would check yourself, and also they had a fear of you that they would be sentenced to death, thence they brought the milk."

Let us just apply the theme of the above moral story to our context of pollution,

- Everyone of us is contributing for the pollution, thinking that our contribution is negligible
- Everyone thinks that there won't be much difference to cause by his/her act.
- None of us has fear of the sin of spoiling the environment and the nature.
- Everyone of us has an inhibitive notion that no one is there to check
- Every individual's behaviour when alone is different from that when in a group
- All are culprits but no one is ready either to accept it or to change themselves
- Everyone becomes a 'judge' for other's mistake, but 'lawyer' for his own mistake
- Comfort and convenience are dominating over the concern for pollution and contamination
- Everyone of us is under an opinion that one alone cannot change the society.

All the above can be proved to be fallacies if we observe that every great journey started with only one (first) step. And remember, the next generation will not excuse us but curses us for our sins. So, come on! Let's gear up for creating a pollution-free environment and contribute by controlling ourselves not to add any pollutants.

(Continued)

Why don't we start now?

One more step ahead for Pollution-free environment (*Aur ek kadam swachatha ke liye!*)

As we have a responsibility and accountability toward our next generation, we must to give

- good water to drink
- good air to breath
- good food to eat
- good environment to live and
- whatever the best possible

SAVE NATURE - HAVE FUTURE.

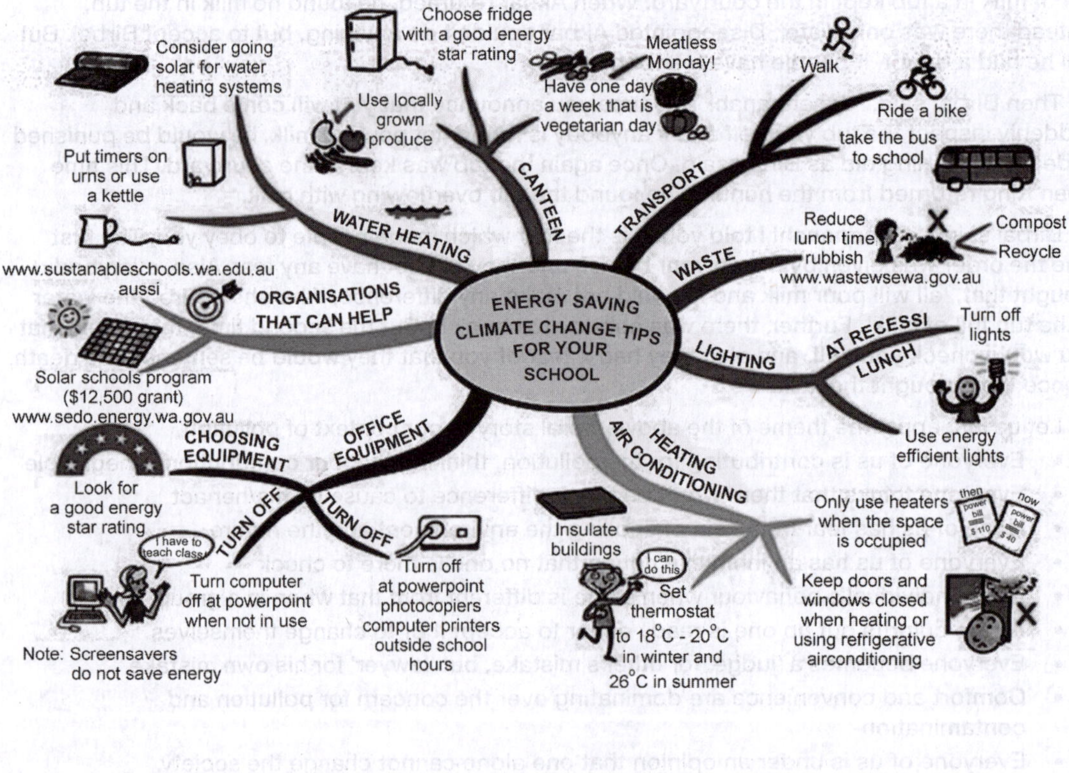

13.1 THE CONCEPT OF POLLUTION AND POLLUTANTS

The most pressing of today's environmental issues is the pollution of the air we breathe, the water we drink, the food we eat and the environment we live in. Many types of pollution contributing to problems range from human health issues to climate change.

As per the history known, air pollution as an urban problem was first recognized in England in the 9th century, when coal was discovered. However, the possible damage to human health through chronic respiratory ailments by inhalation of coal smoke was noticed by John Evelyn in 17th century.

Pollution

Pollution is the induction of contaminants into the natural environment by which human life is affected adversely. Pollution can take the form of chemical substances or energy, such as noise, heat or light.

Pollutants

A pollutant is a waste material that pollutes air, water or soil. In other words, these are the components of pollution, which can be either foreign substances/ energies or naturally occurring contaminants. Three factors determine the severity of a pollutant: its chemical nature, the concentration and the persistence.

Pollution Vs Civilization

Pollution and civilization have been always together one influencing the other. Pollution started from prehistoric times when man created the first fires. This is evident from the "Soot" found on ceilings of prehistoric caves that the high levels of pollution were associated with poor ventilation of open fires. The samples of glaciers also indicate the pollution associated with Greek, Roman and Chinese metallic era; however the pollution during those days was relatively small and was handled by nature itself.

Smog Pollution

Till the Industrial Revolution, coal and wood were used as fuels for cooking, while horses, bullocks for transportation. The world experienced air pollution through soot and smoke by burning of coal, while water and surrounds were polluted by the urine and manure of horses and animals making even towns and cities the cesspits. King Edward I of England banned the burning of sea-coal by proclamation in London in 1272, after its smoke became a problem.

> **O My God!**
>
> **The intolerable primitive conditions for a world national capital?**
>
> In 1870, the sanitary conditions in Berlin were the worst in Europe. August Bebel recalled "Waste-water from the houses emitted a truly fearsome smell. There were no public toilets in the streets or squares. Visitors, especially women, often were desperate for nature's calls. In the public buildings sanitary facilities were unbelievably primitive. Berlin as a metropolis did not emerge from a state of barbarism into civilization until 1870".
>
> The German govt. engaged its scientists, engineers and urban planners to not only solve the deficiencies but to emerge as the world's model city. A British expert in 1906 concluded that Berlin represented "the complete application of science, order and method of public life, a marvel of civic administration, the most modern and perfectly organized city"

Of course, Industrial Revolution solved this problem but gave birth to environmental pollution as we know it today. As historian Martin Melosi notes, the generation saw "miracles of cleanliness" by automobiles replacing the horses. By the 1940s, however, automobile-caused smog (smoke + fog) was a major issue in Los Angeles.

But, the development of factories required huge quantities of coal that gave rise to unparalleled air pollution as well as the large quantities of chemical discharges in addition to the increasing untreated human waste. Perhaps, Chicago and Cincinnati were the first two American cities identified the crux of the problem and enforced laws to ensure cleaner air in 1881 as air pollution became a chronic issue in US in the early 20th century due to coal burning, while water pollution due to bad sanitation. Streets of American cities in 1900, suffered pollution by large amounts of urine and manure of the 3 million horses. Los Angeles, Pennsylvania also witnessed the extreme smog events in the late 1940s. Pollution drew major public attention in the US between the mid-1950s and early 1970s, when Congress passed the Noise Control Act, the Clean Air Act, the Clean Water Act and the National Environmental Policy Act.

London also witnessed one of the extreme cases of water pollution problems with the Great Stink on the Thames in 1858 that led to construction of the London sewerage system and raised the demand for sewer systems, and clean water. Air pollution has been posing a challenge to England, especially from the industrial revolution, till date including event of the recent past with the Great Smog of 1952, which killed at least 4000 people. This prompted UK to bring up environmental legislation, The Clean Air Act-1956.

13.1.1 Sources of Pollution

Pollution is sourced from both natural as well as manmade (anthropogenic).

(A) ***Pollution due to Natural Disasters:*** The after math natural disasters are often associated with pollution of air, water and/or soil. Sometimes the environment also experiences considerable damage.

- Cyclones, hurricanes, tsunamis often involve water contamination from sewage, and petrochemical spills from ruptured boats or automobiles. Larger scale and environmental damage is common if coastal oil rigs or refineries exist.
- The destructions of structures and constructions by earthquakes generate lot of solid waste, debris and dust.

- The volcanic eruptions cause soil contamination as well as the air pollutions (SOx).
- Landslides, mudslides and rock slides also can raise the dust into air causing pollution.
- Floods often pollute water bodies and soils also.
- Nuclear power plants or oil tankers can produce widespread and potentially hazardous releases if accidents (natural/ manmade) occur.

(B) ***Pollution due to Human Activity:*** Man-made pollutants generate from combustion, construction, mining, agriculture and warfare and are significant contributors to the air pollution and are increasing day by day.

- Motor vehicle emissions are one of the leading sources of manmade air pollution. China, US, Russia, India, Mexico, and Japan are 'the world leaders' in air pollution emissions.
- Stationary pollution sources include chemical plants, coal-fired power plants, oil refineries, petrochemical plants, nuclear waste disposal activity, incinerators, large livestock farms (dairy cows, pigs, poultry, etc.), PVC factories, metals production factories, plastics factories, and other heavy industry.
- Agricultural air pollution comes from contemporary practices which include clear felling and burning of natural vegetation as well as spraying of pesticides and herbicides.

While ~400 million metric tons of hazardous wastes are generated each year, the US alone produces ~250 million metric tons. Astounding fact is that Americans with only < 5% of the world's population, produce ~25% of the world's CO_2, and generate ~30% of world's waste. Of course! In 2007, China overtook the US as the world's biggest producer of CO_2, but still far behind based on per capita pollution - ranked 78th.

In Feb 2007, the Intergovernmental Panel on Climate Change (IPCC), with 2,500 scientists, economists, and policymakers from >120 countries, reported that humans have been the primary cause of global warming since 1950, and concluded that humans have ways to cut greenhouse gas emissions to avoid the consequences of global warming. But the transition from fossil fuels like coal and oil should take place within decade to change the climate.

In the case of noise pollution the vast majority (90%) is contributed by the motored vehicles.

13.1.2 Forms of Pollution

Pollution is often classed as point source or nonpoint source pollution. But this classification cannot suffice to explain all the forms of pollutions. The major forms of pollution are listed below along with the particular contaminant relevant to each of them:

- **Air pollution**: This kind of pollution is caused by the release of chemicals and particulates into the atmosphere produced by industries and motor vehicles. Common air pollutants include
  - Oxides of carbon (CO_x): Carbon monoxide (CO) and carbon dioxide (CO_2),
  - Oxides of sulphur: (SO_x) Sulphur dioxide (SO_2), and sulphur trioxide (SO_3),
  - Oxides of nitrogen (NO_x): Nitric oxide (NO), Nitrogen dioxide (NO_2) etc.,
  - Hydrocarbons (HCs): Methane, Ethane like organic gases
  - Chloro-fluorocarbons (CFCs),
  - Gaseous carbon,
  - Dust, dirt and soot and so forth.

Photochemical ozone and smog are created as nitrogen oxides and hydrocarbons react to sunlight. Particulate matter or fine dust is characterized by their micrometre size (PM_{10} to $PM_{2.5}$).

- **Water Pollution:** This kind of pollution is caused by wastewater from domestic or commercial or industrial source. This happens in the following ways.
  - discharges of untreated domestic sewage, and/or chemical contaminants;
  - the discharge of wastewater from commercial and industrial waste (intentionally or through spills) into surface waters;
  - agricultural runoff containing chemical fertilizers and pesticides into flowing waters;
  - release of urban waste and contaminants into surface runoff or flowing waters;
  - waste disposal and leaching into groundwater;
  - eutrophication and littering.
- **Soil Pollution:** Soil pollution is caused due to chemicals released by spill or underground leakage. Some important soil contaminants include hydrocarbons, heavy metals, methyl tert-butyl ether (MTBE), herbicides, pesticides and chlorinated hydrocarbons.
- **Visual Pollution:** This form of pollution refers to the presence of overhead power lines, motorway billboards, open storage of trash, municipal solid waste or space debris and scared landforms (as from strip mining).

Some facts about Air Pollution

Air pollution is a worldwide epidemic that is much worse in some countries than in others.

- In 2009, the 27 members of European Union (EU) reported a cumulative drop in SO_2 by roughly 80% since 1990.
- The WHO reported in national geographic news states that air pollution in China causes ~656,000 deaths every year.
- WHO also reported that on an average of 2 million deaths worldwide are due to air pollution
- In India almost half of all monitored cities have above-average or critical levels of particulate matter below 10 μm.

- **Plastic Pollution:** This is the most adversely affecting pollution on humans and nature, even wildlife caused by the accumulation of plastic products in the environment.
- **Littering:** This type of pollution is caused by criminal throwing of inappropriate man-made objects and unresolved, onto public and private properties.
- **Noise Pollution:** This pollution includes noise of roadways, aircrafts, industrial equipment as well as high-intensity sonar.
- **Light Pollution:** Light pollution is caused by light trespass, over-illumination and astronomical interference.
- **Thermal Pollution:** It is the temperature change in natural water bodies caused by human influence, such as use of water as coolant in a power plant.
- **Radioactive/ Radiation Pollution:** The radiation is the latest type took birth during 20th century as a result of researches and developments of atomic physics and electronics such as nuclear power generation and nuclear weapons research, manufacture and deployment. (See alpha emitters and actinides in the environment), mobile phones, electronic gadgets

The World's Most Worst Polluted Places		
No.	Place	Country
1.	Agbogbloshie	Ghana
2.	Chernobyl	Ukraine
3.	Citarum River	Indonesia
4.	Dzershinsk	Russia
5.	Hazaribagh	Bangladesh
6.	Kabwe	Zambia
7.	Kalimantan	Indonesia
8.	Matanza Riachuelo	Argentina

SELF ASSESSMENT INTERMISSION (SAI – 13.1)

1. Define the terms pollution and pollutants.
2. Give various sources of pollution.
3. Describe different forms of pollution.
4. Distinguish between Climate and Weather.
5. What is littering?
6. What are the common air pollutants?
7. Give a brief account of pollution due to natural disasters.
8. List out different pollutants.
9. Pollution and civilization have been always together one influencing the other. Discuss
10. Did Industrial Revolution solve the pollution problems? Explain.

13.2 AIR POLLUTION

Air is said to be polluted when it is contaminated with harmful gases, dust, fumes or odour that affects health or comfort of humans and animals or could

O My God!

Ten Worst Industries?

The Pure Earth, an international non-for-profit organization dedicated to eliminating life-threatening pollution in the developing world, issues an annual list of some of the world's most polluting industries. The top ten are:

1. Lead-Acid Battery Recycling
2. Industrial Mining/ Ore Processing
3. Lead Smelting
4. Tannery Operations
5. Artisanal Small-Scale Gold Mining
6. Industrial/Municipal Dumpsites
7. Industrial Estates
8. Chemical Manufacturing
9. Product Manufacturing
10. Dye Industry

cause damage to plants and materials. More specifically, the undesirable gases, liquid or solid substances present in air in sufficient concentration, for a sufficient time, and under certain conditions, often called 'air pollutants', tend to interfere with human comfort, health or welfare and cause environmental damage.

13.2.1 Air Pollutants

Well known and the major air pollutants are carbon monoxide, sulphur dioxide, nitrogen oxides, ozone, particulate matter and lead. They usually occur as a result of discharges of factories, motor vehicles, industrial exhaust and volcanic eruptions. Of course, there are also natural sources such as wind-blown dust and smoke from fires. For the ease of study, the air pollutants are classified under two categories as follows:

(a) Primary pollutants

(b) Secondary pollutants

(a) **Primary pollutants:** These are the pollutants released into atmosphere (air) and directly pollute the air. These are major contributors of the air pollution. Examples: carbon monoxide (CO) released from vehicle exhausts, factory exhausts due to incomplete burning; sulphur dioxide (SO_2) released during the combustion of coal.

(b) **Secondary pollutants:** Further pollution can occur due to the compounds formed when primary pollutants undergo chemical reactions. These pollutants are known as secondary pollutants. Example: Photochemical smog, petro chemicals etc.

Major Outdoor Air Pollutants

There are some major outdoor air pollutants that affect humans as well as environment as listed below:

- Particulate matter
- Ozone
- Nitrogen dioxide
- Carbon monoxide
- Sulphur dioxide
- Lead

The major sources and the health effects of the above pollutants are summarized and tabulated below Table 13.1.

Table 13.1 Air Pollutants: Causes and effects.

No.	Pollutant	Source/cause	Health Effects
1.	Particulate matter 	• Power plants and industries • Motor vehicles • Domestic coal burning • Natural sources (volcanoes, dust storms) • Small particles form surface for acid aerosol formation	• Increased mortality • Decreased lung growth and functions • Increased acute respiratory morbidity (Pneumonia, Asthma)
2.	Ozone 	• Secondary pollutants • Formed by photo chemical reaction of VOC's, NO_2+O_2	• Lung irritation and inflammation • Impaired pulmonary function • Eye, nose, and throat irritation
3.	NOx 	• Power plants, industries • Motor vehicles • Natural sources (volcanoes, lightening, bacteria)	• Emphysema in animals • Decrements in lung function • Increased airway reactivity • Increased susceptibility to infection
4.	CO 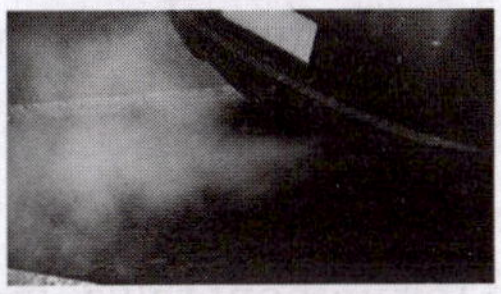	• Incomplete combustion of fuels • Vehicle exhaust • Industry fires	• Combines with haemoglobin in blood • Reduces oxygen carrying capacity • At higher risk: children with anaemia, heart disease, or chronic lung diseases and foetuses
5.	SO_2 	• Combustion of sulphur containing coal or oil • Industrial processes, smelting of sulphur ores • Natural sources (volcanoes) • Combines with water to form H_2SO_4 (acid aerosol, acid rains)	• Gas is upper way irritant - Primarily affects naso pharynx and proximal airways • Acid aerosol reaches distal airways - Bronchi constriction - Slowing bronchial clearance - Chronic bronchitis
6.	Lead	• Tetra ethyl lead (TEL) in petrol • Mining and smelting of lead ores • Industry • Waste incineration • Dust (Examples: homes with old lead based paint, battery, recycling, smelters)	• Interferes with many enzyme systems - Heart synthesis - Neuro-toxic effects - Blood pleasure • Most severe effects in infants and in young children
7.	Biological Pollutants	• Moulds • Pollens • Caster/ Soya bean dust	- Bronchi constriction - Slowing bronchial clearance - Chronic bronchitis

O My God!

Pea Souper (London Smog)?

The London Smog of 1952 was so thick that road, rail and air transport were almost standstill and a performance at the Sadler's Wells Theatre suspended the shows as fog in the auditorium was intolerable for the audience and the performers. The fog was so thick that the pedestrians could not find their way at night. People couldn't see even their own feet. This type of fog is known as "Pea Souper". It is not known how many people died as a direct result of the fog.

O My God!

The Major Pollution outbreak in India?

One of the worst industrial/ pollution/ chemical disasters occurred without warning early on the morning about 3 am of Dec 3, 1984, at Union Carbide's pesticide plant in Bhopal, India. While most people slept, a leak, caused by a series of mechanical and human failures, released a cloud of lethal methyl iso-cyanate (MIC) over the sleeping city. Some 2000 people immediately and another 8000 died later. Health officials, not informed about chemicals at the factory, were completely unprepared for the tragedy

13.2.2 Forms of Air Pollution

As per American Lung Association, there are two main forms of air pollutions most harmful to humans. These are

- Ozone or Smog, and
- Particle pollution or soot

Ozone or Smog Pollution

The pollution combined by smoke and fog is often termed as Smog (**Smoke+Fog)** or Ozone pollution, formed by chemical reaction between sunlight and the vapours emitted by the burning of carbon based or fossil fuels. Ozone pollution is highest during the sunniest months of the year. These pollutants in short term exposure cause irritation to skin, and the respiratory system, and long term exposure can lead to more serious health problems, like impaired lung function, inflammation of the lung lining, and higher rates of pulmonary diseases.

Soot or Particle Pollution

This is the most dangerous and very wide spread throughout the environment that consists of solid and liquid particles made up of ash, metals, soot, diesel exhaust, and chemicals. This mainly occurs due to burning of coal in power plants and other industries, and/or by using of diesel fuel in passenger vehicles, cargo vehicles, and heavy equipments. Burning wood is also a source of particle pollution. Lung cancer and premature birth are probable serious health effects. It also irritates respiratory system, including asthma and sneeze, cough, wheeze, and even shorter life spans.

13.3 CAUSES OF AIR POLLUTION

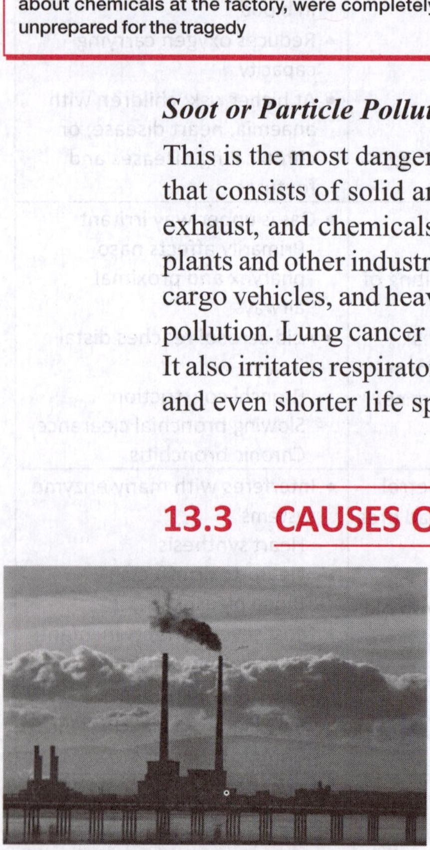

- Exhaust from factories/ industries and vehicles in Traffic
- Burning of fossil fuels
- Agricultural activities
- Mining operations
- Indoor air pollution
- Solid waste mismanagement

- Chemical incidents and spills
- Atomic/ nuclear accidents and Radiations/ radio activity

13.3.1 Exhaust from Factories/ Industries and Vehicles in Traffic

The exhaust from factories and industries including the combustion of fossil fuels by industrial plants and vehicles in traffic cause the outdoor pollution, which commonly contain carbon monoxide, sulphur dioxide, particulate matter, nitrogen oxides, hydrocarbons and others. However, the composition and characteristics of emissions may vary for each specific industry (e.g. Smelting, fermentation, food processing, Paper production, Refining etc.).

13.3.2 Burning of Fossil Fuels

This is yet another most contributing source of causing air pollution. When fossil fuels are burnt, nitrogen oxides are released in to the atmosphere, which contribute to the formation of smog and acid rain. Ammonia is another nitrogen compound emitted to the air, primarily from agricultural activities but also from fossil fuels.

Fossil fuels cause air pollution in the following ways:

- The formation of carbon dioxide (CO_2) released in to the atmosphere can absorb infrared radiations emitted by the earth and re-radiate it back, called 'greenhouse effect'.
- Combustion of coal, gasoline, and other fossil fuels in insufficient supply of oxygen produces carbon monoxide (CO) and unburnt hydro carbons. This is highly dangerous, as CO combines with hemoglobin in the blood to form carboxy-hemoglobin and obstructs oxygen flow. Thence, many hydrocarbons being carcinogenic cause serious health hazards.
- Coal contains some compounds of sulphur and nitrogen, which are oxidized (SOx and NOx) during combustion are corrosive and poisonous. Subsequently, during rains these oxides dissolve in rain water to cause 'acid rains'.

13.3.3 Agricultural Pollution

Agricultural pollution occurs in the following ways:

- Ammonia is the major pollutant released from pesticides and fertilizers to contribute to the air pollution, and others include the oxides of sulphur and some organic compounds.

- Pesticides and insecticides sprayed, mix with the water and seep into ground while some may mix up in air and the rest be absorbed by the plant itself. During the local streams of water from the ground contaminate, thence harm the animals that graze these crops and plants.
- Pollution can be caused by soil erosion and sedimentations. Though, soil is comprised of many layers, only the topmost layer is used for farming or grassing due to insufficient farming practices. This layer of soil, since is left open for erosion by water or wind, leads to decline in fertility each year on one hand while the pollution on the other.

13.3.4 Mining Operations

Mining operations often cause air pollution in its surrounds. Before the excavation, the upper layer of the earth crest often referred to as 'overburden' is removed. This is done by first blasting and then removed by shovels. While blasting and shovelling lot of dust rises up and pollutes the atmospheric air that has high potential of causing bronchitis, respiratory problems and other serious health hazards to the employees as well as the residents of surrounding areas. Therefore, the mining companies are required to follow certain environmental and rehabilitation codes. In addition to the health hazards, the environmental impact of mining includes

- Soil erosion,
- Formation of sink holes,
- Loss of bio diversity
- Contamination of soil,
- Polluting ground water, surface water by chemicals from mining
- Environmental damage due to leakage of chemicals
- Effect on the public health

13.3.5 Solid Waste Mismanagement and its Effects

The more common soil contaminants are chlorinated/ fluorinated hydrocarbons (CFH), heavy metals such as chromium, cadmium (in rechargeable Ni-Cd batteries), and lead (in batteries & paints), aviation fuel, gasoline, MTBE, zinc, arsenic and benzene. The municipal landfills are the source of several chemicals entering the soil and groundwater from the wide variety of refuse accepted, particularly the illegally discarded substances and also some unusual releases of polychlorinated dibenzodioxins (in short called *dioxins*).

Effects of solid waste management

- The decomposition of waste is also a cause of local environmental pollution. Particularly, this is a chronic problem in developing countries such as India. [Realizing this fact, the Prime Minister of India, Mr. Narendra Modi announced a program "Swach Bharat (Clean India)", "Ganga Prakshalan (Cleaning of Ganges)" and so on].
- The problem is usually associated with rapid urbanization.
- A major environmental problem is by the gases released during decomposition of garbage.
- Methane is a by-product of the anaerobic respiration of bacteria.
- Another problem is the enhanced greenhouse gas effect and climate change.
- There is every chance of spreading mosquitoes and micro-organisms to cause an epidemic.

13.3.6 Chemical Incidents and Spills

Chemicals can be corrosive, toxic, reactive or even explosive. So, chemicals can be hazardous anywhere and anytime by their very nature, or during their manufacture, or while storage, and when they are under transport, the effects of which can be disastrous, for both humans and the environment. Thus their contribution to the environmental pollution is significant.

The petroleum and its products (often referred to as organic chemicals) take lion's share chemical accidents, particularly while refining or acting as fuels. Other sources include the building blocks of plastics, paints, dyes, inks, polyester, and many of the products. The inorganic chemicals such as acids, caustics, cyanide, and metals are yet another important class of chemical pollutants.

13.3.7 Atomic/ Nuclear Accidents and Radiation/ Radio Activity

Atmospheric pollution was widely recognized after WW-II, with fears of radioactive fallout from atomic warfare and testing. Lake Karachay, named by the World Watch Institute as the "most polluted spot" on earth, served as a disposal site for the SU throughout the 1950s and 1960s. Chelyabinsk, Russia, is considered the "Most polluted place on the planet".

Testing of nuclear weapons continued in the Cold War (about 40-50 yrs after WW-II). Though extreme care is taken, the potential for disaster suggested by incidents occurred at 'Three Mile Island and Chernobyl explosion -1986' and the recent explosion of the 1999 Takaimura atomic power plant explosion in Japan. (Ref: Chapter 11, article 11.6.4 for more details)

Further, the international catastrophes such as the Bhopal disaster in 1984 and the wreck of the Amoco Cadiz oil tanker off the coast of Brittany in 1978 are still ringing the warning bells for putting large scale efforts to address them.

In addition to these, the world is seriously concerned on the implication of pollution due to the following issues

- Consequences and complications on a planetary level with the issue of global warming
- Depletion of ozone layer due to use of prohibitive chemicals
- Pollution due e-waste and the problem of their disposal
- The persistent organic pollutant (POP) group of chemicals such as PBDEs and PFCs
- The spread of invasive species and new viruses
- Human ingestion of toxic chemicals
- Pollution introduced by light at night became a global problem, more severe in urban centres, but nonetheless contaminating also far away from towns.
- A recently discovered problem is the Great Pacific Garbage Patch, a huge concentration of plastics, chemical sludge and other debris, collected into a large area of the Pacific Ocean by the N. Pacific Gyre.

SELF ASSESSMENT INTERMISSION (SAI – 13.2)

1. What do you understand by 'Air Pollution? What are various primary and secondary pollutants?
2. List out major air pollutants. Give their causes (sources) and effects.
3. Write a short note on 'smog' pollution.
4. Give a brief account on 'soot' pollution.
5. Describe different forms of air pollution.
6. Enumerate the causes of air pollution.
7. Explain about the air pollution caused by exhaust gases.
8. Write short notes on the air pollution caused by the following.
   (a) Burning of fossil fuels (b) Agricultural waste (c) Mining operations
9. What are the various sources of causing radiation? Discuss about the air pollution due to radiation.
10. What do you understand by solid waste management? Describe its connection with air pollution.
11. Discuss the relation between air pollution and chemical incidents or spills.

13.4 EFFECTS OF AIR POLLUTION

Air pollution can even create global problems, such as depleting the upper atmospheric ozone layer and hence causing global warming. However, this is somewhat complicated worldwide issue and needs the serious attention, co-operative efforts to find solutions and sincere implementation on the international platforms.

***Example*:** In the late 1990s, forest fires in Indonesia, caused a haze of smoke to hang for months over neighbouring south-east Asian countries. Schools were forced to close, while local hospitals reported large numbers of haze-related illnesses in young children.

Air pollution can effect in multiple ways and are even interactive and inter-dependent. Some of the major effects are listed below:

- On Plants and trees
- On Wildlife and Animals
- Eutrophication
- Respiratory and Heart problems
- Global Warming
- Acid Rain
- Depletion of Ozone layer

Plant dead from air pollution

13.4.1 Impact of Air Pollution on Plants

The most affected species on the earth due to the air pollution are plants, gardens and trees. Alas! They cannot even runaway from pollution, but for silently bearing the consequences.

The pollutants enter the plants and oxidize their tissues, leading to discoloration of leaves, which look like burnt or bleached. Similar problems can be caused by soot and other air pollution agents. The effect on the plants can be observed through

- Relatively fewer/ faded leaves and smaller roots.
- Reduced yield and/or drop earlier in the season than healthier plants do.
- Groundnut is one of the highly affected plants with pollution
- Plant dead from air Pollution

13.4.2 Effect on Wildlife and Animals

Animals are affected by air pollutants through three paths:

1. Nose-Inhalation of gases or small particles,
2. Mouth-Ingestion of suspended particles in food or water.

3. Skin-Absorption of gases.

Usually, invertebrates/ soft bodied (e.g. earthworms), or animals with thin, moist skin such as amphibians are most affected by the pollutants.

13.4.3 Eutrophication

The deposition of nitrogen compounds helps forest growth but leads to the chemical disruption of ecosystems on land and in sea that can ruin bio diversity. The following are main reasons of eutrophication.

- In fresh water environments eutrophication is almost always caused by phosphates, since phosphorous usually limits biological growth.
- On land and in the sea, nitrogen is the limiting factor in the majority of cases. The deposition of nitrogen-originating from emissions of nitrogen oxides and ammonia, acts as a fertilizer.
- Nitrate ends in the ground water where it causes problems in the production of portable water.

13.4.4 Effect on Human Health

Health effects on humans from common types of pollution.

The polluted air can kill many organisms including humans. The major effects of pollution on human health are listed below.

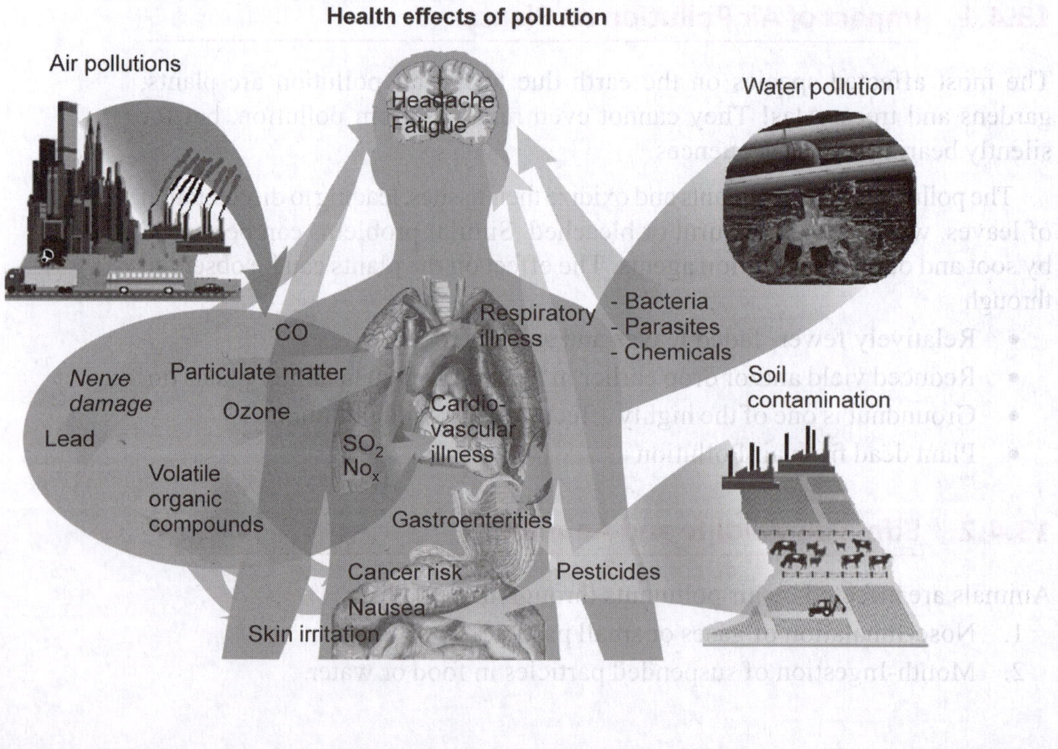

- Air (Ozone) pollution can cause respiratory disease, cardiovascular disease, throat inflammation, chest pain, and congestion.
- Heart and lungs are the parts of human body attacked by diseases induced by air pollution.
  - Older people and children are at major risk
  - Those with heart or lung disorders are at additional risk.
  - Lead and heavy metals cause neurological problems.
  - Mercury causes developmental deficits in children and neurologic symptoms.
- Noise pollution induces loss of hearing, high BP, stress and sleep disturb.
- Oil spills can cause skin irritations and rashes.
- Chemical and radioactive substances can cause cancer and as well as birth defects.
- Water pollution can cause several diseases to affect any part of the human body.

13.4.5 Effect on Environment

Pollution has a number of effects on environment a few are listed below;

- The emission of greenhouse gases leads to global warming, affects ecosystems in many ways.
- As CO_2 can dissolve, it can cause ocean acidification, decreasing the pH of Earth's oceans.
- SOx and NOx can cause acid rain which lowers the pH value of soil and reduces the yield.
- NOx removed from air by rain can also alter the species composition of ecosystem.
- Smog reduces the sunlight received by plants for photosynthesis and leads to the production of troposphere ozone which damages plants.
- The toxins such as heavy metals levels are increasing exponentially.
- Invasive plants can contribute debris and biomass that can spoil soil and its chemical compositions of an environment, often reducing native species competitiveness.

O My God!

Pollution is silent killer?

Pollution is killing humans silently. In developing countries, the contaminated drinking water is killing ~ 14,000 deaths/day. An estimated 500 million Indians have no access to a proper toilet. Over 10 million people in India fell with waterborne illnesses in 2013, and 1,535 died, most of them children. Nearly 500 million Chinese lack access to safe drinking water. In last decade about 1.2 million died prematurely each year in China due to air pollution. The WHO estimated in 2007 that air pollution causes ½ million deaths/yr in India. The pollution deaths annually in US are >50,000.

- Soil can become infertile and unsuitable for plants that affects other organisms in the food.

13.4.6 Effect on Worker Productivity

A number of studies show that pollution has an adverse effect on the productivity of both indoor and outdoor workers.

A litter trap catches floating waste in the Yarra River, east-central Victoria, Australia

13.5 AIR POLLUTION CONTROL

We know that the waste products from overconsumption, heating, agriculture, mining, manufacturing, transportation and other human activities, whether they accumulate or disperse, will degrade the environment. So, we need to control these, if not be stopped completely.

13.5.1 Pollution Control Activities

Pollution control involves activities and the efforts to control of emissions, pollutants and effluents into air, water or soil. In the hierarchy of controls, the following are the practices used.

- Recycling
- Reusing
- Waste minimisation
- Mitigating
- Preventing
- Compost

Air pollution control system, known as a Thermal oxidizer, decomposes hazard gases from industrial air streams at a factory in USA

13.5.2 Pollution Control Devices

The following equipment/ devices are popularly used for pollution control.

- Air pollution control
  - Thermal oxidizer
- Dust collection systems
  - Bag-houses
  - Cyclones
  - Electrostatic precipitators

A dust collector in Pristina, Kosovo

- Scrubbers
  - Baffle spray scrubber
  - Cyclonic spray scrubber
  - Ejector venturi scrubber
  - Mechanically aided scrubber
  - Spray tower
  - Wet scrubber
- Sewage treatment
  - Sedimentation (Primary treatment)
  - Activated sludge bio-treaters (Secondary treatment; also used for industrial wastewater)
  - Aerated lagoons
  - Constructed wetlands (also used for urban runoff)
- Industrial wastewater treatment
  - Oil-water separators
  - Bio-filters
  - Dissolved air flotation (DAF)
  - Powdered activated carbon treatment
  - Ultra-filtration
- Vapor recovery systems
- Phyto-remediation

Gas nozzle with vapor recovery

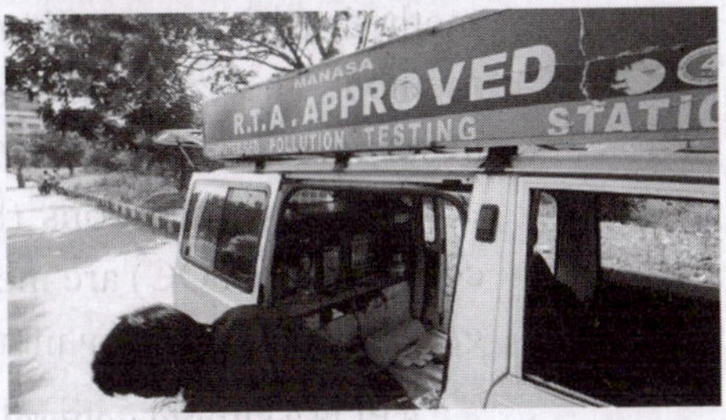

A Mobile Pollution Check Vehicle in India.

13.5.3 Air Pollution Measurement

The Air Pollution is measured using an Index value called Air Pollution Index (API) or Air Quality Index (AQI) based on the level of 6 atmospheric pollutants, namely sulphur dioxide (SO_2), nitrogen dioxide (NO_2), suspended particulate matter >10 im in aerodynamic diameter (PM_{10}), suspended particulate matter >2.5 im in aerodynamic diameter ($PM_{2.5}$), carbon monoxide (CO), and carbon dioxide (CO_2). Air quality measurement is commonly reported in terms of: micrograms per cubic meter ($\mu g/m^3$) or parts per million (ppm) or parts per billion (ppb).

The concentration of each individual component is measured by a specific method. SO_2 concentration is measured by the *ultraviolet fluorescence method,* where the analysed sample is exposed to UV-lamp irradiation with energetic excitation of SO_2 molecule. NO_x concentration is measured by *chemiluminescence analyzer/coulometric method* using the principle based on the nitrogen molecule excitation by ozone. The PM_{10} concentration is measured by, the *gravimetric* or *radiometric method* based on beta-ray absorption in a sample captured on filtering material. CO concentration is measured by *IR-correlation absorption spectrometry*, while Ozone concentration measurement is based on *UV absorption photometry*. The concentration of SO_4^{2-} in SPM is measured by *X-ray fluorescence (XRF)* method using paper filters while NH_3 and NH_4^+ are measured by Berthelot method. The *concentration of metals* in air can be analyzed by the *atomic absorption spectrometry (AAS)* while the amounts of other pollutants such as aromatic hydrocarbons (benzene, toluene, xylene etc.) or volatile organic compounds (VOC) are measured by BTX analyzers and suitable probes using *gas chromatography* methods.

API is a simple generalized way to describe the air quality and is computed by taking several sets of air pollution data. It was formerly used in China, Hong Kong and later Malaysia. In China the API was replaced by an updated Air Quality Index (AQI) in early 2012 and on 30 Dec 2013 Hong Kong changed to a health based index.

API scale is devised from zero to 500 and above, zero being no pollution and 500 indicates hazardous (shown in the adjacent table). If the API exceeds 500, a state of emergency is declared in the reporting area, which means - except for essential services, all services are suspended, including commercial, private, industrial activities in the reported area excluding the food sector.

API	Pollution Level	Effect	Color Code
0 - 50	Good	Minimal Impact	Green
51 - 100	Moderate	Minor Breath trouble to sensitive	Yellow
101 - 200	Unhealthy	Breath trouble to Asthma/Heart patients	Brownish Yellow
201 - 300	Very unhealthy	Breath trouble to most of people	Reddish Brown
301 - 400	Severe	Difficult to breath	Thick Brown
401-500	Hazardous	Respiratory illness	Dark Brown
500+	Emergency	Illness leading to death	Black

Like how temperature, humidity, and rainfall are measured, the pollution level is also measured by the meteorological (weather) department at a given area. For example, in India, Lucknow in November, 2017 reached hazardous level (408) while Delhi and nearby surrounding cities (Faridabad, Noida etc.)

including the north Indian cities such as Jodhpur, Varanasi, Agra recorded severe level (300^+), and the pollution level in south state capitals Bengaluru, Trivandrum, Chennai, and Hyderabad were below 100. The highest API value ever recorded was level 1,986 in Palangka Raya (Indonesia) on 22 Sep 2015.

13.5.4 Role of Individual and Society in Air Pollution Control and Self Control

The role of an individual is to assert himself as a leader of his fellow citizens by supporting the Air Pollution Control program. The participation of an educated citizenry in air pollution control is probably more important, because a human can live for days without food, and water but only a few minutes without air. Air is ubiquitous.

The several opportunities seem to be as follows:

1. As a common man, exhibit an exemplary attitude on air pollution control because 'Prevention avoids the need of cure' and 'Dilution is no solution to pollution'.
2. As an employer of a business and industry, one should motivate staff in pollution control cooperation.
3. As an employee of an organization, encourage and participate in programs leading to a better general understanding pollution control problems.
4. As an educated, interact with pollution control boards, and other volunteer groups supporting programs in execution.
5. Support the adoption and enforcement of appropriate ordinances of the state.

13.5.5 Regulation and Monitoring

To protect the environment from the adverse effects of pollution, many nations around the globe have enacted legislation to regulate various types of pollution as well as to mitigate the adverse effects of pollution. A separate wing ISO-14000 is established by International Organization for Standardization (ISO) to certify and look-after environmental related issues.

13.5.6 Greenhouse Gases and Global Warming

The two terms 'Greenhouse' and 'Global Warming' are often spoken almost every day by intellectual to laymen.

What is 'Greenhouse effect'?

How do the 'Green house gases' cause 'Global warming'?

Let us understand this first.

Greenhouse Gases

The mixtures of gases carbon dioxide, methane, and nitrous oxide emitted from natural sources into the air are called 'Greenhouse gases'. In fact, these are very much necessary to moderate the climate of the earth, helping to livelihood and survival. However, they can produce the greenhouse effect, leading to global warming and climate change.

The Sanskrit saying, '*Ati Sarvatra Varjayet*' means 'excess anywhere/ anything should be avoided'. This is applicable to nature also, may it be applied to good or bad, useful or useless things.

For example sugar tastes good, but excessive consumption causes diabetes. No food tastes good without salt, but higher levels result in hyper tension (High BP)

So also, carbon dioxide is vital for photosynthesis and is essential for life-cycle and ecosystem. But, excess or raised levels of CO_2 in the atmosphere affect the Earth's climate. Recent studies reveal the potential for long-term rising levels of atmospheric carbon dioxide to cause critical increases in the acidity of ocean waters, and the possible effects of this on marine ecosystems.

Global Warming

Greenhouse gases form a layer of reflective and absorbent materials in the atmosphere that prevent some of the heat radiated by the sun, thence keep environment sufficiently warm for plant and animal life to survive. However, with the addition of manmade greenhouse gases, too much heat can be reflected back into the atmosphere, giving rise to the current fears what is known as 'Global warming'.

Effects of Greenhouse Gases Given an Oblique Global Warming

Greenhouse gases lead to a variety of detrimental environmental effects. A few of these are

- increased force and severity of hurricanes/ cyclones, and tropical storms,
- increased frequency of storms and storm activity,

- the melting of polar ice,
- raising ocean levels,
- flooding costal and other low lying areas,
- severely altered ecosystems,
- extinctions of plant and animal species,
- increase the probability of acid rains,
- lowering the pH of oceans and thence affecting the oceanic ecosystem and aquatic life.

O My God!

Acid Rain pH<5.2?

The chemical nature of substances is classified under one of the 3 categories as acidic or neutral or basic, which is measured by the Hydrogen ion [H^+] concentration. The pH scale devised by Sorenson, is the logarithm of the H^+ concentration that directly determines the acidic/ basic level of a substance. The pH is of the range 0 to 14. A pH< 7 is acidic while >7 are basic. The pH values near to 7 are considered to be very weak and =7 is neutral. The rain water having pH value <5.2 generally is considered to be as acid rain.

SELF ASSESSMENT INTERMISSION (SAI – 13.3)

1. Discuss the effect of air pollution on plants and animals.
2. Explain the impact of air contamination on plants.
3. How are forests and forest floor affected by air pollution?
4. Describe the effect of air pollution on environment.
5. Explain the impact of air pollution on humans.
6. List out various pollution control devices.
7. How is air pollution measured? Explain.
8. What is air pollution index? Explain how it indicates air quality.
9. What do you understand by 'Greenhouse effect' and 'Global Warming'? Discuss.
10. What are greenhouse gases? What are its effects?
11. Explain the role of individuals in controlling air pollution.
12. Write short notes on the air pollution caused by the following.
    (a) Eutrophication (b) Solid waste Vs. Air Pollution (c) Global Warming

13.6 ACID RAINS

Acid rains are yet another type of exogenous disasters occurs from the clouds above atmosphere. As per records, the term 'acid rain' was first introduced in 1872 by Scottish chemist Robert Angus Smith who noticed this phenomenon during his investigation of rain water chemistry near industrial cities in England and Scotland.

Definition

Acid rain is a rain or any other form of precipitation that is more acidic than it should be.

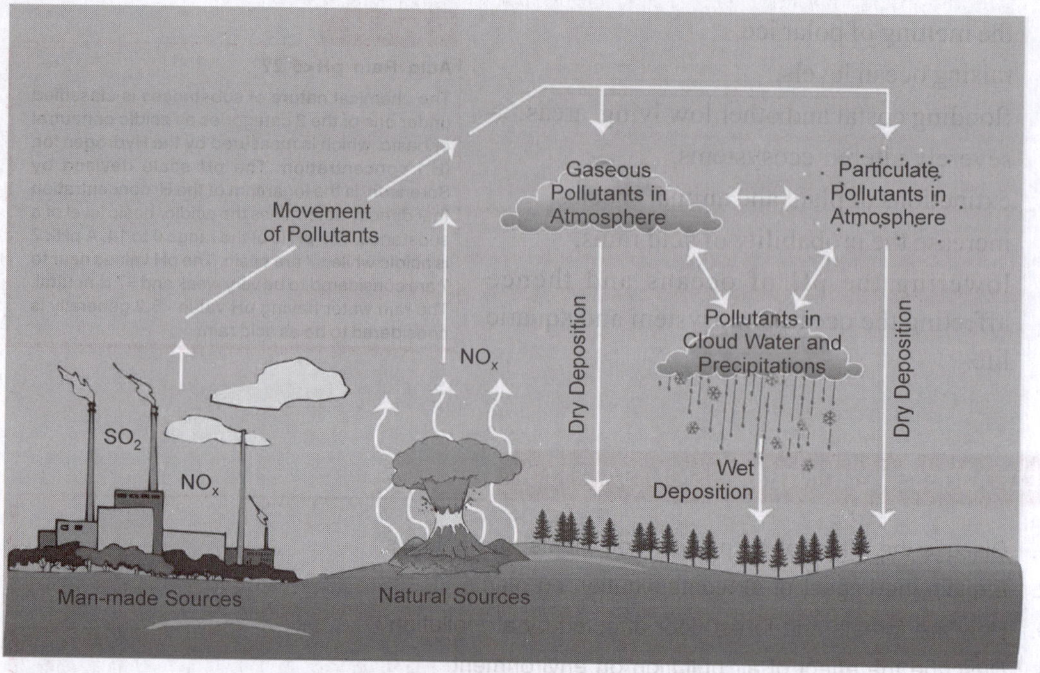

13.6.1 Causes for Acid Rains

Acid rain may occur categorically via two ways viz. natural causes or manmade causes. These are briefed out here below:

Natural Causes

- When a thunderstorm produces lightning, Nitrogen and Oxygen of air react due to the extreme heating of air to form Oxides of Nitrogen (NOx). These oxides mix with rain water and turn to be an acid rain.
- Sulphur dioxide (sulphur burnt) is discharged from erupted volcanoes and rotten vegetation produces sulphurous acid on mixing with rain water or moisture in air and thence the acid rain.

Manmade Causes

Some fuels contain Nitrogen and Sulphur compounds, such as the fuels derived out of public utilities, industrial boilers, motor vehicles and chemical plants etc. When such fuels are burnt, they go into the air and can dome as acid rain.

13.6.2 The Acid Precipitation Process

As known from the hydrological cycle, water goes up through the air from streams, lakes, oceans, and water bodies of troposphere and atmosphere. Water

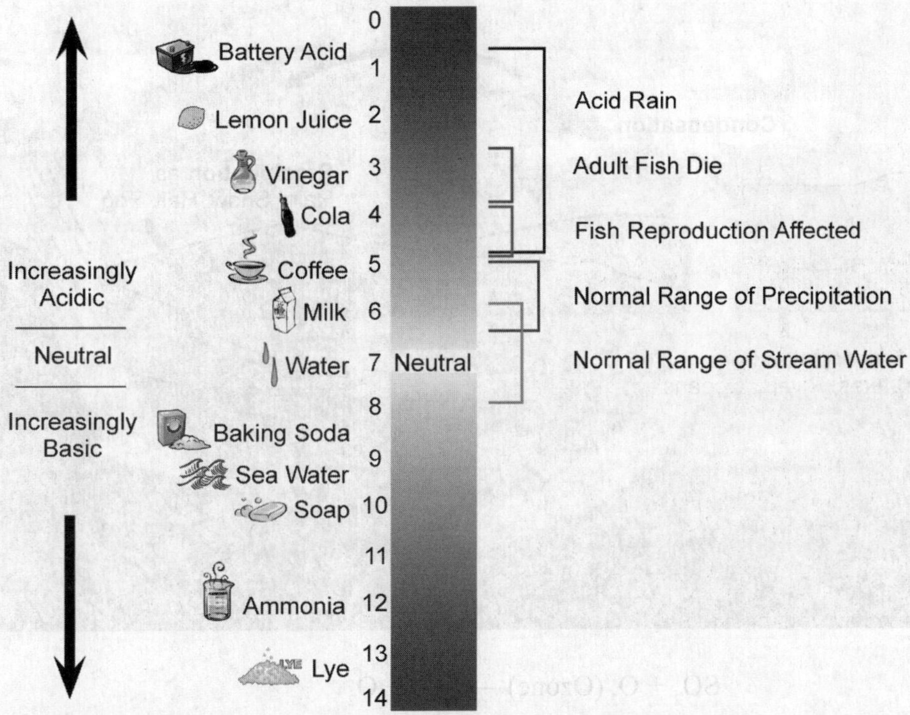

thus went, condenses to form into clouds which release back to the earth in the form of rain, sleet, hail, snow or fog. Even clean and unpolluted air may contain dust particles along with carbon dioxide in minute quantities. The interaction between the water droplets and the CO_2 in the atmosphere could make the rain slightly acidic up to the pH 5.6.

An acid rain can also occur when the rain in the air gets polluted by the pollutants such as

- sulphur dioxide (SO_2),
- carbon dioxide (CO_2),
- nitrogen oxides (NO_x), and
- the bi-products from
  - burning fuels in electric appliances and
  - other industrial and/or natural sources in the atmosphere.

These chemicals react with atmospheric water, oxygen, carbon dioxide, under sunlight to produce acids in rain water. The following reactions are expected to occur.

$SO_2 + H_2O \rightarrow H_2SO_3$ (Sulphurous acid)

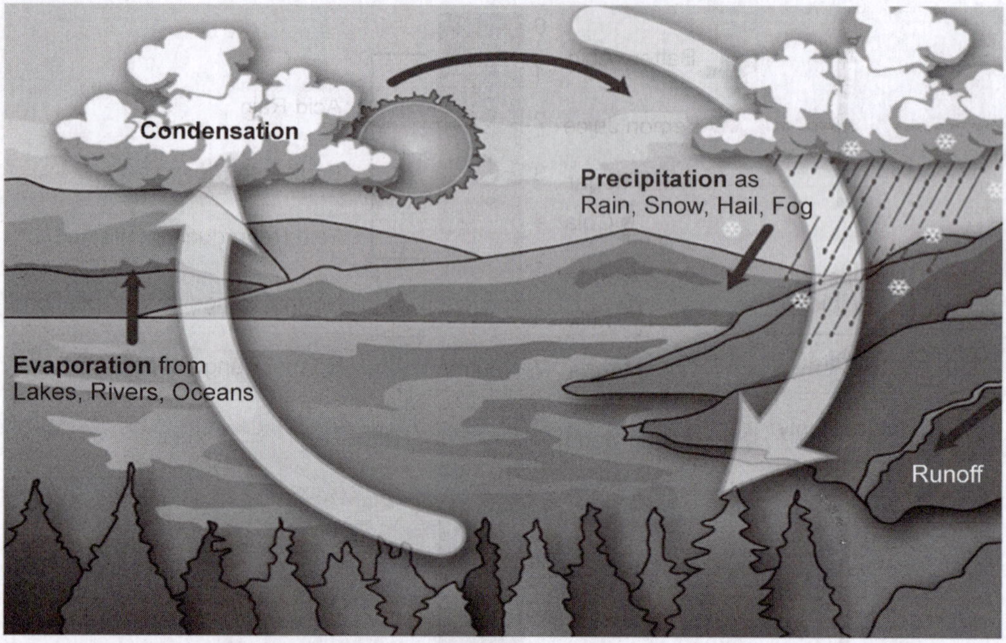

$$SO_2 + O_3\ (\text{Ozone}) \rightarrow SO_3 + O_2$$

$$SO_3 + H_2O \rightarrow H_2SO_4\ (\text{Sulphuric acid})$$

$N_2 + O_2 \rightarrow 2NO$ (when lightning occurs)

$2NO + O_2 \rightarrow 2NO_2$

$NO_2 + O_2 \rightarrow NO + O_3$ (Ozone) or/and

$2NO_2 + H_2O \rightarrow HNO_3$ (Nitric acid) + HNO_2 (Nitrous acid)

The sulphuric acid and nitric acid exist in vapour state when the temperature is high. And when the condensation starts with the fall of temperature, they mix with the rain, fog or snow and thence the acidity increases.

13.7 EFFECTS OF ACID RAIN

Of course, the chemical reactions that cause acid rains take several hours to occur because winds take away these pollutants for 100's of kilometres before they react with water drops. Owing to this reason, the areas far away from the sources of pollution are also affected. The effects acid rains are multi-fold. Among them, some are described below.

13.7.1 Effect on Ecosystems

An ecosystem is all the interactions among the living and nonliving things of all sizes in an area of interest. An ecosystem may be considered as a single tree or entire forest or even entire Earth. Ecology is the study of ecosystems.

All the elements of ecosystem are interconnected, and interactive. Thence, there is a huge interdependence among the organisms. For instance, the acid rain falling on an agricultural land affects the soil and results in the crop failure or burn off causing the food scarcity to humans and cattle. Thus entire system is affected. Therefore, even though acid rain may damage a few organisms in an ecosystem, others may be indirectly affected and the damage caused may take years, or even decades to reverse or recover.

13.7.2 Effect on Forests

Though forests are part of the ecosystem, they need a special mention here as the acid rains directly affect the plants, the primary producers in the ecosystem as a whole. Primary producers are organisms that produce their own food and energy through photosynthesis by making sugars using water and sunlight. Thus the green plants having this ability would become vital to ecosystems as they feed everything else, and provide habitat for other animals and hence have significant role to play.

Acid rain can damage and/or decrease the growth of trees in forests including some sensitive once. (Red Spruce and Sugar Maple, two species of trees found mainly in the East and in New England, are very susceptible to acid rain damage). Acid rain reacts with the minerals to dissolve such as calcium, zinc and magnesium in the soil and in the leaves of trees which are essential for growth of the trees. Further after dissolving, the rain washes away these and thence the trees and plants cannot grow. In addition, the acid rain takes away other minerals and nutrients also from the soil in a similar way, causing nutrient deficient and hence weakens the trees, which in turn and makes them more sensitive to the cold, vulnerable to insects and susceptible diseases. In fact, a well-nourished tree in healthy soil can survive in a very cold winter with difficulty, but a tree already weakened by a mineral/ nutrient deficiency dies during a cold winter.

Moreover, the acid rains liberate the substances like aluminium from the soil that harms the trees and plants, and even can kill fish. The pollution (smog) also reduces the amount of light available for plants to use in photosynthesis, the base of the food chain. Acid fogs are more damagers since the fog can wear away the protective waxy coating on the leaves causing brown spots and making them incapable to photosynthesis.

13.7.3 Effect on Forest Floor and Agricultural Land

Yet another direct effect of acid rains can be observed on forest or agricultural soils. A spring shower in the forest washes leaves and the rain falls through the trees to the forest floor below. Some of this water soaks into the soil while some seeps over the ground and some run into a stream, river, or lake.

Some salts in soil may also act as buffers that resist changes in pH. This ability of the soil to resist pH change is known as buffering capacity. Without buffering capacity, soil pH would change rapidly. Further, the natural sources of acids in forest soils make the soils more sensitive.

pH Toolerance Chart on Aquatic Life

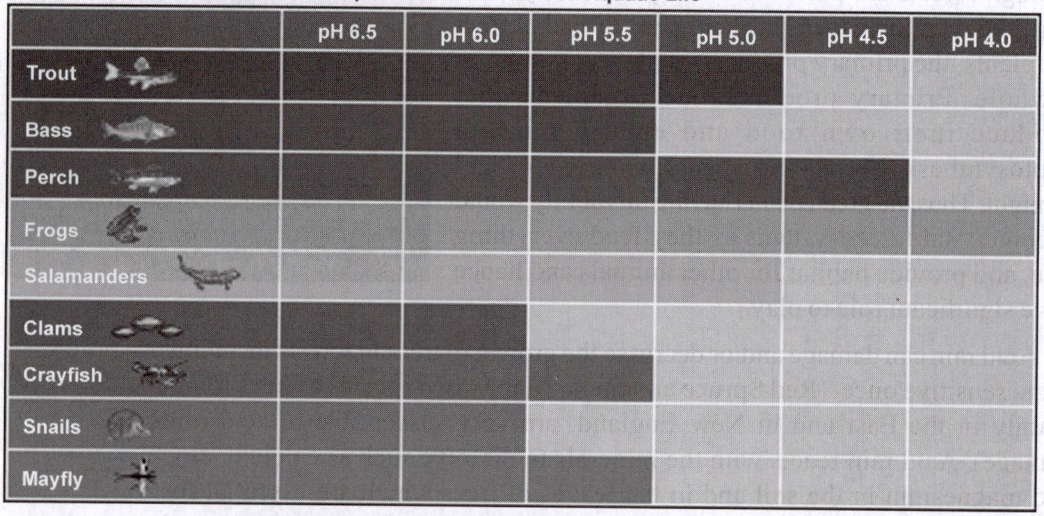

13.7.4 Effect on Ponds, Lakes and Streams

The impacts of acid rains are more clearly visible in aquatic environments such as streams, lakes, and marshes. Forests, fields, buildings, and/or roads, where so ever the rainfall may be, they flow to streams, lakes, and marshes, (Or the rain also may fall directly on aquatic habitats).

Usually, most lakes and streams have a pH between 6 and 8, which may be considered as almost neutral or very weak (negligible) acid or base. The buffering capacity of soil generally neutralizes slightly acidic, clean rain.

Now, if lakes/ streams are already weakly acidic, then acid rain makes it more acidic i.e. the pH value comes so down that even the surrounding soil cannot buffer the rain enough to neutralize it.

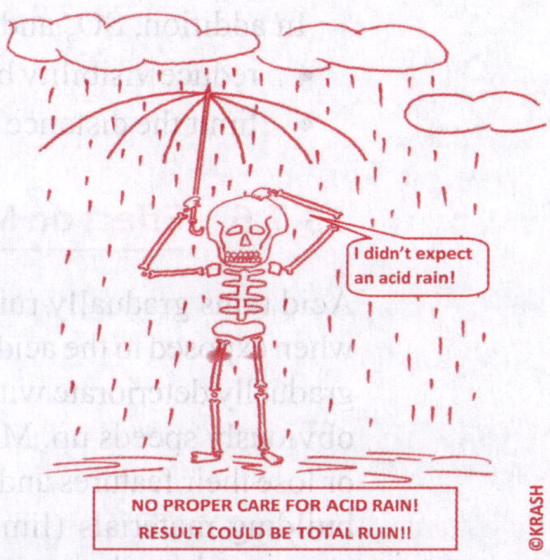

In the lakes with poor in buffering capacity and/ or naturally acidic (even without acid rain), the fish and other aquatic plants and animals cannot survive. At pH 5 most fish eggs cannot hatch. Further, the substances like aluminium flowing into water from the soil can also harm and kill fish. However, some species of plants and animals are able to tolerate acidic waters.

13.7.5 Effect on Humans

Acid Rain is the major cause for the Gradual change in the color of the Taj Mahal's white marble

Acid rain cannot be easily differentiated from clean rain because both look, feel and taste same. Walking is so easy in acid rain just like in a clean rain without any problem. Even swimming in an acid lake also feels as similar as in clean water. What is more dangerous is inhaling the air that contains the pollutants that cause acid rain. In fact, the acidic oxides like sulphur dioxide (SO_2), nitrogen oxides (NOx), particulate matter, and ozone irritate or even damage human lungs. Particularly, these effects are more serious, hazardous and highly vulnerable to children, old-aged and to those already affected by respiratory illness.

Ozone and particulate matter are dangerous pollutants for respiratory system, particularly in the summer. The following effects can occur with exposure to ozone.

- respiratory illnesses, such as asthma, emphysema etc.,
- worsen bronchitis,
- reduced resistance to bacterial/ viral infections,
- coughing,
- chest pain with
  - deep breathing,
  - chest tightness, and
  - shortness of breath,
- permanent damage to the lungs or
- breathlessness and/or death

In addition, SO_2 and NO_X can affect vision. These can

- reduce visibility by scattering light
- limit the distance of vision (far-vision)

13.7.6 Effect on Manmade Materials

Acid rains gradually ruin any material even a stone, metal, paint and so forth, when exposed to the acidic weather in a long run. Generally, man-made materials gradually deteriorate with rains even unpolluted, and if it is acid rain, the process obviously speeds up. Metals rust, stones get eroded, marble statues fade away or lose their features and so forth, because most of the stones including marbles, building materials (limestone, cement, bricks etc.) are made up of metallic compounds such as calcium carbonate, which can react or dissolve in acidic medium. Many buildings and monuments are hence get damaged to irreparable state or prohibitively expensive to regain as original ones. It is impossible to get back the historical monuments such as the Tajmahal in Agra, Lincoln Memorial in Washington, D.C. etc., which are fading away due to acidic environment.

13.7.7 Control Measures

Many possible solutions are available to prevent and/or control acid rains; a few among them are given below:

Burning coal thoroughly: This has double advantage. It greatly reduces air pollution, thereby lessening the possibilities of developing acid rain atmosphere on one hand and utilization of fuels to their full extent burning, thence raising the efficiency and productivity.

- **Scrubbers:** As the industrial power plants are the chief contributors to develop the acidic environment (produce acidified water droplets in the atmosphere), the devices called, 'scrubbers' have to be arranged in the chimneys, which can absorb smoke and acidic fumes. This would control the air pollution from sulphur up to 95%. Further, this equipment along with the chimneys and exhaust pipes should be inspected at regular intervals and serviced.
- **Implementation and Compliance of Standards:** The emission standards must be made mandatory and strictly implemented on all the vehicles and cars. Further, fitting catalytic converters into the exhaust pipes of vehicles is advisable to reduce the amount of SO_2 produced by the vehicles.
- **Educating the People:** Remember! All these acid rain solutions would be fruitful when and only when the people are educated and the awareness about the ill-effects and harms of acid rain is given. So, a

widespread awareness programs are made nationwide through discussions, seminars, demonstrations etc.

- **Self Control by Individuals:** The acid rain solutions find a good rate of success if every individual gets a feel of responsibility toward the control of the acidic environment actually.

13.7.8 Role of Individuals

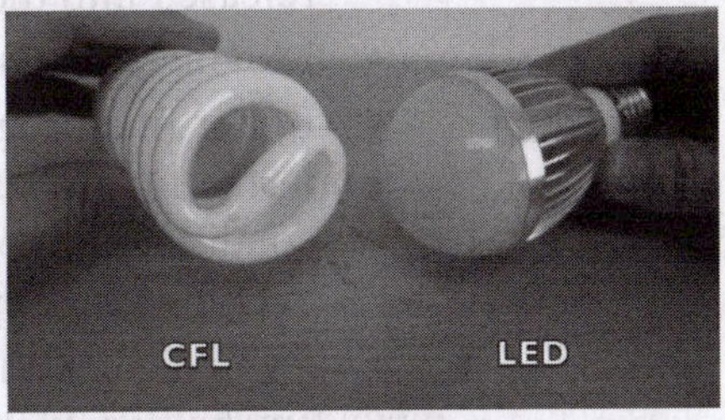

CFL/LED Bulbs

1. Optimizing (Reducing) Fuel Consumption

- One of the major reasons for acid deposition is attributed to consumption of fossil fuel, which is used for energy generation, heating, and transportation. One good idea to reduce acid deposition is to save energy by turning off lights, appliances, electronics, and other devices whenever they are not in use, and use only when they are really required. Even when they are turned off, electronic devices still consume trace amounts of power. Therefore, when you leave the house for a long period of time, it is better turning off and unplugging the electronic devices and appliances. This not only reduces the power bills for an individual, but also reduces the demand and thereby reduces the pollutive/ acidic environment.
- When it is time to replace older appliances – such as the refrigerator, washer, dryer, furnace, air conditioner, and dish washer – upgrade to energy efficient ones. Energy-efficient appliances reduce not only your energy (electricity) consumption bills but also the probabilities of acid rain. The following tips may help in this direction.
  - Ask for the Energy Star logo on a product that ensures that the product is energy-efficient.
  - Replace burnt out incandescent bulbs/ tubes/ fans with Light Emitting Diode (LED) or at least with compact fluorescent lamps (CFL) systems (bulbs/tubes/fans).
  - Purchase new appliances based on exact household needs but not for prestige. For instance, when you have to replace refrigerator, buy one that is sized properly for the space, energy saving and your consumption pattern, but not a bigger one for the show off. Similarly, only required number of bulbs may be arranged outside the house, instead of many/ high consuming bulbs.
- Reducing energy usage is yet another way, which can be achieved by adding extra insulation for walls, attic and basement, and putting weather stripping around windows and doors etc.

- Not only is it great to add plants and trees to the planet absorb carbon dioxide (CO_2), but grows food and also further reduce dependence on the fossil fuels associated with food transportation.
- Trucks, planes, cars, trains and boats that are powered by fossil fuels are big contributors to SO_2 and NO_X that cause acid deposition. By marketing locally can control the transportation-related acid rain emissions released into the atmosphere.
- Moving away from gas appliances is a direct way to reduce acid rain.
- Better fit a programmable thermostat that can save money and energy in the long run. It can be preset on a timer such that the heat or air-conditioning does not run if nobody is at home, and turns off when everyone is sleeping.
- Avoid or ban the use of rubber and plastics. To reduce plastics, don't buy bottled water, invest in reusable shopping bags, purchase food items in bulk, opt for items that are packaged in glass or earthen instead of plastic, and support companies that limit their packaging.
- May not be affordable to everyone to use an electric car, but can change driving habits to use less fuel. Green driving habits include:
  - Keeping the air pressure in your vehicle tyres at the proper level.
  - Braking and accelerating gradually.
  - Using the air-conditioning sparingly.
  - Roll down the windows instead to conserve gas.
- By and large the acid rain emissions are caused during power generation because, while power is used the gas or coal used in the devices contribute to acid rain. Feeling the responsibility towards the society, one can mitigate this impact by using less power, some of which are exemplified below:
  - Natural drying of clothes instead of using a drier.
  - Washing clothes and dishes by hand instead of using washing machine or dish water.
  - All family members can have breakfast/lunch/dinner together instead of one at time
  - Using Air Conditioners sparingly, whenever really essential.
  - Reading a book instead of watching television or playing on the computer.
  - Cooking multiple meals or multiple batches of food at a time.

2. Using Alternative Energy and Transportation

- The majority of the world's energy comes from fossil fuels— in the form of natural gas, coal, and oil—but there are companies focus exclusively on providing energy from renewable sources. (Renewable energies: nuclear, hydropower, solar and wind, geothermal).

- Whatsoever the kind of car you have, consume less fuel and less energy as far as possible. There are plenty of public transit options available in many cities, including buses and trains. Or, consider starting a carpool group with people to your work place or travel with often.
- You can completely eliminate your need for transportation-related emissions by getting around on foot, a bike, rollerblades, or even a skateboard. Let our own body power our movements, and our health and the environment will appreciate the effort.
- Of course, it may not be possible for switching to a green energy provider, but still can reduce the dependence on energy-related fossil fuels. Small wind turbines can be installed in a backyard, or you can install solar panels on your roof to generate electricity for personal use.
- Prefer to buy car powered by an electric or solar or hybrid that has low-emission. This can reduce fossil fuel use and help reduce acid rain.
  - Another option that is cheaper than buying a new car is converting existing one to propane (though it is a fossil fuel, it doesn't emit the acid-rain causing pollutants).
  - If it's not feasible to buy a new car or convert to propane, maintain car properly and make sure of its emission is within the limits.

3. Encouraging and Educating Others

- **Write to industry leaders and government:** Let your government know how you feel about acid rain, and tell them if you think they should be doing more. You can even petition industry leaders and business owners if you feel they could be doing a better job of cleaning up their acts. Suggest the government to give wide publicity and educate through news-papers and electronic media including Radio and TV in the interest of public welfare. For industries that do contribute lots of sulphur dioxide and nitrogen oxides into the atmosphere, explain to them and governments to regulate by ensuring:
  - Using chemical scrubbers to remove pollutants from their smokestacks.
  - Seeking out alternative fuels.
  - Switching to green technologies that don't require fossil fuels.
- **Get your family involved:** Tell them why this issue is important to you and why it should be important to them by explaining what kinds of impacts acid rain can have on the environment and our future.
  - Motivate your family to adopt the same eco-friendly practices such as reducing energy consumption, replacing light bulbs with CFL/LED, and minimizing the use of electronics and appliances.
  - When it comes to transportation, explain how their pocketbooks or notes (and waistlines) can help them for being more active.

- **Inform others:** Explain to those who're willing to listen, including friends, coworkers, and schoolmates that acid rains damage lakes, streams, soils, forests, and the plants and animals those live in those ecosystems. Tell them that acid deposition also causes the premature decay of buildings, homes, and works of art, and has a negative impact on human health and animal life.
    - Use social media such as Whatsapp, Short Message Services (SMS), imo, twitter, e-mails etc. and send the messages, related articles or short video clips etc. to bring the awareness.
    - Tell other people about the steps you've taken to reduce acid rain, and show them how easy it can be for them to adopt some of those same practices.
    - Universities and educational institutions should adopt a policy or a programme of educating at least ten people in a village and submit a report on this as a mini project or at least as a camp under National Service Scheme or National Swayam Sevak (NSS) activities.

SELF ASSESSMENT INTERMISSION (SAI – 13.4)

1. What is an acid rain? Explain.
2. Describe the acid precipitation process during acid rain.
3. Explain how air contamination can produce acid rain.
4. What are the causes of acid rains?
5. How are agricultural lands, forests and forest floor affected by acid rain?
6. Describe the effect of acid rain on environment and eco-system.
7. Explain the impact of acid rains on humans and manmade materials/ monuments.
8. What is the effect of acid rains on lakes, ponds and water bodies?
9. Discuss the role of each individual in preventing/ controlling acid rains.
10. Enumerate various control measures to reducing/ preventing acid rains.
11. How is acid rain measured?

Raw sewage and industrial waste in the New River as it passes from Mexicali to Calexico, California

13.8 WATER POLLUTION

Water pollution is the contamination of water bodies of any form such as streams, rivers, wells, ponds, lakes, seas, oceans, aquifers and groundwater. This environmental degradation occurs when pollutants directly or indirectly enter bodies without adequate treatment to remove harmful compounds.

Water is referred to as polluted when it is spoiled by anthropogenic contaminants and either does not support a human use for drinking, or unable to support biotic communities, such as fish. Natural pheno men a such as volcanoes, algae blooms, storms and earth quakes/ tsunamis also can cause major changes in water quality and ecological status.

Water pollution affects the entire biosphere. Plants, birds, animals and humans cannot live without these bodies of water. If this water is contaminated, the survival of any biological species is difficult.

Needless to say that water pollution is a global issue that needs to be viewed seriously. It requires ongoing evaluation and revision of water resource policy at all levels right from individual aquifers and wells to international level oceans. The water pollution is the worldwide leading cause of deaths and diseases.

Pollution in the Lachine Canal, Canada

O My God!

It is estimated that >14,000 deaths are occurring daily in the world, while in India 580 people die of water pollution related illness every day. About 90% of the water in the cities of China is polluted, as of 2007, half a billion Chinese had no access to safe drinking water. In addition to developing countries, developed countries also struggle with pollution problems. Recent national report in US, 44% of stream miles, 64% of lake acres, and 30% of bays and estuarine sq. miles were polluted. In 2007 that ¼th length of China's 7 main rivers were so poisoned the water harmed the skin.

13.8.1 Resources of Water and Sources of Pollution

Water resources are broadly classified as Surface water and groundwater, which are interrelated. The seepage of surface water through the soil and becomes groundwater. Conversely, groundwater can also feed surface water sources. Through the view point of the source and origin, the surface water pollutions are studied by categorizing into two types Viz. Point source and Nonpoint source.

- ***Point Sources (PS) Water Pollution:*** If contaminants enter a waterway from a single, identifiable source, such as a pipe or ditch, it is called point source water pollution. For examples, discharge from a sewage treatment plant, a factory, or a city storm drain.
- ***Non-Point Sources (NPS) Water Pollution:*** If contamination does not originate from a single discrete source, but from many points, it is called nonpoint source (NPS) water pollution. NPS pollution is often the cumulative effect of small amounts of contaminants gathered from a large area. Examples include runoffs in storm water over an agricultural field or a forest, leaching out of nitrogen compounds from fertilized agricultural lands.

The storm water gets contaminated while washing off of parking lots, roads and highways, (often called urban runoff), is sometimes classed under NPS pollution. However, usually this runoff is typically channeled into storm drain systems and discharged through pipes to local surface waters, whence it becomes a point source.

Point source pollution at a shipyard in Rio de Janeiro, Brazil.

Groundwater Pollution: Groundwater pollution cannot as easily be classified as surface water pollution because by its very nature, groundwater aquifers are vulnerable to pollution by several sources. Moreover, the interactions between groundwater and surface water are complex. So, the distinction of point vs. non-point source seems to be meaningless. For example, a spill or chemical or radio-nuclide contaminants into soil may not create point or non-point source pollution but can still contaminate. Further, the hydrological transport is another source of groundwater contamination and also depends on soil characteristics and site geology, hydrogeology, hydrology, and the nature of the contaminants.

A manhole cover unable to control a sanitary sewer overflow

Human activities leading to the pollution of water sources

13.9 CAUSES FOR WATER POLLUTION

The water pollution is mainly caused due to

- Chemicals
- Pathogens
- Physical changes
- Thermal effects
- Macroscopic materials (Floatables)

The above causes are interrelated and interdependent and interactive also. Some even appear in two or more classes. For instance, the plant leaves and grass etc. may be assumed as a chemicals as well as macroscopic contaminants. Similarly, certain pathogenic contaminants may be chemicals too and some chemicals react to produce thermal pollution or a physical change or a secondary effect.

These are elaborated through the following paragraphs.

13.9.1 Water Pollution by Chemicals

Many of the chemicals and substances that lead to water contamination naturally occur such as calcium, sodium, iron, manganese, etc. Higher concentrations of naturally occurring substances can have negative impacts on aquatic ecology. So, the concentration is the key in determining if it is a natural component or a contaminant. But not to forget that many of the chemical substances even in small concentrations are toxic and reactive to form new hazardous substances.

The chlorinated hydrocarbons are best examples to describe the effect of reacting chemicals. The trichloroethylene (used in industrial metal degreasing and electronics manufacturing) and tetra-chloro-ethylene are used in the dry cleaning industry. Both of these chemicals undergo partial decomposition reactions, leading to new hazardous chemicals like dichloro ethylene and vinyl chloride.

Yet other types of chemicals are oxygen-depleting substances, which may be either natural materials such as plant matter (e.g. leaves and grass) or man-made chemicals. The natural and anthropogenic substances may cause turbidity (cloudiness) in still water bodies, which blocks light and disrupts plant growth and clogs the gills of some fish species, while cause congestion or obstruction to the flow of water in streams in addition to polluting the water.

Further, there are a variety of secondary effects not from the original pollutant, but a derivative condition. For example silt-bearing surface runoff can obstruct the sunlight hampering photosynthesis in aquatic plants.

13.9.2 Water Pollution due to Physical Changes

The physical chemistry of water may be changed which can make the water body unusable. The physical changes in waters may occur by

- Eutrophication
- Human wastes, drainage mixing
- Change in pH value,
- Acid rains,
- Discoloration,
- Temperature

Eutrophication (refer: article 13.4.3 in this chapter) is an increase in the concentration of chemical nutrients in an ecosystem to an extent that increases the primary productivity of the ecosystem. The degree of eutrophication, determines the consequent adverse environmental effects such as anoxia (oxygen depletion) and also the reductions in water quality affecting aquatic and animal populations. All the above factors are already explained in the above paragraphs of this chapter. Therefore it is felt redundant.

13.9.3 Water Pollution by Thermal Effects

Thermal pollution is the change in temperature of a natural water bodies influenced by humans. A common cause of thermal pollution can be mainly attributed to the usage of water as a coolant in power plants and industrial manufacturers.

Thermal pollution varies the physical properties of water. The higher temperatures of water lowers oxygen levels, and hence suffocate aquatic life, vary food chain composition, lows down species biodiversity, and even invades new thermophilic species.

At occasions the urban runoff may also increase temperature in surface waters. Interestingly, the thermal pollution can also be resulted by the release of very cold water from the base of reservoirs into warmer rivers.

13.9.4 Water Pollution by Pathogens

Disease-causing microorganisms are called pathogens that can produce waterborne diseases in either human or animal hosts.

In fact, only a few pathogenic bacteria cause diseases and the vast majority of bacteria are either harmless or beneficial. Coliform bacteria, which are not an actual cause of disease, are often used as a bacterial indicator of water pollution. The common microorganisms, we come across in surface waters that affect human health are:

- *Burkholderia or Bacillus pseudomallei (causes melioidosis in humans, animals and plants)*
- *Cryptosporidium parvum (causes diarrhoea, cryptosporidiosis, intestinal infections)*
- *Giardia lamblia (causes intestinal infection, giardiasis)*

- *Salmonella (causes typhoid, diarrhoea)*
- *Norovirus and other viruses (cause Vomiting, gastroenteritis)*
- *Parasitic worms including the Schistosoma type (cause blood flukes, pains, worms in stomach)*

High levels of pathogens are due to

- poor sanitation systems (septic tanks, pit latrines)
- inadequately treated sewage discharges
- leakage in infrastructures (pipes, pumps, valves)
- overflows of discharges of untreated sewage during rain storms
- Silt (sediment) from sewage discharges
- poorly managed livestock operations.

13.9.5 Water Pollution due to Macroscopic Materials

Macroscopic pollution is caused by large visible items polluting the water, often termed as "floatables" usually found in urban storm water or marine debris on the open seas. This pollution is caused due to trash or garbage (e.g. paper, plastic, or food waste) irresponsibly discarded by people on the ground or into water bodies or streams or even drainages. Of course, it may be accidental or intentional dumping of rubbish, that are washed by rainfall into storm drains and eventually discharged into surface waters, but they cause lot of inconvenience to others as well as clogging/ chocking the free flow of streams besides being polluting water body. Small ubiquitous waterborne plastic pellets and shipwrecks, large derelict ships etc. are yet other classed pollutants under this category. The contaminants may be organic and inorganic substances. Some common macroscopic contaminants are listed below (the list is not exhaustive)

Common Organic Water Pollutants

- Food waste and packaging materials such as plastic covers, wrappers etc.
- Chemical compounds found in personal hygiene and cosmetic products
- Insecticides and herbicides, organohalides and other organic compounds
- Petroleum hydrocarbons, including fuels (gasoline, diesel fuel, jet fuels, and fuel oil)
- Fats and grease including oxygen-demanding substances
- Lubricants (motor oil), and fuel combustion by-products, from storm water runoff

- Disincentive by-products found in chemically disinfected drinking water, such as chloroform
- Volatile organic compounds, such as industrial solvents due to improper storage
- Drug pollution involving pharmaceutical drugs and their metabolites
- Chlorinated solvents are dense and so, go down to the bottom of reservoirs and generally are not miscible with water. Examples are listed below.
    - Polychlorinated biphenyl (PCBs)
    - Trichloroethylene
    - Tetra chloro ethylene
    - Vinyl chloride

Common Inorganic Water Pollutants

- Acidity caused by industrial discharges (e.g. sulphur dioxide from power plants)
- Fertilizers containing nutrients - nitrates and phosphates in storm water runoff from agriculture, as well as commercial and residential use
- Heavy metals from motor vehicles (through urban runoff) and acid mine drainage
- Silt (sediment) in runoff from construction sites, logging, slash etc.
- Packing materials, packets, tins, boxes, mutilated covers etc.
- Detergents and soapy froth from run off
- Ammonia from food processing waste
- Chemical waste as industrial by-products
- Secretions of the aquatic ecosystem
- Ashes from poor burn practices
- Remains of land clearing sites
- Ship wrecks, derelict ships

13.10 MEASUREMENT AND CONTROL OF WATER POLLUTION

Water pollution may be analyzed through several methods: physical, chemical and biological. The samples collected are tested analytically in laboratory while some methods may be conducted *in situ*, without sampling, such as temperature. Government agencies and research organizations have published standardized, validated analytical test methods.

13.10.1 Physical Testing

Common physical tests of water include temperature; solids concentrations e.g., total suspended solids (TSS) and turbidity.

13.10.2 Chemical Testing

Water samples may be tested using the principles of analytical chemistry. Commonly used methods are the tests for pH, biochemical oxygen demand (BOD), chemical oxygen demand (COD), nutrients (nitrate and phosphorus compounds), metals (including copper, zinc, cadmium, lead and mercury), oil and grease, total petroleum hydrocarbons (TPH), and pesticides.

13.10.3 Biological Testing

Biological testing involves the use of plant, animal or microbial indicators to monitor the health of an aquatic ecosystem.

In case the water is suspected to cause any outbreak or found to be serious pathogenic contamination or can be disastrous otherwise, then a disaster manager needs to perform the following activities:

- Outline the risk factors for outbreaks after a disaster,
- Review the communicable diseases likely to occur,
- Prioritize to address communicable diseases in disaster settings,
- Put all the efforts to prevent,
- Bring awareness in the people,
- Use mitigation methods to overcome.

13.11 CONTROL OF WATER POLLUTION

Controlling water pollution requires understanding both technical and environmental factors in relation to the causes and effects of water pollution. The following are some aspects to be considered while taking decisions of pollution control.

- the type and degree of treatment
- the controllability of wastes
- the disposal methods
- the use of adequately treated wastewater
- the technical factors of each drainage basin (dimension/ run off/ flow rate/ capacity)

- the amount and probability of contamination
- the level of harm to the environment.

13.11.1 Controls at Sewage Treatment

Deer Island Wastewater Treatment Plant serving Boston, Massachusetts.

In developed countries, domestic sewage is treated by centralized sewage treatment plants. Some plants have additional systems to remove nutrients and pathogens. The following points help better control:

- utilizing a green infrastructure approach to improve storm water management capacity throughout the system, and reduce the hydraulic overloading of the treatment plant
- repair and replacement of leaking and malfunctioning equipment
- ensuring overall hydraulic capacity of the sewage collection system

A house or business may have an individual septic tank, if not served by a municipal treatment plant that pre-treats the wastewater on site and infiltrates it into the soil.

13.11.2 Control Over Industrial Wastewater Treatment

Dissolved air flotation system for treating industrial wastewater.

Government mandates the industries that generate wastewater with high concentrations of conventional pollutants (e.g. oil and grease), toxic pollutants (e.g. heavy metals, volatile organic compounds) or other non-conventional pollutants such as ammonia, to install specialized treatment systems. There should be a mechanism to strictly monitor these industries. However, the industries producing wastewater with lesser quantities of pollutants may have to be insisted to install a pre-treatment system to remove the toxic components, and then send the partially treated wastewater to the municipal system. Some industries have been successful at redesigning their manufacturing processes through pollution prevention processes to reduce or eliminate pollutants.

The thermal pollution generated by power plants or manufacturing plants may be controlled with:

- cooling ponds, man-made bodies of water designed for cooling by evaporation, convection, and radiation

- cooling towers, to transfer waste heat to the atmosphere through evaporation or heat transfer
- cogeneration, i,e, recycling waste heat for domestic or industrial heating purposes.

13.11.3 Controlling Agricultural Wastewater Treatment

As discussed above, the sources of pollution may be either from a point or nonpoint source. *Non point source controls* are to be concentrated on sediment (loose soil) washed off fields to reduce runoff flows since this is the largest source of agricultural pollution. Common controlling techniques are contour ploughing, crop mulching, crop rotation, planting perennial crops and installing riparian buffers.

Nutrients (nitrogen and phosphorus) are generally supplied to agricultural lands by applying commercial fertilizer, animal manure, or spraying of municipal or industrial wastewater (effluent) or sludge. These nutrients enter runoff from crop residues, irrigation water, wildlife, and atmospheric deposition. This nutrient pollution can be reduced by developing optimal nutrient management plans.

Similarly pesticide impacts also can be minimized using integrated pest management techniques.

Point source wastewater treatment has to focus on areas with large livestock and poultry operations, often referred to as *feedlots*. Anaerobic treatment is to be ensured on animal slurries before disposal. Constructed wetlands may also be used to treat animal wastes. Some animal slurries are treated by mixing with straw and composted at high temperature for bacteriological sterilization and friable manure for soil improvement. Pollution Control Board or Agricultural Development Departments should take a lead role in this aspect and educate farmers.

Silt fence installed on a construction site.

13.11.4 Controlling at Construction Sites

The following tabulated techniques will help pollution control at construction sites

No.	Pollution Cause/Controlling Aspect	Techniques
1.	Erosion control	Mulching, Hydro-seeding
2.	Sediment control	Sediment basins, Silt fences
3.	Discharge of toxic chemicals such as Motor fuels, concrete washout etc.	Spill preventers, Spill controllers, Specially designed containers, Structures to control overflow, Stream diversion

13.11.5 Control of Urban Runoff (Storm Water)

Urban runoff can be effectively controlled by reducing the velocity and flow of storm water on one hand, and reducing pollutant discharges on the other hand. To reduce the effects of urban runoff, several storm water management techniques are available. Some focus on water quantity control, while others focus on improving water quality, and some perform both functions. The following practices/ methods will help reducing/ avoiding pollution problems.

Pollution prevention practices	Thermal pollution by Runoff mitigation systems
• low-impact development techniques, • installation of green roofs and • improved chemical handling (e.g. motor fuels & oil, fertilizers and pesticides)	• infiltration basins, • bio-retention systems, • constructed wetlands, • retention basins and similar devices.

Mitigation

The risk for outbreaks after natural disasters is low, particularly when the disaster does not result in substantial population displacement. Communicable diseases are common in displaced populations that have poor access to basic needs such as safe water and sanitation, adequate shelter, and primary healthcare services. These conditions, many favorable for disease transmission, must be addressed immediately with the rapid reinstatement of basic services. It is very important to assure the primary healthcare and access to safe water. The absence of these should be treated as the early warning to detect epidemic-prone disaster-affected areas. The risk assessment reports to communicable disease can prioritize the need for immunization and vector-control.

Disaster-related deaths are overwhelmingly caused by the initial traumatic impact of the event. Disaster-preparedness plans, appropriately focused on trauma and mass casualty management, should also take into account the health needs of the surviving disaster-affected populations. The health effects associated with the sudden crowding of large numbers of survivors, often with inadequate access to safe water and sanitation facilities, will require planning for both therapeutic and preventive interventions, such as the rapid delivery of safe water and the provision of rehydration materials, antimicrobial agents, and measles vaccination materials.

Challenges to mitigation

- Surveillance in affected areas is basic requirement to understanding the effect of natural disasters on communicable disease, illness and death. Of course, getting this information is often challenging.

- The reorganizing of the pre-existing public health infrastructure can sometimes weaken pre-disaster systems of response.
- Experienced surveillance officers and public health workers if died or missing, it becomes difficult to get information as in case of Aceh in 2004.
- Population displacement can disfigure the census information. This creates confusion and makes the calculation of rates for comparison difficult.
- Healthcare in emergency phase is often delivered by a wide range of national and international agencies, which often creates coordination challenges.
- Lack of pre-disaster baseline surveillance information poses to difficulties in distinguishing epidemic from background endemic disease transmission.
- Although post disaster surveillance systems are designed to rapidly detect cases of epidemic-prone diseases, interpreting this information can be hampered by the absence of baseline surveillance data and accurate denominator values.
- Detecting cases of diseases that occur endemically may be interpreted (because of absence of background data) as an early epidemic.

The priority in these settings, however, is rapid implementation of control measures when cases of epidemic-prone diseases are detected. Despite these challenges, continued detection of and response to communicable diseases are essential to monitor the incidence of diseases, to document their effect, to respond with control measures when needed, and to better quantify the risk for outbreaks after disasters.

SELF ASSESSMENT INTERMISSION (SAI – 13.5)

1. Define water pollution and explain its sources.
2. Explain the impact of water contamination on plants.
3. What do you understand by point source and non-point source of pollution? Discuss.
4. List out the causes of water pollution? Explain.
5. Describe the how water is polluted by pathogens.
6. Describe the how groundwater is polluted.
7. Explain the impact of chemicals on causing water pollution.
8. Explain the thermal effects on causing water pollution.
9. How is water pollution caused by physical changes? Explain.
10. List out various organic and inorganic pollutants that can contaminate water bodies.
11. What is the impact of macroscopic materials in causing water pollution? Explain its effects.
12. List out and explain briefly the control measures of water pollution.

(continued)

13. What are the challenges posed to mitigation to pollution control in disaster prone areas?
14. What steps do you suggest for controlling pollution in urban runoff?
15. Discuss the role of individuals in controlling water pollution.
16. Write short notes on the water pollution caused by the following.
    (a) Eutrophication (b) Solid waste and plastics
    (c) agricultural waste (d) chemicals
17. Write notes on controlling the water pollution due to the following.
    (a) Agricultural waste (b) Construction sites
    (c) Industrial waste water (d) Sewage

MINI-PROJECTS / CASE STUDIES

1. Prepare teams to bring awareness in pollution controlling in the your nearby areas with reference to
   (a) plastic usage (b) sanitation methods (c) waste disposal systems (d) personal healthcare practices (e) adapting paperless systems
   Monitor the teams and prepare the progress reports every month for one year.
2. Prepare a documentary film or a power point presentation on the various pollution causing issues in your vicinity.

CHAPTER 14

Accidents in Transport

(The Manmade Disasters)

O'MY SILENT INNER VIBES (O'M S I V – 14)

Sometime back I received a message from a friend through one of the social media networks. It was quite interesting and somewhat relevant here, so I thought I would share it. It runs as follows.

A priest and a pilot were neighbors in a colony.

The priest used to worship the God everyday with utmost faith in God and also used to preach and deliver the discourses on spiritual issues to the people who visited the temple where he had been working.

The pilot had no faith in prayers. He did believe all this was a waste of productive time. He used to believe that God, if exist, should treat all equally, whether prayed or not without any prejudice and partiality.

The priest and the pilot died after some days. Both went to the Heaven

The priest was surprised to see the pilot in the Heaven, how he could come to Heaven.

Priest asked the God, "O God! I prayed and preached about Your greatness hundreds of times and made hundreds of people to chant Your name thousands of times. Despite the pilot never did so, how he could come to the Heaven".

The God replied with a smile, "My dear son! Praying was your duty, and you did it with care and respect, likewise, taking people safely to their destinations was his duty, so he did it, with same respect. Additionally, he saved people several times. Although, he never took my name, he made hundreds of people praying me, while he was rescuing those hundreds of lives of people during his duty".

The God further said, "My son! While you were preaching, some praying people slept, but when he was rescuing, the slept people also woke up and started praying". "I like rescuing people rather than those praying", the God added.

***

May it be a myth or a fabricated story, but we can certainly find an element of truth. Hundreds of lives are in the hands of a pilot directly, while another thousands indirectly in the form of family members of the passengers. So also the drivers of trains, buses or even the bike riders for that matter are at risk of lives of people depending on them, and around them directly or indirectly.

Of course! Nobody would like driving to die, but most times the overconfidence, carelessness and exhibitionism predominate for heroic deeds or amusement or fun, particularly in youth. Even for those who treat life as 'a play', it is a knock out game and there is no second chance to play. And your 'LIFE' is not only yours. So, just a little concern to the safety for self, fellow beings in surround and toward the environment makes rest of the life and entire world happy. Because, once gone, no one can get 'LIFE' back. Thrilling should not be at the cost of killing. Just think for a while!

SPEED THRILLS – BUT KILLS.

Think a while! Suicide Is Not The Solution To Any Problem…

A student jumped into a river as he could not pass the exam. Due to love failure a young girl hanged herself in her hostel room.

Such news has become so common today…

I read a report in 2013 that out of the 1.28 million deaths; about 8,42,000 were attributed to self-harm (suicide), while 4,05,000 to interpersonal violence, and 31,000 to collective violence (war) and legal intervention. Of my silent inner vibes produced in my heart, a few, which need to be answered before one attempts a suicide, are…

Who will appreciate this? **None...**

What are you going to achieve with this coward action? **Nothing...**

Would your problem be solved by your suicide? **No, it will further grow...**

Think of your Mother, who has taken lot of pains to bring you onto this earth.

Think of your Father, due to whose shed of blood and sweat you have grown.

Think of your Gurus, who taught you how to live.

Think of your Friends who shared all your laugh and grief.

What are you giving them in return? And what right you have to through them in troubles in all dimensions...

An object seen through convex lens, looks big, while through a concave, looks small. It is due to the glass you see but not in the object.

Suicide never gave solution to any problem rather enhanced and generated new ones.

Please pay attention, try to listen, help or at least inform to nearest adults or call helpline given below, if you find any of the following Warning Signs of Suicide in your friends.

- Talking about suicide/dying, no care for health, agitating/ aggressive mood
- Failure in love or relationship, parting out/ break up with a close associate
- Recent loss related to death, divorce, money, job, business, valuables etc.
- Change in personality, behaviour, attitude, not talking to anyone, moody etc.
- Change in sleep patterns (Sleeplessness, excessive sleep), eating habits
- Excessive drinking (alcohol), smoking, consuming drugs and tranquilizers
- Weight loss, weight gain, and diminished sexual interest, no care for valuables
- Loss of interest or pleasure in usual activity, no reaction for others actions
- Buying articles used for suicide such as knife, gun, sleeping pills, poisons etc.
- Fear of losing control, fear complex for very small issues, doubting everything
- Insults, threatens, feels unmotivated, (feel of) trapped/ blackmailed/cheated
- Raped, Accused of some crime such as theft, ragging, eve teasing, victimized etc.
- Low self esteem, feeling worthlessness, sensitive even to small warnings
- Fatigue, severe mood swing, loss of energy, despair and loneliness
- Disinterest in life, No hope for future and Depression, victim of oppression

DECIDE - TO PREVENT SUICIDE

14.1 ACCIDENT-DEFINITION AND CONCEPT

Accident is an undesired, unusual sudden event that may cause damages to assets, injuries and even deaths.

An **accident** is defined as an undesirable, incidental and unplanned unintentional injury or event that could have been prevented and acted upon, prior to its occurrence.

14.1.1 Physical and Non-Physical Accidents

Accidents may be broadly classified into two categories as physical and non-physical accidents. Physical accident means unintended motor/engine driven vehicle collisions or falls or failures that cause injuries or death by touching something sharp, hot, electrical or ingesting poison. Non-physical are unintentionally revealing a secret or otherwise saying something incorrectly, or forgetting an appointment, etc.

Physical accidents are further studied under the following types

1. Transport accidents (Road/Rail/Marine/Air)
2. Fire accidents and Explosions (Bombs/crackers/cell phones/atomic/nuclear)
3. Industrial hazards (Machine handling/operation)
4. Chemical hazards (Leakage/spillage/contamination etc.)

[We shall discuss transport accidents in details in this chapter, while other types of accidents are already discussed in the previously chapter 11].

14.1.2 Transport Accidents

Transport accidents are further classified under four types as

(a) Road Accidents
(b) Rail Accidents
(c) Marine Accidents
(d) Air accidents

These are discussed in the paragraphs to follow

14.2 ROAD ACCIDENTS

Right from the invention of wheel (industrial revolution era) there has been a great development in the new modes of transport as well as the speed and due

to increased traffic the world has been witnessing many road accidents. Road accidents can occur with 2-wheelers (bicycle, motor cycles, bikes, scooters and mopeds), or 3-wheelers (Rickshaws, auto rickshaws and tricycles), 4-wheelers (cars, jeeps, small trucks, goods carriers etc.) and heavy vehicles both public carriers (Vans, Buses, double deck buses, trailers, and coaches etc.) and goods carriers (Lorries, trucks, trailers, trolleys, vehicles, container, dumpers, tuskers etc.).

The great majority of accidents that are on record so far have occurred on roads only. Road accidents are very frequent and most of them are damaging, even fatal in many cases. The large majority of these are caused by human error. Research has shown that driver error accounts for over 80% of all fatal and injury crashes on roads.

Roads are common man's transporting medium and are cheaper as well as safer. But, they may result in higher costs in the case of poor maintenance; poor design and poor operations (speed dumps which damage tyres) lead to accidents particularly for motorcyclists. However, wearing helmet can enhance the safety. Cars are much safer with seat belts advanced braking system, electronic stability control etc. However, safety for pedestrians is still lagging behind. Further, it is becoming more and more challenging issue to governments, security, traffic departments as the vehicles are continuously increasing on roads day by day.

14.2.1 Statistics of Road Accidents

Increasing incidents of road accidents is the global concern, because it is associated with deaths, disability and thence the loss of manpower, altogether the economic losses inflict upon the society and also the nation. Believe it or not! 'Road accidents' as a cause of death has been placed one among the top ten (9th position) in 1990. The forecasts and analysis of data suggests that by the year 2020, it may move up to 6th position. The road accidents for the last 3 decades in India indicate that these have gradually increased from about 1 to 4 lakhs and the number of people injured in road accidents has risen from 70 thousand to nearly 4 lakhs. The road accidents on the mountainous terrain are relatively more fatal.

The gravity of the problem and the seriousness of the issue of road accidents can be understood from the from the following statistical facts occurred on Indian roads (Ref. Fig. 14.1).

- Over 1,37,000 died on roads in 2013 alone, which is more than the number killed in all wars together in India.
- On average 16 children died on Indian road daily.
- About 5 lives end on Delhi road every day.
- There is one death every 4 minutes due to road accidents in India.
- Drunken driving is one of the leading causes
- On average, 1214 road crashes occur every day in India.
- Two wheelers account for 25% of total road crash.
- 20 children under age of 14 die every day due to road crashes.
- Hyderabad is rated 8th position among the top 10 cities with highest number of road crash deaths.

Together with the terrain the fatalistic nature of road accidents is contributed to the delay in response and the lack of post accident medical care for victims.

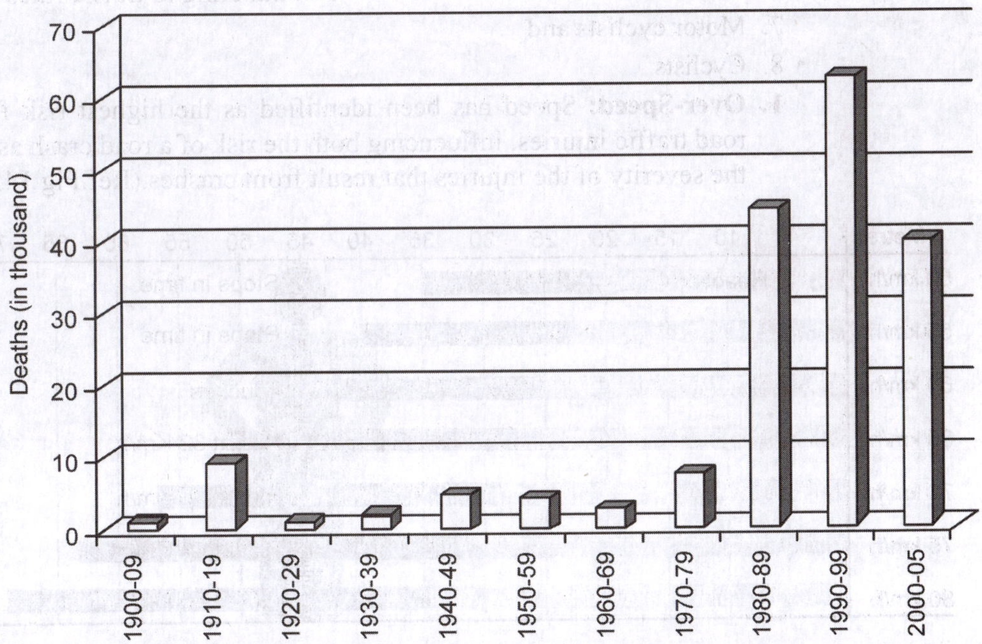

Fig. 14.1 Deaths of road accidents in the last century in India.

14.2.2 Causes of Road Accidents

Vehicle collisions and skids/falls are the most common causes of fatal injuries. Many people are being killed as a consequence of inexperience, speeding, intoxication through drink or drugs or just plain recklessness.

Of all these reasons, the primary reason for these road accidents is attributable to the negligence of driver. Perhaps! Due to the great freedom given to the drivers, accidents involving heavy vehicles occur too frequently, resulting in many deaths. Accidents occur even to the people who are careful, but many accidents may be avoidable if adhered to rules correctly.

The main reasons for road accidents are in the following order

1. Over-Speed
2. Alcohol and Drugs
3. Mobile phones and driving
4. Fatigue by driving long durations
5. Overloaded auto-rickshaws
6. Not adhering to traffic rules
7. Motor cyclists and
8. Cyclists

1. **Over-Speed:** Speed has been identified as the highest risk factor in road traffic injuries, influencing both the risk of a road crash as well as the severity of the injuries that result from crashes.(Ref.Fig 14.2)

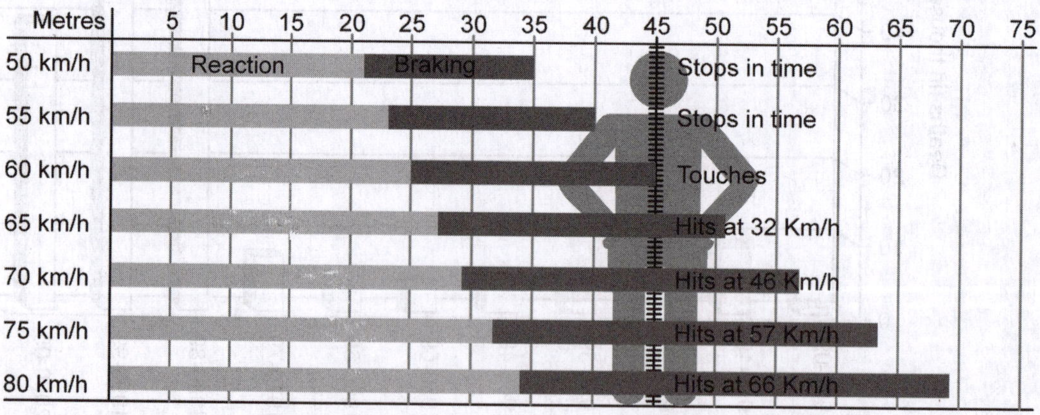

Fig. 14.2 Braking (at various speeds) and Its likely impact.

Accidents due to excessive speed driving account as much as 28% of killing collisions and 18% of those results in serious injury. Youth particularly, are craze of driving at over speeds. "***Speed Thrills-But Kills***".

Every year people are killed because drivers are travelling too fast. The drivers, especially young must be given awareness of stopping distance, speed, rules and regulations. Adverse road conditions and a heavy vehicle also increase braking distance, so one should have the knowledge about the facts and should maintain an optimum speed.

> **O My God!**
>
> **Think about this: There's no such thing as safe speeding**
>
> Choose your speed and you choose your consequences.
>
> In a 60 km/h zone, travelling at...
>
> - 65 km/h, you are **twice** likely to have a serious crash
> - 70 km/h, you are **4** times likely to have a serious crash
> - 75 km/h, you are **10** times likely to have a serious crash
> - 80 km/h, you are **32** times likely to have a serious crash than if you drive at 60 km/h.
>
> In rural/ sub-urban areas, travelling just 10 km/h faster than the average speed of other traffic, you are **twice** as likely to have a serious crash.

Excess speed is defined as exceeding the speed limit, while *inappropriate speed* is defined as driving at a speed unsuitable for the prevailing road and traffic conditions. Both excess and inappropriate speeds are responsible for a high proportion of the mortality and morbidity that result from road crashes. Controlling vehicle speed can prevent crashes happening and can reduce the impact when they do occur, lessening the severity of the injuries sustained by the victims.

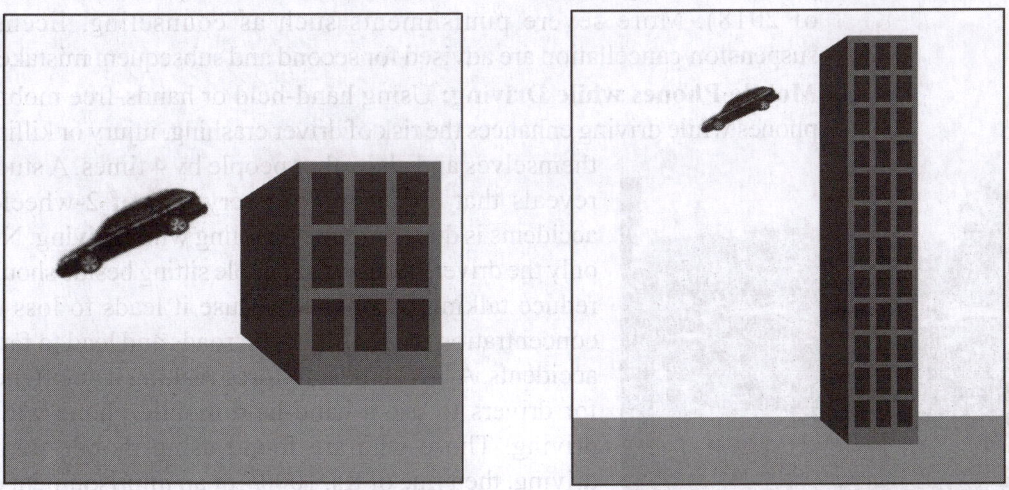

crashing at 50km/h is equivalent to dropping from three (3) storeys

crashing at 100km/h is equivalent to dropping from twelve (12) storeys

Fig. 14.3 Road crashes and their equivalents.

Speed is the single biggest factor contributing to road deaths in Ireland. Over 40% of fatal collisions are caused by excessive or inappropriate speed. A 5kmph difference in speed could be the difference between life and death for a vulnerable road user like a pedestrian.

A study on the effect of hitting pedestrians is as follows:

- Hit by a car at 60 km/h, 9 out of 10 pedestrians will be killed
- Hit by a car at 50 km/h, 5 out of 10 pedestrians will be killed
- Hit by a car at 30 km/h, 1 out of 10 pedestrians will be killed

The effect of crashing at high speeds can be compared as below

- The crashing at 50 km/h is equal to dropping from the top of a 3 storey building (Ref. Fig. 14.3)
- The crashing at 100 km/h is equal to dropping from the top of a 12 storey building (Ref. Fig. 14.3)

2. **Alcohol and Drugs:** Alcohol and drugs consumption makes person to lose his state of mind, co-ordination and concentration. It affects driver's sense of judgment of speed, time and distance. Some people even may also become overconfident or aggressive. Further, the driver's health conditions also impair driving. There is one death every 4 minutes due to drunken driving in world. There are many rules which prohibit 'Drink and Drive' and severe punishments are imposed. Though some countries are strictly following them, by and large India is failing in implementation. In India there is a special police squad for checking the content of alcohol in drivers and those who are found consumed alcohol, then a fine of Rs. 1000/- or an imprisonment of 6 months or both are imposed in India (as of 2018). More severe punishments such as counseling, license suspension/cancellation are advised for second and subsequent mistakes.
3. **Mobile Phones while Driving:** Using hand-held or hands-free mobile phones while driving enhances the risk of driver crashing, injury or killing themselves and also other people by 4 times. A study reveals that about one in every two of 2-wheeler accidents is due to mobile handling while driving. Not only the driver, but also the people sitting beside should reduce talking on phone because it leads to loss of concentration of the drivers on roads and lead to fatal accidents. A law came into force making it an offence for drivers to use a hand-held mobile phone while driving. Those who are found using mobile while driving, then fine of Rs. 1000/- or an imprisonment of 6 months or both are imposed in India (as of 2018).

4. **Fatigue by Driving Long Duration:** Having driven for longer durations continuously, a driver gets fatigue, which can impair the driving abilities.

Even the official vehicles of politicians, government officers and celebrities may have to travel for longer durations and their drivers seldom get rest pause for a good sleep. Several accidents took place of this reason particularly in the last decade.

5. **Overloaded Auto-Rickshaws (3-Wheelers):** Most of the Indian public depends on auto-rickshaws (3-wheelers) owing to its economic nature (cheaper and easy accessibility/ availability) for their local transport. The drivers of such vehicles try to extract more or exploit the situation by overloading with the people than the capacity of the vehicle and often subjected to the accidents, particularly at the turnings and curvy/ bumpy roads. These kinds of accidents are more frequently occurring in rural areas in India.

6. **Motor Cyclists (Bikes) and Auto-Rickshaws:** Motor cyclists are extremely vulnerable and represent 21% of road fatalities. It is compulsory to wear helmet while driving which is very beneficial to the driver to protect from severe injuries. In India, owing to its convenience, and ease, most of the people, particularly middle class (youth and middle aged) prefer motorcycles to reach their destination (schools/ colleges/ offices), and being in hurry, it results in severe accidents. Though it won't be the motorcyclist's mistake, due to collision with heavy vehicles the bikes may lose their balance easily and lead to deadly accidents. Proper motorcycle leathers contain some body armor but this is still a little protection compared to the other heavy vehicle.

7. **Cyclists:** Cyclists are killed or injured in reported road in urban areas. Steepness or the gradient of the road is another physical parameter that is distinct to the hill roads and together with the sinuosity makes hill driving prone to hazards. The hypothesis can thus be expanded to include that the accident proneness of the mountain roads increases with increasing gradient of the roads. Cycle pathways can give some benefit to cyclists.

SELF ASSESSMENT INTERMISSION (SAI – 14.1)

1. Define 'Accident'? What are different types of accidents? Explain briefly.
2. What are different types of transport accidents? Describe briefly.
3. List out various causes for road accidents.
4. Discuss the effect of speed in causing road accidents.
5. 'Speed thrills-But kills'. Discuss.
6. Describe briefly the effect of alcoholism with reference to road accidents.
7. How does mobile phone be reason for causing a road accident? Discuss.
8. Write a note on the accidents with three wheelers and two wheelers.
9. What is a fatigue? Do you agree that fatigue can cause an accident? Justify your answer.

14.2.3 Driving in Fog

Fog can be considered as ground level cloud. It forms when the temperature drops to dew point i.e. the temperature at which air is saturated, and invisible vapour in the air condenses to form suspended water droplets. Sometime, it may be formed due to pollution. Fog lowers visibility, thence creates hazardous driving conditions. If trip cannot be postponed until dense fog lifts (usually by late morning or the afternoon), the following trips may be useful:

- High beams generally produce reflection back off the fog and actually impair visibility even more. So better drive with lights on low beam.
- Fog can create a visual illusion of slow motion when you actually are in speed. So lowdown your speed and watch speedometer.
- Often you cannot listen to the traffic, which you cannot see. So open your window a little, to hear well.
- For clear and maximum visibility, use wipers and defrosters as and when necessary.
- Use the left edge (in India) of the road or painted road markings as a guide.
- Be patient. Do not pass lines of traffic.
- Do not stop on a motorway or heavily travelled road.
- Fog lamps may be used only in dense fog. In clear weather conditions they are liable to cause glare or dazzle and must be turned off.

14.2.4 Bad Driving Habits and Road Safety

There are several drivers who extremely irritate and may become a cause for a danger. A few of such bad habits that frequently occur and very annoying are bad tailgating, poor lane discipline, not indicating, over taking and so forth. Apart from the inconvenience to other road users, this kind of inconsiderate driving is also very dangerous. A brief discussion on these bad habits is here below:

1. **Tailgating (Closely Following and 'Rear-Door' Efforts):** Probably some of the greatest offences are that most among us as drivers are extremely impatient. Some drivers without thinking, just follow traffic and get close, but then they back off as you accelerate way. Some drivers tailgate deliberately knowingly that are the most dangerous. They sit behind you buzzing horn or flashing headlights in an effort to move you, but of course there is nowhere to go as you are in the process of overtaking and thus irritate. Yet another act of tailgating is rear-door efforts for overtaking (from wrong side) or crossing marginally or creating congestion in the path or entering path of pedestrians to overtake and so forth. All these can be causes of accidents, small or big.

A NEW DESIGN OF SEAT BELT TO PREVENT ACCIDENTS

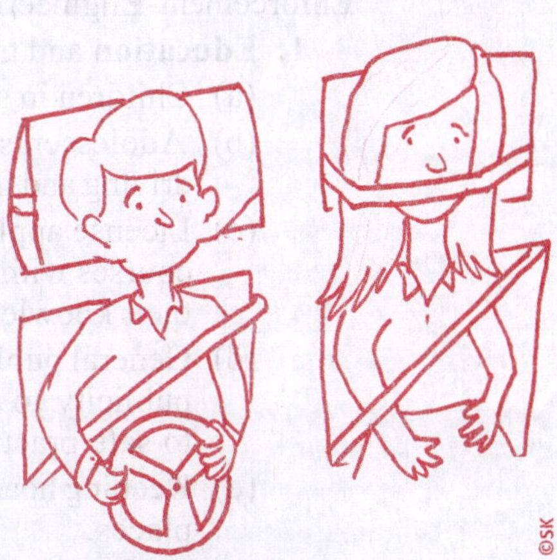

2. **Over/undertaking:** Tailgaters who don't get their way will often resort to overtaking if they can. Yes, there are also selfish individuals go outside lane. They have no concern to the queue of traffic waiting to get past them. Probably, this is because they live in their own tiny world with no more thoughts than to plan for their dinner of the day. This perhaps causes some individuals to lose their patience and over/undertake.
3. **Poor lane discipline:** Some drivers move all over the road and they don't seem to realize where they are supposed to stay in between those white dashed lines. Particularly, the drivers of 2-wheelers in India ride erratically and move between the cars and heavy vehicles without following the lane discipline. This act confuses road-users leading to fatality on innocents.
4. **Indicators and Horn:** Some people seem to have no idea what the orange flashing lights and horns are actually for! They move here and there and go wherever they like without any thought of letting the rest of the road users know what their intentions are.

The above are just a few of the habits of drivers that can be particularly irritating other drivers. Below are some other annoyances.

- Cutting corners, particularly at junctions
- Sudden stopping/turning
- No headlights in conditions that require them
- Throwing cigarettes/ empty bottles/ wastes out of the window
- Leaving main beam on, or dipping only at the last minute

- Uncontrolled engine sound (silencer not working) that causes irritation to others
- Inappropriate use of the horn
- Polluting the air by using adulterated fuel (like adding kerosene to diesel/ petrol)
- Unnecessary flash lighting
- No half shades for head lights and thence cause over flashing on opposite drivers
- Impatient people pushing in ahead of a queue of traffic.

14.2.5 Mitigation Strategies – E.E.E. Approaches

There are 3-main approaches employed to preventing accidents **E**ducation-**E**nforcement-**E**ngineering (abbreviated as **E-E-E** Approaches)

1. **Education** and training approach is used on
   (a) Children in schools by road-traffic instructors and school teachers
   (b) Adolescents in colleges to give awareness on the principles of safe driving and in good driving attitudes
   (c) License applicants (new/renewal) and older drivers with refresher courses with driving principles to bring home safe- and to refresh their knowledge of traffic law
   (d) General public by means of newspaper, radio, television, and other publicity, to draw the attention of all road users both to dangers and to safe practices on the road
   (e) Keeping hoardings, sign boards, instructions on roads at appropriate places.
2. **Enforcement** strategy applied by
   (a) Adopting reasonable and enforceable traffic laws which at the same time are best designed to prevent accidents
   (b) Concentrating the time and energy of traffic officers on the offences, locations, and times that feature frequently in accidents
   (c) Thoroughly testing new drivers to ensure they will not be liable to cause accidents
   (d) Adhering to the rules and regulations and strictly implementing
   (e) Maintaining the safety rules such as use of helmets (2-wheelers) and seat belts (4-wheelers)
   (f) Awarding punishments strictly on those who violate traffic rules such as rash driving, drunken-drive etc.
3. **Engineering** of vehicles and roads through
   (a) Regular inspection for a "warrant of fitness" to ensure that the main components of the vehicle are safe
   (b) Improving the design of the vehicle to give ease of vision and control to the driver so as to reduce the likelihood of injury in an accident

(c) Fitting safety equipment, such as seat belts
(d) Designing and placing speed breakers at appropriate places
(e) Redesigning, repairs and renovation of roads etc.
(f) Redesigning the speed breakers at high traffic areas. There is a recent technique of drawing the 3-D speed breaker (three dimensional zebra cross lines or any figures), which appear like real objects from a certain distance. These can considerably set an illusion from sufficiently far distance, which when seen by the driver would reduce speed (slow down). As the driver approaches them, they appear as normal zebra cross lines. An example is shown in the adjacent figure.

14.2.6 Road Accident Prevention and Rescue Measures

As described above, the main causes of death and injury on roads are speeding, drunken driving and non-wearing of safety equipment such as helmet/seat-belts. Since the traffic accidents depend on several factors, the probability of accidents can be reduced in a number of different ways. The following activities can help preventing or at least reducing the accidents that would normally result from increases in traffic density.

Preventive Measures

(a) A continuous road or traffic reengineering that comprises of the design of new roads that are inherently safe (separating opposing traffic flows, eliminating cross traffic, and providing wide shoulders and traffic lanes and good visibility);
(b) Improving existing roads by realignment, improving vision, and resurfacing slippery surfaces;
(c) Regulating traffic movement by installing traffic signals, traffic islands, road markings, and regulatory signs such as "stop", "bus bay" and "give way" signs; and zebra lines along with traffic signals at junctions and wherever there is a probability of people cross the roads;
(d) Assisting the driver with warning and destination signs to avoid danger and confusion.

Rescue Measures

- The control of all accidents is, in the first instance, the responsibility of the chief and personnel of the effected means of transport.
- It is up to them to limit the resulting damage as much as possible.
- Passengers must obey the directives of the personnel on board and behave as instructed.
- The area where the accident occurs will determine the person in-charge at the disaster side.

14.2.7 Guidelines for Accident Situations

The accident occurrence need not of one's own mistakes, but sometimes accidents occur by other due to which the innocents will be victimized. There are several incidences that the pedestrians have lost lives due to rash drivers on road, derailed trains coming onto roads, air crashes near urban areas or near airports etc. The following are some guidelines to act in such situations.

- In case of air disaster occurring on or in the vicinity of an airport (generally within 5 km radius), the control of the incident is the responsibility of the airport authorities, since control of air traffic and control tower is responsibility of airport.
- If the incident occurs outside the area under control of airport authorities, the political authorities of the affected area will be the in-charge.
- In case of rail accidents, the alarm, the reconnaissance and rescue will be controlled by the regional traffic control of the railways or by the nearest station.
- The red alert for rail road disasters can be activated by higher political authorities.
- As regards to exclusive road accidents it is important to make the distinction between those occurring motorways and taking place on other roads, bearing in mind the special regulations that may govern certain communications, routes and sensitive areas.
- The rescue means will be supplied by the rescue centre and by the neighboring emergency services.
- If needed specialist in dealing with dangerous substances (radioactive chemicals, hydrocarbons etc.) and the health services (helicopter/ambulances) can also be called upon to help.
- In general a special plan drawn up has a precaution will be activated.
- Non-availability of trained, highly mobile and well equipped search and rescue personnel at crucial locations often cause delay in rescue operations that reduce the probability of survival of the accident victims. So, it is essential requisite keep trained personnel ready at any time and standby teams if required.
- Non-availability of adequate post-accident medical care for the accident victims often results in deaths. The victims are referred to far off medical

colleges or referral hospitals and seriously injured accident victims are usually unable to cope up with this. So all nearest hospitals should be instructed by the government to obey the orders of road transport authorities concerned, as and when required.

- Sufficient powers should be delegated to the transport authorities in the interest of observing safe environment.

1. General Principles and Precautions to Road Users

- Beware and be aware of the dangers involved in using various types of transport.
- Study the regulations and suggested rules published by the transport authorities.
- In case of imminent danger, make sure that you know the protection and rescue apparatus.
- Do not park vehicles on pavements; this puts pedestrians at risk by increasing their need to walk on the road.
- Broken down vehicles should be moved off the roads, hazard warning light should be switched on.
- Be aware of your speed while driving, watch your speedometer and concentrate on your limits.
- Do not overload your vehicle.
- Do not drive under the influence of alcohol and drugs.
- Do not use hand-held phones whilst driving.
- The correct seatbelt or child restrained should be used.

2. While an Accident Occurs or just occurred?

- Keep calm and avoid panic; to the extent possible help family and neighbor who are in difficulty
- Follow the driver's instructions and those of crew, if you are a passenger
- Keep identity card/ papers and important personal documents (medical and vaccination certificates and details of blood type) and any personal medicine along with you. Now-a-days, the governments have introduced a mobile application which can store such information in your mobile
- Soon after the crash occurs try to free yourself from the cabin, as there is a danger of fire or leaks
- If possible activate the rescue process by alerting the local security or special services (special telephone networks and numbers)

- In case of a major accidents occurring in road with traffic, direct the traffic while taking care of the own safety (signal and mark the accident spot).
- Do not touch or move the seriously wounded unless there is the risk of fire
- It is the duty of witness to alert the rescue services and to give them
  1. The exact location and the nature of accident
  2. Type of vehicle involved
  3. The characteristics of any dangerous substances involved
  4. The likely number of victims.
- Witness should also give their names and addresses in the interest of serving the fellow beings.

3. After Occurrence of the Accident

- Follow the instructions of the intervening bodies and of the rescue personnel.
- keep calm and avoid panic.
- If possible and if necessary collaborate with the rescuers and with the judicial authorities and experts in charge of the investigation.

Trespassing railway tracks

SELF ASSESSMENT INTERMISSION (SAI – 14.2)

1. How does fog affect driving? What measure do you take while driving in fog?
2. What are the bad driving habits with reference to road safety? Discuss
3. What do you understand by the terms 'tailgating' and 'rear-door efforts' in driving?
4. Describe briefly the wrong and right ways of using brakes, indicators and horn while driving a vehicle.
5. Explain the E-E-E approaches so as to employ as mitigation strategies to road accidents?
6. How do you fit the terms 'Education, Enforcement and Engineering' for road safety?
7. Suggest some prevention and rescue measures in the case of road accidents.
8. Enumerate the guidelines for road accident situations.
9. List out general principles of road safety to be observed by road users to avoid road accidents.
10. Explain how you act when you see an accident just occurred on a road.

14.3 TRAIN (RAIL) ACCIDENTS

Railways transportation is the cheapest and largest mass transport mode. Particularly, it is the common man's transport for underdeveloped and developing countries. Indian public largely depend on this kind of surface transport. We can understand its importance and role in Indian economy by the fact that it had a separate ministry and has a separate budget till 2015 since its independence.

Whatsoever the mode of transport used, accidents take place without our knowledge. Generally accidents are attributed to the negligence or mistakes of humans. But the cost of those mistakes is lasting forever. There have been many accidents which took place all over the world which are caused either by human or due to the aggression of nature.

Summarily, train accidents (for that matter any types of accidents) occur mainly due to three reasons. They are

- Technical problems
- Human errors or negligence
- Natural (environmental)

A small mistake can consume several lives and the loss may be unimaginable. Train accidents are the worst accidents in nature, since a train generally would have not less than 600 passengers. Had anything gone wrong, there won't be sufficient source for the rescue of the passengers.

14.3.1 Types of Train Accidents

Like road accidents, the rail accidents (also called the train accidents or train crash or train wrecks) also do occur, and cause casualties, deaths and damages. Trains and the people travelling on them are vulnerable to all kinds of accidents. However, most of these can be avoided completely by taking certain measures. The only way to avoid these ill-fated accidents is to maintain a good safety culture on-board and to be completely aware of the one's personal safety.

There are several types of train accidents and categorizing them is somewhat difficult because of interfering causes and some are unique in nature. These train crashes mostly occur due to the miscommunication between the signal men and the driver, or by derailment of train i.e., when the train wheel jumps off the track. They also occur due to the collision of the trains (i.e., one train hits the other on the same track) or sometimes, as a result of boiler explosion. Further the train wrecks may also occur due to the mechanical and civil failures in design and construction, braking system failure, improper functioning of the engine, explosion of the boiler and many other reasons.

Train crashes happen even by the change in climatic conditions such as in winter, fog makes difficult for the driver to see the track and results in derailment. In rainy seasons also, due to accumulation of the water over the tracks the driver may feel difficulty in the operation. Even sometimes due to human activities i.e., terrorist may hijack the train by firing and bombing etc.

The railway accidents can be better understood in terms of causes as well as effects, which will become a valuable information in studying rail (and other) accidents to help in forestalling similar ones not to occur in the future.

14.3.2 Types of Railway Accidents based on Causes

Schneider and Mase (1971) proposed a classification by causes as listed below.

1. Driver's Errors,
2. Signalmen's Errors,
3. Mechanical Engineering Failures,
4. Civil Engineering Failures,
5. Acts of Other People.

The figure14.4 clearly describes the possible causes against each type of train accidents.

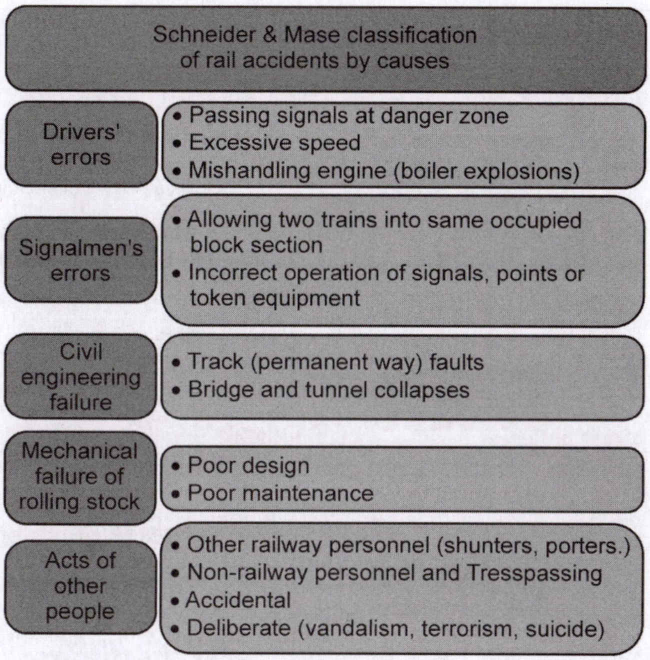

Fig 14.4 Classification of rail accidents based on causes.

14.3.3 Types of Railway Accidents based on Effects

Ludwig Von Stockert (1913) proposed a classification of accidents by their effects (consequences). According to this classification, the railway accidents may be broadly categorized as follows:

1. **Collisions:** Head-on/ Rear/ Due to Buffer stops/ Obstructions
2. **Derailments:** Plain track/ Curves/ Junctions
3. **Others**

The associated figure (14.5) explains the types of train accidents and how they may occur.

1. ***Collisions:*** A collision is defined as the interaction between two or more bodies simultaneously causing change in motion of bodies due to internal forces acted between them. The collision often causes derailment due to the mechanical failure of the tracks such as broken rails or failure of the wheels.
2. ***Derailment***: A derailment means a vehicle such as train runs off its rail. This does not necessarily mean that it leaves its track.
3. ***Others***: The other contributory factors include
   - Strength of rolling stock
   - Fires resulting from accidents

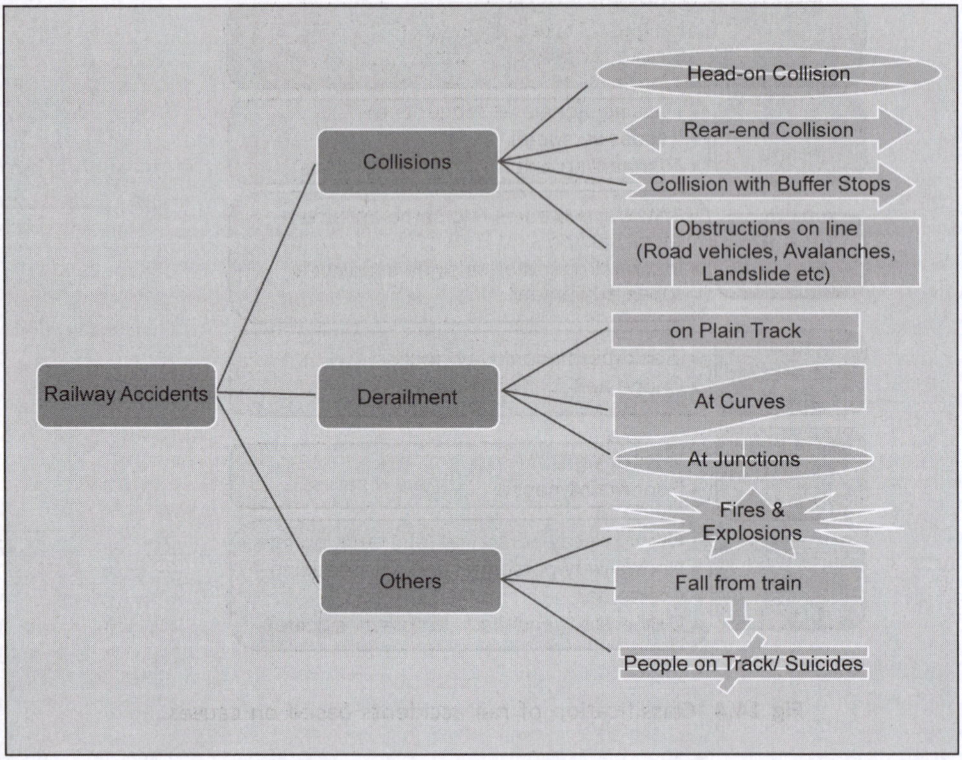

Fig. 14.5 Classification of Rail Accidents based on effects.

- Effectiveness of brakes
- Poor track or junction layout
- Inadequate rules
- Level crossing misuse

14.3.4 Adverse Effects

The train accidents are often fatal and cause a huge damage to the people, national assets and environment directly or indirectly. Particularly, these are more disastrously effect the environment, if they carry hazardous or polluting or inflammable substances such as coal, petro-products Vinyl chloride, Acids, Caustics, Cyanides, Aluminium nitride and so forth. The spilling of these materials may even result in huge fires if a small ignition takes place and it has the ability to damage the entire nearby and surrounding areas and can create losses in business of those respective towns, cities and states even. Due to the train accidents many people may lose their lives, some may be severely injured, or lose their family income and any ways people may suffer due to many reasons, which cannot be consoled in any aspect.

14.3.5 Instructions for Common People

Everyone of us who use or likely to use trains as a medium of transport or otherwise, should

- have the basic knowledge of the dangers involved while travelling
- know/ study the rules and regulation and follow them
- act as per the rules of the government
- know the ways to escape from the compartment and land safely in case of emergency

While the train accident occurs or just has occurred

- not be panic and keep calm to the extent possible
- strictly follow the instructions of the authorities and of rescue teams
- help family and neighbours who are in need and difficulty
- ensure that documents are in a safe zone
- in case of fire accidents, evacuate the compartment as early as possible to avoid loss
- not touch or move the seriously wounded unless there is a risk of fire or toxic fumes
- call the rescue services and to give them the exact location
- call the ambulance as early as possible

After the accident

- Do not panic - keep calm
- Follow the instructions of the authorities
- If possible collaborate with rescue team and with authorities and experts of the investigation

Role of individual in preventing train accidents

- Do not smoke in the trains
- Do not allow any one smoke or drink in the trains
- Do not let anyone stand near the tracks
- Do not allow anyone to stand at the doors
- Do not climb upon the trains
- If anything goes wrong then immediately inform the authorities or else take some precautions
- If any suspicious person enters the compartment immediately inform the authorities
- Help the needy and those in difficult

14.3.6 Government Intervention and Rescue Measures

The train accidents can be avoided by taking suitable preventive and protective measures to minimize the technical and human failures. Further, the malicious attacks can be prevented. The rescue measures involve the installation of a reliable alarm security system and regular surveillance of rail installations and equipment.

- At the outset, the regional traffic control centre of the railways will use alarm reconnaissance and initiate rescue measures. The local authorities take control of first aid for the victims. Measures by coordinating the sources available like police, fire brigades, civil defence, health services, rescue plan or red alert are activated by higher political authorities.

Role of government in preventing the train accidents

- Proper signalling should be maintained between the train driver and the signal operator
- In case of fog or heavy rains the trains must be delayed
- If water enters the track it must be cleared off immediately and till then the trains must be delayed
- Drivers without proper experience should not be allowed to drive the trains
- Ensure the signals are working properly
- Ensure the engine working properly or else the fault should be detected and respective measures should be taken

The train accidents due to technical and human errors can be avoided completely by taking preventive measures. Thence, authorities should take all the preventive measures and check the tracks frequently. Prevention is always better than cure.

SELF ASSESSMENT INTERMISSION (SAI – 14.3)

1. Classify train accidents on the basis of their causes of occurrence.
2. What are various technical reasons for train accidents?
3. What are various human errors that can cause train accidents?
4. Enumerate various types of causes of train accidents involving civil and mechanical engineering.
5. Discuss different types of train accidents with reference to the effects.
6. Give short notes on train accidents due to (a) collisions (b) derailment
7. What are the adverse effects of train accidents?
8. What are the general principles one should follow in trains so as to avoid/prevent the accidents?
9. Discuss the role of an individual in preventing train accidents
10. Discuss the role of government in preventing and mitigating the train accidents.
11. Discuss the rescue measures in the event of train accidents.

14.4 MARITIME ACCIDENTS

It is known fact that, most accidents occur all over the world either by human mistakes or by the aggressive nature. As like the road/rail accidents and the aircraft crash landings, the marine accidents (also called the maritime or ship accidents or ship wrecks) also do occur in wide variety of types.

Ships are exposed to numerous hazards leading to the loss of human lives as well as aquatic life, including environment pollution and many more. Even the ships on shore will be prone to many incidents such as ship breaking and crane mishaps while loading and unloading.

14.4.1 Types of Marine Accidents

Some of the various types of marine accidents are listed below:

- Accidents in shipyards
- Crane mishaps
- On crude oil tankers and cargo ships
- Explosion and fire
- Capsizing/ keeling over and Righting
- Rigging
- Foundering
- Grounding
- Scuttling
- Collision
- Wrecking
- Stranding
- Steering
- Scrapping Missing
- Maritime accidents due to drugs/ alcohol
- Breaking/ Dismantling
- Accidents on Barges
- Accidents on tugboats

The above list includes both types of accidents, the sailing ships and steady ships. Let us now discuss about these in brief.

1. **Accidents in Shipyards:** Ship yards are the most dangerous workplaces where the operations like repairing, overhauling, dismantling and scrapping vessels are involved using hazardous chemicals, dangerous equipment and heavy materials. So, while performing these operations, the workers are subjected to an environment vulnerable to accidents.

2. **Crane Mishaps:** A majority of marine accidents, particularly in shipyards and ship decks are due to improper crane and lifting operations performed by unskilled or inexperienced workers. The officials must vacate all the people at loading/ unloading process except only those workers, trained with required safety precautions.
3. **Accidents on Crude Oil Tankers/ Cargo Ships:** Though utmost care is taken while handling an oil tanker (ocean vessel) to transport petroleum, it may explode due to several reasons such as, faulty ship structure, incorrect loading/unloading practices and '*acts of God*' such as stormy weather, gale force winds and lightning which can cause disastrous loss of natural resources and the marine life.
4. **Explosion and Fire:** Generally fire accidents happen when
   - Explosive materials/ hazardous chemicals are carried
   - Improper packing of explosive materials or hazardous chemicals
   - Improper functioning or error in engine functioning
   - Thermal radiation and hence the chemicals explode.

   These result in environmental pollution and also pose threat to human and marine life loss. About $\frac{3}{4}^{th}$ of the ship accidents are mainly caused due to explosions.
5. **Capsizing and Righting***:* When a ship or boat turn*s* upside down or to its side it is called *'capsizing' or 'keeling over'* while *'righting'* is the

act of reversing a capsized vessel. If a capsized vessel has enough flotation to prevent sinking, it may recover on its own (if it is unstable inverted). Self-righting are the vessels of this design.

In dinghy sailing (small vessels) the act of being knocked down is called capsizing while the act of being inverted is called turtling. Capsizing is quite common in dinghy sailing. Of course! Even the large vessels may be capsized or rolled during storms.

6. **Rigging:** During sailing in a strong wind or bad weather, running rigging is often subjected to parting. Generally the brace on the weather side is under strain, and its parting would allow the whole yard to swing free for about a length of 30 m. The modern ships or stays have preventers while warships are equipped themselves with stoppers of rigging/ fighting. These are ropes of small lengths which are attached to shrouds quickly and then tightened.

7. **Foundering:** A ship is said to be foundering if it is tipping on its side due to instability caused by the centre of mass of the ship rising above the meta-center. Foundering may lead to sinking, if the openings on the upper side are not water-tight at the time of capsizing. Generally violent weather, rouge waves and navigation errors leads to severe foundering.

8. **Grounding:** Ship grounding is said to be occurred, when the bottom of the ship's hull scrapes through the ocean bed. About 1/3rd of ship accidents are attributed to ship grounding either intentional (e.g. beaching to land screw or cargo and careering for several reasons like poor maintenance/ repairs) or unintentional (e.g. tides, wind, depth of water, ship speed may destroy the hull).

9. **Scuttling:** This is sinking the ship deliberately by allowing the flow of water into the hull of the ship. This occurs due to several reasons as listed below
   - Opening the valves or hatchets into the sea.
   - Holes may be ripped into the hull with brute force or with explosives.

   Sometimes scuttling is deliberately done to perform the following tasks:
   - To prevent vessel from becoming navigational hazard.
   - To dispose an abandoned/ old/ captured vessel.
   - To provide an artificial reef for the marine life and divers.
   - To prevent ship from being captured by enemy force (self-destruction).

10. **Ship Collision:** The structural impact of a ship with another or a floating or still-object (e.g. iceberg) is called ship collision (e.g. Titanic ship). These accidents are significant as they result hugely in
    (i) Loss of human life.
    (ii) Financial loss to the owning company or country.
    (iii) Damage to the infrastructure.
    (iv) Impact on environment if oil tankers are involved.
11. **Ship Wrecking:** Ship wrecking is the event of the striking of something that causes sinking or stranding of ship. The wreck generally occurs by rocks, land, poor maintenance, violent weather, navigation errors, instability of the ship, powerful waves (developed by bad weather or tsunami), design errors etc.
12. **Stranding and Bleaching:** When a vessel runs aground accidentally it is termed as stranding. If the ground is rocky, the double bottom area of the vessel will probably suffer considerable damage. Physically, bleaching is similar to stranding. But the difference is that bleaching the vessel is an intentional action and under comparatively controlled conditions, while stranding is accidental where the ship is driven on shore by winds and waves.
13. **Steering:** While sailing, ships are often subjected to difficult conditions such as storms and are vulnerable to capsizing or hitting a shoal or rock or icebergs if the steering fails.
14. **Ship Breaking/ Dismantling:** Ship breaking, also called ship demolition is a type of breaking of ship either intentionally or due to heavy tides if the ship is not strong enough to withstand the forces. Generally the life of a ship is 25-30 years before corrosion and after this life span, ship breaking may be deliberately done either to scrap or to recycle or to reuse or for raw material. This may also be done to sell the used old ships to poorer countries which do not have the capacity to build their own new ships because of their economic status.
15. **Accidents on Barges:** Barge is a large flat-bottomed self-propelled or towed boat used mainly for river and canal transport of heavy goods or bulk cargo. Usually, the towed barges are accompanied by tugboats as they are not self-propelled, they don't move quickly or go through dangerous waters. The most common accidents are slip and fall due to several reasons such as tripping hazards, ice, fluids, lack of non-skid applications, faulty repairs, inflammables and explosives.
16. **Accidents in Tugboats:** The tugboats are specialized vessels used to help ships or other maritime structures moving from one place to another on water. Usually, a tugboat is equipped with the sturdy and powerful engines, a hawser and thick cable used to heavy loads. Therefore, they

are often used as fire fighters and ice breakers and even help the disabled ships out at sea in emergencies. Depending on the place of use, we come across three types of tugboats, namely Oceangoing, Harbor and River tugboats

Sometimes these tugboats and their crews also get into accidents leading to serious injuries and deaths mainly due to capsizing, mechanical breakdown, hazards on board, vessel collisions.

14.4.2 Role of Government in Preventing Maritime Accidents

- Government should license to only those companies which strictly follow all the norms.
- Ensure the emergency exits are provided in sufficient number.
- Heavy loads should not be allowed to be carried.
- If it is compulsory to carry hazardous / explosive materials, utmost care should be taken.
- Check if petrochemicals and explosives are packed properly and handled with utmost care.
- Ensure proper signaling system is given to the ships to avoid collisions.

14.4.3 Role of Ship Manufacturers in Preventing Maritime Accidents

- Companies should maintain safety measures to avoid the marine accidents.
- A provision is to be given for escaping in case of any fire accidents
- The ships should be made with a view to have a long life
- The rigidity criteria and impact loads caused by the powerful waves have to be considered while designing and manufacturing. Suitable simulation techniques may be used to study design lapses.
- The materials should be non-corrosive and high temperature resistant for different weather conditions.
- The materials used should contain all the mechanical properties such as fatigue resistance, rigidity, hardness, strength, thermal resistance and so forth.
- The hull should be of greater strength and should be double lined.
- The safety norms issued by the government or international standards should be strictly adhered

Though the ship manufacturer takes all care while designing and manufacturing, yet marine accidents can occur due to '*Acts of God*'. So, we need to be careful as far as possible and rest may be left to God. There should not be any lapses in '*Human Efforts*' till the last possibility to overcome the situation before giving up. Whatsoever the means of transport is, one should be careful in every aspect while travelling.

SELF ASSESSMENT INTERMISSION (SAI – 14.4)

1. List out various types of marine accidents.
2. What are capsizing and righting? Discuss
3. Discuss the concept of rigging and scuttling with reference to maritime accidents.
4. What are foundering and grounding with reference to maritime accidents.
5. What are various types of accidents possible to occur on shipyard and ship deck? Describe briefly.
6. What are ship wreck, ship breaking and dismantling? Discuss.
7. Give short notes on barges and tugboats?
8. What are stranding, bleaching and steering with reference to marine accidents?
9. What are the adverse effects of marine accidents? Briefly describe.
10. Explain the role of government in preventing/ mitigating the marine accidents.
11. Explain the role of ship manufacturers in preventing/ mitigating the marine accidents. What are the precautions they have to take while manufacturing.

14.5 AIR ACCIDENTS

Accidents do occur in air also. The crashes/failures of flying transport vehicles such as aeroplane (airplane), aircraft, helicopter etc, are often referred to as air accidents. Air accidents are more disastrous than those on land, since air bus carries hundreds of people and costs more than 100 times to that of a land bus.

Like the road/rail/marine accidents, these also may occur because of equipment malfunction or human error or by nature. In fact, small airplanes often pose a greater risk than large aircraft with regard to the causes and effects of accidents. The airplane crashes at high speeds and/or higher altitude result in serious injuries and deaths while those at low speed and/or at lower altitude are minor. Whatsoever, a crash can be emotionally and physically devastating for passengers as well as crew.

14.5.1 Technical Causes of Aircraft Crashes

There are number of interfering factors or errors that can result in a plane-crash. The most common causes are listed below:

1. **Engine Failure/ Mechanical Failure:**This is one of the frequently heard causes of air accidents. The engine failures may be attributed to several reasons. Some examples of engine failures occurred in the history along with the chief cause are listed in the associated Table 14.1.

Table 14.1 Technical Failures caused Flight Crash

Reason for Technical Failure	Example of Flight Crash
Manufacturing defect in engine	Qantas32, Delta Airlines Flight 1288
Improper maintenance	American Airlines Flight 191
Pilot error (Miscommunication)	Pinnacle Airlines Flight 3701
Structural Failure/ Metal fatigue	China Airlines Flight 358
Foreign Object Damage	US Airways Flight 1549
Fuel starvation/ exhaustion	British Flight 38, Gimli Glider
Failure of a second engine	US Airways Flight 1549
Damage to other aircraft systems	United Airlines Flight 232
Material failure (Delamination)	Yakovlev (Yak-9s)
Stalling of aerofoils	UAF553, Air France Flight 447
Spatial disorientation/ pilot error	Bell-430, Helicopter, India (2009)

As the safety requirement, the aircrafts are provided with a second or multi engine. In a multi-engine aircraft, if a failure occurs on one of the engines, as a precautionary measure, it is usually landed at a diverted airport instead of continuing to the intended destination. It may result in the aircraft crashing, if an emergency landing is not possible.

2. **Structural failure of the aircraft:** Material fatigue, structural failures and manufacturing defects can cause a catastrophe. Hence, the manufacturer should be very careful and is to be tested very meticulously, strictly, scrupulously and thoroughly.

In present days, the manufacturers of aircrafts are widely using composite materials owing to their light weight and high strength besides being non-corrosive. Composite materials consist of layers of fibers embedded in a resin matrix. However sometimes, when subjected to cyclic stress, the layers of the material may separate from each other (delaminate) and lessen strength, thence developing a failure (refer Table 14.1) inside the material, but nothing visible on the surface. A rigorous inspection and non-destructive testing (NDT) procedures can detect internal defects and can avoid such structural failures.

3. **Stalling:** Stalling an aircraft (increasing the angle of attack to a point at which the wings fail to produce enough lift) is dangerous and can result in a crash if the pilot fails to make a timely correction.

Of course, the systems like stall warning horns (now standard on all powered aircrafts), stick shakers, and voice warnings devices are available to warn the pilot when the aircraft's speed is decreasing close to the stall speed. Stalls occur mostly when pilot allows the airspeed to be too slow for the particular weight and configuration at the time. Further, stall speed is higher when ice/frost sticks to th e wings and/or tail stabilizer and increases with more severe the icing. This is not only because smooth airflow over the wings increases the difficulty, but also due to the additional weight of the accumulated ice. Examples of crashes caused by a full stall of the airfoils (refer table14.1): British European Airways Flight 548 and UAF553 in 1972, Aeroflot 7425 and Arrow Air Fight in 1985. The year 2009 witnessed 3-crashes viz. Colgan-3407, Turkish-1951 and Air France-447.

4. **Electromagnetic interference:** The electronic equipment usage is partially or totally prohibited as it might interact/ interfere with aircraft operation, such as causing disturbance to signal, compass deviations etc. Use of some types of personal electronic devices is prohibited when an aircraft is below 10,000', taking off, or landing. Use of mobile phone, laptops, tablets, book-tops and all such electronic gadgets is prohibited on most flights because in-flight usage may create problems with ground-based cells.
5. **Control Tower Communication and Pilot Error:** Air traffic controllers may get aircraft courses wrong or relay incorrect instructions to pilots, which can cause a crash. Sometimes, the plane may go out of control of tower with a spatial disorientation. This may occur due to environmental problems also, such as rain storm. For example, the Bell-430, helicopter crash on Sep 2, 2009 killed Dr. Y S Rajashekhar Reddy, the then Chief Minister of AP state along with four other government officials at Rudrakonda, India after the communication was lost due to heavy rain. The flight crew decided to go slightly left of their planned route as soon as the pilot noticed weather worsening. Shortly the flight crew encountered a problem with the transmission oil pressure. The pilots were engaged in emergency procedures but in vain. Though the co-pilot continually called out "go around", expecting a crash but due to loss of control and high rate of descent, it crashed by impacting the ground in a steep left bank.

14.5.2 Environmental Causes of Aircraft Crashes

One cannot escape from the 'Acts of God'. Environment created by God can influence to any extent. The lightning, ice/snow, and strong winds can blow a plane off to cause the pilot to lose control of the aircraft and may result in a crash.

Some of the environmental effects are described below.

1. **Lightning:** Boeing studies reveal that airliners are struck by lightning twice per year on average. However, aircrafts mostly withstand lightning strikes without damage. The dangers of more powerful positive lightning were not recognized until the destruction of a glider in 1999. Earlier also such accidents happened such as the crash of Pan Am Flight 214 in 1963, but aircrafts were not designed to withstand lightening strikes during those days because their existence was unknown and not clear.

   The effects of lightning on traditional metal-covered aircraft are well understood now. The Boeing 787 (dreamliner), whose exterior is carbon-fibre-reinforced polymer (FRP) showed no damage from a lightning strike during testing.

2. **Ice and Snow:** Ice and snow can play a major role in causing air accidents. Just a small amount of icing or coarse frost would suffice to impair the wing to develop adequate lift and that is why ice/ snow/ frost on the wings or tail is prohibited. Therefore, in icing conditions of weather, the airlines and airports ensure proper de-icing before takeoff. For example, Air Florida Flight-90 crashed on takeoff in 1982 due to ice/ snow on its wings. In 2005, Southwest Airlines Flight 1248 killed one child on the ground due to heavy snow conditions as it slid off the end of a runway after landing. However, modern airliners are designed to prevent ice build-up on wings, engines, and tails.

   The accumulation of ice during flight can also be catastrophic. This is proven by the crashes of American Eagle Flight-4184 in 1994, and Comair Flight-3272 in 1997. Both were turboprop with straight wings susceptible to in-flight ice accumulation, than are swept-wing jet airliners.

   In order to help pilots for avoiding the in-flight icing conditions, the airline administration requires monitoring the progress of weather along the routes of their flights, and also to be equipped with an ice detector so as to warn pilots about ice accumulation areas, before the situation becomes critical. The modern airplanes and helicopters are provided with "Pitot Heating" to prevent accidents like Air France Flight 447 caused by the pitot tube freezing and giving false readings.

3. **Rain Storm and Hailstorm**: The sudden changes in weather and the rainy conditions often pose difficulty to the aircrafts. Most of the crashes occurred due to environmental causes are due to bad weather conditions including hailstorms and rain storms in addition to lightening. (e.g. The Bell-430 helicopter crash, on 2nd Sep, 2009)

4. **Volcanic Ash:** An active volcano with its plumes of volcanic ash can damage propellers, engines and cockpit windows. For example, in 1982,

British Airways Flight-9 when flew through an ash cloud temporarily lost power from all 4-engines. It was badly damaged, with all leading edges scratched, front windscreens so badly "sand blasted" and could not be used to land the aircraft. Volcanic Ash Advisory Centers enable liaison between meteorologists, volcanologists, and the aviation industry.

5. **Foreign object debris (FOD):** The air accidents by foreign object debris (FOD) may occur because of either natural or manmade causes. The natural causes include hailstorm or dust-devil or tornado or dust in air etc. The manmade causes include items left in the aircraft structure during manufacture/ repairs, debris not cleared on the runway and some solids encountered in flight, which can damage engines and other parts of the aircraft. A strange incident! Air France Flight 4590 crashed due to hitting a part that had fallen from another aircraft.

14.5.3 Human Factors for Air Accidents

Most of the air accidents occurred due to human errors or negligence. The human factors involved in air accidents may be attributed to the errors or mistakes of the pilots and crew or due to the wrong or misleading communication given by the persons at ground controlling. Most common causes occurred hither to in air accidents are listed below.

> **O My God!**
>
> **CRM?**
>
> Much progress in applying human factors analysis to improving aviation safety was made around the time of WW-II by such pioneers as Paul Fitts and Alphonse Chapanis. However, there has been progress in safety throughout the history of aviation, such as the development of the pilot's checklist in 1937. CRM, or Crew Resource Management, is a technique that makes use of the experience and knowledge of the complete flight crew to avoid dependence on just one crew member.

1. **Pilot Error:** Human factors such as pilot errors and miscommunication are yet another potential set of factors, most commonly found in aviation accidents. A pilot may interpret readings incorrectly, miss certain instructions, or otherwise cause the plane to crash. Accidents of this kind can occur in the air (e.g. 1978 Pacific Southwest Airlines Flight 182) or on the ground (e.g. 1977 Tenerife disaster). The communication lapses have internal and external factors. The ability of the flight crew is a critical human factor in air safety. The skill of pilot is crucial particularly, during take-off and landing.

   Example:

   (i) Pilot error (improper maintenance also): American Airlines Flight-191 on landing (1972).

   (ii) Pilot's improper monitoring of instruments crashed Eastern Air Lines Flight-401 (1972).

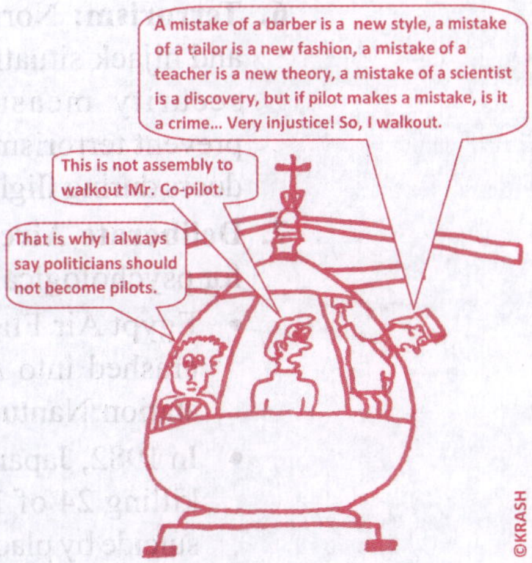

2. **Pilot Fatigue:** The International Civil Aviation Organization (ICAO) defines fatigue as, "A physiological state of reduced mental or physical performance capability resulting from sleep loss or extended wakefulness, circadian phase, or workload".

   Fatigue poses great risk on the crew as well as passengers as it can significantly enhance the probability of pilot errors. Generally, fatigue is prevalent among pilots because of unexpected working hours, longextended duty periods, circadian disruption, difference in temperature pressure conditions and insufficient sleep and so forth. These factors can occur together to produce a combination of sleep deprivation, circadian rhythm effects, and 'time-on task' fatigue. However, the fatigue may be reduced by limiting the working hours and allowing flying as per human comfort.
3. **Pilot Intoxicated:** Rare but it is possible that flight crew members may be in intoxicated condition. If found so, they are arrested or subjected to disciplinary action for being drunken on the job. There are quite a few incidents occurred in this regard. Some examples are given below:
   (i) In 1990, three drunken crew members flying in Northwest Airlines were sentenced to jail. In 2001, Northwest fired a pilot for failing breathalyzer test after a flight.
   (ii) In July 2002, both pilots of America West Airlines Flight-556 were arrested, fired and licences revoked just before flying for drinking alcohol.
   (iii) A fatal accident by drunken pilots of Aero Flight-311 crashed at Koivulahti, Finland, killed all 25 on board in 1961.
4. **Crew Negligence:** There are a few incidents attributed to a little negligence. The cargo door was not closed properly on Turkish Airlines Flight-981 in 1974, led to loss of the aircraft (of course, design of cargo door latch was also a major factor). The improper repair of previous damage on Japan Airlines Flight-123, resulted in explosive decompression of the cabin that destroyed the vertical stabilizer and all (4) hydraulic systems, which power all the flight controls.
5. **Misleading or lack of information:** A pilot wrongly communicated by a document (manual, map, etc.), or a faulty instrument or indicator (in the cockpit or on the ground), or inaccurate instructions or information from flight or ground control can lose spatial orientation, or make another mistake, and consequently lead to accidents or near-misses.

6. **Terrorism:** Normally aircrew are trained to handle terrorism attacks and hijack situations. Particularly, after the Sep 11, 2001 attacks, strict security measures are in practice at airports and airlines to prevent terrorism, such as security checkpoints and locking the cockpit doors during flight.
7. **Deliberate Aircrew Actions:**Although most air crews are screened for psychological fitness, some have taken suicidal actions.
   - Egypt Air Flight-990 (1999), it seems, the first officer deliberately crashed into Atlantic Ocean while the captain was away from his station Nantucket, Massachusetts.
   - In 1982, Japan Airlines Flight-350 crashed at Tokyo Haneda Airport, killing 24 of 174 on board by a mentally ill captain who attempted suicide by placing inboard engines into reverse thrust, while the aircraft was close to the runway. The first officer had not enough time to countermand before the aircraft stalled and crashed.
   - Silk Air Flight-185 (1997) suddenly went into a high dive from its cruising height with so high speed that the aircraft broke apart before it crashed near Palembang, Sumatra. The 3-yr investigation of Indonesia couldn't find cause, finally, US NTSB concluded as deliberate suicide by the captain.
   - On Mar 24, 2015, German wings Flight-9525 (Airbus A320-200) crashed 100 km (62 mi) northwest of Nice, in French Alps, after a constant descent from cruise altitude. All 144 passengers and 6 crew members died. The crash was intentionally caused by the co-pilot, Andreas Lubitz. Having been declared "unfit to work" without telling his employer, he reported for duty and during the flight locked the pilot out of the cabin. In response to the incident, Canada, New Zealand, Germany and Australia implemented new regulations that two authorized personnel to be present in cockpit at all times. Three days later, European Aviation Safety Agency issued a recommendation to ensure at least two crew members, including at least one pilot, are in the cockpit at all times. Several airlines already adopted similar policies voluntarily.
8. **Controlled Flight Into Terrain (CFIT):** *Controlled flight into terrain* (CFIT) accident is said to have occurred when an aircraft is flown under control into terrain or man-made structures. CFIT accidents may result from pilot error or of navigational system error. In Dec 1995, American Airlines Flight-965 tracked off while approaching Cali, Colombia and hit a mountainside although a terrain awareness and warning system (TAWS) in the cockpit warned and desperate pilot attempt to gain altitude.

Another tool is the Minimum Safe Altitude Warning (MSAW) system to monitor aircraft altitudes by comparing with system definedminimum safe altitudes. In this system, the air traffic controller receives an acoustic / visual warning, when the aircraft islower, or to be lower than the minimum safe altitude, and who in turn can alert the pilot.

9. **Military Action:** Passenger planes have rarely been attacked in both peacetime and war. However, there are some occasions happened in the history of air accidents. A few examples are given below.
   - In 1955, Bulgaria shot down El Al Flight 402.
   - In 1973, Israel shot down Libyan Arab Airlines Flight 114.
   - In 1983, SU shot down Korean Air Lines Flight 007.
   - In 1988, US shot down Iran Air Flight 655.
   - In 2001, Ukrainian Air Force accidentally shot Siberia Airlines Flight-1812 during an exercise
   - In 2014, Malaysia Airlines Flight 17 was shot down.

14.5.4 Fire Accidents in Aircrafts

We know that fire and its toxic smoke can cause accidents. Of course! Safety regulations control aircraft requirements through automated fire safety systems. The boarders are strictly prohibited from carrying the fire producing materials/ inflammables. Therefore, the possible cause of fires in airplanes may be due to electrical wiring problems. Following are some of the possible causes

- wires with breached insulation touch each other
- by water dripping on wires or (improperly insulated/ breached) electrical systems
- short circuits

These are difficult to detect when the aircraft is on the ground. However, reflectometry can feasibly test live wires on aircraft during flight. Some examples are given below:

(i) An electrical fire on Air Canada Flight 797 in 1983 caused the deaths of 23 of the 46 passengers.

(ii) In 1985, a fire on the runway caused the loss of 55 lives, 48 from lethal toxic gas and smoke in the British Air tours Flight 28M accident.

(iii) South African Airways Flight 295 was lost in the Indian Ocean in 1987 after an in-flight fire in cargo hold (The cargo holds are now equipped with automated fire extinguishing systems to combat a fire that might occur in baggage holds).

(iv) In May 1996, ValuJet Flight 592 crashed into the Florida Everglades a few minutes after takeoff due to a fire in forward cargo hold, killing all 110 people on board.

14.5.5 Bird Strike

Bird strike is the term used in aviation for a collision between a bird and an aircraft. Several fatal accidents occurred by bird ingestion and bird strikes breaking cockpit windshields. The weight and numbers of birds that can be ingested without hazarding the safe flight of the aircraft are related to the engine intake area.

The effect of ingestion depends on the number and weight of birds and where they strike, the fan blade span or the nose cone. Core damage often occurs by impacts near blade root or on nose cone.

The highest risk of bird strike is near airports during takeoff and landing, and during low-level flying by military aircraft, crop dusters and helicopters.

Some countermeasures to bird strike are given below:

Active countermeasures

- Person with a shotgun through recorded sounds
- Planting poisonous grass that is not palatable to birds/ insects that attract insectivorous birds

Passive countermeasures

- sensible land-use management
- avoiding conditions attracting flocks of birds to the area (e.g. landfills)
- let the grass at airfield grow taller (~12 in or 30 cm) as birds generally won't land if they cannot see one another

O My God!

baggage hit brought aircraft down?

The depressurization occurred on Alaska Airlines Flight 536 in 2005 due to a baggage handler hit the side of aircraft with a tug towing a train of carts during ground services. This damaged metal skin of the aircraft, which was not reported and the plane departed. On rising to 26,000 ft (7,900 m), the damaged section of skin gave way due to difference in pressure between the inside (of craft) and outside air. The cabin explosively depressurized necessitating a rapid descent to denser (breathable) air and an emergency landing. Post landing examination revealed a 12 in (30 cm) hole on the right side of the airplane

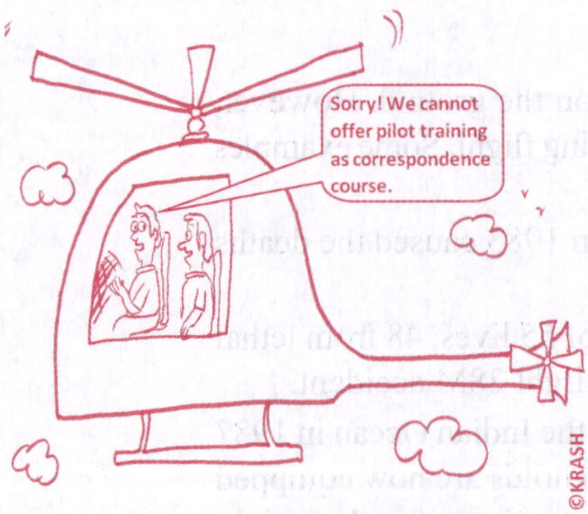

14.5.6 Ground Damage and Runway Accidents

Various ground support equipment which operate in close proximity may cause damage to wings occasionally in the form of scratches, erasing paint or small dents in the skin which subsequently might corrode if goes unnoticed. However, all damages are inspected, measured, and possibly tested to ensure within safe tolerances.

Runway Accidents

There are four types of runway accidents as follows.

- **Runway excursion:** Only a single aircraft making an inappropriate exit from the runway (e.g. American Airlines Flight-191)

- **Runway overrun:** a type of excursion where the aircraft does not stop before the end of the runway (e.g., Air France Flight 358)
- **Runway incursion:** incorrect presence of a vehicle, person, or another aircraft on the runway (e.g., Tenerife airport disaster)
- **Runway confusion:** crew misidentification the runway for landing or take-off (e.g., Comair Flight 191, Singapore Airlines Flight 6)

14.5.7 Roles of various People in Preventing Air Accident

Air accident prevention is the responsibility of every individual involved in the system ranging from government through airport authorities to the passengers. The following paragraphs briefly describe the roles of those involved.

Government

Airport design and location can have a large impact on aviation safety. Many older airports do not meet the standard. The facilities and designs have to be updated and modernized by the government as per the standards as when required on war footing.

Airport Authorities

The airport authorities have to inspect and audit time to time for updating and making it accident free zone. Frequent inspections can avoid accidents considerably and makes all the difference. Any lacunae should be reported to the control room and higher officials for suitable action. The control tower should be alert 24×7, and give instructions to the concerned without any confusion and ambiguity.

Pilots and Crew

- Check the weather very frequently
- Always check the equipment in advance before they use
- Follow the instructions about the course of action time to time given by control tower
- If something is wrong with the aircraft, do not try to fly and inform the same to control tower
- Confirm instructions from the control tower with the readings on navigational instruments.
- If you feel something is wrong during flight, communicate the problem immediately to the crew and to the control tower and make an attempt to land the plane as soon as possible.

Passenger

- Don't be panic and stay calm
- Follow crew instructions

- Keeping calm and listening to directions can mean the difference between life and death in the emergency.

SELF ASSESSMENT INTERMISSION (SAI – 14.5)

1. Classify air accidents with reference their cause of occurrence.
2. What are various technical reasons for air accidents?
3. What are various human errors that can cause air accidents?
4. What are various environmental factors that can trigger an air accident?
5. Enumerate various types of air accidents involving human errors.
6. Write a short note on stalling with reference to air accidents.
7. What type behaviour and attitude lead to a aircraft crash? How? Give examples.
8. How does a bird strike cause the aircraft crash? Suggest some methods to prevent it.
9. What is the effect of the following in causing air accidents? Give examples
   (a) Rain storm and lightning (b) Volcanic eruption
   (c) Ice and Snow
10. What is the effect of the following in causing air accidents? Give examples
    (a) Pilot errors (b) terrorism (c) fatigue
11. Give short notes on air accidents due to (a) bird strike (b) fire
12. What are the adverse effects of air accidents? What measures do you suggest to the passengers to prevent the air mishaps?
13. Explain briefly about the ground damage and runway accidents.
14. What do you understand by controlled flight into terrain (CFIT)? Explain.
15. What are the general principles one should follow in planes so as to avoid/prevent the accidents?
16. Discuss the role of pilots and the crew in preventing air accidents.
17. Discuss the role of government in preventing and mitigating the air accidents.

MINI-PROJECTS / CASE STUDIES

1. Choose a road of your choice and identify the accident prone area. Take the past data and analyze the causes. Suggest some methods to prevent.
2. Prepare a presentation with causes and effects of top 10 of (a) air crashes and (b) maritime accidents (c) train accidents.

15 CHAPTER

Violence, Terrorism and Wars

(The Manmade Disasters)

O'MY SILENT INNER VIBES (O'M S I V – 15)

The Hindu mythological stories from Bhagavatam, Ramayan and Maha Bharat manifest several big wars. If these are considered to have happened in the history, they could be the earliest wars. The end of Dwapar Yug witnessed the largest World War called Maha Bharath War. [It is the earliest recorded war in the known history occurred in the Mesolithic age, about 14,000 years ago]. Lord Krishna tried to prevent the war, but in vein. However, He fought to establish the Dharma and Shanti (the peace).

The Holy Quran has several references of wars. The one to quote is the history behind Muharram. Though Muharram is the 1st month of the Islamic calendar, marked as the New Year, it is commemorated to remember the brutal assassination of Hazrat Imam Hussain Ali, the grandson of Prophet Muhammad (SAS), at the battle of Karbala. The month of Muharram is observed as a period of mourning by all the Muslims, the central theme of which is only peace, As Husssian (AS) told "Be like flower that gives fragrance to even the hand that crushes it'.

Even the Bible says, the Lord Jesus, the son of God came on to the Earth to establish peace and to redeem humanity. He cleansed the human sins with His bloodshed and gave a message that blood can be used for peace not for violence. He preached us what the real sacrifice is.

The Saints, Sages (Rishis) and Gurus of all religions advocate the same.

Lord Sai Baba, the Avadhoot, used to utter the words 'Sab Ka Malik Ek' and advised the world to observe 'Shradha and Saboori' (The peace and patience).

Samrat Ashoka, the Great Emperor of Mourya Dynasty was upset and mentally disturbed with aftermath of kalinga war and adapted Buddhism to establish peace.

The leaders like Mahatma Gandhi, Khan Abdul Gaffar Khan (Frontier Gandhi), Mother St. Theresa, Nelson Mandela and so forth, fought for the peace and laid the path of non-violence. Even Alfred Nobel wanted to use his dynamite for peace, but not for violence.

Whatsoever the religion, creed, clan or caste is, the ultimate theme says 'wellbeing of human being'. Violence and wars never did any good to mankind in any history.

Yes! Nations neither require any security forces nor weapons if humans observe peace. The huge money, efforts, and energy spent on producing the weapons, employing the soldiers and maintaining the department of defense otherwise could have been better used, and for development of mankind.

But, can we imagine without security force? How great the day it would be, if a country does not require any security force.

So, one should never forget, due to whose day and night endless and untiring labour and efforts, we are safely enjoying our days and sleeping in night without any fear. Yes! It is the soldiers (Jawans), security forces and the police. Let us salute to our protectors. Let this chapter be a tribute to those who have sacrificed and have been sacrificing their lives in providing safety and security to the people of their country to live in peace.

JAI JAWAN!

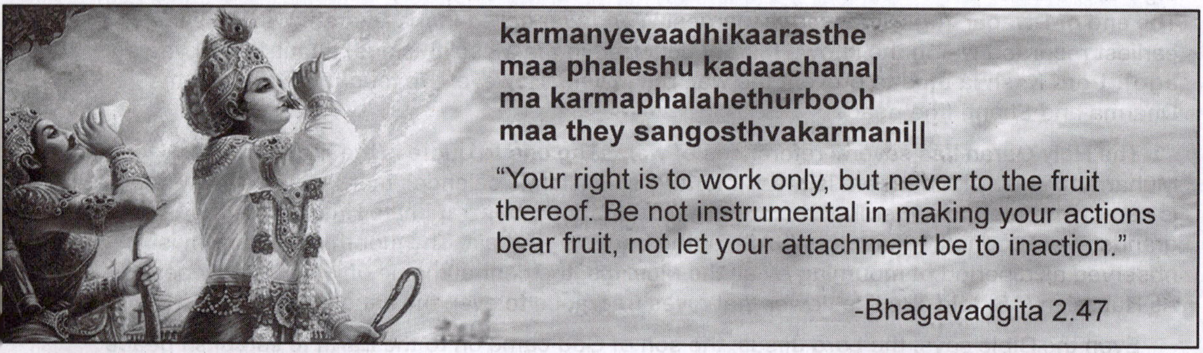
karmanyevaadhikaarasthe
maa phaleshu kadaachana|
ma karmaphalahethurbooh
maa they sangosthvakarmani||
"Your right is to work only, but never to the fruit thereof. Be not instrumental in making your actions bear fruit, not let your attachment be to inaction."
-Bhagavadgita 2.47

"The most merciful person is the one who forgives when he is able to take revenge."
- Imam Hussain (as)
Be Like the flower that gives its fragrance to even the hand that crushes it
Imam Ali (A.S)
The most generous of people, is the one who gives to those from whom he was no hope of return.
imam Hussain (as)

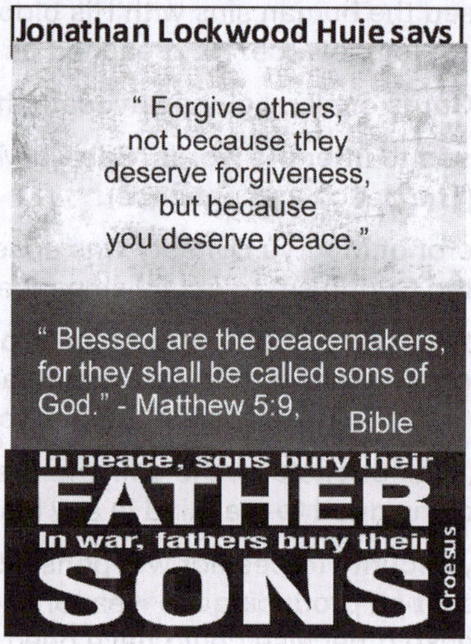
Jonathan Lockwood Huie says
" Forgive others, not because they deserve forgiveness, but because you deserve peace."
" Blessed are the peacemakers, for they shall be called sons of God." - Matthew 5:9,
Bible
In peace, sons bury their
FATHER
In war, fathers bury their
SONS
Croesus

If you don't fight
for what you want,
don't cry
for what you lose.
Buddhism
There was never a good
WAR
or a bad
PEACE
Benjamin Franklin

15.1 VIOLENCE – CONCEPT AND DEFINITION

Violence of many forms is preventable since it is a manmade disaster. Of course! The levels of violence strongly related on modifiable factors such as concentrated poverty, income and gender inequality, the harmful use of alcohol, and the absence of safe, stable, and nurturing relationships among people, especially between children and parents. Therefore, strategic addressing of the underlying causes of violence can prevent violence effectively.

Definition

The WHO defines **Violence** as "*the intentional use of physical force or power, threatened or actual, against oneself, another person, or against a group or community, which either results in or has a high likelihood of resulting in injury, death, psychological harm, maldevelopment, or deprivation*".

15.1.1 Concept of Violence

The violence can occur by/on an individual or a group. Thus it can be differentiated by how it is inflicted i.e. by a person upon self or by another individual or by a small group of individuals, or by larger groups such as states, organized political groups, militia groups and terrorist organizations.

> **O My God!**
>
> **Gun Culture in USA?**
>
> **In USA and Africa, out of every 100,000 people, each year an estimated 61 die a violent death. Corlin, the former president of American Medical association (AMA) said: "The US leads the world in the rate of children deaths from firearms. He concluded: "Gun violence is a threat to the public health of our country"**

Violence may be featured through physical, sexual, psychological and/ or emotional setbacks or any combinations of these setbacks.

15.1.2 Types of Violence

For the sake of understanding, let us classify the violence into three broad categories based on the persons inflicted:

- self-directed violence – includes Suicide (individual to self)
- interpersonal violence – includes Homicide (one to one; one to many)
- collective violence – includes terrorism, wars (groups to groups)

Truly speaking, the dividing lines between the different types of violence are not always so clear. For example, the 'war on drugs', rather than increasing the health and well-being of at risk demographics, most often results in violence against these vulnerable people through imprisonment and police brutality. It is very difficult to categorize such violence. Further, some types of violence have unique characteristics and distinguishable features from others while some others overlap. For example, a violence started as interpersonal may turn out as collective violence.

– A case study on Telangana Movement (1969 & 2000-2010)

Although India is named for 'Unity in Diversity', sporadically incidents have been taking place not only on communal basis, but also on non-communal platforms, of which the noteworthy is 'Telangana Movement'. It took about 369 lives in its 1st phase (1969-72), while more than 1200 lives (almost all the cases are suicides) during the 2nd phase (2009-12).

Seeking the separate state, people of Telangana region (The Hyderabad state under Nizam's rule before independence till 1956), against people of Andhra revolted in 1969. The govt. suppressed it, while 369 people were killed and many injured in firing. Again, in 1972, the Jai Andhra movement by people of Andhra region revolted and was subsided.

But, later, in the year 2000, the revolution re-emerged under Telangana Rashtriya Samithi (TRS) party, led by Mr. K. Chandra Shekhar Rao (KCR), guided and theorized by Prof. K. Jaya Shankar. The movement was calm and peaceful for about 6 years. Though not attributed to violence, it suffered both Telanganites and Andhrites during 2009-12. On 9th Dec 2009, the then Minister for Finance (UPA Govt), Mr. Chidambaram announced the state in response to KCR's fast unto death, but was taken-back by the political forces of Andhra leaders and their motivated Samaikyandhra movement. Both the movements are pacified temporarily with formation of Sri Krishna Committee. Finally, the movement led by Mr. KCR of TRS, Prof. Kodandaram of Telangana Joint Action Committee (T-JAC) supported by all National political parties and all sections of people, ended with the formation of the new 29th Indian state, Telangana on 2nd June 2012. Though sporadic incidents of violence by police actions took place (such as that in Osmania University), there was no communal rioting no interpersonal and no collective violence; however, movement was vigorous and went on peaks during 2009-2011, which consumed about 1400 young lives through suicides (mostly students) in Telangana and a few in Seema-Andhra. The sacrifice (by self burning) of a student Srikanthachary motivated many students towards suicides. However, the role of students in the movement is noteworthy in the agitation and the success of formation of Telangana state on 2nd June 2014.

Can we consider it as a case of violence? Is it a peaceful agitation?

Let us now understand the above in detail.

1. **Self-directed Violence:** Self-directed violence is subdivided into suicidal behaviour and self-abuse i.e. suicidal thoughts, attempted suicides (also called *para-suicide* or *deliberate self-injury*) and self-mutilation.

   Among young people are now at highest risk in the 3rd world, in both developed and developing countries. In the last 45 years, suicide rates have increased by 60% worldwide. For example, almost all the cases (about 1200 youngsters) at various times and places of Telangana state in India have sacrificed their lives during the Telangana movement-2007-11.

   In the recent past, the suicides in youth have increased. The suicides are increasingly occurring among farmers due to loans, school and college students due to failures in love or studies and unemployed youth out of frustration.

   Suicide is one of the 3rd leading causes of death among the age group 15–44 yrs while 2nd leading cause in the 10–24 yrs age group. These figures do not include suicide attempts which are up to 20 times more frequent than completed suicide. Suicide was the 16th leading cause of death worldwide in 2004 and is projected to increase to the 12th in 2030.

2. **Interpersonal violence:** Interpersonal violence can be one of the following forms

   - **Intimate Partner Violence:** This is the violence caused usually, on the family or intimate partner (e.g. spouse), business partner, on elderly persons such as father or mother, or child maltreatment, sexual abuse, eve teasing, women harassment and so forth, though not exclusively at home. When interpersonal violence occurs in families, through physical aggression, sexual coercion, psychological abuse and indifferent behaviour, its consequences can also affect parents, children, and their relationship in long- and short terms physical, mental, sexual and reproductive health problems for victims and for their children, and lead to high social and economic costs. These include both fatal and non-fatal injuries, depression and post-traumatic stress disorder, unintended pregnancies, sexually transmitted infections, including HIV.

Forms of violence such as child maltreatment and intimate partner violence are highly prevalent. Nearly 20% of women and 5–10% of men report being sexually abused as children, while 25–50% of all children report being physically abused. The WHO study revealed that between 15–71% of women reported experiencing physical and/ or sexual violence by an intimate partner at some point in their lives.

- **Homicides:** Frustrated unemployed youth, ill-treated/ maltreated child in his/her youth, suppressed people, maniacs, individuals influenced by a community or a proved by some activity etc. are categorized under this class. The homicides have been common and regular feature in almost all parts of the world. Poorer countries, especially those with large difference between rich and poor, show higher rates of homicide than wealthier countries. Homicide rates differ markedly by age and sex. For 15-30 age groups, male rates were nearly 6 times those of female while for remaining age groups, it is 2-4 times.
- **Community Violence**: This type of violence occurs between individuals who are unrelated, and who may or may not know each other, generally taking place outside the home on the communal grounds or a specific motive. This also includes youth violence, random acts of violence, rape or sexual assault by strangers and violence in institutional settings such as schools, workplaces, prisons and nursing homes.

3. **Collective Violence:**Unlike the other two broad categories discussed above, the collective violence would have certain motives for violence committed by larger groups of individuals or by states. Collective violence is further classified into two sub-categories as follows.

- **Structured violence:** Collective violence that is committed to advance a particular social agenda includes, for example, terrorism, crimes of hate committed by organized groups and mob violence. Political violence includes war and related violent conflicts, state violence and similar acts carried out by larger groups.
- **Economic violence:** It includes attacks by larger groups motivated by economic gain – such as attacks carried out with the purpose of disrupting economic activity, denying access to essential services, or creating economic division and fragmentation. Clearly, acts committed by larger groups can have multiple motives.

15.1.3 Violence with Specific Features

As a matter of fact, it is very difficult to classify the violence because; some are overlapping while some others need to be addressed under separate head owing to their extremity of features of violence or distinctly different nature. The following are a few of them.

(A) War: *"War is a state of prolonged violent large-scale conflict involving two or more groups of people, usually under the auspices of government".*

Though it is classified as a kind of collective violence, it is categorized under a separate head as it is the most extreme form due to which the term violence cannot suffice to describe it. It is fought generally for

- resolving territorial and other conflicts,
- as war of aggression to conquer territory or loot resources,
- in national self-defense or liberation, or
- to suppress attempts of part of the nation to secede from it

We know also ideological, religious and revolutionary wars.

WW-I casualties were over 40 million and WW-II casualties were over 70 million.

(B) Communal Violence: *"This kind of violence occurs on communal grounds and may have both structure as well as economic objective".*

This is inflicted by a certain community of people instigated or led or organized by a person or group or organization. This also includes wars, battles and attacks on communal basis. Due to its significance, this is elaborated in the next sections to follow in this chapter.

(C) Child Maltreatment: Though this violence is classified under interpersonal violence by intimate person, it may be even due to unknown person also. Further, this is a global problem with serious lifelong consequence, which is complex and difficult to study.

Child maltreatment is defined as *"the abuse and neglect that occurs to children under 18 years of age. It includes all types of physical and/or emotional ill-treatment, sexual abuse, neglect, and commercial or other child exploitation, which results in actual or potential harm to the child's health, survival, development or dignity in the context of a relationship of responsibility, trust, or power. Exposure to intimate partner violence is also sometimes included as a form of child maltreatment".*

Consequences of child maltreatment include impaired lifelong physical and mental health, and social and occupational functioning (e.g. school, job, and relationship difficulties). These can ultimately slow a country's economic and social development. Prevention of child maltreatment is possible but needs a multi-directional approach. Effective prevention programmes support parents and teach positive parenting skills.

(D) Youth Violence: The WHO defines youth as *"people between the ages of 10 and 29 years"*.

Youth violence is defined as *"the violence occurring among youths, and includes acts that range from bullying and physical fighting, through more severe sexual and physical assault to homicide"*.

Worldwide 2.5 lakh homicides occur among youth each year, which is comprises 41% of the total homicides (WHO-2008). For each young person killed, 20-40 more sustain injuries. Youth violence causes a serious, often lifelong, impact on a person's psychological and social functioning has a great impact on costs of health, welfare and criminal justice services. Further it reduces the national productivity, the value of property and national economy.

(E) Elder Maltreatment: Elder maltreatment may be *"a single or repeated act, or lack of appropriate attention toward the old persons (e.g. parents or grandparents), that causes distress in them involving a violation of human rights and includes physical, sexual, psychological, emotional; financial and material abuse, abandonment, neglect and serious loss of dignity and respect"*.

Most unfortunate is that the older people are often afraid to report cases of maltreatment to family, friends, or to the authorities. Information on the extent of the problem can be obtained from hospitals, nursing homes, old-age homes and other long-term care facilities, however the records are scarce. Elder maltreatment can lead to serious physiological and psychological problems.

To prevent elder maltreatment and mitigate its consequences, the governments could plan the following three strategies

- public and professional awareness campaigns,
- screening (of potential victims and abusers) and take suitable action,
- encourage caregiver support interventions (e.g. stress management), adult protective services and self-help groups.

(F) Sexual Violence: Sexual violence is defined as *"any sexual act, attempt to obtain a sexual act, unwanted sexual comments or advances, or acts to traffic, or otherwise directed against a* *person's sexuality using coercion, by any person regardless of their relationship to the victim, in any setting. It includes rape, defined as the physically forced or otherwise coerced penetration of the vulva or anus with a penis, other body part or object".* This violence is a serious problem all over the world including developed and developing countries.

Sexual violence poses serious short and long-term consequences on physical, mental, sexual and reproductive health for victims and for their children as described above. Further, if perpetrated during childhood, it can lead to risky sexual behaviours in later life. Every country is paying a special attention and made legal acts to address this problem. Yet it is not sufficient and so, to achieve lasting hange, it is important to enact legislation make modifications, amendments. and develop policies that protect women; address discrimination againstwomen and promote gender equality; and help to move the culture away from violence.

(G) Targeted Violence: Several painful episodes of assassination, attempted assassination and school shootings took place at elementary/ middle/ high schools, colleges and universities (particularly in US). Even the highest powers of their countries such as president of America (e.g. John F. Kennedy), Prime Ministers of India (e.g. Indira Gandhi, Rajiv Gandhi) were also the victims of such brutal acts. The studies (1995–2002) investigated named such attacks as "targeted violence," and laid out suggestions for law enforcement. A major point from these research studies is that targeted violence does not just "come out of the blue".

(H) Non-Physical Violence: Violence need not be physical handling, but can be by a result of exercising power, such as threats and intimidation, blackmail, neglect or acts of omission and so forth. Many forms of violence against women, children and the elderly, result in physical, psychological and social problems that do not necessarily lead to injury, disability or death. Such non-physical violence has a wide range of outcomes – encompassing psychological harm, deprivation and depression. These consequences can be immediate, as well as latent, and can last for years after the initial abuse. Outcomes solely defined in terms of injury or death, limits the understanding of the full impact of this kind of violence. Truly speaking, this violence is mostly invisible and sometimes beyond the reach of law.

The Hyderabad Riots

Hyderabad recorded a history of Hindu-Muslim violence, in 1984 and early 1990s. In fact, a land dispute unrelated to religious matters caused the killing of Sardar, a Muslim auto-rickshaw driver, by two Hindus. But in light of the Babri mosque controversy, people saw it as a Hindu-Muslim conflict. In response to Sardar's killing, Muslims killed 4 Hindus in different parts of the city. BJP workers then attacked Majid Khan, an influential Muslim leader in the Sabzi Mandi area. As false rumours about his death spread, Muslim mobs came out in open, followed by the Hindu mobs, and the violence spread. The violence lasted for 10 wks, and resulted in 200-300 deaths; 1000s were injured. Not a single rioter was arrested. CM Marri Chenna Reddy, of IN Congress, claimed that the riot had been engineered by his rivals in his own party, who wanted to oust him.

15.1.4 Triggering Factors

Various triggers and factors associated with their perpetration and experiencing of one or more of the aforesaid types of violence are

- demographic characteristics
  - low levels of education
  - age related feelings
  - income group (rich for perpetration and poor for vulnerability)
- cultural factors
  - the community/ parental over restrictions
  - boundaries posed by caste or community
- biographic and biological factors
  - genetic disorders
  - history of violence as a perpetrator
  - family history and background
- psychological factors
  - psycho behaviour
  - antisocial personality disorder
  - perversions and maniacs
  - effect of corporal punishments at childhood
- personal factors
  - marital discord
  - a victim or a witness of parental violence
  - extra-marital relations
  - dissatisfaction over the partner
- Social factors
  - use of drugs and tranquilizers
  - harmful level of consumption of alcohol
  - friendships and moving circles
- personality and behavioural factors
  - low level of understanding or immaturity
  - attitudes that are accepting of violence
  - frustrations and depressions/ distress
  - having multiple partners, and

The above list is not exhaustive and most of the listed factors are overlapping. Further, no single factor can suffice to explain the trigger for causing violence, because the causes are quite complex and happen at different levels. To understand this complexity, we need to refer the ecological or socio-ecological model.

15.1.5 Ecological Model

The version of the ecological model comprises of following four-levels to study of violence

Level-1: The first level explores biological and personal factors that influence how an individual behaves and how such factor enhance the likelihood of becoming a victim or perpetrator of violence. The inputs for analysis at this level can be obtained by scanning the demographic characteristics (age, education, and income), personality disorders, genetics, brain lesions, substance abuse, and a history of experiencing, witnessing, or engaging in violent behaviour.

Level-2: The second level of analysis focuses on close relationships, such as those with family and friends. In youth violence, for example, having friends who engage in or encourage violence can enhance a young person's risk to become a victim or perpetrator of violence. In the case of intimate partner violence, this level advocates through marital conflict or discord in the relationship, while in case of elder maltreatment, the important factors could be the stress due to the nature of the past relationships between the abused person and the care giver.

Level-3: The third level identifies through community context — i.e. neighbourhoods, schools, workplaces and also the vulnerable environments. Risk at this level may be affected by factors such as the existence of a local drug trade, the absence of social networks, and concentrated poverty. All these factors have been shown to be important in several types of violence.

Level-4: Finally, the fourth level looks at the broad societal and cultural factors that help to create a climate in which violence is encouraged or inhibited. At this level analysis focuses on responsiveness of the criminal justice system, the flaws in laws, parent-child relationships, social/ cultural norms regarding gender roles, income inequality, the strength/ weakness of the social welfare system, the social acceptability, the availability of weapons, the exposure to violence in mass media, and political instability.

15.1.6 Violence Prevention Approaches and Strategies

There are several approaches to preventing the violence, of which the most used strategies all over the world are Public health approach and Human rights approach.

(A) Public Health Approach : Public health is one of the major concerns in respect of the causes and effects of violence both physiological (injuries) and psychological (stresses and shocks). From a public health perspective, prevention and controlling strategies can be classified into three types:

- Primary prevention approaches – aim at prevention of violence before it occurs.
- Secondary prevention approaches – focus on immediate responses to violence, such as pre-hospital care, emergency services, psychotherapy, treatment for sexually transmitted infections following a rape and so forth.
- Tertiary prevention approaches – concentrate on long-term care, such as rehabilitation and reintegration, and lessen trauma or reduce long-term disability associated with violence.

Prevention is always better than cure. Thence, it is obvious that the public health approach should focus on the primary prevention of violence, i.e. stopping them from occurrence. However, sensing or identifying is the most critical element since it is either asymptomatic or with invisible symptoms. Whatsoever, approaches to prevent violence, whether targeted at individuals or entire communities, must be properly evaluated for their effectiveness and the results shared.

The public health approach may be adapted through a systematic and evidence-based process that is directed through the following four-step path (**DISA - D**efine, **I**nvestigate, **S**et up and **A**ssess):

1. **D**efine the problem conceptually with the statistics that describe
   - the nature and scale of violence,
   - the characteristics of those most affected,
   - the geographical distribution of incidents, and
   - the consequences of exposure to such violence.
2. **I**nvestigate the reasons for occurrence and explore the factors that
   - increase or decrease the risk of its occurrence,
   - can be modified through intervention,
   - can find the ways and means to prevent the problem.
3. **S**et up through designing programmes by using above information that are
   - legally permitted,
   - scientifically proven,
   - practicable and effective.
4. **A**ssess the effectiveness of programmes through outcome based evaluations that should include
   - Circulate the information to execute through proven effective programmes,
   - Adapt the programmes to local contexts and implement them,
   - Monitor to ensure the effectiveness and/or re-evaluate in the new setting.

(B) Human Rights Approach: The human rights approach is built on the obligations of states to respect, protect and fulfil human rights and thence to prevent, eradicate and punish violence. It recognizes violence as a violation of many human rights of which most important are:

1. the rights to life, liberty, autonomy and security of the person;
2. the rights to equality and non-discrimination;
3. the rights to be free from torture and cruel, inhuman and degrading treatment or punishment;
4. the right to privacy; and
5. the right to the highest attainable standard of health.

These human rights are respected in international as well as regional treaties and included in national constitutions and laws, which stipulate the obligations and include mechanisms to be accountable. An autonomous body, Human Rights Commission (HRC) is set up by the nations, to look after these issues.

The government should take all appropriate legislative, administrative, legal, social and educational measures to protect the child and woman from all forms of physical or mental violence, injury or abuse, neglect or negligent treatment, maltreatment or exploitation, including sexual abuse. The courts of law, educational institutions and social groups should cooperate and conduct the programmes in this direction in coordination with HRC.

15.1.7 Prevention Programmes

Prevention programmes to be effective or to have promise to reducing youth violence include

- schools-based anti-bullying or prevention programmes; and
- life skills and social development programmes with an objective to
    - reduce access to alcohol,
    - reduce use of illegal drugs,
    - reduce access to weapons and guns,
    - manage anger and emotions,
    - resolve conflict, and
    - develop the necessary social skills to solve problems.
- prohibiting corporal punishments
- create positively significant neighbourhood effects
- intervention involving relocating families to better or less poor environments
- urban renewal projects such as business improvement districts

- creating employment or developing industrial corridors to keep youth busy in work
- programmes designed to help children and adolescents
- programmes on parenting and counselling parents at appropriate stage
- adapting strategies to support gender equality such as
  - providing reservations in facilities and services
  - microfinance or subsidies to weaker sections like women and downtrodden
  - tax rebates/ concessions to females and elders.

SELF ASSESSMENT INTERMISSION (SAI – 15.1)

1. Define Violence. What are its types? Explain briefly.
2. Can suicide be considered as violence? Discuss.
3. Discuss the Telangana Movement – 2009-12 in light of violence.
4. Explain the interpersonal violence and collective violence.
5. Write short notes on wars and communal violence.
6. Describe the violence caused due to maltreatment on children, women and elders.
7. List out the triggers of violence.
8. Explain ecological models to describe violence.
9. Discuss the public health approach end human rights approach in preventing and controlling the violence.
10. What are the preventing measures of violence?

15.2 COMMUNAL VIOLENCE

It is the violence that occurs on communal lines by victimizing a certain community associated with conflicts, riots between groups of different religious faith. Every nook and corner of the world in its history has seen this type of violence with different titles such as ethnic violence, non-state conflict, civil unrest, minority's unrest, mass racial violence, inter-communal violence and ethno-religious violence and so forth. The characteristics of communal violence are distinctly different from other types of violence in terms of emotions, exclusive perpetrators/ motivators/ leaders, high frequency of occurrence, huge damages associated with it and so forth. Therefore this kind of violence needs to be addressed separately.

Definition

UNO defines the communal violence as "any conflict and form of violence between communities of different religious groups, or sects/tribes of same religious group, clans, ethnic or national origin. However, this excludes conflict between two individuals or two families".

The Indian law defines communal violence as, "any act or series of acts, whether spontaneous or planned, resulting in injury or harm to the person and or property, knowingly directed against any person by virtue of his or her membership of any religious or linguistic minority, in any State in the Union of India, or Scheduled Castes and Scheduled Tribes within the meaning of clauses (24) and (25) of Article 366 of the Constitution of India".

15.2.1 Causes for Communal Violence

Colm Campbell, after studying the events in S. Africa, Palestina and N. Ireland, proposed the following common causes for communal violence

- when the state fails to provide order, security and equal justice, it leads to mass mobilization, followed by radicalization of anger among one or more communities,
- targeted mass violence by a few from one community against innocent other,
- communal violence follows when the rule of law is degraded,
- refusal to arrest members of other community in conflict,
- imprisonment of people of a single community,
- perceived or actual prisoner abuse,
- killing peaceful demonstrators,
- suppression of complaints,
- refusal to prosecute
- psychological.

In addition, some types of violence caused by ***psychos and maniacs*** will have no specific reason.

O My God!

Catholics Vs Protestants

In 1561, Huguenots in Toulouse went on a procession to express Protestant ideas. After few days, the Catholics hunted the leaders of the procession and burnt them. In the French town of Pamiers, communal clashes between Protestants and Catholics were routine, particularly during holy celebrations where the Catholics took out a procession with a statue of St. Anthony, sang and danced while Protestants used to disrupt the festivities by pelting stones. In 1566, when the Catholic procession reached a Protestant neighborhood, the Protestants chanted "kill, kill, kill!!" and numerous fatalities followed. In 1572, 1000's of Protestants were killed by Catholics in the cities - Paris, Aix, Bordeaux, Bourges, Lyon, Meaux, Orleans, Rouen, Toulouse, and Troyes.

15.2.2 Communal Violence in World History

History experienced number of episodes of communal violence. The list is so large that this is not sufficient. Few noteworthy events continent wise are given below.

In Europe

Almost every page of European history is filled with communal riots and wars particularly, in Russia, France, Italy, England and Germany with clashes between Protestants and Catholics; Christians and Muslims; violence against Jews and Roman minorities. The birth of Jesus Christ, who is believed to have come onto Earth to establish peace and love, itself is a big example for existence of communal violence.

In Africa

Nigeria witnessed centuries of violence between Christian south and Islamic north. In 1964, after independence from British rule, widespread violence on religious lines, between Arabs and Africans, consumed 20,000 humans and overthrown the Sultan of Zanzibar.

In the annals of Uganda during late 1960s and early 1970s, Kenyans and Asians saw huge number of thefts, physical assault and sexual violence, followed by expulsions by Idi Amin, whose justification was his religion for his actions and violence.

Coptic Christians suffered communal violence in Egypt for decades.

In Asia

East, South and Southeast Asia have recorded large number of incidents of communal violence. In 20th century, Singapore registered communal violence between Malays and Chinese while all through its history, Indian subcontinent has been recording large amount of communal violence between inter religions such as Hindus & Muslims, Hindus & Christians as well as intra religions such as Sunni and Shia (sects of Islam), Vaishnava & Shaiva (main sects of Hinduism), Catholics & Protestants (sects of Christianity) and so forth, more so between 18th–20th centuries (British colonial era) during processions related to religious celebrations.

The height of communal violence is witnessed by S. Asia after the 1st partition of Bengal in 1905, when segregation, unequal political and economic rights were imposed on Hindus and Muslims by Lord Curzon, based on religion. Both the sides thought the colonial rule is favoring the other side, led to riots. It effected to withdraw the decision and in 1911 Bengal partition is reversed to its re-unification.

In 1919, British General Dyer ordered to fire on unarmed protestors in Amritsar, consumed 380 lives, thence communal violence followed in India against British settlements.

100's of communal violence happened during the first half century of 1900, causes attributed to religious, political sovereignty including partition of India on religious lines into East Pakistan, West Pakistan and India. The 1946-1947 witnessed million deaths, particularly near the borders of India-Pakistan and India-Bangladesh. Examples: Direct Action Day, Noakhali riots and the Partition riots in Rawalpindi.

In Americas

Americas are not exception for the so called Mass racial violence (also called race riots) some of which occurred in US are given below for sample

- racial based communal conflict of African Americans took place after American Civil War
- conflict between Americans and recent European immigrants in 19th and 20th centuries
- attacks on Native Americans and Americans over the land
- frequent fighting among various ethnic groups in major cities in the Northeast and Midwest US throughout the late 19th and early 20th century
- violence connected with Latin American immigrants in 20th century
- Mass violence and looting in Afro-American, Mexico-American and Puerto Rican American communities during the Civil Rights Movement in the 1960s and 1970s
- 1967-68 nationwide deadly riots in most major US cities led >100 deaths following the assassination of Martin Luther King, Jr
- Violent protests and riots resulting from potential cases of police brutality against Afro-American and the tensions ignited after particular incidents such as the killings of Trayvon Martin (2012), Michael Brown, Jr (2014) and Freddie Gray (2015).

Almost all parts of South America have witnessed race-riots as a regular feature. Since the list so big, they are not given here.

15.3 COMMUNAL VIOLENCE IN INDIA

In India, communal violence has been occurring between the followers of different religions or philosophies. In recent times, it involved Hindus and Muslims, although incidents of violence have also involved Christians and Sikhs. Despite the secular and religiously tolerant constitution and also powerful autonomous bodies such as National Human Rights Commission of India, National Commission for Minorities and Non-governmental organizations, sporadic (even serious sometimes) incidents of communal violence have been occurring in India.

> **O My God!**
>
> **Asoka Vs Ajivikas (Jains)**
>
> As per ancient texts of Ashokavadana/ Divyavadana, a picture drawn by a non-Buddhist (Ajivika) in Pundravardhana showing the Buddha bowing at the feet of Nirgrantha Jnatiputra (Mahavira, the founder of Jainism) made the emperor Ashoka Mourya furious to arrest him, and to kill all the Ajivikas (around 1800). Later, Ashoka burnt another follower of Nirgrantha in Pataliputra and his entire family alive in their house for a similar drawing. He further announced an award of one dinar (silver coin) if anyone brings the head of a heretic of Nirgrantha. As a result of this order, his own brother, Vitashoka, was mistaken for a heretic and killed by a cowherd. Their ministers advised the suffered Ashoka to guarantee the security of all beings, whence, Ashoka stopped such executions.

During 2005–2010 period, on average 130 deaths of communal violence are recorded (0.01per lakh population), with Maharashtra reported the highest death toll while Madhya Pradesh highest rate per year per lakh populations.

15.3.1 In Ancient India

Ancient Indian history has tons of pages filled with wars and mass violence, but most of them are not recorded. Some are recorded by archeological department while some are predicted/ epitomized by historians. Some samples are given below.

- Ashoka, emperor of Mourya dynasty, fought a violent war of which the most violent was Kalinga war that changed him to take Budhism.
- Emperor Ashoka killed many non-Budhists (Jains), but after his brother was a victim of his own orders, he changed and stopped communal violence.
- In south India, several incidents of communal violence took place between Vashnavas (followers of Lord Vishnu) and Shaivas (followers of Lord Shiva).

15.3.2 Medieval India

Most of these records are available in history. Some notable events are given below.

- Hindus were persecuted during Islamic rule between 1000 -1500 AD which reduced Hindus population by 80 million (according to Prof. K.S.Lal)
- Communal violence happened with the raids by Turko-Mongol, Persian and Afghan armies, aggravated during Delhi Sultanate, Mughal Empire.
- Religious violence also happened in Portuguese rule of Goa in 1560.
- A regular feature of the Mughal Empire was the riots attested by Delhi Sultanate, and was so frequent that the Muslim League in 1905 for the Muslims and the Hindu Sabha (later Mahasabha) in 1915 were founded exclusively to work on these.
- During the British period, religious communities became political constituencies.
- Gigantic riots out broke in 1947, when M. A. Jinnah became 1st Governor General of Pakistan and the new border was demarcated.

15.3.3 Violence in Indian History

Violence on religious lines has been a regular feature with a high frequency from the ages until India became independent. Even independent India recorded sporadic communal riots despite having one of the world's best constitutions. We shall have a quick look on various notable episodes recorded on the timeline of Indian history.

Muhammad Bin Qasim – Minority Dynasties (8th - 10th century)

As per the records, large disturbances on religious ground in India occurred from the 8th century, when Islamic armies attacked the Hindu and Buddhist kingdoms from the northwest parts of Indian subcontinent (the now Pakistan and parts of Gujarat, Rajasthan and Punjab). Md bin Qasim with his army, destroyed temples, monasteries and attacked many towns to rob wealth and enslave Buddhists and Hindus and in some places, mosques/ minarets were on the ruins. About $1/5^{th}$ of the booty and slaves were sent as khums tax to Hajjaj and the Caliph. Delhi Sultanate destroyed the Hindu Martand (Sun) Temple in Kashmir in this period only.

The repeated destruction of the Hindu Temple at Somnath stand as the best evidence for the Islamic invasions (mainly focused on destruction of Hindu temples), started with Umayyad Caliphate in Sindh in 711 AD. In the late 8th century, Abu Jafar al Mansur attacked Hindu kingdoms in Baroda and Kashmir, and enslaved many children and women. As sympathized, Shias were expelled by Sunnis after these raids. The 3rd, 4th fitna and other civil wars raged in Arab and Persia between Sunni and Shia sects.

Lines by Abu Nasr Mohd ibn Mohd al Jabbaru-l'Utbi, Táríkh Yamini about Ghazni's invasion

Swords flashed like lightning amid the blackness of clouds and fountains of blood flowed. Noon had not arrived when the Muslims wrecked their vengeance on the infidel enemies of God, killing 15,000 of them, spreading them like a carpet over the ground, and making them food for beasts and birds of prey. God bestowed upon Sultan's friends such an amount of booty beyond all bounds and calculation, including 5 lakh slaves, beautiful men and women. The Sultan returned to his camp, having plundered immensely, by God's aid that took place on 27th Nov 1001.

Mahmud Ghazni (11th century)

Perhaps! The most repeatedly used name in the texts to exemplify repeated attempts to succeed a task is Mahmud Ghazni from Afghanistan who invaded Indian subcontinent 17 times during the early 11th century to loot and destruct Hindu temples such as at Mathura, Dwarka, and others. Numerous Muslims also died along with 1000's of Hindus. On his 6th raid (1008 AD), the Hindu kingdoms of Ujjain, Gwaliar, Kalinjar, Kanauj, Delhi and Ajmer formed a coalition to resist. Hindu women sold their jewelry to assist war needs. 1000's of Turk-Afghans were killed within an hour of their entry through Punjab. However, armies fled in chaos in different directions and many Hindus were hacked to death. About 50,000 lives were lost in Gujarat and Sindh in Ghazni's 16th raid (1024 AD), where Ghazni personally stripped of the gold and destroyed the Shiva lingam of 3rd Somnath temple.

Delhi Sultanate – Mohammed Ghori (1173-1206 AD)

India experienced extensive religious violence through raids and invasions for 320 years (1206-1526 AD) and the victims were Hindus, Buddhists, Jains as well as Shia and Sufi Muslims by Sunni Muslims. In medieval India *Somnath Temple in Gujarat witnessed repeated destruction by Muslims, followed by repeated reconstruction by Hindus.* Constructions of new Hindu, Jain and Buddhist temples, as well as the repairs of desecrated temples were banned during Delhi Sultanate. Mohammed Ghori raided N. India at the end of 12th century (1st attack in 1194) and destroyed Hindu temples and idols such as at Varanasi.

Qutb-ud-din Aibak (1206-1287 AD)

According to historian Maulana Hakim Saiyid Abdul Hai, Mamluk dynasty ruler Qutb-ud-din Aybak is 1st Muslim king of Delhi throne, who built 1st mosque, "Quwwat al-Islam" in Delhi, with demolished parts of 20 Hindu and Jain temples after a great violence.

Khilji Dynasty (1290-1320 AD)

Violence continued on religious basis in the reign of Jalaluddin Firoz Shah Khilji and Allauddin Khilji. Riots by Hindus erupted in today's Punjab, Gujarat, MP, UP with mass executions, where all men and even boys of age 8 were killed.

The Muslim army led by Malik Kafur, made 2 violent raids on S. India, (1309-11), against Hindu kingdoms of Devagiri (MS), Warangal (TS) and Madurai (TN). Slaughtering 1000's, the temples (including Halebid), cities and villages were looted. 1000 camels were deployed to carry it to Delhi. In the booty from Warangal was the Koh-i-Noor diamond. Malik Kafur attacked Srirangam temple in 1311, massacred resisted Brahmin priests for 3 days, robbed temple treasury and destroyed many religious icons. In 1323 Ulugh Khan invaded Srirangam to desecrate icons and killed 12,000 Hindus. The Vaishnava philosopher Sri Vedanta Desika, hid in corpses with the manuscript of Srutaprakasika, the magnum opus of Sri Sudarsana Suri whose eyes were plucked out, and also of his 2 sons.

The extreme rule of 'Kill'ji

Nusrat Khan, a general of Khilji, imprisoned all women and children and publicly humiliated the wives of suspects. The children were cut into pieces before their mothers. Even the *kazis*, *muftis* and court officials of Allauddin endorsed it on religious grounds. Kazi Mughisuddin of Bayánah advised Allauddin to "keep Hindus in subjection, as a religious duty, as they are the most inveterate enemies of Prophet, who commanded us to slay, plunder, and make them captive; convert to Islam or kill or enslave them and spoil their wealth and property."

Lines of FS Tughlaq's autobiography *Futuhat-i Firoz Shahi*

Some Hindus erected a new idol-temple in Kohana village and assembled to perform their idolatrous rites. They were seized and brought before me. I ordered to proclaim this wickedness publicly and put them to death before the palace gate, also the infidel books, the idols, and the vessels used should all be publicly burnt. The others were restrained by threats and punishments, as a warning to all men, that no zimmi could follow such wicked practices in a Musulman country.

Tughlaq Dynasty (1321-1394 AD)

After Khiljis, Tughlaqs assumed the power and continued religious violence. Feroz Shah Tughlaq imposed the mandatory Jizya tax on Hindus and were

arrested, brought to the palace and executed for practicing their religious acts. When Firoz Shah died, slaves in his service were mass killed/ burnt live particularly the Brahmin priests who refused to convert to Islam. However, his successor, Mohammed Bin Tughlaq was great emperor who was an artist, multilingual person, philosopher and philanthropist, but has become an icon of intelligent fool for his failed experiments such as changing the capital from Delhi to Daulatabad and back several times (and many more of similar decisions). Though his idea was good for administrative comfort, it presented security problems in the north border. He also wanted to invade China, but taken back as he lost most of his soldiers while passing Himalayas (Ignorance of geographical knowledge). He changed currency coins from silver to Bronze, due to shortage and for cost reduction, but futile experiment. He experimented on tax systems also but in vain.

Timur's Massacre of Delhi (1398 AD)

The Turko-Mongol ruler Timur attacked India massively and all Hindus were looted (but excluded muslim areas), killed or imprisoned and enslaved about 1 lakh Hindus during last years of 14th century.

Sikandar the Iconoclast (1399-1416 AD)

After Timur, in the early 15th century, Muslim Sultans scattered in various areas. Kashmir Sultan Sikandar was crazy for religious violence for which he was named *but-shikan* (idol-breaker) after destruction of Hindu and Buddhist temples, shrines, ashrams, hermitages and other holy places. In his reign, most Hindus left with only 3-options: converting to Islam, leaving Kashmir, ending the life.

Sayyid Dynasty (1414-1451 AD)

After Timur, Delhi Sultanate was anarchical and in chaos. Sayyid dynasty ruled northern parts of India, and Hindus retaliated, attacked and forts seized, e.g. Jalandhar (1431) was retaken by Hindus and all Muslims inside fort were imprisoned.

Lodi Dynasty (1451-1526 AD)

Religious violence again rose during the period of Bahlul Khan Lodi and Sikandar Lodi. Sikandar entirely ruined the temples of Mathura, and all the Hindus (in Mathura) were strictly prohibited from shaving their heads and beards.

Mughal Empire-Babur, Humayun, Suri Dynasty (1526-1556)

In 1526 Babur killed Ibrahim Lodi, the last of Lodi dynasty, and ruled for 4 yrs and his son/successor Humayun (taken over by Suri dynasty temporarily).

During their 3 decade rule, religious violence was day-to-day issue, particularly, against Sikhs which was faced by Guru Nanak, who commented upon them in 4-hymns.

Lines from '*Tuzak-i-Babari and Babur nama*'

The northwest India was targeted on Sikh and non-Sunnis where 1000's were killed and built as "towers of skulls". In 1545, Sher Shah Suri, led a religious violence across western and eastern parts. He attacked the Hindu fort of Kalinjar, captured it, killing every Hindu infidel inside the fort.

Akbar (1556-1605 AD)

Akbar's reign had somewhat communal/ religious harmony. He has introduced a new religion "Din-i-lahi". However, the early years saw religious violence such as the massacre of Hindus of Garha in 1560 AD, under Mughal Viceroy Asaf Khan. As per the historian Maulana Ahmad, the battle at Chitor (also Rantambore) fort killed 40,000 (peasants) + 8,000 (Rajputs), many imprisoned and properties looted.

Lines from 'Tabakat-i-Akbari'...

Historian Nizamuddin Ahmad wrote on violence a t Nagarkot (present Himanchal). "an idol temple of Mahámáí, was taken by Muslim, however, some Rajputs, fought till they were all cut down. A number of Brahmins, those served the temple were killed. Nearly 200 black cows in the struggle crowded for shelter in the temple while some Turks' arrows and bullets fell like rain, to kill the cows. They then took off their boots and filled them with the blood, and spilled upon roof and walls of temple"

Jahangir (1605-1627 AD)

Nur-ud-din Mohammad Salim (Jahangir), the 4th Mughal Emperor also targeted at Hindus, Jains and Sikhs.

Lines from 'Intikháb-i Jahangir-Shahi'

A companion of Jahangir and historian, described the religious violence: One day at Ahmedabad, many superstitious *Seoras* (Jains) of Gujarat made several splendid temples and placed their false Gods. Emperor Jahangir ordered to banish and demolish. Their idol was thrown down on the uppermost step of the mosque so that it might be trodden upon by those who came for daily prayers, by which they were highly disgraced, and Islam exalted.

Jahangir's orders to torture and execute Guru Arjun, in 1606, turned out Sikh history to focus on militancy with religious violence against Mughals to protest against Islam and to protect their faith. It flared thereafter, and led to introduce *khalsa* (military brotherhood) in 1699 by the 10th Sikh guru, Gobind Singh.

Shah Jahan (1627-1658 AD)

Jahangir's son and his successor of the Mughal empire, Shah-Jahan (built Tajmahal in memory of his wife Mumtaj Begum) has established a communal peace and secularism. People quote his reign (1627-1658 AD) as a golden era.

Aurangzeb (1658–1707 AD)

Aurangzeb, the cruelest Mughal emperor, dethroned and jailed his father Shah Jahan, and eldest brother Dara Shikoh for favoring secularism. He then, poisoned the children of Shikoh to death. Aurangzeb banned Diwali, re-introduced *jizya* (tax) on non-Muslims, destroyed Hindu temples, arrested and killed (shaheed) the 9th Sikh guru Tegh Bahadur. He also killed the 4 sons of the tenth guru Gobind most cruelly. India saw a scale of religious violence that lists as 23rd in 100 deadliest episodes of atrocities in human history. The world witnessed the worst of worst events with 4.6 million deaths (the world record death toll from communal violence).

In Islamic rule (80 campaigns), >60000 temples were destroyed of which some were destroyed completely, while in others restructured or modified as mosques. Idols were smashed, and the city of Mathura was temporarily renamed as Islamabad. Aurangzeb destroyed major Hindu pilgrim sites in Varanasi, Mathura and Somnath, Mosques were built on these sites. (e.g. Mosque replaced Kesava Deva Temple in Mathura).

Aurangzeb on his death bed repented in writing that he had "***greatly sinned***" and "it should not happen that Muslims be killed and the blame for their death rest upon him".

Sikh Rule- Dogra Raid of Yasin and Hunza

In 1837, after seizing control and suppressing Yousaf-zahis, Maharaja Ranjit Singh appointed Gulab Dogra as the Hindu governor of Jammu and Kashmir (J&K) who demolished the Jama Masjid of Srinagar. 1000's of Muslims were killed and few 100s of women were sold as slaves in Jammu. After getting J&K through the Treaty of Lahore and Treaty of Kashmir, Ranbir Dogra invaded Yasin and Hunza to punish Muslim rebels in 1863. Genl. Hoshiara Singh with 3,000 troops attacked and killed 1000's of Muslims. Caught Yasin is driven to Srinagar forced to labour and women were made harems of Dogra Soldiers.

Tippu Sultan, King of Mysore (1782–1799 AD)

The King of Mysore, Tipu Sultan regarded as anti-Christian, caught about 60,000 out of 67000 (92%) Catholics of Mangalore at Seringapatam (Srirangapatnam), between 24 Feb 1784 and 4 May 1799. They were forced to march through the jungles and mountains of the Western Ghat range. Forcibly 30,000 of them converted to Islam and the women (& girls) were made wives of the Muslims. The resisted/ escaped were defaced of their noses, upper lips, and ears, even hands and legs.

Immediately after the Treaty of Mangalore (1784), Tippu took control on Canara and seized Christians, robbed their properties, and sent to Seringapatam, through the Jamalabad fort route. He destroyed 27 Catholic churches (except The Church of Holy Cross at Hospet, due to resistance of Jain Chauta Raja of Moodbidri) including churches in Malabar & Cochin.

Tippu raided British soldiers (1780-1784) and on defeating Battle of Pollilur (1780), 7,000 Britishers captured, over 300 were circumcised, given Muslim names and several British regimental boys were forced to dance to entertain the court. The Netravati River flew with blood and dead bodies that the local residents left their riverside homes.

Tippu didn't leave even Hindus, especially the Nairs and Kodavas, who were either forcibly converted to Muslim or tortured to death. Nair trooped from Travancore, with the help of the East India Company (EIC) after defeating Tippu in 3rd Anglo-Mysore War. In 1783, the Kodavas revolted and Runmust Khan, the Nawab of Kurool, attacked the Kodavas resulting 500 deaths and over 40,000 Kodavas ran to the woods and hid in the mountains.

Tippu wrote on non-muslims...

In 1788, whence Tippu ordered Sher Khan, his governor of Calicut to convert Hindus to Islam, in July, 200 Brahmins were forcibly converted and fed beef. Tippu's letter on 19 Jan 1790 to the Governor of Bekal, Budruz Zuman Khan, reads, "Don't you know I have achieved a great victory recently in Malabar and over 4 lakh Hindus were converted to Islam? I am determined to marchagainst that cursed Raman Nair (*Raja* of Travancore) very soon". The translation of an inscription on the stone at Seringapatam in the fort, reads, "Oh Almighty! dispose the whole body of infidels! Scatter their tribe, cause their feet to stagger! Overthrow their councils, change their state, and destroy their very root! Cause death to be near them, cut off from them the means of sustenance! Shorten their days! Infest them with diseases, deprive their eyes of sight, make black their faces (i.e., bring shame)."

Indian Rebellion of 1857

In 1813, the EIC started promoting Christianity, belittling Hinduism and Islam due to which the resentment and fear of forced conversions began among Indian soldiers as well as civilians resulting in the revolt, seeking independence from British rule. The Indian soldiers of EIC revolted when the British introduced new rifle cartridges, rumoured to be greased with pig and cow fat, which is an abhorrent concept to Muslims and Hindus respectively, for religious reasons, finally resulted in killing more than 1 lakh.

Partition of Bengal (1905)

The British, since the 18th century had been using 'divide and rule' policy on Hindus and Muslims in every aspect. They initially favoured Muslims to impress Mughal India, but shifted after the 1857 revolt. A series of riots in 1891, 1896 and 1897 in Calcutta, concerned British and risen political movement for independence of India, forced to the first attempt to partition Bengal, the most significant province of India in 1905, along religious lines - a Muslim majority state (East Bengal) and a Hindu majority state (West Bengal). But, it was deeply resented, both groups found British favoritism to the other side. The continued riots through 1907 worsened to revert in 1911. Nevertheless, it hardly calmed the violence as riots geared up between Muslims and Hindus till 1930s.

Annie Besant wrote on Moplah Rebellion

"Moplahs murdered and plundered hugely, and killed or drove away all Hindus who would not apostatize. About a lakh of people were driven from their homes with nothing but their clothes they had on, stripped of everything. Malabar has taught us what Islamic rule still means, and do not want to see another specimen of the Khilafat Raj in India."

Moplah Rebellion (1921)

The Anti-Hindu rebellion by the Muslim Mappilas (British spelt Moplah) of Kerala in 1921, motivated by the Khilafat movement and Karachi resolution killed over lakh Hindus, forcibly converted and/or driven out of their homes and property, later occupied by Mappilas. (This is why today's Malappuram district has Muslim majority). The Mappilas revolted due to rivalry on the Hindu landlord Nair, Nambudiri Jenmi backed up by British latter. Finally, Mohd Haji, the Caliph of Moplah Khilafat declared Ernad & Walluvanad as Khilafat kingdoms.

Partition of British India (1947)

Though not exclusively attributed to communal, the violence has been common in the end-years of British rule, such as those during Salt Satyagraha at Dandi, Quit India Movement, Swadeshi Movement and Jalianwalah Bagh action by General Dier and so forth. However, in 1947 there was massive religious violence, Kolkata and Indo-Pakistani Punjab border being the most affected. Believe it or not! On Direct Action Day, (16 Aug 1946) alone, nearly 3000 dead and 17000 injured.

As a matter of fact, after the Rebellion of 1857, British used divide-and-rule policy and exploited communal lines successfully to prevent revolts. On the same lines, Mohd Ali Jinnah was motivated to lead Indian Muslims to have a cultural and political identity of Muslims. The partition plan was executed to make India and Pakistan independent, whence about 14.5 million crossed borders to ensure their safety in an increasingly lawless and communal grounds. The new governments were totally unequipped to deal with migrations, massive communal violence and slaughter on both sides recorded above 5 lakh deaths.

Bahmani Sultanate

The **Bahmani Sultanate**, a Muslim state of the Deccan in S. India was one of the major medieval Indian and 1st independent Muslim kingdoms in South India, established by Turkic Genl. Ala-ud-Din Bahman Shah revolting against Md. bin Tughlaq. Their capital (1347-1425) Hasanabad (Gulbarga) was later moved to Muhammadabad (Bidar). The Vijayanagara Emperor Krishnadevaraya defeated the last remnant to collapse Bahmani Sultanate. After 1518 it broke up into 5 states: Nizamshahi of Ahmednagar, Qutb Shahi of Golconda (Hyderabad), Baridshahi of Bidar, Imadshahi of Berar, Adilshahi of Bijapur, collectively known as the "Deccan Sultanates". A lot of bloodshed, looting and violence occurred during this period, specifically against Hindus.

15.3.4 Nizams in the Princely State of Hyderabad

Huge violence on communal ground manifested in one of broken state of Deccan Sultanate after Bahmani was Qutb Shahi of Golconda, also called the princely state of Hyderabad, a Hindu-majority (85%) state ruled by the Muslim Nawabs, the Nizams. In 1926, Md Nawaz Khan, founded the Majlis-e-Ittehad-ul-Muslimeen (MIM), with an objective to unite the Muslims in support of Nizam and to reduce the Hindu majority by large-scale conversion to Islam. MIM had a storm troopers **Razakars**, a private militia headed by Qasim Razvi to support the rule of Nizam Osman Ali Khan, Asaf Jah VII and also resisted the integration of Hyderabad State into independent India in 1947 (like all the other Princely states, the Hyderabad State was also given the choice of joining India or Pakistan, but Nizam wanted neither, but to remain independent. Finally he entered standstill agreement with India on 29 Nov 1947 to maintain status quo). The Razakars misused the special powers taken from Nizam, who was helpless but to abide by their dictates. Countless Hindu women were victims of rape and kidnap by Razakars. 1000s jailed who braved the cruelties of the oppressive administration and 1000s of Hindus had to flee to Vijaywada or Bombay while lakhs have been killed.

To counter the Razakars, Telanganites under the leadership of Swami Ramanand Tirtha formed the Andhra Hindu Mahasabha seeking integration with India. Eventually, the Indian Army routed the Razakars during Operation Polo, "the police action", under the directions of Sardar Vallabhbhai Patel, the Indian Minister for Home Affairs. Qasim Razvi who tried to integrate with Pakistan, was arrested and jailed but allowed to move to Pakistan where he was granted asylum.

SELF ASSESSMENT INTERMISSION (SAI – 15.2)

1. Define Communal Violence. What is its meaning? Do you consider it as a disaster? What is its significance in disaster management?
2. Enumerate the causes for communal violence.
3. Give a brief history of violence occurred in Asia and Africa.
4. Give a brief history of violence occurred in Europe and Americas.
5. Discuss about the violence occurred on communal basis in ancient and medieval India.
6. Describe Mohammad Ghazni's attacks on India and the communal violence caused.
7. Describe Mohammad Ghori's attacks on India and the communal violence caused.
8. Discuss the violence caused in India during the period of Khiljis and Tughlaqs.
9. Explain the rule of Mughals in light of communal aspects.
10. Give a brief account of communal violence caused by Delhi sultans of Mughal dynasty.
11. Describe how Babur's and Humayun's rule bothered Hindus.
12. Discuss about the communal harmony during Akbar's and Shah Jahan's rule.
13. 'Aurangzeb was the world's cruelest ruler ever'. Support the statement with some examples.
14. Give on account of communal issues during Tippu Sultan's reign.
15. Discuss the communal disturbances occurred in British India.

15.4 COMMUNAL VIOLENCE IN MODERN INDIA

Since independence, though India has always been maintaining secularism as a constitutional commitment, yet, sporadic large-scale Hindu-Muslim communal violence has been occurring. The major incidences are

- The 1969 Jai Telangana/ 1972 Jai Andhra movement
- The 1969 Gujarat riots,
- The 1980 Communal riots in 1980's of Hyderabad
- The 1984 Anti-Sikh Riots (Operation Blue Star)
- The 1989 Ethnic Cleansing and Bhagalpur riots
- The 1992 Ram Janma Bhoomi-Babri Masjid issue
- The 2002 Godhra Hindu-Muslim Communal riots

Furthermore, now and then certain incidents have been occurring such as in 2010, when Taslima Nasrin's article (published in a local newspaper) was viewed offensive to Islam by some people leading to religious violence in Shimoga Karnataka and other places of India with widespread looting, 2 deaths and 100 injuries.

We shall now have a glance on Such incidents.

15.4.1 Gujarat Hindu-Muslim Communal Riots (1969)

In Sep–Oct 1969, Gujarat witnessed the most deadly Hindu-Muslim riots after the 1947 partition violence. Starting after an attack on a Hindu temple at Ahmedabad, extended to major cities/towns of Gujarat, included the attacks on Muslim chawls by Dalit Hindu neighbours. It continued for a week, and then restarted a month later with a death toll of 660 (430 Muslims, 230 Hindus), injuries of 1000+ and property loots for 48,000+ people.

15.4.2 Anti-Sikh Riots – Operation Blue Star (1984)

In the 1970s, Punjabi Sikhs sought autonomy and complained against domination by the Hindu, but the government led by Mrs. Indira Gandhi suppressed it, particularly during Indian Emergency, when India's constitution was suspended, 1.4 lakh were arrested of which 40,000 were Sikhs without due process. After lifting the Emergency, during elections, she supported Jarnail Singh Bhindranwale, a Sikh leader to undermine Akali Dal, the largest Sikh political party. However, Bhindranwale began opposing the central government and moved his base to the Darbar Sahib (the Golden temple) in Amritsar, provoked Sikhs to demand for making Punjab as a new country. In June 1984, by the orders of Mrs. Indira, Indian army attacked the Golden temple (named Operation Blue Star) with tanks and armoured vehicles, whence made a bloodshed with the death 1000's of innocent Sikhs. In retaliation, she was assassinated on 31st Oct 1984 by her own two Sikh bodyguards, Satwanth Singh and Bianth Singh.

The assassination provoked mass rioting against Sikhs (the 1984 anti-Sikh pograms) in Delhi, where the Government and police aided worker gangs of

Indian National Congress party "strategically, methodically and systematically" targeted Sikhs and Sikh homes resulting in 15–17 thousands of Sikhs burnt alive or killed and suffered massive property damage, displacing at least 50,000 Sikhs.

15.4.3 Ethnic Cleansing of Kashmiri Hindus

About 300 Kashmiri Pandits were killed between Sep 1989-90. In early 1990, local Urdu newspapers *Aftab* and *Al Safa* raised jihad against India and ordered the expulsion of all Hindus and own Kashmir. Ultimatums (notices) 'to leave within 24 hours or die' were pasted on the houses of all Hindus resulting in migration of about 3-5 lakh pandits Kashmir. Consequently in the next few days (June 1990), the masked men running in the streets started firing against Hindus (who didn't want to leave Kashmir) with AK-47. Many Kashmiri Pandits were killed by Islamic terrorists, (often referred to as 'ethnic cleansing') in the Wandhama massacre and the 2000 Amarnath pilgrimage massacre.

15.4.4 Anti-Muslim Violence – Ram Janma Bhoomi Vs Babri Maszid (1992)

On 6 Dec 1992, Vishva Hindu Parishad (VHP) and Bajrang Dal destroyed the 430-year-old Babri Mosque in Ayodhya claiming that the mosque was built over the birthplace of the ancient deity Rama (in 2010 Allahabad court ruled that the site was indeed a Hindu monument before the mosque was built there, based on evidence submitted by the Archaeological Survey of India). The action humiliated Muslims resulting religious riots with >1200 deaths. Since then the GoI blocked off at the sites and referred to court. No sooner than the incident, the riots blew out in cities and towns (even some villages also) of entire country.

Examples: Law & order was out of control due to the acid attacks at Hyderabad, and the AP Govt. had to impose curfew for >15 days, 5 burnt alive at Bainganwadi in Mumbai, 4 dead in a fire in the Asalpha timber mart at Ghatkopar, and a couple pulled out of a rickshaw and burnt to death and the list is so big.

15.4.5 Godhra (Gujarat) Hindu-Muslim Communal Riots (2002)

Many buildings in Ahmedabad were set on fire during 2002 Gujarat violence. Closing doors and burning Hindus alive by Muslims in Godhra train, led to the 2002 Gujarat riots in which mostly Muslims were killed. The United Progressive Alliance (UPA) Govt. declared in the parliament on 11 May 2005 that 790 Muslims and 254 Hindus were killed, 2,548 injured, 223 missing. It was also reported that 919 widows and 606 children were orphaned. Nevertheless, the

Gujarat Govt. and Sangh Parivaar claimed the violence as spontaneous communal clash and uncontrollable reaction, the GoI implemented the recommendations of the Sachar Committee to help Muslims.

15.4.6 Anti-Christian Violence

Human Rights Watch reported religious violence on Christians in India, by Hindu organizations due to forcible reconversion of converted Christians to Hinduism in 1999, which involved in distribution of threatening literature and destruction of Christian cemeteries. An Australian missionary was burnt to death while sleeping in his station wagon at Manoharpur in Keonjhar district in Odisha in Jan 1999. In 2003, Dara Singh was convicted of leading the gang responsible. The other incidents include…

- In 2007, foreign Christian missionaries were targeted.
- Begun in Dec 2007, attack on Christians in Kandhamal and other districts of Odisha, resulted in 2-Hindu and 1-Christian deaths, and the destruction of houses and churches. Hindus claim that Christians killed a saint Laxmananand, and thence retaliated, but the claim has no conclusive proof. 20 people were arrested for the attacks.
- Similar incidents occurred in Karnataka from 14 Sep 2008.
- In Jabalpur, M.P., 2-Statues inside St Peter and Paul Church were set on fire, in 2008.

15.4.7 Anti-Hindu Violence

Religious violence, in general is less in many towns, particularly very less in villages in India. As per the 2012-records of riot rates per lakh, Kerala reported the highest while Punjab and Meghalaya reported zero riot incidence rates.

However, in the recent times, Hindus and their temples are attacked by Muslim militants. Some notable incidents include the 1998 Chamba massacre, the 2002 fidayeen attacks on Raghunat and Akshardham Temples by Islamic terrorists Lashkar-e-Toiba and the 2006 Varanasi bombings (suspected Lashkar-e-Toiba), Marad massacre and the Godhra train burning, which resulted in many deaths and injuries. Some more noteworthy incidents are briefed out below.

- During 1992 Bombay riots, 275 Hindus died. In retaliation to the killing of 3-Muslims were killed by Rashtreeya Sevak Sangh (RSS), on 2nd May 2003, 8-Hindus were killed and one of the attackers (Mohd Ashker) also died in chaos.
- In Aug 2000, Swami Shanti Kali, (Hindu priest) was shot dead in his ashram in Tripura. Police identified 10 Christian terrorists of National

Liberation Front of Tripura (NLFT) as responsible. On 4 Dec 2000, (3 months after his death), their other ashram at Chachu Bazar near the Sidhai police station was raided by Christian militants of NLFT and killed 11 priests, and ashrams, schools, and orphanages in the state were closed down.

- The separatist group NLFT banned Hindu worship including celebrations of Durga and Saraswati Puja (2004) and killed resisting tribal leaders and raped some tribal women. The Baptist Church of Tripura supported NLFT and arrested two church officials in 2000, one of them for possessing explosives.
- On 3rd & 4th Jan 2002, 3-Hindus and 2-Muslims were killed in Marad, near Kozhikode due to scuffles between 2 groups began due to dispute of drinking water. The National Development Front (NDF), an Islamist organization, was suspected for the Massacre.
- In Oct 2005-Mau (UP) Hindu-Muslim riots, triggered by the proposed celebration of a Hindu festival, 5 persons died.
- Communal riots in Hyderabad in 1984 and early 1990s killed/ injured 100's of people.
- In Sep 2008, Swami Laxmanananda, a Hindu Guru was killed along with 4 disciples by unknown assailants (Maoists later claimed responsibility). Police arrested 3 Christians in this connection.
- In the 2010 Deganga riots in West Bengal, 100's of Hindu shops and residences were looted, destroyed and burnt; dozens of Hindus were severely injured and several Hindu temples desecrated and vandalized by the Islamists led by Haji Nurul Islam (MP of Thrinamul Congress). Again after 3-years (the 2013 Canning riots), 100's of Hindu businesses were destroyed.
- 254 Hindus were killed in 2002 Gujarat riots, half of which are due to police firing.

Communal Violence in films and literature

Communal violence in India have been a topic for several films and novels. A few are listed below (Regional films not given):

- *Garam Hawa*: by M.S.Sathyu based on partition written by Ismat Chugtai.
- *Gandhi* (1982) shows the Direct Action Day and Partition riots.
- *Tamas*: on partition based on a book by Bhishm Sahni
- *Bombay* (1995): the period of Dec 1992 - Jan 1993 in India, and the controversy of the Babri Mosque in Ayodhya.
- *Maachis*: by Gulzar about Punjab terrorism
- *Earth* (1998): displayed Partition violence in Lahore.
- *Fiza* (2000): a setup amidst Bombay Riots.
- *Hey Ram* (2002): semi-fiction related to Partition of India.
- *Mr. and Mrs. Iyer* (2002): on relationship between 2 characters Meenakshi Iyer and Raja amidst Hindu-Muslim riots in India.
- *Firaaq* a film set in the aftermath of the *2002 Gujarat riots*.
- *Final Solution* (2003): on 2002 Gujarat violence (ban in India)
- *Hawayein* (2003): struggles of Sikhs during 1984 anti-Sikh riots.
- *Black Friday* (1993): Derected by Anurag Kashyap on the 1993 Mumbai serial bomb blasts.
- *Amu* – An award-winner about a girl orphaned during the 1984 Anti-Sikh riots.
- *Train to Pakistan*, a novel and also film by Khushwant Singh on the Partition of India
- Toba Tek Singh, a satire by Saadat Hasan Manto based on the Partition of India.
- *Parzania* – a 2007 film about the 2002 Gujarat riots

(Hindutva groups in Gujarat threatened to attack theatres and so purposely not released in Gujarat since theatre owners and distributors refused to screen fearing retaliation)

SELF ASSESSMENT INTERMISSION (SAI – 15.3)

1. List out major incidents of communal violence occurred in Modern India (after independence). Explain causes and effects of any one.
2. Despite being one of the best secular countries, Modern India has been facing several issues on communal grounds. Discuss giving some examples.
3. Discuss the causes and effects of Ram Janma Bhoomi – Babri Masjid issue.
4. Write a note on the Godhra incident.
5. Write a note on anti-Sikh violence in India after independence.
6. Write a note on anti-Muslim violence in India after independence.
7. Quoting some incidents, discuss the anti-Hindu violence occurred in independent India.

15.5 TERRORISM

Terrorism, is a threat to society and a big crime targeted intentionally, deliberately and indiscriminate violence associated with political, religious, or ideological motives, (often referred to as 4th generation warfare), thence illegal under anti-terrorism laws.

15.5.1 The Concept & Meaning

The term "Terrorism" is originated from French word *terrorisme* (also in Latin *terrere* means "to frighten"), and referred specifically to state terrorism as practiced by the French government during the 1793–94 Reign of Terror. The *terror cimbricus* was a state of emergency in Rome against the Cimbri tribe in 105 BCE that the Jacobins cited as a precedent when imposing the 'Reign of Terror' during the French Revolution. After the Jacobins lost power, the word "terrorist" became a term of abuse, later to the killing of innocent people for political purposes or to create a sensation. Some noted terrorist events are given below:

- During 1st century AD, Sicarii Zealots in Judaea Province targeted against Jewish "collaborators", even temple priests, Sadducees, Herodians, and other wealthy elites, who were called terrorists.
- In Jan 1858, Italian patriot Felice Orsini (named as terrorist) threw 3 bombs to assassinate French Emperor Napoleon III, but killed 8 bystanders and 142 injured.
- The 1st organization used modern terrorist techniques was the Irish Republican Brotherhood, founded in 1858, carried out revolutionary attacks in England, [It is pictured in "The Fenian Guy Fawkes" by John Tenniel].

- Modern terrorism shaped up by Nuclei Armati Rivoluzionari, neo-fascists with deadliest massacre of Italy with 85 deaths in Bologna railway station attack on 2 Aug 1980.
- Baghdad bus station had a triple car bombing in Aug 2005 that killed 43 people.
- About 35,000 Pakistanis died of terrorism in recent Islamabad Marriott Hotel bombing.
- Worldwide non-state terrorist incidents 2000–2015 as per the Global Terrorism Database, 61,000+ incidents of non-state terrorism consuming about 1.5 lakh lives.
- Most worst hither to, is United Airlines Flight 175, hijacked, hit the South Tower of the World Trade Center (WTC) on **11th Sep 2001**, in NY. It is the height of the terrorism

15.5.2 Definition

Some of the well accepted definitions are given below:

- A political violence in an asymmetric conflict that is designed to induce terror and psychic fear (sometimes indiscriminate) through the violent victimization and destruction of noncombatant targets (sometimes iconic symbols) meant to send a message from an illicit clandestine organization - Carsten Bockstette
- The criminal acts intended to provoke a state of terror in the public, a group of persons for political purposes, but in any circumstance unjustifiable, whatsoever may be the factors of a political, philosophical, ideological, racial, ethnic, religious or any other nature that may be invoked to justify them.
- The US Task Force defines terrorism as "a tactic or technique by means of which a violent act or the threat thereof is used for the prime purpose of creating overwhelming fear for coercive purposes, premeditated, politically motivated violence perpetrated against noncombatant targets by sub-national groups or clandestine agents, usually intended to influence an audience". - US Code Title 22 Chap 38, Sec 2656f(d)
- In Nov 2004, UN Secretary-General narrated terrorism as "an act intended to cause death or serious bodily harm to civilians or non-combatants with the purpose of intimidating population or compelling a government or an international organization to do or abstain from doing any act".
- Terrorism can be described by its activities involving in violence or danger to
  - human life that violate federal or state law;

- intimidate or coerce of a civilian population;
- influence the policy of a government by intimidation or coercion; or
- affect the conduct of a government by mass destruction, assassination, or kidnapping.

Some official/governmental definitions of terrorism use illegitimacy or unlawfulness of the act to distinguish between actions of government (thence "lawful"), individuals and small groups.

The term terrorism has been defined differently in the legislations of various nations and the controversy is still continuing because even the international community also could not yet formulate legal and universally agreed definition of this crime.

For example,

A strategic bombing on an enemy city, even though designed to affect civilian life, would not be considered terrorism if it were authorized by a government. Nevertheless, it is not universally accepted, as it denies the activity of terrorism. Thus same act may or may not be treated as terrorism depending on whether it is sponsored by a government and on the perspective of one government or another; and it diverges from the historically accepted meaning and origin of the term.

15.5.3 Characteristics of Terrorism

Is 'Act of Terror' same as 'Terrorism'?

18 USC§2331 defines "international and domestic terrorism" for purposes of Chapter 113B of the Code, entitled "Terrorism".

Barrack Obama, the then US President on the Boston Marathon bombing of Apr 2013, declared that "Anytime bombs are used to target innocent civilians, it is an act of terror". Critics pointed out to distinguish between "act of terror" and "terrorism", particularly when used by the White House.

After understanding the above definitions, terrorism is characterized by:

- Embedded political aims and motives;
- Influencing the targeted audience(s) to reach short/midterm political goals and/or desired long-term end states;
- Political, philosophical, ideological, racial, ethnic, religious or a similar back drop;
- Media may be purposefully exploited and used as an amplifier/multiplier so as to achieve maximum attainable publicity;
- Violent, or equally threatening of violence;
- Long range psychological repercussions beyond the immediate victim or target;
- Perpetrated by a sub-national group or non-state entity.
- Structured and conducted by
- an organization with an identifiable chain of command or

- conspiratorial cell structure (members wear no uniform or identifying insignia) or
- individuals or a small group influenced/motivated/inspired by the ideological aims or
- some existent terrorist movement and/or its leaders.

15.5.4 The Mirror Image of Terrorism

"***The terrorist of one man is the freedom fighter of another***". The terms 'terrorism' (and so the term 'terrorist') is used in a negative sense which indicate indiscriminate, immoral, unjustified, condemnable activity on one side while on the other side it is assumed by their opponents as separatist, freedom fighter, liberator, revolutionary, vigilante, militant, paramilitary, guerrilla, rebel, patriot, or any similar words in various languages and cultures. Thus the similarly meant Arabic words Jihadi, Mujaheddin, and Fedayeen have entered the English dictionaries.

- During WW-II, the Malayan People's Anti-Japanese Army was allied with the British, but during the Malayan Emergency, its successor (the Malayan Races Liberation Army), were branded "terrorists" by the British.
- US President Ronald Reagan met Afghan Mujahideen leaders in the Oval Office in 1983, called "freedom fighters" during the Soviet–Afghan War, but 20 yrs later, their fight against foreign powers was labeled "terrorism" by George W. Bush.
- The leaders involved in a "liberation" struggle, marked as "terrorists" by the Western governments or media, later in the liberated nations, are called "statesmen".

Examples: the Nobel Peace Prize laureates Nelson Mandela and Menachem Begin.

- WikiLeaks editor Julian Assange was also called a "terrorist" by Sarah Palin and Joe Biden
- Sometimes, the states for reasons of history, culture and politics differ if certain organizations are terrorists, e.g. for many years, US government refused to label Irish Republican Army (IRA) as terrorists while UK (closest ally of US) branded as terrorism.

15.5.5 Classification of Terrorism

Depending on the country, the political system, and the time in history, the disorders and terrorism can be classified in several ways.

Based on the Intent/ Content of Violence

1. **Civil disorder** is a mass or group violence that disturbs the peace, security, and normal functioning of the community.
2. **Political terrorism** is violent criminal behaviour that creates fear in the community with a political objective.
3. **Non-Political terrorism** is not aimed at political purposes but consciously designed to generate and maintain a high degree of fear for coercive purposes (the end is individual or collective gain rather than the achievement of a political objective).
4. **Quasi-terrorism** is an incidental violence similar to terrorism i.e. the same purpose (to induce terror in the immediate victim), same modes and techniques and also produces similar consequences and reaction but lacks the essence.
5. **Limited Political Terrorism** is a genuine political terrorism characterized by a revolutionary approach limited to and committed for ideological or political motives but not part of a concerted campaign to capture control of the state.
6. **Structural Terrorism (or Official or State Terrorism)** is carried out by governments in pursuit of political objectives, often as part of their foreign policy. In other words, it is nations rule based on fear and oppression similar to terrorism or such proportions.

Based on Area/ Location

1. **International Terrorism** is an international political driven terrorism where the victims belong to different nation(s) from that of the terrorists.
2. **Domestic Terrorism** occurs within the country and the terrorists as well as the victims both belong to same nation.

Based on Causes and Effects

1. **Political Terrorism** is driven by political interests and social objectives. It can be further classified as
   - **(A)** Sub-state terrorism,
   - **(B)** State terrorism and
   - **(C)** Sponsored terrorism.

   A brief discussion on these is given in the paragraphs to follow:

   - **(A)** **Sub-state terrorism:** This happens by groups or individuals motivated by social revolution or rooted by faith on religious grounds with an aim to either spread or enforce the belief. Depending on the situation and root cause of the violence, this is further categorized into 5 kinds as given below:

(a) Social revolutionary terrorism
(b) Nationalist-separatist terrorism
(c) Religious terrorism
  - Religious fundamentalist terrorism
  - New religions terrorism
(d) Right-wing terrorism
(e) Left-wing terrorism

(B) State Terrorism : This is committed by government agents or forces involving state's foreign policies like using its military to terrorism.

Examples: German bombing of London, Japanese bombing of Pearl Harbor, British firebombing of Dresden, US atomic bombing of Hiroshima (WW II).

(C) State-sponsored Terrorism: A state can sponsor terrorism by funding or harboring. But when states provide funding for groups treated are terrorists, rarely acknowledge them as such. Some examples are given below:

1. Palestine Liberation Organization, Democratic Front for the Liberation of Palestine and other groups considered to be terrorists, were funded by SU.
2. The Islamic State in Iraq received "private donations from Gulf states".
3. Italian Beirut Fascists funded Stern Gang to fight on British Mandate for Palestine.
4. Pakistan has created and nurtured terrorist groups as policy for achieving tactical objectives against its neighbours, especially India.

O My God!

The Height of Terrorism

The **9/11 disaster** was a series of 4 coordinated attacks by Islamic terrorists, al-Qaeda on the US on Tuesday, Sep 11, 2001, killed 2,996 people, injured >6,000 and at least $10 billion in infrastructure/ property damage. Four passenger airlines departed from California were hijacked by 19 al-Qaeda terrorists. Two planes (United Airlines Flight 175 and American Airlines Flight 11) were crashed into the North and South towers of the World Trade Centre (WTC) complex in NY to collapse both 110-story towers within 102 min. The debris and resulting fires continued to collapse all other buildings including the 47-story 7 WTC tower, and significant damage to 10 large surrounding structures. The 3rd plane, American Airlines Flight 77, was crashed into the Pentagon (HQ of US Defense) in Arlington County, Virginia, leading to a partial collapse of the building's western side. The 4th plane, United Airlines Flight 93, was initially steered toward Washington, D.C., but crashed into a field in Stony Creek Township near Shanksville, Pennsylvania, as its passengers tried to overcome the hijackers. 9/11 was the single deadliest incident for fire-fighters and law enforcement officers in the history of US, with 343 and 72 killed respectively. Suspecting al-Qaeda, US launched War on Terror and invading Afghanistan to depose Taliban that sheltered al-Qaeda. Many countries strengthened their anti-terrorism legislation and expanded the powers of law and intelligence to prevent terrorist attacks. Though initially denied, al-Qaeda's leader, Osama bin Laden, in 2004 claimed responsibility for the attacks citing the US support to Israel, the presence of US troops in Saudi Arabia, and sanctions against Iraq as motives. After evading capture for almost a decade, Osama bin Laden was killed by SEAL Team 6 of US Navy in May 2011.

The destruction of WTC caused serious damage to the economy of Lower Manhattan and a significant effect on global markets, resulting in the closing of Wall Street until Sep 17 and the civilian airspace in US and Canada until Sep 13. Many closings, evacuations, and cancellations followed, out of fear of further attacks. Cleanup of the WTC site was completed in May 2002, and the Pentagon was repaired within a year. On Nov 18, 2006, construction of One WTC began and was officially opened on Nov 3, 2014.

Democracy Vs Domestic Terrorism

It is difficult to define the relation between democracy and domestic terrorism. Terrorism is most common in nations with intermediate freedom, while uncommon in the most democratic nations (the suicide attack is an exception). Some examples are...

Non-democratic

- ETA in Spain under Francisco Franco (terrorism increased after Franco's death)
- Ukrainian Nationalists in pre-war Poland,
- Shining Path in Peru under Alberto Fujimori,
- the Kurdistan Workers Party when Turkey was ruled by military leaders and
- the ANC in South Africa.

Democratic – Japan, UK, US, Israel, India, Indonesia, Spain, Germany and Philippines

Source of funding for sponsored terrorism

"Revolutionary tax" is major form of funding, and essentially a euphemism for "protection money". These are extorted from businesses including farms cultivating illicit drugs and they also "play a secondary role as other means of intimidating the target population". Other major sources are kidnapping for ransoms, fraud, smuggling, wildlife smuggling, dacoit and robbery.

Non-state groups

Groups not part of the state apparatus of in opposition to the state are most commonly referred to as a "terrorist" in the media.

2. **Criminal Terrorism:** Violence on lower by higher on the hierarchy is nearly always invisible, or unnoticed, but when noticed, it is fully rationalized. However, the violence by lower on the hierarchy on higher is unthinkable, and when occurs, it is a shock, horror of the victims. — *Derrick Jensen*

Examples:

1. US Arizona (BB-39) burnt by Japanese surprise attack on Pearl Harbor, Dec 7, 1941
2. The anthrax mailed inside letters to US politicians was the work of a *lone wolf*.
3. Civilians were trapped in a London underground train after a bomb exploded further down the train at Russell Square Tube station on 7 July 2005
4. St Paul's Cathedral after the German bombing of London, 1940.

3. **Intimate (Pathological) Terrorism:** Intimate Terrorism (IT) involves emotional or psychological abuse and is generally aims the control by one partner over the other. It escalates over time and involves serious injuries. IT could be in two types:
   - "Generally-violent-antisocial" associated with general psychopathic and violent tendencies
   - "Dysphoric-borderline" emotionally dependent on the relationship.

15.5.6 Motives and Targets of Terrorists

The terrorist organizations don't choose terrorism for its political effectiveness, and the individual terrorists are motivated by a desire for social solidarity than political or strategic objectives, which are often murky and undefined. Mostly terrorists would have long-range goals that too, in large-scale, often due to unresolved political conflict. Of course, the types of conflicts vary largely. Hither to, the history witnessed one or more of the following causes (sometimes they are interrelated also) for the terrorism.

- A territory to form a new sovereign state or become part of a different state
- Dominance of territory or resources by various ethnic groups
- Imposition of a particular form of government

- Economic deprivation of a population
- Opposition to a domestic government or occupying army
- Religious fanaticism

Generally, terrorist attacks are often targeted to frighten public using explosives or poison or weapons of mass destruction. They usually employ methodical and strategic plans to attacks in advance through trained participants, undercover agents, and raise money from sympathizers or supporters or through organized crime. Communications may take place either through modern telecommunications or through old methods such as couriers.

Most general strategies and the motives of terrorists are seen in the following ways.

- ***Attacks on 'collaborators'***

  Terrorize people and stop cooperating with the state so as to undermine state control.

  Example: Used during their independence struggles in Ireland, Kenya, Algeria and Cyprus
- ***Attacks on high-profile symbolic targets***

  To polarize the population and also to draw international attention to struggles unreported.

  Example: Used by Al-Qaeda on the WTC and the Pentagon in the US on Sep 11, 2001, attack on Indian Parliament.
- ***Attacks on high traffic areas***

  Revenge or retaliating against a state for its actions against its citizens or to show their identity or with a special motive of belief

  Example: Dilsukhnagar (Hyderabad) bomb blasts
- *Attack on tourists and places of tourism*

  Terrorism and tourism are closely related. In the 1970s, the targets of terrorists were politicians and chiefs of police while now international tourists and visitors are selected as main targets of attacks.

  Examples: Mumbai attack (Hotel), attack on Indian Parliament, the Luxor massacre in Egypt, the attacks on the WTC and the Pentagon on Sep 11, 2001, were the symbolic epicenter.

15.5.7 Role of Perpetrators in Initiating

Perpetrators are the individual(s) or group(s) or state(s), who initiate and execute the acts of terrorism, operating from inside or outside the state. However, it is carried out by small and secretive cells, highly motivated to serve a particular cause and many of the most deadly operations in recent times, such as Rajiv Gandhi's assassination, the Sep 11 attacks, the London bombing, 2008 Mumbai attacks, the 2002, Bali bombing and Dilsukhnagar (Hyderabad) bomb blast, were planned and made use of close friends, family members and other strong social networks.

The physical and behavioral aspects of the terrorist would be almost like any normal person so as to avoid detection. Particularly, till the assigned mission is executed, a terrorist will look, dress, and behave normally and very difficult to differentiate from normal person. For example, the Wall Street bombing at noon on Sep 16, 1920 killed 38 and injured many 100's but, the perpetrators were not caught hither to and will never be (because by now, the perpetrators might have naturally died also).

Some argue that identification of terrorists based on personality, physical or sociological traits are not possible and efforts would be futile. But, it is not completely true, since certain traits can be traced significantly indifferent and unique to distinguish. For example, the majority of attacks carried out were by the men aged 16–40, most of them had cruel and cunning, watching eyes.

15.5.8 Role of Governments to Defending

Terrorism is defended by the government in wide range of methods. The following are some specific types of defending methods that were successful in the past and recommendable to future.

- Targeted laws, criminal procedures (anti-terrorism acts)
- Deportations, and enhanced police powers
- Alerting the concerned through all possible methods
- Target hardening such as locking doors/ in-gates
- Adding traffic barriers and frisking the entrants
- Preemptive military action
- Reactive, proactive & pre-active police actions
- Increased intelligence and surveillance activities
- Preemptive humanitarian activities
- More permissive interrogation, detection and detention policies.

SELF ASSESSMENT INTERMISSION (SAI – 15.4)

1. Define Terrorism. What is its meaning? How is the term derived?
2. Do you consider terrorism as a disaster? What is its significance in disaster management?
3. What are the characteristics of terrorism?
4. What are the types of terrorism? Brief out each type.
5. Classify the terrorism on the basis of causes and effects.
6. Enumerate the causes for terrorism.
7. What are motives of terrorists?
8. 'A terrorist of one man is a freedom fighter of other'. What do you understand by this statement? Explain.
9. Discuss the role of perpetrators in initiating terrorism.
10. Explain the role of government to defend terrorism.

15.6 WAR AND WARFARE

War is defined as *"a state of armed conflict between societies and is characterized by extreme aggression, destruction, and mortality, using regular or irregular military forces"*. An absence of war is usually called "peace".

Warfare refers to *"the common activities and characteristics of wars in general, and is not restricted to purely legitimate military targets, and can result in massive civilian or other non-combatant casualties"*.

15.6.1 The Worse of Wars

The following are some facts recorded in the war history of the world

- The deadliest war in known history, in terms of total deaths, is the WW-II (1939-1945), with 60–85 million deaths, followed by the Mongol conquests with > 41 million.
- The most destructive in modern history is War of the Triple Alliance (Paraguay casualties).
- Richard Smalley(2003) wrote, war is 6th of 10 biggest disasters for next 50 yrs.
- Conway W. Henderson observed ~14,500 wars from 3500 BC till date, costing 3.5 billion lives, leaving only 300 yrs of peace.
- Crusades were a series of religious wars sanctioned by Latin Church in medieval period.
- Wars killed >3,640 million while post war diseases killed >1,240 million. About 1680 million people died from infectious diseases in 20th Century itself.
- US Bureau of the Census (1894) says, Indian Wars of 19th century consumed ~50,000 lives.
- The Spanish Civil War (1937) was Europe's bloodiest and most brutal civil war.
- Nuclear warfare (Aug 1988), lowered population by 1,850 (5,150 to 3,300) million within a year, without considering "the nuclear winter". It exceeds the 14th Century Black Death.
- The 2-WWs, followed by the 2nd Sino-Japanese War (treated as part of WW-II) are the 3 of top 10 most costly wars & in high death toll, all occurred in the last century.
- Other than top 3, most of the others involved China or its neighbors.

Ongoing Conflicts

Several ongoing armed conflicts are prevailing around the world, the deadliest of which is the Syrian Civil War. The others include, Afghanistan wars, Iraq conflicts, Mexican Drug War, India-Pakistan (Kashmir issue), Israel–Palestine, Eritrea-Ethiopia border conflicts, and Civil wars/ internal conflicts in Somalia, Sudan, Libya, Egypt, Peru, Columbia (S. America), Thailand, Myanmar, Bangladesh and so forth.

The Top Ten Largest by Death Toll		
Deaths (millions)	**Period**	**War**
100	1939–1945	WW-II & 2nd Sino-Japan
60	13th century	Mongol Conquests
40	1850–1864	Taiping Rebellion
39	1914–1918	WW-I
36	755–763	An Shi Rebellion
25	1616–1662	Qing dynasty conquest on Ming dynasty
20	1370–1405	Conquests of Timur
16	1862–1877	Dungan revolt
5–9	1917–1922	Russian Civil War
4-7	1803-1815	Napoleonic Wara

15.6.2 Types of Wars

Wars are often described in the following types

- **Asymmetric warfare** is a conflict between two populations of drastically different levels of military capability or size. Example: Wars between Ghazni and Indian Kings.
- **Biological warfare**, or germ warfare, is the use of weaponized biological toxins or infectious agents such as bacteria, viruses, and fungi. Example: Chinese, Mangolians, Turks spread plague/ cholera in their warfare, Japan developed breeds of flees to spread plague during WW-II.
- **Chemical warfare** involves the use of weaponized chemicals. Poison gases were used during WW-I, and resulted in over a million casualties (>1 lakh civilians).
- **Civil war** is a war between forces belonging to the same nation or political entity. Example: Russian, French Revolts.
- **Conventional warfare** is declared war between states in which biological, nuclear or chemical weapons are not used or see limited deployment.
- **Unconventional warfare**, the opposite of conventional warfare, is an attempt to achieve military victory through acquiescence, capitulation, or clandestine support for one side of an existing conflict.

- **Cyber warfare** involves the actions by a nation-state or international organization to attack or attempt to damage another nation's information systems (by virus/ malware).
- **Nuclear warfare** is warfare which uses nuclear weapons as the primary or a major, method of achieving surrender.
- **War of aggression** is for conquest or gain rather than self-defense; this is treated as war crime under customary international law.
- **Total war** is warfare by any means possible, disregarding the laws of war, placing no limits on legitimate military targets, use of weapons and tactics resulting in significant civilian casualties, or demanding a war effort to significant sacrifices by friendly civilian population.

15.7 THE WORLD WARS

The invention of gun and the technological advances led to modern warfare. At the end of each of the last two WWs, maximum efforts were made to get a greater understanding of the war dynamics and the consequences and thence resulted in formation of Nations League and its successor, the United Nations Organizations (UNO) to prevent wars, thence to attain global peace. Let us have a quick look at these world wars.

15.7.1 First World War I (WW-I)

One of the deadliest conflicts in history, the **World War I (WW-I)**, also called the **Great War**, or the **War to End All Wars**, was originated in Europe on 28 July 1914 and ended on 11 Nov 1918 that mobilized about 70 million (85% Europeans) military personnel while killed over 9 million combatants and 7 million civilians. It brought major political changes and revolutions in many nations and the unresolved rivalries lasted for 2 decades to trigger World War-II.

The war was between the world's economic great powers, in two opposing alliances: the Allies (the Triple Entente of the Russian Empire, the French 3rd Republic, and UK & Ireland) versus the Central Powers of Germany and Austria-Hungary. The alliances later got reorganized and expanded when more nations joined: Italy, Japan and US joined the Allies, while the Ottoman Empire and Bulgaria joined the Central Powers.

The trigger for the war was the assassination of Archduke Franz Ferdinand, the heir to the throne of Austria-Hungary, by Yugoslav nationalist Gavrilo Princip in Sarajevo on 28 June 1914. This set off a crisis when Austria-Hungary gave an ultimatum to the Kingdom of Serbia, invoking the previous issues. Within weeks the major powers were at war, and the conflict soon spread around the world. On 28th July the Austro-Hungarians declared war on Serbia and on next day Russia declared mobilization while on 30th July Germany's ultimatum to demobilize was refused, it declared war on Russia on 1st Aug. Russia urged its Triple Entente ally France to open up a 2nd front in the west. To retake Alsace-Lorraine (lost by France in the Franco-Prussian War in 1870) France accepted Russia's plea, to mobilize forces (1st Aug) and Germany declared Germany war (3rd Aug) on France. Violating Belgian neutrality, Germany invaded Belgium and Luxembourg before moving towards France from the north that led UK to declare war on Germany on 4th Aug. Thus it flared up and continued. The Ottoman Empire (in Nov 1914) and Bulgaria (in 1915) joined the Central Powers while Italy (in 1915), Romania (in 1916) and US (in 1917) joined the Allies.

As Russian govt. collapsed in March 1917, and a revolution in November followed by a further military defeat, brought Russians to terms with Central Powers via the Treaty of Brest Litovsk, which granted Germans a significant victory. On 4th Nov 1918, the Austro-Hungarian empire agreed to armistice, and on 11th Nov 1918 Germany also due to its own trouble with revolutionaries ended the war in victory for the Allies.

By the end of the war or soon after, German, Russian, Austro-Hungarian and Ottoman Empires ceased to exist. National borders were redrawn, with several independent nations restored or created. During the Paris Peace Conference of 1919, the Big Four (Britain, France, US and Italy) imposed their terms in a series of treaties. The League of Nations was formed with the aim of preventing any repetition of such a conflict. But, this effort failed, and economic depression, renewed nationalism, weakened successor states, and feelings of humiliation (particularly in Germany) eventually perpetrated to the start of World War II.

15.7.2 Second World War II (WW-II)

Yet another deadliest conflict in history, **World War II (WW-II)**, during 1939-1945, involved >100 million people from the vast majority of the world's countries (>30) including all of the great powers—eventually forming 2-opposing military alliances: the Allies and the Axis. It took away about 85 million lives, mostly civilians in SU and China. The disastrous violence included massacres, deliberate genocide of holocaust, strategic bombing, starvation, diseases and the first use of nuclear weapons in history.

In fact, Japan aimed to dominate Asia and Pacific through war with China in 1937. But the world war is said to have begun on 1 Sep 1939 with the invasion of Poland by Nazi Germany and subsequently by France and UK on Germany. With series of campaigns and treaties, supplied by SU during 1939-1941, Germany conquered or controlled much of Europe, and formed the Axis alliance with Italy and Japan. The war continued mainly between the European Axis powers and the Allies of UK and British Commonwealth, with campaigns. In 1941, on 22nd June, the Axis powers invaded SU, while in Dec, Japan attacked US and European colonies in the Pacific Ocean, and quickly conquered much of W. Pacific. The Axis halted a little in 1942 when Japan lost the critical Battle of Midway, and Germany and Italy were defeated in N. Africa.

The war in Europe concluded with an invasion of Germany by the Western Allies and SU, capture of Berlin by Soviet, the suicide of Adolf Hitler and the subsequent German unconditional surrender on 8 May 1945. Following the Potsdam Declaration by the Allies on 26 July 1945 and the refusal of Japan to surrender under its terms, US dropped atomic bombs on Hiroshima and Nagasaki on 6th and 9th Aug respectively. Japan finally surrendered on 2 Sep 1945, ending the war.

WW-II changed the political alignment and social structure of the world. The United Nations Organization (UNO) was established to foster international co-operation and prevent future conflicts. The victorious great powers (China, France, SU, UK, and US) became permanent members of UN Security Council. The SU and the US emerged as rival superpowers (The Cold War lasted for the next 46 yrs).

15.7.3 War Ethics

While I was writing this topic, one of my friends asked me, what I was writing about. I said 'War Ethics'.

He suddenly jumped up out of his seat, with a big laughter and asked 'War?' or 'Ethics?' After looking at my mixed feeling face, he asked me 'How can ethics exist on an enemy, when there is a war? And when there are ethics, there is no chance for a war'.

I was a bit confused for a while, but I was clear. Then I said, 'Yes! Ethics must exist and ethics would exist in war. Ethics existed in all wars to much extent if not total'. I started giving examples.

Punjab King Jaipal – Ready to die for peace

Sultan Yamin-ud Mahmud and Amir Sabuktigin attacked Punjabi Hindus (986 AD). After several battles, the Hindu King Jaipal sent message to Sultan to avoid war. But Sultan wanted complete victory to his zeal for the honor of Islam. Jaipal then sent a new message to Sultan and Amir, "You have seen impetuosity of Hindus and their indifference to death. If you insist on war to plunder elephants and slaves, then we have no alternative but to destroy our property, take the eyes out of our elephants, cast our families in fire, and commit mass suicide, leaving you to conquer stones and dirt, dead bodies, and scattered bones". Amir then promised peace in exchange for a large ransom. However, his soldiers burnt the Hindu villages and towns, demolished idol-temples, and looted the wealth of the Hindu homes and king's treasure.

All is fair in love and war...

©SSRK

In the ancient wars, men never used to fight with women. For friendship or enmity, they used to see equivalence. Bhishma Pithamaha in Maha Bharat war dropped down his weapons when he saw Shikhandi (trans-gender) before him on Arjun's chariot in the war, following war ethics of not to fight with women, impotents, children and weaker. War ethics did not permit to fight after sunset. For killing Jayadhrat (King of Sindhu) before sunset, Lord Krishna made all the difference with His holy Discus (Chakra) covering the sun for some time (It could be solar eclipse also). There are several incidents to prove war ethics in the epics. Some events seem to be unethical, but they are clearly justified by many intellectuals.

Most of the wars in the history also followed such war ethics. The story of wars between Alexander and King Purushotham, Sindhu King Jaipal against Sultan Yamin ud-Muhmad are some examples.

Of course! Everything is fair in love and war. As long as it is justified by majority and if intellectuals get convinced, war is fair. After seeing the most disastrous two world wars, the UNO identified the significance of the war ethics.

15.7.4 Just War Theory

Just War Theory was founded by the UN and the International Laws regulate legitimate war after the bitter experiences of WW-II. The 'Just War Theory' prescribes war ethics under two principle aspects:

1. Jus ad bellum (Right to War) and
2. Jus in bello (Right in War)

1. **Jus Ad Bellum (Right to War):** This principle provides criteria for the unfriendly acts and situations that can justify declaring war on another nation. There are 6 main criteria that a 'just war' declared should
   - be by a lawful authority
   - have just and righteous cause to substantiate to merit large-scale violence
   - be just with rightful intentions i.e. aimed to betterment and curtail evil
   - have a reasonable chance of success
   - be a last resort and
   - have the goals proportional to means being used.

2. **Jus In Bello (Right in War):** This is the set of ethical rules during ongoing war. There are two main principles namely, proportionality and discrimination.
    - Principle of proportionality refers to the forces needed that can morally appropriate to achieve targets and the injustice suffered.
    - Principle of discrimination specifies the legitimate targets of war, and determines the combatants whether to kill or not.

Failure to follow these rules can result in the loss of legitimacy for the just-war-belligerent.

15.8 THEORIES FOR MOTIVATION TO WAR (WHY, WHEN AND WHERE WAR GENERATES?)

15.8.1 Psychoanalytic Theories

Psychoanalysts use psychology as motivators for war of which the three theories most commonly cited are:

1. According to psychoanalysts E.F.M. Durban and John Bowlby, human beings are inherently violent and the act of bias and hatred against in terms of sentiments, races, religions, nations or ideologies flairs up and aggravates.
2. Franco Fornari, psychoanalyst of Italy, theorizes that violence develops out of our "love need" i.e. attachments, and thence can result in war out of willingness of human beings to die for their love, may it be mother, father, wife or lover or a place or race, or even nation.
3. Another theory says that war is often caused by leaders who seek war (e.g. Napoleon and Hitler) drag common people for their powers of crisis when the populace opts for a decisive leader, who then leads the nation to war.

For obvious reasons, the common people don't want war; may it be America, England, Russia, China, Japan or Germany or any country for that matter. After all, it is the leaders of the country who determine the policy and no matter whether it is a democracy or a Parliament or a fascist dictatorship or a Communist dictatorship.

15.8.2 Evolutionary Theory

Though several theories exist on evolutionary basis, the following are two main schools:

- Organized warfare developed in or after the Mesolithic, through complex social organization due to larger population density and thence competition over resources;

- Ancient human practices derived from animal tendencies, such as territoriality and sexual competition like the behavior patterns of chimpanzees and ants (group wars).

15.8.3 Economic Theory

This theory sees war as international growth in economic competition. It believes that war begins as a pursuit of markets for natural resources and for wealth. For example, Kuwaiti oil wells were on fire, during the Gulf War, 1 March 1991. This theory links up war with economic development as viewed by historians and economists, capitalists, world leaders, including Presidents of US and US Generals.

> **O My God!**
>
> **Hermann Gõring at the Nuremberg trials, April 18, 1946 said,**
>
> ... the people can always be easily trapped to emotional burst by the leaders. All they do is tell them they are being attacked and denounce the pacifists for lack of patriotism and exposing the country to danger. It works the same way in any country.

15.8.4 Marxist Theory

This says that all modern wars are caused by competition for resources and markets between imperialist powers. It believes that war disappears by world revolution by over-throwing free markets and class systems. Rosa Luxemburg, Marxist philosopher argues imperialism is the result of capitalist countries requiring new markets. So, expansion of production is possible if and only if there is relative growth in consumer demand. As capitalist economy cannot fill this, producers have no option than to spread out into non-capitalist markets to find consumers, thence resulting imperialism.

> **O My God!**
>
> **Pope Urban-II on the eve of 1st Crusade (1095) spoke**
>
> For this land which you now inhabit, shut in on all sides by the sea and the mountain peaks, is too narrow for your large population; it scarcely furnishes food enough for its cultivators. Hence it is that you murder and devour one another, that you wage wars, and that many among you perish in civil strife. Let hatred, therefore, depart from among you; let your quarrels end.

15.8.5 Demographic Theories

Demographic theories present two views, Malthusian and youth bulge.

- ***Malthusian theory:*** Thomas Malthus (1766–1834) says that populations always increase until they are limited by war, epidemic, or famine. It believes rising populations and limited resources raise violent activities resulting in wars.
- ***Youth bulge theory:*** Heinsohn, proposed youth bulge theory according to which a youth bulge occurs when 30-40% of the males of a nation belong to 15-30 yrs (fighting age). It will follow periods with total fertility rates as high as 4–8 children per woman with a 15–30 yr delay. The theory is substantiated by the prominent historical events such as French

Revolution (1789), Nazism in Germany (1930s), Rwandan Genocide (1994) and many more. However, this theory is criticized as leading to racial, gender and age discrimination.

15.8.6 Rationalism/ Neo-realism Theory

Rationalism and Neo-realism (international relations) theory assumes that international actors are rational, seek the best possible outcomes for themselves, and desire to avoid the costs of war. As per Game theory approach, all actors can bargain better if war did not occur, but yet war occurs. According to philosopher Iain King, "Most instigators of conflict overrate their chances of success, while most participants underrate their chances of injury". James Fearon gave 3 explanations for why some countries engage in war:

1. ***Issue Indivisibilities*** occurs when the thing for which the two parties are fighting cannot be shared between them, and only one of them owned entirely, thence the two parties cannot avoid war by bargaining.
2. ***Information Asymmetry (Incentives to Misrepresent)*** occurs when two nations maintain confidentiality upon their individual capabilities, and do not agree on either.
3. ***Commitment Problems*** may influence bargaining due to the states' promises and commitments.

15.8.7 Political Science Theories

The political science theories use the concepts of system, societal, and individual levels of analysis of causes for war. This kind of division was first proposed by Kenneth Waltz in *Man, the State, and War* and has been often used by political scientists since then.

- ***System-level theories*** are interpreted through several different schools of thought, of which, the two main sub-theories are balance of power and transition of power. These two theories are not mutually exclusive, and can be used situational.
- *Societal-level theories or Diversionary theory or scapegoat hypothesis*, **says that political power uses war as a diversion.**
- ***Individual-level theories*** suggest differences in people's personalities, decision-making, emotions, belief systems, and biases determine if the conflicts get out of hand.

15.9 EFFECTS OF WAR

The result of war is certainly a significant destruction in almost every aspect. The list of effects of war is given below, and list is not exhaustive.

- Loss of human lives, especially youth
- Injuries and physical disablements
- Mental stress to civilians
- Loss of assets/ properties of both public and private
- Death of cattle and animals
- Economic crisis and recess
- Destruction of forests
- Destruction of infrastructure
- Deterioration of the ecosystem
- Decrease in social speding
- Ruined Foreign relations
- Occurrence of famine
- Spoilage of environment and effect on the weather due to pollution of air/water/soil
- Large-scale emigration from the war zone
- Post-traumatic stress disorder to the soldiers
- Mistreatment of prisoners of war or civilians

Though the effects of war are numerous and severe to affect the human life, some last for longer time and affect the generations also. For example, the bombing in Hiroshima and Nagasaki, the effect is found in Japan today even after in the 8th decade. These effects are directly visible, nevertheless, some go unnoticed, but cause considerable loss to the country. We shall now discuss some of such effects.

O My God!

Richard Gabriel* wrote in his *No More Heroes

In every war in which American soldiers have fought in, the chances of becoming a psychiatric casualty – a consequence of the stresses of military life – were greater than the chances of being killed by enemy fire.

15.9.1 Effect on Military Personnel

The first and foremost effect of the war is on military and soldiers that go unnoticed or least attended and treated less important. Military personnel in war often suffer mental and physical injuries, including depression, post-traumatic stress disorder, disease, injury, and death.

Examples:

- As per Indian history, Samrat Asoka, a great emperor of Mourya dynasty was upset and mentally disturbed with after math of Kalinga war and adopted Buddhism to establish peace. If this is the Samrat's status, imagine the civilians, soldiers and their families.

- One-tenth of American men were hospitalized for mental disturbances during 1942- 1945, and after 35 days of uninterrupted combat, 98% of them manifested psychiatric disturbances in varying degrees.
- 18 - 54% of Vietnam-war veterans suffered from Post Traumatic Stress Disorder.
- Based on 1860 census, 8% of all white males aged 13-43 died in the American Civil War, including about 6% in the North and approximately 18% in the South. This caused a severe shortage of male population.
- During Napoleon's retreat from Moscow, of the 4.5 lakh soldiers who crossed the Neman on 25 June 1812, less than 40,000 returned. More military personnel died (1500 – 1914) by typhus than from military action by the Russians. Further, had there been no medical advancement, there would be 1000's more killed by the diseases and infections.
- During the 7 Years' War, the Royal Navy reported it conscripted 184,899 sailors, of whom 133,708 died of disease or were missing.
- Swank and Marchand's study on WW-II revealed that after 60 days of continuous combat, 98% of all military survivors became psychiatric casualties, fatigue cases, hysteria, anxiety, confusion/ obsession/ compulsive states, and character disorders.

15.9.2 Effect on Civilians

The result of any war in the history is recorded with significant loss of life, along with destruction of infrastructure and led to famine, disease, and death in the civilians. Some examples are given below:

- The Holy Roman Empire population was reduced by 15-40% during the 30 Years' War, Further, the survivors suffered psychological after-effects of witnessing the destruction.
- In WW-II around 60 million people died, of which 40 million were civilians.
- Soviet Union (SU) suffered about 27 million death toll of WW-II of which vast majority were young men who had not yet fathered, thence population growth in the postwar SU drastically fell down.
- In about 9 million on the territory of Soviet Belarus in 1941, about 1.6 million were killed by the Germans in actions away from battlefields, including about 7 lakh prisoners of war, 5 lakh Jews, and 3.2 lakh counted as partisans (the vast majority were unarmed civilians).

Of course! During some wars there was increased revenue by weapon manufacturers.

O My God!

Mao & Einstein on Wars

Mao Zedong in the socialist camp told not to fear nuclear war with US since, even if "half of mankind died, the other half would remain while imperialism would be razed to the ground and the whole world would become socialist." In 1947, in concern of the consequences and costs of the rapid modern destructive warfare with the atom bomb, Albert Einstein famously stated, "I know not with what weapons WW-III will be fought, but WW-IV will be fought with sticks and stones."

15.9.3 Effect on the Economy

War generally stimulates some country's economy while damages others. Nations lost in war are often required to pay war reparations to the nations won and in certain cases land is ceded. Overall, the economy of any nation would be disturbed and causes a severe recess after war.

Examples

- Alsace-Lorrain territory was traded 3-times between France and Germany.
- After WW-I, the Russian economy almost collapsed and contributed greatly to the Russian Revolution of 1917.
- WW-II was costliest conflict in history with cumulative expenditure was trillion USD
- By the end of the war, 70% of European industrial infrastructure was destroyed.
- Assets damage in the SU was estimated at 679 billion rubles.
- The total damage of WW-II includes destruction of 1,710 cities/ towns, 70,000 villages, 2,508 church buildings, 31,850 industrial establishments, 64,374 km (40,000 mi) of railroad, 4100 railroad stations, 40,000 hospitals, 84,000 schools, and 43,000 libraries.

15.9.4 Effect on Arts and Culture

Wars motivate and enforces migration of large displacements of population which contains large number of experienced, experts, artists, and creative people, thence causing curtails the country's creative potential as well as the culture in the long-run. War also has a negative effect on an artists' individual life-cycle output.

Example: The spread Muslim culture in Indian sub-continent occurred after Mughal wars and Muslim attacks.

Finally, we shall conclude this chapter (Violence, Terrorism and Wars) with the famous quote of Benjamin Franklin "THERE IS NEVER A GOOD WAR OR A BAD PEACE."

SELF ASSESSMENT INTERMISSION (SAI – 15.5)

1. Define the terms 'War; and 'Warfare'. What is its meaning? Do you consider it as a disaster? What is its significance in disaster management?
2. What are the types of wars? Enumerate the causes.
3. Discuss the causes and effects of First World War.
4. Write a detailed note on Second World War referring to the causes and effects.

(continued)

5. What are the effects of a war? Explain referring WW-II as an example.
6. Discuss about the major wars took place in the world history.
7. Why, when and where does war generate? List and briefly explain the theories of war.
8. Whatsoever the country may be, the common citizens of any country will never want a war. Do you support the statement? Justify your answer.
9. What do you understand by 'war ethics'? Explain the Just Theory of war.
10. Discuss the effects of war in economics, tourism and arts.
11. Explain the effects of war on civilians and military personnel.

MINI-PROJECTS / CASE STUDIES

1. In the Indian context, write a report on violence against the following weaker sections. Analyze the causes and effects. Quote some examples occurred in the near past.
   (a) women, (b) children, (c) older people (d) scheduled castes & Scheduled Tribes (e) Backward Communities (f) Economically Backward classes
2. Write a report on terrorists attack on (a) Indian Parliament (b) Mumbai Hotel (c) Bomb blast at Dilsukhnagar, Hyderabad
3. Choose any the present ongoing war, collect data and prepare a report on causes, development and the present status.
4. Collect data and present a report on the wars between India and Pakistan since independence till date. Critically analyze the Kashmir issue.

List of important battles fought in India from 1000 CE up to 1757 CE.

Name of Battle	Date	Place	Winner	Loser	Effect
Battle of Tarain	1191	Tarain	Prithvi Raj of Chauhan Dynasty	Muhammad Ghori	-
2nd Battle of Tarain	1192	Tarain	Md Ghori	Prithvi Raj Chauhan	Ghori entered India
Battle of Chandawar	1194)	Chandawar	Md Ghori	Jaichandra, King of Kanauj	Ghori extended his empire in India
Battle of Panipat	(11-Apr - 1526)	Panipat	Babur	Sultan Ibrahim Lodhi	Babur expanded small principality to empire
Battle of Khanwa	17-Mar -1527	Khanwa	Babur	Rajputs under Rana Singh	
Battle of Chanderi	(1528)	Chanderi	Babur	Medini Rai of Chanderi	-
Battle of Ghagra	(6-May - 1529)	Ghagra	Babur	Afghans	Afghans are defeated
Battle of Chausal	(7-Jun-1539)	Chausal	Shershah	Humayun	-

(continued)

Name of Battle	Date	Place	Winner	Loser	Effect
Battle of Kanauj or Billgram	(17-May-1540)	Kanauj	Shershah	Humayun	Agra was occupied by Sher shah
Battle for Delhi	7 Oct 1556	Tughlaqabad Fort Area	Hemu	Akbar	Hemu defeated Akbar &titled 'Vikramaditya'
Battle of Panipat	(5-Nov-1556)	Panipat	Akbar	Hemu	Akbar reoccupied Delhi.
Battle of Tallikota	(23-Jan-1565)	Tallikota	Ali Adilshah and four others	Aliya Rama Raya	Vijayanagara empire starts declining
Battle of Haldighat	(1576)	Haldighat	Raja Man Singh (Genl. of Mughal emperor Akbar)	Rana Pratap Singh of Mewar	-
1st Carnatic	(1745–48)	Carnatic of South India	French East India Company	British East India Company	-
2nd Carnatic War	(1749–54)	Carnatic of South India	British East India Company	French East India Company	French lost expanding opportunities. Continued as trading
3rd Carnatic War	(1756–63)	Carnatic of South India	British East India Company	French East India Company	-
Battle of Plassey	(Jun-1757)	Plassey	British under Robert clive	Siraj ud-Daulah	British won major war and later ruled India.
Battle of Buxar	(1764)	Buxar	Sir Hector Munro commander of British forces	Shuja-ud-Daula Mir Qasim Shah Alam II	-

CHAPTER 16

Bio-hazards

(Bacterial, Protozoan and Fungal Epidemics)

O'MY SILENT INNER VIBES (O'M S I V – 16)

After 1910 AD there was an epidemic of cholera in Shirdi, India. The administration tried everything they could to alleviate. At last some people approached Sai Baba to help. The Fakir went to a nearby house, picked up a grinding stone and spread a sack on the floor; and thereon set a grinding stone and then started grinding the wheat by putting few handfuls of wheat. Immediately, this news spread into the village, and at once men and women ran to the *Masjid* and flocked to see Baba's act. Four women, from the crowd, forced their way up and pushing Baba aside, took forcibly the peg (handle) into their hands and singing ***Baba's Leelas*** (Divine play) started grinding. At first Baba was enraged, but on seeing the women's love and devotion, he was pleased and began to smile. While they were grinding, they began to think that Baba had no house, no property, no children, none to look after, and he lived on alms, and so he did not need any wheat-flour for making *roti;* what would he do with this big quantity of flour? Perhaps as Baba is very kind, he will distribute the flour amongst us. Thinking in this way, they finished the grinding and divided the flour into 4 parts and took one each. Baba, calm and quiet thither to, got wild and started abusing them, "Have you gone mad? Whose father's property are you looting away? Did I borrow any wheat from you? Now do this, "Take the flour and sprinkle it on the village borders". On hearing this, the women felt abashed and whispering amongst them, went away to the outskirts and spread the flour as directed by Baba.

Baba furiously ordered cholera to go away.

Then onward the cholera epidemic started to subside, patients recovered and Shirdi was completely free from the doom of cholera. What earthly connection was there between wheat and cholera and how to reconcile their significance? The incident seems to be inexplicable and a part of Baba's limitless powers.

So have faith in the God, who can do anything possible, because He is G-O-D, the Generator, the Operator and the Dissolver.

Even Jesus said "Rise and go; your faith has made you well." Matthew 8:1–4, Mark 1:40–45 and Luke 5:12–16

The New Testament describes instances of Jesus healing people with tzaraath (leprosy) (Luke 5:10). [*Talmud* (Sifra 63) clarifies that *tzaraath* refers to various types of lesions or stains in ritual impurity and occurs on cloth, leather, or houses, as well as skin]. According the Biblical narration...

When Jesus came down from the mountainside, large crowds followed him. A man with leprosy knelt before him and said, "Lord, if you are willing, you can make me clean". Jesus touched him "I am willing, Be clean!" Immediately he was cleansed of his leprosy. Then Jesus said, "See that you don't tell anyone. But go, show yourself to the priest and offer the gift Moses commanded, as a testimony to them."

Then, Jesus travelled to Jerusalem along the border between Samaria and Galilee. As was going into a village, 10 men with leprosy met Him. They stood at a distance and called out in a loud voice, "Jesus, Master, have pity on us!" When He saw them, He said, "Go! Show yourselves to the priests". And as they went, they were cleansed.

One of them, when He saw He was healed, came back, praising God in a loud voice. He threw himself at Jesus' feet and thanked Him—and he was a Samaritan.

Jesus asked, "Were not all ten cleansed? Where are the other nine? Has no one returned to give praise to God except this foreigner?" Then He said to him, "Rise and go; your faith has made you well".

So believe in yourself and have faith in God. Your faith will make you well.

16.1 CONCEPT AND DEFINITION OF EPIDEMIC

An **epidemic** (means "above people" in Greek) is the rapid spread of infectious disease to a large number of people in a given population within a short period of time, usually within 2-weeks. Epidemics could be the consequence of disasters such as earthquakes, tropical storms, floods, droughts, etc. Epidemics may also attack animals, and thence transmit the disease to humans causing local economic disasters and affect public health.

The Red Cross society, the World Health organization (WHO), and the Center for Disease Control (CDC) and Prevention, US are putting their best efforts in creating awareness, advocating effective action, control, prevention, social mobilization, volunteer activities and logistics support such as transport, warehousing and so forth.

16.1.1 Definition

An ***epidemic*** is defined as "*the unusual increase in the number of cases of an infectious disease due to wide spread of an already existing disease in a certain region*".

An epidemic may be restricted to one location; however, if it spreads to other countries or continents and affects a substantial number of people, it may be termed a ***pandemic***.

16.1.2 Causes

The fundamental reasons for the occurrence of epidemics are

- Increased virulence
- Introduction into a novel setting
- Changes in host susceptibility to the infectious agent

An epidemic disease need not be contagious, e.g. West Nile Fever and the Obesity Epidemic (as per the WHO). The conditions for an epidemic are usually-

- infected food supplies such as contaminated drinking water and
- the migration of populations of certain insects or animals, like rats or mosquitoes, which act as disease vectors.

Certain epidemics like whooping-cough (in spring) occur in certain season, whereas measles produces two epidemics, one in winter and one in summer. Influenza, the common cold, and other infections of the upper respiratory tract, such as sore throat, occur predominantly in the winter.

16.1.3 The Concept of Outbreak

If individuals are affected by a common agent it is called ***common source outbreak***. If the exposure is singular and all of the affected individuals develop the disease over a single exposure and incubation course, it is termed a ***point source outbreak***. If the exposure is continuous or variable, it is termed a ***continuous outbreak*** or ***intermittent outbreak***, respectively.

In a ***propagated outbreak***, the disease spreads person-to-person. Affected individuals may become independent reservoirs leading to further exposures.

Many epidemics will have characteristics of both common source and propagated outbreaks. For example, secondary person-to-person spread may occur after a common source exposure or environmental vectors may spread a zoonotic diseases agent.

16.1.4 Transmission

Transmission is the spreading of infection of disease from one person or animal to other. This occurs in many routes and forms as listed below.

- **Airborne transmission:** This is the spread of infection by droplet nuclei or dust in the air through short distances (10 - 20 ft).

- **Arthropod transmission:** This occurs either mechanically through acontaminated proboscis or feet, or biologically when there is growth or replication of an organism in the arthropod.
- **Biological transmission:** This occurs through a biological process, i.e. developing through an infecting agent in an intermediate host.
- **Colostral transmission:** This is a form of vertical transmission through successive generations.
- **Contact transmission:** Here, the disease agent is transmitted by contacting directly by biting, sucking, chewing or indirectly by inhaling droplets, drinking of contaminated water, travelling in contaminated vehicles (via touching).
- **Cyclopropagative transmission:** In this type, the agent undergoes both development and multiplication in the transmitting vehicle.
- **Developmental transmission:** In this transmission, the agent undergoes only some development in the transmitting vehicle.
- **Fecal-oral transmission:** The infectious agent is shed by the infected host in feces and acquired by the susceptible host through ingestion of contaminated material.

- **Horizontal transmission:** Lateral spread to others in the same group and at the same time; spread to contemporaries.
- **Mechanical transmission:** The transmitter is not infected in that tissues are not invaded and the agent does not multiply.
- **Propagative transmission:** The agent multiplies in the transmission vehicle.
- **Vertical transmission:** From one generation to the next, perhaps transovarial or by intrauterine infection of the foetus. Some retroviruses are transmitted in the germ line, i.e. their genetic material is integrated into the DNA of either the ovum or sperm.

16.1.5 Risk Factors Leading to Epidemics after Natural Disaster

The relationship between natural disasters and communicable diseases is often misinterpreted. There will be usually chaos after a natural disasters and a fear likely to develop in people due to the dead bodies and infections that may be a curtain-rise for epidemics. Natural disasters are catastrophic events with atmospheric, geologic, and hydrologic origins. The risk factors for outbreaks after disasters may be attributed to the following factors:

- Population displacement
- Degree of crowding
- Availability of safe water
- Sanitation facilities
- Underlying public health status
- Resistance power of the population
- Availability of healthcare services
- Interactions within the local diseases
- Ecological influences
- Diseases in dead and affected people
- The type of virus/bacteria or disease
- The environmental conditions

16.1.6 Population Displacement: A Primary Concern

As understood from the above factors, the risk of transmission of communicable disease after disasters is fundamentally depends on

- size of population displacement
- characteristics of population displacement,

O My God!

Isolation and Quarantine?

Isolation is to separating the sick people from those who are not. Quarantine refers to separating those who may have been exposed to a disease until they either show signs of the disease or are no longer at risk. To decrease spread effectively, Governments often quarantine the epidemic areas or people who may transmit.

There is an exclusive hospital named "Quarantine Hospital" (people call with a nick 'Quaranty') at Nallakunta, Hyderabad, Telangana state Capital, specially built for quarantined fever patients.

Other associated reasons include

- proximity of safe water
- availability of well functioning hygienic sanitation,
- nutrition status of the displaced population
- level of immunity to vaccine-preventable diseases (e.g. measles)
- access to healthcare services.

16.1.7 Diseases Associated with Crowding

Crowding helps the transmitting communicable diseases. A few examples are given below.

1. **Measles:** Measles transmission after a natural disaster, depends on immunization among the affected population; specifically children <15 years are susceptible. More so, in crowded living conditions and so needs even higher immunization to prevent outbreaks.
2. **Neisseria Meningitidis:** Meningitis is transmitted from person to person, particularly in situations of crowding. Example: Cases and deaths from meningitis among those displaced in Aceh and Pakistan.
3. **Acute Respiratory Infections (ARI):** These majorly cause of illness and death among displaced populations, particularly in children <5 yrs age. Risk factors include crowding, exposure to indoor cooking with open flame, and poor nutrition. Lack of access to health services and to
   - ARI increased 4-fold in Nicaragua in the 30 days after Hurricane Mitch in 1998.
   - ARI accounted for the highest number of cases and deaths after tsunami in Aceh in 2004
   - After the 2005 earthquake in Pakistan.

O My God!

Disease due to Dead Bodies is a Myth

The sudden appearance of large numbers of dead bodies in the disaster-affected area obviously enhances the fear and concern of disease outbreaks. But strictly speaking, there is no evidence that dead bodies pose a risk for epidemics after natural disasters.

Yes! It may be surprising and may be unbelievable. When death is directly due to the natural disaster, human remains do not pose a risk for outbreaks.

Historically, fears of major disease outbreaks in the aftermath of natural disasters have shaped the perceptions of the public and policymakers. These expectations, misinformed by associations of disease with dead bodies, created fear and panic in the affected population and led to confusion in the media and elsewhere.

Of course! Dead bodies only pose health risks in a few situations that need specific precautions, such as deaths from cholera or hemorrhagic fevers etc. Further, the proper sanitation, and scientific disposal of dead bodies (electrical cremation, burying) can minimize the risk. Deaths during/ after natural disasters (especially rapid-onset disasters) are overwhelming due to blunt trauma, crush-related injuries, or drowning. Believe it or not! Deaths from communicable diseases after natural disasters are less common.

While researches, scientific studies and the history too, reveal these facts, the risk for outbreaks after disasters is often exaggerated by both health officials and the media which create a havoc and chaos in the common public. Imminent threats of epidemics remain a recurring theme of media reports from areas even recently affected by disasters, regardless of attempts to dispel these myths.

16.2 CLASSIFICATION OF EPIDEMICS

Epidemics may be broadly categorized as

- the epidemics after disasters and
- the natural epidemics

16.2.1 Epidemics after Disasters

The following are the common natural and man-made disasters which may be followed by the epidemic outbreak

Natural

- earthquakes and tsunamis
- volcanic eruptions
- landslides/rockslides/mudslides
- floods
- heat and cold waves
- drought
- cyclones

Man-made

- wars and military actions
- civil wars
- bomb blasts
- chemical hazards
- Terrorism/Activities of extremists
- catastrophic accidents

Examples:

- An outbreak of ***diarrheal disease*** after flooding in Bangladesh in 2004 involved >17,000 cases due to *Vibrio cholera* (O1 Ogawa & O1 Inaba) and enterotoxigenic *Escherichia coli*.
- Floods in Mozambique in Jan–Mar 2000 led to an increase in the incidence of diarrhoea.
- A large (>16,000 cases) 1998-***cholera epidemic*** (O1 Ogawa) in W. Bengal preceded floods.
- Floods in Indonesia in 1992–1993, caused diarrheal illnesses due to *Salmonella enteric* serotype Paratyphi A (paratyphoid fever).
- After the 2005 earthquake in Pakistan, >1,200 cases of acute jaundice, and hepatitis E, and clusters of measles (>400 clinical cases in 6 months after eq) occurred in areas of unsafe water.
- Clusters of both hepatitis A and hepatitis E were noted in Aceh after the Dec-2004 tsunami.
- Outbreaks of leptospirosis occurred in Taiwan, Republic of China, after Typhoon Nali in 2001.

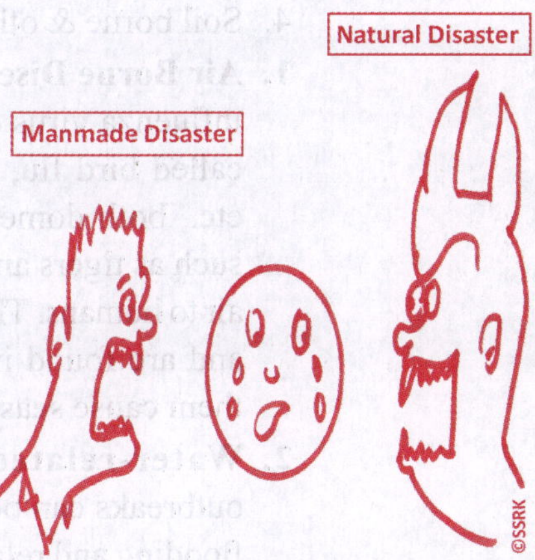

- Flood-related outbreaks of leptospirosis in Rio de Janeiro, Brazil (1996), Krasnodar, Russian Federation (1997), Argentina (1998) and Mumbai, India (2000) after floods.
- An earthquake in Costa Rica's Atlantic Region in 1991 changed habitat that favoured breeding and extreme rise in malaria cases.
- Periodic flooding clubbed with El Niño–Southern Oscillation encouraged malaria epidemics in the dry coast of Peru.
- A measles out broke in Philippines (1991) by eruption of Mt. Pinatubo involved >18,000 cases.
- After the tsunami in Aceh, a cluster of measles in 35 cases occurred in Aceh Utara district, and continuing sporadic cases and clusters were common despite mass vaccination campaigns.

16.2.2 Classification based on Mode of Transmission

Based on the transmission of disease the epidemics may be divided as

1. Air borne: Influenza (Flu, Dog Flu, Horse Flu, Swine Flu, Avian Influenza or Bird Flu)
2. Water borne: Diarrhoea, Cholera
3. Vector borne: Malaria, Dengue
4. Soil borne & others: Anthrax, TT

1. **Air Borne Diseases:** The lion's share of air borne diseases is taken by influenza virus causing flu and avian flu, or avian influenza (AI), also called bird flu, which primarily affects birds (chickens, ducks, geese etc., both domestic and migratory), but also sometimes other species such as tigers and pigs (often called Swine flu) and transmitted through air to humans. Though rare, bird flu can cause severe infections in humans and are found in many strains or varieties, the flu virus being one of them cause seasonal outbreaks in humans around the world every year.
2. **Water-related Communicable Diseases:** ***Diarrheal disease*** outbreaks can occur by contaminated drinking water, particularly after flooding and related displacement.

   Hepatitis A and E are transmitted by oral route, often associated with lack of access to safe water and sanitation. Hepatitis A is endemic in most developing countries, mostly with children and infants at high risk, while hepatitis E–endemic areas frequently experience heavy rains and floods. However, the illness is usually mild, but in pregnant women more risk with a fatality rate of 1 in 4.

   Leptospirosis is yet another epidemic-prone zoonotic bacterial disease transmitted by direct contact with contaminated water. Rodents release leptospires in their urine in large quantities which enter through skin and mucous membranes with water, damp soil or vegetation (such as sugar cane), or mud. Flooding motivates the spread.

3. **Vector borne Diseases:** Natural disasters, particularly meteorologic events such as cyclones, and flooding, can affect vector-breeding sites and thence disease transmission. While initial flooding may wash away existing mosquito-breeding sites, standing water caused by heavy rainfall or overflow of rivers can create new breeding sites. This situation can result (with typically some weeks' delay) in an increase of the vector population and potential for disease transmission. The crowding of infected and susceptible hosts, a weakened public health infrastructure, and interruptions of ongoing control programs are all risk factors. ***Malaria*** and ***Dengue*** outbreaks after flooding, rainfall and humidity are a well-known phenomenon. However, transmission is not directly associated with flooding, but high risk for transmission is due to increased vector's breeding sites (mostly artificial containers such as improperly disposed tea-cups) caused by disruption of basic water supply and solid waste disposal services. The risk for outbreaks can be influenced by other complicating factors, such as changes in human behavior (increased exposure to mosquitoes while sleeping outside, movement from dengue-non-endemic to endemic areas, paused disease control activities, overcrowd) or changes in the habitat promote mosquito breeding (landslide, deforestation, river damming, and rerouting of water).

4. **Soil borne and other Diseases:** These diseases are caused by the micro-organisms which are deposited in the soil. Sometimes the organisms present in the excretions of infected animal/ humans may be mixed with soils and when the ambient conditions prevail, these may flair up and enter the human body through opened parts such as eroded skin, cuts and wounds.

16.2.3 Classification based on Causing Micro-Organism

The natural epidemics may be classified on the basis of the disease causing microorganisms or mode of transmission.

Based on the cause of infection the epidemics can be categorized as:

1. **Bacterial:** Anthrax, Cholera, Diphtheria, Plague, Typhoid Fever, Typhus, Meningitis, Tetanus (TT), Tuberculosis (TB- Tubercle Bacillus)
2. **Protozoan:** Malaria
3. **Fungal:** Meningitis

4. **Viral:** Influenza (Flu, Dog Flu, Horse Flu, Swine Flu, Avian Influenza or Bird Flu), Ebola, Infantile Paralysis or Poliomyelitis or Polio, Measles, Smallpox, Chickenpox, Chikungunya, Dengue, HIV/AIDS, Japanese Encephalitis, Meningitis, Yellow Fever, Zika etc.

[This chapter focuses on the diseases caused by bacteria mainly, and a few others like protozoan, fungal and others, while the viral diseases are discussed in the next chapter].

SELF ASSESSMENT INTERMISSION (SAI – 16.1)

1. Define epidemic. What are the causes to occur epidemics? Do you consider it as a disaster? What is its significance in disaster management?
2. What is an outbreak? Enumerate different types of outbreaks.
3. What are the types of epidemics? Enumerate the causes.
4. Distinguish the terms endemics, epidemics and pandemics. Give examples.
5. What are the causes which lead to result in epidemic? Classify epidemics based on causing micro-organisms. Give examples.
6. Explain various forms of transmission to cause diseases.
7. List out the risk factors leading epidemics after a natural disaster. Give examples.
8. How is public displacement responsible to cause epidemics?
9. Do you think epidemics are caused due to dead bodies after epidemics? Discuss.
10. What are water borne, air borne, vector borne and soil borne diseases? Explain briefly.
11. With examples, explain how crowding can communicate diseases.

16.3 ANTHRAX (SOIL BORNE)

Anthrax is a rapid spreading disease in most animals due to the bacterium *Bacillus Anthracis* or *B. anthracis*. It is known by variety of names, like Siberian plague, Cumberland disease, charbon, splenic fever, malignant edema, woolsorter's disease, and la maladie de Bradford.

16.3.1 Mode of Infection

It can be transmitted through contact with infected meat. Anthrax can occur in three forms:

- Skin (cutaneous),
- Lungs (inhalation), and
- intestinal (ingestion)

The genus bacterial spores are soil-borne and can survive in tough conditions also for decades or even centuries. It can be found on all continents, including

Antarctica. They get reactivated and multiply rapidly when inhaled, eaten, or contacted with broken skin. Not a surprise to know that a disturbed grave site of infected animals caused infection over 70 years after the animal's death.

Usually infection develops in herbivores on eating or breathing in the spores while grazing and carnivores get infected by eating the infected animals. Thus anthrax can spread in humans from infected animals, either through direct contact or by eating raw or undercooked meat. Surprisingly, Anthrax is rare in dogs and cats, which is evident from 2001 anthrax attacks (only one case was reported). Anthrax outbreaks occur in some wild animal populations with some regularity.

Inhalational (Lungs)

Though infection by humans breathing is relatively rare, it may get initiated with cold (or flu-like symptoms) for several days, followed by pneumonia and severe respiratory collapse. Mortality is about 85% but early treatment (as in 2001 anthrax attack), can reduce it to 45%. The pulmonary anthrax causes severe respiratory illness and treatment should not be delayed.

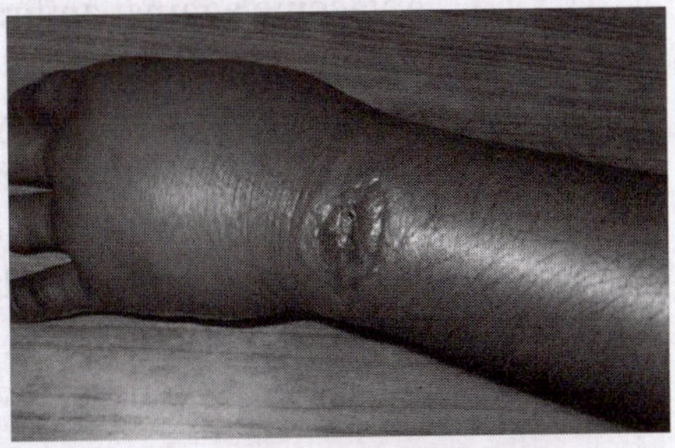

Skin lesion by anthrax

Inhalational anthrax, also called woolsorters' disease was an occupational hazard for wool sorters, is now rare as almost no infected animals remain. The last fatal case occurred in California, US in 1976, when a weaver died after working with infected wool imported from Pakistan. To reduce spread, the deceased was sealed in plastic bag within a metal container for autopsy.

Gastrointestinal (GI)

Eating anthrax-infected meat causes infection resulting in serious gastrointestinal (GI) difficulty, blood vomits, severe diarrhoea, acute inflammation of the intestinal tract, loss of appetite, and lesions in the intestines/mouth/throat. It makes toxins in the bloodstream and can be fatal ranging from 25-60% depending on starting the treatment. GI anthrax is very rare but, in Dec 2009, an outbreak (14 deaths) occurred amongst heroin addicts in Glasgow, Scotland.

Skin (Cutaneous)

Cutaneous Anthrax, also known as **Hide Porter's Disease**, is found on the skin in humans in the form of boil-like pains but itching/irritating lesions which finally turn as ulcers with a black centre (eschar). It enters human body through wounds or cuts on the skin, if exist, while they handle infected animals and/or animal products such as skin, meat, leather, wool etc. Cutaneous anthrax is rarely fatal if treated.

A Mystery in Anthrax History

During Dec 2009, New Hampshire Dept. of Health and Human Services confirmed a case of anthrax in a woman, which she could contract from an African drum used by the woman in a drumming circle. The woman apparently inhaled anthrax [in spore form] from the drum. She became critically ill, but surprisingly, with gastrointestinal anthrax rather than inhaled anthrax, which is unique in American medical history. Jodie Dionne-Odom, epidemiologist, described it a mystery and really didn't know why it happened".

16.3.2 The Causing Bacteria

Bacillus anthracis, a rod-shaped, Gram-positive, aerobic bacterium about 1/9 μm in size, was isolated by Robert Koch (1905 Nobel Prize winner in Medicine for the bacterium causing tuberculosis) in 1876 from a blood sample of an infected cow and put into a mouse. It normally rests in endospore form in the soil, and can survive for decades. Herbivores are often infected whilst grazing, especially when eating rough, irritant, or spiky vegetation: perhaps the vegetation causes wounds within the GI tract and allows the endospores into the tissues. This in open wound multiplies inside and kills the host within a few days. The endospores germinate at the site of entry into the tissues and then spread by the circulation to the lymphatics, where the bacteria multiply.

16.3.3 Vaccines

A vaccine against anthrax, from Pasteur's 19th century work with cattle (the 2nd effective vaccine ever) to protect American troops in biological warfare, is controversial. 20th century used modern product (BioThrax, 5-dose series licensed by the FDA). Human anthrax vaccines developed by SU in late 1930s and in UK in 1950s, while the current FDA-approved US vaccine was formulated in the 1960s. Currently administered vaccines are acellular (US) and live spore (Russia) varieties. All anthrax vaccines show reactogenicity (erythema, induration, soreness, fever).

The First Vaccine

Anthrax posed a major economic challenge in France during 19th century. Horses, cattle and sheep were highly vulnerable, and entrusted Louis Pasteur to investigate for a vaccine, after his successful work to protect the wine and silk industries. In May 1881, Pasteur with his assistants Jean-Joseph Henri Toussaint, Émile Roux et al demonstrated public experiment at Pouilly-le-Fort. He prepared 2 groups of 25 sheep, a goat, and several cows. One group was injected with Pasteur's vaccine twice, with a gap of 15 days; and other group unvaccinated. 30 days later, both groups were injected with a culture of live anthrax bacteria. All the unvaccinated died, while the vaccinated survived. However, the vaccine was unsuccessful when challenged by Australia. A more robust cell-free vaccine was developed by John Gunn and Mc Garvie Smith instead of the live-cell Pasteur-style used for veterinary. The vaccine was available from 1970.

16.3.4 Treatment and Precaution

Anthrax cannot be spread directly from person to person, but clothing and body may be contaminated with anthrax spores. Decontamination can be effective by a thorough wash with antimicrobial soap and water. Waste water should be treated with bleach or any antimicrobial agent. Articles used by them have to be boiled in water for 30 minutes or longer. Chlorine bleach is ineffective in destroying spores, but formaldehyde is effective. Burning clothes is best to destroy spores. After decontamination, there is no need to immunize, treat, or isolate contacts of persons who are ill with anthrax unless they were also exposed to the same source of infection.

Early antibiotic treatment is essential and delay reduces the probability of survival. Large doses of I.V. and oral antibiotics such as fluoroquinolones

(ciprofloxacin), doxycycline, vancomycin, erythromycin, or penicillin are suggested. If death occurs from anthrax, the body should be isolated to prevent possible spread. Burial does not kill anthrax spores.

If a person is suspected as having died from anthrax, every precaution should be taken to avoid skin contact with the potentially contaminated body and fluids exuded through natural body openings. The body should be put in strict quarantine. A blood sample should then be collected and sealed in a container and analyzed in an approved laboratory to ascertain if anthrax is the cause of death. Then, the body should be incinerated.

16.3.5 Anthrax Bio-hazard

During early days of this century, anthrax has become focal point of biohazards, as the anthrax spores can be cultivated with minimal equipment and knowledge. (But, to make in large scale for biological warfare, it needs extensive practical knowledge, training, and highly advanced equipment). Yes! Concentrated anthrax spores were used for bioterrorism in the 2001 anthrax attacks in the US, delivered by mailing postal letters containing the spores. The letters were sent to several news media offices and two Democratic senators:

Tom Daschle of S Dakota and Patrick Leahy of Vermont. As a result, 22 were infected and 5 died. Only a few grams of material were used in these attacks and in Aug 2008, the US Dept. of Justice announced that Dr. Bruce Irvins, a senior bio-defense researcher employed by the US govt, was responsible. The events also spawned many anthrax hoaxes and the US Postal Service installed 'biohazard detection systems' at its distribution centres to scan for anthrax being transported through the mail. They even sterilized some mails using gamma irradiation and/or treated with a proprietary enzyme formula supplied by Sipco Industries Ltd.

A scientific experiment performed by a high school student, later published in *The Journal of Medical Toxicology*, suggested a domestic electric iron at its hottest setting (at least 400°F) used for at least 5 minutes destroys all anthrax spores in a common postal envelope.

16.4 TETANUS OR TT (SOIL BORNE)

The name **Tetanus** (or **lockjaw** or **trismus** or **Sceptic),** the most popularly called **TT,** came from Greek, means 'taut'/ 'to stretch'. It is characterized by muscle spasms starting at jaw and then progress to rest of the body with a frequency of 3-4 weeks. Symptoms appear in 1-3 weeks after infection but recovery takes months and 10% deaths also.

The bacterium *Clostridium tetani*, found in soil, dust, rust and manure causes TT by entering through cuts/ breaks/ puncture/ wounds in the skin to produce toxins that interfere with muscle contractions. Blessing in disguise! TT is not contagious and so, does not spread between people.

It can be prevented by the vaccine. The wound should be cleaned, any dead tissue should be removed and muscle relaxants may be used to control spasms. Ventilation may be needed if breathing is affected. Tetanus can occur in any part of the globe but hot and wet climates are more vulnerable, particularly where the soil has lot of organic matter.

16.4.1 Types of Tetanus

The following are the four different forms of tetanus as per clinical experiences.

O My God!

The WHO certifies a country eliminated neonatal TT, if it has < 1 in 1000 live births in at least 2 yrs, e.g: In 1998, Uganda recorded >3000 TT cases while 2400 died. After a serious public health program, Uganda in 2011 got certified as eliminated

O My God!

Despite of the cause known and vaccine developed (in 1924 by Giorgio Rattone at University of Turin), it still caused about 3.6 lakh deaths in 1990 while it reduced to 60000 in 2013. The mortality is higher in unvaccinated and in over 60 yrs of age.

Generalized Tetanus: It is the most common type (80% of TT cases) usually in a descending pattern.

Neonatal Tetanus: It is in newborns to unvaccinated mothers. Hope, to hear the good news of declaring this TT eradication worldwide very shortly!

Local Tetanus: It is an uncommon form that persists when contraction of muscles for many weeks before gradually subsiding, occur in the area of an injury.

Cephalic Tetanus: It is the rarest (1–3% of cases) form pertaining to head muscles/ nerves that occurs after trauma to head area, skull fracture, eye injury and dental extraction.

16.4.2 Causes and Symptoms

TT is caused by the bacterium *Clostridium tetani* (*C. Tetani*), associated with rusted and corroded materials like rusty nails and the objects at outdoors or scrap yard etc. Strictly speaking, rust does not cause tetanus nor does it contain *C. Tetani* bacteria, but the rough surface of rusty metal merely provides a prime habitat for the spores to reside, and the nail like sharp materials can become the means to puncture skin and make way to enter the body at the wound. *C. Tetani*, being an anaerobic bacterium, chooses an environment that lacks oxygen. May it be rusty or not, nail like materials provide good shelter for tetanus infectors, as low-oxygen area on the object (due to oxidization and same object can puncture wound), can inject endospores to its ambient environment for growth. Heroin users, particularly those inject subcutaneously are at high risk.

Symptoms begin with mild spasms in the jaw muscles, extends to facial muscles. chest, neck, muscles that help breath, abdominal muscles, buttocks/ back muscles, hand/ foot arching spasms (called opisthotonos), drooling, excess sweat, fever, difficult to swallow, irritability, suffocation, heart attack, breath problems, irregular heartbeat and uncontrolled urination or defecation. Prolonged action causes sudden painful muscle contractions, called "tetany", leading to fractures and muscle tears.

16.4.3 Diagnosis & Treatment

Presently, there is no specific blood test for diagnosing TT, but is based on its symptoms. However, "spatula test" is one that involves touching the posterior pharyngeal wall with a soft-tip to observe the effect. An involuntary contraction of the jaw (biting down on the "spatula") confirms TT positive while a gag reflex attempting to expel the foreign object indicates TT negative. *The American Journal of Tropical Medicine and Hygiene* supports the spatula test's high specificity (Not false-positive) and high sensitivity (94% of infected are positive to test).

Unlike many infectious diseases, recovery is neither fast nor easy. However, vaccine can prevent TT. Adults need a booster every 10 yrs, but may not prevent a fatal case. For children < 7 yrs, TT vaccine is given in combination with Diphtheria and Pertusis (DPT/DTaP) vaccine. For adults and children > 7 yrs, the Td vaccine (TT & diphtheria) or Tdap (TT, diphtheria & acellular pertussis) is used while TT toxoid (TIg) can be given to suspected cases.

Mild TT can be treated with TT antibodies (TIg) or TT antitoxin and antibiotics while severe TT needs intensive care. Good ventilation and proper nutrition are essential to survive TT infection. Intake must be 3.5–4 kcal and >150 g of protein/day through a Ryle's tube directly into the stomach or into a vein due to increased metabolic strain and full recovery of muscles, may take 4-6 wks.

SELF ASSESSMENT INTERMISSION (SAI – 16.2)

1. What are soil borne epidemic diseases? Describe any one of your choice.
2. How is anthrax caused? Explain its modes of infection.
3. What are the precautions and treatments referred for persons infected by anthrax?
4. "Anthrax was the focal point of biohazard during the early days of this century." substantiate the statement with some evidential supports.
5. What are the causes of tetanus (TT)? What are the symptoms of TT infection?
6. What are various types of TT? How do you treat a TT infected person?
7. Why do rusted materials cause TT? Explain the mechanism of TT infection.
8. "May it be rusted or not, nail like material can cause TT". Do you agree? Justify your answer.

16.5 CHOLERA (WATER BORNE)

The word **Cholera** is from Greek *kholera* (from *kholç* means "bile"). It is of the bacterium *Vibrio cholerae* that infects the small intestine. The symptoms are large amounts of watery diarrhoea for a few days sometimes followed by vomiting and muscle cramps. Diarrhoea may lead to severe dehydration and electrolyte imbalance within few hours and skin may turn bluish and even result in sunken eyes, cold skin, decreased skin elasticity, and wrinkling of the hands and feet. Symptoms may be seen from 2 hrs to 5 days after exposure.

Cholera is caused by variety of *Vibrio cholerae*, some produce severe, some other less. Humans are the only animal affected. It is spread mostly by contaminated water/ food with human feces containing the bacteria. Undercooked seafood is also a source. Risk is high with poor sanitation, unclean drinking water, and poverty. Cholera is diagnosed by a stool test and rapid dipstick test.

John Snow, England, was 1st to identify the importance of contaminated water as its cause in 1854. So, improved sanitation and purified water supply can forestall to a large extent. Oral vaccines provide reasonable protection for about 6 months, which have an additional advantage of protecting against another type of diarrhoea caused by *E. coli*. The treatment is oral rehydration therapy—the replacement of fluids with slightly sweet/salt solutions, preferably rice-based solutions and Zinc supplementation (for children) and in severe cases, I.V. fluids, such as Ringer's lactate and antibiotics.

Cholera is affecting around 3–5 million people every year worldwide causing ~1½ lakh deaths. Children are mostly affected. Africa and south-east Asia are most vulnerable.

16.5.1 Symptoms

Suddenly starting with a fishy odour, for ½ to 5 days after ingestion of the bacteria and then vomiting of clear fluid are the primary symptoms. If untreated, patient produces 10-20 litres (3-5 gal) of diarrhoea a day, leading to life-risk dehydration and electrolyte imbalance. Cholera has been nicknamed the "blue death" as the skin turns bluish-gray due to huge loss of fluids.

Cholera usually will not have fever, if at all there is; it is due to a secondary infection. The following common characteristics can be found in cholera patients.

- Diarrhoea (rice water)
- Vomiting
- Electrolyte imbalance
- Patients are lethargic
- Dry mouth
- Peripheral pulse, rapid
- Sunken eyes
- Difficult breathing
- Urine output decreases with time
- Wrinkled hands and feet
- Deep & labored breathing pattern
- Muscle cramping and weakness
- Cold clammy skin
- Dehydration
- Altered consciousness, seizures
- Decreased skin turgor
- Low B.P. due to dehydration
- Even coma due to electrolyte loss

Credit : Care Hospitals, Hyderabad

16.5.2 Cause and Transmission

Transmission is mostly via the fecal-oral route of contaminated food or water caused by poor sanitation. About 100 million bacteria are needed to cause cholera in a normal healthy adult, and a little less in those with gastric acidity. Children (2-4 yr) are more susceptible. The susceptibility to cholera depends on blood group also, for example, 'O' group is most susceptible. Persons of lower

> **O My God!**
>
> **Famous persons died of cholera**
> - Sadi Carnot, Physicist, a founder of thermodynamics (1832) & IC Engines
> - Charles X, King of France (1836)
> - James K. Polk, 11th US President (1849)
> - Carl von Clausewitz, Prussian soldier and German military theorist (1831)
> - Elliot Bovill, Chief Justice of the Straits Settlements (1893)

immunity (such as AIDS), and/ or malnourished children are more vulnerable.

Most cases in developed countries are affected by seafood (shellfish and plankton), while in the developing world by water. Cholera infected people can transmit and spread if the untreated diarrheal discharge gets into waterways, groundwater or drinking water supplies. Eating any foods washed in such waters, drinking any infected water, eating shellfish from affected waterway, can be cholera-prone but very rare to spread directly from person to person.

In fact, most bacteria do not survive the acidic conditions of the human stomach. The few surviving bacteria whence leave the stomach and reach the small intestine, propel through the thick mucus that sticks on the intestinal walls, and no longer need the flagella to move. The bacteria stop the energy conserving protein production (flagellin), and start producing the toxic proteins that enforces the watery diarrhoea.

16.5.3 Diagnosis and Prevention

Quick treatment reduces mortality rate to <1%; while untreated rises to 50–60%. For certain genetic strains of cholera, death occurs within 2 hrs, e.g. 2010 Haiti and 2004 Indian outbreak

A rapid dipstick test can detect *V. cholerae* which can be confirmed by other antibiotic resistance tests. In epidemic situations, a patient history is recorded with a brief examination. Stool and swab samples collected in the acute stage of the disease, before antibiotics are started.

The WHO recommends focus on prevention, preparedness, and response to face the spread of cholera. Prevention is possible with good practices of sanitation. There are several points along the cholera transmission path to halt its spread, as listed below.

1. Sterilization

- Disposal of infected fecal waste water and all contaminable materials (e.g. clothing, bedding etc.).
- All materials used by the patients must be sanitized by washing in hot water and chlorine bleach.
- Hands touched cholera patients or their clothing, bedding, etc., should be thoroughly cleaned and disinfected with chlorinated water or other effective antimicrobial agents.

2. Sewage

- Antibacterial treatment of general sewage by chlorine, ozone, ultraviolet light or other effective treatment before it enters the waterways or underground water supplies.
- Prevent undiagnosed patients from inadvertently spreading the disease.

3. Sources

- Warn about possible water contamination sources and direct how to decontaminate the water (boiling, chlorination etc.) for possible use.
- Hand wash with soap and/or ash after visiting toilets and before handling food or eating.

4. Water purification

- All water used for drinking, washing, or cooking should be sterilized.
- Boiling, chlorination, ozone water treatment, UV light sterilization (e.g. solar water disinfection).
- Antimicrobial filtration in any area where cholera may be present.
- Chlorination and boiling are least expensive and most effective ways to stop transmission.
- Cloth filters or sari filtration, though very basic, have significantly reduced the occurrence of cholera when used in poor villages in Bangladesh that rely on untreated surface water.
- Better antimicrobial filters, like those present in advanced individual water treatment hiking kits.
- Public health education and adherence to appropriate sanitation practices.

5. Surveillance

- Surveillance and prompt reporting allow for containing cholera epidemics rapidly.
- It is a seasonal disease in many endemic countries, occurs annually mostly during rainy seasons.
- Surveillance systems can provide early alerts to outbreaks, thence coordinated response and assistance in preparation of preparedness plans.
- Efficient surveillance systems can also improve the risk assessment for potential cholera outbreaks.

O My God!

Yellow Flag on Ship?

In the past, a yellow quarantine flag was flown if any crew members or passengers were suffering from cholera. No one aboard with flying yellow flag would be allowed ashore. Of course, now, in modern sets of international maritime signal flags, the quarantine flag is yellow and black.

Signal flag "Lima" called the "Yellow Jack" which when flown in harbor means ship is under quarantine. A simple yellow flag (also called "Yellow Jack") had historically been used to signal quarantine, but now indicates the opposite, as a signal of a ship free of disease that requests boarding and inspection

- Understanding the seasonality and location of outbreaks provides guidance for improving cholera control activities for the most vulnerable.
- For prevention to be effective, it is important that cases be reported to national health authorities.

6. Vaccination

A number of safe and effective oral vaccines for cholera are available.

- Dukoral, an oral vaccine, has an 52% efficacy during 1st yr and 62% in 2nd yr, with minimal side effects. It is available in over 60 countries (but not currently recommended).
- An injection vaccine is effective for 2-3 yrs.
- Russian-Jewish bacteriologist Waldemar Haffkine developed the 1st cholera vaccine in July 1892.

7. Sari filtration

- To filter drinking water, an effective and cheapest method is to use *sari* (a long cloth garment that Indian traditional Women Wear) folded 4-8 times. In Bangladesh this practice reduced cholera nearly 50%.

16.5.4 Treatment

- According to the WHO, eating and drinking fluids speeds up the recovery of normal intestinal function, that reads "Continue to breastfeed your baby if the baby has watery diarrhoea, even when travelling to get treatment. Adults and older children should continue to eat frequently".
- Highly effective, safe, simple and most successful treatment of cholera is oral rehydration therapy. Severe cases need I.V. rehydration with "Ringer's lactate" with added potassium in large volumes.
- Despite widespread beliefs, fruit juices and commercial fizzy drinks like cola, are not ideal for rehydration of people with serious infections of the intestines,
- The too high sugar (in certain fruit juices) content may even harm water uptake.
- If commercial ORS is expensive or difficult to get, it can be made with 1 ltr of boiled water, ½ ts of salt, 6ts of sugar, added with mashed banana for potassium and to improve taste.
- While the dehydration is corrected, potassium levels may reduce rapidly, so eating foods high in potassium like bananas or green coconut water will revive the situation.
- Antibiotic treatments for 1-3 days may reduce the severity and lowers fluid requirements.
- However, patient can recover even without antibiotics, if enough hydration is given.

- WHO recommends antibiotics only in case of severe dehydration, such as Azithromycin, Doxycycline, Cotrimoxazole, Erythromycin, Tetracycline, Chloramphenicol, Fluoroquinolones or Ciprofloxacin and Furazolidone.
- Zinc supplements can reduce the duration and severity of diarrhoea.

16.6 DIPHTHERIA (WATER BORNE)

Diphtheria (Greek: *diphthera* means leather) is an infection caused by *Coryne bacterium diphtheriae*. After 2-5 days of exposure, symptoms appear (sore throat and fever). As it becomes severe, a grey/white patch develops in the throat, which can block the airway and create a barking cough. The neck may swell due to large lymph nodes and skin, eyes and/or genitals also may be affected. Untreated cases may lead to myocarditis, inflammation of nerves, kidney problems, and bleeding problems due to low blood platelets and thence an abnormal heart rate and/or paralysis.

Nearly 1 lakh cases reported in 1980, drastically (95%) reduced to just 5000 in last 3 decades. Mostly it affects children and is currently seen in some regions of Sub-Sahara Africa, Indonesia and India. It is rare in developed countries due to widespread vaccination. The disease was first described in the 5th century BC by Hippocrates but the bacterium was discovered in 1882 by Edwin Klebs. It usually spreads by direct contact or contaminated objects or through the air and mortality is 5-10%. There are 3 main types of *C. diphtheriae* with different severities and the symptoms are caused by toxin generated by the bacteria. Diagnosis is made by the throat appearance while culture can confirm.

During childhood, Diphtheria toxoid is an effective vaccine for prevention. 3-4 doses along with tetanus toxoid and acellular pertussis vaccine and every 10 years further doses are recommended. Protection can be verified by the antitoxin level in blood. Antibiotic erythromycin or penicillin-G can be used to treat and surgery (tracheostomy) is needed to open the airway in severe cases.

16.6.1 Symptoms & Diagnosis

An adherent, dense, grey pseudo-membrane covering the tonsils is classically seen in diphtheria

The symptoms of diphtheria usually begin 2-7 days after infection. Symptoms of diphtheria could be

- Fever of 100.4°F (38°C) or above

- Chills & shivering
- Headache
- Bloodstained nasal discharge
- Barking cough
- Fatigue/tiresomeness
- Difficulty swallowing
- Pain while swallowing
- Sore throat
- Swollen neck/throat
- Bull neck
- Body pains
- Cardiac arrhythmias
- Difficulty breathing
- Rapid breathing
- Cranial & peripheral nerve palsies
- Lymphadenopathy
- Myocarditis

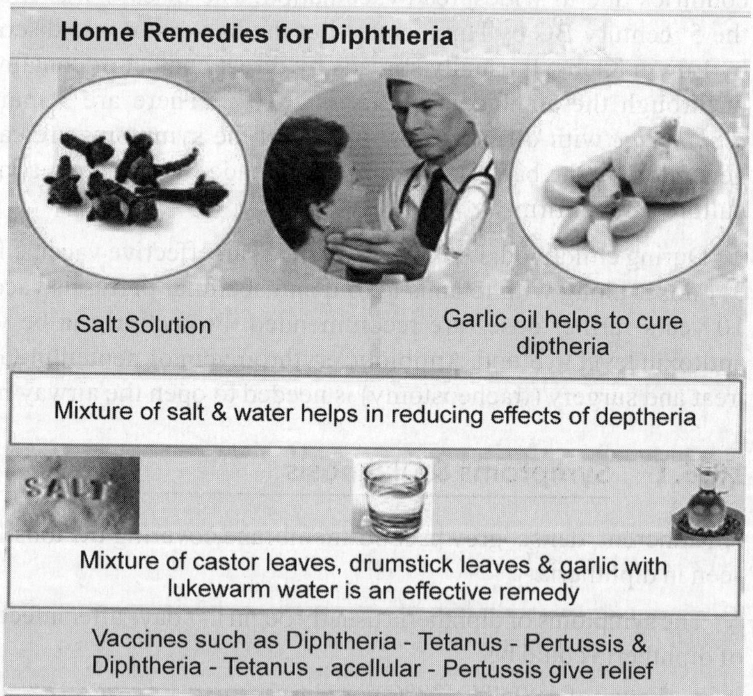

- Bluish skin coloration (cyanosis)
- Foul-smelling
- Hoarseness

Diphtheritic Croup

Laryngeal diphtheria can be characterized by swollen neck/ throat, or "bull neck", often associated with a serious respiratory problem, "barking" cough, hoarseness, and difficult breathing, and usually referred to as "diphtheritic or true croup", or simply "croup". The croup is very rare in countries which made diphtheria vaccination customary.

As per CDC of US, diagnosis of diphtheria is based on both laboratory and clinical criteria.

Laboratory criteria	Clinical criteria
• Isolation of *C. diphtheriae* from a gram stain	• Upper respiratory tract illness with sore throat
• Throat culture from a clinical specimen	• Rarely low-grade fever (>102°F or 39°C)
• Histo-pathologic diagnosis by a stain called "Albert's Stain".	• An adherent, dense, grey pseudo-membrane covering the posterior pharynx, which can extend to entire trachea-bronchial tree.

16.6.2 Prevention and Treatment

Diphtheria vaccine is usually combined with tetanus (Td), and pertussis (DTP, DTaP, TdaP) vaccines. Quinvaxem (pentavalent vaccine), a mix of 5 vaccines is widely used on infantile children.

Severe cases should be given diphtheria antitoxin and kept in acute medical care, as throat obstruction may need intubation or a tracheotomy. It can even paralyze the eye, neck, throat, or respiratory muscles. The following antibiotics may be used (particularly for *C. Diphtheria*).

- Metronidazole
- Erythromycin (orally or by injection) for 14 days (40 mg/kg per day with a max. of 2 g/d), or
- Procaine Penicillin-G for 14 days (300 KU/d for children of <10 kg & 600 KU/d for >10 kg).
- Rifampin or Clindamycin for those allergic to penicillin-G or Erythromycin

In case throat infection is neglected, the diphtheria toxin spreads through the blood and can lead to complications of heart and kidneys. It can also cause nerve damage leading to paralysis.

16.7 TYPHOID FEVER (WATER BORNE)

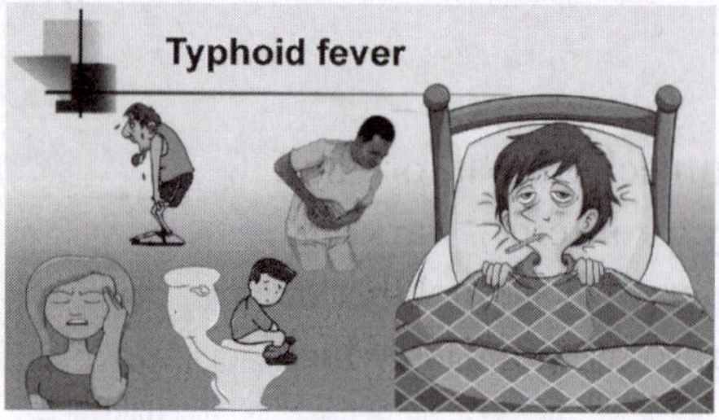

Typhoid, (means "resembling typhus" due to the similarity in symptoms) is a bacterial infection due to *Salmonella typhi*, (also called *Salmonella enteric*) that grows in the intestines and blood. The symptoms (mild or severe) usually appear in 1-4 weeks after exposure in the form of high fever for longer period with weakness, abdominal pain, constipation, body pains and headache. Uncommon, but diarrhoea and vomiting may also occur. Some people develop a skin rash with rose coloured spots. Some people carry the bacterium without being affected; but, they still can spread the disease to others. Thus it is also known as a type of **enteric fever** along with paratyphoid fever.

Typhoid is spread by contaminated food or water with the feces of an infected person. Unhygienic environment and poor sanitation raise the risk. Travellers should be very careful with reference to their food and drinks. Blessing in disguise! It does not spread through animals and pets, that is to say, only humans can be infected. But be careful! The flying insects (like house flies, mosquitoes) may carry and transmit the bacterium on to the eatables and drinks.

It can be diagnosed by either culturing the bacteria or detecting its DNA in the blood, stool, or bone marrow. A typhoid vaccine can prevent about 30-70% of cases up to 2 - 7 years. Other efforts to prevent are by providing clean drinking water, better sanitation, and hand-wash. Ensure no infection for the cook or chef or persons, before preparing food for others. Antibiotics (azithromycin, fluoroquinolones or cephalosporins) work well, but if resistance develops, treatment becomes very difficult. So, *frequent use of antibiotics should be avoided*.

Typhoid is most common in India, particularly, in children. In 2000, typhoid fever caused an estimated 22 million illnesses and >2 lakh deaths mostly

O My God!

Typhoid Mary?

Mary Mallon, popularly known as Typhoid Mary, was the most destructive and notorious carrier of Typhoid. In 1907, she was the first carrier to be identified and traced in US. She was a cook in NY who is closely associated with 53 cases and 3 deaths. Health authorities told Mary to give up the job as cook or have her gall bladder removed, as she had a chronic infection and being the carrier of the disease. Mary quit her job, but returned later under a false name. After another typhoid outbreak, she was detained and quarantined forcibly in 1907 for 3 yrs and then again from 1915 until her death in 1938. She died of pneumonia after 26 years in quarantine.

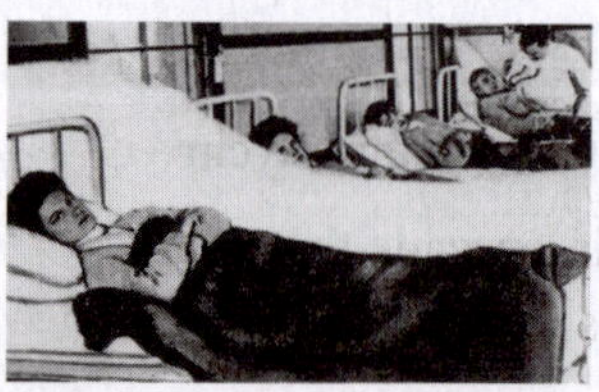

Typhoid Mary on hospital bed

children and young adults (5-19 yrs). All over the world, in 2013, about 11 million new cases reported and >1.61 lakh died. The risk of death may be 25% if untreated, but can be reduced to 1-4% if treated.

16.7.1 Symptoms & Features

The typhoid fever when untreated undergoes 4-stages, each lasting about a week with the following symptoms.

The major symptom: The fever usually rises in the afternoon during 1st and 2nd week.

1st Stage: Body temperature rises slowly, fever fluctuates with malaise, headache and cough and in some cases bloody nose and/or abdominal pain. A decrease in white blood cell count; blood cultures are positive for *S. typhi* or *S. paratyphi*. Widal test is negative in 1st week.

2nd Stage: Too tired to get up, with high fever ~104°F (40°C), frequent delirium, usually calm, but sometimes agitated, hence called with the nickname "nervous fever". Rose spots appear on lower chest and abdomen, diarrhoea (5-8 per day) in green, like pea soup with a characteristic smell and frequent constipation. The spleen and liver enlarge and tender. Widal test is strongly positive (blood cultures sometimes positive).

3rd Stage: Number of complications occur in this stage like, platelet count goes down slowly, risk of bleeding rises, intestinal haemorrhage due to bleeding in congested, Peyer's patches (serious, but not fatal) and Intestinal perforation (No warning signs but very serious and fatal).

4th Stage: Fever subsides but any of above complication(s) may start. It may be fatal if neglected. Death risk is about 25%. If the fever is still very high, dehydration ensues. Patient is delirious (typhoid state). Some get macular rash on trunk, delirium/coma/Neuropsychiatric, with picking at bedclothes or imaginary objects.

O My God!

Typhoid killed great people

- **No Jokes!** Arnold Bennett, English novelist, drank a glass of water in a Paris hotel to prove it was safe, but died after 2 months, in 1932.
- **Remember!** In memory of Leland Stanford, Jr., who died of typhoid in 1884, his parents founded Stanford University, one of the top 10 in the world.
- **Be Careful!** Claypole, British scientist, died in 1915, acquired while preparing vaccinations for WW-I troops, despite she vaccinated herself.
- **Couldn't fly out!** Wilbur Wright, the older of the Wright brothers, died of typhoid on May 30, 1912

16.7.2 Transmission & Prevention

As bacterium spread is promoted by poor hygiene habits, bad public sanitation, and feeding on feces by flying insects, the best way to control is by educating public to wash their hands before and after handling food.

Since typhoid affects only humans but not animals, it can only spread in environments when the human feces or urine contact with food or drinking water. Thence, good care during food preparation (hot and well cooked), along with good hygienic habits (washing hands/improved sanitation) can prevent. The chlorinated drinking water can drastically reduce in the transmission as proven in the US. Today, drinking water is purified by modern scientific methods such as heating and cooling, and filtering by reverse osmosis etc.

Two typhoid vaccines are licensed: (1) Oral type – Ty21a vaccine and (2) Injection Type – typhoid polysaccharide vaccine. Both are recommended for the travellers to typhoid endemic areas. Boosters are recommended every 5 yrs for the oral vaccine and every 2 yrs for the injection form.

16.7.3 Diagnosis & Treatment

Diagnosis is made by demonstrating antibodies against *Salmonella* antigens

- Blood test
- Widal test
- Bone marrow test
- Stool culture

Widal test is time-taking and it is too late to wait till diagnosis. Properly treated typhoid is not fatal. The oral rehydration therapy can better treat diarrhoea associated with typhoid. Use of antibiotics (ampicillin/ amoxicillin/ ciprofloxacin/ cefixime) reduces the fatality rate to about 1%. Resistance to ciprofloxacin is an increasing problem, particularly in Indian subcontinent (India, Pakistan, Bangladesh), Thailand, Vietnam and S. America. For these, azithromycin is suggested.

O My God!

- The disease is referred by various names, often based on symptoms, such as gastric fever, enteric fever, abdominal typhus, infantile remittant fever, slow fever, nervous fever, and pythogenic fever.
- Industrialization, particularly, the invention of automobile, greatly reduced typhoid, as it eliminated the public health hazards associated with cattle, bullock and horse manure in the public street that led to large number of flies.
- Often we get confused between Typhus and Typhoid having names and symptoms similar but, they are different.
- The British bacteriologist Almroth Edward Wright 1st developed an effective typhoid vaccine at the Army Medical School in Netley, Hampshire.

O My God!

TYPHOID is different from TYPHUS (Vector Borne)

Typhus, (means smoky or hazy in Greek that describes mind of the affected) is caused by *Rickettsia* bacteria resembles many diseases. *Rickettsia* is an intracellular parasitic bacterium transmitted to humans via external parasite such as lice (on humans), fleas (on rats) and ticks (on others), and cannot survive for long outside living cells. Typhus is distinctly different from typhoid fever caused by different genera of bacteria. Beginning with sudden fever, chills, headache, and other flu-like symptoms about 1–3 weeks after infection, in 5-9 days, a rash starts on the trunk and spreads all over body except face, palms and soles. Also, meningo encephalitis begin the 2nd wk i.e. photophobia, delirium or coma. Typhus is prevented by inoculated typhus vaccine series before travelling to endemic areas, and avoid contact with lice. If untreated, up to 60% may die, and over age 60 yrs are at highest risk. Doxycycline may prevent death. Some need oxygen and IV fluids. DDT was used to kill the lice on millions of refugees and displaced persons. The 1st vaccine was developed by Polish zoologist Rudolf Weigl. Better, safe and cheap vaccines were developed during WW-II. Since then, only few epidemics occurred in Asia, Europe, the Middle East, and Africa.

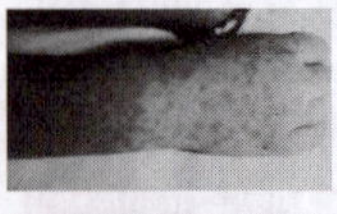

Rash by epidemic typhus

Charles Nicolle, the 1928 Nobel Prize in Medicine for identifying of lice as transmitter of epidemic typhus

SELF ASSESSMENT INTERMISSION SA 16

1. What are water borne bacterial epidemic diseases? Describe any one of your choice.
2. How is cholera caused? Explain its mode of infection.
3. What are the precautions and treatments referred for persons infected by cholera?
4. What are various methods to prevent the spread of cholera?
5. How is diphtheria caused? Explain its mode of infection.
6. What are the precautions/prevention and treatments for diphtheria?
7. How is typhoid caused? Explain its mode of infection and various stages.
8. What are the prevention and treatments referred for persons infected with typhoid?
9. Distinguish between typhus and typhoid. Explain each briefly.
10. What are the causes of typhoid? What are the symptoms of typhoid?
11. Why is typhoid called with various names such as enteric fever, nervous fever etc.?
12. Who is Typhoid Mary? Explain why she is so named.

16.8 TUBERCLE BACILLUS (TB) OR TUBERCULOSIS (AIR BORNE)

Tuberculosis (**TB**) is an infectious disease of lungs caused by *Myco-bacterium tuberculosis* (MTB). TB can be found in two types, viz. active and latent. Again, the active TB can be either pulmonary (lung infection) or extra-pulmonary (infection to other than lungs). About 10% of latent infections progress to active in which about 50% if untreated may die.

Chest X-ray with advanced TB: Infection (white arrow-heads), and the formation of a cavity (black arrows).

TB spreads through the air when person having active TB coughs, spits, speaks, or sneezes. However, people with latent TB do not spread the disease. People with HIV/AIDS and smokers are more susceptible. TB is diagnosed by chest X-rays, microscopic examination and culture of body fluids. Diagnosis of latent TB depends on the tuberculin skin test (TST) or blood tests.

16.8.1 Symptoms

The symptoms are fever, chills, night sweats, weight loss, loss of appetite and fatigue. Nail clubbing may also occur.

Pulmonary TB: About 90% cases are pulmonary with chest pain and prolonged cough with sputum, of which $\frac{1}{4}^{th}$ may be asymptomatic. Blood cough may occur. The upper lung lobes are more affected by TB than the lower ones.

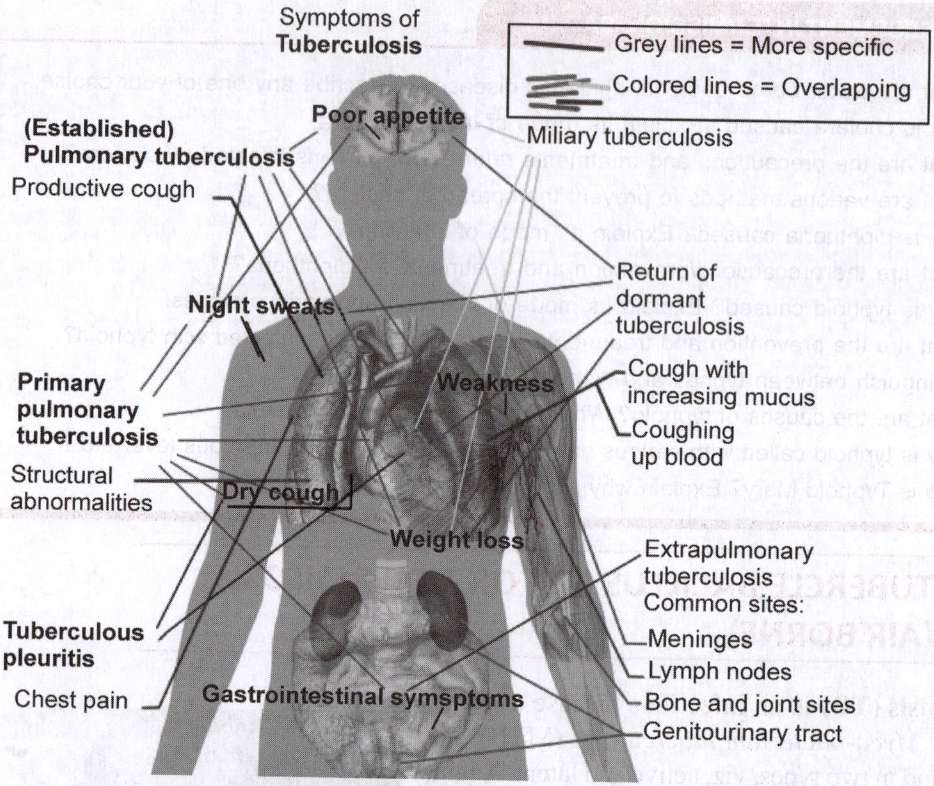

Extra-pulmonary: In 15–20% of active cases, the infection spreads outside the lungs such as pleura (TB pleurisy), central nervous system (TB meningitis), lymphatic system (scrofula of neck), the genitourinary system (urogenital TB), and the bones and joints (Pott disease of spine and Osseous TB) collectively called "extra-pulmonary TBs, usually occur in immune-suppressed or young or those with HIV. More serious, widespread form of TB is "disseminated or Miliary TB".

16.8.2 Causes & Transmission

The main cause of TB is *Mycobacterium tuberculosis*, a small, aerobic, non-motile bacillus. It divides at very slow rate (once in every 16 to 20 hrs) as compared to other bacteria (@>1hr). MTB can be detected by sputum (phlegm).

By cough, sneeze, speak, sing, or spit, active pulmonary TB patients expel infectious aerosol droplets 0.5-5.0 Öμm. A single sneeze can release up to 40,000 droplets, each of which can transmit the disease (the inhalation of <10 bacteria may infect). A person with active but untreated TB may infect 10–15 others per yr. Blessing in disguise! The transmission can occur from only with active TB – but not with latent TB. The transmission depends on several factors, such as

- The number of infectious droplets expelled by the carrier,
- The effectiveness of ventilation,
- The duration of exposure,
- The virulence of the *M. Tuberculosis* strain,
- The level of immunity in the uninfected person, and others.

It is not contagious usually, after 2 wks of effective treatment. To be infected, it takes 3-4 wks.

16.8.3 Risk Factors

- Most risky factor globally is HIV (13% of TBs have HIV), mostly, in sub-Saharan.

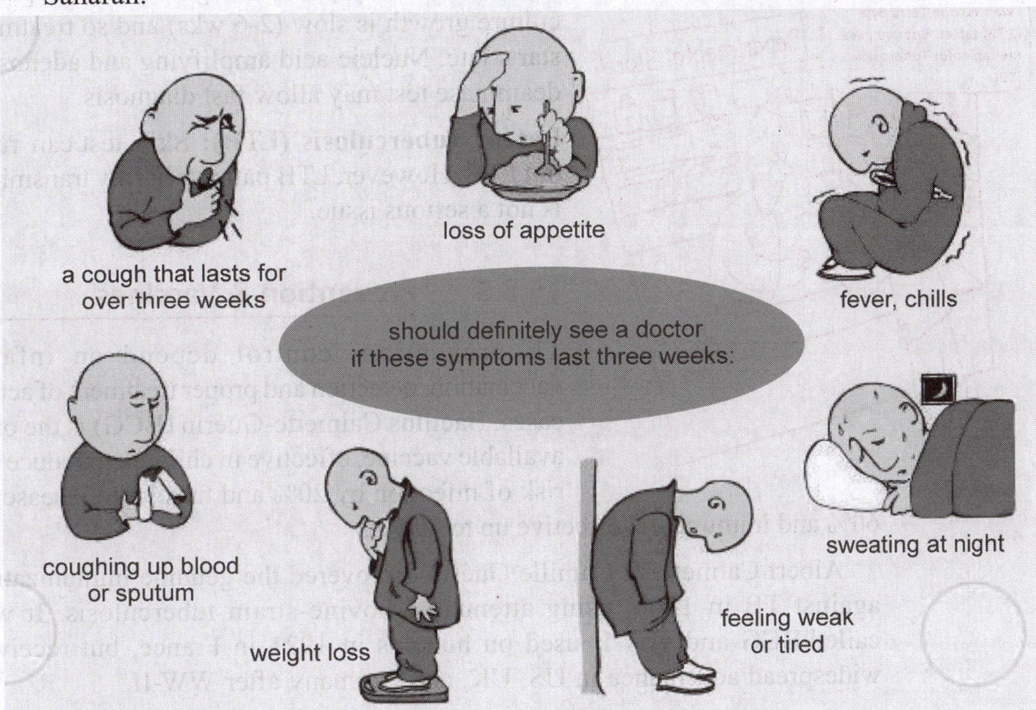

- Children in close contact with high-risk patients, and caretakers serving the patients
- Vulnerable people (e.g. prisoners, beggars and homeless)
- Medically underprivileged and resource-poor communities
- Overcrowding and malnutrition
- Injection of illicit drugs/inhabitants
- High-risk ethnic minorities

O My God!

Koch's Mar-24 is World TB day?

The MTB was identified on 24 Mar 1882 by Robert Koch (Nobel Prize in physiology/ medicine in 1905). He didn't believe bovine (cattle) and human TB were similar. Later, the transmission from animal source was greatly reduced by pasteurization process. Koch identified a glycerine extract of the tubercle bacilli as a remedy for TB in 1890, called "tuberculin". As it was not effective, it was later adapted as screen test for pre-symptomatic.

- Alcoholism
- Diabetes mellitus (3-fold increased risk)
- Chronic lung diseases
- Silicosis (risk is about 30-fold)
- Genetic susceptibility
- Smoking (twice risky than non-smokers)
- Medications like corticosteroids & inflixim

16.8.4 Diagnosis

Active Tuberculosis (ATB): The symptoms lasting for 2-wks can be ATB. A chest X-ray and multiple sputum culture for acid-fast bacilli or tissue biopsy can diagnose. Blood/ sputum culture growth is slow (2-6 wks) and so treatment starts late. Nucleic acid amplifying and adenosine deaminase test may allow fast diagnosis.

Latent Tuberculosis (LTB): Skin test can rule-out LTB. However, LTB patients hardly transmit, it is not a serious issue.

16.8.5 Prevention & Vaccines

TB prevention/ control depend on infant-vaccination, detection and proper treatment of active cases. Bacillus Calmette-Guérin (BCG) is the only available vaccine, effective in children to reduce the risk of infection by 20% and turning to disease by 60% and immunity is effective up to 10 yrs.

Albert Calmette & Camille Guérin discovered the genuine immunization against TB in 1906, using attenuated bovine-strain tuberculosis. It was called BCG and was 1st used on humans in 1921 in France, but received widespread acceptance in US, UK, and Germany after WW-II.

16.8.6 TB in Animals

Mycobacteria infect many different animals, including birds, rodents, and reptiles. A fruitful effort was made to eradicate bovine TB caused by *M. bovis* from the cattle and deer herds of New Zealand. As of 2015, TB is widespread among elephants in US. The animals originally received the disease from humans (called *reverse zoonosis*). Since the disease is air-borne and both humans and other animals can be infected, it is a public health concern affecting circuses and zoos.

16.9 LEPROSY (AIR BORNE)

Leprosy, also known as **Hansen's disease (HD)**, is a long term infection caused by the bacteria *Mycobacterium leprae/lepromatosis*.

The name comes from the Latin word *lepra*, (=scaly), while "Hansen's disease" is named after G. A. Hansen. Initially, it is asymptomatic (for 5-20 yrs). Symptoms if develop, could be in nerves, respiratory tract, skin, and loss of eyesight and/or sensitivity of touch and so, due to repeated injuries/ infection ignored wounds, the parts may also be lost. Leprosy spreads through respiratory droplets, cough or contact with nasal fluid of an infected.

Contrary to popular belief, it is not very contagious. The 2 main types of disease are based on the number of bacteria present or poorly pigmented, numb skin patches: pauci-bacillary (5 or few) and multi-bacillary (>5). The diagnosis is confirmed by finding acid-fast bacilli in a biopsy of the skin or by detecting the DNA using polymerase chain reaction (PCR).

There were 4 strains of *M leprae* with specific regions; Strain 1 in Asia, Pacific region and E Africa; strain 4, in W. Africa and the Caribbean; strain 3 in Europe, N. Africa, and Americas; and strain 2 only in Ethiopia, Malawi, Nepal/ N. India, and New Caledonia.

16.9.1 Cause & Transmission

Leprosy is caused by *M. leprae* and lepromatosis (isolated in 2008). Being not possible to culture *in vitro*, it is grown in animals such as mice and armadillos for study. Natural infection also is reported in nonhumans, like African chimpanzee, sooty mangabey and red squirrels. Persons in close contact with a leper are at highest risk. Malnutrition,

O My God!

Leprosy Movies?

Though there are plenty of scenes related to leprosy appeared in several movies, some are noteworthy and watch worthy. St. Damien DeVeuster, a Roman Catholic priest from Belgium; Vietnamese poet Hàn M□c Tí and Baldwin IV, a Christian king of Latin Jerusalem, afflicted with leprosy. The effects of Baldwin's disease were portrayed in the film *Kingdom of Heaven*. Forough Farrokhzad made a 22-minute documentary about a leprosy colony in Iran in 1962 called *The House Is Black*. The film humanizes the people affected and opens by saying that ***"there is no shortage of ugliness in the world, but by closing our eyes on ugliness, we will intensify it."***

O My God!

Using the term 'Leper' is Offence?

Leprosy has been affecting 'humanity' for 1000s of years. Persons with leprosy are often discriminated. Depending on the level of disfigurement, a person with leprosy receives varying stigma and ostracism. They are paid less. Leprosy mothers are not allowed to go close to their children out of fear of infecting. In a report, 50% women with leprosy stopped breast-feeding, though doctors are seriously educating. It is treated using the term "leper" is offence, as it is generally thought that the term alienates people owing to its use as a term for the shunned. So, it is recommended to address as "persons affected with leprosy". To bring awareness, World Leprosy Day (started in 1954) is observed on Jan, 30 or nearest Sunday in commemoration of Gandhiji's death.

Among the new cases registered in 16 countries, India stands highest (> 50%). Separating people by keeping them in leper colonies is still occurring in places such as India, China, and Africa. However, most colonies have closed since leprosy is not very contagious.

other illnesses may reduce the immune function and increase the risk. Surprise is that HIV does not increase the risk of developing leprosy.

Leprosy transmits by nasal droplets during close contact with infected. It is neither sexually transmitted nor highly infectious. It may be present in 3 species of non-human primates also be transmitted to humans by armadillos. Two routes of *M. leprae* from the human body are the skin and the nasal mucosa. The skin route favours the respiratory route. However, immune systems can eliminate leprosy during the early stage. It is unclear why some people develop lepromatous type while others develop other types of leprosy.

16.9.2 Symptoms & Diagnosis

Leprosy is basically a granuloma disease of peripheral nerves, mucosa of upper respiratory tract and skin lesions (patches), untreated leads to permanent damage of the skin, nerves, limbs and eyes. Contrary to folklore, leprosy does not cause body parts to fall off, though they become numb or diseased as a result of secondary infections, which can result in tissue loss causing finger/toes to be shortened/ deformed, as cartilage is absorbed into the body.

According to the WHO, it is diagnosed by

- **Skin lesions:** macules (flat), papules (raised), or nodular with loss of sensation or weakness.
- **Positive skin smears:** acid-fast leprosy bacilli are diagnostic clinically.

The symptoms are runny nose, dry scalp, eye problems, skin lesions, muscle weakness, reddish skin, smooth shiny diffuse thickening of facial skin, ear and hand, loss of sensation in fingers and toes, thickening of peripheral nerves, and flat nose due to destruction of nasal cartilage. Also, phonation and resonation of sound occurs during speech. Often, atrophy of testes/ impotency happen.

O My God!

Some facts about leprosy

- Leprosy was once believed to be highly contagious and was treated with mercury
- Many early cases thought to be leprosy could actually were syphilis.
- Until the introduction of MDT in the early 1980s, the disease could not be diagnosed and treated successfully.
- Japan still has sanatoriums
- Schäffer(1898) recognized Nasal mucosa transmission
- As of 2013, 14 countries have leprosy cases topped by India (59%) followed by Brazil (14%), Indonesia (8%), Tanzania, Madagascar, Mozambique and the W Pacific.

16.9.3 Prevention

Early detection is important, since physical and neurological damage may be irreversible even if cured. Medications can decrease the risk. However, the problem is with resistance, cost, and disclosure of a person's infection status when following-up. The WHO recommends examining for leprosy, and treated only if symptoms are present. BCG vaccine can protect in addition to TB (better 2 doses).

O My God!

Indian formulated medicine for Leprosy?

The oldest evidence of leprosy was found in Harappa and was also discussed by Hippocrates in 460 BC. Interpretations of leprosy are made on the basis of descriptions in Indian Atharvan Veda and Kausika Sutra, Greek, and Middle Eastern documentary sources.

The Indian scientist Shantaram Yawalkar and his colleagues formulated multidrug therapy (MDT) clubbing all 3 drugs recommended by the WHO in 1981 and supplying free of cost, is no longer infectious after 1st monthly dose. It is safe and easy and cured >16 million worldwide in last 2 decades.

SELF ASSESSMENT INTERMISSION (SAI – 16.4)

1. What are air borne bacterial epidemic diseases? Describe any one of your choice.
2. How is TB caused? On what factors spread of TB depends?
3. What are the types of TB? Explain its mode of infection.
4. What are the precautions and treatments TB patient?
5. What are various methods to prevent the spread of TB? What are the risk factors?
6. How is Hansen's disease (leprosy) caused? Explain its mode of infection.
7. What are the precautions/prevention and treatments for leprosy?
8. Why is using the term 'leper' an offence? Discuss.

16.10 PLAGUE (AIR & VECTOR BORNE)

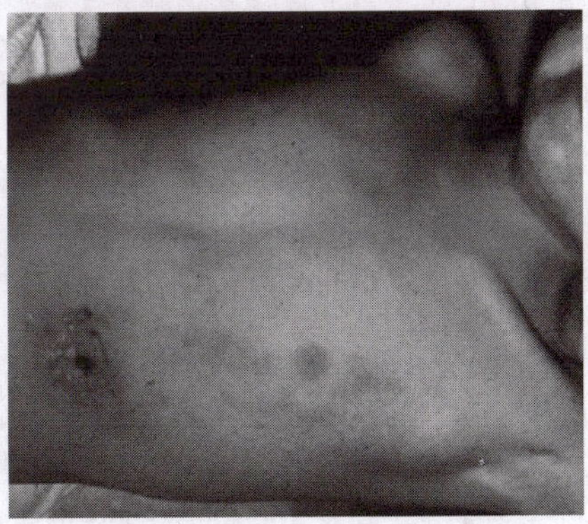

The word *"plague"* perhaps, came from Latin *plâga* ("blow, wound") or German *Plage* (=infestation). It is an infectious disease caused by the bacterium *Yersinia pestis*, named after the French-Swiss bacteriologist Alexandre Yersin. Till June 2007, plague, cholera and yellow fever were the 3-major epidemic diseases to the WHO. It is treatable if detected early. Plague swept through Eurasia with very high death rates and caused major cultural changes.

16.10.1 Cause & Transmission

The oriental rat flea (Xenopsylla cheopsis) after a blood meal. Both male and female fleas feed on blood and can transmit the bubonic plague.

Transmission of *Y. pestis* to uninfected individual is possible by any of the following means.

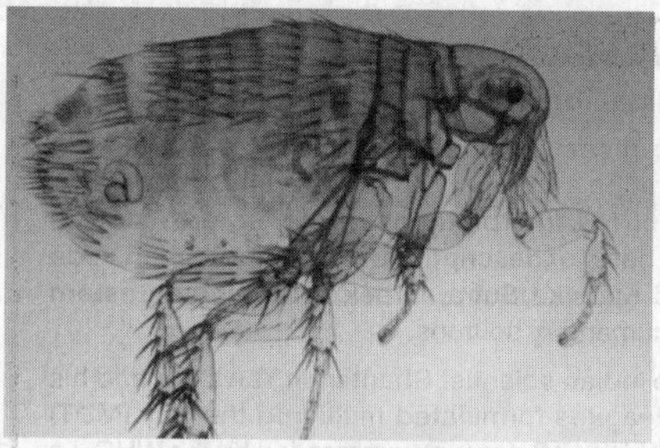

- ***droplet contact*** – coughing or sneezing on another person
- ***direct physical contact*** – touching an infected person, including sexual contact
- ***indirect contact*** – usually by touching soil contamination or a contaminated surface
- ***airborne transmission*** – if the microorganism can remain in the air for long periods
- ***fecal-oral transmission*** – usually from contaminated food or water sources
- ***vector borne transmission*** – carried by insects or other animals.

Y. pestis circulates in animal reservoirs, particularly in rodents (rats, mice, squirrel, beaver, porcupine etc.). The plague spreads in temperate latitudes between the parallels 55°N and 40°S.

Contrary to popular belief, rats are not direct spreaders of the bubonic plague, but due to fleas (*Xenopsylla cheopis*) that infect the rats, making them the first victims of the plague. Human is infected by bite of a flea that has been

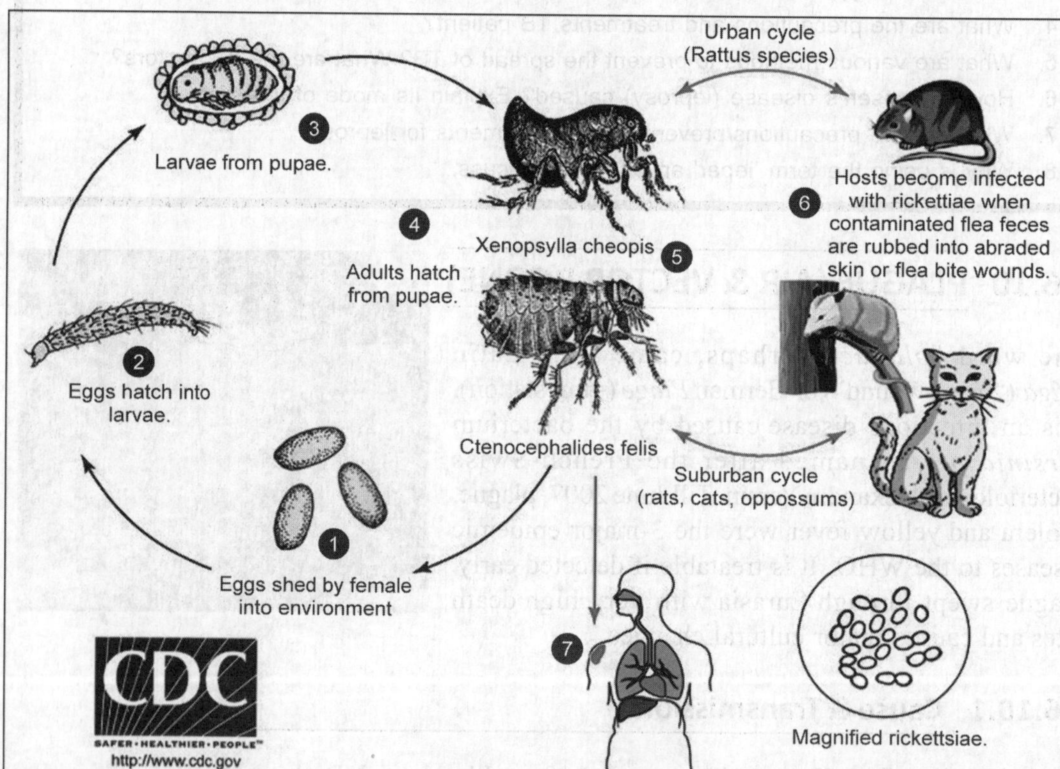

infected by biting infected rodent. The bacteria multiply inside the flea, sticking together to form a plug that blocks its stomach and causes it to starve. The flea then bites a host and continues to feed, even though it cannot quell its hunger, and consequently the flea vomits blood tainted with the bacteria back into the bite wound. The bubonic plague bacterium then infects a new victim, and the flea eventually dies from starvation. Serious outbreaks of plague are usually started by other disease outbreaks in rodents, or a rise in the rodent population.

Thought Plague – But Not?

In 2nd yr of Peloponnesian War (430 BC), Thucydides described an epidemic begun in Ethiopia, passed through Egypt and Libya, then to Greek. In the Plague of Athens, the city lost 1/3 of its population for which Plague was the suspected factors along with typhus, smallpox, measles etc. but later clarified that it is due to **typhoid**.

In 1st century AD, Rufus of Ephesus, a Greek anatomist, refers to an outbreak in Libya, Egypt and Syria. It was thought to be **plague.**

In 2nd century, the city *Antonine Plague* also called Plague of Galen was named after family name of (Antoninus) *Marcus Aurelius*, and the disease assumed as plague. But in fact, the actual disease was smallpox

In 1894, two bacteriologists, Alexandre Yersin (France) and Kitasato Shibasaburô (Japan), independently isolated the bacterium responsible for the 3rd Pandemic in Hong Kong. Yersin named it *Pasteurella pestis* in honor of the Pasteur Institute, where he worked, but in 1967 it was moved to a new genus, renamed *Yersinia pestis* in honor of Yersin.

16.10.2 Types of Plague

Depending on lung infection, or sanitary conditions, plague can spread in the air, by direct contact, or very rarely by contaminated undercooked food. The symptoms of plague depend on the areas of infection on the body. The three main types of plague are:

- Bubonic plague (in lymph nodes),
- Septicemic plague (in blood vessels),
- Pneumonic plague (in lungs)

O My God!

Charminar is Memory of End of Plague?

The **Charminar** is a monument and mosque in Hyderabad, India. The structure was built in 1591 AD. It is the most famous building of Hyderabad and also in India. It was built by Muhammad Quli Qutb Shahi to celebrate the end of a deadly plague.

Charminar
Pride of Hyderabad

Bubonic Plague: *Y. pestis* spreads through the lymphs of the infected human until it reaches a lymph node, where it stimulates severe hemorrhagic inflammation that expands the lymph nodes causing a characteristic "bubo". The infection may pass into bloodstream/ lungs to form *secondary septicemic/ pneumonic plague.*

Septicemic Plague: This occurs when lymphatic drain occurs into the bloodstream and move to almost all parts of the body. In septicemic plague, bacterial endotoxins cause tiny clots throughout the body and tissues die. So, bleeding into the skin and other organs can occur and cause red and/or black patchy rash and also coughing up/ vomiting of blood (hemoptysis/ hematemesis). The bumps look like insect bites; usually red and sometimes white in center.

Untreated, septicemic plague is usually fatal, often die on the same day, however, early treatment with antibiotics reduces mortality rate to 4-15%.

Pneumonic plague: This arises from infection of the lungs and causes coughing/ sneezing and thence produces airborne droplets containing bacterial cells and is likely to infect the inhaler within 2-4 days, or even just a few hrs. The symptoms such as headache, weakness and spit/ vomit of blood are not easy to differentiate from several other respiratory illnesses. The disease is rapid and if undiagnosed soon (few hrs), death may follow within 6 days. Untreated cases have ~100% mortality.

Pharyngeal plague: This is an uncommon form of plague that resembles tonsillitis found in cases of close contact of patients with other forms of plague.

Meningeal plague: This form of plague occurs when bacteria cross the blood-brain barrier, leading to infectious meningitis.

Other forms: There are a few other rare forms including asymptomatic plague and abortive plague. *Cellulocutaneous plague* results in infection of skin and soft tissue, often around the bite site of a flea.

16.10.3 Treatments and Immunization

Waldemar Haffkine, a doctor worked in Bombay, India, was the 1st to invent and test a plague vaccine against bubonic plague in 1897. If detected in time the various forms of plague are highly responsive to antibiotics. Since this disease is rare in most parts of the world, routine vaccination is not needed unless otherwise has high risk of exposure. The vaccination is recommended for:

- all lab and field personnel working with *Y. Pestis*
- people engaged in aerosol experiments with *Y. pestis*;
- people operating in areas with enzootic plague.

16.10.4 Plague as a Biological Weapon

China, Medieval Europe, Xiongnu/ Huns, Mongols, Turks used infected bodies (dead or alive) of animals such as cows or horses, and human corpses to contaminate enemy water supplies. Han Dynasty General Huo Qubing died of such a contamination in warfare against the Xiongnu. In 1347, Mongol army used the infected corpses as a biological weapon by catapulting over the city walls, infecting the inhabitants. The Genoese traders fled and transmitted, thence spread the

O My God!

Plague was in Bronze Age?

Y. Pestis is detected in archaeological samples of teeth of Bronze Age, about 5000 yrs ago (3000 BC), in the Afanasievo & Andronovo cultures in Siberia, the Corded Ware culture in Estonia, the Sintashta culture in Russia and the Unetice culture in Poland.

plague (Black Death) through their ships into the south of Europe. During WW-II, Japan developed weaponized plague, by breeding and releasing of large numbers of fleas. During the Japanese occupation of Manchuria, Unit 731 deliberately infected Chinese, Korean, and Manchurian and prisoners of war with the plague bacterium. Ishii (Japan) used innovative bombs containing live mice and fleas, with very small explosive loads, to deliver the weaponized microbes, during WW-II. After WW-II, both US and SU (USSR) developed means of weaponizing pneumonic plague. Of course, plague could be easily treated with antibiotics, whence US was ready with large supplies on hand if such an attack occurs, and thence making the threat less severe.

16.10.5 Plague in India, 1994 Surat Epidemic

The 1994, pneumonic plague epidemic in Surat, India recorded 52 deaths and a large internal migration of about 3 lakh residents due to unhygienic conditions and a number of uncleared animal carcasses after heavy monsoon rains with clogged sewers, leading to massive flooding. Some countries, such as those nearby Gulf, cancelled some flights and paused the shipments from India because of the widespread fear of people spreading to other parts of India and the world, but that scenario was averted. Thanks to Indian health authorities for quick response and effective actions for public health.

> **O My God!**
>
> **Plague Pandemics?**
>
> The history of plague outbreaks are described under 3 pandemics by Joseph P. Byrne of Belmont University as follows.
>
> **1st Pandemic** (541 to ~750), spread from Egypt to Merranean (starting with the Plague of Justinian) and N-W Europe
>
> **2nd Pandemic** (~1345 to ~1840): spread from Central Asia to Merranean (Now France) & Europe (starting with the Black Death), and China
>
> **3rd Pandemic** (1866 to 1960s): spread from China to various places around the world, notably India and W Coast of US.

16.10.6 Recent Cases

- July 16, 2013, a squirrel trapped in the Table Mountain Campgrounds of Angeles National Forest, found positive of plague, led to the closing of the campground.
- Aug 26, 2013 Temir Isakunov, Kyrgyzstan, a teenage boy, died of bubonic plague.
- Dec 2013 Pneumonic Plague epidemic in Madagascar, large bush fires forced rats into towns.
- July 13, 2014 a Colorado man was diagnosed with the pneumonic plague
- July 22, 2014, Yumen, China sealed off quarantined 151, as bubonic plague killed a man.
- Nov 21, 2014, the WHO reported 40 deaths and 80 infected in Madagascar.

16.11 MENINGITIS (AIR AND VECTOR BORNE)

The word meningitis (in Greek *méninx*, means 'membrane' and medical suffix -*itis*, 'inflammation') means an acute inflammation of the protective membranes on the brain and spinal cord (collectively known as meninges). It may be caused by bacteria or virus or fungus or other micro-organism infection. The most common symptoms are fever, headache and neck stiffness. Other symptoms include confusion or altered consciousness, vomits, and inability to tolerate light (photophobia) or loud noises (phonophobia). Young children exhibit nonspecific symptoms, like drowsiness, irritability or poor feeding. The meningitis due to meningococcal bacteria may get a rash.

Meningitis is life-threatening medical emergency owing to the inflammation near to the brain and spinal cord. A lumbar puncture diagnosis is done by inserting a needle into the spinal canal to collect a sample of cerebrospinal fluid (CSF) to test. Some forms of meningitis are preventable by immunization with vaccines. The acute meningitis is treated with antibiotics, sometimes antiviral drugs and corticosteroids. If not treated quickly, meningitis can lead to serious consequences like deafness, epilepsy, hydrocephalus, or cognitive deficits.

Sub-Saharan Africa has been named the "meningitis belt" due to its large epidemics of this pathogen, the largest ever recorded in history swept the entire

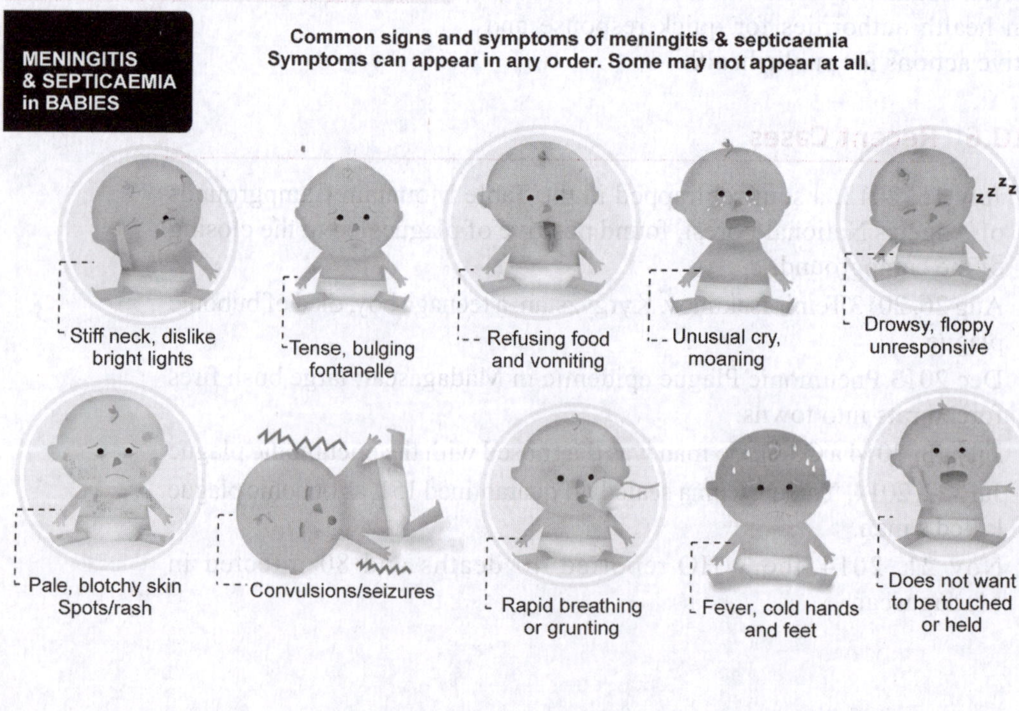

region in 1996–1997, causing 2.5 lakh cases and 25,000 deaths. Epidemics often occur in dry season (Dec-Jun) and this occurs in areas where many people (crowd) live together for the first time, such as army barracks while mobilizing, college campuses, the annual Hajj pilgrimage and so forth. Usually pigs and cranes act as reservoirs while mosquitoes are carriers. It generally does not spread human to human.

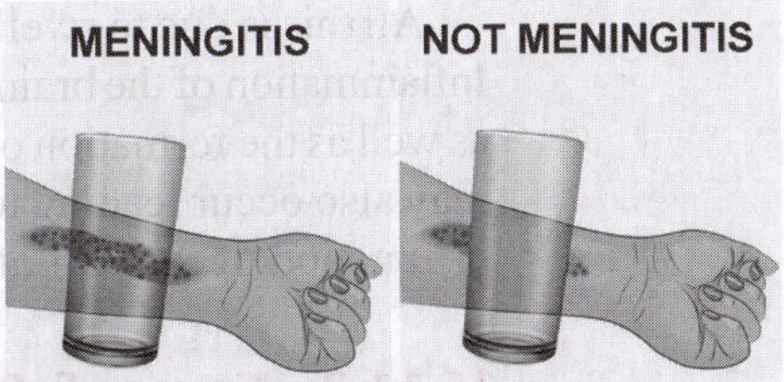

16.11.1 Factors favouring Meningitis

The factors associated with the development of epidemics in the meningitis belt include:

- medical conditions (immunological susceptibility of the population),
- demographic conditions (travel and large population displacements),
- socioeconomic conditions (overcrowding and poor living conditions),
- climatic conditions (drought and dust storms), and
- concurrent infections (acute respiratory infections).

16.11.2 Symptoms

A person is asked to rapidly rotate the head horizontally, if it does not make the headache worse, meningitis is unlikely. Symptoms are nuchal rigidity, sudden high fever with severe headache, and altered mental status, photophobia and phonophobia in adults (not in children), and may be irritable and look unwell with leg pain, cold extremities, and abnormal skin colour. Further, the fontanel (the soft spot on the top of a baby's head) can bulge in below 6 months infants. The bacterium meningococcal meningitis causes a rapidly spreading petechial rash, with numerous small, irregular purple/red spots (petechiae) on the trunk, lower extremities, mucous membranes, conjuctiva, and the palms of the hands or soles of the feet, fall of BP, fast heart rate, high or abnormally low temperature, and rapid breathing, leading to insufficient blood supply to other organs, the excessive clotting obstructing blood flow to organs and increase the bleeding risk. It may lead to haemorrhage of adrenal glands and Waterhouse-Friderichsen syndrome, often fatal.

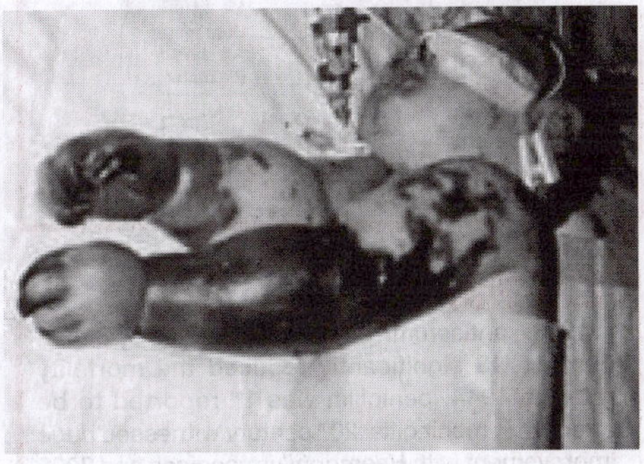

Adult Neck stiffness, Texas meningitis epidemic of 1911–12. The child with meningococcal meningitis & petechial rash, survived, became poster child for the vaccination campaign in NZ.

All this is due to swell in brain tissues by increased pressure inside the skull. Inflammation of the brain (encephalitis) or its blood vessels (cerebral vasculitis), as well as the formation of blood clots in the veins (cerebral venous thrombosis), may also occur leading to weakness, loss of sensation, or abnormal movement or function of the part of the body.

16.11.3 Causes & Diagnosis

Meningitis is an infection caused due to micro-organism (virus/ bacteria/ fungi/ protozoa) when reaches the meninges, e.g. in bacterial meningitis, bacteria reach meninges through the bloodstream or direct contact between meninges either through nasal cavity or the skin.

Bacterial Meningitis: vary according to the age group. Neonates contract from mother before birth, Children (<5) by HiB while in older children and adults 80% are due to *meningococcus* & *Streptococcus pneumonia*. More risky with >50 yrs age. The risk can be lowered by pneumococcal vaccine in both children and adults. It is also encountered in persons with immune problems, such as AIDS.

Viral Meningitis: by varicella zoster virus (cause of chickenpox/shingles), mumps virus, and HIV.

Fungal Meningitis: by organ transplantation, HIV/ AIDS, and the loss of immunity (with age), but is uncommon with a normal immune system.

Parasitic Meningitis: Amoebic meningitis or cerebral malaria (malaria infecting the brain) by amoebae (Protozoa) such as *Naegleria fowleri*, contracted from freshwater sources.

O My God!

Your Head is Protected by Meninges?

The meninges are 3-membranes, (pia mater, arachnid mater and dura mater) along with the cerebrospinal fluid which protect the central nervous system (brain & spinal cord). The pia mater is a very delicate impermeable membrane, firmly adheres to the surface of the brain including all the contours, nooks & corners. The arachnoid mater (so named due to its spider-web-like appearance) is a loose fitting sac on top of the pia mater, filled with cerebrospinal fluid in sub-arachnoid space. The outermost i.e. dura mater, is a thick durable membrane, attached to both the arachnoid and the skull.

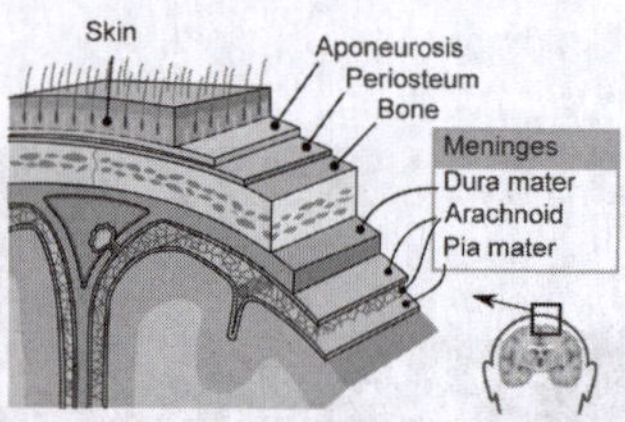

O My God!

In 1906, antiserum produced in horses by Simon Flexner, US significantly reduced the mortality rate. In 1944, penicillin was 1st reported to be effective in meningitis. 20th century witnessed huge improvement with *Haemophilus* vaccines and 2002 evidenced steroids to improve the situation.

Meningitis is diagnosed based on blood tests such as C-reactive protein, CBP, blood cultures, CT or MRI scan, CSF by lumbar puncture (LP-spinal tap). Various other specialized tests are available in specific cases. Identification of Meningitis after death can be checked by inflamed pia-mater and arachnoid layers of the meninges.

16.11.4 Prevention & Vaccination

Meningitis can be prevented through vaccination (long term), or with antibiotics (short term). Bacterial and viral meningitis are contagious, not as serious as the common cold or flu. Both can be transmitted through droplets of respiratory secretions while kissing, sneezing or coughing, but cannot be spread by just breathing nearby. The risk reduces by '***behavioural control***'.

Since the 1980s, many countries are immunizing against *Haemophilus influenza* type B in their routine childhood vaccination schemes. Meningococcus vaccines exist against groups A, B, C, W135 and Y. A quadrivalent vaccine combines all 4-vaccines [ACW135Y vaccine is now a visa-requirement for Hajj]. Pneumococcal conjugate vaccine (PCV) is active against 7 common serotypes while pneumococcal polysaccharide vaccine (PPV) covers 23 strains. BCG can reduce tuberculous meningitis. Antibiotics (rifampicin/ ciprofloxacin/ ceftriaxone) reduce the risk for short term, but can't protect against future infections. The treatment suggested for various types of meningitis are antibiotics and steroids (Bacterial), supportive therapy (Viral) and Lumbar Puncture/ Drain (Fungal meningitis). Untreated, bacterial meningitis is always fatal. Viral meningitis, in contrast, tends to resolve spontaneously and is rarely fatal. Fungal meningitis is rare to occur.

16.12 MALARIA (VECTOR BORNE)

Perhaps! In 1829, the term malaria originated from Italian: *mala aria*—"bad air"; while the disease was formerly called *ague* or *marsh fever* due to its association with swamps and marshland. It is a mosquito-borne infectious disease caused to humans and animals by protozoa (single-celled parasitic micro-organisms) belonging to the *Plasmodium* type. While biting, the infected *Anopheles* (female) mosquito transmits the disease by inducing the parasite-contained saliva into the person's blood. These parasites travel to the liver where they mature and reproduce. The symptoms appear after 10-15 days of mosquito bite, as fever with fatigue, headache and vomiting. If untreated, it becomes chronic, resulting in yellow skin, seizures, coma or death.

Malaria is diagnosed by the microscopic test using blood films. The risk can be reduced through preventing mosquito bites by using mosquito nets and repellents or control measures like spraying insecticides and draining standing waters. Hither to, there is no effective vaccine, and so treated by anti-malarial drugs (chloroquine phosphate, mefloquine, sulfadoxine/ pyrimethamine etc.)

Malaria is widespread in the tropical and subtropical regions around the equator (Sub-Sahara, Asia, and Latin America). In 2015, ~44 million died out of ~214 million cases infected worldwide (90% in Africa).

Malaria is often associated with poverty and has a major negative effect on economic development through

- prevention costs,
- health care expenditures and
- reduced revenue on tourism and so forth.

16.12.1 Classification

Malaria can be classified in several ways. A few are discussed below.

I. Based on Severity Malaria is of 2 types-Severe and uncomplicated.

As per the WHO, Malaria is found to be either "severe" or "uncomplicated" and is deemed severe when any of the following criteria are present, otherwise uncomplicated.

> **O My God!**
>
> **malERA?**
>
> Malaria Eradication Research Agenda (malERA) is the process of identifying the areas of R&D for the worldwide eradication of malaria. MPs that infect rodents are widely used for research. About 200 parasitic Plasmodium species are identified that infect birds, reptiles and mammals of which about 30

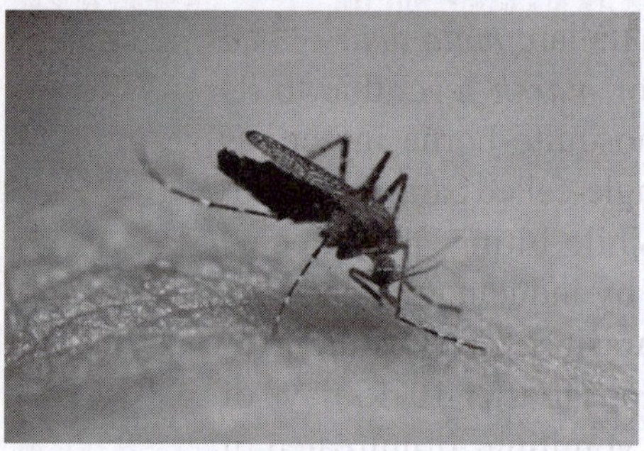

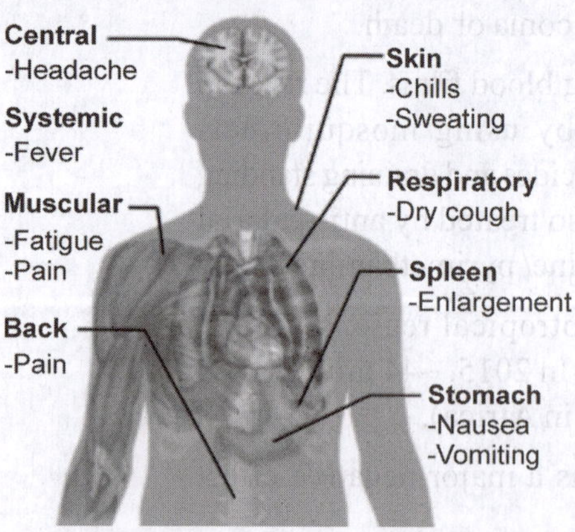

- Decreased consciousness
- Too weak to walk
- Parasite level > 1lakh/µL
- Breathing problems
- Two or more convulsions
- Acidosis or lactate levels >5 mmol/L
- Pulmonary oedema
- Bleeding problems
- Haemoglobin < 50 g/L
- Kidney failure
- Haemoglobin in urine
- Blood glucose < 2.2 mmol/L

Example: Cerebral malaria is severe malaria

II. Based on infection area and its development Malaria is considered in 2 kinds (phases)

1. Exoerythrocytic phase that involves the liver and
2. Erythrocytic phase that involves red blood cells, or erythrocytes.

III. Based on type of plasmodium, it is classified into 5 types

There are 5 species of *Plasmodium*, namely,

1. *Plasmodium Falciparum (dangerous & can cause death)*

2. *Plasmodium vivax (milder form)*
3. *Plasmodium ovale (milder form)*
4. *Plasmodium malariae (milder form) and*
5. *Plasmodium Knowlesi (rarely causes disease)*

Anopheles stephensi mosquito feeding blood meal (expelling surplus blood droplet)

Sir Ronald Ross (himself a malaria survivor), received 1902 Nobel prize for discovering medicine for Malaria when he was working in PGH Calcutta, India

In Apr 1894, a Scottish physician Sir Ronald Ross visited Sir Patrick Manson at his house on Queen Anne Street, London, for 4-yr-research collaboration. Ross in1898, in the Presidency General Hospital in Calcutta, explained the complete life-cycle of the MP in mosquitoes and proved malaria is mosquito-borne by isolating MP from the salivary glands of mosquitoes that had fed on infected birds for which he was awarded the 1902 Nobel Prize in Medicine. After resigning the Indian Medical Service, Ross worked at newly founded Liverpool School of Tropical Medicine to direct malaria-control in Egypt, Panama, Greece and Mauritius. His findings, implemented in 1900 by William C. Gorgas as health measures during Panama Canal construction, saved 1000's of lives and helped develop methods to future public-health campaigns.

16.12.2 Symptoms and Causes

Main symptoms of malaria

After the mosquito bite, the symptoms begin within 1-4 weeks depending on resistive power of the bitten, the length of exposure and use of anti-malarial medicine as prevention. Initial signs are common to all types of malaria; similar like flu or gastroenteritis or viral diseases, such as headache, fever, shivering, joint pain, vomiting, jaundice, haemolytic anaemia, haemoglobin in urine, retinal damage, and convulsions. The noteworthy symptom of malaria is paroxysm—i.e. a cyclical occurrence of sudden coldness followed by shivering and then fever & sweating, occurring every 2 days (tertian fever) in *P. Vivax/ P. Ovale* infections, and every 3 days (quartan fever) for *P. Malariae*. *P. Falciparum* infection can cause recurrent fever every 1–2 days, or almost continuous. Severe cases of *P. Falciparum* (in 1-4 weeks after infection) may turn up as cerebral malaria, often exhibit neurological symptoms, such as abnormal posturing, conjugate gaze palsy (failure of the eyes to turn together in the same direction), seizures or coma or death.

About 75% infections and large majority of deaths are due to *P. Falciparum*, while about 20% are due to *P. Vivax*. However, in recent days, *vivax* is also posing life-threats. Global warming is likely to affect malaria transmission, but the severity is unclear.

16.12.3 Recurrent Malaria

Often malaria patients stop medication after they get free from the fever. Perhaps! This is due to the problem of vomiting sensation caused by anti-malarial drugs. This may prove to be more dangerous because it can recur and become more resistive to the medicines. So, doctors advise the malaria treatment even after the primary dosage is completed and the patient should take a complete course including the secondary course as per the advice of the doctor. The recurrence depends on the type of parasite, resistance of the individual, effectiveness of previous treatment, exposure period, number of bites, and so forth. This recurrence can be found in 3 ways as follows:

1. **Recrudescence:** This is the recurrence after a symptom-free period due to survival of parasite in blood in case of inadequate or ineffective treatment.
2. **Relapse:** The symptoms reappear after the parasites have been eliminated from blood but persist as dormant hypnozoites in liver cells that may return within 2–6 months (often with *vivax/ ovale*).
3. **Reinfection:** In this case, the parasite caused the past infection is eliminated from the body but a new parasite is introduced within 2 weeks of treatment for the initial infection. Usually, this may confuse between reinfection and recrudescence, as often it is attributed to treatment failure.

Nobel Prize Winners

1. 1902, Sir Ronald Ross: Life cycle of MP & Mosquito
2. 1907 Charles Louis Alphonse Laveran: MP in RBC
3. 1927 Julius Wagner-Jauregg: Malaria inoculation
4. 2015 Tu Youyou: CholoroQuin from Artemisia Annua

O My God!

Females only are dangerous?

Only female Anopheles mosquitoes feed on blood, that too, in the night; male mosquitoes feed on plant nectar, and do not transmit the disease. The females usually start searching for a meal at dusk, and will continue throughout the night until taking a meal. Though rare, blood transfusion can also transmit mp.

16.12.4 Origin & Research

The *P. Falciparum* malaria might have been originated from gorillas and chimpanzees. Hippocrates (2700 BC) described periodic fevers labelled tertian, quartan, sub-tertian and quotidian. Malaria contributed to the decline of Roman Empire and so, known as the "Roman fever". Charles Louis Alphonse Laveran, a French army doctor was awarded, 1907 Nobel Prize for Physiology/ Medicine for finding MP in red blood cells in 1880. A year later, while treating yellow fever patients in Havana, Carlos Finlay (Cuba) found evidence of mosquitoes as carriers. The work was followed by Josiah C. Nott and Sir Patrick Manson, the "father of tropical medicine", on transmission of filariasis. Dr. Ronald Ross (UK) proved the lifecycle of malaria parasite and mosquito as vector which earned him the Nobel Prize in 1902.

Artemisia annua, source of the Antimalarial drug Artemisin

Malaria was first (1677) effectively treated with the bark of cinchona tree (grows on the slopes of Andes, Peru) that contains quinine, which Europe recognized as an antimalarial treatment. In 1940s, chloroquine replaced quinine to treat all malarias, and was used until 1980s. In 1970s Artemisinins isolated from the plant *Artemisia annua*, by the 2015 Nobel winner, Tu Youyou et al (China) became the recommended treatment for *P. Falciparum* malaria.

Malaria treats Syphilis!

During 1917-40s, the MP (*P. Vivax*) used to be injected deliberately (malaria therapy) to induce fever to combat certain diseases like tertiary syphilis for which Julius Wagner-Jauregg, Austria, received the 1927 Nobel Prize in Physiology or Medicine. It is no longer in use as it was too dangerous to claim 15% deaths.

16.12.5 Diagnosis & Prevention

Since the symptoms are not specific, diagnosis of malaria in non-endemic areas needs thorough analysis. Following are common symptoms raise the curtain for suspecting malaria.

- enlarged spleen,
- low number of platelets in the blood, and
- recent travel history,
- higher-than-normal levels of bilirubin in blood
- fever and headache,
- chills and shiver
- fatigue and body pains
- abdominal pain

Malaria is usually confirmed by the microscopic blood test or by antigen-based rapid diagnostic tests (RDT). Simply speaking, "***fever means malaria unless proven otherwise***".

Since there is no vaccine for malaria, mosquito control or elimination and thence mosquito bite avoidance is the only best way of prevention of malaria.

For individual protection from mosquito, the most effective are:

- Repellents available in various forms such as a cream to apply on human skin, a burning coil that spreads the fumes, a paper when burnt produces fumes, a solid mat on slow heating diffuses invisible repellent gas, a liquid repellent vaporizes on slow heating and so on.
- Net is affordable & durable. Insecticide-treated mosquito net (ITN) is powerful & double effective.
- Electronic devices produce so high frequency sounds as to repel the female mosquitoes away.
- Mosquitoes usually rest on a nearby wall/ surface to digest the blood-meal squeezed from humans, whence the walls of houses are sprayed

O My God!

DDT was the 1st pesticide used for indoor residual spraying used exclusively to combat malaria in the early days. Later, its widespread applications quickly spread to agriculture and other areas.

O My God!

FILARIASIS (PHILARIASIS) or FILARIA is caused by Mosquito borne Roundworms?

Filariasis (or **philariasis**) is a parasitic disease caused by roundworms of the Filarioidea type (helminthiases), spread by blood-feeding black flies and mosquitoes (Culex). It was the 1st disease discovered to be transmitted by mosquito bite. Humans can host 8-filarial nematodes, divided into 3-groups:

- Lymphatic filariasis, caused by the worms *Wuchereria bancrofti*, *Brugia malayi*, and *Brugia timori*, occupy lymphatic system; leads to *elephantiasis*
- Subcutaneous filariasis caused by *Loa loa* (the eye worm), *Mansonella streptocerca*, and *Onchocerca volvulus* (causes river blindness), occupy subcutaneous fat layer of skin.
- Serous cavity filariasis (abdomen), caused by *Mansonella perstans* and *Mansonella ozzardi*.

The life cycle of filarial nematode worms consists of 5-stages. In 1st stage female worms mate with male to produce 1000's of micro-filariae, taken up to 2nd stage by the vector insect (intermediate host) during a blood meal, where they develop into 3rd-stage (infective) larvae. While taking another blood meal, it injects the infectious larvae into skin (stage-4), which in ~1-year, mature into adult worms.

Symptoms: Common symptom of lymphatic filariasis is elephantiasis—edema with thickening of skin and underlying tissues. Often, it affects the lower extremities, but different species can affect different parts of body e.g *W.Bancrofti*: legs, arms, vulva, breasts, scrotum (hydrocele), *B. Timori* rarely affects genitals. *O.Volvulus* affects eyes (river blindness).

Diagnosis & Treatment: By Microfilariae in blood film smears & finger prick test. For *W. bancrofti*, (vector: mosquito) blood is collected in night while day for *Loa loa's* (vector: deer-fly). *M. Streptocerca* & *O. volvulus*, produce microfilarae not in blood; but in skin and so, tested by skin snips, and so at any time. Filaria is treated by albendazole with diethylcarbamazine. Doxycycline for elephantiasis. In 2015 William C. Campbell and Satoshi Ômura were Co-awarded the Nobel prize in Physiology/ Medicine.

Filariasis can also affect cattle, sheep, horses, dogs and donkeys.

with insecticides so that the resting mosquitoes can be killed before they go for a next bite to transmit the MP. Mosquito repellents/ insecticides such as DDT, cyfluthrin, deltamethrin etc, called 'Indoor Residual Spray (IRS)' are available.

- Efforts to reduce mosquito larva by decreasing the open water where they develop.

Other methods

- Community participation
- health education on malaria & control measures
- Awareness to cover over areas of stagnant, still water, like water tanks that are ideal to breed the parasite by mosquito.
- Diagnose in early stages can forestall fatality.
- Preventive therapy on pregnant women, infants and preschool children.

The people visiting areas of malaria take Chloroquine/ mefloquine/ doxycycline etc., 1-2 weeks before arriving and 4 weeks after leaving.

16.12.6 Challenging Issues

Drug resistance is growing problem in 21st century (now to all anti-malarial drugs), due to

- Naturally the parasite is getting resistance over a period of time.
- Self medication by some people and hence acquiring the resistance.
- Under/over dosage given by some doctors.
- Common people have poor knowledge on the causes & effects of malaria parasites and mosquitoes.
- Half knowledge treatment by some private medical practitioners (PMP).
- Major epidemic of slums affecting the country's economy to spend more on public health.
- It affects the tourism department of a country and hiders its economic development.
- Malaria is the worst hazard for military personnel, particularly during military actions.

SELF ASSESSMENT INTERMISSION (SAI – 16.5)

1. What are vector borne bacterial epidemic diseases? Describe any one of your choice.
2. How is plague caused? On what factors spread of plague depends?
3. What are the types of plague? Explain its mode of infection.
4. What are the precautions and treatments against plague?
5. Write a short note on 1994- Plague Epidemic occurred at Surat, India.
6. What are various methods to prevent the spread of plague? What are the risk factors?
7. How is meningitis caused? Explain its mode of infection.
8. What are the precautions/prevention and treatments for meningitis?
9. What are the types of meningitis? Explain briefly.
10. What are the symptoms of meningitis? How do you treat?
11. How is malaria caused? On what factors spread of malaria depends?
12. What are the types of malaria? Explain its mode of infection.
13. What are the precautions and treatments against plague?
14. Write a note on research and development with reference to Malaria
15. What are the methods to prevent malaria? What are the challenging issues regarding controlling malaria, particularly in the Indian environment?
16. What is recurrence malaria? Discuss different possibilities of recurrence.
17. Why do doctors recommend continuing malaria treatment even after fever is controlled?
18. Write a note on filarial with reference to cause, mode of infection, symptoms and treatment.

MINI-PROJECTS/CASE STUDIES

1. Visit nearest hospital and conduct a survey on the outbreaks such as malaria, typhoid etc. in your locality. Analyze the situation with causes and effects. Suggest some improvements.
2. Visit your nearest Primary Health Centre (PHC), investigate if the facilities and medical care and cleanliness are adequate. Submit a report to the authorities concerned, with due suggestions.

Summary of Biohazards (Bacterial Epidemics)					
Disease	**Symptoms**	**Causes**	**Carrier**	**Effect**	**Treatment**
Anthrax	Cold (or) flu symptoms	Bacillus Anthracis	Soil borne	Effects on lungs, skin, intestinal ingestion	Biothrax vaccine
Tetanus (a) Generalized (b) Neo-natal (c) Local (d) Cephalic	Mild spasms in jaw & facial / head muscles	Clostridium Tetani	Soil borne	Effects on muscles, eye, nerves	Td vaccine, TT with diphtheria & pertusis (DPT/Dtap) vaccine
Cholera	Watery diarrhoea, muscle cramps, sunken eyes	Vibrio Cholera	water borne	Causes dehydration, lethargy, water electrolyte imbalance.	Rehydration, IV fluids, antibiotics
Diphtheria	Fever, nasal discharge, head ache, body pains	Coryne Bacterium Diphtheria	Water borne	Effects on respiratory tract, skin, throat	Vaccine with tetanus (Td) & pertusis (DTP, Dtap, Tdap) pentavalent vaccine
Typhiod	Fever, headache, weakness	Salmonella Typhi	Water borne	Inflammation of heart muscles, severe illness	Antibiotics and fluids
Tuberculosis (a) Pulmonary TB (b) Extra pulmonary	Fever, loss of appetite and fatigue	Myco-Bacterium TB (MTB)	Air borne	Effects lungs	BCG vaccine
Leprosy	Muscle weakness, dry scalp	M.Leprae & Leproma-tosis	airborne	Causes neurological damage	Mycobacterium indicus pranii (MIP)
Plague (a) Bubonic plague (b) Septicemic plague (c) Pneumonic plague (d) Pharyngeal plague (e) Meningeal plague	Fever, chills, headache, muscle ache	Yersinia Pestis	Air& vector borne	Effects lymph nodes, blood vessels	Antibiotics as streptomycin, gentamycin, IV fluids.
Meningitis (a) Bacterial (b) Viral (c) Fungal (d) Parasitic	Adult neck stiffness	Bacterial Meningitis	Air& vector borne	Effects on gastrointestinal and skin	Haemophilus vaccine
Malaria	Head ache, fever, jaundice	Plasmodium Parasite	Vector borne	Effects on abdomen, muscles	Artemisinin combined theraphy (ACP)

CHAPTER 17

Bio-hazards: Viral Epidemics

O'MY SILENT INNER VIBES (O'M S I V – 17)

In the olden days there was a little distinction between the measles, smallpox and chickenpox and all these are believed to be the curses of the 'Village-Goddess' or 'Local Goddess'. Thus, various measles/smallpox/chickenpox goddesses have been worshipped throughout parts of the Old World, for instance, the Hindu goddesses ***Shitala Mata,*** *Pochamma, Maisamma, Maridamma, Poleramma, Mahankali, Ammavaaru and so forth [the names vary village to village depending on the local importance].*

Even Chinese worship goddess T'ou-Shen Niang-Niang to prevent/cure smallpox. They pray for her mercy, by treating smallpox pustules as "beautiful flowers" as a euphemism to avert offending the goddess. In the New Year's Eve, the children of the house wear ugly masks during sleep, so as to conceal any beauty and thereby avoid attracting the goddess, who would be passing through sometime that night. If smallpox occurs, shrines would be set up in the homes of the victims to worship. If the victim recovers, the shrines are carried away in a special paper chair/boat and burnt otherwise the shrine is destroyed and cursed, so as to expel the goddess from the house.

The Hindu goddess Shitala is both worshipped and feared during her reign as she is both evil and kind and inflicts victims when angered, while can calm the fevers of the already afflicted. Portraits show her holding a broom in her right hand to sweep out the disease and a pot of cool water in the other hand to soothe victims. In some areas in India, there will be branches of Neem-tree instead of broom. Shrines were created where many India natives, both healthy and not, worship to protect themselves from this disease. To gain mercy of Shitala, Indian women, offer cooling foods and pots of water on the roofs of their homes. In south India, the people worship with leaves of Neem tree, lemons, turmeric, saffron, ashes and sandal powder etc. which are supposed to give coolness. Further, in some places, the victims of pox believe that the Goddess wants a sacrifice of goat, sheep or chicken for measles, smallpox, chickenpox respectively and so offer its blood by cutting throat of the respective animal ('bali') before the goddess.

(Continued)

At least 7-religious deities have been specifically dedicated to such diseases, such as the god ***Sopona*** in the Yoruba religion in Japan. Smallpox/Chickenpox/Measles are not clearly described in either the Old or New Testaments of the Bible or in the literature of the Greeks or Romans whereas a similar reference can be found in India's medical book (AD 400). In some cultures, such as Japan, Europe, Africa etc., smallpox is believed as act of demons, who are accordingly blamed. Nearly all such cultures also believe that the demon is afraid of red colour and so, red treatment is given to victim by decorating their rooms in red, including offering the red blood in some regions. Believe it or not! This was even practiced by Charles–V of France and Elizabeth–I of England.

Belief gives people relief.

But as long as the belief is blind, it could be a superstition. Most unfortunate is that most of Indians still superstitious when comes to these types of infections and reluctant to visit the doctors, even in this 21st century.

Have faith in the power of the Supreme, but at the same time, have trust in power of science, because 'even God will not help without human effort'.

Doctor treats...and the God cures... (*Vaidyo... Naaraayano... Hareeh...*)

Thence, we should understand about such diseases, how they occur, how to prevent, diagnose and treat and so forth.

17.1 MEASLES (AIR BORNE)

Measles, caused by the measles virus (MV) is a highly contagious airborne infection spreads by cough/ sneeze, through saliva or nasal secretions. The symptoms develop in 1-2 weeks after exposure and last for 7–10 days, usually begin as fever (>104°F or 40°C), cough, runny nose and inflamed eyes and after 2-3 days, small white spots appear inside the mouth (called Koplik's spots) followed by a red, flat rash on the face and then to rest of the body within 3-5 days. Complications occur in about 30% with diarrhoea, blindness, inflammation of the brain, pneumonia etc. German measles (Rubella) and roseola are different diseases.

Blessing in disguise! People usually do not get this disease more than once.

No specific treatment is available, but vaccine is effective preventing deaths. Measles affects about 20 million/yr, mostly in Africa and Asia. Most of the infected/ died (1lakh in 2013, 5.5 lakh in 1990) are < 5 yrs old. The risk of death among infected is 0.2% but goes up to 10% in case of malnutrition. It is not believed to affect other animals.

17.1.1 Symptoms and Causes

The symptoms are: fever of 4-Day-3C's —Cough, Conjunctivitis (red eyes) and Coryza (cold with headache, fever 104°F/40°C, sneeze) along with rashes (Koplik's spots) for about a week. Described as red maculopapular rash, starting on the back of ears, in few hours, spreads to head, neck and then to the body, often with itching, appears up to 8 days (called "stain") changing colour from red to dark brown, before disappearing. The infection usually resolves after

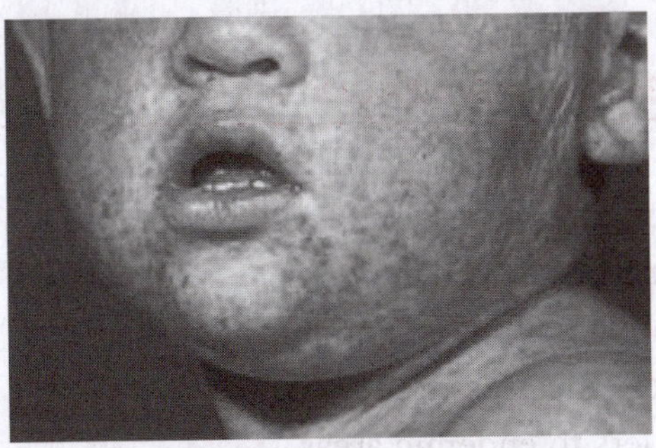

Child with measles

Skin infection 3rd day

MV Micrograph

O My God!

Lanka 'A Crank'?

In 2011, German anti-vaccination campaigner and HIV/ AIDS denialist Stefan Lanka posed a challenge on his website and offered € 100,000 to the one who proves scientifically that measles is caused by a virus and finds the diameter of the virus. He assumes the measles virus does not exist and the illness is psychosomatic. Overwhelming scientific evidence was provided from various medical studies and by German physician David Barden, but was not accepted by Lanka that forced Barden to appeal in court. The case caught wide global attention and ended with the ruling that Lanka to pay the prize. The clinical neurologist, well-known medical advocate Dr. Steven Novella called Lanka "a crank".

3 weeks. Negligence may complicate and may turn to diarrhoea, pneumonia, acute brain inflammation bronchitis (viral/ bacterial), and corneal ulcer, and are often more severe in adults.

Measles caused by a single-stranded, negative-sense, enveloped RNA virus of the genus *Morbillivirus* within the family *Paramyxoviridae,* was 1st isolated in 1954 by Nobel Laureate John F. Enders and Thomas Peebles. *There are no other animal reservoirs than humans.* It is highly contagious spread by cough or sneeze via close personal contact or direct contact with secretions.

17.1.2 Risk Factors and Prevention

- Immunodeficiency caused by HIV/ AIDS
- Immune-suppression after organ/ stem cell transplant
- Alkylating agents/ corticosteroid therapy
- Loss of inherited antibodies before immunization
- Travel to areas where measles is endemic
- Contact with travellers to endemic areas

Maurice Hilleman 1st developed measles vaccine. Licensed vaccines are available from 1963 and an improved one from 1968. Children are immunized against measles between 6-12 months, generally as part of the 3-part MMR vaccine (measles, mumps, and rubella) and a 2nd dose between the ages of 4-5 yrs, to increase rates of immunity. Life-threatening adverse reactions are very rare (one in million).

17.1.3 Diagnosis and Treatment

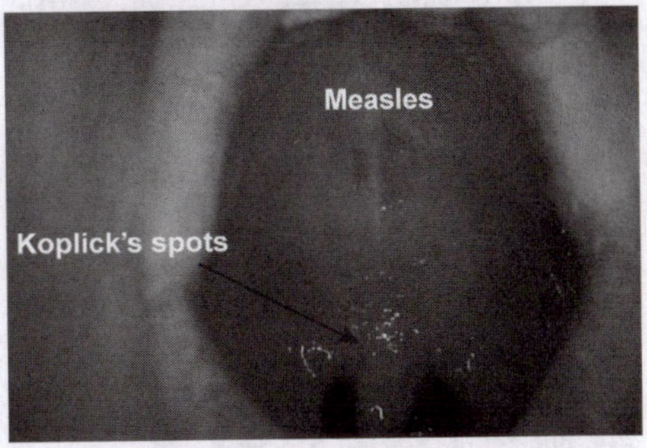

Koplik's spots 3rd day

Clinical diagnosis of measles needs a background of fever for at least 3 days, and one of the 3C's (Cough, Coryza, Conjunctivitis) followed by Koplik's spots, confirmation by IgM/IgA antibodies or isolation of measles virus RNA from respiratory specimens/ saliva/ sputum.

No specific treatment, but for rest and support with oral rehydration (sweet/ salty fluids), healthy food are given. Vitamin-A supplementation is advised to reduce the risk of blindness. Some may develop pneumonia or ear infections or bronchitis (viral/ bacterial) or brain inflammation; while no specific treatment for brain inflammation but, antibiotics are used to treat bacterial pneumonia, sinusitis and bronchitis. Ibuprofen or Paracetamol can be used to reduce fever and pain and, if needed, dilate the airways for cough. Aspirin raises the risk of developing Reye syndrome.

17.2 SMALLPOX (AIR BORNE)

> **O My God!**
>
> **Smallpox still exist?**
>
> In March 2004 smallpox scabs were found inside an envelope in a book on Civil War medicine in Santa Fe, New Mexico.
>
> In July 2014 several vials of smallpox were discovered in FDA lab at National Institute of Health in Bethesda, Maryland.

Smallpox is an infectious disease caused by either of the two variants of virus, *Variola major* and *Variola minor*, named after Latin disease *Variola vera*, (*varius*=spotted or *varus* = pimple). The disease was originally known in English as the 'pox' or 'red plague'; the term 'smallpox' was 1st used in Britain in 15th century to distinguish from the "great pox" (Syphilis)

Beginning in small blood vessels of skin, mouth and throat, the infection spreads as maculopapular rash and emerges as fluid-filled blisters. *V. major* is more serious (mortality 30–35%) while *V. minor* is a milder (mortality 1%). It is also known as ***alastrim*, *cottonpox*, *milkpox*, *whitepox***, and ***Cuban itch***.

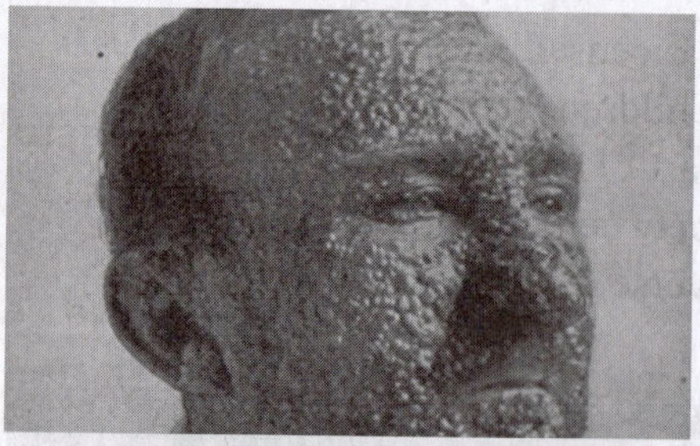

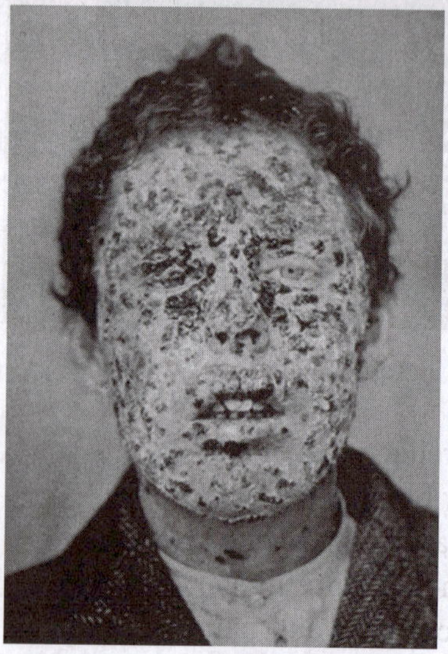

17.2.1 Symptoms

Rash due to smallpox (variola major)

The inhaled variola major attacks the oropharyngeal (mouth & throat) or respiratory mucosa and migrates to regional lymph nodes to multiply which spreads by 12th day. The virus enters the bloodstream in large numbers (called viremia) and then to spleen, bone marrow, and lymph nodes. Initially, cold +fever (at least 101°F/38.3°C), muscle pain, malaise and headache, later nausea and vomiting and backache often occur. 12th–15th day lesions, small reddish spots called enanthem—appear on mucous membranes of mouth, tongue, palate and throat, and temperature falls near normal. The lesions rapidly enlarge and rupture, releasing large amounts of virus into saliva. The virus causes characteristic pimples (called macules), begin on forehead, rapidly spread to the whole face, proximal portions of extremities, the trunk, and lastly to distal portions within 2 days, later no new lesions appear.

At this point variola major infection can take different courses, resulting in 4 types namely, ordinary, modified, malignant (or flat) and hemorrhagic (or Black Pox). Most (90%) of the unvaccinated cases are ordinary. Modified smallpox is often confused with chickenpox. The malignant and hemorrhagic forms are usually fatal.

3-Former directors of Global Smallpox Eradication Program read the news that smallpox had been globally eradicated, 1980—***WHO, Resolution WHA33.3***

17.2.2 Causes and Transmission

4-orthopox viruses infect humans: variola, vaccinia, cowpox and monkeypox of which variola causes smallpox (in 2-varieties v. major/ minor) only in humans while others can infect animals too.

Variola is airborne and is transmitted by inhaling (oral, nasal, or pharyngeal mucosa) or prolonged face-to-face (within 6 ft or 1.8 m), direct contact with infected body-fluids or contaminated objects such as bedding or clothing. The virus transmits throughout the illness period, but more frequent during 1st week, when the skin lesions are intact. It is highly contagious till the last scab falls off, but spreads more slowly and less widely, perhaps because it needs close contact, that too, after the onset of rash. In temperate areas, the infection is highest in winter, where as throughout the year in tropical areas. *Smallpox is not transmitted by insects or animals.*

17.2.3 Prevention-Vaccination

In the early days, smallpox was prevented by inoculation (named as variolation after the introduction of vaccine to avoid confusion), which likely occurred in India, Africa, and China. In 1796, Dr. Edward Jenner, Berkeley, UK, discovered the immunity by inoculating with lesion of cowpox (one of the other orthopox variants) and named it 'vaccine', (*vaccai* = cow in Latin). Being safer, it soon became popular all over the world. However, in 19th century, it was replaced by vaccinia virus (belongs to the same family but is genetically distinct), which uses a 2-pronged needle dipped into the vaccine solution and pricked several times in a few seconds into the skin at the upper arm. If successful, a red and itchy bump develops in 3-4 days. In the 1st week, the bump turns as large blister (called "Jennerian vesicle"), fills with pus, and begins to drain. During the 2nd week, it dries up to form as scab, falls off in 3rd week, leaving a small scar.

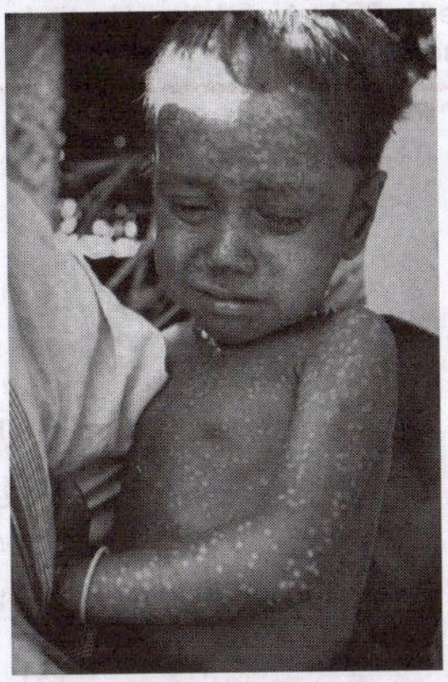

2-yr-old Rahima Banu of Bangladesh, the last person *V. Major* infected naturally in 1975

The success was 95% and offered high immunity for 3-5 yrs, and even more if revaccinated. After declared 'eradicated' by 1986, routine vaccination had been ceased in all countries. It is now recommended for laboratory workers at risk for occupational exposure.

17.2.4 Biological Warfare

The British used smallpox as a bio-weapon at Siege of Fort Pitt during the French and Indian Wars (1754–1763) against France and its allies. As per historians, "it was deliberate British policy to infect the Indians with smallpox". On June 24, 1763, William Trent, a local trader and commander of the Fort Pitt militia, wrote, "I hope it will have the *desired effect*". How inhuman they were!

The smallpox was used as a weapon during the American Revolutionary War (1775–1783). During WW-II also, UK, US and Japan (Unit 731 of the Imperial Japanese Army) used it. In 1947, SU established a smallpox weapons factory in the city of Zagorsk, 75 km to the northeast of Moscow. An outbreak of smallpox weapon occurred during testing at a facility on an island in the Aral Sea in 1971. General Prof. Peter Burgasov, Chief Sanitary Physician of Soviet Army described the incident.

O My God!

In March 2004 smallpox scabs were found inside an envelope in a book on Civil War medicine in Santa Fe, New Mexico.

In July 2014 several vials of smallpox were discovered in FDA lab at National Institute of Health in Bethesda, Maryland.

17.2.5 Notable Examples of Smallpox

- Mummy of Lakota Chief Sitting Bull, Ramses V of Egypt
- Guru Har Krishan, 8th Guru of the Sikhs, in 1664,
- In Europe, deaths of smallpox often changed dynastic succession. Edward VI, the only survived son of Henry VIII, died without male successor to the throne (his 2-immediate successors were both women, and both had it but survived).
- King Louis XV of France succeeded his great-grandfather Louis XIV through a series of deaths of smallpox or measles among the earlier in the succession line. He also died of the disease in 1774.
- Soviet leader Joseph Stalin was victim at the age of 7 and so, his face was badly scarred. He later had photographs retouched to make his pockmarks less apparent

17.3 CHICKENPOX (AIR BORNE)

It seems funny and surprise why the term chicken has been given to this diseases because it is neither caused nor carried by chicken. Further, it does not affect the chickens also. However, some people give reasons as given below:

- It is relatively mild disease like how chicken is mild among all the non-vegetarian foods.
- The designation *chicken* is for tenderness such as a child (i.e., literally 'child pox'),
- It is believed to be derived from *chickpeas*, based on resemblance of the vesicles to chickpeas, or to come from the rash resembling chicken pecks.
- The idea that the disease may have originated in chickens.
- A corruption of *itching-pox*,

Chickenpox (or **Varicella**) is highly contagious caused by Varicella Zoster Virus (VZV), on skin as rash with small itchy blisters, which finally scab over. It often starts on the chest, back and face, then spreads all over the body. Other symptoms are fever, tiredness and headache. Symptoms begin 1-3 weeks after exposure and last for 5-10 days. It is more severe in adults than children.

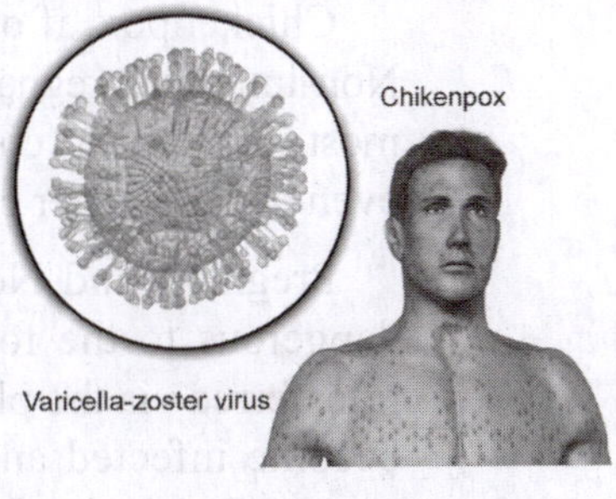

Chickenpox is an airborne disease that spreads through the cough/ sneeze. It is diagnosed by the symptoms and confirmed by polymerase chain reaction (PCR) test of the blister fluid or scabs.

Blessing in disguise! ***People got the disease once, usually do not get again.***

Since the vaccine protects up to 90%, routine immunization is recommended in many countries. Vaccination within 3-days of exposure works better in children. Paracetamol for fever, Calamine lotion for itching can help while short fingernails can reduce/ prevent injury from scratching.

17.3.1 Symptoms and Diagnosis

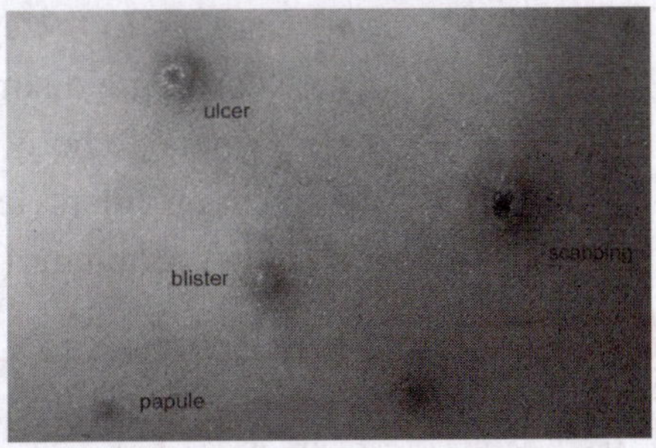

In children it stars with itchy rash or spots in oral cavity while in adults, it begins with nausea, loss of appetite, muscle pains and headache followed by rash or oral sores, malaise and low fever. The rash begins as small red dots on face, scalp, upper arms and legs, and turn to small bumps, blisters and pustules within 10–12 hrs, later as scabs. Blisters may also occur on the palms, soles, and genital area with severe itching. The enanthem (internal rash) and exanthem (external rash) can occur one after the other in 1-3 days or may be simultaneous. The symptoms appear 10-21 days after exposure, who becomes contagious with running nose/ enanthem/ exanthem persist till all vesicular lesions dry out to scabs (4-5 days). The infection usually resolves within 2-wks but rash takes a month.

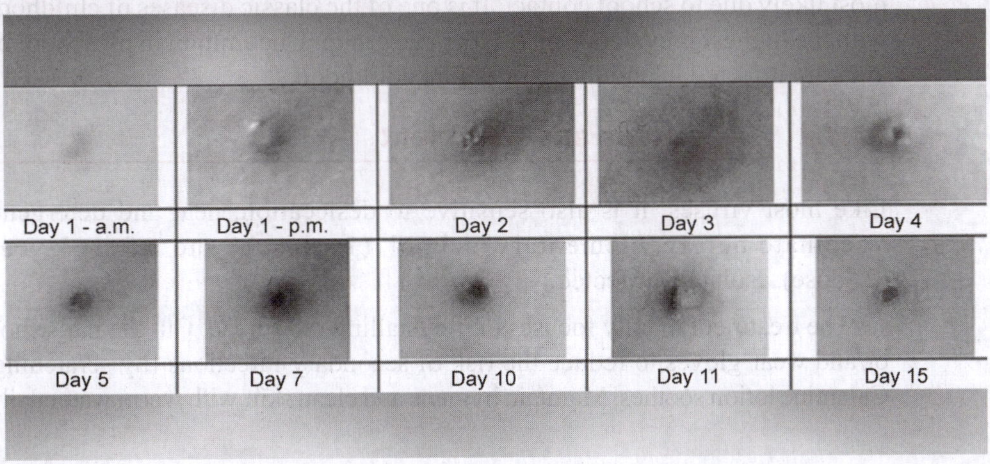

Chickenpox, if occurs, is more severe in men than in women or children. Non-immune pregnant and immune-suppressed persons are at highest risk. The most common late complication is shingles (herpes zoster), caused by reactivation even decades after childhood infection.

Pregnant and Neonates: The first 6-months pregnancy period is more dangerous to the foetus if infected with VZV. For pregnant, antibodies are transferred via the placenta to the foetus. However, immunized woman cannot become infected and need not worry about self or infant. But, if infection occurs during the first 28 weeks of gestation, it can result in foetal varicella syndrome (also known as *congenital varicella syndrome*). The other possible effects could be

- Damage to brain (e.g. encephalitis)
- Damage to the eye (e.g. cataracts, blind)
- Neurologic disorder (e.g. Horner's syndrome)
- Damage to body (e.g. dysfunction)
- Skin disorders (lesions, hypo-pigmentation)
- Other problems (toes/fingers/anal/bladder)

Maternal infection is associated with premature delivery. *Neonatal varicella*, the infection in gestation or soon after birth is highly risky to the baby particularly, if exposure is within 7 days before or after delivery. The baby may also be exposed to the virus via infectious siblings or other contacts, but of less concern if mother is immune. Diagnosis by PCR test of amniotic fluid has risk of abortion.

O My God!

Shingles?

After a chickenpox infection, the virus still remains in the nerve tissues. The immune system protects from the virus, but in later days, whenever it becomes weak, virus gets reactivated and results in different form of the viral infection called shingles (also known as herpes zoster). Every adult above 60 yrs is advised for the *herpes zoster* vaccine. Shingles probably affects 20% of chickenpox infected children at their adult phase. Stress can also enhance Shingles

Children: In temperate areas, it is basically a disease of children, mostly during winter/ spring, most likely due to school contact. It is one of the classic diseases of childhood, with the highest prevalence in 4–10 yr age group. Uncommon in preschool but 90% are infected in childhood or before adulthood.

17.3.2 Prevention and Treatment

Like most viruses, it is also sensitive to desiccation, heat and detergents. Vaccinate before elementary school (1st dose), and after 5-years (2nd dose). Isolate if infected.

The treatment mainly focuses on forestalling the spread. Cut the nails short, or/and wear gloves to reduce the risk of secondary infections (by scratching). Calamine lotion soothes. Maintain hygiene and clean skin with warm water daily.

Use Paracetamol for fever but not Aspirin, due to the risk of the serious (even fatal) damage to liver and brain, Reye syndrome. Antiviral drugs are used sometimes but not advisable for age between 1 month and 12 yrs. Oral acyclovir drug reduces the symptoms within 24 hrs, but not recommended as no effect on complication. Adults are advised to take lot of water to reduce dehydration and to relieve headaches. Antihistamines, being sedative can be used if itching is severely disturbing.

17.3.3 Distinction between Smallpox and Chickenpox

Chickenpox was commonly confused with smallpox in the post-eradication era. A few distinctions are given below.

No.	Small pox		Chicken pox
1.	Pustule size is nearly of same as they progresses more uniformly	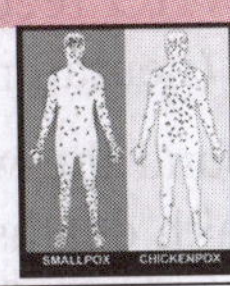	Pustules are of varying size due to variations in timing of pustule eruption
2.	Affects palms and soles of feet		Usually does not affect palms and soles
3.	Occurs all over and more at limbs		Mostly on torso, spreads less to limbs

SELF ASSESSMENT INTERMISSION (SAI – 17.1)

1. What are air borne viral epidemic diseases? Describe any one of your choice.
2. Write a detailed note on measles, with reference to the mode of infection, diagnosis, symptoms, treatment, prevention and vaccination.
3. What are the precautions and treatments referred for those dealing with persons infected by measles?
4. What are various methods to prevent the spread of measles?
5. Why is smallpox so called? What are its other names? How is it caused? Explain its mode of infection.
6. Explain how variola virus and its other forms used to eradicated smallpox.
7. How is chickenpox caused? Why is it named chickenpox? Explain its mode of infection.
8. What are the prevention and treatments for chickenpox in an epidemic environment?
9. Distinguish between smallpox and chickenpox. Explain each briefly.
10. What are the causes and symptoms of chickenpox? What are the preventive methods?
11. Give a short note on shingles.

17.4 INFLUENZA OR FLU (AIR BORNE)

The term *Influenza* (="influence" in Italian) refers to the cause of the disease; initially, attributed to 'unfavourable astrological influences'. Influenza, commonly known as "**flu**", is an infection by influenza virus (*Not to be confused with Haemophilus influenza*). with common symptoms as: runny nose, sore

> **O My God!**
>
> **Stomach (or 24 Hr) Flu?**
>
> Nausea and vomiting occur more commonly in the unrelated infection gastroenteritis, which is sometimes inaccurately referred to as "stomach flu" or "24-hour flu". Complications of influenza can occur as sinus infections, viral or secondary bacterial pneumonia and worsen previous health problems leading to asthma or heart failure.

throat, high fever, muscle pains, headache, cough and tiredness, which begin within 2 days after exposure to the virus and last less than a week. The cough, however, may last for more than 2 weeks. In children, there may be nausea and vomiting but not common in adults.

3-types of influenza viruses affect people, called Type A, B, and C. Usually, the virus spreads through the air from cough/ sneeze at short distances and by touching virus contaminated surfaces and then the mouth/ nose/ eyes. The infection is diagnosed by testing the throat, sputum or nose.

Wearing a surgical mask and frequent hand wash lowers the risk (soap inactivates virus). The WHO recommends vaccinating yearly to persons at high risk. Antiviral drugs (neuraminidase inhibitor) are used to treat.

Influenza spreads around the world in about 3-5 million cases of severe illness and about 2.5-5 lakh deaths, mainly in winter while near the equator, outbreaks may occur at any time of the year. Death occurs mostly in too young, too old and other ill-healthy people. Pandemics are less frequent. In the 20th century 3-pandemics occurred: Spain (1918), Asia(1958), and Hong Kong(1968), each claimed more than a million deaths. The WHO declared an outbreak of a new type A/H1N1 pandemic in June 2009. Influenza may also affect other animals such as pigs, horses, dogs and birds.

17.4.1 Symptoms & Treatment

About 1/3rd of people with flu are asymptomatic and begin suddenly 1-2 days after exposure. Usually the 1st symptom is fever of 100-103°F (38-39°C) with chills & aches and pains. Other symptoms are:

- Fever and extreme coldness (chills shivering, shaking rigor)
- Body aches, pains in joints and throat
- Reddened eyes, facial skin, mouth, throat and nose
- Cough
- Runny nose
- Irritated, watering eyes
- Nasal congestion
- Sneezing
- Petechial rash

Though it is difficult to distinguish between the common cold and influenza in the early stages, flu can be identified by a sudden high fever and extreme fatigue. Diarrhoea is uncommon in adults, except in H5N1 "bird flu", that too, a symptom in children.

Flu patients have to take lot of rest, drink plenty of liquids, avoid using alcohol and tobacco and if necessary, take acetaminophen (paracetamol) to relieve the fever and muscle pains. Children and teenagers with flu must avoid aspirin (particularly for B), as it can lead to Reye's syndrome or fatal disease of liver. As flu is caused by a virus, antibiotics are not effective, but antiviral drugs may be effective, and mostly recoverable in 1-2 wks.

17.4.2 Types of Virus

There are 3 types of influenza viruses whose RNA viruses make up 3 of 5 genera of the family Orthomyxoviridae:

- Influenza virus A
- Influenza virus B
- Influenza virus C

A 4th family of viruses proposed as influenza D, was isolated in 2012. Of the 3-genera of influenza viruses (A, B and C) that cause human flu, influenza A is common in pigs while C being rare, B has not been reported in pigs. Further, influenza C does not infect birds.

Influenza virus A: A large variety of 'A' is naturally hosted by wild aquatic birds and transmitted to poultry or cause pandemics. The type-A, the most virulent is subdivided into different serotypes based on antibody responses as listed below

H1N1: Caused Spanish Flu in 1918, and Swine Flu in 2009

H5N1: Caused Bird Flu in 2004

H3N2: Caused Hong Kong Flu in 1968

H2N2: Caused Asian Flu in 1957

H1N2: Endemic in humans, pigs and birds

H7N7: Unusual zoonotic potential

Other influenza viruses: **H7N2; H7N3; H7N9; H9N2; H10N7**

Swine flu is caused most commonly by influenza-A subtypes H1N1, H1N2, H2N3, H3N1, H3N2 and H7N9. The death of 61-year Madison County, Ohio is the first, with a new swine flu strain, which she contracted with hogs at the Ross County Fair.

Influenza virus B: This single species genus mostly infects humans (seal and ferret only are other susceptible) and is less common and mutates slower (2–3 fold) than type-A, so, pandemics are rare.

Influenza virus C: This also has one species, which can infect humans, dogs and pigs, but not birds, with severe illness and local epidemics. Of course, it is less common than the others and usually causes only mild in children.

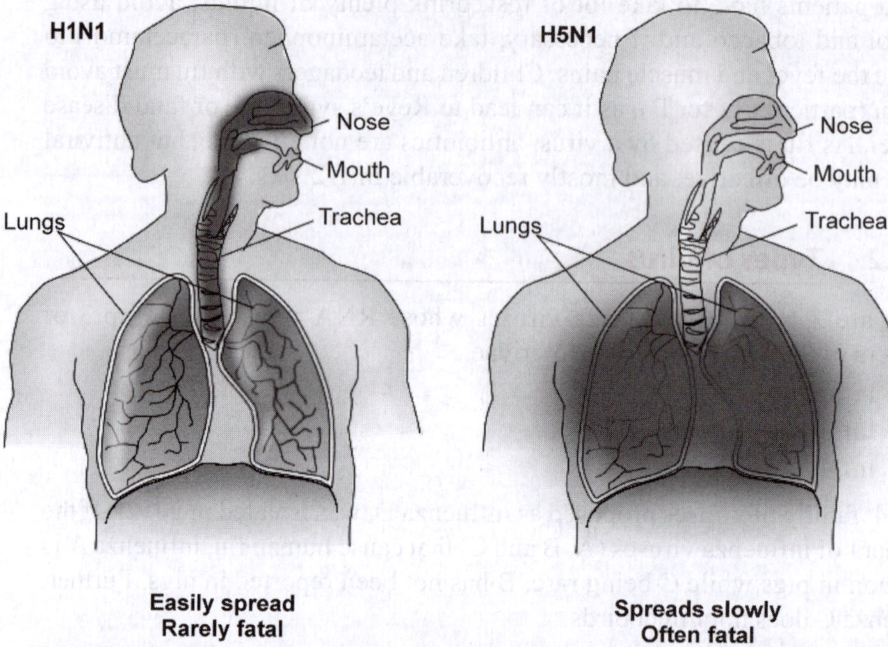

Fig. 17.1 The routes and infection of seasonal H1N1 and avian H5N1.

17.4.3 Transmission

Influenza can develop in ½ -1 day after infection, peaks on 2nd day and persists for 5-10 days. Children are more vulnerable and persist up to 2 weeks. Influenza can spread mainly in 3 ways:

1. ***Direct transmission:*** If infected one sneezes mucus directly into the eyes/ nose/ mouth of another
2. ***Airborne route:*** By aerosol inhalation of an infected while coughing, sneezing or spitting.
3. ***Indirect way:*** Through hand-to-eye/nose/mouth transmission, either from contaminated surfaces or direct personal contact such as a hand-shake.

In the airborne route, inhaling just one droplet (general size is ϕ0.5-5 μm) is enough. Though a single sneeze releases up to 40,000 droplets, most of which are quite large, and so quickly settle down. The survival of influenza airborne droplets depends on humidity and UV radiation or sunlight.

Structure & nomenclature of Influenza virus

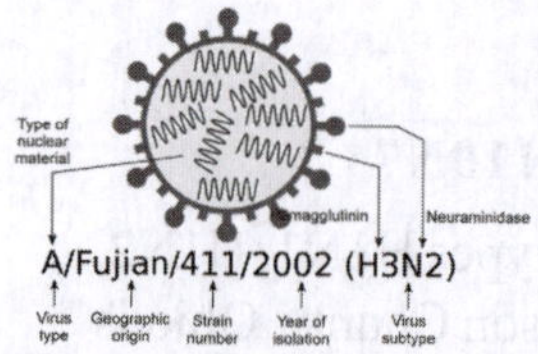

Influenza viruses A, B and C are very similar in overall structure. The particle of virus is roughly spherical with Ö80–120 nm. The filamentous form is common in influenza C, with cordlike structure up to 500 μm long. Hemagglutinin (HA) and Neuraminidase (NA) are the 2 large glycol-proteins on the outside of the viral particles, and form the basis of the *H* and *N* distinctions, e.g. *H3N2*. There are 16H and 9N subtypes known, but only H 1, 2 and 3, and N1 and 2 are commonly found in humans.

As the influenza virus survives outside of the body, it can be transmitted by contaminated surfaces such as banknotes, doorknobs, light switches and other household items. The virus survival period on a surface varies; 1-2 days on hard, non-porous surfaces such as plastic or metal, for about 15 minutes from dry paper tissues, and only 5 minutes on skin. However, the virus present in mucus lasts for longer periods (up to 15 days on banknotes) and indefinitely when frozen. They become inactive by heating to 56°C (133°F) for a minimum of 60 minutes, and by acids (at pH <2).

17.4.4 Prevention & Control

The WHO and US-CDC recommend vaccine for high-risk groups, such as children, old, health care workers, people chronically ill (asthma, diabetes, heart disease), immuno-compromised, HIV/AIDS, cancer, and post organ transplant. The high mutation rate of virus doesn't allow influenza vaccine to protect for longer period. So, it is recommended to vaccinate every year.

Spread of influenza can best be reduced by good personal health/hygiene habits such as: not touching eyes, nose or mouth; frequent hand washing (with soap and water, or with alcohol-based hand rubs); Avoiding spitting; covering coughs and sneezes; avoiding close contact with sick people; and staying home if sick. Wearing face masks prevent transmission both ways, for self and the community. Smoking raises the risk of catching flu as well as aggravating.

Since influenza spreads through both aerosols and contacting contaminated surfaces, sanitizing surface prevents infections to a large extent. Quaternary ammonium compounds and bleach are used in hospitals as they last long and effective, while diluted chlorine bleach is sufficient for a home. Alcohol is also effective sanitizer.

During past pandemics, closing schools, churches and theatres slowed the spread but could not show much effect on the overall death rate. Perhaps! This could discourage public gathering and might reduce transmission, but not on control. When less numbers of people are infected, isolating the sick might reduce the risk.

17.4.5 Seasonal Variations

There are 2 different flu seasons (winter & summer) each year and the 2 hemispheres of earth (see Fig. 17.2) experience in opposite ways; so, the

WHO recommends 2 different vaccine formulations every year; one for the Northern, and one for the Southern Hemisphere. As influenza is caused by a variety of species and strains of viruses, in any given year some strains can die out while others create epidemics, while yet another strain can cause a pandemic.

Fig. 17.2 Seasonal risk areas for influenza: Nov–Apr (blue), Apr–Nov (red), and year-long (yellow).

Outbreaks of the flu usually occur seasonally. Perhaps, because people are indoors more often during the winter, and also are in close contact, thence promote transmission. Another reason could be cold temperatures keep air dry, which may dehydrate mucus, preventing the body from expelling virus. Moreover, virus survives longer on surfaces at colder temperatures and aerosol transmission of the virus is highest in cold environments (less than 5°C) with low relative humidity. The lower air humidity in winter is the main reason for seasonal influenza transmission in temperate regions.

Also, seasonal changes affect infection rate in tropical regions, particularly, some countries experience the peaks of infection during the rainy season. Further, school terms are a major factor in childhood diseases such as measles and pertussis, along with the flu. H5N1 exhibits seasonality in both humans and birds.

The effect of vitamin D (solar UV radiation) levels on immunity is proposed by Robert Edgar Hope-Simpson in 1965 for seasonality of flu and explained why influenza occurs mostly in winter and tropical rainy season, when people stay indoors, away from the sun, and their vitamin-D levels fall.

17.4.6 Virus in Animals

All the known sub-types (HxNy) of influenza virus with 16 forms of ***Hemagglutinin*** and 9 forms of ***Neuraminidase*** have been identified in birds, but many subtypes are endemic in humans, pigs, dogs, horses, monkeys, camels, ferrets, cats, seals and whales. However, the main variants named conventionally are: *Avian or bird flu, human flu, swine flu, horse flu and dog flu*. (Cat flu generally refers to feline viral rhinotracheitis or feline calicivirus and not infection from an influenza virus). The symptoms are similar in humans, pigs, horses and dogs.

An outbreak of influenza in harbour seals caused about 500 seal deaths at New England coast in 1979–80. Outbreaks in pigs are common but mortality is not severe. Vaccines are developed to protect poultry from avian influenza.

17.5 SWINE FLU (AIR BORNE)

Sub types of Influenza A			
H \ N	N1	N2	N3
H1	*	*	
H2	*		*
H3	*	*	

Swine influenza or **swine flu** or **pig influenza**, **pig flu**, or **hog flu** is an infection caused by any of several types of **Swine Influenza Virus** (**SIV**) among the subtypes of influenza-A as shown with asterisks in adjacent diagram (H1N1, H1N2, H2N1, H2N3, H3N1 and H3N2) and influenza C that are endemic in pigs worldwide. Transmission from swine to humans is uncommon and does not always lead to human flu, but result only in the production of antibodies in blood. If transmission causes human flu, it is called *zoonotic swine flu*. People with regular exposure to pigs are at high risk. Symptoms of zoonotic swine flu are similar to influenza viz. chills, fever, sore throat, muscle pains, severe headache, cough and weakness.

17.5.1 Swine Flu in Swine

Pigs with flu show the symptoms as fever, lethargy, sneeze, cough, breathlessness, loss of appetite, weight loss (12 lb in 3-4 weeks) and poor growth, causing loss to farmers.

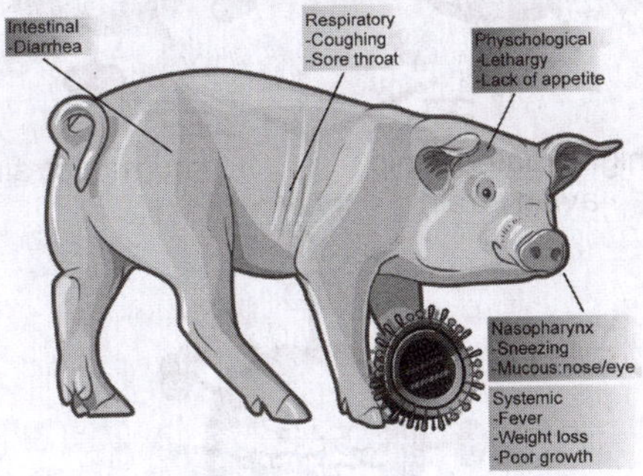

Fig. 17.3 Symptoms of swine influenzas

17.5.2 Swine Flu in Humans

Zoonotic swine flu is rare. In all, 50 cases occurred since 1958, only 6 died (1-pregnant, 1-leukemia, 1-Hodgkin's lymphoma and only 2 healthy). The 2009 H1N1 virus is not zoonotic, as it is not Swine-to-Human but Human-to-Human transmission, through airborne droplets. H1N1 swine flu is similar to influenza with same symptoms. Fatalities are more likely in young children and the old, and if occurs, may be due to high fever (leads to neuro-problems),

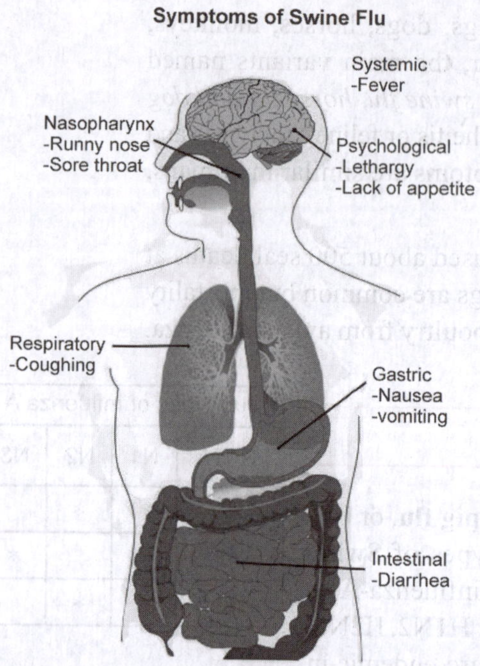

Fig. 17.4 Symptoms of Swine Flu

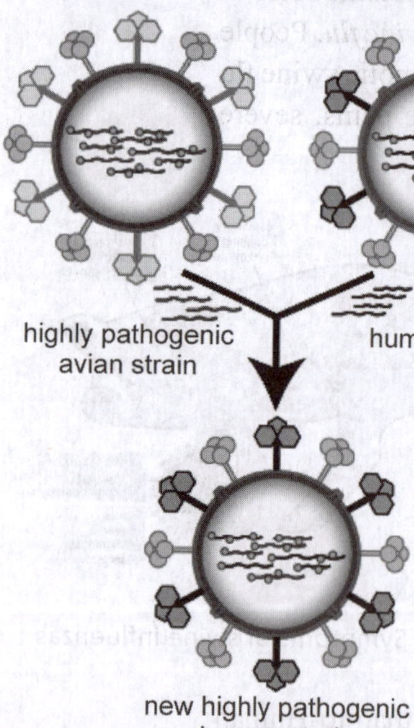

Fig. 17.5 Re-assortment & evolution of new strain

dehydration (vomits and diarrhoea), respiratory failure, pneumonia (leads to sepsis), electrolyte imbalance and kidney failure.

17.5.3 Transmission and Prevention

As the swine flu transmits in 3-ways, (S to S, S to H and H to H), the prevention also has 3 components, i.e. prevention (i) in swine, (ii) transmission to humans, and (iii) its spread in humans.

A. Swine to Swine (S to S)

The direct contact between animals occurs during animal transport, feeding and farming either by touching noses, or through dried mucus. Airborne transmission occurs through the aerosols of pigs when they cough or sneeze.

Prevention in Swine: The spread of flu among swine can be prevented by facility management, herd management, and vaccination. Facility management refers to using disinfectants and maintaining ambient temperature as they are unlikely to survive outside living cells for more than 2-weeks, except in cold but above freezing conditions, and are readily inactivated by disinfectants. Herd management refers not to add infected pigs to uninfected as carrier pigs are usually responsible for infection.

B. Swine to Humans (S to H)

Intense exposure while working in swine (poultry for bird flu) has high risk of hosting zoonosis and re-assortment and so, vaccination is essential for them. Infected pigs can usually infect 3 species (pigs, birds and humans) and exchange genes to produce new and dangerous strains and re-assortment, e.g. Avian influenza virus H3N2 evolved from H2N2 by antigenic shift, similarly H5N1 in pigs (found in China). Blessing in disguise! Swine flu is not spread by pork products, because the transmission of virus does not occur through food.

Prevention of S to H: Swine can be infected by both avian and human flu strains, and so hosts the antigenic shifts to create new influenza strains. Risk factors are smoking and, not wearing gloves when working with sick animals, thereby increasing possibility of subsequent hand-to-eye/ nose/ mouth contact. So farmers and veterinarians are advised to use face masks and hand gloves. Better, vaccinate swine.

> **O My God!**
>
> **2015 India outbreak:** Sudden outbreak of swine flu occurred in the winter season of 2014-15 in India, the highest infections and deaths being recorded in Rajasthan, Gujarat, Madhya Pradesh, Maharashtra, Delhi, and Telangana. The circulating strain was the same as that of global pandemic in 2009 (A/H1N1). Out of 31,156 infected, 1,841 died as of Mar 19, 2015. The sudden spurt in the season left the Indian govt unexplained but concerned. The instructions were issued to investigate into reasons, and issued directives to all states to
>
> (a) Screen of influenza A/H1N1 cases,
> (b) Describe of A/H1N1 for identification, detection, and distinction from (similar) common cold,
> (c) Clinically manage protocol of Pandemic A/H1N1
> (d) Provide home care,
> (e) Collect of human samples and study.

C. Humans to Humans (H to H)

The infected people cough or sneeze, and when others breathe in or touch it and then touch their own face, this transmission occurs. The swine flu in humans is most contagious during first 5 days of the illness, and for children up to 10 days. The greater majority of transmission is due to H to H only. Swine flu caused in 2009 flu pandemic is not endemic to pigs and not transmitted from S to H, but from H to H.

Prevention of H to H: Prevention among humans calls standard infection control methods i.e. frequent washing of hands with soap and water or with alcohol-based hand sanitizers, and also by disinfecting household surfaces, diluted chlorine bleach solution. Also, avoid touching eyes, nose or mouth, stay away from people infected, and avoid large gatherings, stay home.

17.5.4 Treatment

The treatment to humans is already discussed in the above paragraphs under the influenza (human flu). The same is applicable to swine-flu also. This also is rarely fatal, so, no much treatment than rest and supportive care is needed. Instead, it is better to focus on prevention of the spread in farm(s). Vaccination, veterinary management, and antibiotics may prevent other related diseases.

17.6 AVIAN INFLUENZA OR BIRD FLU (AIR BORNE)

Flu symptoms in birds are not specific, but a small reduction in egg production, or weight loss with minor respiratory disease, may appear (difficult to diagnose). Strains like Asian H9N2 are highly virulent to poultry with high mortality (100% within 2 days) causing huge losses to poultry farmers. Also the

> **O My God!**
>
> **US Public Refused Vaccination?**
>
> The 1976 US outbreak (Jan-Feb) highly concerned the President G. Ford urged on every person in US be vaccinated. Due to PR problems, the program began late on Oct 1, but 3 Sr citizens died soon after the injections. Media outcry, the vaccine was the cause. Science writer Patrick Di Justo, wrote, "The govt had long feared mass panic about swine flu—now they feared mass panic about the swine flu vaccinations. The public refused to trust a govt-operated health program that killed old and crippled young people".

avian-adapted, highly pathogenic strain of H5N1 called "highly pathogenic avian influenza (HPAI) virus, commonly known as "avian influenza" or simply "bird flu" is endemic in many bird populations, particularly in SE Asia. It is epizootic (an epidemic in non-humans) and panzootic (a disease affecting animals of many species), killing tens of millions of birds.

17.6.1 Spread

Most of the avian flu cases in humans are due to either handling dead infected birds such as chickens or turkeys or from contact with infected fluids (on contaminated surfaces or drops). There is a large threat in Asia with infected poultry due to low hygiene and close quarters.

> **O My God!**
>
> **Highly Pathogenic Subtypes?**
> There are 144 subtypes (16HX9N) of influenza viruses, but highly pathogenic in humans are only some strains of 5 subtypes: H5N1, H7N3, H7N7, H7N9, and H9N2. An old woman in Jiangxi, China, died of pneumonia in Dec 2013 the 1st human fatality caused by H10N8 strain, poses challenge to the world that some more can add to the list in future.

HPAI or A/H5N1 is spread by bird to bird (B to B) and bird to human (B to H), but not human-to-human (H to H). However, in future, it may re-assort into a strain of H to H transmission.

H5N1: H5N1 (subtype of HPAI), killed millions of poultry (mortality rate 60%) and 100's of humans throughout Asia, Europe, and Africa. The Thai outbreak caused huge losses to poultry as infected birds were culled and slaughtered. The chicken consumption drastically fell down as the public lost confidence in poultry products. Further, adding fuel to fire, the spread of the virus was aggravated by bird migration, cool temperature (apt for virus survival) and several festivals during that time. Since 1987 (the 1st H5N1 outbreak), there has been growing number of A/H5N1 (B-to-H) transmissions. Though A/H5N1 does not transmit H to H easily, in 1997 Hong Kong outbreak, 6 of 18 died, none of whom worked with poultry. But the 1st H-to-H transmission was noticed, when 7 family members of Sumatra got infected as one family member worked with infected poultry. So, it may cause another pandemic if it reoccurs. Thence, the prevention and control of avian flu must be treated as top priority. The WHO recommends protective clothes for poultry workers and isolating flocks.

H7N9: H7N9 is another recently noticed new HPAI virus subtype when 1st human infection reported in 2013 in China. A month later, >100 people were infected, of those 20% died, 20% recovered in few days, and the rest were critically ill. As of Jun 30, 43 (of 133 infected) died and many of them had link with birds, and there is no H-to-H transmission; but experts reported instances of H to H infection. As this virus does not kill poultry, surveillance is difficult. Presently no vaccine exists, but antiviral drugs may work. The WHO quotes H7N9 as "an unusually dangerous virus for humans".

17.6.2 In Domestic Animals

Many domestic animals like cats, dogs, ferrets, pigs and birds are infected with H5N1 virus.

Birds: Quite often, HPAI is contracted by domestic birds in addition to poultry flocks. Less pathogenic viruses are controlled by vaccines and veterinary management.

Seals: A recent strain of virus infects the lungs of seals.

Cats: Cats show a variety of symptoms that usually lead to death. Cats get infected by either eating an infected bird or contracting from another infected cat.

17.6.3 Prevention

People not in regular contact with birds are not at risk. The workers of poultry and animal control, wildlife biologists, and ornithologists are at high risk and so, better get vaccinated at regular intervals. Flocks must be isolated from outside birds, particularly wild birds and their waste. The infection can be lowered with proper care, personal hygiene and personal protective equipment (PPE) for eyes, nose, mouth, head & hands, such as aprons, goggles, gloves, shoes, head/ hair cover (preferably disposable)

SELF ASSESSMENT INTERMISSION (SAI – 17.2)

1. How is flu caused? Explain its mode of infection.
2. What are the precautions and treatments referred for persons infected by flu? What are precautions and prevention methods you suggest to those who work with flu infected?
3. What are various methods to prevent the spread of influenza?
4. How is swine flu caused? Explain different paths of transmission and their control methods.
5. Discuss the measures to prevent swine flu epidemics by S-S, S-H and H-H transmission.
6. What are the precautions/prevention and treatments for swine-flu?
7. How is bird flu caused? Explain its spread and various strains of avian influenza virus.
8. What are the prevention and treatments of avian influenza?
9. Distinguish between swine flu and bird flu. Explain each briefly.
10. What are the causes of avian influenza? What are its symptoms?

17.7 EBOLA VIRUS DISEASE (DIRECT CONTACT)

Ebola Virus Disease (EVD) or **Ebola Hemorrhagic Fever (EHF)** or simply **Ebola**, a viral hemorrhagic fever caused to humans and other animals is named after River Ebola, Africa, as the first 2-outbreaks occurred simultaneously in 1976, one in its nearby village Yambuku and another in Nzara in Africa. The

O My God!

The story of Ebola?

The 1st infected in Zaire outbreak was a school headmaster Mabalo Lokela, showed symptoms on 26th Aug 1976 after returning from a trip to N. Zaire & the Ebola River during 12-22 Aug. In fact, quinine was given thinking as malaria. Condition worsened, admitted to Yambuku Mission Hospital on 5th Sept, and finally died on 8th (after 14 days). Soon after Lokela's death, others who were in contact also died, and entire Yambuku was panic. The country's Health Minister and Zaire President Mobutu Sese Seko quarantined Yambuku and capital, Kinshasa. No one was permitted to enter or leave the area; the roads, waterways, and airways were under martial law; schools, businesses and social organizations closed. Researchers of CDC, Peter Piot, co-discoverer of Ebola and others were also affected. Inadvertently given unnecessary vitamin injection to pregnant women with unsterilized syringes and needles by Belgian nuns led to the 26-day-outbreak & 2 week quarantine with a toll of 318 cases and 280 deaths (88% fatal). The cause was thought Marburg virus, but later knew as a new type related to Marburg. The virus strains isolated were named after the 'Ebola' River, near the original outbreak site in Zaire. Though thought the 2 outbreaks were connected, later realized that they were caused by 2 distinct Ebola viruses, SUDV and EBOV.

largest outbreak hither-to, was the epidemic (11000 died/ >28000 infected) in W. Africa, during Dec 2013 to Jan 2016.

The airborne spread between animals is not proven. But, the direct contact with body fluids is suspected. Since, EVD also resembles malaria, cholera, meningitis and other viral hemorrhagic fevers, thence the blood samples are tested for RNA or antibodies or for the virus itself to confirm.

Control of outbreaks needs fast detection, trace of infection, quick access to lab, proper healthcare and disposal of the dead through cremation or burial. The spread from infected animals to humans can be controlled by thorough cooking of meat and wearing protective clothes etc. No specific treatment or approved vaccine is available. Supportive treatment with oral rehydration therapy (or sweet/ salty water) or I.V. fluids can improve.

17.7.1 Causes and Symptoms

In humans, EVD is single -stranded, non-infectious RNA genomes caused by 4 of 5 viruses of the genus *Ebola virus* namely, Bun-Di-Bugyo Virus (BDBV), SUDan Virus (SUDV), TAï Forest Virus (TAFV) and the most deadly, simply called EBOla virus (EBOV, formerly Zaire Ebola). The 5th, RESTon Virus (RESTV), affect other species but not humans.

The symptoms begin in 2 to 20 days of contracting as influenza-like fever (>101°F/ 38.3°C), weakness, tiredness, reduced appetite, muscular & joint pains, headache and sore throat, often followed by vomits, diarrhoea and abdominal pain along with reduced function of liver and kidneys. Next, breath difficulty and chest pain may occur, along with swell, headache and confusion. Nearly half the cases develop maculo-papular rash and/or flat red area with small bumps in the skin after 5-7 days. Also, internal and external bleeding or decreased blood clotting may occur. It may cause blood in vomits/ cough/ stool or into the whites of eyes and/or skin. Within 1-2 weeks, the patient may either recover or go into coma or die with low BP due to fluid loss or bleeding. Those who survive often contract muscular/ joint pain, liver inflammation, weakness, loss of vision/ hearing/ appetite/ weight.

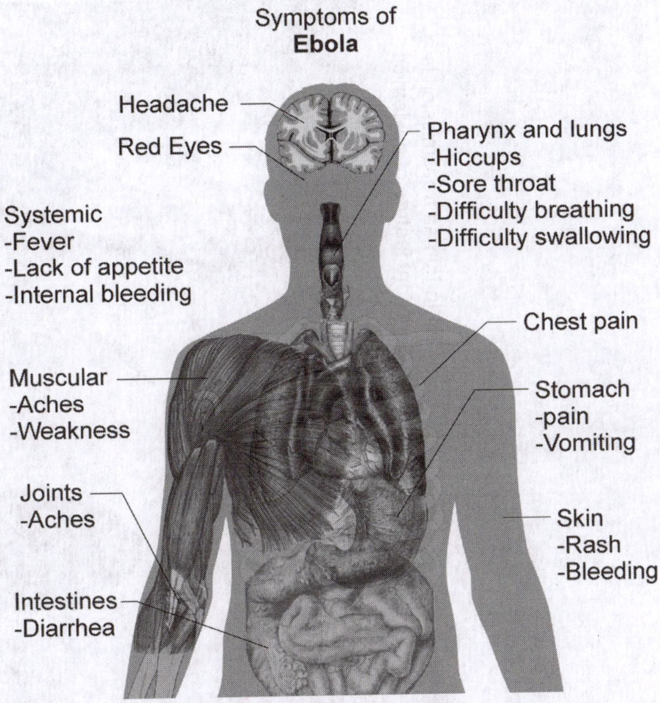

Fig. 17.6 Symptoms of Ebola.

17.7.2 Transmission

Ebola spreads only by direct contact with the blood or other body fluids such as saliva, mucus, vomit, feces, sweat, tears, breast milk, urine and semen of an infected person.

As per the WHO, input points being nose, mouth, eyes, open wounds, cuts and abrasions, EVD spreads through blood, feces, vomit, needles and syringes, and only 'very sick' people can spread in saliva and large aerosol droplets, but not sweat. The virus can survive for a few hours on dry objects, few days in body fluids outside of a person. It can persist for >3 months in semen after recovery, whence can infect through intercourse. It may also occur in the breast milk, but not known how long it is unsafe after recovery. Surprisingly, in 2014 Ebola virus was found in eyes of a patient even after 2 months of virus clearance in his blood. Though H-to-H transmission by air is not a serious issue, risk of health workers can be reduced by masks, gowns, gloves, goggles etc.

Another chief source is from dead bodies, which still remain infectious (e.g. The 2014 Guinea outbreak). People must be very careful while burial/ cremation. Electric cremation can lower the risk.

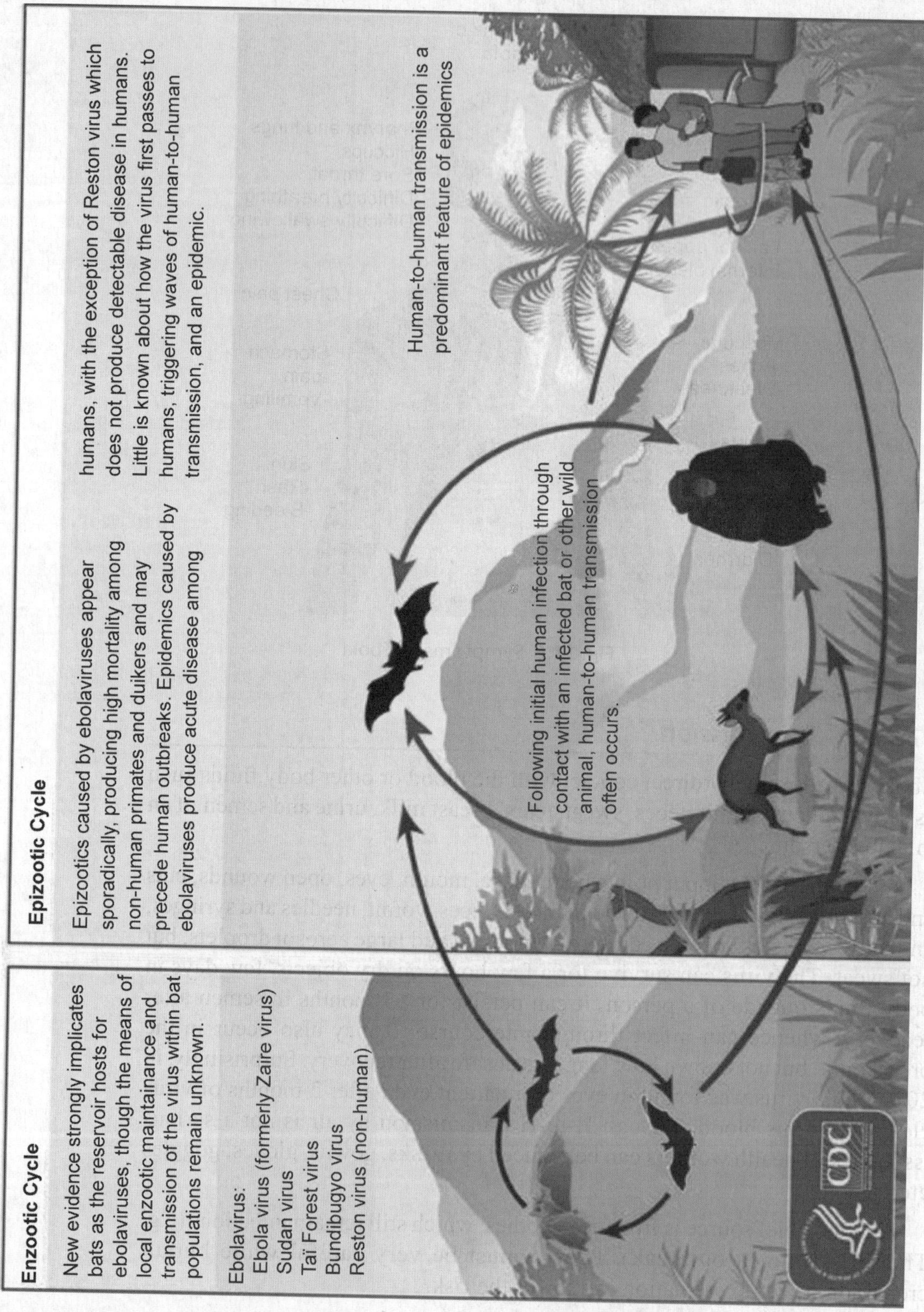

Fig. 17.7 Enzootic and Epizootic Cycles of Ebola.

In Africa, wild animals hunted for food (referred to as bush-meat) are doubted as animal-to-human transmitters of diseases. Though not clear, spread of Ebola occurred from birds/ animals to humans might be due to direct contact with an infected wild animal or fruit bat. Other wild animals Ebola are several monkey species, chimpanzees, gorillas and baboons after eating the virus carrying bats. Spread of EVD is not found by water/ food except bush meat hither-to. Also, mosquito & other insect bites are too insufficient to infect. However, pigs can spread through droplets in the air or on the ground by sneeze or cough.

Plants, arthropods and birds are suspected to be possible viral reservoirs. Pet dogs can also be infected, but do not show symptoms when carry virus. The involvement of dogs and other animals during the outbreak of EBOV are not known.

17.7.3 Diagnosis and Treatment

Information about travel/ work history, along with the exposure to wildlife, helps diagnosing. The diagnosis parameters include low platelet and WBC count, abnormalities in liver enzymes and blood clot/bleed time.

No specific treatment is approved hither to. Supportive treatment and early care with oral/ I.V. rehydration helps. Paracetamol is advised for pain, fever, nausea and anxiety but not aspirin or ibuprofen due to the bleeding risk. Blood products like RBC, platelets or frozen plasma may be given. Anti-malarial drugs and antibiotics are often used before diagnosis. Hospital care is better; if not feasible, use bleached towels while moving with infected bodies and bleach on stains. Caretakers have to wash hands with bleach and cover their mouth and nose.

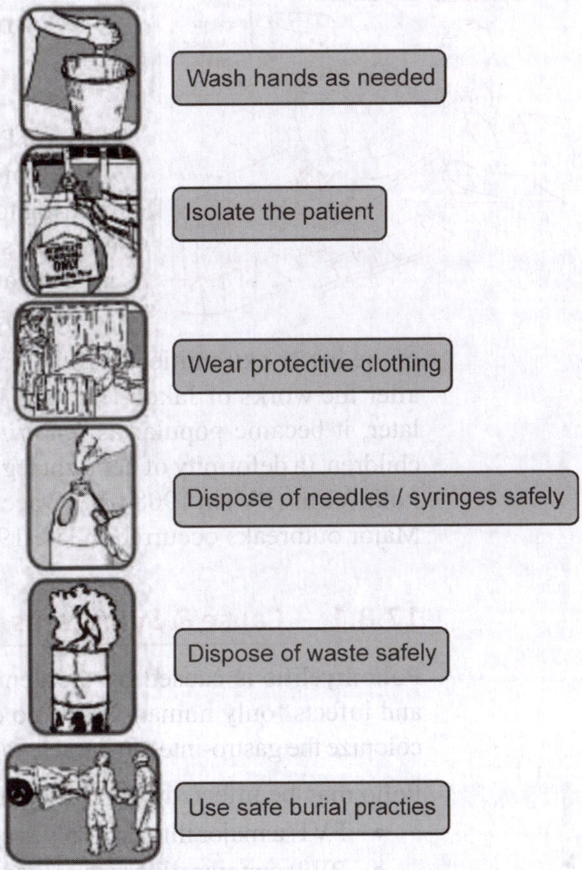

Fig. 17.8 Precautions to attendants

In Sep 2014, a vaccination n-Ebola found to show immune without getting sick. In Jul 2015, a trial vaccine VSV-EBOV was also effective. But, none had yet been approved by the US Food & Drug Administration (FDA) for clinical use in humans.

17.7.4 Ebola as a Bio-weapon

Ebola is assumed as a bio-safety level-4 agent and Category-A bioterrorism agent by US (CDC). It has the potential to be weaponized in bio-warfare, but difficult to make as a mass destructive weapon as it turns ineffective quickly in open air.

Oops! Fake emails in 2014 were misused to spread computer malware.

17.8 INFANTILE PARALYSIS OR POLIOMYELITIS OR POLIO (DIRECT CONTACT)

The term **Poliomyelitis**, or simply **Polio** is from Greek *poliós*, means 'grey', *myelós* means 'marrow', referring to the grey matter of the spinal cord, and the medical suffix *-itis*, denotes inflammation, i.e., 'inflammation of the grey matter in spinal cord'.

In 1789, Michael Underwood 1st described it as "debility of the lower extremities". Of late, it was called *Heine–Medin disease,* named after the works of Jakob Heine in 1840 and Karl Oskar Medin in 1890. But, later, it became popular as *infantile paralysis*, due to its tendency to affect children. (a deformity of her right leg due to polio). Karl Landsteiner 1st identified Polio Virus (PV) in 1908 while vaccine was developed in 1950s by Jonas Salk. Major outbreaks occurred in late 19th century in Europe and US.

17.8.1 Cause & Symptoms

Poliomyelitis is caused by the genus *enterovirus* known as Poliovirus (PV) and infects 'only humans' and 'no other animal'. The group of RNA viruses colonize the gastro-intestinal tract—specifically the oropharynx and the intestine.

Polio may be infected in the following 3 serotypes: PV1, PV2 and PV3

- PV1: a major illness involves central nervous system (CNS), and paralytic.
- PV2: a major illness involves CNS non-paralytic.

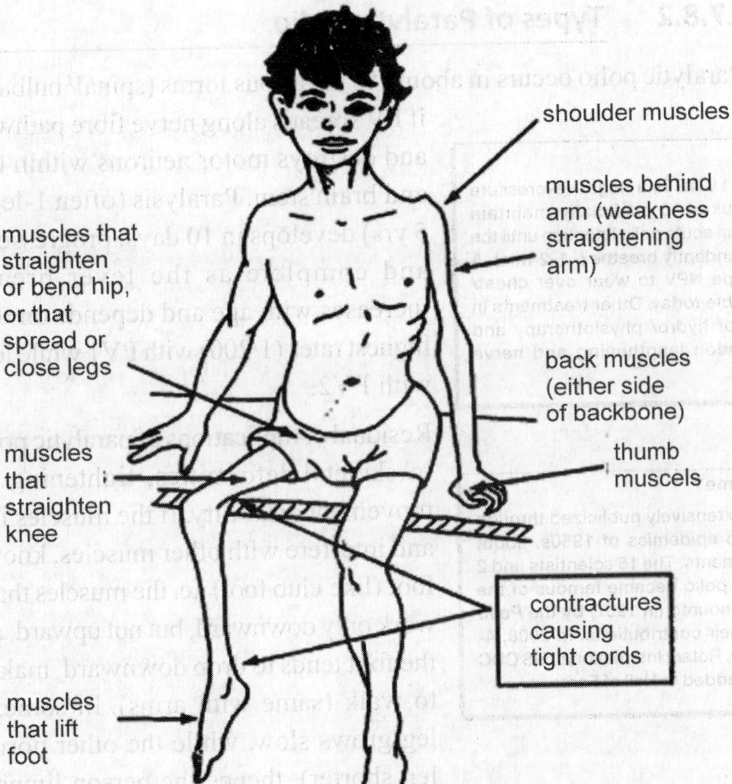

Fig. 17.9 Polio Symptoms

- PV3: a minor illness which does not involve CNS, also called abortive poliomyelitis.

All the 3-serotypes of PV are extremely virulent with same symptoms but preventable with the vaccine and boosters for travellers. After immunization with vaccine, IgA antibodies stop virus replication in the tonsils and gastrointestinal tract, while IgG and IgM antibodies prevent the spread. However, one serotype of PV does not provide immunity against the other, and full immunity to each serotype is essential.

In most people PV is asymptomatic. Rarely, symptoms are seen in upper respiratory tract (sore throat & fever), gastro-intestinal (nausea, vomit, abdomen pain, constipation) and influenza-like illness (ILI). It causes the weakness to legs; many but not all fully recover. PV usually spreads (H-to-H) through mouth with food/ water but uncommon by infected saliva. Spread may be up to 6 wks even without symptoms.

Polio existed for 1000's of yrs- A polio victim in Egypt carving (1403–1365BC)

17.8.2 Types of Paralytic Polio

Paralytic polio occurs in about 1% in various forms (spinal/ bulbar/ bulbospinal) if PV spreads along nerve fibre pathways, replicates and destroys motor neurons within the spinal cord and brain stem. Paralysis (often 1-leg in children < 5 yrs) develops in 10 days; progresses for 2-3 days, and complete as the fever breaks. The risk increases with age and depends on the type of PV; highest rates (1/200) with PV1 while lowest (1/2000) with PV2.

Residual complications of paralytic polio often occur in skeletal deformities, tightening of joints and movement disability. If the muscles in the limb sag and interfere with other muscles, known as equinus foot (like club foot) i.e. the muscles that pull the toes, work only downward, but not upward, and eventually the foot tends to drop downward, making it difficult to walk (same with arms). In some, the affected leg grows slow, while the other normally (so one leg shorter), thence the person limps and leans to one side, leading to deformities of spine, osteoporosis and chance of bone fractures. It may cause loss of function of veins in legs, due to blood pool in paralyzed lower limbs.

O My God!

Iron Lung?

Historically, IRON LUNG is a negative-pressure ventilator (NPV) used to artificially maintain respiration during an acute polio infection until the patient can independently breathe (~1-2 wks). A modern jacket-type NPV to wear over chest/ abdomen is available today. Other treatments in history are electro/ hydro/ physiotherapy and surgeries like tendon lengthening and nerve grafting.

O My God!

Polio Hall of Fame?

The disease was extensively publicized through media during polio epidemics of 1950s, about scientific advancements. The 15 scientists and 2 laymen worked on polio became famous of the century and are honoured (in 1957) by the ***Polio Hall of Fame*** for their contributions. In 2008, 4-organizations (WHO, Rotary International, US CDC and UNICEF) were added to Hall of Fame

O My God!

The nerves affected by polio?

Critical nerves affected are *the glosso-pharyngeal nerve* (controls swallowing & throat functions, tongue movement & taste), *the vagus nerve* (controls over heart, intestines & lungs), and *the accessory nerve* (controls upper neck movement), the *trigeminal nerve and facial nerve* (controls cheeks, tear ducts, gums & muscles of face), leading to double vision, chewing difficulty & abnormal respiratory rate, depth & rhythm (finally respiratory arrest).

Spinal polio occurs by viral invasion of the motor neurons or the ventral (front) grey matter in spinal column.

Bulbar polio occurs in ~2% of cases if PV destroys nerves within the bulbar region (white matter connects cerebral cortex to brain stem) and weakens the muscles supplied by cranial nerves and show symptoms of encephalitis i.e. hard to breath, talk and swallow.

Bulbospinal Polio is found in 20% of all paralytic polio cases with both, bulbar and spinal symptoms, so named bulbospinal (or respiratory) polio. The virus affects upper part of cervical spinal cord to paralyze the diaphragm resulting in hard or impossible to breathe without ventilator and leads to paralysis of the arms/ legs and also affects throat and heart.

17.8.3 Transmission & Diagnosis

Polio is highly contagious via fecal-oral (intestinal) and oral-oral (oro-pharyngeal) routes through contaminated food/ water. It is seasonal in temperate climates, peak in summer with incubation of 1-3 wks, most infectious within a week and transmits until the virus remains in saliva or feces. After entering mouth, infects the pharynx and intestinal mucosa, then hijacks the host cells to replicate. It splits within gastrointestinal cells for a week and spreads to tonsils, intestines to multiply abundantly. Then it enters bloodstream to multiply and survive long up to 17 wks.

> **O My God!**
>
> **India is Polio-Free country from 2014?**
>
> If there are no cases of polio for 2 or more years in a country, it is declared as a polio-free. So far declared, polio-free are Americas (1994), Europe (2002), 37 Western Pacific countries, including China and Australia (2000). Despite eradication 10 yrs prior, an outbreak was confirmed in China in Sep 2011 (due to Pakistan). On 1st Sep 2015 WHO confirmed 2 cases of PV1 in Ukraine. The last case in the region was in India in Jan 2011 and since then, no cases reported in India, and so in Feb 2012 India was taken off the list of polio endemic countries. On Mar 27, 2014, WHO announced the eradication of polio in the South-East Asian Region, (11 nations), Bangladesh, Bhutan, Korea, India, Indonesia, Maldives, Myanmar, Nepal, Sri Lanka, Thailand and Timor-Leste. As of 2015, polio is endemic in only 2 countries: Pakistan and Afghanistan.

Diagnosing a stools or a swab of the pharynx and analyzing CSF taken by a lumbar puncture (spinal tap) reveals WBC & protein level. PCR amplification confirms "wild or vaccine type"

17.8.4 Prevention & Treatment

By early 20th century, the improvement in community sanitation, sewage disposal, public sanitation and water supplies etc. in developed countries drastically reduced the risk of paralytic polio infection.

No cure for polio but for relieving of symptoms and preventing complication by giving antibiotics for infections, analgesics for pain along with exercise and nutritious diet. Treatment needs long-term rehabilitation, physiotherapy, corrective shoes and sometimes surgery.

> **O My God!**
>
> **Post-Polio Syndrome (PPS)?**
>
> 25-50% paralytic polio recovered in childhood, after decades also, can develop symptoms like new muscle weakness and extreme fatigue, which is called post-polio syndrome (PPS). The risk of PPS is more with age by loss of neurons, the permanent residual impairment, and disuse/ overuse of neurons. It is not infectious to spread PV, but a slow progressive with no treatment

Most polio cases get only temporary paralysis and comeback in a month, but full recovery takes 6-8 months. Paralysis remaining for 1 year is likely to be permanent, though recovery of muscle strength is possible 1-1½ yr after infection.

17.8.5 Vaccine

Two vaccines are in use to induce immunity to polio, blocking H-to-H transmission of wild PV, thence protecting both individual and the community (so-called herd immunity). In fact, Hilary Koprowski developed the 1st polio vaccine on 27 Feb 1950, which was in use during 1950s. At University of Pittsburgh, Jonas Salk developed the inactivated polio vaccine (IPV) in monkey

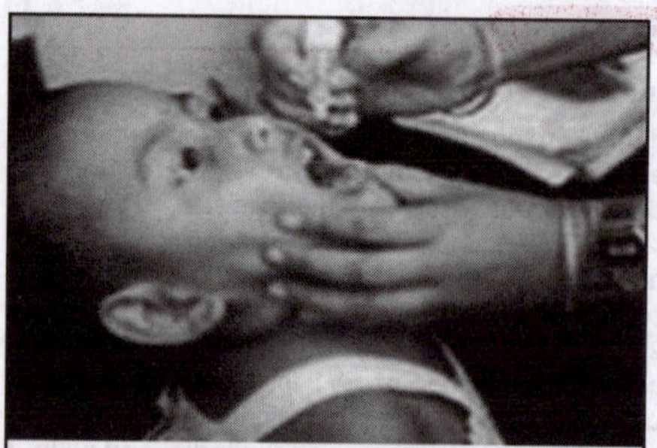

A child receives OPV

Drop Polio from the nation with a Drop of Polio vaccination

kidney tissue culture, inactivated with formalin, in 1952, announced to the world on 12 Apr 1955. After 2 doses (injection), 90% develop protective antibody to all 3 PVs, and at least 99% with 3 doses.

Albert Sabin in 1957 developed another live, oral polio vaccine (OPV), produced by the repeated passage of the virus through nonhuman cells at sub-physiological temperatures. OPV is the best choice to control polio as it is cheap, easy to use, and produces excellent immunity to all 3PVs in the intestine with single dose in about 50% of recipients while >95% with 3 doses.

World Polio Day (24 Oct) was established by Rotary International to commemorate the birth of Jonas Salk, who led the 1st team to develop the vaccine. Salk's IPV and Sabin's OPV led to establish Global Polio Eradication Initiative (GPEI) in 1988, which reduced polio worldwide by 99%.

17.9 HIV/AIDS (DIRECT CONTACT)

Human Immunodeficiency Virus (HIV) infection causes Acquired Immune Deficiency Syndrome (AIDS), prolonged and asymptomatic. The advanced stage hampers the immune system, increases the risk of opportunistic infections including TB (usual) to tumours (rare) and weight loss.

There are lot of fears and confusions about transmission of HIV/AIDS. The following table clarifies.

HIV / AIDS may be transmitted by	HIV / AIDS is not transmitted by

• Unprotected sex
• Hypodermic needles
• Contaminated blood transfusion
• Transplantation
• Mother to child during
  • Pregnancy
  • Delivery
  • Breastfeeding
	• Saliva
	• Tears
	• Kissing
	• Hugging
	• Biting
	• Coughing
	• Sneezing
	• Sharing plate/glass
	• Spitting
	• Using public toilet seat

Methods of prevention include safe sex, male circumcision, use of sterilized needles and careful blood transfusion and so forth. In case of disease transmitting from mother to child, both the mother and child have to be treated with antiretroviral medication, otherwise, the average survival time is 10 yrs.

In 2014 about 37 million people were living with HIV and resulted in 1.2 million deaths, most of them were from in sub-Saharan Africa. Since its discovery, it killed 39 million worldwide.

HIV/AIDS has a great impact on society in many ways, like public health, culture, economy and social discrimination. There are many misconceptions about HIV/ AIDS. It was topic of many controversies involving religion including the Catholic Church's decision not to support condom use as prevention.

17.9.1 Symptoms and Stages

Main symptoms of acute HIV infection and AIDS

There are 3 main stages of HIV infection: acute infection, clinical latency and AIDS.

Acute infection: The initial period (usually 1-2 weeks) from the contraction of HIV is called acute/ primary HIV or acute retroviral syndrome. It appears as an influenza-like illness. The symptoms in most cases are fever, throat inflammation, rash, headache, and/or sores of mouth and genitals. Gastrointestinal symptoms like nausea, vomiting or diarrhoea, neuropathy or Guillain-Barre syndrome also may occur.

The symptoms are not specific and often unable to identify. Even family doctor or regularly attended hospital often misdiagnose as one of the many

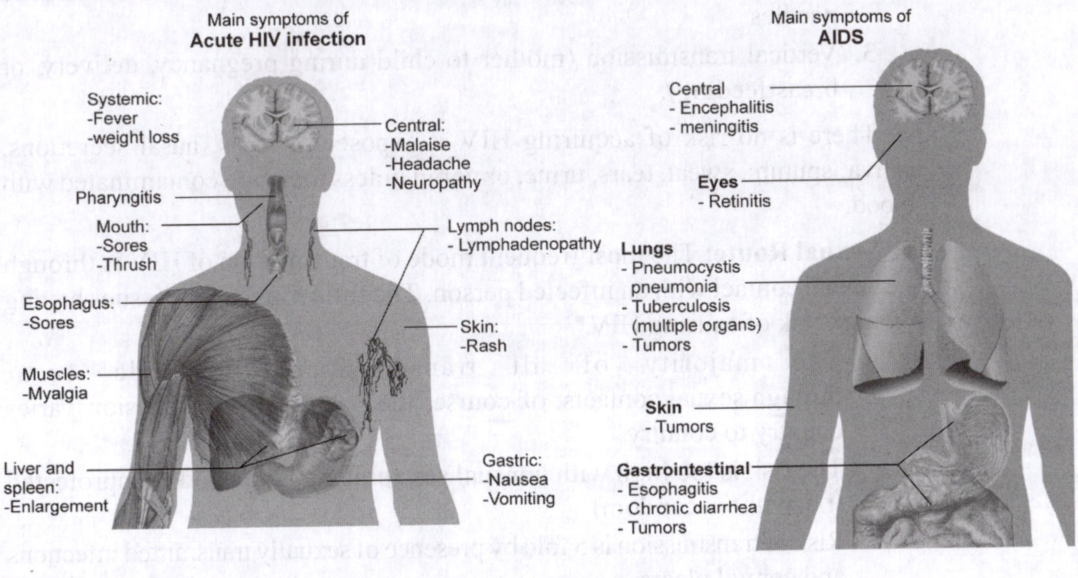

Fig. 17.10 Symptoms of HIV/AIDS.

common infections with overlapping symptoms. Therefore, the doctors and hospitals have taken it as a mandatory check up for any case to rule out HIV risk factors for the infection.

Clinical latency: The 2nd stage, called clinical latency, asymptomatic or chronic HIV, if untreated can live ~3-20 yrs (average 8 yrs). Either few or no symptoms at first, but at the end, many people experience fever, weight loss, gastrointestinal problems and muscle pains. About 50-70% of people experience non-painful enlargement of lymph nodes for over 3-6 months.

Acquired Immune Deficiency Syndrome (AIDS): AIDS is defined in terms of $CD4^{+}$ T cell count <200 cells/µL. If untreated, ~50% of HIV turns as AIDS within 10 yrs. The presence of AIDS can be suspected by pneumonia (40%), HIV wasting syndrome (20%), and candidiasis and recurring respiratory infections and diarrhoea (90%).

The immune deficiency may raise curtain for opportunistic infections, caused by bacteria, viruses, fungi, and parasites that are otherwise controlled by immune system. AIDS raises risk of developing various viral-induced cancers, including Kaposi's sarcoma, lymphoma and cervical cancer.

17.9.2 Transmission and Risk

HIV is transmitted by 3 routes:

1. Sexual contact (unprotected)
2. Body fluids or tissues including blood transfusion and use of unsterilized needles
3. Vertical transmission (mother to child during pregnancy, delivery, or breastfeeding).

There is no risk of acquiring HIV if exposed to feces, nasal secretions, saliva, sputum, sweat, tears, urine, or vomit unless these are contaminated with blood.

1. **Sexual Route:** The most frequent mode of transmission of HIV is through sexual contact with an infected person. The following are the issues having high risk of causing HIV.
   - The majority of all transmissions worldwide occur through sexual contacts; of course, the pattern of transmission varies country to country.
   - The risk is too high with unusual sex (oral/anal etc.) and if unprotected (i.e. without condom)
   - Risk of transmission is 5 fold by presence of sexually transmitted infections and genital ulcers

- The sexually transmitted diseases (STD), like Gonorrhoea, Chlamydia, Syphilis, Bacterial Vaginosis and Trichomoniasis also increase the risk of transmission.
- Commercial sex workers (including those involved in pornography) have higher rate of HIV.
- Rough sex is yet another factor to enhance risk of transmission.
- Sexual assault is also believed to carry greater risk of HIV transmission as condoms are rarely worn, physical trauma to the vagina or rectum is likely, and have a risk of concurrent STD.

2. **Body fluids Route:** The second most frequent mode is through blood and blood products. The following are various possibilities transmission in this mode
   - Blood or blood product transfusion from an infected person.
   - Body parts (such as eyes, kidney etc) transfusion from infected person.
   - Needle-sharing during intravenous drug use (risk is 2.4% per act).
   - Needle stick injury, (risk is 0.8% per act).
   - Medical injections or surgery with unsterilized equipment.
   - Contact of infected blood with cuts, burns, any opened up areas that oozes blood in body.
   - Mucous membrane exposure to infected blood (risk is 0.1% per act).
   - Invasive procedures in assisted delivery, and dental care.
   - Giving or receiving tattoos, piercings, and scarification are theoretically at risk of infection but no confirmed cases have been documented hither to.
   - It is not possible for mosquitoes or other insects to transmit HIV.

3. **Vertical Transmission (Mother-to-Child):** The third most common way in which HIV is transmitted from mother to child during
   - Pregnancy (risk 40%)
   - Delivery/Child birth (risk 20%)
   - Breast feeding (risk 40%)

When mother is detected with HIV, risk may be reduced by caesarean section, avoiding breastfeed, and treating newborn with antiretroviral.

O My God!

It is estimated that AIDS would kill more people this decade than all the wars and disasters in the past 50 yrs. So far, 25 million died and >40 million are with HIV/ AIDS (5 million in 2001 alone,). ~70% of HIV-infected are in sub-Sahara, Africa and in Zimbabwe and Botswana, >25% are of age group of 15-49. It is spreading rapidly in S. Asia, countries of former SU and Caribbean.

Criminal Transmission

Criminal transmission refers to intentional or deliberate or reckless infection of a person with the HIV. Some countries have laws that criminalize HIV transmission or exposure.

17.9.3 Diagnosis and Treatment

HIV screening is recommended for people of all ages. Currently, there is no cure or effective HIV vaccine. Hither to, the supposed most effective vaccine, RV 144-2009, (trials are still going on) found a success of 30% only. So, irrespective of CD4 count, Highly Active Anti-retroviral Therapy (HAART) is advised by the WHO for all ages including pregnant soon after the diagnosis. The desired outcome comes out long term.

Diet: The WHO recommends nutrient requirements in HIV/AIDS.

- A general healthy diet with micronutrient supplements and selenium.
- The vitamin A supplement in children to reduce mortality and improve growth.
- Higher intake of vitamin A, zinc, and iron can produce adverse effects. in adults, and so not recommended unless there is documented deficiency.
- Multivitamin supplement to improve pregnant/lactating women and the children.

17.9.4 Origin

The 3-African animals shown in the associated figure, (L to R: African Green Monkey, Sooty Mangabey and Chimpanzee) were the sources of SIV, HIV-2 and HIV-1 respectively. The unsafe medical practices in Africa after WW-II, such as unsterile reuse of syringes during mass vaccination, antibiotic and anti-malaria treatment, were causes of spread.

The epidemic rapidly spread among high-risk groups during late 1960's. Unexpected number of homosexuals developed a rare skin cancer, Kaposi's sarcoma whence, CDC of US formed a task force to monitor the outbreak. HIV/AIDS became a global pandemic by 2001.

O My God!

AIDS was called "4-H & GRID"?

In early days, the CDC did not officially name it AIDS, but termed it as "the 4H disease", since it seemed to affect Homosexuals, Hemophiliacs, Heroin users, and Haitians. However, the general press publicized the term "GRID", (Gay-Related Immune Deficiency). But after disproving it not just connected to gays, so, GRID was misleading, the term AIDS was proposed in Jul 1982, and CDC started referring to the disease as AIDS officially from Sep'82.

17.9.5 Misconceptions

There are many misconceptions about HIV and AIDS, which are untrue. The most common misconceptions which neither cause nor spread nor cure AIDS are given below.

- kissing
- sharing a glass/ plate
- coughing
- spitting
- using public toilet seat
- sneezing
- AIDS can spread through casual contact such as hand shake/hug
- Sexual intercourse with a virgin will cure AIDS (the most worst misconception)
- HIV can infect only gay men and drug user
- Any act of anal intercourse between two uninfected gay men
- Open discussion of HIV and homosexuality in schools leads to increased rates of AIDS.

SELF ASSESSMENT INTERMISSION (SAI – 17.3)

1. How is ebola caused? Explain its symptoms.
2. What are the precautions and treatments referred for persons infected by ebola?
3. How is ebola transmitted? What are various methods to prevent the spread?
4. Write a short note on ebola as a bio-weapon.
5. How is polio caused? Explain its mode of infection.
6. 'It infects only humans-No other animals', which disease is it? Explain.
7. What are the precautions/prevention and treatments for polio?
8. What are the different serotypes of polio? Briefly describe.
9. Explain different types of paralytic polios.
10. Write a short note on polio vaccination.
11. How is AIDS caused? Explain its mode of infection and various stages.
12. What are the prevention and treatments referred for persons infected with AIDS?
13. List out various possibilities of causing HIV/ AIDS through
    (a) sexual route (b) Body fluids route (c) vertical transmission.
14. What are the misconceptions about HIV/ AIDS?
15. Discuss about the discriminations of people with HIV/ AIDS in society.

17.10 CHIKUNGUNYA (VECTOR BORNE)

Chikungunya (means "that which bends up" in Makonde language,) is caused by the chikungunya virus with sudden fever 2-4 days after exposure and usually lasts 2-7 days, along with severe joint pains last for weeks or months, even sometimes years.

The disease was 1st described by Marion Robinson and W.H.R. Lumsden in 1955, following an outbreak in 1952 on the Makonde Plateau at the borders of Mozambique and Tanganyika (present Tanzania) in Africa, but 1st recorded outbreak is in 1779. Since 2004, the disease has occurred in outbreaks in Asia, Europe and Americas.

The virus transmits to humans by 2-species of mosquito of the genus *Aedes (A)* namely, *A. albopictus* and *A. aegypti*. Animals like monkeys, birds, cattle etc. act as reservoirs of the virus. The best way to prevent and control Chikungunya is to avoid mosquitoes and their bites. To some extent this is achieved through repellents, nets, fumes, sprays and so forth which can keep mosquitoes away. Though, no specific treatment is known, supportive care is recommended, including rest, fluids and medications to reduce fever and joint pain.

17.10.1 Causes and Symptoms

CHIKV, a member of *alphavirus* genus, is transmitted by arthropods in general and hence called arbovirus (**ar**thropod-**bo**rne virus), mosquitoes in particular. Although mosquito is the main medium of transmission, it may occur vertically also from mother to child during pregnancy or at birth. It can also occur via infected blood or organ transplantation, however, no such case is registered hither to. CHIKV spreads through bites of *Aedes(A)* mosquitoes, namely, *A. aegypti* (the most common vector) and *A. albopictus,* also called Asian Tiger Mosquito. Other potential transmitters are *A. furcifer-taylori*, *A. africanus*, and *A. Luteocephalus*.

Chikungunya virus in short called CHIKV, emerges within 12 days after a mosquito bite and may be asymptomatic also. In 70-90% of the cases, the symptoms are fever accompanied by strong joint pains (usually wrists, elbows, shoulders, knees, ankles, and all finger joints, muscles and ligaments) or stiffness and last for weeks or months, or even for years. The joint pain can be debilitating, often resulting in near immobility of the affected joints. In 40-50% of cases, maculopapular rash occurs after 2-5 days. In few cases, abdominal pain, nausea, vomiting or diarrhoea, may also occur. No surprise! Chronic CHIKV can induce arthralgia, arthritis and rheumatological diseases in long term.

Examples: After La Reunion outbreak-2006, 50% of 40+ age reported long-term musculoskeletal pain while in France 60% suffered from arthralgia 2-years after acute infection. In Italy, 66% of people reported muscle pains, joint pains, or asthenia after one year.

17.10.2 Diagnosis & Prevention

Acute high fever and severe joint pains indicate chikungunya and can be confirmed if the patient has travelled through or spent time in the potential areas within the last 12 days (the incubation period). However, a definitive test needs viral isolation, clinical tests and serological diagnosis, but it takes 1-2 wks and large amount of blood.

Since no approved vaccine exists, the best way is to prevent and protect against contact with such disease-carrying mosquitoes and/or control mosquito population by limiting their habitat. Mosquito control focuses ***eliminating the standstill waters*** where mosquitoes lay eggs and develop their larva; if elimination of the standstill water is not possible, insecticides/ germicides/ repellents or biological control agents such as DDT, PMD (p-menthane-3,8-diol, a substance derived from the lemon eucalyptus tree) can be spilled/sprayed provided they do not cause any chemical hazard. Wearing bite-proof long sleeves and trousers and treating garments with pyrethroids (e.g. mosquito coils/ scent) are also effective in protecting from mosquitoes.

Females Are Dangerous...But Not Males

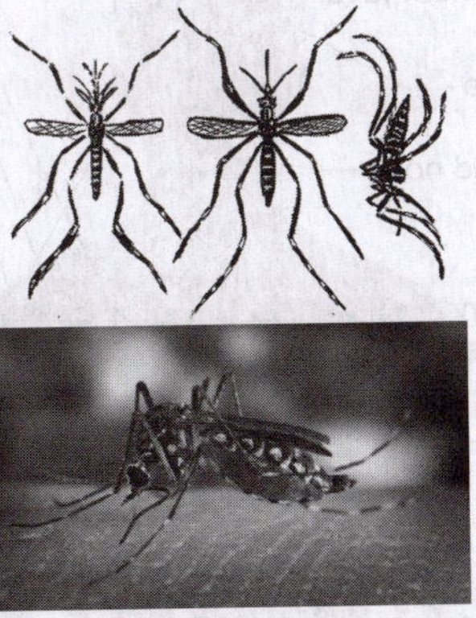

1. Adults of the yellow fever mosquito *A. aegypti*: The male is on the left, females are on the right. Only the female mosquito bites humans to transmit the disease. 2. Female *Aedes aegypti* feeding (squeezing).

17.10.3 Treatment

Strictly speaking, no specific treatment is available and supportive care is only alternative. Thence fever and joint swelling are treated with non-steroidal anti-inflammatory drugs such as Paracetamol and fluids, but not Aspirin (the risk of bleeding) and Corticosteroids (cause immune-suppression and can worsen). Analgesics can be a simple solution for partial symptom relief.

17.10.4 Biological Weapon

Chikungunya was one of more than a dozen researched as potential biological weapons.

17.11 DENGUE FEVER (VECTOR BORNE)

> **Zika or Dengue!**
> After the detection of Zika virus in Brazil in April 2015, (the 1st ever in the Western Hemisphere), it is now thought that some Chikungunya and Dengue cases could in fact be Zika virus cases or co-infections.

Perhaps! The Spanish word *dengue*, derived from *dinga* (Swahili phrase *Ka-dinga pepo*, means caused by an evil spirit). W. Indian slaves with dengue were said to have the posture and gait of a dandy and so the disease was also known as *dandy fever*. The term *break-bone fever* was used by Benjamin Rush, US Founding Father in 1789 referring to 1780 epidemic in Philadelphia. Other names read in the history are, *breakheart fever, la dengue, infectious thrombocytopenic purpura*, and *Philippine/ Thai/ Singapore hemorrhagic fever.*

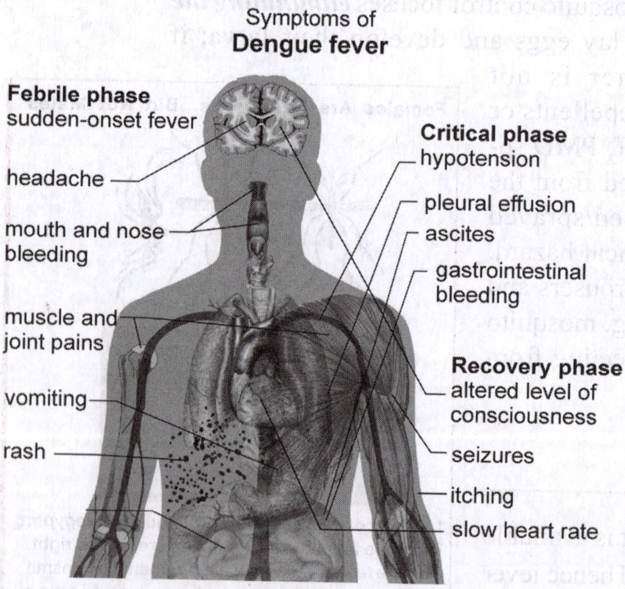

Fig. 17.11 Symptoms of Dengue fever.

17.11.1 Dengue Fever – Dengue Virus

It is a mosquito-borne infectious tropical disease caused due to dengue virus (in short DENV) whose symptoms appear in 3-15 days after infection as high fever, headache, vomiting, muscle/ joint pains, and a typical rash. Recovery takes < 2-7 days; rarely, turns as fatal *dengue hemorrhagic fever* (bleeding, reduced platelets and blood plasma leakage), or *dengue shock syndrome* (dangerously low BP)

17.11.2 Causes & Symptoms

DENV, the cause for dengue fever is spread by several species of mosquito of *Aedes* type (mainly *A. Aegypti*). This virus is found in 5 varieties; surprisingly, infection with one type usually immunes lifelong to that type, but only short-term immunity to the others. Hence, subsequent infection with another type increases the risk of severe complications.

> **O My God!**
>
> **ARBOVIRUS means ARthropod-BOrne VIRUS**
>
> DENV is an RNA virus of the family *Flaviviridae*; genus *Flavivirus*. Other members of the same genus cause yellow fever, Omsk hemorrhagic fever West Nile, St. Louis encephalitis, Japanese encephalitis, tick-borne encephalitis and Kyasanur forest disease. Most are transmitted by arthropods (mosquitoes or ticks) and are so named arboviruses.

Mostly dengue virus is asymptomatic (80%) and the incubation ranges from 3-14 days, but often within a week. So, travellers returning from endemic areas are unlikely to think of dengue. Symptoms in children are similar to those of the common cold and gastroenteritis (vomiting and diarrhoea).

The symptoms of dengue start suddenly with fever, headache (typically located behind the eyes), muscle and joint pains and a rash. The *breakbone fever* is so named owing to its associated muscle and joint pains. The infection process can be understood by dividing into 3-phases:

1. Febrile phase
2. Critical phase
3. Recovery phase

1. **Febrile phase:** High fever around 104°F (40°C) along with body pains and headache usually for 2-7 days, nausea and vomits and in 50–80% cases measles-like rash occurs (flushed skin on 1st/ 2nd day and later as rash) like "white islands in a red sea".
2. **Critical phase:** Fever resolves; leakage of plasma from blood vessels for 1-2 days and fluid accumulates in chest and abdomen, low blood supply to vital organs. So, gastrointestinal organs dysfunction and severe bleeding may occur.
3. **Recovery phase**: This occurs when the leaked fluid into bloodstream gets absorbed within 2-3 days. This is often associated with severe itching and a slow heart rate. However, another rash may occur either maculopapular or vasculitic followed by peeling of skin. Fatigue lasts for weeks.

If recovery does not take place, the low blood circulation lowers B.P. and insufficient blood supply to the vital organs such as liver, kidneys, head etc. Further, dysfunction of the bone marrow due to infection leads to reduced platelets that are essential for blood clotting, thence raises other complications.

17.11.3 Transmission

Dengue is transmitted through

(i) Mosquito (*Aedes*) bite (major contributor)
(ii) Infected blood transfusion
(iii) Infected organs transplantation.
(iv) Vertical transmission (mother to child) during pregnancy or at birth
(v) Other (person-to-person) modes of transmission (rare)

> **O My God!**
>
> **Mosquitoes have a time to bite?**
>
> Yes! Specific timings are maintained by mosquitoes.
>
> 1. Anopheles bites only in the nights but not days. This night biter carries Bactaria (M. Palcifarum) that causes Malaria.
> 2. Aides Aegypti/ Albopictus bite during the daytime. These day-biters are the carriers of CHICKV, DENV, YF and ZIKV to cause Chikungunya, Dengue, Yellow and Zika fever.
> 3. Culex bites only between 6pm to 9pm which carries nematodes (parasites) to cause phylariasis/ elephantiasis or JEV to cause Japanese Encephalitis

Though *Aedes Aegypti* (originated from Africa) is the chief transmitter of Dengue, the other *Aedes* species such as *A. albopictus*, *A. polynesiensis* and *A. scutellaris*, can also carry DENV. These are found between the latitudes of 35°N and 35°S up to a height of 1km (3300 ft) above the earth. They usually bite during the early morning and in the evening, but they may also bite any time of day. Humans get infected even by a single bite and host the virus.

A *female* mosquito takes a blood meal from a dengue infected person, (during the initial 2–10 day febrile phase) and becomes itself infected. After 8–10 days, the virus spreads all over the tissues of mosquito including its salivary glands. When the mosquito takes another blood meal, it releases some enzyme into human skin so as the blood will not clot. During this process, virus enters human body and spreads, Surprisingly, the virus has no effect on the mosquito, though remains infected for life. *A. aegypti* lays its eggs on stagnated waters and artificial water containers (e.g. small disposable tea-cups) and live in close proximity to humans.

17.11.4 Diagnosis

It is very difficult to differentiate from other viral infections. Usually dengue is suspected with the symptoms of fever plus two or more of the following:

- High temperature (fever)
- Nausea and vomiting
- Rash
- Generalized pains
- Low WBC count
- Low platelet count
- Positive tourniquet test

> **O My God!**
>
> **June-15: International Anti-Dengue Day**
>
> June 15 is observed to be the International Anti-Dengue Day, with the goals to increase public awareness, mobilize resources for its prevention and control and, to demonstrate the Asian region's commitment in tackling the disease. The idea was agreed in series of meetings, with the first event held in Jakarta (2010), Indonesia (2011), Yangon, Myanmar (2012) and Vietnam (2013).

- Other warning signs
- Worsening abdominal pain
- Continuous vomiting
- Liver enlargement
- Mucosal bleeding
- Lethargy or restlessness
- Serosal effusions

Dengue fever and Chikungunya are so similar viral infections with many same symptoms that it is very difficult to distinguish. Even malaria, leptospirosis, viral hemorrhagic fever, typhoid fever, measles, meningococcal disease, influenza, Zika fever also have similar symptoms. Hence, the test for low WBC count, low platelets and metabolic acidosis are better ways to confirm the dengue. The WHO in 2009 categorized dengue as uncomplicated and severe. Severe dengue is associated with bleeding, organ dysfunction or plasma leakage and all other cases are uncomplicated.

17.11.5 Prevention and Control

Efforts by the WHO: Prevention depends on controlling and protecting from the mosquito bites. The WHO advises Integrated Vector Control program consisting of 5 elements:

1. Advocacy, social mobilization and legislation to strengthen public health bodies and communities
2. Collaboration between the health and other sectors (public and private)
3. An integrated approach to disease control to maximize use of resources
4. Evidence-based decision making to ensure any interventions are targeted appropriately and
5. Capacity-building to ensure an adequate response to the local situation.

Initiatives by Government/communities/societies

- Educate the people to practice cleanliness, particularly those who live in endemic areas.
- Control Mosquito (*A. aegypti*) by eliminating its habitats.
- Get rid of open sources of water.
- Spill insecticides or biological control agents to the areas of stagnated water.
- Spray with organophosphate or pyrethroid or suitable insecticides.
- Reduce open collections of water through environmental modification.
- Give the concern for negative health effects from insecticides.

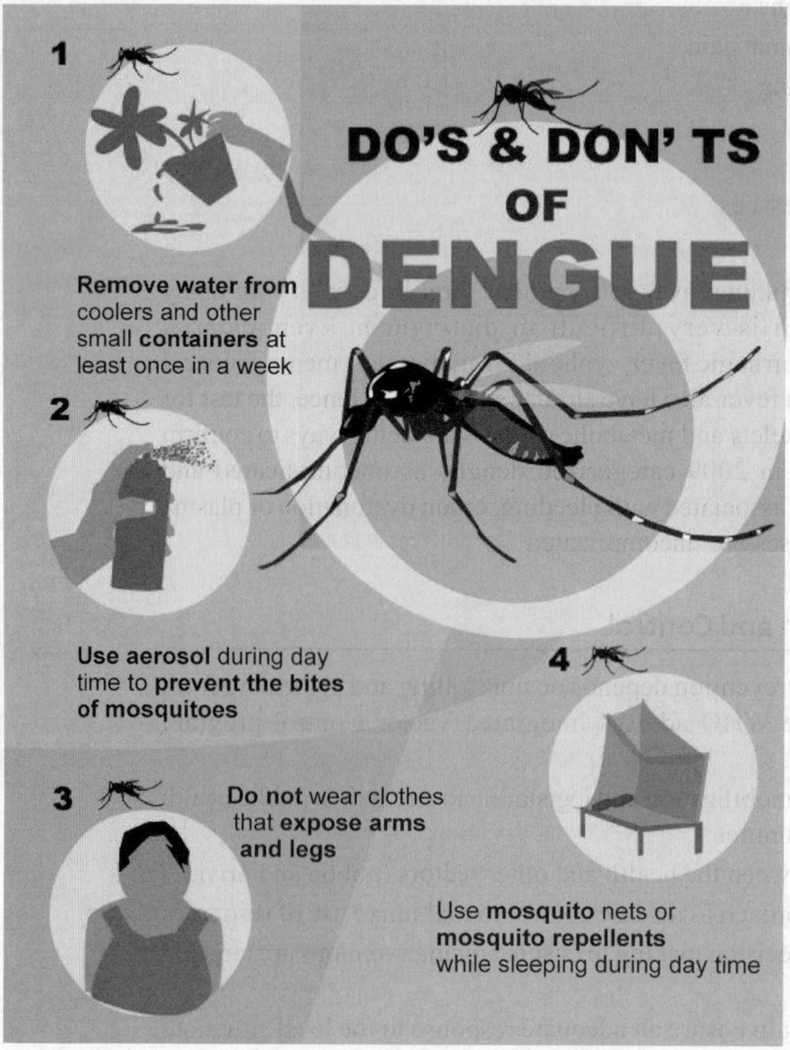

Fig. 17.12 DO's & DONT's of Dengue.

Responsibilities of People (individuals)

- Keep the surroundings and environment clean.
- Wear clothing that fully covers the skin.
- Use mosquito netting while resting/sleeping.
- Spread/diffuse mosquito repellent fumes.
- Apply insect repellent (DEET is most effective).

17.11.6 Treatment/Management

> **O My God!**
>
> **Vaccine for Dengue!**
>
> Though, a vaccine for dengue, (Dengvaxia produced by Sanofi) is made available in Mexico, Philippines, and Brazil in early 2016, as of now (2016) there is no commercially available vaccine, particularly in India. The ongoing research trials through infecting the mosquito population with bacteria of the *Wolbachia* genus are quite encouraging to dengue virus resistance.

In fact, there are no specific antiviral drugs for dengue, maintaining proper fluid balance is only better way. The treatment depends on the symptoms and warning signs.

- Those who are able to drink, pass urine, have no "warning signs" and are otherwise healthy can be managed at home with daily follow up and oral rehydration therapy.
- Those who have other health problems have "warning signs" and so, be careful.
- Those who cannot manage regular follow up should be cared in hospital.
- In those with severe dengue care should be provided in an area where there is access to an intensive care unit (ICU).

Paracetamol (acetaminophen) should only be used for fever. Better blood transfusion rather than waiting, in case of unstable vitals of a decreasing *hematocrit*.

17.12 JAPANESE ENCEPHALITIS OR JE (VECTOR BORNE)

Encephalitis is sudden inflammation of brain with symptoms as headache, fever, confusion, drowsiness, and fatigue, sometimes even seizures or convulsions, tremors, hallucinations, stroke, and memory problems. The word is from Greek, *enképhalos* (brain), of *en* (=in) and, *kephalé* (= head, even in Sanskrit-Kapaala), with medical suffix *–itis* (=inflammation).

Japanese Encephalitis (JE), is mosquito-borne (*Culex tritaeniorhynchus* and *Culex vishnui*) Japanese encephalitis virus (JEV) from the family Flaviviridae (closely related to West Nile virus). Horses, domestic pigs and wild birds are reservoirs while transmission to humans may be serious.

17.12.1 Symptoms and Diagnosis

JEV has an incubation of 5-15 days and mostly asymptomatic; only 0.04% infections develop into encephalitis. Fever (100–105°F or 38–41°C), headache and malaise are other non-specific symptoms may last for 1-6 days. Acute stage may have stiff neck, convulsions and mental retardation. Lifelong neurological defects such as deafness, nausea, and swelling of the testicles may occur.

Antibodies in serum and CSF by IgM capture, ELISA is usually detectable in 3-8 days but persist for 1-3 months. Other clinical tests are...

- Brain scan, MRI to check inflammation and differentiate from other possible causes.
- EEG, in monitoring brain activity, encephalitis will produce abnormal signal.
- LP (spinal tap) helps determine via testing CSF, obtained from the lumbar region.
- Blood test and Urine analysis

In fatal cases, nucleic acid amplification and virus culture of autopsy tissues can be used.

17.12.2 Prevention and Treatment

Vaccine is available for JE, but contraindication to Pertussis immunization is to be observed. Currently 3-vaccines based on the genotype III virus, are available: SA14-14-2, IC51 ChimeriVax-JE. In Sep-2012 the Indian firm Biological E. Ltd has launched an inactivated cell culture derived vaccine based on SA 14-14-2 strain.

There is no specific treatment, but need support for feeding, breathing or seizure control. It is not transmitted from person to person and so no need to isolate and following drugs help.

- Antiviral drugs (if virus is cause)
- Antibiotics (if bacteria is cause)
- Acetaminophen for fever
- Sedatives for restlessness
- Steroids to reduce brain swell
- Physical therapy (if brain is affected post-infection)

Rural endemic locations are at high risk, but not urban areas. Some countries experienced JE epidemics, but controlled by vaccination, like China, S. Korea, Japan, Taiwan and Thailand while, periodic epidemics are still occurring in Vietnam, Cambodia, Myanmar, India, Nepal and Malaysia. Human, cattle, horses and swine act as an amplifying host. Infection in swine is asymptomatic.

O My God!

Asia is at Risk of YF?

In Mar 2016, China confirmed the 1st imported case in a 32-yr man who had been to Angola during an ongoing outbreak of YF. On 28, Mar 2016, ProMED-mail issued a warning that the YF outbreak might spread further and the countries where dengue and the mosquito vector prevail are at risk. Beware! Authorities are warning that a spread to Asia could be more serious since vaccine stockpiles are insufficient.

17.12.3 Other Types of Encephalitis

1. Viral Encephalitis
2. Bacterial Encephalitis
3. Limbic encephalitis
4. Autoimmune encephalitis
5. Encephalitis lethargic

17.13 YELLOW FEVER (VECTOR BORNE)

Carlos Finlay

Walter Reed

Yellow Fever (YF) belonging to *Flavivirus*, is spread by the bite of an infected female mosquito of *Aedes aegypti* species (vector of ZIKV, CHIKV & DENV also). The disease is difficult to identify, unless the blood sample is tested with PCR. Though, safe and effective vaccine against YF is available, reducing the transmitter mosquito is the best way to prevent.

YF is common in tropical areas (S. America and Africa), fortunately not in Asia. Yearly, it is infecting 2 lakh of which 30,000 fatal (nearly 90% in Africa)

17.13.1 Cause and Symptoms

In 1881, Dr. Carlos Finlay (Cuba) proposed YF as mosquito borne but not by direct human contact. Ezekiel Stone Wiggins, the Ottawa Prophet, proposed in 1888, was astronomical. Finally, huge loss of lives of soldiers due to YF, during the Spanish–American War (1890s), compelled Walter Reed to prove Finlay's "mosquito hypothesis" in 1900. YF was the 1st virus shown to be transmitted by mosquitoes. Though *Aedes aegypti*, is main, the tiger mosquito (*A. albopictus*) can also act as vector of arboviruses. The physician William Gorgas applied these concepts and eradicated YF from Havana (along with malaria) during construction of Panama Canal.

Symptoms of YF appear within 3-6 days, causing a mild infection with fever, headache, chills, back pain, fatigue, loss of appetite, muscle pain, nausea and vomiting, which last only 3-4 days and about 15% cases enter a toxic 2nd phase with recurring fever, along with jaundice due to liver damage and abdominal pain, bleeding in the mouth, eyes, and gastrointestinal tract will cause blood vomits, hence called, *vomito negro* (= black vomit in Spanish). Mortality exceeds

O My God!

Do you Support Deforestation?

According to the historian McNeill, ecologic disruption caused by sugar plantations created the conditions for mosquito and viral reproduction and subsequent outbreaks of YF. Deforestation reduced insectivorous bird populations and other creatures that fed mosquitoes and their eggs

O My God!

Napoleon gave up war to YF!

During the Napoleon Wars, postings for soldiers to W. Indies were nightmares due to YF. To recoup France's New World Empire, and to regain control on sugar trade in St. Domingue (Hispaniola), Napoleon sent an army led by his brother-in-law to control after a slave revolt. The historian J.R. McNeill wrote that YF claimed about 45000 lives of forces during the war. Only 1/3rd troops could return to France. Napoleon gave up and Haiti declared independence in 1804 as the 2nd republic in Western Hemisphere.

50%, in severe epidemics, but ***surviving the infection provides lifelong immunity***, and normally there is no permanent organ damage.

17.13.2 Transmission & Diagnosis

The process of virus entering from mosquito to human is same as that of dengue (DENV) disease. Epidemiologically, there are 3-different infection transmission cycles from mosquitoes to humans, particularly in Africa and S. America. These are:

A. Urban Cycle

B. Intermediate or Savannah Cycle

C. Jungle or Forest or Sylvatic Cycle

A. Urban Cycle involves only the YF mosquito i.e. *A. Aegypti*, which is well adapted to urban areas and can also transmit other diseases, such as Zika, Dengue and Chikungunya. The urban cycle is responsible for the major outbreaks of YF in Africa.

B. Intermediate or Savannah cycle occurs between the jungle and urban cycles. Different mosquitoes of the genus *Aedes* are involved. In recent years, this has been the most common form of transmission of YF in Africa.

C. Jungle or Forest or Sylvatic cycle is present, where *Aedes Africanus* (in Africa), mosquitoes of the genus *Haemagogus* & *Sabethes* (in S. America) serve as vectors. In the forest, the mosquitoes infect non-human primates, which infect the people in the jungle who carry the virus to urban areas, where *A. aegypti* acts as a vector. Thus YF cannot be eradicated due to jungle cycle. In S. America, the forest cycle is the only way to infect humans.

The virus growth in blood culture can be observed, but it takes 1-4 weeks. However, reverse transcription PCR can confirm. But it also takes 6-10 days. Liver biopsy can verify inflammation and detect viral antigens, but, due to the bleeding tendency, it is only advisable for *post mortem* to confirm the cause of death. Of course! Other viral fevers, like Ebola must be excluded to confirm.

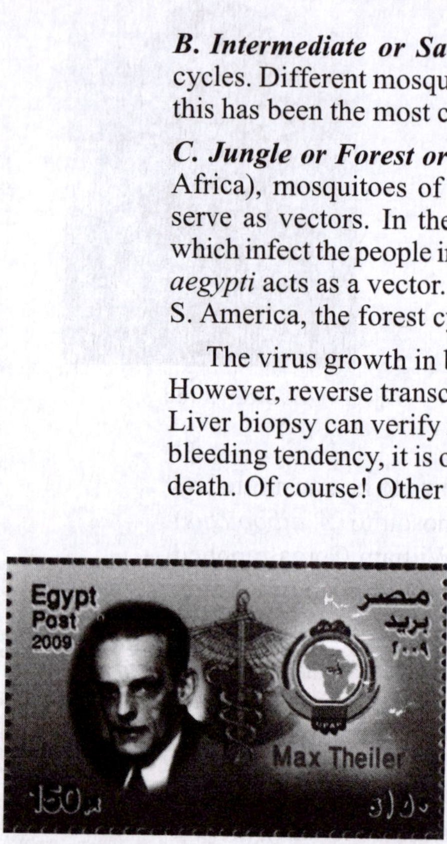

17.13.3 Prevention and Vaccination

Though vaccination is available, avoidance of mosquito bites is better way, particularly, in areas where YF is endemic, because, a vaccination can protect only YF while mosquito control can save total area.

The vaccine 17D, widely used by the US Army during WW-II, was developed by S. African microbiologist

Max Theiler (Nobel Prize in 1951) at Rockefeller Institute, NY by culturing in chicken eggs. A French team also developed French Neurotropic Vaccine (FNV) from mouse brain tissue, but not recommended due to incidences of encephalitis. The vaccine eradicated in S. America (urban cycle), but was unsuccessful in Africa (sylvatic cycle). In 2013, the WHO stated, "a single dose vaccine is sufficient for life-long immunity against YF."

If infected, hospitalization and intensive care is necessary owing to rapid deterioration. Rehydration and pain relief with paracetamol, but not Acetylsalicylic acid (aspirin) is advisable.

17.13.4 Vector Control and Treatment

Control of *A. aegypti* is essential, especially because the same mosquito can also transmit dengue and chikungunya. It breeds preferentially ***in water, in domestic waste, tires, cans, plastic bottles and used improperly disposed tea-cups.***

Two main strategies are employed to reduce mosquito populations.

(i) to kill the developing larvae, using larvicides, larvae-eating fish and copepods

(ii) to reduce populations of the adult YF mosquito using insecticide-treated mosquito nets, curtains and lids of water tanks are effective.

17.14 ZIKA VIRUS (VECTOR BORNE)

ZIKa Virus (ZIKV) also belongs to *Flaviviridae* family and *Flavivirus* genus, related to yellow fever, dengue, Japanese encephalitis and West Nile virus, spread by ***daytime-active*** *Aedes* mosquitoes, such as *A. aegypti* and *A. albopictus*. It is named after the Zika Forest of Uganda, where the virus was 1st isolated in 1947 by the scientist of Yellow Fever Research Institute. Since 1950s, it is limited to a narrow equatorial belt of Afro-Asia, but during 2007-2016, it spread eastward, across Pacific Ocean to the Americas, and by 2015–16 Zika reached pandemic levels. The reason for the pandemic is perhaps urbanization and globalization.

Zika Rash on arm

17.14.1 Symptoms & Diagnosis

Zika fever often causes no or only mild symptoms. Symptoms (if appear) could be fever, red eyes, joint pain, headache, and rash, which last less than a week. No deaths reported yet with initial infection.

The presence of Zika virus can be determined by testing the blood, urine, or saliva when the person is sick. As of 2016, there is neither specific treatment to cure nor any vaccine nor preventive medicine, but paracetamol and rest may help. Admission to hospital is rarely necessary.

17.14.2 Transmission

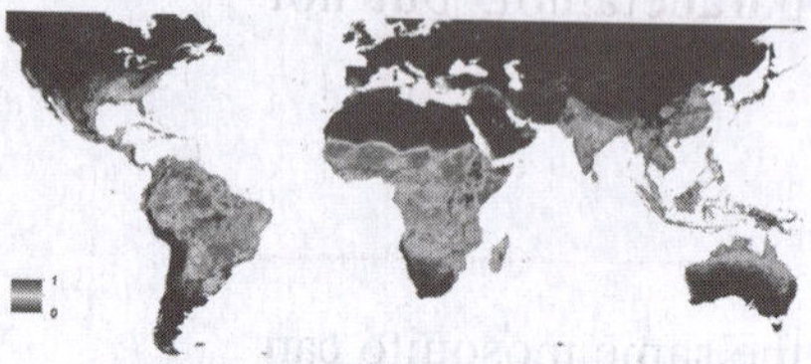

A. aegypti occurrence distribution (Blue=none, Red=highest)

The transmission cycle is similar to those of CHIKV, DENV and YFV & even mosquito is also same. In addition to mosquito borne, ZIKV can also be transmitted horizontally (intercourse) as well as vertically (mother to child) that can result in severe brain malformation, microcephaly & other birth defects in children and rarely Guillain–Barré syndrome (GBS) in adults.

O My God!

Zika can live in Semen?

In 2014, ZIKV was found in the semen at least 2-weeks (possibly up to 10 weeks also) after a man fell ill with Zika fever. In 2011 a US biologist bitten many times while studying mosquitoes in Senegal, developed symptoms after 6-days returning and his wife not travelled outside the US, also caught ZIKV in few days, raising the doubt of sexual transmission and it is found true. In early Feb 2016, it is reported that a man from Texas not travelled abroad, but infected after his male monogamous sexual partner had anal penetrative sex with him a day before and after onset of symptoms. As of Feb 2016, 14 such cases are investigated, but it is not known if women can transmit ZIKV to their sexual partners.

Mosquito: Zika is basically spread by the day-biter female *A. aegypti*, researchers found other Aedes genus such as *A. albopictus*, (the tiger mosquito), *A. africanus*, *A. apicoargenteus*, *A. furcifer*, *A. hensilli*, etc., and also even *Anopheles coustani*, *Mansonia uniformis*, *Culex perfuscus*,

Sexual: Zika can be transmitted from a man or woman to their sexual partners. The virus is infectious for longer period (2-10 weeks) when it is via semen. As of April 2016 sexual transmission of Zika has been documented in 6-countries during the 2015 outbreak.

In March 2016, the CDC updated its recommendations about precautions for couples, and advised that heterosexual couples with men confirmed with ZIKV or its symptoms must use condoms or not involve in penetrative sex (i.e., vaginal intercourse, anal intercourse, or fellatio) for at least 6 months after symptoms begin. This includes men who live in or visited the areas with Zika. Men who traveled, even if not developed symptoms of Zika, should use condoms or not have sex for at least 8 weeks after their return in order to minimize risk.

Pregnancy: ZIKV can spread from an infected mother to her foetus during pregnancy or at delivery.

Blood transfusion: As of April 2016, 2-cases of Zika transmission through blood transfusions are reported from Brazil, after which the US-FDA recommended to screen blood donors for 4 wks.

17.14.3 Prevention and Treatment

Prevention involves avoiding mosquito bites and proper use of condoms. Efforts to prevent bites include the use of insect repellent, covering much of the body with clothing, mosquito nets, and getting rid of standing water where mosquitoes reproduce.

Women in affected zones by the 2015–16 Zika outbreaks are advised to put off pregnancy and pregnant women not to travel to these areas.

SELF ASSESSMENT INTERMISSION (SAI – 17.4)

1. What are vector borne viral epidemic diseases? Describe any one of your choice.
2. How is Chickungunya caused? Explain its mode of infection.
3. What are the causes and symptoms of chickungunya?
4. Discuss the diagnosis, prevention and treatments for chickungunya epidemic?
5. What are various methods to prevent the spread of dengue?
6. How is dengue caused? Explain its mode of infection and various stages.
7. What are the precautions/prevention and treatments for dengue?
8. How is Japanese Encephalitis (JE) caused? Explain its mode of infection.
9. What are the symptoms and causes of Japanese Encephalitis (JE)? What prevention and treatments do you refer to a person infected with JEV?
10. Distinguish between day biters and night biters among mosquitoes. Explain each briefly.
11. What are the causes of yellow fever? What are the symptoms and causes?
12. List and explain the cycles of yellow fever spread? Give the preventive methods.
13. What are the symptoms and causes of Zika fever?
14. How is Zika transmitted? What are various modes of transmission? What prevention and treatments do you suggest?
15. Write a short note on Aedes Aegypti with reference to its activities as reservoir, transmitter of various diseases.

MINI-PROJECTS / CASE STUDIES

1. Adopt two or three villages in your vicinity and conduct awareness camps on causes, and precautions to be taken for various diseases such as HIV/AIDS, Measles, Flu etc. Prepare a questionnaire to interview some people on misconceptions. Clearly explain them the truths and myths.

2. Conduct some awareness camps or workshops on sanitation and best health practices.

Summary of Biohazards – Viral Epidemics					
Disease	**Symptoms**	**Causes**	**Carrier**	**Effect**	**Treatment**
Measles	Cough, Sneeze Runny nose, Inflamed Eyes Followed by a red, flat rash on face and body	Measles Virus	Airborne	Occur in about 30% with diarrhoea causes blindness, inflammation of brain, pneumonia	No specific treatment
Small pox	Attacks mouth and Nose	Variola major/ minor virus vaccinia, cowpox and monkey pox virus	Air borne	Effects on respiratory mucosa and migrates to lymph nodes. Effects on blood steam bone marrow and lymph nodes	Vaccina virus
Chicken pox	skin rash, itchy blisters, scabs on chest, back, face & all over body	Varicella Zoster Virus (VZV)	Air borne	Fever, tiredness and headache (children/ pregnants more vulnerable)	Vaccinate 1st dose for neonates, 2nd dose 5th yr. Treat with antiviral drugs
Ebola virus	Muscle &joint pains	Ebola virus	Direct contact	Effects on functioning of liver & kidneys	Trial vaccine VSV-EBOV
Poliomyelitis (or) Polio PV1/PV2/PV3	Major illness	Polio virus	Direct contact	Effects on central nervous system	Live oral polio vaccine(OPV)
HIV/AIDS	Acute infection, rash, fever	Human Immuno-deficiency Virus	Direct contact	Hampers immune system	HIV screening, Anti retroviral therapy
Chikungunya	Sudden fever	Chikungunya virus	Vector borne	Effects wrists, elbow, shoulder	Non – steroidal, anti-inflammatory drugs
Swine flu H1N1/H2N2/ H3N3	Diarrhoea, nausea, vomits	Swine influenza virus	Air borne	Effects on respiratory tracts, kidneys &leads to neuro problems	Flu vaccination
Dengue fever	Fever, head ache	Flavi virus	Vector borne	Causes bone fever	CYD-TDV vaccine
Yellow fever	Fever, fatigue, loss of appetite	Flavi virus	Vector borne	Effects on liver/ kidneys leading to jaundice	Yellow fever vaccine(live)
Zika fever	Fever, headache, skin rash	Zika virus	Vector borne	Effects on muscles and joints	Zika virus vaccine

CHAPTER 18

Mruthyormaa Amrutham Gamaya

The Response, Rescue and Mitigation

O'MY SILENT INNER VIBES (O'M S I V – 18)

There was a great devotee, living in a small village. Once, that village was attacked by tremendous floods. The government had announced evacuation and asked everyone to leave the village immediately. Everybody was leaving with fear except the devotee, who said, "The God comes to save me. I have faith". As the water level rising up, a bus came to evacuate the villagers; the devotee refused and said, "The God comes to save me. I have faith." As the water level rising up more, he climbed a big wall of his house then a boat came to him to save. Again he refused and said "The God comes to save me. I have faith". The water level rising up further, he climbed the roof of his house. This time a helicopter came to rescue him, but he said, "The God comes to save me. I have faith". Finally, he got drowned. When he reached the Lord, he burst into tears and questioned. "Why didn't you come to save me? I had a full faith in you", the Lord replied with a smile, "Who do you think that the bus, the boat and the helicopter sent to you?"

The moral of the story is that the God is there everywhere. He is Omnipresent, Omniscient, and Omnipotent. He may come in any form may it be living thing or non-living thing to rescue you, if you have faith. But, without human effort, even the God cannot save you. In fact, the human effort itself is the form of God.

Lord Sri Krishna says,
(In the Verse 7 and 8, Chapter 4)
The Gnyana Yoga of Bhagavad-Gita,
Yada yada hi dharmasya glanirbhavati bharata
Abhyuthanamadharmasya tadatmanam srijamyaham
Paritranaya sadhunang vinashay cha dushkritam
Dharmasangsthapanarthay sambhavami yuge yuge
The meaning of these two verses (slokas) is-
Whenever there is decay of righteousness, O Bharata!
And when there is exaltation of unrighteousness, and then I Myself come forth;
For the complete protection of the good, for the total destruction of evil-doers,
For the sake of firmly establishing the righteousness, I am born from age to age.

I have been listening to this meaning of the verses, but never observed keenly. But today, some vibes are inherently produced silently inside my heart to understanding the verses as :

1. *Yada-Yadahi* means whenever; This indicates that the God comes not just 'when' needed, but every time 'whenever' needed
2. *Abhyuthanamadharmasya*, here, *Adharma* (unrighteousness) *Uthanam* (means bouncing) is sufficient to use; but it was told *Abhyuthanam,* which stresses that it is exalting. (God will not come just for every small issue, but comes when it is a disaster)
3. *Paritranaya,* here *tranaya* (saving) could make equal sense, but it is not just saving, it is more than that i.e. 'Complete Protection'
4. *Vinashay*, which means 'total destruction', but not simple *nashay* (destruction)

(Continued)

5. *Dharma Sangsthapanarthay,* here, *Sthapana* (installation) could have been enough, but it is *Sangsthapana*, which means establish, but not just install the *dharma* (righteousness)

So, now we can analyze the above verses, and can be applied to the present context.

For example, if you are not well, say feverish, you don't generally bother to visit doctor than taking a little rest; but if the fever is severe, then you would consult a doctor and take medicines. Thence, when the system (Dharma) of the body is decayed (Adharma) by exaltation of some evil pathogen like virus or bacteria (evil doer), the God creates himself in the form of medicine. So also, He may come as a vaccine if an epidemic attacks; or as a boat when floods inundate and so forth.

Whatsoever the ***Disaster*** (Destruction of Dharma) may it be, the ***GOD*** comes in the form of ***Mitigation Manager*** without expecting anything in return.

Let us bow down to those RESCUERS! Hats off!! Jai Ho!!!

18.1 MITIGATION – THE CONCEPT AND MEANING

Mitigation refers to all actions taken *before a disaster to reduce its impacts.*

Definition/ Meaning

Mitigation is the effort to reduce loss of life and property by lessening the impact of disasters.

In other words, the **disaster mitigation** refers to eliminate or reduce the impacts and risks of hazards through proactive measures taken before an **emergency** or the **disaster** occurs.

In order that mitigation to be effective, the action is to be initiated well in advance to the occurrence of the disaster—to reduce human and financial consequences later (analyzing risk, reducing risk, and insuring against risk). It is important to know that disasters can happen at any time and any place and if we are not prepared, consequences can be fatal.

18.1.1 The Concept and Significance of Mitigation

It is well known fact that nobody knows when a disaster can occur. We know that-

- Disasters can happen at anytime and any place.
- The human and financial consequences of disasters are hard to predict.
- The number of disasters each year is increasing.

The above three points necessitate the conduct of disaster mitigation programs because, they help reducing the impact of disasters. However, effective mitigation requires understanding local risks, address the hard choices, and invest in long-term community well-being. In addition to the risk analysis, it is needed to understand the vulnerability of the region. Whatsoever! Without mitigation actions, the safety, financial security and self-reliance may be jeopardized.

18.1.2 Objectives of Mitigation

The following are the major objective of disaster mitigation.

1. Develop plans that will aid the implementation of techniques for mitigation of the natural and manmade hazards of given region.
2. Conduct public education, outreach and awareness programmes to help local citizens to better understand the hazard mitigation and the ways to protect the lives and properties from the impact of a disaster when it occurs.

3. Undertake the cost effective structural projects those will benefit reducing the effect of disasters if they occur.
4. Implement sound hazard mitigation policies and preventive methods into a framework of local government operations across the region.

18.1.3 Strategies of Mitigation

To achieve the above objectives to prevent or mitigate disasters, the following four Strategies are employed

- Hazard management and vulnerability reduction
- Economic diversification
- Political intervention and commitment
- Public awareness

The first two apply exclusively to disasters caused by natural phenomena while the latter are used to mitigate any other hazards.

18.1.4 Types of Mitigation

Disaster mitigation measures can broadly be classified into two types as

1. Structural
2. Non-structural

1. ***Structural Mitigation*** involves the construction projects which reduce economic and social impacts.

Examples of Structural Mitigation

- After the Chennai Floods, Tamil Nadu state government announced financial support to any new project aimed at reducing the risks of floods.
- After Super cyclone 1999, Odisha government determined to construct multipurpose cyclone shelters along Odisha coast to the vulnerable people during floods and cyclones.
- Building flood dikes, flood gates etc.

2. ***Non-Structural Mitigation*** involves the policies and practices which raise awareness of hazards or encourage developments to reduce the impact of disasters

Examples of Non-Structural Mitigation

- In Oct 2015, 11 mountain states of India viz. Arunachal Pradesh, Assam, Himachal Pradesh, Jammu and Kashmir, Manipur, Meghalaya, Mizoram, Nagaland, Sikkim, Tripura and

Uttarakhand adopted a building code separate from the rest of India via a resolution.

- Land–use zoning, Land Hazard Zonation

Various mitigation activities include:

- Reviewing building codes and building use regulations
- Vulnerability analysis updates
- Zoning and land-use management and planning
- Implementing preventative health measures
- Educating businesses and the public on simple measures they can take to reduce loss or injury, for instance fastening bookshelves, water heaters, and filing cabinets to walls to keep them from falling during earthquakes.

18.2 FUNCTIONS OF DISASTER MITIGATION AND MANAGEMENT

As already discussed in chapter-2 of this book, the disaster mitigation management is mainly concerned with the six important functions. Of these, the first three mitigation functions (Awareness, Prevention and Preparedness) are performed before the occurrence of the disaster while the last three managerial functions begin just after the occurrence of the disaster.

1. **Awareness:** This function of disaster managers is concerned with spreading information and giving wide publicity to keep people aware of their roles in mitigating the expected disaster. The government and local bodies or ministry or the organizations (private/ government/ PSU) may advertise in the public interest in the news channels of TV and Radio, and newspapers and also other possible social media. Announcements also may be made at the places of community gatherings such as bus stands, railway stations, airports, traffic centres, shopping malls, theatres etc.
2. **Prevention:** This function is concerned with how to stop, or prevent or postpone a disaster to occur. The manmade disasters may be preventable but most of the natural disasters cannot be prevented. In such case, evacuation may be one solution so as to save the lives and some valuables.
3. **Preparedness:** Whether or not the disaster is preventable, one should be ready to face the occurrence of the event. The wise idea is to be prepared by following the specified precautions/ mitigation measures to eliminate/ reduce the impact, what is known as preparedness.
4. **Response:** While the disaster unpreventable hits suddenly, it should be attended immediately and initiate rescue measures so that damages and

losses may be minimized. How fast you respond depends on the communication system, transportation system and the rescue mechanisms.

5. **Rehabilitation:** Under this function, the disaster managers are concerned with sheltering, clothing and providing living conditions to the victims of disasters. The government also often takes help of certain non-government philanthropic organizations and humanitarians as well as the taxes and earnings (such as one day wages of employees) to re-establish the disaster hit area.
6. **Recovery:** How to recover the loss and revive the situation, What are the roles of individuals, communities, and societies as well as the local, state and central governments. There are the prime concerns of the disaster managers. It is also connected with insurance claims, and compensations for property renovation and the ex-gratia etc. Though lives cannot be brought back, we can try for normal living conditions to reinstitute. The governments often pay the money in terms of ex-gratia and some schemes to compensate the losses or damages incurred.

18.2.1 Activities of Mitigation

In addition to the above functions, the disaster/ emergency managers are entrusted with the activities such as risk evaluation, vulnerability study, and forward planning.

Mitigation activities should incorporate the measurement and assessment of the evolving risk environment. Activities may include the creation of comprehensive, proactive tools that help to decide where to focus funding and efforts in risk reduction.

Some of activities of mitigation measures include:

- Hazard mapping
- Adoption and enforcement of land use and zoning practices
- Implementing and enforcing building codes
- Construction of cyclone shelters/ rehabilitation centres
- Cyclone relief fund pooling and disbursement plan
- Flood plain mapping
- Seismic maps/ weather change monitoring
- Reinforced tornado safe rooms
- Epidemic prevention measures
- Burying of electrical cables to prevent ice pile-up
- Raising of homes in flood-prone areas
- Disaster mitigation public awareness programs
- Insurance programs.

18.2.2 Common Instructions Universally Applicable to Mitigation of All Types of Disasters

The following instructions are universally applicable and have to be added to the mitigation plans of all disasters. [Since these are common to all, these are not given again at mitigation plan of each disaster in the texts to follow in this chapter. These may be included for each type disaster as required].

- Do not lose energy by crying and getting tensed.
- Do not be panic, be calm. Think how to mitigate.
- Identify safe places indoors and outdoors.
- Know emergency telephone numbers (such as doctors, hospitals, police, fire station etc.)
- Educate your yourself, family members and friends. Share the information and instructions through social media.
- Repair defective electrical wiring and leaky gas connections or those are potential of fire risks.
- Store weed killers, pesticides, and flammable products securely in closed cabinets with latches and on bottom shelves.
- Plan and practice evacuation routes from your home, school, workplace, or any other place at risk.
- Know your escape route at night and during inclement weather. Familiarity may save your life.
- Practicing your plan makes the appropriate response more of a reaction, requiring less thinking during an actual emergency situation.
- Plan in such a way that you should be able to reach your safe location on foot within 15 min.
- Use Weather Radio or a local radio/ TV News channel for updated emergency information.
- Use protective clothing and other safety equipment (e.g. head covers, nose masks, goggles etc.).
- Use social media to spread the information.

Disaster Emergency Kit

- Battery operated torch with extra batteries
- Battery operated radio
- First aid kit and manual
- Emergency food (dry items) and water (packed and sealed)
- Candles and matches in a waterproof container and a knife
- Chlorine tablets/ powdered water purifiers
- Can opener
- Essential medicines
- Identity card/ Passport and copies of important documents
- Cash and credit cards
- Thick ropes and cords
- Sturdy shoes.

- Cover your mouth with a handkerchief or clothing.
- Local emergency management officials can advise the best route to safety and likely shelter locations.
- Talk to your insurance agent.
- Avoid areas of disaster and also those vulnerable.
- Store extra drinking water in suitably covered vessels.
- Use phone only for emergency calls. Telephone lines are frequently overwhelmed in disaster situations. They need to be clear for emergency calls to get through.
- If someone needs to be rescued, call professionals with the right equipment to help.
- Follow the instruction by radio. Keep some extra batteries for transistors.
- Keep a hurricane lantern filled with kerosene, battery operated torches and enough dry cells or any appropriate equipment.
- Keep some dry non-perishable food always ready for use. Make arrangement to get extra food in emergency, which can be eaten without cooking. Make provision for children and old people requiring special diet.
- Ignore rumours and do not spread them; this will help to avoid panic situations.
- Call and inform Fire & Emergency Services (101), Police (100) and Medical Services (108) in India.

18.2.3 Help Your Community

- Publish a special section in your local newspaper with emergency information on earthquakes. Publicize the information by printing the phone numbers of local emergency services offices and hospitals.
- Announce "Do's and Don'ts" and other required information frequently through electronic media as well as radio and other private sources.
- Conduct week-long series on locating hazards in the home.
- Work with local emergency services and officials to prepare special reports for people with mobility impairment on what to do during an earthquake.
- Provide tips or conduct disaster drills in the home or at community gatherings.
- Interview representatives of the gas, electric, and water companies about shutting off utilities.
- Work together in your community to apply your knowledge to building codes, retrofitting programmes, hazard hunts, and neighbourhood and family emergency plans.

- Help people who require special assistance— Infants, elderly people, those without transportation, large families who may need additional help in an emergency situation, people with disabilities, and the people who care for them.
- Sometimes, your presence might congest the place and hamper rescue and other emergency operations and also put you at further risk from the residual effects (such as contaminated water, crumbled roads, landslides, mudflows, flash floods, and other hazards). Vacate space for other.

SELF ASSESSMENT INTERMISSION (SAI – 18.1)

1. What is mitigation? What is its meaning and significance in disaster management?
2. What are the types of mitigation? Briefly describe with examples.
3. Give the list of items in an emergency kit.
4. What do you understand by the terms 'Structural' and 'Non-Structural' mitigation?
5. Enumerate the functions of disaster manager in managing and mitigating the emergency situations.
6. What are the objectives and strategies of disaster mitigation?
7. List out some activities of disaster management?
8. Suggest some universally applicable disaster prevention and mitigation measures.
9. List out what you do to help your community to facing disaster emergency situations.

18.3 DISASTER MITIGATION PLANS BASED ON CAUSES AND EFFECTS

Based on their cause of occurrence, we have broadly classified the disasters into two categories as natural and manmade (refer chapter 2, for classification). However based on the impact/ effects, each of these may be sub-divided into two types each i.e. Major and minor. Thus we can understand the disasters into four categories as shown the table 18.1.

Disaster mitigation plans vary from one type to the other since, each disaster is a unique and the characteristics of one disaster are entirely different from the other. However, some disasters gain more importance in view of the damage or life loss they cause. Further, the occurrence and causes of some disasters are not known and they are not in our control, such as earthquake, cyclone etc. In view of the causes and effects, the major natural disasters (shown in the top left window in table 18.1) are given more importance while the next importance is given to major manmade disasters.

Table 18.1 Types of Disaster based on Causes/ Effects

Disaster	Major (Effect)	Minor (Effect)
Natural (Cause)	Earthquake/ Tsunami Cyclone/Hurricane/Typhoon Floods/ Urban Floods Volcanic Eruption Drought/ Famine	Landslides/ Mudslides Rainstorm/ Thunderstorm Heat waves/ Cold waves Hailstorm/ Snow storm Avalanche/ Blizzard
Manmade (Cause)	Nuclear Explosion/ Radiation Chemical/ Industrial Hazards Wild Fire/ Deforestation Wars/ Terrorism Epidemics/ Bio-Hazards Air/ Water/ Soil Pollution Air/ Train/ Marine Accidents	Road/ Rail Accidents Communal Violence/ Riots Food Poisoning/ Pollution Industrial Accidents/ Crisis Fire / Chemical spills Smog/ Littering Acid rain

18.4 GUIDELINES FOR MITIGATION OF MAJOR NATURAL DISASTERS

18.4.1 DO's and DON'Ts for Earthquake

Before an Earthquake

1. Get an expert advice if there are any signs of structural defects.
2. Follow codes (e.g. BIS codes) relevant for building standards.
3. Repair deep plaster cracks in ceilings and foundations, if any.
4. Fasten shelves securely to walls.
5. Anchor overhead lighting fixtures to the ceiling.
6. Place large or heavy objects on lower shelves.
7. Store breakable items such as bottled foods, glass and porcelain material in low and closed cabinets with latches.
8. Don't hang heavy items such as pictures and mirrors near beds, sofa and anywhere that people sit.
9. Brace overhead light and fan fixtures.
10. Secure water heaters, LPG cylinders etc., by strapping them to the walls or bolting to the floor.
11. Store weed killers, pesticides, and flammable products securely in closed cabinets with latches and on bottom shelves.
12. Identify safe places indoors and outdoors, such as...
    - Under strong dining table or bed
    - Against an inside wall
    - Away from where glass could shatter around windows, mirrors, pictures

- Away from where heavy bookcases or other heavy furniture could fall over
- In the open, away from buildings, trees, telephone and electrical lines, flyovers and bridges

13. Educate you yourself, family members and friends. Share the information and instructions through social media such as WhatsApp, Facebook, Twitter, Instagram, SMS etc.,and use the following.
    - Awareness Generation Resources for Earthquake Disaster Management
    - Disaster (Earthquake) Resistant Construction Practice
    - Techno Legal Regime for Safe Construction Practice
    - Past Programmes/Projects, Resource Materials on Earthquake Risk Management.

Develop an emergency communication plan

- In case family members are separated from one another during an earthquake (a real possibility during the day when adults are at work and children are at school), develop a plan for reuniting after the disaster.
- Ask an out-of-state relative or friend to serve as the 'family contact' after the disaster; it is often easier to call long distance. Ensure everyone in the family knows the name, address, and phone number of one another.

During an Earthquake

As far as possible, stay safe during an earthquake. Be careful! Some earthquakes could be foreshocks and a larger earthquake might occur. Limit your movements to a few steps that reach a nearby safe place and stay indoors until the shaking stops and make sure exiting is safe.

If indoors

- **DROP** to ground; take **COVER** by keeping under a robust table or any such furniture; and **HOLD** ON until the quake stops.
- If you don't find any table or desk near you, then cover your face and head with your arms crossed over and stoop down at a corner of the room.
- Protect yourself by staying under the **lintel** or **within inner door frame**, in the **corner of a room**, **under a table** or even **under a bed**.
- Go away from windows, glass, outside doors and walls, and any object that could fall, like lighting fixtures or furniture.
- Stay in bed and protect your head with a pillow if you are on it, when earthquake occurs.

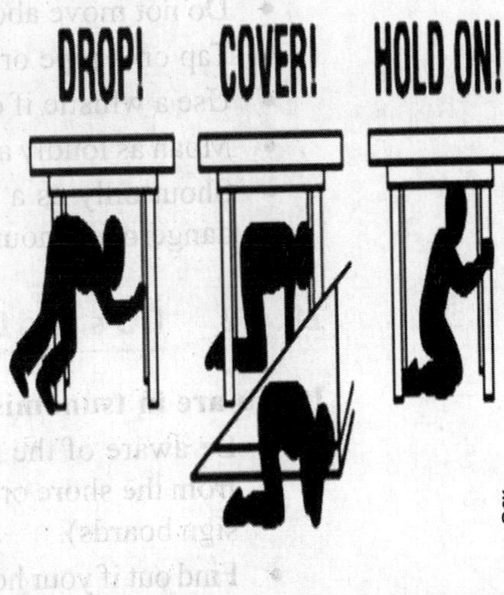

- To the nearest safe place, move away from heavy light fixture that could fall.
- Use a doorway for shelter only if it is in close proximity to you and if you know it is a strongly supported, load bearing doorway.
- Keep inside until the quaking stops and ensure it is safe to go outside. Most injuries occur when people inside try to move to different locations inside the building or try to leave.
- Beware and be aware that electricity may turn off and fire alarms may turn on.

If outdoors

- Get away from constructions, structures and buildings (particularly, more risky if they are old),
- Stay away from trees, streetlights and utility wires.
- Do not move from where you are, if it is a safe place (better open land).
- If you are in open space, stay there until the shaking stops.
- The greatest is the danger directly outside buildings particularly at exits; and alongside exterior walls. Most casualties occur from collapsing walls, flying glass, and falling objects.

If in a moving vehicle

- Stop as early as safety permits and stay in the vehicle.
- Do not stop near or under buildings, trees, overpasses, and utility wires.
- Proceed cautiously once the earthquake has stopped.
- Avoid roads, bridges, or ramps that might have been damaged or cracked.

If trapped under debris

- Do not light a match.
- Do not move about or kick up dust.
- Tap on a pipe or wall so rescuers can locate you.
- Use a whistle if one is available make any sound.
- Moan as loudly as possible without opening mouth.
- Shout only as a last resort, because shouting can cause you to inhale dangerous amounts of dust.

18.4.2 DO's and DON'TS for Tsunami

If you are in tsunamis

- Be aware of the height of your street above sea level and the distance from the shore or other high-risk waters. (Local administration may put sign boards).
- Find out if your home, school, workplace, and frequently visited locations are at tsunami risk.

- If your children's school is in an identified inundation zone, check up the school evacuation plan.
- Find out if you need to pick your children up from school or from another location. Telephone lines during a tsunami watch or warning may be overloaded and traffic jams might occur.
- Go as high or far as you can. Every meter inland or upward can make a difference.
- After a disaster, roads may become blocked or unusable. Footpaths normally lead uphill and inland, while many roads parallel coastlines.
- Be prepared to evacuate on foot if necessary. Follow post-tsunami evacuation routes; these will lead to safety.
- Everyone, who resides near shores, or tsunami prone areas, must have knowledge of what to do in a tsunami situation. So, discuss with your family about tsunamis and what are the Dos and DON'Ts.
- Discussing tsunamis in advance can reduce fear and save life as well as the valuable time in an emergency.
- Discuss flood (associated with tsunami) safety and preparedness measures with your family.
- Read the terms and conditions of insurance schemes available (browse the websites of insurance providing companies) and understand them. In case of any doubts call (Toll free) the customer care / customer support officers to get clarified.
- Discuss with your insurance agent. Considering acts of God, some policies connected with home loans / House-ownership policies may not cover floods, earthquakes, tsunami, volcano etc. Thoroughly understand by questioning the Insurance Agent about the benefits from Multi-Hazard Insurance Schemes and choose appropriate scheme. Inform the same to all your family members.

If you are visiting Tsunami-risk area

- Ask hotel reception for tsunami evacuation information and know about the warning system.
- Well before a warning is issued, it is very much essential to know designated routes to escape.
- An early warning signal of a tsunami is that the sea water precedes several metres, exposing fish on beaches or shallow areas. If such scene is seen, leave the beach immediately and go to higher ground far away from the beach.
- Observe the code of constructions. Most tsunami waves are < 3 m, thence, elevate house to reduce damage to property.

- Avoid building or living in buildings within 200 m of the high tide coastline. These areas are more vulnerable to tsunamis, strong winds, or coastal storms.
- Protect your property by using appropriate scientific methods while building the structures.
- Consult the civil engineering experts if it requires any alterations to make tsunami-resistant.
- Make a list of items to bring inside if tsunami warning is issued.
- Make a list that will help you in a tsunami situation. Paste it on any wall of your home. Also keep a copy of it in your mobile.
- Be prepared and take all precautions to prevent flooding.
- Ensure your pet animals can escape and be able to move to higher ground if tsunami strikes.

What to Do if You Feel a Strong Coastal Earthquake

If you are in a coastal area and feel an earthquake for 20 sec or more, then:

- Drop, cover, and hold on. Follow all the instructions given under earthquake. (Refer the above section 18.4.1- Dos and DON'Ts of earthquake)

When the shaking stops

- Gather all your family members and move as early as possible to higher ground away from coast because tsunami may strike within minutes. Thank God! It gives at least few minutes of time unlike an earthquake
- Avoid downed power lines, High Tension wires and cables
- Keep away from damaged buildings and bridges which may fall during foreshock or aftershock.

If you are on land

- Read books or browse during your free time to know all truths and myths of tsunami, which could save your life during your free time.
- Use social media to share this knowledge with your relatives and friends, which could save their lives!

If you are in school and hear a tsunami warning

- Follow the advices of teachers and other school personnel
- Follow the warning instruction through weather reports in radio or TV Channels.

If you are at home and hear a tsunami warning

- Make sure that all the family members are aware of the warning.
- Vacate house if you live in the evacuation zone.
- Move calmly in an order and safe manner to any safe place.

- Follow the instructions and advices of local emergency and law enforcement authorities.

If you are at the beach or near the ocean and feel the earth-shake

- No sooner than you hear or feel or suspect the earth shake, move to higher ground.
- Don't wait for the announcement of tsunami warning. You may not find much lead time after announcement.
- Go away from rivers and streams leading to ocean just like how you would go away from a beach.
- Tsunami generated in distant locations generally gives sufficient lead time to move to higher ground. But, for locally-generated tsunami, when ground shake is felt, you may have a very few minutes only.
- High, multi-storied, reinforced concrete hotels are located in many coastal areas. The upper floors of such hotels can be safe places to find refuge
- Should there be a tsunami warning and if you cannot move quickly inland to higher ground, go onto top floors of constructions or structures.
- Homes and small buildings are generally not designed to withstand tsunami impacts. So, do not stay in these structures, if there is a tsunami warning.
- Stay away from low-lying areas immediately if tsunami warning is issued.

If you are on a boat

- Tsunami wave activity is quite imperceptible in Open Ocean; therefore, do not return to port because tsunami warning has been issued to that area.
- Tsunamis do produce quick changes in water level and thence unexpected dangerous currents in harbours and ports.

If there is time to move your boat or ship from port to deep water (After a tsunami warning has been issued)

- Most of the harbours and ports have control of a harbour authority and/ or a vessel traffic system. When a tsunami is expected, try to contact the harbour / port and seek the direction.
- For owners of small boats, it is safest to leave their boat at the dock and physically move to higher ground, particularly if tsunami is locally-generated.
- Severe weather conditions (turbulent sea outside harbour) indicate a greater hazard to small boats, then there no other good option than physically moving to higher ground.
- Before returning to port, contact to verify and ensure the safe conditions with the harbour authorities for navigation and berthing.

What to do after a Tsunami

Before re-entering your own house after a tsunami, you must be very cautious and check each and every corner of your house. The chief areas to check include, civil/ construction related issues such as foundation, walls, flooring etc., fire catching materials, electrical wiring/ equipment, gas line leakages, plumbing/ sewage lines, and poisonous bio-species (snakes/ scorpions/ centipedes/ insects) and so forth. Let us go into details of these issues.

General	▪ Beware! Tsunami might have damaged roads, culverts, bridges, or other places. Know the status with local transport/ municipal authorities before travelling to that area. ▪ Check yourself for injuries if so, get first aid before helping injured or trapped persons. ▪ The most common injury following a disaster is cut feet. So, better wear long trousers, a long-sleeved shirt, and sturdy shoes.
Structural/Civil related	▪ If you are re-entering buildings or homes, be extra cautious. Flooding due to tsunami could have damaged buildings. Mind your every step with utmost care. ▪ Shovel out mud/ sand/ silt before it solidifies. ▪ Do not stay in a building if water remains around it. Tsunami water also, like floodwater, can weaken foundations that may result as sunken buildings, cracked floors, or collapsed walls. ▪ Inspect walls, floors, doors, staircases, and windows thoroughly to ensure the building is not in risk of collapsing. ▪ Watch for loose plaster, drywall, and ceilings that could fall. ▪ Inspect foundations for cracks or other damage which can make building uninhabitable.
Fire Related	▪ Use battery-powered lanterns or flashlights while inspecting buildings because, battery-power is the safest and easiest. In respect of fire hazards, it poses less risk to user, occupants, or building. ▪ DO NOT USE CANDLES. There is risk of catching fire if any inflammable material or liquid or gases might have crept in with floods or otherwise. ▪ Check for fire hazards. Due to the earthquake, there may be broken/ leaking gas lines, and the tsunami flooded electrical circuits, or submerged furnaces or electrical appliances and so forth. ▪ Check if flammable/ explosive materials might have come by tsunami driven flooding. Fire is the most frequent hazard following floods
Gas leaks	▪ Check for gas leaks. If you smell gas or hear a blowing or hissing noise, open the windows/ doors and everyone rush outside quickly. Turn off the gas using the outside main valve if you can. Call the gas company from a neighbour's home. If you have turned off the gas for any reason, get it turned back on by a professional only or under the expert's supervision.
Electrical	▪ Check physically the electrical system for any damages. If you find sparks or broken/frayed wires, or if you smell burning insulation, turn off the electricity at the main fuse box or circuit breaker. ▪ If you have to step in water to reach the fuse box or circuit breaker, call an electrician first and take suggestion. Electrical equipment should be dry enough before it is returned for service. ▪ Use electricity only after thorough check by the electricity department professionals. There is every possibility of short circuit due to wet walls and may lead to fire hazards.

Sewage/ Water line	▪ Check for damage to sewage and water lines. If you have any doubt of sewage lines damage, avoid using the toilets and call a plumber. ▪ Turn off the main water valve before draining water from these sources. Use tap water if and only if local health officials advise it is safe. ▪ If water pipes are damaged, contact the water providing agency/ municipal office. If there is a leakage, turn off the main valve and arrest the leakage, also avoid using water from the tap. ▪ Safe water can be obtained from undamaged water heaters or by melting ice cubes if were made before the tsunami hit.
Biosphere related	▪ Watch out for wild animals, particularly poisonous snakes, scorpions, centipedes and insects that may have come into buildings with the water as tsunami floodwater flushes snakes and animals out of their homes. Use a stick to poke through debris. ▪ Watch your animals closely. Keep all your animals under your direct control. Hazardous materials abound in flooded areas. Pets usually will behave strangely and cry with characteristic sounds different from normal sounds before tsunami or earthquake. ▪ Pets may escape from home or through a broken fence. Pets may become disoriented, particularly because flooding usually affects scent markers that normally allow them to find their homes. The behaviour of pets may change dramatically after any disruption, becoming aggressive or defensive, so be aware of their well-being and take measures to protect them from hazards, including displaced wild animals, and to ensure the safety of other people and animals.
Food	▪ Any food that has come in contact with floodwater may be contaminated, so throw it away. Throw away the food stored before tsunami at your home, unless otherwise perfectly secured. The tsunami flooding might have wetted and damaged or poisoned it. ▪ Check stored food thoroughly before using it. ▪ Check the food supplies even it is bought out.
Recovery	▪ Take pictures of the damage in all angles, both of the building and its contents, for insurance claims. ▪ Open the windows and doors to help dry the building. ▪ Contact your insurance company evaluator valuation of damage ▪ Contact your nearest government official to seek the ex-gratia / aid from government for recovery/ rehabilitation
Others	▪ Anticipate aftershocks. If the earthquake is of large magnitude (8 to 9+ on Richter scale) and located nearby, some aftershocks could be as large as magnitude 7+ and capable of generating another tsunami. The number of aftershocks will decrease over the course of several days, weeks, or months depending on how large the main shock was.
Details	For further details- visit official website of National Disaster Management Authority http://ndma.gov.in/en/2014-08-07-11-24-51/national-policy/70-citizens-corner/natural-disaster/tsunami/541-do-s-and-don-ts.html

SELF ASSESSMENT INTERMISSION (SAI – 18.2)

1. What precautions would you suggest to the people living in an earthquake prone area?
2. How do you act when you sense the tremors of an earthquake?
3. What measures would you take to reduce the impact of an earthquake?
4. How do you act when an earthquake occurs and if you are in the following situations?
   (a) at home (b) walking on a road (c) driving a car
   (d) in school/ office
5. How do you act after an earthquake has occurred?
6. Describe briefly the DOs and DON'Ts in the event of an earthquake.
7. What precautions would you suggest to the people living in a tsunami prone area?
8. How do you act when you sense strong tremors of an earthquake when you are at seashore?
9. What measures would you take to reduce the impact of a tsunami before it occurs?
10. How do you act when a tsunami occurs and if you are in the following situations?
    (a) at home (b) walking on a beach (c) in a boat (d) outdoors
11. How do you act after a tsunami has occurred?
12. Describe briefly the DOs and DON'Ts in the event of a tsunami.

18.4.3 DO's and DON'Ts for Cyclone/ Storm/ Hurricane/ Typhoon/Depression

The depressions are very common in the monsoon seasons and they travel on the shores. When depression is formed in the ocean, the coastal areas get strong winds and rains also. If a depression becomes stronger and converts to cyclone/ storm, it may cause a lot of damage to the coast while rainstorms may occur on the upper/farer areas to coast.

The mitigation procedures are almost same as that with tsunami, therefore it is felt redundant to mention again. However, there are certain points noteworthy, in the mitigation process of cyclones because, unlike tsunami, the cyclones are associated with strong winds and rains. After reading the mitigation process given under tsunami, the below points also may be noted.

Before the Cyclone Season

- Demolish condemned buildings.
- Check for any loose tiles in the house and get it repaired.
- Check doors and windows including bolts and fasteners and get repaired, if any.
- Remove hay/ dead branches/ dying trees/ any debris close to the house;
- Remove or anchor removable objects such as lumber piles, loose tin sheets, loose bricks, garbage cans, sign-boards etc. which can fly in strong winds.

- Keep some wooden boards ready so that glass windows can be boarded if required.

Cyclone Stages for actions

The actions that need to be taken in the event of a cyclone threat can broadly be divided into:

1. Before the cyclone season
2. When cyclone alerts and warnings are issued
3. When evacuations are advised
4. When the cyclone has crossed the coast.

When the Cyclone starts

- Keep monitoring weather reports and warnings. This helps you prepare for a cyclone emergency.
- Believe only in the official information and pass this information only to others.
- When a cyclone alert is on for your area, work normally, but be alert to the radio warnings
- Stay alert for the next 24 hrs as a cyclone alert means that the danger is within 24 hrs.

When your area is under cyclone warning get away from low-lying beaches/ areas close to coast

- Leave early for high ground, otherwise shelter gets flooded
- Switch off the electrical mains in your house.
- Do not delay and run the risk of being marooned
- Board up glass windows or put storm shutters in place.
- Provide strong suitable support for outside doors.
- If you do not have wooden boards handy, paste paper strips on glasses to prevent splinters. However, this may not avoid breaking windows.
- If you have to evacuate the house move valuable articles to upper floors to reduce flood damage.
- Ensure working condition of your hurricane lantern, torches, emergency lights; keep them handy.
- Small and loose things, which can fly in strong winds, should be stored safely in a room.
- Ensure the window/ door can be opened only on the side opposite to the one facing the wind.
- If the centre of the cyclone is passing directly over your house there will be a lull in the wind and rain lasting for half an hour or so. During this time do not go out; because immediately after that, very strong winds will blow from the opposite direction.

When Evacuation is Instructed

- Do not worry about your property.
- Remain in the shelter until you are informed to leave.
- At the shelter follow instructions of the person in charge.
- Pack essentials for yourself and your family to last a few days.
- Carry medicines, special food for babies and children or elders.
- Head for the proper shelter or evacuation points indicated for your area.

Post-Cyclone Measures

- Remain in the shelter until informed that you can return to your home.
- Strictly avoid any loose and dangling wires from lamp posts.
- Report the correct losses to appropriate authorities.
- Clear debris from your premises immediately.
- Get inoculated against diseases immediately.
- Drive carefully, if you have to.

18.4.4 DO's and DON'Ts for Floods/ Urban Floods/ Rainstorms

What to do before a flood

To prepare for a flood

- Avoid building in flood prone areas unless you elevate and reinforce your home.
- Elevate the furnace, water heater, and electric panel if susceptible to flooding.
- Install "Check Valves" in sewer traps to prevent floodwater from backing up into the drains of your home.
- Contact community officials to find out if they are planning to construct barriers (levees, beams and floodwalls) to stop floodwater from entering the homes in your area.
- Seal the walls in your basement with waterproofing compounds to avoid seepage.

If a flood is likely to hit your area

- Be aware that flash flooding can occur. If there is any possibility of a flash flood, move immediately to higher ground. Do not wait for instructions to move.
- Be aware of streams, drainage channels, canyons, and other areas known to flood suddenly. Flash floods can occur in these areas with or without such typical warnings as rain clouds or heavy rain.

If you have to prepare to evacuate

- Secure your home. If you have time, bring in outdoor furniture.
- Move essential items to an upper floor.
- Turn off utilities at the main switches or valves if instructed to do so.
- Disconnect electrical appliances.
- Do not touch electrical equipment if you are wet or standing in water.

If you have to leave your home, remember these evacuation tips

- Do not walk through moving water.
- Six inches of moving water can make you fall.
- If you have to walk in water, walk where the water is not moving.
- Use a stick to check the firmness of the ground in front of you.
- Do not drive into flooded areas.
- If floodwaters rise around your car, abandon the car and move to higher ground if you can do so safely. You and the vehicle can be quickly swept away.

For Urban Floods

Before floods

1. Do not litter waste, plastic bags, plastic bottles in drains.
2. Try to be at home if high tide and heavy rains occur simultaneously.
3. Listen to messages by Municipal bodies from time to time and act accordingly.
4. Evacuate low lying areas and shift to safer places.
5. Ensure that everyone has emergency kit and necessary documents while evacuating or shifting.
6. Make sure that each family member has identity card.
7. Put all valuables at a higher place in the house.

In the Flood Situation

1. Obey orders by government and shift to a safer place.
2. Be at safe place and then try to collect correct information.
3. Switch of electrical supply and don't touch open wires.

DO's

1. Switch off electrical and gas appliances, and turn off services off at the mains.
2. Carry your emergency kit and let your friends and family know where you are going.
3. Avoid contact with flood water it may be contaminated with sewage, oil, chemicals etc.

4. If you have to walk in standing water, use a pole or stick to ensure that you do not step into deep water, open manholes or ditches.
5. Stay away from power lines as electrical current can travel through water,
6. Report power lines that are down, to the power company.
7. Look before you step-after a flood, the ground and floors are covered with debris, which may include broken bottles, sharp objects, nails etc. Floors and stairs covered with mud and debris can be slippery.
8. If the ceiling is wet shut off electricity.
9. Place a bucket underneath the spot and poke a small hole into the ceiling to relieve the pressure.
10. Use buckets, clean towels and mops to remove the water from the afflicted rooms.
11. Place sheets of aluminium foil between furniture and wet carpet.

DON'Ts

1. Don't walk through flowing water - because water currents can be deceptive and shallow fast moving water can knock you off your feet.
2. Don't swim through fast flowing water – because you may get swept away or there may be any poisonous snakes or species may bite or struck by an object in the water.
3. Don't drive through flooded area – because you may not be able to see abrupt drop - offs and only half a meter of flood water can carry a car away. Also driving through flood water can damage the engine of car/ bike and even the nearby property.
4. Don't eat any food that has come into contact with flood water. It might cause food poisoning.
5. Don't reconnect your power supply until a qualified engineer has checked it. Be alert for gas leaks
6. Don't smoke or use candles, lanterns, or open flames.
7. Don't scrub or brush mud and other deposits from materials, this may cause further damage.
8. Never turn on ceiling fixtures if ceiling is wet. Stay away from ceilings those are sagging.
9. Never use TVs, VCRS, CRT terminals or other electrical equipment while standing on wet floors, especially concrete. Use battery powered transistor radio for listening to news and instruction from government or officials concerned.
10. Don't attempt to remove standing water using your vacuum cleaner.
11. Don't remove standing water in a basement too fast. If the pressure is relieved too quickly it may put undue stress on the walls.

18.4.5 DO's and DON'Ts for Volcanic Eruptions

Volcanoes can damage the facilities and utilities like roads, bridges and agricultural fields etc. volcanic eruptions may create other natural disasters also. Some mitigation strategies are given below:

Before volcanic eruptions

- Be prepared for the other natural disasters those are often accompanied by volcanic eruptions such as
    - Mudslides/ Land slide/ Rock falls
    - Flash floods/ mud flows/ lava flow
    - Ash fall/ Acid rains
    - Earthquakes/ Tsunami.
- Be alert and secure your house and keep an eye on the volcano if you are nearby it.
- Strengthen roofs against ash loads.
- Constructing slope roofs like inverted 'V' shape is better as the ashes can run down.
- Retrofit air intakes in emergency vehicles
- If you feel eruption or a smell of it, immediately inform the emergency services such as fire, police, health centre etc.

If warning sign of volcanic eruption is issued

- Don't come out unless instructions are given by officer in charge of the locality.
- Follow instructions of local radio and local announcements.
- Close doors and windows secured and air tight.
- If evacuation is instructed, close all doors, windows and ventilators and all openings.
    - Determine which areas should be evacuated or avoided when eruptions occur.
    - Study the locations of community areas such as schools, theatres, hospitals, bus stands, railway stations etc. in light of volcanic eruptions and plan accordingly.
    - Conduct evacuation drills
    - Prepare evacuation plan and routes of escape
    - Prepare and circulate the instructions to follow if eruption takes place

Necessary actions to be taken by government/ local bodies or people nearby

- Volcanic eruptions often release lava which can cover villages nearby.

- Pour cool water or ice blocks. In Iceland, the villages have poured cold water to slow down the lava flow, which saved the fishing port of Heimay.
- Drill holes near the volcano. In Sicily, on Mt. Etna, engineers have blasted holes and lava flow turned away into the holes which saved from swallowing the villagers. A similar technique may be planned, and executed in advance.
- Prepare a valley or wells and the guide ways from all sides near a volcano.

Indonesia, Philippines and Japan are the countries with highest possibilities of volcanic eruptions while India has least probability.

18.4.6 DO's and DON'Ts for Drought/ Famine

Mitigation Strategies

- Cloud seeding
- Lift irrigation schemes
- Desalination of sea water for irrigation and/or drinking
- Drought monitoring – continuous observation of levels of rain fall
- Crop diversification towards low water requiring crops
- Land use optimization by careful planning and advising for crop rotation so as to minimize the soil erosion
- Rain water harvesting structures; Inter basin water transfer; Integrated basins planning (e.g. Mission Kakateeya and mission Bhageeratha of Telangana state, India).
- Recycling water i.e. purifying/ treating waste water/ sewage for reuse.
- Constructing canals or redirecting rivers though drought areas.
- Water use restrictions/ creating water consciousness.

SELF ASSESSMENT INTERMISSION (SAI – 18.3)

1. What precautions would you suggest to the people living in coastal area to face cyclones?
2. How do you act when you get a cyclone warning?
3. What measures would you take to reduce the impact of a cyclone?
4. How do you act when an earthquake occurs and if you are in the following situations?
   (a) Indoor (b) walking on a road (c) driving a car (d) in a beach
5. What are post-cyclone measures? Discuss.
6. Describe briefly the DOs and DON'Ts in the event of a cyclone.
7. What precautions would you suggest to the people living in a flood prone area?
8. What measures would you take to reduce the impact of floods?

(continued)

9. How do you act when floods occur and if you are in the following situations?
   (a) at home (b) walking on a road (c) driving on road (d) outdoors
10. How do you act when evacuation is instructed due to floods?
11. Describe briefly the DOs and DON'Ts in the event of volcanic eruption is (a) likely to occur (b) while occurring (c) just occurred.
12. Describe briefly the mitigation strategies for drought/ famine.

18.5 GUIDELINES FOR MANAGING MINOR NATURAL DISASTERS

18.5.1 DO's and DON'Ts for Landslides/ Rockslides/ Mudslides

We cannot stop disaster but minimize its impact by preparing ourselves better for landslides. The Government of India has made plans to identify the areas where landslides occur repeatedly through Landslide Hazard Zonation (LHZ) maps which demarcate areas by different colours. National Disaster Management Authority (NDMA), India has published a guideline on Landslides and Snow Avalanches as given on its website. Following are the precautionary measures for landslides in the form of "Do's and Don'ts"

Do's

- Prepare tour to hilly region as per the information given by weather department or news channel.
- Move away from landslide path or downstream valleys quickly without wasting time.
- Keep drains clean. Keep surrounds clean and neat.
- Inspect drains for - litter, leaves, plastic bags, rubble etc. and inform authorities concerned.
- Keep the weep holes open.
- Grow more trees that can hold the soil through roots.
- Check the areas of rock fall and subsidence of buildings, cracks that indicate landslides and move to safer areas.
- Check the river water. Even muddy river waters indicate landslides upstream.
- Notice such signals and contact the nearest Tehsil or District Head Quarters.
- Ensure that toe of slope is not cut, remains protected.

- Listen for unusual sounds such as trees cracking or boulders knocking together.
- Stay **Alert, Awake and Active (3A's)** during the impact or probability of impact.
- Locate and go to shelters.
- Try to stay with your family and companions.
- Check for injured and trapped persons.
- Mark path of tracking so that you can't be lost in middle of the forest.
- Know how to give signs or to communicate in emergency to flying helicopters and rescue team.

Don'ts

- Do not touch or walk over loose material and electrical wiring or pole.
- Don't uproot trees unless re-vegetation is planned.
- Avoid construction and staying in vulnerable areas.
- Do not build houses near steep slopes and near drainage path.
- Do not drink contaminated water directly from rivers, springs, wells but rain water if collected directly is fine.
- Do not move an injured person without rendering first aid unless the casualty is in immediate danger.

18.5.2 DO's and DON'Ts for Heat Wave/ Fire Hazards/ Summer Hazards

Heat Wave conditions can result in physiological strain, which could even result in death. The vulnerable people (particularly, children, old age people, sick or weak) often suffer from heat/ sun strokes in hot summers most generally. In addition to this, fire accidents are very common in summers.

To tolerate and resist the impact during the heat wave and to prevent serious ailment or death because of heat stroke, the following measures are recommended.

DO's

- Visit doctor immediately, if you feel faint or ill.
- Consume/ give oral rehydration syrup (ORS), or homemade drinks like lassi, torani (rice water), lemon water, buttermilk, etc. which helps rehydrating the body.
- Keep onion with you and either eat or smell it as frequently as possible.
- Let your pet animals be in shade and keep plenty of water available to them to drink.

- Keep windows open at nights.
- Use fans, damp clothing and take bath in cold water frequently.
- Drink sufficient water and as often as possible, even though you are not thirsty
- Wear lightweight, light-coloured, loose, and porous cotton clothes.
- Wear heat protective equipment such as goggles, umbrella/ hat, shoes or chappal while going out in sun.
- Do carry water with you, while travelling.
- Let your home be cool, by using curtains, shutters or sunshade
- If you have sufficient place in front yard/ backyard, make a shed or a canopy or a hut with leaves of coconut tree or palm tree or any grass etc. This provides coolness by convection process.
- If your house is having a roof, get it painted with white cement or a cool paste etc. The white colour has least absorption and so reflects the heat/ light back.

DON'Ts

- Don't leave children or pets in parked vehicles.
- Don't do strenuous activities when temperature is high outside.
- Don't work outside between 12 noon and 3 pm.
- Don't go out in the sun, particularly, between 12 noon and 3 pm.
- Don't consume alcohol, tea, coffee and carbonated soft drinks. They dehydrate the body.
- Don't eat high-protein food and stale food. They kill apatite or prevent you having sufficient energy or may cause diarrhoea.
- If you have to necessarily work outside, use a hat or an umbrella and also a damp cloth on your head, neck, face and limbs.

Tips for Treatment of Person Affected By Sunstroke/ Hot Wave

- The most important is to bring down the temperature of the body.
- Keep the person laid in a cool place, under a shade.
- Go on wiping his/her entire body with a wet cloth.
- If possible wash the body frequently.
- Pour normal temperature water on the head (no ice because sudden cooling is not advisable).
- Give the person ORS to drink or lemon sarbat/ torani or whatever is useful to rehydrate the body.

- Drive the person immediately to the nearest hospital/ health centre.
- The patient needs immediate hospitalisation, as heat strokes could be fatal.

Acclimatization

People who have come from a cooler climate to a hot climate are more vulnerable and at high risk. If such a person(s) visit your family during the heat wave season, advise them not to move in open field for a period of one week or till the body is acclimatized to heat and should drink plenty of water. Acclimatization is attained by gradual exposure to the hot environment during heat wave.

Fire Fighting

- Avoid carrying flammable materials. If it is a compulsion, then pack them carefully and securely. Label such container clearly as "INFLAMMABLE".
- Use protective clothing and protective equipment.
- Use white or light coloured pure cotton clothes.
- Help fire fighters.
- Inform fire department (Dial 101 in India).
- Do not smoke near fire catching materials such as LPG, Oxy-Acetylene cylinders, Petro products, oils & volatile chemicals etc.

18.5.3 DO's and DON'Ts for Cold Waves/ Winter Hazards/ Blizzards/ Hailstorms

Some Safety Tips

Clothing

- Wear layers of clothing to stay warm. Loose-fitting is more effective of insulation.
- Gloves and hat/ monkey cap will prevent losing body heat
- Use rugs/ thick bed sheets on bedding to provide warmth

At home

- Insulate pipes outdoors by wrapping with insulators so as not to burst.
- Let your faucets drip to prevent freezing water from causing pipes burst.
- Close off unneeded rooms and cover gaps (under the door) and cracks with towel like cloth.
- If you use a space heater, place it on level, hard surface like glass or metal.
- Don't forget to turn off space heaters when your leaving the room.

- If you use a fire place, cover it with hard surface like glass or metal so as to prevent sparkles.
- Never use a stove or oven to heat your room
- Keep any flammable items at least 3ft away from your bed/ sofa/ curtains/ clothes/ wardrobes.
- Check your children and elderly people as they are more vulnerable to adverse effects of cold
- Bring in your pets or otherwise ensure they are sheltered so as not subjected to cold weather.
- Bring in your outdoor plants (in pots) or covers them with plastic or insulation.
- Have a flash light with extra batteries. Avoid using candles
- Ensure your cell-phone fully charged.

If have to travel by car

- Check your car battery and condition.
- Keep your car fuel tank full.
- Carry the winter kit (Flash light, water, blankets, high-calorie snacks, jumper cables, etc.)

18.6 GUIDELINES FOR MAJOR MANMADE DISASTERS

The major man made disasters include nuclear, Chemical, Industrial and biohazards. We shall now discuss about the mitigation measures of these disasters in the paragraph to follow.

18.6.1 DO's and DON'Ts for Nuclear Hazards and Radiation

Preparedness at Nuclear Plants

- Ensure negligibly small probability of a major accident at nuclear plant leading to the release of large quantities of radioactivity into the environment.
- If by chance, there is a major release into the environment, prepare the prompt and effective implementation plan of countermeasures that can reduce the radiological consequences for the public and the environment.

Preparedness for Nuclear/Radiological Emergencies

The management of nuclear emergencies needs coordination among various service groups. In the case of potential radiological consequences in the public domain, all the authorities at the three levels, i.e., district (local), state and central, play a vital role and assist the offsite officials in effectively responding to and keeping the public informed on the precautions to be taken.

Major Responsibilities of Nuclear Power Plant Operators

- promptly classify and characterize an emergency,
- prepare a plan to mitigate the emergency,
- notify and recommend protective actions off site compliant with international guidelines,
- protect people those on site,
- plan for obtaining off-site assistance,
- conduct environmental monitoring of the affected area and
- assist off-site officials in keeping the public informed.

Major Responsibilities of Off-Site Officials

This includes the arrangements required to promptly implement protective actions and countermeasures in the affected area.

Emergency Preparedness for Nuclear Power Plants

A comprehensive emergency preparedness plan for proper implementation of counter-measures can significantly reduce the consequences of an emergency situation, and is mandatory for all nuclear facilities to obtain a license for the operation of a nuclear facility. Emergency Response Manuals are prepared for the three main types of emergencies, viz., plant, on-site and off-site, and that the plans are in place to handle these types of emergencies. The operators of nuclear facilities must make an assessment of the type and quantum of release of radioactivity under various accident conditions and the extent to which it can spread into the environment.

Plant Emergency

When a plant boundary or a section of the plant is subjected to the radiological consequences of an abnormal situation, it is described as a plant emergency. Nuclear facilities in the country have the following provisions for the detection, classification, notification and mitigation of any emergency situation:

1. Emergency operating procedures for assessment of an emergency condition and its mitigation.
2. Pre-identification of facility-specific, abnormal situation for classifying plant/ site emergency.
3. Facility-specific, approved nuclear emergency response plans of all the functionaries who have been assigned roles during the emergency.
4. Alerting the plant personnel by the emergency siren and making an emergency announcement.
5. Adequate means for communicating a notification to the emergency response organisations at the facility, the district and state authorities, and the central government authorities.
6. Identified assembly locations for plant personnel and casual visitors for their accounting, and assessment of persons trapped in the radiological areas.

7. Formation of rescue teams and activation of a treatment area and decontamination centre.
8. Radiation survey around the plant and outside the plant and site boundaries.
9. Assessment of wind speed, wind direction and the affected sector around the nuclear facility.
10. Provision of the services of the ambulance and paramedical staff at its site, whenever needed.
11. Equipment and materials for handling a nuclear emergency are kept at a designated place of the nuclear facility and ERC (Emergency Response Centre).

On-Site Emergencies

An accidental release of radioactivity or the potential of release of activity extending beyond the plant, but confined to the site boundary, constitutes a site emergency condition. In addition to all the provisions applicable in a plant emergency, the following additional provisions are ensured:

1. Extensive radiological survey for assessment of radiological conditions within the site boundary.
2. Suitable prophylaxis to all assembly areas for administration to plant personnel, if needed.
3. Identification of temporary shelters within the site for shifting plant personnel, when required.
4. Provision of a fleet of vehicles for evacuation of plant personnel from the site to a safer place.
5. Provision of fixed/ portable contamination monitors to check personnel/ vehicles leaving the site.
6. On sensing the potential of release of radioactivity that can transgress into public domain, the district authorities are alerted to be on standby for emergency operations in the public domain.
7. Radiological monitoring of the environment (16 km radius around the plant).

Off-Site Emergencies

On recognising the potential for an uncontrolled release of radioactivity into the public domain, the district authorities concerned are alerted to be on standby for emergency response operations. In addition to all the provisions applicable in plant emergency and site emergency, the following additional provisions are to be ensured for handling a nuclear emergency in the public domain:

1. Pre-identification of plant condition, which can lead to an emergency in the public domain.

2. An assessment of the radiological status at the site boundary and in the public domain.
3. For handling of an off-site emergency condition in an NPP, there is an off-site emergency committee headed by the district magistrate of the district and supported by the district sub-committee, which include chiefs of all public service departments relevant in the district and also the Head of the Site Emergency Committee of the nuclear facility for technical advice.
4. This committee takes decisions pertaining to the handling of a nuclear emergency outside the site boundary and ensures implementation of countermeasures such as sheltering, prophylaxis and evacuation and resettlement, including maintenance of law and order and civil amenities.
5. All the activities pertaining to the handling of an off-site emergency are guided and coordinated from a pre-designated emergency response centre located outside the boundary of nuclear plant.
6. The information and broadcasting department of the district, in association with an authorised officer, ensures the correct information flows to media to avoid panic and spreading of rumours.

18.6.2 DO's and DON'Ts for Chemical Hazards and Industrial Accidents

Precautions to be taken during and after the Chemical (Industrial) Accidents

1. Evacuate calmly and quickly perpendicular to wind direction through the designated escape route
2. Keep a wet handkerchief or piece of cloth/ sari on face during evacuation.
3. Keep the sick, elderly, weak, handicapped and other people who are unable to evacuate inside house and close all the doors and windows tightly.
4. Do not consume the uncovered food/ water etc open to the air, drink only from bottle.
5. Change into fresh clothing after reaching safe place/ shelter, and wash hands properly.
6. Inform Emergency/Essential Services.
7. Listen to PA (Public Address) System of the plant/ factory, local radio/ TV channels for advice from district administration/fire/health/police and other concerned authorities.
8. Provide correct and accurate information to government official and inform at public gathering places (like schools, colleges, shopping centres, theatres, parks, bus stands, railway stations etc.).

General Precautions during Normal Time

1. Do not smoke, lit fire or spark in the identified hazardous area.
2. Sensitize the community living near the industrial units.
3. The living areas should be more vigilant about the nature of industrial units and associated risks.
4. Keep the contact numbers of nearest hazardous industry, fire station, police station, control room, health services and district control room, for emergency use.
5. Avoid housing near the industries producing or processing the hazardous chemicals, if possible.
6. Participate in all the capacity building programmes organized by the government/ voluntary organizations / industrial units.
7. Take part in preparing disaster management plan for the community.
8. Identify safe shelters along with safe and easy access routes and share with disaster management committee.
9. Prepare a family disaster management plan and explain it to all the family members.
10. Make the family/ neighbours aware of the basic characteristics of various poisonous/ hazardous chemicals and the first aid required to treat them.
11. Adequate number of personal protective equipments needs to be made available, to deal with emergency situation.
12. Prepare an emergency kit of items and essentials in the house, including medicines, documents and valuables.

18.6.3 DO's and DON'Ts for Bio-Hazards/ Epidemics

Before Disaster

A. Plan for Family Biological Disaster.

B. Preparation by ensuring prevention measures:

(a) Personal cleanliness - daily bath, don't grow long nails and wear clean clothes.

(b) Follow Hand Hygiene (Wash hands with soap and water before preparing food or eating, after passing urine or stools, coughing or sneezing).

(c) Eat nutritious and balanced food.

(d) Immunization status should be up to date.

(e) Prevent overcrowding.

(f) Have good ventilation for house.

(g) Protect from hot and cold weather.

(h) You and your family members should have health education.

(i) The areas under risk should be kept under surveillance.

C. Take a First Aid and Cardio-Pulmonary Resuscitation (CPR) training.

D. Subscribe to a Medical Insurance Plan.

DO's & DON'TS

A. Diarrheal Group of Diseases Including Cholera

Do's

1. Follow Hand Hygiene.
2. Encourage drinking of water from a safe source or that has been disinfected (chlorinated).
3. Add bleaching powder in all community wells at regular intervals.
4. Use water pumped out from standard pumps (In India Mark II hand pumps), if installed in the village/ community.
5. Drink potable water in an emergency that has been boiled for at least 15 minutes up to a temperature not less than 60°C (bubbling temperature) and consumed it the same day.
6. Store water in narrow mouthed container.
7. Cook food thoroughly especially meat, poultry, eggs and seafood until it is steaming and eat it while it is still hot.
8. Ensure the meat and poultry is safe and no part of the meat discolored or foul smelt, or in the case of egg, their shells are not cracked.
9. If food is not eaten immediately, reheat cooked until it is steaming hot prior to serving.
10. Keep food items covered.
11. Increase fluid intake as soon as diarrhea starts by drinking ORS solution or home-made preparation of Table Salt 5g (1ts) in and 20g (4ts) of Sugar dissolved in 1 litre of drinking water.
12. Encourage banana eating, which provides potassium.
13. Continue feeding children when they are sick (breastfeeding if the child is being breast fed).
14. Refer the diarrhea case to the nearest health facility in case of the child is
    - irritable, restless or lethargic or unconscious
    - drinking poorly or not drinking
    - marked thirst

- having fever for long time
- blood in stools

Don'ts

1. Do not drink water from unsafe sources.
2. Do not eat uncooked food unless it is peeled or shelled.
3. Do not leave cooked food at room temperature longer than 2 hrs.
4. Do not consume cut fruits from vendors.
5. Do not defecate in open area.
6. Do not give access to rats and houseflies in your premises.

B. Air-borne/ Respiratory Diseases (Tuberculosis, Influenza, Chickenpox, Meningitis etc.

Do's and Don'ts:

1. Respiratory Hygiene/ Cough Etiquette:

   (a) Cover the nose/ mouth with a handkerchief/ tissue paper when coughing or sneezing which should be disposed off in dustbins;

   (b) Perform hand hygiene (e.g. frequent hand wash with soap and water, alcohol-based hand rub, or antiseptic hand wash) and thoroughly dried preferably using disposable tissue paper/ towel after having contact with respiratory secretions and contaminated objects/ materials.
2. Triple layer surgical mask of standard and certified make should be worn by suspected/ probable/ confirmed cases of influenza or by the care provider in home care settings and close family contacts of such cases undergoing home care.
3. Don't have close contact with people who are having respiratory illness.
4. Don't allow the sick person going into the community. They should stay at home.
5. Sick persons at home should keep distance from others.
6. Don't go to school/office, public places for at least 24 hrs after symptoms have resolved.
7. If sick persons must have to go into the community (e.g. to seek medical care), then they should wear a face mask or use a handkerchief or tissues to cover any coughing and sneezing so as to reduce the risk of spreading the infection in the community.

8. Get good sleep, be physically active, manage your stress, drink plenty of fluids, and eat nutritious food. Avoid smoking.
9. Persons who have difficulty in breathing or shortness of breath should seek immediate medical attention and report to nearby hospital.
10. Immunization status should be up to date as per National Universal Immunization Program.

C. Mosquito Borne Diseases (Malaria, Dengue, Chikungunya etc.)

Do's

1. Follow "sun-down sleeves-down" approach. Wear clothes that cover arms and legs.
2. Prevent water collections on ground and other places to prevent malaria breeding.
3. Empty water containers at least once a week and wash the containers thoroughly.
4. Remove water from coolers from time to time and clean.
5. Cover and seal any septic tanks.
6. Use all mosquito repelling/ preventing/ killing agents.
7. Change brand/ type/ dosage time to time if mosquitoes get resistance
8. Use Mosquito Nets, preferably, Insecticide Treated Bed Nets (ITBN).
9. Apply insect repellants while sleeping to keep away mosquitoes.
10. Seek medical advice in case of rashes, mental irritation or unconsciousness..

Don'ts

1. Don't encourage children/ old aged people to wear shorts and half sleeved clothing.
2. Don't permit water stagnation. Clean water tanks at regular intervals.

3. Don't permit accumulation of discarded items such as tires, tubes, empty coconut shells, household items and objects wherein water may collect.
4. Don't litter or throw ***disposable tea-cups/ water tumblers*** outside of a dustbin or at road side. They will collect water during rains or through any opportunity and become a nice home for mosquitoes, especially (Aida Egyptie) that causes dengue/ chikungunya.
5. Don't bathe/ swim in village ponds and/or allow cattle to take bath in the same pond.

18.7 GUIDELINES FOR MANAGING MINOR MANMADE DISASTERS

Various types of accidents are categorized under this group. Some mitigation tips are given here under.

18.7.1 DO's and DON'Ts for Road Accidents

1. General Principles and Precautions to Road Users

- Beware and be aware of the dangers involved in using various types of transport.
- Study the regulations and follow the traffic rules given by the transport authorities.
- Do not park vehicles on pavements putting pedestrians at risk by increasing their need to walk on road.
- Broken down vehicles are to be moved off the roads, hazard warning light must be switched on.
- Be aware of your speed while driving, watch your speedometer and concentrate on your limits.
- Do not overload your vehicle.
- Do not drive under the influence of alcohol and drugs.
- Do not use hand-free or hand-held phones whilst driving.
- The correct seatbelt or child restrained should be used.

2. While Accident Occurs or Just Occurred.

- Keep calm and avoid panic; to the extent possible help who are in difficulty
- Follow the driver's and crew's instructions, if you are a passenger
- Keep identity card/ papers and important personal documents (medical and vaccination certificates and details of blood type) and any personal medicine along with you. Now-a-days, the governments have introduced a mobile app., to store such information in your mobile.
- Soon after a crash occurs try to free yourself from the cabin, as there is a danger of fire or leaks
- If possible activate the rescue process by alerting the local security or special services (special telephone networks and numbers)
- In case of a major accidents occurring in road with traffic, direct the traffic while taking care of the own safety (signal and mark the accident spot).

- Call 108 (Ambulance/ medical service). Now-a-days, you need not give your personal details, but witness should alert the rescue services by giving them.

  1. The exact location and the nature of accident
  2. Type of vehicle involved
  3. The characteristics of any dangerous substances involved
  4. The likely number of victims.
- Witness may give his/her name and address (optional) in the interest of serving the fellow beings.

18.7.2 DO's and DON'Ts for Rail Accidents

Everyone who uses or likely to use trains as a medium of transport or otherwise, should

- know/ study the rules and regulation and follow them
- act as per the rules of the government
- know the ways to escape from the compartment and land safely in case of emergency

While the train accident occurs or just has occurred

- strictly follow the instructions of the authorities and of rescue teams
- help family and neighbours who are in need and difficulty
- ensure that your documents are in a safe zone
- in case of fire accidents, evacuate the compartment as early as possible to avoid loss
- call the rescue services and to give them the exact location

Role of individual in preventing train accidents

- Do not smoke in the trains and do not allow any one smoke or drink in the trains
- Do not let anyone stand near the tracks and at the doors
- Do not climb upon the trains
- If anything goes wrong then immediately inform the authorities or else take some precautions
- If any suspicious person enters the compartment immediately inform the authorities
- Help the needy and those in difficult

[Most part of the information is taken from official website of National Disaster Management Authority (NDMA) of India. Should you need further information, you may visit http://ndma.gov.in/]

SELF ASSESSMENT INTERMISSION (SAI – 18.4)

1. What precautions would you suggest to the people living hillside where landslides or rockslides are likely to occur?
2. How do you act when you get a landslide warning?
3. What measures would you take to reduce the impact of a heat wave?
4. How do you act when a cold wave occurs and if you are in the following situations?
   (a) Indoor (b) driving a car (c) outdoors
5. What are mitigation strategies and measures you suggest for the accidents likely to occur in (a) chemical (b) Industrial (c) nuclear environments? Discuss.
6. Describe briefly the DOs and DON'Ts in the event of a industrial accidents.
7. What precautions would you suggest to the people living in a nuclear plant?
8. What measures would you take to reduce the impact of
   (a) Heat wave (b) Cold wave?
9. How do you act when epidemics occur? Discuss the mitigation measures.
10. How do you act if you are in the following situations?
    (a) Earthquake occurs when you are at home
    (b) Rockslide occurs when you are walking hillside
    (c) An accident occurs while you are driving on a road
    (d) When you are moving along nuclear/ chemical hazardous area
11. How do you act for the following biohazards/ epidemic?
    (a) Airborne (b) Mosquito borne (b) water borne
12. Describe briefly the DOs and DON'Ts in the event of (a) cholera (b) dengue (c) influenza
13. Describe briefly the mitigation strategies for train accidents.

MINI-PROJECTS / CASE STUDIES

1. Conduct campaigns and drills on various mitigation and safety procedures in and around your society.

Om tryambakam yajâmahe sugandhim pushtivardhanam
urvâ rukamiva bandhanath mruthyor mukshiya mâmruthath

Sarve Janah Sujano Bhavanthu
Sarve Sujanah Sukhino Bhavanthu

Index

A

B

C

D

E

F

G

I

J

K

L

M

N

O

P

Q

R

S

T

U

V

W

Y

Z